TH

GHALIB

Mirza Asadullah Khan Ghalib (1797–1869), noble, poet, and wit of nineteenth-century Delhi, is the most famous and popular of the Urdu poets that the Indian subcontinent has produced. His life spans the years of the twilight of the Mughals, the Revolt of 1857, and the terrible aftermath. This complete Ghalib anthology comprises poetry and prose translated from both Persian and Urdu, as well as biographical details, and provides a context within which modern-day English-speaking readers can read and understand his poetry.

New translations from Ghalib's Urdu and Persian ghazals form a significant part of the volume. A note on translating Ghalib, a survey of his Urdu and Persian poetry, and a detailed explanatory index provided to guide the readers, complete the volume. The first-ever compendium of Ghalib's oeuvre, *The Oxford India Ghalib* is a collector's item for aficionados of Urdu literature and especially of its poetry.

Ralph Russell, eminent Urdu scholar, was Reader in Urdu at the School of Oriental and African Studies (SOAS), University of London. He has previously published *Ghalib: Life and Letters* (OUP 1994) and *Three Mughal Poets* (with Khurshidul Islam, OUP 1993). He edited the collection of essays, *Ghalib: The Poet and his Age* (OUP 1997), and has since published *The Pursuit of Urdu Literature: A Select History*; *An Anthology of Urdu Literature*; *The Famous Ghalib*; and *How Not to Write the History of Urdu Literature and other Essays on Urdu and Islam* (OUP 1999).

The Oxford India Collection is a series which brings together
writings of enduring value published by OUP.

Other titles include

Forthcoming

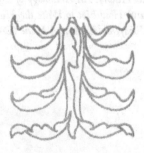

THE OXFORD INDIA

GHALIB

Life, Letters and Ghazals

edited by
RALPH RUSSELL

OXFORD
UNIVERSITY PRESS

OXFORD
UNIVERSITY PRESS

Oxford University Press is a department of the University of Oxford.
It furthers the University's objective of excellence in research, scholarship,
and education by publishing worldwide. Oxford is a registered trademark of
Oxford University Press in the UK and in certain other countries

Published in India by
Oxford University Press
22 Workspace, 2nd Floor, 1/22 Asaf Ali Road, New Delhi 110002, India

First Edition published in 2003
Oxford India Paperbacks 2007
22nd impression 2023

ISBN-13: 978-0-19-569238-9
ISBN-10: 0-19-569238-1

Typeset in Aldine 10.5/12
by Excellent Laser Typesetters, Pitampura, New Delhi 110 034
Printed in India by Manipal Technologies Limited, Manipal

Contents

Preface

THIS BOOK IS FOR READERS who know of Ghalib's greatness as a man, as a writer and as a poet, and who want to know him better, but cannot read Urdu and Persian, the languages in which he wrote. They can however approach him through the medium of English and this book attempts to present in English, within the range of a single convenient volume, a great part of his most significant work, both in prose and in verse. It includes much previously published material, the bulk of which is the joint work of Khurshidul Islam and myself; and even that which appears under my name alone owes an immense debt to him, because in our forty years' collaboration I acquired an understanding of Ghalib which I could never have acquired on my own. Two essays by other writers, from a collection which I edited, are also included.

The rationale of the book is as follows: *Ghalib: A Self-portrait*, was the obvious choice to put first. Then comes *Ghalib: Life and Letters* (abridged to fit into the compass of this volume) which covers all of Ghalib's most significant prose writing, both in Persian and in Urdu. Percival Spear's essay adds a fuller picture of the Delhi of Ghalib's day, the city where he spent most of his life.

This is followed by a section on the verse. *Getting to Know Ghalib* surveys that large part of his verse which he wrote in the *ghazal* form. It is illustrated mainly by quotations from his Urdu, but is equally applicable to his Persian ghazals. But while all of his Urdu verse is in the ghazal form, his Persian contains a great deal written in other genres, and A. Bausani's essay gives a useful and revealing survey of these. I have included it because my translations are of verses taken only from the ghazals.

A substantial selection of the verse is being published for the first time. Added to the previously published selection of the prose, this volume constitutes the most comprehensive compendium of Ghalib's work.

RALPH RUSSELL

Introduction
Ghalib: A Self-portrait*

Ralph Russell

ON 15 FEBRUARY 1969 IT WAS exactly a hundred years since Ghalib died. It seems to me fitting that in celebrating his centenary we should begin by remembering him not as a great poet of Urdu and Persian—although he *is* that—and not as a great writer of Urdu and Persian prose—although he is that too—but as a man; and that is why in this paper I propose to present a portrait of him as a man, a portrait which one can draw almost entirely in extracts from his own writings. I must confess that there are other reasons too for this choice of subject. I am addressing myself to an audience part of which knows Ghalib's poetry well, and part of which knows it not at all. The British element in my audience has not reached that desirable stage of cultural development which would enable it to appreciate Ghalib's poetry without a good deal of explanation, and a paper in which Ghalib is first introduced is not, I think, one in which I should launch into such a venture. On the other hand, even Urdu speakers may find in the picture which I present at any rate *some* features with which they are not already familiar—features

* Lecture delivered in 1969, the centenary of Ghalib's death.

which, I hope, will enhance still more their enjoyment of his poetry. I hope, therefore, that this self-portrait may be of interest to all.

I propose to portray Ghalib mainly in terms of extracts from his prose writings, both Persian and Urdu,[1] and I should perhaps explain at the outset that there are considerable differences between his Persian and his Urdu prose styles. His Urdu is in general almost conversational in its style; his Persian on the other hand, is prose of a highly formal, stylized kind, to which he devoted as much care as he did to his poetry. It is markedly rhythmical, often rhyming, with much alliteration and play upon words. Critics have tended all too often to assume that it is somehow lacking in sincerity and in natural appeal. That is a view which I emphatically do not share. At any rate, in translating it I have tried to reproduce something of the character of the original. I must leave it to you to decide how far it makes its intended impact.

Ghalib, as many of you will know, came from a family of soldiers—men of Turkish stock who had emigrated to India from an area that now falls within the territory of the Central Asian republics of the Soviet Union. It was an ancestry of which he was inordinately proud, and Hali is echoing Ghalib's own words when he writes:

> His ancestors traced their pedigree back to Tur, the son of Faridun [a legendary king of ancient Persia]. When the Kayyanis conquered all Iran and Turan, and the power and majesty of the Turanis departed from this world, the line of Tur was for a long time stripped of its dominion and its wealth. But the sword never fell from its hand, for among the Turks it was an age-old tradition that when a man died, the son inherited only his sword, and the rest of his property and wealth and home went to the daughter. At length, after many years, during the period of Islam, by the power of this same sword the Turks restored their fallen fortunes, and in the Seljuk dynasty the foundation of a mighty empire was laid. For several centuries it ruled over all Iran and Turan, and over Syria and Rum [i.e. Asia Minor], until at last after many years the Seljuks' empire came to an end, and their sons were scattered and dispersed abroad. One of them was Tarsam Khan, a man of noble birth, who made his home in Samarkand. And it was from this Tarsam Khan that Ghalib's grandfather...was descended.[2]

---

[1] All quotations are taken from Ralph Russell and Khurshidul Islam, *Ghalib, Life and Letters*. Page references in subsequent footnotes are to this book.

[2] p. 36.

Ghalib, I think, often regretted that he could not follow in their footsteps. He was the first to break with their tradition. His grand-father, he tells us, had served under Emperor Shah Alam. His own father had lived a soldier's life, and indeed had been killed in battle.[3] But for Ghalib himself a different destiny was intended. He writes in one of his Persian letters:

> Alas for my fate! born to be struck down by misfortune and to see my granaries reduced to ashes! I had not the means to ride to war like my ancestors... nor the capacity to excel in knowledge and ability like Avicenna and the wise men of old. I said to myself, 'Be a darvish and live a life of freedom.' But the love of poetry which I had brought with me from eternity assailed me and won my soul, saying, 'To polish the mirror and show in it the face of meaning—this too is a mighty work. The command of armies and the mastery of learning is not for you. Give up the thought of being a darvish, and set your face in the path of poetry.' Willy-nilly I did so, and launched my ship upon the illusory sea of verse. My pen became my banner, and the broken arrows of my ancestors became my pens.[4]

He was born in Agra, in December 1797, and spent his boyhood there, until at the age of thirteen he was married to a bride of eleven and shortly afterwards made his permanent home in Delhi. Late in life he recalled his early days there. He writes to a young Hindu friend:

> [Your grandfather] and I were about the same age—there may have been a year or two's difference one way or the other. Anyway, I was about nineteen or twenty and he was about the same. We were close friends and used to play chess together; we would often sit together until late into the night. His house was quite near mine and he used to come and see me whenever he liked. There was only Machia the courtesan's house and the two by-lanes between us. Our big mansion is the one that now belongs to Lakhmi Chand Seth. I used to spend most of my time in the stone summer-house near the main entrance. I used to fly my kite from the roof of a house in one of the lanes nearby and match it against Raja Balwan Singh's.[5]

He remembered Agra for rather less innocent pleasures too, to which he refers in a suitably vague and delicate way in a Persian

[3] p. 32.
[4] p. 37.
[5] p. 145.

letter written to his wife's kinsman Ziya ud Din Ahmad, perhaps not many years after he had settled in Delhi. Ziya ud Din Ahmad was visiting Agra, and Ghalib writes to him:

> Twin soul of mine, may Agra's air and water, distilled from hapless Ghalib's sighs and tears, rejoice your heart. Though we are far apart, yet the power of thought of my far-ranging mind has brought our oneness to the point where distance dares not to draw near. Granted that you have gone on a far journey and that the thought is near to you that you are far from me; and yet while you stay in the city of my birth, then truly we are near to one another. And I rejoice because my love that sees afar has sent my eyes and heart with you upon this journey, that I too, held in this place of exile [Delhi], may pay due tribute of joy at the sight of the city of my birth. Let no man look upon Agra as of slight account, but as he passes through her roads call on God's preserving and protecting power to hold her in its keeping. For she...was once the playground of my love-distracted heart. There was a time when in her soil only the mandrake grew, and, save the heart, her trees would bear no other fruit, and the drunken breeze of morning ranged through her gardens to lift up and to bear away men's hearts so that the drunkard longed no longer for his morning draught, so that the pious bent his mind no more to prayer. To every grain of dust of that land in flower my body sends it message of love, and on every leaf in those fair gardens my soul calls benedictions to rain down.[6]

Though he was only in his teens when he came to Delhi to live, he had already acquired some reputation as a poet, and it was a reputation which he maintained and enhanced as the years went by. But it was not only his poetry that made him popular, for he was a remarkable man in many ways—remarkable for his personal appearance, for his frankness, for his friendliness, for his originality and for his wit. There is plenty of independent evidence to support what he has written about himself in this sort of connection, but I shall quote mainly his own words. In 1861 he wrote to a friend who had had his portrait done and sent it for Ghalib to see:

> Your auspicious portrait has gladdened my sight. I must have said some time in the company of friends, 'I should like to see Mirza Hatim Ali. I hear he's a man of very striking appearance.' And, my friend, I had often heard this from Mughal Jan. In the days when she was in Nawwab Hamid Ali Khan's service I used to know her

[6] p. 38.

extremely well, and I often used to spend hours together in her company. She also showed me the verse you wrote in praise of her beauty.

Anyway, when I saw your portrait and saw how tall you were, I didn't feel jealous because I too am noticeably tall. And I didn't feel jealous of your wheaten complexion because mine, in the days when I was in the land of the living, used to be even fairer, and people of discrimination used to praise it.

In the same letter he speaks of his aversion to following current fashions. The day came, he says, when he decided to grow a beard:

> But remember that in this uncouth city [Delhi] everybody wears a sort of uniform. *Mullahs*, junk-dealers, *hookah*-menders, washermen, water-carriers, innkeepers, weavers, greengrocers—all of them wear their hair long and grow a beard. The day your humble servant grew a beard he had *his* hair shaved off—but God save us! what am I prattling about?[7]

The reference to the lady in the extract I quoted a moment ago indicates quite frankly one of the features of his life at this time. The terms in which he writes of her show quite clearly that she was a courtesan. He himself tells us that somewhere about this time he was in love with a *domni*, that is, one of a Hindu caste of singing and dancing girls. More than forty years later he was to speak of the grief he felt when she died:

> It is forty years or more since it happened, [he writes] and although I long ago abandoned such things and left the field once and for all, there are times even now when the memory of her charming ways comes back to me and I shall not forget her death as long as I live.[8]

A Persian letter written many years earlier refers perhaps to this same woman. And it describes not only his grief but the philosophy of love and of life which he formed at the time and to which he adhered for the rest of his life. The letter is written to a friend who, it seems, had recently suffered a similar loss. Ghalib writes:

> In the days of my youth, when the blackness of my deeds outdid the blackness of my hair, and my head held the tumult of the love of fair-faced women. Fate poured into my cup too the poison of this pain, and as the bier of my beloved was borne along the road, the dust rose from the road of that fortitude which was my essence. In

[7] p. 158.
[8] p. 185.

the brightness of broad day I sat on sack-cloth and clad myself in black in mourning for my mistress, and in the black nights, in the solitude of sorrow, I was the moth that flew to the flame of her burnt-out candle....

Yet though grief tears at the soul and the pain of parting for ever crushes the heart, the truth is that to true men truth brings no pain; and amid this tearing of the soul and this crushing of the heart we must strive to ponder: Where is the balm that can banish this distress? ...A man must amid the sorrow that melts the soul, set out to learn the lesson of fortitude.... The nightingale, notorious for love, pours forth his melody for every rose that blooms, and the moth to whose great passion all men point, gives his wings to the flame of every candle that makes radiant her face. Truly, the candles radiant in the assembly are many, and roses bloom in the garden abundantly. Why should the moth grieve when one candle dies? When one rose fades and falls why should the nightingale lament? A man should let the world of colour and fragrance win his heart, not bind it in the shackles of one love. Better that in the assembly of desire he draw afresh from within himself the harmonies of happiness, and draw into his embrace some enchanting beauty who may restore his lost heart to its place and once more steal it away.[9]

Where Ghalib can write frankly of matters such as these it is hardly surprising that he made no secret of the fact that he never kept the more troublesome commandments of his religion—never said the five daily prayers, never kept the Ramzan fast, had no ambition to perform the pilgrimage to Mecca, and broke the prohibition on wine. Hali wrote of him:

From all the duties of worship and the enjoined practices of Islam he took only two—a belief that God is one and is immanent in all things, and a love for the Prophet and his family. And this alone he considered sufficient for salvation.[10]

Ghalib continued to live in Delhi until he was nearly thirty, when, for reasons that need not concern us here, he went to Calcutta. He was away for nearly three years, and though he did not achieve what he went for, he enjoyed travelling and he liked Calcutta very much. For some extraordinary reason, if my Bengali friends will excuse me for saying this, he even liked the Calcutta climate. And in a short poem he wrote after his return he speaks

[9] pp. 50–1.
[10] p. 44.

of the other things he liked about it—its greenery, its pretty women, its fruits, and its wines:

> Ah me, my friend! The mention of Calcutta's name
> Has loosed a shaft that pierces to my very soul.
> Its greenery and verdure take away your breath;
> Its women's charms are such that none escapes them whole.
> Their glances pierce the armour of the stoutest breast;
> What heart withstands the blandishments of forms so fair?
> All freshness and all sweetness are its luscious fruits;
> Its mellow wines are pleasing beyond all compare.[11]

When he speaks of 'its luscious fruits', what he has first and foremost in mind are undoubtedly mangoes. Like all men of sound taste he had a passion for mangoes. And, again like all men of sound taste, he knew the proper way to eat them:

> I once said how I wished I could get to Marahra during the rains and eat mangoes to my heart's content and my belly's capacity. But where shall I recover the strength I once had? I neither have the same appetite for mangoes nor the same capacity to hold so many. I never ate them first thing in the morning, nor immediately after the midday meal; and I cannot say that I ate them between lunch and dinner because I never took an evening meal. I would sit down to eat them towards evening, when my food was fully digested, and I tell you bluntly, I would eat them until my belly was bloated and I could hardly breathe. Even now I eat them at the same time of day, but not more than ten to twelve, or, if they are of the large...kind, only six or seven.[12]

He returned from Calcutta to Delhi, and so life went on. He was generally in debt, for he lived in a style a good deal more lavish than his regular income could support, and all his attempts to supplement it were for years together almost without result. In general he did not let this depress him unduly, though there were certainly times when he felt it keenly and wrote bitterly about it. But in 1847, when he was in his fiftieth year, he suffered a terrible and quite unexpected blow. He was charged with keeping a gambling establishment at his house, was convicted, and spent three months in jail. More painful to him even than this was the way in which all his friends and admirers deserted him at this crisis.

[11] p. 57.
[12] p. 182.

Only one—Mustafa Khan Shefta—stood by him in his need. His wife's relatives, who had been his friends and great admirers of his poetry, would have nothing to do with him at this time. All this is reflected in a poem which he wrote from jail. I give a much shortened version of some of its verses. He begins:

> Here within prison walls confined I tune the lute of poetry
> That sorrow bursting from my heart, transmuted into melody,
> May sing a song to draw forth blood—that even from captivity
> I may work wonders in the world, and build a tavern for the free.
>> Thus shall I labour hard; hard labour consorts with imprisonment.
>> Bonds shall no longer choke my voice, and I will sing my heart's
>> lament.

He continues with two verses in which he speaks with bitter irony of his self-styled 'friends':

> Old friends, you must not incommode yourselves to come and visit me,
> And knock upon my door—I cannot open it as formerly.
> Imprisoned thieves are now my friends, and bow to my supremacy.
> I still their clamour, telling them, 'Outside there is no loyalty.'
>> The sentence passed upon me, true, is not for all eternity,
>> But from the world I look no more for joy that makes man truly
>> free.

And in contrast, he greets his new companions in prison and expresses the warmest gratitude to Shefta—Mustafa Khan Shefta—who alone stood by him:

> But prison warders, prison guards, assemble here, for I am come.
> Open the gates to welcome me as I draw near, for I am come.
> Friends, prisoners in your narrow cells, be of good cheer, for I am come.
> A poet's words, a poet's wisdom you shall hear, for I am come.
>> When friends and kinsmen all have turned away from me in my
>> disgrace
>> Why should I not find comfort here from strangers, captive in this
>> place?
> It was no policeman sent me here, no magistrate, no power of earth—
> This suffering, this imprisonment, was written in my fate at birth.
> And what of that? One noble man, Mustafa Khan, despite this dearth
> Of noble men, asks after me, and makes me see my own true worth.
>> He is God's mercy, God's compassion, sent in human form for me.
>> And if I die I shall not grieve, knowing that he will mourn for me.[13]

[13] p. 71.

His experiences taught him something he never forgot. It showed him how different were the values which respectable men professed from those which they practised when it came to the test, and convinced him that those few who, like himself, really practised the standards of conduct which society proclaimed, were calling down misfortune upon their own heads. It must have been with the experience of 1847 very much in mind that he wrote to one of his friends fourteen years later:

> Glory to God! I find that in so many things you and I have shared the same fate—ill-treatment from our relatives, grievance against our kin.
> ...You are a prey to grief and sorrow, but...to be the target of the world's afflictions is proof of an inherent nobility—proof clear, and argument conclusive....[14]

But after his release from jail, his fortunes took a turn for the better. He was befriended by men who had influence with the Mughal king, Bahadur Shah, and who secured for him what in many years of effort he had not been able to secure for himself, the patronage of the Mughal court. Three years later, in 1850, he was commissioned to write a history of the Mughal dynasty. In succeeding years he became the *ustad*—the mentor in poetry—of the king, gained the patronage of the heir-apparent and, briefly, a stipend from the king of Oudh. At no time in his adult life was he materially so well off as he was in these years. But, as a poet and writer, this was not primarily what he wanted. He saw himself above all as a great Persian poet, but what the king demanded of him was Persian prose, Urdu poetry, and even—most deplorably of all—Urdu prose. He is pretty blunt in expressing some of these feelings in the preamble to the history he was writing for the king.

> One night I said to my frenzied heart—a heart more wise than I: 'Grant me the power to speak, and I will go into the presence of that King whose court and its wondrous works rank with the garden of Iram, and will say, 'I am the mirror of secrets, and should be made to shine; I am the creator of poetry and should be cherished.' It said: 'O foolish one, these were words for another occasion; the time for them has passed. Now if you still have words to say, say, "I am bruised and need balm for my wounds; I am dead and need life to revive me."'

[14] p. 199.

Having thus made it clear that what the king has given him is very much a second preference he goes on to say how fortunate he is to be writing for the king, and then, being Ghalib, goes straight on to add how fortunate the king is to have Ghalib writing for him:

> ...I cannot feel too great a pride in my happy fate, that I have a master such as you to direct my labours; and as I would lay down my life for you I swear that you too must feel pride in the great kindness of fortune, that you possess a slave like Ghalib, whose song has all the power of fire. Turn your attention to me as my skill demands, and you will treasure me as the apple of your eye and open your heart for me to enter in.[15]

He was always very free in his behaviour towards the king. To this period belong some of the best-known anecdotes about his attitude to his religious obligations. Ghalib rarely allowed any serious discussion of this, and nearly always turned aside any serious criticism with a joke. When a man read him a lecture against wine-drinking and told him that the prayers of the wine-drinker are never granted, Ghalib replied: 'My friend, if a man has wine, what does he *need* to pray for?'[16] A *ghazal* which he recited before the king ended in the verse:

> Ghalib, you write so well upon these mystic themes of love divine
> We would have counted you a saint, but that we knew your love of
>   wine.

Hali says: 'I have been told that when Ghalib recited this *ghazal*, the king commented on the final couplet, "No, my friend; even so we should never have counted you a saint." Ghalib replied, "Your Majesty counts me one even now, and only speaks like this lest my sainthood should go to my head."'[17]

Once at the end of the Ramzan fast the king asked him: 'Mirza, how many days' fasts did you keep?' Ghalib replied: 'My Lord and Guide, I failed to keep one,' and left it to the king to decide whether this meant he had failed to keep only one or failed to keep a single one.[18]

[15] p. 75.
[16] p. 45.
[17] p. 103.
[18] p. 102.

When the king contemplated making the pilgrimage to Mecca, Ghalib, who was only rarely able to gratify the love of travel which I mentioned earlier, proposed this bargain to him:

> He goes to Mecca; if the King will take me in his company
> Gladly will I transfer to him the merit that accrues to me.[19]

Ghalib's period of relative prosperity did not last very long. In 1857 came the great revolt sparked off by the sepoy mutiny of May, and by the end of September, with the British re-occupation of Delhi, the Mughal court departed from the stage of history, never to return.

Ghalib may or may not have foreseen the revolt, but he did know that the British were moving towards the ending of Mughal power, and he tried to safeguard his livelihood beforehand. In his book one of the recognized functions of royal courts was to maintain good poets, and he therefore drew the attention of the wealthiest royal court in sight to the fact that he would be an eminently suitable recipient of its generosity. In other words, he wrote to Queen Victoria. In case she was not too familiar with the proper forms he explained them to her. He tells us:

> I indicated what my expectations were by saying that the emperors of Rum and of Persia, and other conquering kings, had been accustomed to bestow all manner of bounties on their poets and panegyrists. They would fill a poet's mouth with pearls, or weigh him in gold, or grant him villages in fief or open the door of their treasuries to shower wealth upon him. 'And so your poet and panegyrist seeks a title bestowed by the imperial tongue, and a robe of honour conferred by the imperial command, and a crust of bread from the imperial table.'

He didn't know, poor man, that the British monarchy was a horse of a very different colour from the monarchies *he* knew about. He received a polite reply which much encouraged him, but that was about all he ever did receive.[20]

Throughout the revolt itself Ghalib stayed in Delhi. He himself tells us what he did:

> On 11 May 1857 the disorders began here. On that same day I shut the doors and gave up going out. One cannot pass the days without

[19] p. 103.
[20] p. 113.

something to do, and I began to write my experiences, appending also such news as I heard from time to time.[21]

I think there can be no doubt that he was entirely out of sympathy with the revolt, not, I think, because of any fervent loyalty to the British, but because he was a shrewd and realistic man: he estimated that the revolt was bound to fail, and that failure would bring disaster in its train. Moreover he was a very self-conscious aristocrat, and it was evident to him that it was men whom he regarded as plebeian riff-raff that were the driving force of the revolt. His contempt for them, and his sympathies for the aristocratic elements who suffered at their hands, is evident in what he writes. But if his sympathies were not with the rebels, neither did he condone the excesses which the British committed, especially against the Muslims. He writes in a short poem of the time:

Now every English soldier that bears arms
Is sovereign, and free to work his will....

The city is athirst for Muslim blood
And every grain of dust must drink its fill....[22]

He wrote bitterly of the execution of three Muslim nobles—Nawwabs of three small estates in the neighbourhood of Delhi:

[They] have been taken separately, on separate days, and hung on the gallows tree, that none might say that their blood has been shed.[23]

And the events of 1857 deeply affected his own family—his wife (for whom however, as he bluntly tells us, he had no particular love), his two adopted children and his younger brother. Extracts from his diary here tell their own story.

I am face to face with misfortune, and wild and fearful fancies throng my heart. Formerly I had none to support but my one wife, with neither son nor daughter. But some five years ago, I took to my bosom two orphaned boys from the family of my wife, prime source of all my troubles. They had just learned to talk, and love for these sweetly-speaking children has melted me and made me one with them. Even now in my ruined state they are with me, adorning my life as pearls and flowers adorn my coat. My brother, who is two years

21 p. 114.
22 p. 129.
23 p. 128.

younger than I, at thirty years of age gave sense and reason to the winds and trod the ways of madness and unreason. For thirty years he has passed his life unaware, troubling no man and making no commotion. His house is apart from mine, at a distance of about 2000 paces. His wife and daughter, with the younger children and the maid-servants, saw that their best course lay in flight, and went away, leaving the mad master of the house with the house and all it contained, with an aged doorkeeper and an old maid-servant, to fend for himself. Had I had an enchanter's power I could not in those days have sent anyone to bring the three of them and their goods to me. This is another heavy sorrow, another calamity that has descended on me like an avalanche. Two tender children, tenderly reared and cherished, ask for milk and sweets and fruit, and I cannot give them. Alas! at such a stage the tongue falls silent. We live in anxious thought for bread and water, and die in anxious thought for shroud and grave. Constant care for my brother consumes me. How did he sleep at night? What did he eat by day? And no news comes, so that I cannot even tell if he be still alive or if the weight of constant hardship has broken and killed him....[24]

On Wednesday, 30 September, seventeen days after the taking of the city and the sealing of our lane, news was brought to me that robbers had attacked my brother's house and looted it, and the whole lane had been plundered. But they spared...[his] life and those of the old doorkeeper and old maid-servant....[25]

On 19 October, in the first watch of the day, my brother's doorkeeper with downcast face and dishevelled hair, brought me the joyous news of my brother's death. I learned that he had taken the road to oblivion and walked with hurrying steps: for five days he had burned in high fever, and then half an hour after midnight, had urged the steed of life to leap from this narrow pass. Think not of water and cloths, seek not for corpse-washers and grave-diggers, ask not for stone or brick, talk not of lime and mortar; but say how can I go to him? Where can I take him? In what graveyard can I consign him to the earth? Cloth, from the dearest and finest to the cheapest and coarsest, is not to be had. Hindus may take their dead to the river and there at the water's edge consign them to the fire. But what of the Muslims? How could a Muslim join with two or three of his fellows and, joining shoulder to shoulder, pass through the streets carrying their dead to burial? My neighbours took pity on my loneliness and at length girded their loins to the task. One of the Patiala soldiers went in front, and two of my servants followed. They

[24] p. 143.
[25] pp. 143–4.

washed the corpse, wrapped it in two or three white sheets they had
brought with them, and in a mosque at the side of his house dug
a hole in the ground. In this they laid him, filled up the pit with
earth once more, and came away. Alas for him who in his life of sixty
years passed thirty happily and thirty in sadness...God grant him
His mercy—for in his life he knew no comfort—and send some
angel for his delight and grant his soul to dwell in Paradise for ever.
Alas for this good man of ill-fortune...who in the years of sanity
never showed anger and in the years of madness troubled no
man...but lived his life a stranger to himself...and on the twenty-
ninth of the month of Safar, died.

> Bow down your head and ask for God's forgiveness;
> Where'er you do so, there His threshold is.[26]

A year later, when he looked back on events, what grieved him
perhaps most of all was the loss of so many of his friends. He had
friends in all camps—among the British, among the Hindus,
among the Muslims who aided the British and the Muslims who
supported the revolt—and he mourned all of them deeply and
sincerely.

He once wrote to Tufta:

> I hold all mankind to be my kin and look upon all men—Muslim,
> Hindu, Christian—as my brothers, no matter what others may
> think.[27]

And a year after the revolt he wrote:

> How grievous it is to mourn *one* loved one. What must his life be
> like who has to mourn so many? Alas! so many of my friends are
> dead that now if I should die there will be none to weep for me.[28]

This intense feeling of loneliness never quite left him through-
out the eleven years of life that remained to him. The British re-
took Delhi in September 1857, and at once expelled most of the
population from the city. *Hindu* residents were allowed to return
only three months later, in January 1858. It was more than two
years before *Muslims* were allowed to return and take up permanent
residence. All this time Ghalib was there, but his friends were
scattered far and wide. He comforted himself by writing letter after

[26] pp. 145–6.
[27] p. 107.
[28] p. 134.

letter to them, and the great collection which resulted constitutes, after his poetry, his greatest memorial. He once wrote to Tufta:

> In this solitude it is letters that keep me alive. Someone writes to me and I feel he has come to see me. By God's favour not a day passes but three or four letters come from this side and that; in fact there are days when I get letters by both posts—one or two in the morning and one or two in the afternoon. I spend the day reading them and answering them, and it keeps me happy. Why is it that for ten and twelve days together you haven't written—that is haven't been to see me? Write to me, Sahib. Write why you haven't written. Don't grudge the half-anna postage. And if you're *so* hard up, send the letter unstamped.[29]

From then to his death the situation did not change much in this respect. His friends could not come to Delhi, and he generally lacked the money, and increasingly, the physical health, to leave Delhi to visit them.

Life increasingly became a burden to him, and he repeatedly expressed a longing to die which I think he genuinely felt. Meanwhile it was characteristic of him that he never, to the very end, lost the sense of humour which was his main shield against the afflictions of life. At one time he was convinced that he would die in the Muslim year 1277, corresponding to 1860/1 of the Christian calendar. Two years before that date he wrote:

> You know that when despair reaches its lowest depths there is nothing left but to resign oneself to God's will. Well, what lower depths can there be than this that it is the hope of death that keeps me alive? And my resignation gains strength from day to day because I have only another two to two-and-a-half years to live; and somehow the time will pass. I know you will laugh and think to yourself I am talking nonsense. But call it divine revelation or call it superstition, I have had this verse kept by for the past twenty years....

He then quotes a verse which incorporates a chronogram—a form of words from which a date can be deduced—giving 1277 as the year of his death.[30]

As 1277 approached he looked forward to it more and more:

> How much life is left to me? Seven months of this year and twelve of next year. Then in this very month I shall go to my Master, where

[29] p. 149.
[30] p. 154.

hunger and thirst and piercing cold and raging heat will be no more. No ruler to be dreaded, no informer to be feared, no rent to be paid, no clothes to be bought, no meat to be sent for, no bread to be baked. A world of light, a state of pure delight.

> O Lord, how dear to me is this my wish:
> Grant Thou that to this wish I may attain!

> The slave of Ali, son of Abi Talib,
> Who longs for death's release,

Your servant,
Ghalib[31]

But in due course 1277 came and went, and Ghalib didn't die. One of his friends wrote to ask him why his prophecy had not come true. Ghalib replied pointing out that there had been an epidemic of cholera in Delhi:

> My friend, I was not mistaken about 1277, but I thought it beneath me to die in general epidemic. Really, it would have been an action most unworthy of me. Once this trouble is over we shall see about it.[32]

In other moods he was thankful that he had been spared. He replied to a friend who had written some verses to him congratulating him upon his escape:

> Lord and Master, to what can I compare the couplets you write in my praise and how can I thank God sufficiently for them? It is God's goodness to His servants that makes His chosen favourites speak well of such a disgrace to creation as I am. It seems that this great good fortune was written in my fate that I should come through this general epidemic alive. O God, my God, praise to Thee that Thou hast saved one who deserved death by sword or fire, and then raised him to high estate! I sometimes feel that the throne of heaven is my lodging and Paradise my back garden. In God's name compose no more verses in my praise, or I shall not shrink from claiming Godhead myself![33]

The mention of the cholera epidemic prompts me to say in passing that one of the most interesting aspects of Ghalib's letters is the picture they give of the long tribulations which the people

[31] p. 168.
[32] p. 193.
[33] p. 199.

of Delhi had to suffer during these years—sufferings to which the
events of 1857 were merely the prelude. Ghalib wrote in 1860:

> Five invading armies have fallen upon this city one after another: the
> first was that of the rebel soldiers, which robbed the city of its good
> name. The second was that of the British, when life and property
> and honour and dwellings and those who dwelt in them and heaven
> and earth and all the visible signs of existence were stripped from
> it. The third was that of famine, when thousands of people died of
> hunger. The fourth was that of cholera, in which many whose bellies
> were full lost their lives. The fifth was the fever, which took general
> plunder of men's strength and powers of resistance. There were not
> many deaths, but a man who has had fever feels that all the strength
> has been drained from his limbs. And this invading army has not
> yet left the city.[34]

But more relevant to my present purpose are the letters in which
he speaks frankly of himself, or of how he feels towards his friends.
It is striking how quick he is, despite the heavy burden of his own
troubles, to encourage and sustain them when *they* are in trouble.
Thus he writes to Mihr:

> First I want to ask you a question. For several letters past I have
> noticed you lamenting your grief and sorrow. Why? If you have fallen
> in love with some fair cruel one, what room for complaint have you
> there? Rather should you wish your friends the same good fortune
> and seek increase of this pain. In the words of Ghalib (God's mercy
> be upon him!),
>
>> You gave your heart away; why then lament your loss in plaintive
>> song?
>> You have a breast without a heart; why not a mouth without a
>> tongue?
>
> And if—which God forbid—it is more mundane griefs that beset
> you, then my friend, you and I have the same sorrows to bear. I bear
> this burden like a man, and if you are a man, so must you. As the
> late Ghalib says:
>
>> My heart, this grief and sorrow too is precious; for the day will come
>> You will not heave the midnight sigh, nor shed your tears at early
>> morn.[35]

[34] p. 181.
[35] pp. 185–6.

Two of his most famous letters were written to the same man on another occasion. Mihr had a mistress, a courtesan named Chunna Jan, and he was deeply grieved when she died. Ghalib writes to comfort him:

> Mirza Sahib, I received your letter with its grievous news. When I had read it I gave it to Yusuf 'Ali Khan Aziz to read, and he told me of your relationship with her—how devoted to you she was and how much you loved her. I felt extremely sorry, and deeply grieved.... Friend, we 'Mughal lads' are terrors; we are the death of those for whom we ourselves would die. Once in my life I was the death of a fair, cruel dancing-girl. God grant both of them His forgiveness, and both of us, who bear the wounds of our beloveds' death, His mercy...I know what you must be feeling. Be patient, and turn your back on the turmoil of earthly love...God is all-sufficient: the rest is vanity.[36]

We have no means of knowing how long an interval elapsed between this letter and the next, but it seems that Mihr could not overcome the grief he felt at his mistress's death, and Ghalib adopts quite another tone in an effort to rally him:

> Mirza Sahib, I don't like the way you're going on. I have lived sixty-five years, and for fifty of them have seen all that this transient world of colour and fragrance has to show. In the days of my lusty youth a man of perfect wisdom counselled me, 'Abstinence I do not approve: dissoluteness I do not forbid. Eat, drink and be merry. But remember, that the wise fly settles on the sugar, and not on the honey.' Well, I have always acted on his counsel. You cannot mourn another's death unless you live yourself. And why all these tears and lamentations? Give thanks to God for your freedom, and do not grieve. And if you love your chains so much, then a Munna Jan is as good as a Chunna Jan. When I think of Paradise and consider how if my sins are forgiven me and I am installed in a palace with a houri, to live for ever in the worthy woman's company, I am filled with dismay and fear brings my heart into my mouth. How wearisome to find her always there—a greater burden than a man could bear. The same old palace, all of emerald made; the same fruit-laden tree to cast its shade. And—God preserve her from all harm—the same old houri on my arm. Come to your senses, brother, and get yourself another.
>
> Take a new woman each returning spring
> For last year's almanac's a useless thing.[37]

[36] p. 186.
[37] p. 186.

His friends were indeed very close to his heart. Tufta once wrote saying that he was afraid Ghalib was displeased with him. Ghalib replies:

> What you have written is unkind and suspicious! Could I be cross with you? May God forbid! I pride myself that I have one friend in India who truly loves me; his name is Hargopal, and his pen-name Tufta. What could you write which would upset me? And as for what someone else may whisper, let me tell you how matters stand there. I had but one brother, who died after thirty years of madness. Suppose he had lived and had been sane and had said anything against you: I would have rebuked him and been angry with him.[38]

Very occasionally something happens that provokes an explosion. In 1862 he ends a letter to Alai: 'Stopped drinking wine on June 22nd: started again on 10 July:

> Thanks be to God! The tavern door is open once again!'[39]

He was asked to explain what this was all about, and in his next letter (of 28 July 1862) he does so:

> But these days all I have is the sixty-two rupees eight annas of my pension from the authorities and my hundred rupees from Rampur, and only the one agent from whom I can borrow and to whom I must pay interest and an instalment of the principal month by month. There is income tax to pay, the night-watchman to pay, interest to pay, principal to pay, the upkeep of my wife, the upkeep of the children, the upkeep of the servants—and just the Rs 162 coming in. I was in difficulties, and could hardly make my way. I found I could not even meet my day-to-day needs. I thought to myself, 'What shall I do? How can I solve the problem?' Well, a beggar's anger harms no one but himself. I cut out my morning cool drink, halved the meat for my midday meal, and stopped my wine and rose-water at nights. That saved me twenty rupees or so a month, and I could meet my day-to-day expenses. My friends would ask me, 'How long can you go on without your morning and evening drinks?' I said, 'Until He lets me drink again.' 'And how can you live without them?' they asked. 'As He vouchsafes me to live,' I replied. At length, before the month was out I was sent money from Rampur, over and above my stipend. I paid off the accumulated instalments on my regular debt. That left the miscellaneous ones—

[38] p. 209.
[39] p. 201.

well, be it so. My morning drink and wine at night were restored, and I again began to eat my full quota of meat.

Since your father asked why I had stopped drinking and then started again, read this part of my letter to him....'

He then turns upon one Hamza Khan, a *maulvi* who had once been tutor to Alai in his childhood and had now been ill-advised enough to have Alai write to Ghalib that it was time to act on the words of Hafiz:

Hafiz, old age besets you: leave the tavern now.
Debauchery and drinking go along with youth.

Without even breaking the sentence, Ghalib goes straight on:

...and give my respects to Hamza Khan and tell him:

You who have never known the taste of wine
We drink unceasingly

You see how He vouchsafes me drink? To make a name as a *maulvi* by teaching the *baniyas* and brats of Dariba, and to wallow in the problems of menstruation and post-natal bleeding is one thing: and to study the works of the mystics and take into one's heart the essential truth of God's reality and His expression in all things is another. Hell is for those who deny the oneness of God, who hold that His existence partakes of the order of the eternal and the possible, believe that Musailma shares with the Prophet the rank of the Seal of the Prophets, and rank newly-converted Muslims with the Father of the Imams. My belief in God's oneness is untainted, and my faith is perfect. My tongue repeats, 'There is no god but God,' and my heart believes, 'Nothing exists but God, and God alone works manifest in all things.' All prophets were to be honoured, and submission to each in his own time was the duty of man. With Muhammad (peace be upon him) prophethood came to an end. He is the Seal of the Prophets and God's Blessing to the Worlds.... Then came the office of Imam, conferred not by the consensus of men, but by God: and the Imam ordained by God is 'Ali (peace be upon him), then Hasan, then Husain, and thus onwards until the promised Mahdi (peace be upon him):

In this belief I live, in this I die.

Yes, and there is this more to be said, that I hold free-thinking and atheism to be abhorrent, and wine-drinking to be forbidden, and myself to be a sinner. And if God casts me into Hell, it will not be to burn me, but that I may become added fuel to the flames, making them flare more fiercely to burn those who deny God's oneness and reject the prophethood of Muhammad and the Imamate of 'Ali.... And now you graduate from school-mastering and take up preaching to seventy-year-olds. By dint of repeated fasting you memorize one verse of Hafiz:

Hafiz, old age besets you, etc.

and recite it—and that before one who has written twice and three times as much verse as Hafiz did, to say nothing of prose. And you do not observe that as against this one verse, Hafiz has thousands which contradict it![40]

The letter is interesting also as one of the very few places where Ghalib speaks seriously of his religious beliefs.

Besides letter-writing he spent much of his time in these years correcting and polishing the verses which his many friends who bowed to his poetic superiority submitted to him. It was a task which he enjoyed, and it is evident that he took great pains with it. Tufta, who was a full-time poet, and prolific one at that, once apologized for sending so much at a time for him to correct. Ghalib replied:

Listen, my good sir. You know that the late Zainul Abidin Khan was my son, and that now both his children, my grandsons, have come to live with me, and that they plague me every minute of the day, and I put up with it. God is my witness that you are a son to me. Hence the products of your inspiration are my spiritual grandsons. When I do not lose patience with these, my physical grandsons, who do not let me have my dinner in peace, who walk with their bare feet all over my bed, upset water here, and raise clouds of dust there— how can my spiritual grandsons, who do none of these things, upset me? Post them off at once for me to look at. I promise you I'll post them back to you at once. May God Almighty grant long life to your children—the children of this external world—and give them wealth and prosperity, and may He preserve you to look after them. And on your spiritual children, the products of your inspiration, may He bestow increase of fame and the gift of men's approval....[41]

But if he was kind he was also firm. And he had a very independent approach to the generally recognized authorities on Persian usage and Persian poetry. He once wrote bluntly of the poet

[40] p. 202.
[41] pp. 91–2.

Hazin—and Hazin was one whom he regarded as a *good* poet—that he had used an entirely superfluous word in one of his verses:

> In this couplet [which he has just quoted] Hazin has written one *'hanoz'* too many; it is superfluous and absurd, and you cannot regard it as a precedent to be followed. It is a plain blunder, a fault, a flaw. Why should we imitate it? Hazin was only human, but if the couplet were the angel Gabriel's you are not to regard it as an authority, and are not to imitate it.[42]

One of the tasks of the angel Gabriel, in Muslim belief, has been to convey the words of God to the prophets sent to mankind; he is therefore associated with divine eloquence.

And he once gave him even more general guidance:

> Don't think that everything men wrote in former ages is correct. There were fools born in those days too....[43]

On occasion he helped his pupils and friends to compose odes to various prospective patrons. In his day patronage was still the mainstay of poetry, and the first move for any aspiring poet who wanted the time and opportunity to practise his art was to find himself a patron who would be willing to support him, or at any rate *contribute* to his support. He would compose an ode in such a man's praise, present it to him, and hope for the best. Ghalib not only polished his pupils' odes for them, but sometimes even wrote them for them. He often comments sarcastically when some intended patron doesn't respond as Ghalib thinks he should. Thus he writes to Tufta:

> Listen to me, my friend. The man to whom you addressed your ode is as much a stranger to the art of poetry as you and I are to the problems of our respective religions. In fact you and I, in spite of our ignorance of religious matters, at any rate have no aversion for them while this is a fellow whom poetry makes sick.... These people aren't fit to be spoken of, much less to be praised.[44]

The only consolation in such circumstances was that the ode was generally a paean of praise in such exaggerated and unspecific terms that if it failed to secure the desired response from one prospective

[42] p. 95.
[43] p. 208.
[44] p. 231.

patron, it might, with a few alterations here and there, be made suitable for presentation to another. Ghalib used his odes in this way on at least one occasion. He had written an ode in praise of the last-but-one king of Oudh, Amjad Ali Shah, which for some reason had never been presented. Amjad Ali Shah was succeeded by Wajid Ali Shah. In Urdu and Persian metre the two names scan exactly the same. So when Ghalib had occasion to present an ode to Wajid Ali Shah he just changed the names and used the old ode. He wrote of what he had done: 'I put Wajid Ali Shah in Amjad Ali Shah's place. After all, God Himself did the same.'[45]

While he helped his friends in this way he had nothing much to offer from successful experience of this sort of operation. It was not until he was in his fifties that his own efforts in this direction had produced any very substantial results. Indeed, in one rather sourly humorous passage he reflects that his odes seem to have a disastrous effect.

> No one whom I praise survives it. One ode apiece was enough to dispatch Nasir ud Din Haidar and Amjad All Shah [kings of Oudh]. Wajid Ali Shah [the last king] stood up to three, and then collapsed. A man to whom I addressed ten to twenty odes would end up on the far side of oblivion.[46]

In the last years of his life, writing letters and correcting his friends' verses remained virtually his only occupations. His health was failing. He had started going deaf many years earlier and had sometimes suffered from persistent boils and other maladies which he ascribed to overheating of the blood. In 1863 he fell ill again, and this time it was a painful, long-continued illness which depressed and embittered him. The conduct of his friends at this time distressed him a good deal. He *told* them how ill he was, and asked their forgiveness if he could not reply at once to their letters or correct and return their verses promptly. But it seemed as though they simply refused to register how ill he was. He writes to one:

> Today I got another letter from my lord and master. I have not read it yet, but Shah Alam Sahib has written on the back of it, 'You have not replied to my letter'—although... I have already written to say that I no longer have the strength to write or the quickness of mind to correct verses. Why should I repeat the same thing a dozen

times? I conceive two possible ends to my present state: recovery, or death. In the first case I will inform you myself; in the second, all my friends will know of it from others. I write these lines as I lie in bed.[47]

Even Tufta was no exception, and Ghalib writes to him bitterly:

I wrote to you that I was well, and you believe it and offer thanks to God. I wrote what I had said about the severity of my illness was poetic exaggeration, and I expect you believe that too, although both these things were said ironically. I am sick of lies, and heartily curse all liars. I never tell a lie. But when all my attempts to persuade you I was telling the truth had no effect, then I wrote and told you I was well. And I did so after I had sworn to myself that so long as there was breath in my body, so long as my hand could hold a pen, and so long as I could contemplate correcting your verse, I would send back the very next day every sheet of paper you sent to me. Briefly, I am near to death. I have boils on both my hands and my leg is swollen. The boils don't heal and the swelling doesn't subside. I can't sit up. I write lying down. Your double page arrived yesterday and today I have corrected it lying here and sent it back. Take care that you go on thinking of me as in good health, and send sheet upon sheet to me. I shall never keep it more than a day. If I am near to death, well, what of that?[48]

His memory began to fail him more and more. He lost poems which people sent to him. To one such he writes:

Exalted sir, the *ghazal* your servant brought has gone where I am going—to oblivion. That is, I have lost it....[49]

Despite periods in which his health improved a good deal, he never really got better. His friends continued to pester him, though he even went to the extent of having it printed in the newspapers that he was no longer in a position to accept verse for correction. But, in general, the bitterness disappears from his tone. He writes to his friend Maududi:

Do you know the state I am in now? I am extremely weak and feeble. [My hands] have begun to tremble, my eyesight has got much worse, and my senses are not with me. I have done what I could to serve my friends, reading their pages of verse as I lie here and making

[47] p. 217.
[48] p. 217.
[49] p. 221.

corrections. But now my eyes cannot see properly and my hands cannot write properly. They say of Shah Sharaf Ali Bu Qalandar that when he reached advanced old age God exempted him from his religious duties and the Prophet excused him the prescribed observances. I expect of my friends that they will exempt me from the service of correcting their verses. The letters they write out of love for me I shall continue to answer to the best of my ability.[50]

By February 1869 he was on his death-bed. Hali describes his last days, and his very characteristic last letter:

A few days before his death he became unconscious. He would remain unconscious for hours at a time, coming to for only a few minutes before relapsing again. It was perhaps the day before he died that I went to visit him. He had come to after being unconscious many hours, and was dictating a reply to a letter from... Nawwab Ala ud Din Ahmad Khan [Alai], who had written from Loharu asking how he was. He replied, 'Why ask me how I am? Wait a day or two and then ask my neighbours.'[51]

A few days later he was dead.

He died knowing that men of his own age had not valued him at his true worth; he looked to posterity for the appreciation he deserved, and he was confident that he would one day receive it. He had written:

Today none buys my verse's wine, that it may grow in age
To make the senses reel in many a drinker yet to come.
My star rose highest in the firmament before my birth:
My poetry will win the world's acclaim when I am gone.[52]

I think he was right. His fellow-countrymen now acclaim him as one of their greatest poets, and to the extent that his work can be presented in other languages, the world at large will come to recognize his worth.

---

[50] p. 242.
[51] p. 260.
[52] p. 38.

GHALIB'S
Prose and its Context

PART I

Ghalib: Life and Letters

Ralph Russell and Khurshidul Islam

Family Background,
Boyhood and Youth in Agra

GHALIB'S ANCESTORS WERE OF TURKISH stock and came from Transoxiana—'beyond the river' as the Islamic world called it. But his grandfather emigrated to India in the eighteenth century to seek his fortune at the court of the Mughal emperor, and in India, at Agra, Ghalib was born on 27 December 1797. He has himself given an account of his family background in one of his letters, but in terms which become fully meaningful only if one knows something of the period of Indian history to which it relates.

When Ghalib was born the Mughal empire was dying, and indeed it was already in full decline at the time when his grand-father came to India. A century before that it had been one of the most splendid empires known to world history. Its territory had included all of northern India and had extended far south into the peninsula. Its wealth and splendour were known throughout the civilized world, and its internal stability was ensured by the general prosperity of its subjects. Its capital, Delhi, was, in Percival Spear's words, '...a great and imperial city...with anything between one and two million inhabitants. It was the largest and most renowned city, not only of India, but of all the East, from Constantinople to Canton. Its court was brilliant, its mosques and colleges numerous, and its literary and artistic fame as high as its political renown.' The empire's achievement was above all the work of Akbar, the greatest of the Mughal emperors, who died in 1605 after a reign of nearly fifty years; but during the century which spans the reigns of his successors, Jahangir, Shahjahan, and Aurangzeb, its splendour was maintained, and it drew to India in these years men of talent and ambition from all over the Islamic world, who saw that it was here that their abilities would find their fullest scope.

But this period comes to an end with Aurangzeb's death in 1707, and from that time the decline is catastrophically rapid. The multiplicity of factors which contributed to it makes the story a complex one. The first great blow was struck by the Marathas, a people inhabiting the territory of the present-day state of Maharashtra, whose struggle to throw off the Mughal yoke is perhaps the first which clearly indicates the character of the sub-continent as a land of many nationalities. The development of Maratha nationhood had already become fully evident by the sixteenth century, and the subsequent emergence of a great political and military leader in the person of Shivaji gave it a political cohesion which had hitherto been lacking. From small beginnings Shivaji initiated the struggle for Maratha independence, and so successful was he that by the second half of Aurangzeb's reign the imperial armies were engaged in an unceasing and ultimately fruitless struggle to reduce the Marathas to subjection. Aurangzeb's death left them in virtual control of their own national territories, and they then turned their attention increasingly to the plunder and domination of the territories around them. By 1720 they were raiding far into northern India, and in the course of time they aimed to establish their ascendancy throughout the sub-continent. Meanwhile the empire was itself disintegrating, weakened by fierce successive struggles for the throne between rival claimants, and by the virtual secession of its provinces to form independent states under hereditary dynasties of great nobles whom the centre was no longer able to control. By the mid-century the six provinces of the peninsula—the Deccan—had, in effect, seceded from the empire to form what was to become the princely state of Hyderabad. To the east, in Bengal, the British East India Company had become the real ruler. West of Bengal lay the province of Oudh, by now, in all but name, the hereditary, independent dominion of its governors. Between it and Delhi were a number of smaller dominions, while all the regions southwest, west, and northwest of the capital were either dominated by the Marathas or ruled by independent powers. Aurangzeb's own territory was increasingly restricted to a relatively small region centred on Delhi, and even within this region the real power was not his, but that of dominant groups of nobles who one after the other controlled the emperor until overthrown by more powerful adversaries. Yet Delhi remained a key centre of political development, for all the different powers in the land alike owed formal allegiance to the emperor and alike derived from him their title to power. For this reason the ever-shifting balance of forces brought repeated invasion and despoliation to Delhi, as contending forces fought for the control of the capital and of the emperor's person. In this struggle forces external to India were also engaged. From the northwest came the invasion of the Persian king, Nadir Shah, who in 1739 crushingly defeated the emperor's army, occupied Delhi, and returned home only after systematically despoiling the capital of all its accumulated treasure. After Nadir Shah's death, Ahmad Shah Abdali, the successor to the Afghan part of his kingdom, continued his policy, and from 1748 to 1761 invaded India repeatedly. By 1760 Afghans pressing down from the northwest and Marathas pushing up from the south came into collision, and in 1761 the two armies met in full force at Panipat. The Marathas were so decisively defeated that for ten years they were unable to assert themselves again; yet it was not they but the Afghans who were henceforth to drop out of the contest for the control of Delhi. For while Abdali, beset by growing troubles at home and faced with the sustained rebellion of the Sikhs of the Panjab, was too preoccupied to intervene, the Marathas recouped their strength and by 1771 had once again established their ascendancy. Only the British remained as serious rivals. But British strength was growing. To the control of Bengal, firmly established by the battle of Plassey in 1757, they had in 1765 added that of Oudh, defeating its ruler in battle and imposing a treaty which in effect made him their vassal. As their power continued to increase a contest with the Marathas became inevitable, and in 1803 the issue was settled by the Marathas' defeat and the establishment of a British supremacy which was to last for nearly a hundred and fifty years.

This is the background which alone makes intelligible to the modern reader Ghalib's letter of 15 February 1867, in which he briefly describes the history of his family fortunes:

> I am of Seljuk, Turkish stock. My grandfather [father's father] came to India beyond the river [Transoxiana] in Shah Alam's time.[1] The Empire was already weakend, and he took service with Shah Alam with a command of only fifty horse..., receiving a fertile estate sufficient to provide for his own livelihood and for the upkeep of his troop. But after his death this was lost in the anarchy of those times. My father Abdullah Beg Khan Bahadur went to Lucknow, and entered the service of Nawwab Asaf ud Daula.[2] After a short time he went to Hyderabad and took service with Nawwab Nizam Ali Khan.[3] There he had the command of a force of three hundred cavalry. He stayed there for several years, until he lost his appointment as the result of internal dissensions there. He then decided to move right away to Alwar, where he took service with Rao Raja Bakhtawar Singh [the ruler of Alwar]. There he was killed in some battle. His brother, my uncle, Nasrullah Beg Khan Bahadur was in the Marathas' service as Governor of Agra, and it was he who took charge of me. In 1803 when the action with General Lake[4] took place, the Governorship became a Commissionership, and an Englishman was made Commissioner. My uncle was ordered by General Lake to raise a force of cavalry, and became commander[5] of a force of four hundred. His personal salary was one thousand seven hundred rupees and he was granted in addition, for the duration of his life, land which brought in a hundred to a hundred and fifty thousand rupees. He had not held this position for much more than a year when he died suddenly. The cavalry force was disbanded and the grant of land replaced by a monetary allowance. This allowance I still receive. I was five years old when my father died, and eight years old when my uncle died....

The background which this letter outlines is one of the most important factors in Ghalib's development. His ancestors belonged

[1] Emperor Shah Alam came to the throne in 1759 and died in 1806.
[2] Ruler of Oudh, and nominally Wazir of the Empire from 1775 to 1797. Lucknow was his capital.
[3] Ruler of Hyderabad State from 1762 to 1803.
[4] Lord Lake commanded the British forces which defeated the Marathas in 1803 and replaced them as the controllers of Emperor Shah Alam, the masters of Delhi and Agra, and dominant power in northern India.
[5] Ghalib uses the English word 'brigadier'.

to a medieval world, where a noble entered the service of a more powerful overlord to whom he pledged his allegiance and his service in war in return for the wealth and rank appropriate to his position. But his grandfather migrated to India in a period when the centres of power were for ever shifting and when one's allegiance must shift with them if one was to survive; when, therefore, no commitment to any superior could be much more than provisional, and to engage one's loyalties too deeply was to court disaster. Ghalib's own account makes this clear, if only by implication, and if in his childhood he could not yet understand fully all the implications of the repeated changes of allegiance in his family history, they were nevertheless a part of his heritage, and his own life was to show their influence.

Ghalib's father had married into one of the most distinguished families of Agra. He had never set up house on his own, but had made his home with his wife's parents, and his own children— Ghalib, his brother Yusuf, and a sister known as Choti Khanam ('Little Lady')—grew up there—that is, in the house of their mother's parents. Little is known of the family except that its wealth and its influence were considerable; and occasional references in Ghalib's own writings show that he grew up in conditions where every kind of material comfort was assured to him. Proper provision was also made for his education, and he acquired the subjects traditionally taught to the sons of aristocratic Muslim families—Persian, a little Arabic, the elements of logic, philosophy, medicine, and so on. It was in Persian that his progress was most marked, and by the age of eleven, according to his own account, he was already writing Persian poetry. He had, he says, begun writing Urdu verse some years earlier, and Hali quotes an account which supports this claim:

> Munshi Bihari Lal Mushtaq says that there was a gentleman named Kanhayya Lal, who was a resident of Agra and contemporary of Ghalib's. On one occasion when he visited Ghalib in Delhi he asked him in the course of conversation whether he remembered the masnavi[6] he had written in the days when he used to fly his kite in Agra. Ghalib said he did not. Lala Sahib then said, 'It is an Urdu masnavi and I have a copy of it.' Accordingly he brought it and gave it to Ghalib, who read it with great pleasure. At the end he had put into the mouth of the kite the verse of some classical Persian poet:

[6] A poem in rhymed couplets.

My friend has tied a string around my neck
And leads me everywhere it pleases him.

Lala Sahib used to say that Ghalib was eight or nine years old when
he wrote this poem.

Kite-flying was a popular sport with adults as well as children,
and Ghalib recalled in later years how it had ranked with chess as
one of his favourite pastimes in his early youth. It was often played
as a contest. The kite-strings were treated with powdered glass, and
the object of the game was to fly your kite so that its string sawed
through that of your opponent. Elsewhere he admits indirectly to
less innocent pastimes, speaking in vague poetic terms of a love of
wine, woman and song—a love of which other contemporary writers
speak more directly, if in suitably delicate terms. In his society
these things were a graver offence against conventional morality
than they are in ours, for the drinking of wine is specifically
forbidden by Islam, and the purdah (*parda*) system—that most
drastic form of segregation of the sexes—left association with
courtesans as virtually the only way in which a man could freely
enjoy the company of women. On the other hand, society always
tolerates a good deal in those who have wealth and social status, and
Ghalib's society was no exception to this rule. An early marriage
in 1810, when he was thirteen and his bride eleven, does not seem
to have inhibited these enjoyments in any way.

He did not spend all his time on them. Some of it he devoted
to pursuing his enthusiasm for Persian, in which he continued to
show a most remarkable promise, and his prowess here was
sufficiently marked for him to be mentioned in contemporary
accounts by the time he was in his teens. Thus when a year or two
after his marriage he left Agra permanently to live in Delhi, he was
already something of a public figure.

Ghalib's own later memories of his boyhood and youth in Agra
(for even after he moved to Delhi, he often made prolonged visits
there) were, all in all, pleasant ones, as his writings show. True,
there are passages in which he expresses regret for the sensuous
pastimes of his youth, but these are largely conventional, and the
most that we can legitimately deduce from them is that he regretted
the amount of time he spent in such pleasures rather than the
pleasures themselves. It is when one studies his early work—work
written while he still lived in Agra—that one realizes that there

must have been other experiences that affected him profoundly and received expression in his early verse. For his early work is clearly that of one who knows the meaning of mental and emotional distress and has been forced by his experience to think deeply on the problems of life. To understand it, we are compelled to think of experiences which Ghalib himself preferred to forget. We must recall that he was left fatherless at the age of five, and lived through the rest of his boyhood dependent upon the kindness of others. He must have learned that his father was a man who had never succeeded in making his own way in life, remaining in the last resort dependent upon his wife's parents. In Indo-Muslim society, the position of the wife of such a husband, living in her parents' house, was not an enviable one. That of a young widow was even less so; and the fact that she and her children lived as dependents of a family higher in the social scale than her husband had been did not make things any easier. A sensitive and intelligent child such as Ghalib clearly was must have felt all these things keenly; and this sort of situation was prolonged by his being married, at the early age of thirteen, into one of the aristocratic families of Delhi, a family which, like his maternal grandfather's, was much wealthier and much more socially distinguished than his own. Given the aristocratic values of the society he lived in, it is more than likely that those upon whom he was dependent regarded him (perhaps even without being conscious of it) as an inferior class of being. Ghalib himself knew no other values; indeed, he was to cling to them throughout his life—and he must have felt at one and the same time both a secret sense that their attitude towards him was justified and a resentment that it should be so.

It is safe to say that these less pleasurable experiences combined with the enjoyable ones of which he speaks to form important aspects of his character which continued unchanged throughout his life. When in his teens he left Agra permanently to go to live in Delhi, he was a man who had experienced and enjoyed without any strong sense of guilt the pleasures which life can offer, including the pleasure of using the intellectual and poetic talent which he knew he possessed. A sense of the instability of relationships in the world to which his family belonged perhaps enhanced his sense that all that life can give is to be treasured and enjoyed to the utmost while it lasts, while at the same time it made him cautious of looking too far ahead, or of committing himself unreservedly to any one love for fear of too deep an involvement which might ultimately bring him to grief. This ability to hold himself a little aloof must have been strengthened by his boyhood experience of living in a family (and one which was a microcosm of aristocratic society) and yet never quite being a fully integrated part of it. This, together with his intellectual sharpness, produced a quality of ironic scepticism, and a sense of humour which both enhanced his capacity to enjoy life and armed him against its more bitter experiences. Finally this same early experience produced what is the most noticeable flaw in his character, while at the same time it spurred him to develop his poetic talent to the full. He had felt keenly that others had regarded him as inferior to themselves— all the more keenly because he himself accepted as valid the yardsticks—birth, wealth, profession, rank, and social and political influence—with which they measured him, and knew that he could not compete in these fields. He reacted with a jealous assertion of his worth, and for all one's sympathy with him, one cannot help smiling at some of the ways in which he did so. Thus, he always took an inordinate pride in his ancestry. Hali's words well reflect his feeling on this point:

> References to his family, its origin and its worth occur frequently in Ghalib's own writings. His ancestors were Aibak Turks, who traced their pedigree back to Tur, the son of Faridun [a legendary king of ancient Persia]. When the Kayyanis conquered all Iran and Turan, and the power and majesty of the Turanis departed from this world, the line of Tur was for a long time stripped of its dominion and its wealth. But the sword never fell from its hand, for among the Turks it was an age-old tradition that when a man died, the son inherited only his sword, and the rest of his property and wealth and home went to the daughter. At length, after many years, during the period of Islam, by the power of this same sword the Turks restored their fallen fortunes, and in the Seljuk dynasty the foundation of a mighty empire was laid. For several centuries it ruled over all Iran and Turan, and over Syria and Rum (i.e. Asia Minor), until at last after many years the Seljuks' empire came to an end, and their sons were scattered and dispersed abroad. One of them was Tarsam Khan, a man of noble birth, who made his home in Samarkand. And it was from this Tarsam Khan that Ghalib's grandfather...was descended.

Ghalib, in his best Persian prose style, writes that it was this illustrious forebear who, 'descending like a torrent from the heights into the depths below, left Samarkand and came to India'.

His inordinate pride that 'his ancestors for a hundred generations had been soldiers' recurs again and again in his life, and it was this pride which made him throughout his life live in the style appropriate to a distinguished noble, regardless of the fact that he rarely had the necessary resources to maintain this style of living.

His second assertion of his worth was made in the field of Persian—traditionally for several centuries the language of culture of the whole Islamic world. True, his mother tongue was not Persian, and his ancestors were not Persians but Turks. But he had been taught by a Persian, and his natural aptitude had enabled him to show a prowess which was indeed wholly exceptional. Moreover he took as his models only those poets who had Persian as their mother tongue, treating with contempt most Indian writers and scholars of the language. His contempt was in some measure justified, but there is a quality of exaggeration about it which springs from an awareness of his own exceptional talent and an over-anxious desire to force this upon the attention of others. This same awareness of his talent is perhaps mainly responsible for his view, which he held almost to the end of his days, that Persian was *par excellence* the language of literature, and that Urdu, by contrast, was an inferior medium for poetry and no medium at all for prose. Even his own Urdu poetry he regarded, or professed to regard, as of little or no significance, and whenever it came under attack he tended to reply by an aggressive assertion of his excellence in Persian—thus shifting his ground to a field where he knew that his critics could not easily follow him.

But if in his pride of ancestry and his claims for his Persian work there is sometimes a false and exaggerated note, in his third claim he is on the firmest of firm ground. He rests his final claim to men's esteem on his poetry, and here his claim is justified to the full. He does not hide the fact that a yearning to excel was one of the driving forces which made him strive for perfection as a poet. In the poetic prose of his Persian letters he writes,

> Alas for my fate! born to be struck down by misfortune and to see my granaries reduced to ashes! I had not the means to ride to war like my ancestors... nor the capacity to excel in knowledge and ability like Avicenna and the wise men of old. I said to myself, 'Be a darwesh and live a life of freedom'. But the love of poetry which I had brought with me from eternity assailed me and won my soul, saying, 'To polish the mirror and show in it the face of meaning—this too is

a mighty work. The command of armies and the mastery of learning
is not for you. Give up the thought of being a darwesh, and set your
face in the path of poetry'. Willy-nilly I did so, and launched my ship
upon the illusory sea of verse. My pen became my banner, and the
broken arrows of my ancestors became my pens.

Because he 'brought the love of poetry with him from eternity',
in the course of time he accomplished this 'mighty work' and knew
that he had accomplished it. As he did so he became convinced that
he would never win the universal recognition from his contem-
poraries which his achievement merited, and he reacted to this
realization in ways which are not always admirable. But he was
confident that posterity would recognize his full worth:

Today none buys my verse's wine, that it may grow in age
To make the senses reel in many a drinker yet to come.
My star rose highest in the firmament before my birth:
My poetry will win the world's acclaim when I am gone.

His confidence has proved to be well-founded.

Delhi and Calcutta, c. 1810–29

Ghalib made Delhi his permanent home within a year or two
of his marriage, but for some years he continued to spend long
periods in Agra, and there are letters of his which show with what
affection he still thought of it long after it had ceased to be his
home. Thus he writes to his friend Ziya ud Din Ahmad Khan,
who is visiting Agra:

Twin soul of mine, may Agra's air and water, distilled from hapless
Ghalib's sighs and tears, rejoice your heart. Though we are far apart,
yet the power of thought of my far-ranging mind has brought our
oneness to the point where distance dares not to draw near. Granted
that you have gone on a far journey and that the thought is near to
you that you are far from me; and yet while you stay in the city
of my birth, then truly we are near to one another. And I rejoice
because my love that sees afar has sent my eyes and heart with you
upon this journey, that I too, held in this place of exile [Delhi],
may pay due tribute of joy at the sight of the city of my birth. Let
no man look upon Agra as of slight account, but as he passes through
her roads call on God's preserving and protecting power to hold
her in its keeping. For she...was once the playground of my

love-distracted heart. There was a time when in her soil only the mandrake grew, and, save the heart, her trees would bear no other fruit, and the drunken breeze of morning ranged through her gardens to lift up and to bear away men's hearts so that the drunkard longed no longer for his morning draught, so that the pious bent his mind no more to prayer. To every grain of dust of that land in flower my body sends its message of love, and on every leaf in those fair gardens my soul calls benedictions to rain down.

I think of your good fortune, and...my eye is on the road to see when you will write, and weeps to see no letter ever comes to tell me how the stone horse[7] received my greeting and how the river's ripples made reply.

All the same, as the years passed, his ties with his birthplace gradually weakened and he came to regard himself as a Delhi man. With only one prolonged absence, he was to spend the rest of his life there.

At the time he settled there the city was just emerging, after a century of incessant troubles, into a period of peace. From 1739 to 1803 it had been repeatedly fought over, besieged, fought in and plundered—by Persians, Afghans, Marathas, and by rival aspirants for power within the imperial nobility itself. Much of it was ruined and deserted. Its population had fallen from the nearly two million of Aurangzeb's day to well under a tenth of that figure. Percival Spear has described how a traveller approaching it '...in the sixties of the eighteenth century would...observe not only the deserted tombs and ruined gardens which are to be seen today, but also miles of decaying suburbs, the relics of other Delhis which had been abandoned during the troubles of the mid-century.' It was no longer a great centre of literature. One by one practically all of its poets had left it and moved to less troubled centres farther east, above all to Lucknow, the capital of the British client state of Oudh. But 1803 brought a change. With the British triumph over the Marathas, Delhi and the empire passed into the hands of a power far stronger than it had known for nearly a century. No rival from without could effectively challenge its control, and no force from within could effectively oppose its will. Lawlessness and brigandage were methodically suppressed, and life and property in the city and on the roads leading to and from it were once more secure.

[7] A famous monument in Agra.

In the half-century of internal peace that followed, Delhi experienced something like a renaissance, a flowering of literature and learning to which men of the next generation such as Hali looked back nostalgically. Hali begins his preface to his life of Ghalib by evoking this memory,

> In the thirteenth century of the Muslim era[8] when the decline of the Muslims had already entered its most extreme phase, and, along with their wealth, renown and political power, their great achievements in the arts and sciences had also departed from them, by some good fortune there gathered in the capital, Delhi, a band of men so talented that their meetings and assemblies recall those of the days of Akbar and Shahjahan.... In the days when I first came to Delhi autumn had already come to this garden—some of these men had left Delhi, and others had departed this world. Yet even among those who remained were men whom I shall always feel pride at having seen, men whose like it seems that the soil of Delhi, and indeed of all India, will not produce again. For the mould in which they were formed has changed, and the breezes in which they grew and flowered have veered round....

Characteristically, the Delhi renaissance expressed itself largely in religious forms, for here as in medieval Europe, religion still concerned itself with every aspect of man's existence and prescribed the norms of his social and political behaviour no less than those of his private life. Religious learning was the one major department of intellectual life which had not declined in the city even in its darkest days. Indeed, the family of Shah Waliullah, one of the most important thinkers in the history of Indian Islam, 'had made the plundered capital the centre of the theological sciences' in the latter half of the eighteenth century. He can be regarded as the founder of the radical reforming trend in modern Indian Islam, and from his time dates a long-drawn-out conflict between the traditionalists in religion and the radical reformers who, like the Protestants of the European Reformation, thought of themselves as reviving the original purity of their faith. This conflict was raging vigorously in Delhi when Ghalib settled there. Along with the flourishing of religious controversy went the development of the studies necessary to it and traditionally associated with it—above

---

[8] Corresponding roughly to the nineteenth century of the Christian era.

all, Arabic and Persian. In the early nineteenth century Delhi was a famous centre of these studies, attracting students from as far afield as Balkh and Bukhara (in Central Asia). The period also produced its great hakims, practitioners of the traditional system of medicine inherited from the Greeks and developed and transmitted by the Arabs throughout the Islamic world. Their names are cited by Urdu writers alongside those of other prominent learned men of this period.

Urdu too received a new impetus. Shah Waliullah's son, Shah Rafi ud Din, produced in 1803 an Urdu translation of the Quran, a significant event not only in the history of religious movements, but also in the history of modern Urdu prose, of which it was a pioneer work. The drain of poetic talent to Lucknow ceased, and Delhi again became the centre of a group of distinguished poets, of whom Ghalib was one. This revival of poetry owed a great deal to the encouragement of the Mughal court which, deprived of all far-reaching political powers, turned more and more to cultural interests. It patronized Urdu poetry as its predecessors, before the decline of the empire, had patronized Persian. Indeed, it was an important patron of learning in general; the great royal libraries were well cared for, and there is evidence that they were available not only to the court but to Delhi scholars and students in general. In addition there were fine manuscript libraries in the private possession of individual nobles.

British ascendancy at this juncture did more than provide the security within which this intellectual flowering could take place. The British in India were still at the stage where their rule operated as far as possible through the old Mughal forms. Persian was still the official language; the educational system, the administration of justice, and indeed the administration in general were largely along the traditional lines. Many of the leading intellectual figures among the Muslims held important posts in the judiciary. The British officials themselves were men who were thoroughly at home in the Mughal setting. Many of them knew Persian well and had a genuine enthusiasm for it. They mixed freely, and were often on friendly and intimate terms with the Mughal aristocracy. There were even some who tried their hand at composing Persian and Urdu poetry. Through them their Indian acquaintances came into contact with western ways of thought too, and learned something of the material and intellectual achievement of Europe; and the general atmosphere of intellectual activity in Delhi led also to a widespread interest in western-style education. It was during these years that Delhi College was established. Here, alongside the traditional Arabic and Persian studies of Mughal India, western studies were also provided for, and some of the prominent Muslim divines of the day encouraged Muslims to take an interest in them. It is highly significant that many of the great Urdu writers and leaders of Muslim thought in the second half of the nineteenth century were men who had been connected with Delhi College in their youth. In short, Mughal culture and English culture met in these fifty years on terms of mutual respect. This situation was ended by the upheaval of 1857 and is only now, a century later, again being generally restored. Sleeman, one of the outstanding British officials of the period, and one who served continuously for forty-five years in the country, bore impressive testimony to the enthusiasm of the Indian Muslms for learning, and to the high standards which they attained:

> Perhaps there are few communities in the world among whom education is more generally diffused than among Muhammadans in India. He who holds an office worth twenty rupees a month commonly gives his sons an education equal to that of a prime minister. They learn, through the medium of the Arabic and Persian languages, what young men in our colleges learn through those of the Greek and Latin—that is, grammar, rhetoric and logic. After his seven years of study, the young Muhammadan binds his turban upon a head almost as well filled with the things which appertain to these branches of knowledge as the young man raw from Oxford...and, what is much to his advantage in India, the languages in which he has learnt what he knows are those which he most requires through life.

Sleeman goes on to describe some of the Arabic and Persian classics—works by Ghazali, Tusi, and Sadi—which the Indian Muslim most commonly studied, and concludes, 'These works...are the great "Pierian spring" of moral instruction from which the Muhammadan delights to "drink deep" from infancy to old age; and a better spring it would be difficult to find in the works of any other three men.' This last comment is typical of the sincere respect for oriental learning which characterized the best British officials of the day. Sleeman himself was, we are told, well-versed in Arabic, Persian, and Urdu, and he is not untypical in this respect.

It is not difficult to imagine how congenial this setting was to one of Ghalib's background and attainments. He took his place among the Delhi aristocracy, meeting them on equal terms and living in the same style as they did. 'He jealously maintained his sense of self-respect,' writes Hali, 'and always kept up the style he considered appropriate to his position.... He would never go out except in a palanquin or an open sedan chair. He never called upon those nobles who did not visit him, and never failed to return the visits of those who did.' He was fully involved also in the intellectual life of the city, dominated at this time by the religious controversies between the traditionalists and the radical, militant followers of Sayyid Ahmad Barelavi and Shah Ismail.[9] These controversies were not by any means confined to theologians; all educated Muslims were affected by them and, in general terms, allegiance would be given to one side or the other. Ghalib's own position was characteristically different. His closest personal friend during this period was Fazl i Haq, the main protagonist of the traditionalists and a man whose erudition, particularly in Persian, combined with his integrity and moral courage to win Ghalib's respect and affection. Yet Ghalib did not allow his admiration for the man to dominate his own judgements.

The same independence, the same reluctance to involve himself deeply in religion, and indeed a certain cheerful irreverence towards it is evident in an anecdote of an encounter with his father-in-law, Ilahi Bakhsh Maruf. Maruf was not only his elder; his family was one of the most distinguished among the Delhi aristocracy, and in addition Maruf himself was both a poet of established reputation and deeply religious man whose fame for piety and religious insight brought many to seek his spiritual guidance. But Ghalib was not unduly overawed by these considerations. Hali writes,

Ilahi Bakhsh Maruf... used to accept people as his disciples, and when their numbers swelled sufficiently he would get copies made of his line of spiritual descent through all the principals of his order, and distribute copies to each of them. On one occasion he gave Ghalib a copy of this pedigree and told him to make a further copy. But in the copy he made he wrote alternate names only, including

[9] Often called Wahhabis because of their resemblance to the similar movement in contemporary Arabia. But the Indian movement was in fact of independent origin.

the first and third, but omitting the second and fourth, and so on. When he had finished, he took the original, together with his 'copy' back to Maruf. When he looked at it he was extremely angry and asked him, 'What is this you have done?' Ghalib replied, 'Sir, think nothing of it. The pedigree is really a ladder on which one climbs to God. If you knock out alternate rungs, it merely means that one must put a little more spring into one's step; but one can climb it just the same.' This reply angered Maruf even more, and he tore up what Ghalib had written and had another copy made by someone else. And in this way Ghalib rid himself of this chore for good.

We have no detailed knowledge of the evolution of Ghalib's views on religion. He came of Sunni stock, but at some stage of his life became a Shia,[10] or if not actually a Shia, one closely sympathetic to Shia beliefs. But we do not know of any period of his life when he could have been described, in the conventional sense of the words, as a religious man. He seems to have accepted sincerely enough the main tenets of Islam, and equally, for all practical purposes, to have accepted them alone. As Hali puts it:

> From all the duties of worship and the enjoined practices of Islam he took only two—a belief that God is one and is immanent in all things, and a love for the Prophet and his family. And this alone he considered sufficient for salvation.

Hali might have added that Ghalib's attitude to God Himself was not always one of reverential respect. Thus he himself relates:

> He was lying on his bed at night looking up at the sky. He was struck by the apparent chaos in the distribution of the stars and said, 'There is no rhyme or reason in anything the self-willed do. Just look at the stars—scattered in complete disorder. No proportion, no system, no sense, no pattern. But their King has absolute power, and no one can breathe a word against Him!'

Open and implied criticism of God is common both in his poetry and his prose. He shared the view, expressed by Persian and Urdu poets long before him, that man is a helpless puppet in God's hands, who cannot perform a single act of his own volition, and yet is unfairly accused by God of being free, and hence accountable

---

[10] The two major communities of Muslims. Shias, who are greatly outnumbered by the Sunnis, differ from them mainly in rejecting the legitimacy of Muhammad's first three successors (caliphs) and accepting only that of Ali and his descendants.

to Him for his sins. Such sentiments are usually (but not always) expressed humorously in Ghalib's writings, but something deeper lies beneath the humour.

When Ghalib permitted himself to think of the God of Islam in these terms it is not surprising that he should have rejected Islam's more irksome restrictions, at any rate where he himself was concerned. Thus he had always liked wine, which is not permitted to a true Muslim; but far from attempting to conceal his liking for it, he openly sang its praises, recognizing at the same time, without any evasion, that he was breaking the laws of Islam in so doing. His drinking is usually treated humorously in his verse, and many anecdotes show that this generally was his attitude. He would not be drawn into serious discussions about it, and could rarely resist the temptation to make fun of people who tried to lecture him. Hali quotes one such instance.

> A man, in Ghalib's presence, strongly condemned wine-drinking, and said that the prayers of the wine-bibber are never granted. 'My friend,' said Ghalib, 'if a man has wine, what else does he *need* to pray for?'

It seems that he found wine a stimulus to writing poetry. Hali says,

> He often used to compose his verses at night, under the influence of wine. When he had worked out a complete verse he would tie a knot in his sash, and there would be as many as eight to ten knots by the time he retired to bed. In the morning he would recall them, with no other aid to his memory, and would write them down.... He wrote a pleasant and attractive hand...in the style that most Persians use, and though his letters were well formed, he wrote quickly and continuously.

Just as he never observed the prohibition on wine, so also he never kept the fast of Ramzan,[11] when for a whole month between the hours of dawn and dusk the true Muslim may not eat or drink or smoke or indulge in any other form of physical pleasure. To the orthodox Muslim, fasting is one of the five basic duties of his faith. Hali tells a story of how Ghalib was once visited during Ramzan by a pious Sunni maulvi who was apparently unaware of Ghalib's non-conformity in this respect.

---

[11] We give the word as it is spoken in Urdu. The Arabs call it Ramadan.

It was the middle of the afternoon, and Ghalib told his servant to bring him a drink of water. The maulvi sahib was astonished and said, 'What sir? Are you not keeping the fast?' Ghalib replied, 'I am a Sunni; I break the fast two hours before sunset.'

This is a joke at the maulvi's expense. Needless to say, the Sunnis and Shias alike fast throughout the hours of daylight. But Shias are in some respects more meticulous in the religious restrictions they impose upon themselves, and they do in fact break their fast later than the Sunnis.

In general he would not allow his religion or the lack of it to become a cause of friction in any of his personal relationships with men whom he liked and respected, and he evaded making it an issue either by refusing to be serious or else by saying whatever he thought the other wanted to hear.

Yet despite his avowed unorthodoxy he felt himself to be a part of the Muslim community. Hali writes:

Although he paid very little regard to the outward observances of Islam, whenever he heard of any misfortune befalling the Muslims it grieved him deeply. One day in my presence when he was lamenting some such occurrence, he said, 'I have none of the hallmarks of a Muslim; why is it that every humiliation that the Muslims suffer pains and grieves me so much?'

His intellectual grasp was aided by a remarkable memory, which so long as his faculties were unimpaired made it unnecessary for him ever to buy a book.

He never—or practically never—bought a book. There was a man whose trade it was to bring round books from the booksellers and hire them out on loan. Ghalib always used to get his books on loan from him, returning them when he had finished reading them. Any striking idea or point of substance that he read in a book engraved itself upon his memory, and he never forgot it.

These years in Delhi, and above all his close friendship with Fazl i Haq, brought about an important advance in his development as a poet. His keen intellect, his prowess in Persian and his determination to win himself a distinctive place as a poet had led him to write—whether in Persian or in Urdu—in a highly original, but exceedingly difficult style. Hali quotes one of his early Urdu verses in illustration....

Elsewhere he writes:

Not only were his ideas strange; his language was equally so. He regularly used Persian constructions...in his Urdu verse, and many of his lines were such that by changing a single word one could turn them into Persian. Some of his modes of expression were his own invention, unparalleled by anything that had gone before either in Urdu or in Persian.

Ghalib always did his best to keep clear of the beaten track and as far as he could, avoided ordinary forms of expression; and he was therefore less concerned to make his verse readily intelligible than to express it in an original and striking way.

Not surprisingly, Ghalib's verse came under heavy criticism from the start. During his Agra period he paid little attention to his critics, putting them down as ignoramuses incapable of understanding serious poetry; but he could hardly maintain this attitude when he found that in Delhi too such criticism of him was general. Much of it was conveyed to him through the characteristically Urdu institution of the mushaira. A mushaira was a gathering of poets, usually called together at the invitation of some prominent patron of literature, where each would recite his latest compositions. The proceedings were governed by well-known conventions, but within the conventional forms both appreciation and criticism could be frankly expressed—and in more than one way.

'I have heard,' writes Hali, 'that the poets of Delhi would come to mushairas where Ghalib was present and recite ghazals which sounded very fine and impressive but were really quite meaningless, as though to tell Ghalib in this way that this was the kind of poetry *he* wrote.' Azad[12] relates how on one occasion Hakim Agha Jan Aish, a well-known Delhi wit, recited these lines at a mushaira at which Ghalib was present:

What is the point of writing verse which only you can understand?
A poet feels the thrill of joy when others too can understand;
We understand the verse of Mir, we understand what Mirza wrote;
But Ghalib's verse!—Save he and God, we know not who can understand!

Others conveyed their criticism more privately.

[12] A contemporary of Hali.

On one occasion Maulvi Abdul Qadir of Rampur said to Ghalib, 'There is one of your Urdu verses which I cannot understand,' and there and then made up this verse and recited it to him:

> First take the essence of the rose
> out of the eggs of buffaloes—
> And other drugs are there; take those
> Out of the eggs of buffaloes.

Ghalib was very much taken aback and said, 'This verse is certainly not mine, I assure you.' But Maulvi Abdul Qadir kept up the joke and said, 'I have read it myself in your diwan;[13] if you have a copy here I can show it you here and now.' At length Ghalib realized that this was an indirect way of criticizing him and telling him that verses of this kind could be found in his diwan.

Ghalib would have resisted such criticism longer had not Fazl i Haq criticized him in the same way. Fazl i Haq was a man whom Ghalib both loved and respected. He regarded him as one of the very small number of his contemporaries who had a real command over his beloved Persian and a capacity to appreciate real poetry. Equally, Fazl i Haq felt all these things about Ghalib too. Hali sums up:

> Since Ghalib was basically a very sane man, he learned his lesson from the objections of his critics, and gradually came onto the right path. In addition, as Ghalib's relationship with Fazl i Haq became more and more intimate, he began to dissuade him more and more from writing verses of this kind, so much so that [when Ghalib compiled his Urdu diwan] he discarded at Fazl i Haq's suggestion practically two-thirds of all the Urdu he had written.

Thenceforth, without surrendering any of his originality, he was to express what he had to say in more intelligible form.

Hali's testimony to the great esteem in which Ghalib held Fazl i Haq is borne out by Ghalib's Persian letters. He once wrote to him:

> During these last days I formed the desire to compose a few verses in the manner of Urfi[14] on the oneness of God. Now, when the effort of my poetic power has reached the point where I have excelled both Urfi and myself, I am constrained to lay these verses before one whose true appreciation of verse can sustain a hundred such as me and a hundred thousand such as Urfi, and can indicate to each one of us his station [in Persian poetry].

---

[13] Collection of lyrical verse.
[14] A classical Persian poet.

The controversies around his poetry do not seem for the most part to have been at all acrimonious, for Ghalib was a popular figure in Delhi. Hali writes that he was, in appearance and temperament alike, an attractive man.

> Delhi people who had seen Ghalib in his youth have told me that he was generally regarded as one of the most handsome men in the city, and even in his old age, when I met him for the first time, one could easily see what a handsome man he had been.... Tall and broadly built, and with powerful limbs, he looked even then like a newcomer from Turan.

Many years later Ghalib himself recalls his youthful appearance in a letter to a friend:

> I am noticeably tall...and [in former days] my complexion was [unusually] fair, and people of discrimination used to praise it.... In this uncouth city [Delhi] everybody wears a sort of uniform. Mullahs, junk-dealers, hookah-menders, washermen, water-carriers, innkeepers, weavers, greengrocers—all of them wear their hair long and grow a beard. The day your humble servant grew a beard, he had *his* hair shaved. But, God save us! What am I prattling about?

This well illustrates his aversion to following the common herd, an aversion which made him go out of his way to be different, not only in his poetry, but also, says Hali, 'in his ways, his dress, his diet, and his style of living'. He was a man to whom people quickly felt attracted.

> There was a sincere welcome for all who came to see him, so that anyone who had once met him always wanted to keep up the acquaintance. He was always delighted to see his friends, and felt their joys and their troubles as his own. That is why he had innumerable friends, of every community and creed....

He had a great reputation as an amusing conversationalist, and this too drew people to him.

> In Delhi some people use the word *rath* [a sort of carriage] as feminine, while others make it masculine. Somebody said to Ghalib, 'You tell us, sir; is *rath* feminine or masculine?' Ghalib replied, 'My friend, look at it this way: when the passengers are women it should be feminine; and when they are men it should be masculine.'[15]

[15] He himself used it as masculine in the singular and feminine in the plural.

He was all his life extremely fond of mangoes, but

> one of his closest friends Hakim Razi ud Din Khan did not share
> this taste. One day he and Ghalib were sitting in the verandah of
> Ghalib's house when a man passed by in the lane driving a donkey.
> There were some mango skins lying in the road, but the donkey
> just sniffed at them and passed on. 'You see?' said Razi ud Din, 'even
> donkeys don't eat mangoes.' 'Of course!' said Ghalib, 'donkeys don't
> eat them.' Shefta used to relate how on one occasion Ghalib, Fazl
> i Haq and other friends were discussing mangoes. Everybody was
> expressing his opinion on what qualities a good mango ought to have.
> When everyone else had spoken Fazl i Haq said to Ghalib, 'Why don't
> you give us your opinion?' 'My friend,' said Ghalib, 'in my view there
> are only two essential points about mangoes: they should be sweet,
> and they should be plentiful.'

In short, Ghalib was well liked and had many friends; a number
of them were British, some of whom held important positions in
the British administration.

There are events of these years of which one would like to know
a good deal more. One such was a love affair which influenced
him deeply. Such things are not spoken of in Muslim society, but
Ghalib was an exceptionally frank man, and three times in his life
he wrote of this experience. The most specific detail comes latest,
in a letter, undated, but perhaps written in 1860, in which he says
that the girl was a *domni*—a singing and dancing girl—and that she
died suddenly. 'It is forty years or more since it happened,' he
writes, 'and although I long ago abandoned such things and left
the field once and for all, there are times even now when the
memory of her charming ways comes back to me and I shall not
forget her death as long as I live.' A moving poem written at the
time she died is included in his collected verse, and a Persian letter
to Muzaffar Husain Khan, who, it seems, had suffered a similar
loss, tells both of the grief he felt and of the resolve which he
afterwards made.

> 'In the days of my youth,' he writes, 'when the blackness of my deeds
> outdid the blackness of my hair, and my head held the tumult of
> the love of fair-faced women, Fate poured into my cup too the poison
> of this pain, and as the bier of my beloved was borne along the
> road, the dust rose from the road of that fortitude which was my
> essence. In the brightness of broad day I sat on sackcloth and clad
> myself in black in mourning for my mistress, and in the black

nights, in the solitude of sorrow, I was the moth that flew to the flame of her burnt-out candle. She was the partner of my bed, whom at the time of parting my jealous heart could not consign even to God's keeping. What pain that her lovely body should be consigned to dust! So beautiful she was that for fear of the evil eye of the narcissus, I could not take her to walk with me in the garden. What outrage that her corpse should be borne to the burial ground! When the fowler's prey has broken from his broken snare, what does he know of peace? And when the flower falls from the flower-gatherer's grasp...how can joy come near him? When the beloved one gives herself to her lover—what though an age of toil and torment go before—only a lover knows the measure of the love and kind compassion it betokens. A thousand praises to those loyal beloveds who make in measure more than due, restitution for the lovers' hearts their glance has stolen and give their very lives in love for them!

Yet with all this, though grief at a beloved's death tears at the soul and the pain of parting for ever crushes the heart, the truth is that to true men truth brings no pain; and amid this tearing of the soul and this crushing of the heart we must strive to ponder: Where is the balm that can banish this distress? Who has the strength that can twist the wrist of death? In God's name! A man must not rove far into the valley of these parching, pestilential winds and must, amid the sorrow that melts the soul, set out to learn the lesson of fortitude. You who have eyes to see, think upon this: that all the capital of those who venture all for love...is this one heart, lost now to the supple waist of their beloved, caught now and fettered in the ringlets of her curling locks. But where has a dead body the suppleness of waist to make the heart leap from its place? And where the curling ringlets to catch the soul in their toils? I fear lest this unlawful grief throw dust into the clear eye of the soul or slowly ripen till it bear the fruit of the heart's death. The nightingale, notorious for love, pours forth his melody for every rose that blooms, and the moth to whose great passion all men point, gives his wings to the flame of every candle that makes radiant her face. Truly, the candles radiant in the assembly are many, and roses bloom in the garden abundantly. Why should the moth grieve when one candle dies? When one rose fades and falls why should the night-ingale lament? A man should let the world of colour and fragrance win his heart, not bind it in the shackles of one love. Better that in the assembly of desire he draw afresh from within himself the harmonies of happiness, and draw into his embrace some enchanting beauty who may restore his lost heart to its place and once more steal it away.

Apart from this, the first period of Ghalib's life in Delhi seems to have been a happy one, until in a single year a series of heavy blows befell him. In 1826 his only brother Mirza Yusuf went mad (and was to remain so for the rest of his life); his father-in-law died; and he found himself for the first time in severe financial difficulties, with creditors pressing him hard to pay debts which he could not possibly meet.

In general it is not difficult to see why Ghalib should have found himself heavily in debt. He moved in the highest circles of Delhi society, and his pride would not allow him to live in an appreciably different style, even though he lacked the resources to support it. But the full details of the situation are obscure. In his boyhood and early youth it seems likely that he had had all he wanted from his mother's parents, and he may have continued to fall back on their resources to some extent during his early years in Delhi. But at some stage this source dried up—when and why we do not know—and this left him in the last resort dependent upon a wealthy and influential noble named Ahmad Bakhsh. Ghalib's family had in fact owed its livelihood to him since Ghalib was six years old, when his uncle Nasrullah Beg, who had been in the service of the Marathas, lost everything by their defeat at the hands of the British in 1803. Ahmad Bakhsh was at that time

> ...the agent of the Alwar Raja in his dealings with Lord Lake and the British. He so favourably impressed both the Raja and the British that he was granted the district of Loharu [some 100 miles west of Delhi] in hereditary rent-free tenure by the one and the principality of Firozpur [about 60 miles south of Delhi] by the other.

He was thus a man of considerable influence, and out of regard for the obligations of kinship (for his sister was the wife of Nasrullah Beg) he now used it to get Nasrullah Beg taken into the service of the British and provided with adequate means of livelihood on the sort of scale he had previously enjoyed. And it was Ahmad Bakhsh again who, when Nasrullah Beg died in 1806, intervened with the British authorities to provide indirectly for his dependents. Nasrullah Beg's grants had been, as Ghalib himself tells us in the letter already quoted (p. 32), for the duration of his own life only; but Ahmad Bakhsh now persuaded the British to make an arrangement whereby he was excused his payment of Rs 25,000 a year to them on condition that he made provision for

Nasrullah Beg's dependents and maintained a force of fifty cavalry to be made available to the British in case of need. A month later he got their authorization to reduce by half—from Rs 10,000 to Rs 5000—the amount allotted to the support of Nasrullah Beg's dependents. Ghalib's share under this arrangement amounted to Rs 750 a year.

For many years all went well, and it is more than likely that so long as money was coming in, Ghalib did not bother to enquire where it all came from and how much of it was his by legal right. But in the closing years of his life Ahmad Bakhsh took steps to provide for his sons' position after his death, and these measures, in the long run, spelt trouble for Ghalib. Ahmad Bakhsh had two wives; by the first he had a son named Shams ud Din, while by the second he had two sons, Amin ud Din and Ziya ud Din. (Amin ud Din was one of Ghalib's closest friends.) In 1822, with the consent both of the Raja of Alwar and of the British, he declared his eldest son Shams ud Din his heir. This settlement naturally displeased the two younger sons (the more so because their mother was an aristocrat, while Shams ud Din's mother was a common Mewati woman), and in 1825, at his father's wish, Shams ud Din assigned Loharu as a provision for them. In the following year he took over from his father, and in 1827 Ahmad Bakhsh died. The two younger sons were still very much dissatisfied with the position, and the feud between them and Shams ud Din intensified. It lasted for years, with both sides appealing repeatedly to the British authorities, who gave successive decisions, supporting now one side and now the other. Ghalib's Rs 750 a year was throughout payable by Shams ud Din; the fact that he was a close friend of Amin ud Din would have been quite enough to ensure that Shams ud Din paid Ghalib no more than he was obliged to, and seems in fact to have prompted him to pay him less than was due to him, and that too only at irregular intervals.

All this compelled Ghalib, perhaps for the first time, to examine his legal rights in the matter. To what extent he was already aware of them we do not know. He seems to have known the general tenor of the May 1806 agreement between Ahmad Bakhsh and the British, but not perhaps that of June 1806, which reduced by half Ahmad Bakhsh's liability to Nasrullah Beg's dependants. At all events, in the legal proceedings he now initiated he challenged the validity of the document of June 1806, declaring it to be a forgery.

After a fruitless visit to Firozpur, where Shams ud Din kept him hanging about, treating him with courtesy, but clearly prepared to concede him nothing, Ghalib decided to appeal in person to the British supreme authorities in Calcutta. He set out from Delhi in the spring of 1827, and was away for nearly three years, the greater part of which was spent in the British capital waiting for his case to be decided.

In the experience of these two years, the question of his 'pension' as Ghalib always called it, is of relatively minor significance, and may be cleared out of the way at once. Shams ud Din, his half-brothers, and Ghalib all had influential friends among the British on whose support they could count, and Ghalib had perfectly good reasons for hoping for a successful outcome. But as Hali writes, 'In the end he achieved nothing'. The date of the Governor-General's rejection of Ghalib's claim was 27 January 1831 and throughout his life he never received more than the Rs 750 a year laid down in the document of June 1806.

But if Ghalib did not achieve the purpose for which he set out for Calcutta in 1827, he gained greatly in other ways. The experience of so long and arduous a journey was itself a new and interesting one for him. Large parts of the journey were over unmetalled roads; part of the way he travelled by river; and the final stage, from Banaras (Benares) to Calcutta, he did on horseback. The journey brought him in personal contact with men of letters in all the important centres along his route, and he continued to maintain the contact by letter in the years to come. He first broke his journey for any considerable length of time at Lucknow, where he stayed for several months. From the 1770s it had virtually replaced Delhi as the centre of Mughal intellectual life, and a second generation of Urdu poets and of Persian and Arabic scholars was now flourishing there. Its leading Urdu poet Nasikh now became Ghalib's personal friend, and an appreciable part of Ghalib's early verse shows his influence. Hali writes:

When Ghalib left Delhi on his journey to Calcutta he had not at first intended to stop anywhere on the way. But influential people in Lucknow had long wanted him to visit the city, and when he reached Kanpur (Cawnpore) he decided to do so. In those days Nasir ud Din Haidar was king [of Oudh] and Raushan ud Daula his deputy. Ghalib was given an excellent reception in Lucknow, and was highly spoken of to Raushan ud Daula.

Ghalib had hoped to be granted an audience by the king, and to receive enough from him to defray a substantial part of the expense of his journey to Calcutta. Although his hopes in this respect were disappointed, he stayed on in Lucknow for several months, and his Persian letters show how many contacts he made there. Some of these were to serve him in good stead later on.

In October he went on his way, passing through Banda, Allahabad and Banaras, and finally reaching Calcutta on 20 February 1828—near enough a whole year after he had set out from Delhi. Banaras particularly enchanted him, and he wrote a Persian poem in its praise which he entitled *The Lamp of the Temple* in allusion to its fame as a holy city of the Hindus. More than thirty years later he still remembered it with pleasure, writing on 12 February 1861 to his friend Sayyah:

> What praise is too high for Banaras? Where else is there a city to equal it? The days of my youth were almost over when I went there. Had I been young in those days I would have settled down there and never come back this way.

Calcutta too, he liked. He admired the greenery everywhere, and, less understandably, seemed even to have liked its climate. During his stay there he became involved—for the first time in his life, but by no means the last—in an acrimonious public dispute with Indian scholars of Persian, who were at that time no less numerous in Calcutta than in other centres of Mughal culture. The incident began at a mushaira where poets, Ghalib among them, had gathered to recite their verse. When Ghalib recited his Persian poem, objections were raised to the language of some of his lines, and these were supported by reference to the authority of Qatil, an eighteenth-century Indian poet and lexicographer of Persian who was generally acknowledge by Indian scholars of Ghalib's day as a great authority. Hali writes,

> But except for Amir Khusrau[16] Ghalib did not hold any Indian poet of Persian in esteem. In one of his letters he writes, 'Among the Indians, except for Khusrau of Delhi there is no established master. Faizi's[17] poetry is all right in parts.' For this reason he considered men like Qatil and Waqif of no account whatever. At the mention

[16] A famous Persian poet of thirteenth-century Delhi.
[17] A famous poet of the reign of Akbar (1556–1605).

of the Qatil's name he turned up his nose and said, 'I do not accept the word of Dilwali Singh, the Khatri[18] of Faridabad; only the work of Persians can be accepted as authoritative.' (Mirza Qatil was a convert to Islam. Before his conversion his name had been Dilwali Singh, a Khatri from Faridabad, in Delhi district. After he became a Muslim he went to Lucknow, where he was very highly regarded.) This answer raised a storm among his opponents, and he was inundated with objections.

Although plenty of others in Calcutta took his side in the dispute he thought it politic to retreat before the storm, and wrote a poem entitled *An Adverse Wind*, in which he attempted to placate his opponents while at the same time maintaining (albeit apologetic-ally) his original stand. His reasons for seeking peace were probably largely diplomatic ones, for among those who had sided against him in this dispute were influential men whose support could be valuable to him in fighting his case for his 'pension'. He might have known beforehand that to provoke this kind of dispute would land him in trouble, but his enthusiasm for Persian and his conviction of the rightness of his standards of judgement where Persian was concerned made it impossible for him to hold back. Now and throughout his life his zeal in his own defence led him into exag-gerations; but his position was basically sound, and it is significant that during the Calcutta controversy he was supported by a Persian, an envoy of the Persian prince Kamran who was in Calcutta at the time.

This incident was not his only distasteful experience in Calcutta, and as time went on and he made no discernible progress in his case, he sometimes wrote bitterly of the place. One of his short Persian poems gives an imaginary dialogue between himself and an unnamed adviser:

> I said to him, 'So tell me, then, what is Calcutta like?'
> He said, 'You cannot find its like in all the seven climes.'
> I said, 'What calling would a man do best to follow here?'
> He said, 'There is no calling you can follow free from fear.'
> I said, 'Then tell me, what course would you recommend to me?'
> He said, 'The course of giving up all thought of poetry.'
> I said at last, 'It is in search of justice I have come.'
> He said, 'Then run away! Why beat your head against a stone?'

---

[18] The name of a Hindu caste.

But his subsequent recollections of Calcutta were often pleasant. In a Persian letter written after his return to Delhi he says,

One should be grateful that such a city exists. Where else in the world is there a city so refreshing? To sit in the dust of Calcutta is better than to grace the throne of another dominion. By God, had I not been a family man, with regard for the honour of my wife and children, I would have cut myself free and made my way there. There I would have lived till I died, in that heavenly city, free from all cares. How delightful are its cool breezes, and how pleasant is its water! How excellent are its pure wines and its ripe fruits!

If all the fruits of Paradise lay there outspread before you
The mangoes of Calcutta still would haunt your memory!

Ghalib's love of mangoes alone would have made Calcutta dear to him. There are numberless anecdotes on this point, relating to all periods of his life.

In a short Urdu poem, which the strait-laced Hali does not quote, it is other pleasant recollections which are given more prominence.

Ah me, my friend! The mention of Calcutta's name
Has loosed a shaft that pierces to my very soul.
Its greenery and verdure take away your breath;
Its women's charms are such that none escapes them whole.
Their glances pierce the armour of the stoutest breast;
What heart withstands the blandishments of forms so fair?
All freshness and all sweetness are its luscious fruits;
Its mellow wines are pleasing beyond all compare.

Pleasant memories of mangoes and of pretty women were not Calcutta's only gifts to him. The city was the British capital, a modern city which had grown up under British rule on a site where before their coming there had been only three small villages. English influence, English ways, and English material progress were more evident there than anywhere else in India, and Ghalib's lively intelligence and the strong element of modernity in him which had long since been evident cannot have failed to feed on all these things. He knew neither English nor Bengali, but he had Muslim friends who had been resident there for some time, and Persian was in those days still a medium through which he could converse with appreciable numbers of Muslims, Bengalis, and Englishmen alike. Ram Mohan Roy, the first great intellectual figure in modern Indian history to take up and propagate with enthusiasm much of the outlook of modern Europe, had already made an impact in Calcutta, and *Mirat ul Akhbar* (Mirror of News), the Persian newspaper which he published, was only one of several which were current in Calcutta at the time. Ghalib's Persian letters speak of a number of them. At that time there were no newspapers in Delhi or anywhere else in northern India, and some years were yet to pass before the printing press made its appearance there. Ghalib formed during this period the habit of reading newspapers which remained with him for the rest of his life. From it he gained a range of general knowledge and a widening of his intellectual horizons which his contemporaries in Delhi could not yet attain. Thus his nearly two years' sojourn in Calcutta must have still further strengthened his appreciation of the new which his own temperament and the atmosphere of Delhi in the early days of British rule had already made a part of him.

Delhi, 1829–47

Ghalib arrived back in Delhi on 29 November 1829, with none of his financial difficulties solved; and when fourteen months later the Governor-General rejected his claims absolutely, it was clear that no certain prospect of solving them remained.

It is more than likely that by this time Ghalib had long since resigned himself to the prospect of defeat. At some earlier stage he had written in anger and disgust to Siraj ud Din Ahmad:

> A report on my case has been sent up to a higher court. And, God save me, what a report!—a report involved and involuted as a Negro's curling hair, a report full of tumult and disorder as a lover's distracted heart, a report to encompass the murder of a world of hopes and longings, a report to call forth a decree to dash my honour in the dust.

Ghalib's debts at this time amounted to more than Rs 40,000—that is to nearly sixty times the amount of his regular annual income. But the anxieties which this caused him were only a part of his misfortunes. His adversary Shams ud Din was both influential and popular in Delhi society, and Ghalib's failure to win his case against him gave many people a good deal of satisfaction. He says in one of his letters that he became an object 'of ridicule to all and of censure to some', and for a time he kept very much to himself and avoided the society of others. Within a few years he was subjected to further humiliation when two of his creditors grew tired of waiting and took him to court. The court ordered him to pay Rs 5000 or go to jail. He had no means of paying, but fortunately for him, prominent men were treated with special consideration in the Delhi of those days, and were safe from arrest so long as they kept to their own houses. Ghalib's period of 'imprisonment' amounted therefore to no more than house-arrest. All the same, the indignity would have rankled deeply even with men far less touchy about their honour than Ghalib was, and he writes bitterly to his Lucknow friend and fellow-poet Nasikh, who had written to ask him for news of what was happening. The letter is in Persian, but he writes with a feeling and spontaneity which for the most part leaves him no time to produce the elaborate prose which his Persian letters generally exemplify:

> Four months have passed since I retired to my corner and closed the gates of access on friend and stranger alike. I am not in prison, but I eat and sleep as any prisoner does, and may I be branded as an infidel if in these few days I have not suffered torture and distress more than twofold the torment that the infidel suffers in a hundred years in Hell. Urfi has said:
>
> > The bitter fragrance of the poison Fate poured in my cup
> > Has burnt to ash the heart that could have felt hope and despair.

The letter goes on to speak of a still more painful experience that befell him while he was still undergoing this 'imprisonment'. On 22 March 1835, William Fraser, the British Resident of Delhi, was shot dead. Ghalib was closely involved in two ways. First, he knew Fraser personally, and was genuinely attached to him. Though the details of their relationship are not known, it is easy to see on what it was based. Fraser was, like Ghalib, a proud and independent man, impatient of convention and filled with intellectual curiosity. 'He lived as a solitary among his colleagues, saying that they had no rational conversation. But when he met the botanist Jacquemment, he travelled two days' journey out of his way to enjoy his company.' Jacquemment described him as 'an excellent man with great originality of thought, a metaphysician to boot....' In marked contrast with his lack of interest in his British colleagues was his easy intimacy with the aristocratic families of Delhi, an intimacy based on an insight into and respect for their culture. An Indian contemporary tells us that he possessed a substantial library of Persian and Arabic books. All these things must have won him Ghalib's sincere regard. But the two men were also connected by a further tie, for Fraser had espoused the cause of Ghalib's friends Amin ud Din and Ziya ud Din against their kinsman Shams ud Din. The tone in which Ghalib continues his letter to Nasikh is therefore understandable:

> While I dwelt in this same seclusion and distress, a cruel, ruthless man who knew not the fear of God—may he dwell in eternal torment—in the blackness of the night killed with a musket's shot William Fraser Sahib Bahadur, the Resident of Delhi and unhappy Ghalib's kindly benefactor. My heart felt afresh the grief of a father's death. My soul was shaken within me; a mighty sorrow seized in its grip all my power of thought and burned to ashes the granary of my content and scraped from the page of my spirit all trace of the writing of hope. As chance would have it, far-sighted men saw signs that did not err, and on their foundation [Karim Khan] a horseman in the service of the Lord of Firozpur [Shams ud Din] was seized on a charge of the murder of that officer of lofty rank and noble qualities. The Magistrate of the City already knew me and felt the bond of mutual regard. In the seclusion I have spoken of, when like the owl I flew by night alone, from time to time I went to him at night to pass an hour or two in pleasant converse. When this event took place he made me his partner to pry into the mystery, until at last the crime was brought home to the Lord of Firozpur, and on the Government's command he was made prisoner, along with others who were close to him, and a force of police was sent to his estate. The men of Delhi knew that he and I were at odds, and now all assailed me and laid at my door the seizure of that man of black ingratitude and killer of a just ruler. That is, the men of Delhi, high and low, have spread abroad the slander that Shams ud Din Khan is innocent, and Fathullah Beg Khan and Asadullah Khan [Ghalib] have out of their abundant malice caught the authorities in a web of lies they have woven, drawn them from the path of right, and plunged poor Shams ud Din into disaster. And in all this the best of it is this, that Fathullah Beg Khan is himself the uncle's son of the Lord of Firozpur. In short the stage is come when the slanderers of Delhi repeat their constant curses upon me. At first my heart felt only the grief of William Fraser Sahib's death; but now that the man who killed him is identified, and the slanderers of the city loathe and shun me, I raise my voice each morning in prayer

to that God who strikes down the oppressor and succours the oppressed, and call on Him to speed the day when that ruthless, overweening man shall pay the penalty and be hurled from the heights to the gallows' degradation. And I know that my desire will prevail and my prayer will find acceptance.... Within a month the outcome will be settled....

Things did indeed come to an issue soon after. Investigations showed that Karim Khan, the actual murderer, had acted on the direct instructions of Shams ud Din, and on 3 October 1835, both of them were publicly hanged. In a further letter to Nasikh, Ghalib tells him of this outcome:

> If I am late in sending you his letter do not conclude my affection for you fades. What could I do? For my resolve was set upon a mighty task and my eyes upon a lofty aim, until the turmoil was stilled and each one met the end he merited. The ruler of Mewat [Shams ud Din], like Karim Khan his man, was hanged by the neck and sent into oblivion:
>   The day must come when every man reaps what he sowed.

He goes on to say that the Firozpur estate and all its appendages had been confiscated, but that a full and final settlement had not yet been made. When it was, he hoped to gain by it:

> My eyes still wait to see the token of my triumph. To speak more plainly, what the Lord of Firozpur used to pay me was less than was my due; and if the government pays no more than that sum, I shall not rest content.

Meanwhile he had more immediate difficulties to face. His first letter had not spoken too strongly of the strength of feeling in Delhi over the Fraser murder, and if his love for Fraser made him feel a fierce satisfaction at Shams ud Din's execution, many of his fellow-citizens of Delhi felt differently. Among Shams ud Din's numerous well-wishers there were many who believed him to be innocent and suspected his enemies—and Ghalib among them—of having conspired to get him hanged. The strength of popular feeling may be gauged from the fact that for some years Shams ud Din's tomb was a place of pilgrimage, and that in the 'Mutiny'—twenty-two years later—the insurgents completely destroyed Fraser's tomb, while leaving those of other prominent British officials unmolested.

A letter written about the same time to Mir Azam Ali, who taught in a Muslim seminary in Agra, reflects the same bitterness and distress as his letters to Nasikh, and is of special interest because in it he reviews the whole course of his life since he left Agra for Delhi many years earlier. He writes:

[Your letter] recalled to my mind that the world in former days held a city that I called my birthplace and men I called my friends. Your asking after me was like a dagger, thrust into the very vitals of my mind; and now you may see and wonder at the blood that drips from my lamenting lay. The years of separation which you, my master, reckon at sixteen years and I who write this letter deem to be not less than twenty, have been the sharp point of a knife scraping the writing of all peace and happiness from the page of my heart. When I first came to Delhi, my goblet held still the lees of the wine of heedlessness, and some few days of my life were given up to seek the satisfaction of my sensuous desires. I wandered erring in these ways until my drunken head was reeling, and, lost to myself, my feet strayed from the tavern floor and stumbled in the pit. I rose, with my whole body bruised and broken, and with dust upon my head and face. From one side came the onset of my brother's madness, and on the other rose the angry outcry of my creditors; such turmoil came upon me that my breath lost the way to my lips and my sight the way to the windows of my eyes, and the world lit by the shining lamps of heaven was darkened in my sight. I sewed my lips against speech and closed my eyes to the sight of myself, and set myself to live with my grief through world upon world of ruin and disaster.... Lamenting the injustice of the age I pressed my breast against the edge of the sharp sword and reached Calcutta. Those who held sway there strengthened my spirit with kindness and compassion, bringing me hope that the road that lay blocked before me would be opened up. And the desire to go out into the wilderness and die, which had brought me out of Delhi, departed from me; and the yearning for the temples of the god of fire and for the taverns of Shiraz[19] which tugged at my heart, calling me to Persia, left my soul. Two years I dwelt in that place of radiance, as though it were a shrine and I in constant attendance there. When the Governor-General prepared to go to Hindustan,[20] I hastened before him to Delhi. But the times turned against me, and the building I was building fell to ruin. Six years have passed since then and I have

[19] The ancient religion of Persia was Zoroastrianism. Shiraz was the city of Hafiz, the great classical lyric poet of Persia.

[20] In the more restricted sense of the central region of the northern plains.

thrown to the winds all thought that I might prosper. I give up my heart to the high hope of sudden death and keep to my corner, closing the doors of access on friend and stranger alike.

If in the midst of this grief and sorrow of which I have told you but a part, my letters cease and words fail me and my pen and voice write and speak no more, and I forget the august elders of the city of my birth, then in the realms of justice I go innocent. But what of those who hold high rank in the land of love and loyalty, and care not for those who lie in distant parts, and do not even seek to know whether they live or die? If I should speak of them, then would the steed of grievance course side by side with the steed of speech. If in this field I should contest with you, how will you score against me? And if you ignore so weak an adversary, what answer will you render to God, Who is not weak? None of my countrymen has helped me bear my grief, and I must think that in this world I *have* no country.

He goes on to reject bitterly and emphatically a suggestion that he should come to Agra to plead his case before a court about to assemble there. For the man under whose authority it meets 'is that same self-willed, callous man whose dagger of oppression struck me down, and whose black glances darkened my days. Grant me, O God, that he too suffer loss, and the things that he has made my eyes to see, Fate may compel him too to look upon!'

In all these hardships Ghalib seems to have found his main consolation in writing, and he comforts himself with the idea that his greatness as a poet necessarily means misfortunes without end. One of his poems of this period contains the lines:

I asked the Mind Supreme why Destiny
Decreed for me life-long captivity.
It said, 'Ill-starred one, are you then a crow,
Caught in the snare only to be set free?
You are nightingale, held in a cage
So that the age may hear your melody.

A Persian letter written some years later to his friend Haqir amplifies the same thought.

Words cannot tell of hapless Ghalib's failures. One might say that he has no God to care for him. And intellect bears witness and observation argues that cutting and wounding alone makes beauty and excellence shine forth. That the beauty of the cypress may appear, men cut and wound it. That the wine may be worthy to be passed round, they press and strain it. Until the reed be cut and shaped it cannot be a pen; until the sheet of paper be cut and reduced to pages it cannot be the bearer of a letter. Assuredly in this great workshop of creation and destruction He must needs create in order to destroy, and must needs destroy in order to create. He made me out of earth, and then exalted me to the skies. For some years He had regard for my exalted station; and then He hurled me down to earth, and that too with such force that my whole form made its imprint in the earth—and such an imprint that no knife can scrape this imprint from it. One would think that these accidents of creation and destruction bore me away from the world and brought to it in my place a broken man, a man so broken that death and life, laughter and weeping seem the same to him. O God, grant that this form that made its imprint on the earth and this imprint on the earth that this form made, may soon be removed from the face of the earth and consigned to the bosom of the earth.

It was during these years that he first compiled the volume of his selected Urdu verse, discarding much of his earlier work as has already been described. He also gathered together his Persian verse and prose, and wrote many new Persian ghazals at this time. The Persian prose collection was probably compiled by about 1840 (though it was not printed until 1849), and is in five sections, of which the third and the fifth are the most interesting. In the third section Ghalib quotes selected lines from his Persian verse and instances appropriate contexts where they might be quoted in letter-writing; in the fifth he assembles his Persian letters to his friends. These include letters to many of the most famous names in the literature and scholarship of the nineteenth-century Muslim India, and show how well-established Ghalib's reputation was. It is worth stressing that these letters were written with the most elaborate care—as is clear from some of those already quoted—and Ghalib regarded them as much as any other of his Persian prose writings, as models of literary composition on which he could pride himself.

Some of the best letters are to his Calcutta friend Siraj ud Din Ahmad, a man whom he was to describe many years later as one of the two best friends he had ever had. For years after his return to Delhi, Ghalib continued writing to him. One letter begins with a rebuke to him for not having written:

You whose command Ghalib obeys, and in whose service Ghalib is bound and to whom Ghalib turns in reverence, were it not that a grief possesses my heart, I and my heart alone could tell what new paths of complaint against you we would have opened up, and for what quarrels we would have laid the foundations. It is your gain that I am hapless and helpless. Otherwise, had I the resolve and the strength, I would have grappled with you and fought till your clothes were all torn and my face and head were cut and bruised. Fear God! Ponder well and judge justly: our relations have come to this, that ages pass and not a letter comes to show that you remember me!

I have said that I am bound by the need to lay a new grief before you. What room for complaint is there in a soul that grieves? The few lines I have written had no place on this page, but I wrote them because my reason told me—and writhed in pain to tell me—that perhaps my friend, who is unacquainted with the ways of friendship, might think that I am pleased with him and, so thinking, might neglect to atone for the wrong that he has done me.

Another letter concerns the death in Calcutta of a common friend, Mirza Ahmad Beg.

He used to say, 'I shall be coming to Delhi,' but, unkind man that he was, he forgot his promise and turned into another road, urging his camel swiftly on towards another goal. And, granted that he cared nothing for his friends, why did he not take thought for his little children, that he withdrew his protecting shade from over their heads? Alas for the friendlessness of his friends! and woe for the fatherlessness of his children!

He goes on to speak of the dangers that beset the children—for even the eldest son is no more than a boy—and concludes:

At all events, what is needed now is a trustee, a man who is both prudent and who respects their rights, who will come to their help and comfort them in their fatherless state.... I know what they must feel, for I was myself a child when I lost my father. By God I tell you that the care of these poor children is a prime duty, a binding duty, upon you and Mirza Abul Qasim Khan. You must keep their helplessness ever before your gaze and never be heedless of them.... 'God sees to it that they who do good shall not fail of their reward.'

On another occasion he writes of the resignation from his post and departure from Delhi of his old friend Fazl i Haq. Exactly what happened is not clear from the letter, but it appears that Fazl i Haq, who held a post in the Delhi courts, was unjustly put in a position where he felt that the only honourable course was to resign. Ghalib writes bluntly and indignantly about it.

> Be it known that the ineptitude of the authorities who do not know men's worth, has come to the pitch where that man of unparalleled learning...Maulvi Hafiz Muhammad Fazl i Haq has resigned [his post] and so released himself from shame and degradation. Take Maulvi Fazl i Haq's knowledge and learning and wisdom and character and reduce them all a hundredfold; then measure this hundredth part of them against this post in the civil courts; the post would even then be less than these qualities merited. To be brief, after his resignation Nawwab Faiz Muhammad Khan appointed a monthly sum of Rs 500 for my master's [i.e. Fazl i Haq's] expenses and sent for him. The day Maulvi Fazl i Haq left Delhi I cannot describe what the people of the city felt. The heir-apparent to the throne of Delhi...Mirza Abu Zafar Bahadur sent for him to bid him farewell. He took a shawl from his own personal apparel and laid it upon his shoulders, and the tears came to his eyes as he said, 'As often as you say "I am leaving", I think that there is nothing I can do but bear it patiently. But All-Knowing God knows with what infinite effort I bring the words of farewell from my heart to my tongue.' These were the words of the heir-apparent....

If writing consoled Ghalib, it did not feed him, and his financial position was as acute as ever. But if he badly needed extra income, he would not seek it in any way he thought derogatory to his honour. In this way he missed an opportunity in January 1842 of a professorship in Persian at Delhi College. Hali relates what happened:

> In 1842, when Delhi College was reorganized on new principles, Mr Thomason, Secretary of the Government of India, who later became Lieutenant-Governor of the North-Western Provinces, came to Delhi to interview the candidates. A teacher of Arabic had already been appointed at a salary of Rs 100, and Mr Thomason wished to make a parallel appointment for Persian. The names of Ghalib, Momin Khan and Maulvi Imam Bakhsh had been suggested to him, and Ghalib was the first to be called for interview. When he arrived in his palanquin.... Mr Thomason was informed, and at once sent for him. But Ghalib got out of the palanquin and stood there waiting for the Secretary to come out and extend him the customary welcome. When some considerable time had passed and Mr Thomason had found out why Ghalib did not appear, he came out personally and explained that a formal welcome was appropriate when he attended the Governor's durbar, but not in the present case, when he came as a candidate for employment. Ghalib

replied, 'I contemplated taking a government appointment in the expectation that this would bring me greater honours than I now receive, not a reduction in those already accorded me.' The Secretary replied, 'I am bound by regulations'. 'Then I hope that you will excuse me', Ghalib said, and came away.

It was more in accord with the traditions he knew to take the course open to every poet or scholar of established reputation and seek the patronage of a ruler wealthy enough to provide for his support. Modern opinion too readily assumes that such a relationship necessarily implies subservience of the poet to his patron; but this was certainly not the case. In Mughal society the patronage of learning and letters was one of the accepted social functions of the nobility, and the established poet could look to receive patronage simply because he was an established poet; occasional panegyrics of his patron and odes on special occasions would be expected of him, but this was by no means the most important basis of the relationship, and the poet saw nothing injurious to his self-respect in it, any more than the great noble saw anything dishonourable in his allegiance to his overlord. Ghalib was of all people the least likely to fawn upon a patron, though he readily accepted the composition of panegyrics as a recognized part of the unwritten contract between them. He had made his debut in this line some years ago, when in 1827 he had composed an ode to the ruler of Oudh, hoping to receive in return a substantial contribution to the expenses of his journey to Calcutta. It is significant that in it he had written:

I pledge my faith, and swear I never fawned on kings;
Our independent pride was handed down to us.
We too give bounty, and I need to feel no shame
To come now asking bounty from the bounteous.

This always remained his attitude. It may have been, in part, his financial straits which made Ghalib indulge all the more a fondness for gambling, and this was now to involve him in one of the most distressing experiences of his life. The full circumstances of the incident, which occurred in 1847, are somewhat obscure, and there are several conflicting accounts of it. It appears that Ghalib had always enjoyed gambling, though he had not habitually played for high stakes. It was his misfortune that he was now living in a period when the authorities seem to have felt that gambling had assumed the proportions of a serious evil in Delhi society, and were determined to stamp it out by the most drastic legal penalties. He had already felt the effects of this policy six years earlier, when his house had been raided and he had been fined Rs 100; but he now seems to have thought that he had meanwhile acquired influential friends in the British administration on a sufficient scale to protect him from any drastic consequences even if he were caught. He was soon undeceived. This time when his house was raided he was arrested, brought to trial, and given a heavy sentence. A contemporary newspaper reported: 'Mirza Sahib has been sentenced to a fine of Rs 200 and six months' imprisonment with hard labour; in the event of failure to pay the fine, the period of imprisonment will be extended, while on payment of Rs 50 over and above the Rs 200 he may be excused the hard labour.' This sentence was upheld in higher courts. This was an unexpected and terribly heavy blow to Ghalib, not least because he could not understand how his influential contacts had failed to protect him. Hali writes:

> Ghalib has himself given a brief account of this incident in a Persian letter, which I give here in translation: 'The Chief of Police was my enemy, and the Magistrate did not know me.... Although the Magistrate has authority over the Chief of Police, he behaved, where I was concerned, as though the Chief of Police had authority over him, and issued the order for my imprisonment. The Sessions Judge was my friend; he had always treated me with friendship and kindness, and in most companies where we met, had behaved quite informally with me; yet he too acted now as though he did not know me. An appeal was made to the higher courts, but my case was not heeded and the sentence was upheld....'

The heavy sentence seems to have created a great stir in Delhi, and a good deal of indignation. The newspaper report already quoted continues:

> When it is borne in mind that Mirza Sahib has long been a sick man on a strict diet...we are obliged to say that the distress and the hard labour will be beyond his strength to endure, so much so that his very life may be endangered.... It is contrary to all justice that, for a very ordinary crime, a talented nobleman, whom the public honours and respects profoundly, should have to pay a penalty so drastic that it may well cost him his life.

So great was the concern at Ghalib's arrest that the king, who entertained no very warm feelings towards him, was induced to write to the authorities requesting his release; but he received the reply that this was a matter for the courts, and the administration could not intervene.

Accordingly Ghalib began to serve his prison sentence, and if he had felt deeply humilitated by his 'imprisonment' in his home twelve years earlier, it can be imagined what his feelings were now. The hardships of prison life[21] were not all that was in store for him; even more painful to him was the effect of his sentence on his friends and relations. All except one held aloof from him, apparently thinking it discreditable to continue association with one who was now a convict serving a prison sentence. Two of Ghalib's closest friends from his earliest years in Delhi had been Fazl i Haq and Amin ud Din, who was now Lord of Loharu. Fazl i Haq was no longer in Delhi; Amin ud Din, who had not only been Ghalib's friend but was related to him by marriage, became openly hostile, and when an Agra newspaper mentioned in a report that he was Ghalib's kinsman, he went to the extent of having it made clear in a subsequent issue that the relationship was one by marriage only. His brother Ziya ud Din's conduct was no better. The one exception was Ghalib's fellow-noble and fellow-poet Shefta, whom Ghalib had come to know well later than the others, after his return from Calcutta, and who now did all he possibly could to relieve Ghalib's distress.

Nawwab Mustafa Khan Shefta was nine years younger than Ghalib, having been born in Delhi in 1806. His background was strikingly similar to Ghalib's, except that his ancestors had migrated to India not from Tukestan but from Kohat, in the borderlands of Afghanistan, and were related to the family which early in the eighteenth century established the small principality of Farrukhabad in what is now western Uttar Pradesh. His father served in the Maratha armies as the commander of a regiment, and when the conflict with the British under Lord Lake developed, he used his diplomatic skill to bring about a peaceful settlement between Lord Lake and his own commander. The British rewarded him in 1813 with estates bringing in Rs 3000 a year. This grant was for the duration of his own life, and he provided for his descendants the following year by buying the estate of Jahangirabad in the Meerut district, then being auctioned by the British because the former

---

[21] Though he did not have to eat prison food. His food was sent to him from his home.

owner had failed to pay them the revenue due on it. On his death
the British resumed possession of the estates they had granted
him, but in recognition of his past services appointed a stipend of
Rs 20,000 a year to his successors.

Shefta grew up in Delhi, and received a thorough education in
Persian and Arabic. In his youth he lived in the usual style of the
young Delhi aristocrat; wine and women formed part of his regular
pleasures, and his liaison with a stylish, wealthy and cultured
courtesan named Ramju was well-known. But he later turned to
religion and gave up these things. In this connection the story is
told that he visited Ghalib one day during the cold season when
Ghalib was drinking wine. Ghalib invited him to join him. 'I have
given it up,' said Shefta. 'What?' said Ghalib, 'Even in winter?' In
1839 he set out on the pilgrimage to Mecca, and after an adven-
turous journey during which he was shipwrecked, ultimately
returned to Delhi in 1841.

Though no such reform had taken place in Ghalib, Shefta's
regard for him was unchanged. Poetry was the great bond between
them and each had the highest opinion of the other's work. Mihr
writes:

> Hali used to say that as soon as Shefta heard the news of what
> had happened, he at once took steps to see everyone in authority
> he could think of, and made continuous efforts to get Ghalib
> released. Then came the trial and the appeal. Shefta paid all the
> expenses out of his own pocket. All the time Ghalib was in prison
> he went to visit him regularly every other day. He used to tell people,
> 'My deep regard for Ghalib was never based upon his sobriety or
> his piety, but on his greatness as a poet. Today he is accused of
> gambling, but that he drinks wine has always been known. Why
> should it make any difference in my regard for him that he has
> been charged and sent to prison? His poetic talent is the same today
> as ever it was.'

Ghalib felt a gratitude to him as intense as the bitterness he felt for
the friends who had turned their backs on him, and both feelings
find expression in a long poem which he wrote in prison:[22]

> Here within prison walls confined I tune the lute of poetry
> That sorrow bursting from my heart, transmuted into melody,

[22] It is considerably abridged in the translation that follows.

May sing a song to draw forth blood—that even from captivity
I may work wonders in the world, and build a tavern for the free.
Thus shall I labour hard; hard labour consorts with imprisonment
Bonds shall no longer choke my voice, and I will sing my heart's lament.

Old friends, you must not incommode yourselves to come and visit me,
And knock upon my door—I cannot open it as formerly.
Imprisoned thieves are now my friends, and bow to my supremacy.
I still their clamour, telling them, 'Outside there is no loyalty'.
The sentence passed upon me, true, is not for all eternity,
But from the world I look no more for joy that makes man truly free.

The candle's flame with equal ease puts darkness everywhere to flight
But better that it burn for kings, filling their palaces with light.
Ghalib is precious frankincense; if he must burn, then it were right
To burn him in a costly censer, symbol of a prince's might.
Alas that he lies here where never comes the cooling breeze of morn—
Only the burning, searing wind that scorches even the desert thorn.

But prison warders, prison guards, assemble here, for I am come.
Open the gates to welcome me as I draw near, for I am come.
Friends, prisoners in your narrow cells, be of good cheer, for I am come.
A poet's words, a poet's wisdom you shall hear, for I am come.
When friends and kinsmen all have turned away from me in my disgrace
Why should I not find comfort here from strangers,
     captive in this place?

It was no policeman sent me here, no magistrate, no power of earth—
This suffering, this imprisonment, was written in my fate at birth.
And what of that? One noble man, Mustafa Khan despite this dearth
Of noble men, asks after me, and makes me see my own true worth.
He is God's mercy, God's compassion, sent in human form for me
And if I die I shall not grieve, knowing that he will mourn for me.

Friends, in this garden of the world I am a weed; if I should die
You need not grieve; its cypresses and fragrant flowers are you, not I.
But if you lack the heart to love, still you can raise your voice on high;
I lay this poem before you now; its meed of praise do not deny.
You will not think of me, I know, in one another's company
But still, where men recite their verse, surely you will remember me.

Ghalib did not serve his full sentence, and, so far as is known, did not have to perform hard labour—means were presumably found to pay the Rs 250—but he did serve three whole months in jail. Then, in circumstances which are now quite obscure, and which he himself declared he did not understand, he was released.

The letter quoted by Hali says as much, and continues by describing Ghalib's feelings about the whole affair:

> Then for some unknown reason when half my term had expired, the Magistrate took pity on me and wrote a report to the higher court recommending my release, and the order for my release was handed down.... Because I believe that all that happens, happens by God's will—and there is no fighting against His will—I hold myself free from any stigma in what has happened and resign myself to accept all that the future may bring. Yet to entertain a desire is not to contravene the law of submission to Him, and it is my desire no longer to stay in this world, and if I must stay, then not to stay in India. There is Rum; there is Egypt; there is Iran; there is Baghdad. But these too I pass by. The Kaba itself is the sanctuary of the free, and the threshold of the Prophet,[23] who is God's blessing to all the worlds, is the resting place of His devotees. I await the day when I shall gain release from this bondage of wretchedness, which wears away my soul more than the bondage I have undergone could do, and shall set my face towards the wilderness, not caring where I go. This, then, is what I have suffered, and this is what I desire.

Ghalib and the Mughal Court, 1847–57

His imprisonment is a milestone in Ghalib's life; and the same year of 1847 is memorable also because it marks the beginning at long last of his connection with the Mughal court. He was befriended by Nasir ud Din (generally known by his nickname of Kale Shah, or Miyan Kale Sahib), whom the king had accepted as his murshid, or spiritual guide. On his release from jail Kale Shah put a house at his disposal, where he was able to live rent-free, and it was through his influence that Ghalib at length gained audience with the king. Ghalib joked about his obligation to Kale Shah, whose nickname means roughly 'the Black Saint'. Hali writes: 'One day he was sitting with Miyan Kale when an acquaintance called to congratulate him on his release from prison. "Release? Who's been released?" said Ghalib, "I've come out of the white man's prison into the black man's prison".' Thanks to Miyan Kale, Ghalib now had access to the king, but for another three years no permanent connection was established. Then in 1850, the king's physician, Hakim Ahsanullah Khan, who was an admirer of Ghalib's Persian writing, secured for

---

[23] Medina, where Muhammad is buried.

him a commission to write in Persian prose the history of the Mughal dynasty. For this service he was to receive a stipend of Rs 600 a year. Thus at the age of fifty-two he began to receive, for the first time in his life, a regular income over and above his 'pension'. At the same time the king conferred upon him a ceremonial robe, and the titles Najm ud Daula, Dabir ul Mulk, Nizam Jang (Star of the Realm, Scribe of the State, Marshal of War). This was only a beginning. For the next few years a measure of good fortune continued to come his way. In 1854 he was chosen as the ustad of the heir-apparent, Mirza Fakhr ud Din. Ikram comments, 'The heir-apparent had taken the widow of Shams ud Din,' Ghalib's ancient enemy, into his harem. Clearly, Ghalib's literary fame must have been very firmly established for the heir-apparent to overlook Ghalib's enmity to Nawwab Shams ud Din and make him his ustad.' Ghalib was to receive as ustad a stipend of Rs 400 a year. In the same year (or perhaps a little earlier) he reaped the reward of his panegyrics of the kings of Oudh, and Wajid Ali Shah, the last king, directed that he should be paid a stipend of Rs 500 a year. In 1854, too, Zauq died, and Ghalib, perhaps only because no other poet of comparable standing was now left in Delhi, was appointed to succeed him as the king's ustad. Thus at the end of 1854 his financial position was better than it had been for many years. Besides his pension of Rs 750 a year he was getting Rs 600 from the king, Rs 400 from the heir-apparent, and Rs 500 from the king of Oudh.

If these years mark a certain turn in Ghalib's fortunes, they are also important for another reason. These were the years in which Ghalib, for the most part, gave up writing his letters in Persian and changed over to Urdu instead. Substantial numbers of these Urdu letters have been preserved, so much so that from this point onwards they begin to become the most important source for the story of his life, and it will be increasingly possible to tell that story in his own words. Hali believes that it was his appointment to the task of writing the history of the Mughal dynasty that marked the turning point. He writes:

> It seems that up to 1850 Ghalib always conducted his correspondence in Persian; but when in that year he received the appointment to write the history of the Mughal dynasty and became wholly engrossed in writing *Mihr i Nimroz*,[24] he must, out of necessity, have

[24] The name which Ghalib gave to the first part of his history.

been driven to do his letter-writing in Urdu. He used to compose
his Persian prose works, and most of his Persian letters too, with the
utmost labour, and one sees in them, somewhat more than in his
verse even, the working of his imaginative and poetic powers. Thus
when all his effort was directed to the writing of *Mihr i Nimroz*, it
must have been a burden to him to continue writing his letters in
Persian, and that too in his own characteristic style. We must infer,
therefore, that from 1850 onwards he began writing them in Urdu....

Hali's general inference is probably correct, though as we shall see,
there are on the one hand a number of Urdu letters written as early
as 1848, and, on the other, at least a few Persian ones which were
written after 1850.

The letters show that the enhanced status and the improved
financial position which these years brought did not make Ghalib
by any means completely happy. In the first place the bitter and
humiliating experiences of 1847 continued to affect him deeply. As
late as January 1850 he writes to Haqir:

My kind and compassionate and generous friend and benefactor, I
owe you a reply to your letter. But what am I to do? Heavy grief
and sadness is always with me. I no longer wish to live in this city;
and the difficulties and obstacles in the way are such that I cannot
leave it. In brief, my misery and sorrow is such that only the hope
of death keeps me alive.

He who lives on because he hopes to die
His hopelessness is something to be seen.

Secondly, though money was important to Ghalib, other things
were much more important to him—nor, for that matter, was the
money, welcome though it must have been, enough to solve his
financial difficulties. These continued to oppress him, and it
oppressed him still more to think that the king whose patronage
he had at last won—and not only the king—was incapable of
assessing him at his true worth. Being the man he is, he makes this
perfectly clear in the preamble to the history he is writing for him.
He begins with eloquent praise to Kale Shah, to whose kindness
after his release from prison he owed so much.

I am his neighbour, and the dwellers in the skies lie in my shadow, and
so long as I sit in the dust of his threshold, the angels envy me my high
estate and I am the apple of the eye and the joy of the heart of the
shining stars, and the moon and the heavenly bodies lie at my feet.

But he goes on to speak of his listlessness of spirit, and of the general unawareness of his talent that has reduced him to his present state.

In my body, made of dust, there is no life, as there is no life in the whirling dust-storm that provides a brief spectacle for men's eyes. Perhaps I am the painted picture of the nightingale of the garden; the fragrance from the rose inspires no melody to burst forth from its heart. Or I am the verdure on the tempered sword, which cannot bend before the blowing of the drunken wind. The bond that linked my heart with joy was broken long ago, and the blood still drips unceasingly from my heart. How strong that bond must have been! And with what force it must have been broken! One night I said to my frenzied heart—a heart more wise than I: 'Grant me the power to speak, and I will go into the presence of that king whose court and its wondrous works rank with the garden of Iram, and will say, "I am the mirror of secrets, and should be made to shine; I am the creator of poetry and should be cherished." It said, 'O foolish one, these were words for another occasion; the time for them has passed. Now if you still have words to say, say, "I am bruised and need balm for my wounds; I am dead and need life to revive me."'

...I cannot feel too great a pride in my happy fate, that I have a master such as you to direct my labours; and as I would lay down my life for you I swear that you too must feel pride in the great kindness of fortune, that you possess a slave like Ghalib, whose song has all the power of fire. Turn your attention to me as my skill demands, and you will treasure me as the apple of your eye and open your heart for me to enter in. They say that in the days of—[Emperor Shahjahan], by that open-hearted sovereign's command [the poet] Kalim was time and time again weighed against silver and gold and pearls and rubies. I desire that you command men of discernment to flinch not from the toil and effort, and to weigh my poetry—not many times, but just once—against Kalim's verse.

> Look not upon me slightingly:
> though I am dust beneath your feet
> Men honour this your capital because I dwell in it.

See my perfection, look upon my skill; see how despite the rage that wears away my life, despite the distress that drains away my strength, my rich imaginative power cherishes the muse of poetry and my eloquence surrounds her with all the delights that her heart could wish. I dwelt long with the Source of all Bounty, and drew constantly upon His stores and I excel the poets that came before me because I dwelt longer in His splendid abode. For I was sent down into the world after twelve hundred years,[25] and Sadi and Khusrau appeared after six hundred and fifty. And why talk of the poets of Emperor Akbar's day? My presence bears witness that your age excels his....

And now the age makes new demands of me—me, who have drunk wine my whole life through, and felt its heady exaltation and in that exaltation have spoken nothing but poetry, and if my steps have strayed into the paths of prose, have walked there too with the same drunken gait; now—at this time, when my heart is cleft in twain and my imaginative power destroyed, and my sense and perceptions dulled, and my mind as though no longer in being and my body broken because my soul is sick, and my soul in disarray because of my body's pain and if I set myself to write no more than a page, then before it is completed and I turn the leaf, the joints of my fingers have stiffened and the pen falls from them, and my blood is burnt to nothing in my veins, and my sight in my eyes, and my breath on my lips and my marrow in my bones—even so the age demands of me that I tune the lute of narrative, that it may judge of the quality of the melody I play and put my style of playing to the test.

We can follow the progress of his work in the letters to Haqir. Its final form differed from that which he had originally planned. He describes the general plan thus:

I have named the work *Partawistan* (The Land of Radiance) and divided it into two volumes. The first volume begins with the creation of the world[26] and goes up to Humayun [i.e. to 1556]: I have entitled it *Mihr i Nimroz* (The Sun at Midday). The second volume will begin with...Akbar and go up to the reign of His Majesty, the present king, and will be entitled *Mah i Nimmah* (the Moon at mid-month).

Mihr i Nimroz was completed quite quickly, although, as we shall see, a stage came when Ghalib had to rewrite the first part of it. His stipend for writing it was payable half-yearly in arrears, and as the first half-year came to an end he seems to have been anxious to be able to produce tangible evidence that he had really earned it. This is clear from a letter which he wrote to Haqir on 2 January 1851; and the same letter makes it clear that he had little other motive impelling him to write, for the task was one which did not inspire him. He writes:

Well, my friend, I've completed the account of Emperor Babur [died 1530]...the first six months—July to December 1850—are up. Let

[25] I.e. in the thirteenth century of the Muslim era.
[26] This describes the final form.

me see when I get my first six months' pay. If after I receive it my salary is henceforth made payable monthly then, of course, I'll go on writing. Otherwise I'll bid this job goodbye. I haven't yet sent this account of Babur to His Majesty. I finished the manuscript yesterday, and it is being written out in fair. When the fair copy is ready I shall present it, and at the same time apply to have my salary paid monthly. The six months were nearly up; that is why I concentrated on completing the manuscript. And that is why I have not had time to write to you. God save me, what a life!...The pen is never out of my hand.

Ghalib put forward his request for monthly payments in a poem which is included in his collected Urdu verse. It ends with a couplet which he was to use later repeatedly in addressing other patrons:

May you live on another thousand years
And every year have fifty thousand days!

If the writing of *Mihr i Nimroz* gave him any pleasure at all, it was simply the pleasure of exercising his command of Persian prose, and this was a pleasure which he wished to share with Haqir, of whose literary judgement he had an exceedingly high opinion. Thus the same letter makes it clear that he had a copy of whatever he wrote specially made to be posted to Haqir: 'Write and tell me where the instalment I sent you ends. Write out the last sentence or the last verse—whichever it is—so that I can get the rest copied out from that point and send it to you.' More than once in subsequent months he stressed—in the words of a letter of 4 August 1851—'Rest assured, until what I write reaches you and you read it, I myself don't feel any pleasure in it.'

In another three months he had reached the end of Humayun's reign—that is, the point at which he had planned to bring the first volume to a close. On 28 March 1851, he writes: 'I've completed the account of...Humayun;...now I shall start on Akbar.' But in fact he never managed to get further.

However, his labours even on the first volume were not yet over. He later wrote to Haqir (10 April 1853):

Let me explain what happened. When I got as far as Humayun, by way of excuse—though what I said was no more than the truth—I told the Hakim Sahib [Ahsanullah Khan] that I could not manage the selection of the materials. I asked him to make the selection of relevant materials from the historical texts, get a draft written out

in Urdu, and send it to me. I would put in into Persian and deliver
it to him. He agreed to this, and sent me a draft beginning with the
creation of the universe and of Adam. Now I had, in effect, to write
a new book. [Ghalib had started his history with Timur (Tamerlane)
the ancestor of the Mughal kings.] I prefaced it with a short
introduction, and began to write in a quite distinctive style. The draft
he had sent me covered the period from Adam to Chingiz Khan
['Jengis Khan']. I wrote after my own fashion and handed over my
manuscript to him. From the month of Ramzan up to the present
day—that is, for the last ten months—the drafts have stopped
coming. What I have written must amount to sixty-four pages.
Two or three times I have pressed for more drafts, but I have always
had the same answer—'It's Ramzan'; then 'People are busy with
the Id celebrations'; and so on. I thought, 'What does it matter to
me? Why should I ask to be given hard labour?'—and I stopped
asking them. Hakim Sahib [Ahsanullah Khan] must have got the
sixty-four pages I have written, but I'm not going to ask for them
back. Why should I? Let them be, and good riddance to them. What
have *I* to do when not even the foundation has been laid?

He had already had occasion some months earlier to avow quite
bluntly his lack both of interest and of competence in history. A
Brahmin friend of Haqir had apparently approached him to consult
Ghalib on some point relating to the history of a particular locality
in which he was interested. On 19 November 1851, he had replied:

I am so much a stranger to history and geometry and arithmetic that
I don't even understand them. Employees of the royal offices write
out in Urdu the material I need for the book and send it to me. I
put it into Persian and hand it in. I don't possess a single book; my
only acquisition is that I can write verse and prose according to my
lights. I am no historian:

I have not read the stories of Sikandar and Dara
The tales of love and loyalty are all my stock in trade.

(The verse is a much-quoted Persian couplet. Sikandar and Dara are
the Persian names of Alexander the Great and Darius respectively.)

It is characteristic of Ghalib that even so he had taken pains to
do what he could to help his questioner. He explains at some
length why the question does not fall within the scope of the kind
of history he is writing, and how little help is to be expected from
the inadequate stock of books in the royal libraries. Then, after

explaining his own incompetence in the words already quoted, he continues:

I have a brother [actually a relative by marriage] Nawwab Ziya ud Din Ahmad Khan, son of the late Nawwab Ahmad Bakhsh Khan. He is my shagird in prose and verse. Now he has developed a taste for history, and has acquired an unparalleled knowledge and mastery of the subject. I asked him to investigate the point, so that I could send you something in reply, but he told me that nothing would be found in any book except *Ain i Akbari*—and he has read every book on the subject and carries its gist in his head. So that is how I am placed; this is what he, in whom I have full confidence, tells me; and that is the state of affairs in the royal libraries. Express to him my humble service, and my regret.

Mihr i Nimroz was ultimately printed and published in 1854, on the initiative of the heir-apparent, who in the same year made Ghalib his ustad. Ghalib wrote to Haqir on 15 September 1854:

This time I didn't write a panegyric ode at Id, but finished and presented a volume of the history.... In short, *Mihr i Nimroz* has been completed and presented to His Majesty. Now, if I live long enough, I shall write *Mah i Nimmah*. I have been presented with the king's letter of pleasure—that is, with a document expressing the royal praise and pleasure. I try to look upon it as the equivalent of a robe of honour and an estate.... Well, I must be thankful for my connection with the king. I cannot boast of anyone who appreciates my worth. As the *dom* said, 'When a man understands me, he is my slave; and when he doesn't I am *his* slave.' [The *doms* are a Hindu caste of male singers and dancers, hired by wealthy men on occasions for celebration. The *dom* whom Ghalib quotes means that he can command his own price from the man who really appreciates his art; otherwise he is helpless, and must be content with what he can get.]

Life lies upon you like a yoke upon your neck, Bedil,
And, willy-nilly, you must live it; what else can you do?

In the event it seems probable that *Mah i Nimmah* was never written, or, if written, was never published.

This letter makes it clear that by presenting *Mihr i Nimroz* to the king he escaped the chore of writing an ode in his praise. Repeated references in his letters to Haqir show that the writing of such poems at Id and on other occasions for rejoicing—which would be expected of him as a poet in the king's service—became ever more distasteful to him. The following year (23 June 1855) he wrote to Haqir: 'This Id I didn't even contemplate writing an ode; in fact not even a qata or rubai. I composed two or three couplets on the spot and recited them and I didn't even keep a copy of them.' And three months later, on 24 September 1855, he wrote again:

> I've left off writing odes; and why do I say 'left off'? The fact is that I *can't* write them. I've been writing a qata or a rubai for the two Ids [Id ul Fitr, which follows the Ramzan fast, and Baqar Id, which falls forty days later] and presenting them. On this occasion Hakim Sahib [Ahsanullah Khan] insisted strongly, saying that these were no Id offerings at all—no better than the couple of couplets which schoolboys write to give to their teacher as an Id offering. There was nothing else for it but to write these forty or so couplets in masnavi style and present them.

These remarks come in the course of a letter replying to an enquiry from Haqir. It seems that Haqir had heard of this masnavi and had written to complain that, contrary to his usual custom, Ghalib had not sent him a copy. Ghalib replied:

> My lord and master, do you *understand* what you are writing about, or do you just come forward to complain?...You may put me on oath, and I will swear to it that I never entered these verses in my diwan. It's nothing; so why should I send it to you? I am sorry that you have no inkling of my plight. If you could see me you would know that
>
>> I no more have the heart on which
>> I used to pride myself.
>
> I do not draw breath without thinking of the last breath that I shall ever draw. I am already sixty years old.[27] How much longer have I to live? I have written ten to twelve thousand couplets in Persian and Urdu—ghazals, odes, qatas and rubais. How much longer can I go on writing? Through bad times and good, I have passed my days the best way I could. And now the thought of death occupies me; what will death be like? And what shall I have to face after death?
>
>> I lived my life waiting for death to come,
>> And, dead, I still must see what else I face.
>
> If I didn't send you these verses it was only because I was depressed. Had I included them in my diwan I could not have failed to send

[27] In fact, he was not quite 58.

them. But when I didn't include them, what point was there in sending them to you?

In his next letter, of 3 October 1855, he adds the comment, 'I only wrote the Id masnavi to save money; because if I hadn't presented that I would have had to make an offering of three or four rupees.'

Where poetry was concerned his relations with the king had from the start been of a somewhat ambiguous kind. A delicate situation which arose in December 1851 well illustrates the sort of problems which they posed. In that month Ghalib wrote a prothalamion on the occasion of the forthcoming marriage of the king's youngest son, Mirza Jawan Bakht. Azad relates the story in detail; but Azad was the loyal shagird of Ghalib's rival Zauq, and, consciously or unconsciously, he suppresses things which it is important to know if we are to see the incident in its true perspective. Fortunately we possess Ghalib's own (albeit less circumstantial) account of the early stages, and this throws additional light on the affair. Azad says:

> Nawwab Zinat Mahal [one of the king's wives] was a great favourite with the king, and although her son Jawan Bakht was younger than many of his other children, the king was trying to get him recognized as his heir. On the occasion of this marriage, the most elaborate preparations were made, and Ghalib composed this prothalamion and laid it before His Majesty. [Azad then gives the full text of the poem, but the only significant lines are the last, in which he makes the poetic boast:
>
> As one who knows the worth of poetry—and not as
> Ghalib's partisan—I say
> If you would write a prothalamion, read this of
> his and try to know the way.]

When this last couplet was read out to him, it occurred to His Majesty that it implied a hit at him, as though to say,

No one else can write a prothalamion like this, and since you have made Shaikh Ibrahim Zauq your ustad and Poet Laureate, this shows that you do not "know the worth of poetry" and are merely Zauq's "partisan". Accordingly, that same day, when Zauq presented himself as usual, the king handed him the prothalamion and asked him to read it. Zauq did so and the king then said, "Ustad, you too compose a prothalamion". "Very good, Sire", replied Zauq. "Write it now", said the king, "and consider well the last verse." Zauq sat down there and then and wrote this prothalamion. [The full text follows; the last verse is:

> Take this to those who claim that they are poets;
>   Stand and recite it to them, and then say:
> This is poet's prothalamion:
>   If you would write one too, this is the way.]

In Ghalib's account there are significant differences. First, it appears from it that the prothalamion was a command performance, written at the king's virtual order or, more precisely, at the order of the queen, conveyed through the king, and that even the final rhyme (which Ghalib did not approve) was laid down for him. In the elaborate prose style which he usually prescribed for himself when he wrote in Persian, he wrote (in a letter to Shafaq):

> I have long ceased to tune the lute of Urdu verse. True, to gain the goodwill of that Sovereign before whom Solomon is a simple scribe, I from time to time untimely pour out the strains of Urdu song. And especially at the command of that Queen before whom Bilqis bends in worship, I bent my mind to the writing of rekhta[28] in this unreasonable rhyme. Perchance I may in the concluding couplet have cried the drunken cry of poetic drunkenness. One [Zauq] whom the fancy possesses that he possesses a perfection he does not possess, presumed that it was he of whom I spoke. In the concluding couplet of a poem he struck a note accordingly and stood in the stance of combat, and thought that thus my challenge had been checked. But I did not deign to turn towards him, deeming sheer disdain sheer proof of my distinction.

There follows the passage already quoted in which he laments the fate that barred the paths to martial prowess and to learning and to the wandering life of a darwesh and made him a poet; and he goes on:

> And either in this age there is none with eyes to see, or else there are such, but they will not glance my way. And surely that is why, in the deep darkness of my days, none knows and none acknowledges the wonder of my work. And now in these last days when my teeth are gone and my ears are slow to hear and my hair is white and the wrinkles line my face and my hands tremble and my foot is in the stirrup,[29] what is left of the tumults that once raged in my heart?

[28] An old term for Urdu.
[29] I.e. ready to make my last journey—that is, to die.

I break my daily bread and taste the tortures of approaching death—
and that is all. What shall I reap tomorrow of all I have sown today?

It seems clear that when Ghalib wrote this letter he did not yet
know that Zauq's rejoinder to his original poem had been written
at the king's instance and that it was the king's displeasure as much
as Zauq's that it expressed. However, he soon realized the true
position, for, to continue in the words of Azad's narrative,

> Zauq's poem was at once given to the singers who attended on the
> king and by evening it was being sung in every by-lane of the capital.
> The very next day it appeared in the newspapers. Ghalib was not
> slow in understanding these things. He presented the following
> poem to the king:

An Apology

I write these lines to lay the facts before you
And not to boast my sterling quality.

For centuries my ancestors were soldiers
My standing does not rest on poetry.

Broad-minded, I would live at peace with all men
Friendly with all, with none at enmity.

That I am Zafar's slave is ample honour—
Though without wealth or rank or dignity.

Could I presume to cross the royal tutor?
I could not think of such temerity!

The King's all-seeing eye knows truth from falsehood:
I need no oath to pledge my honesty.

I make no claims to be an Urdu poet:
My object was to please Your Majesty.

I wrote the poem at the royal order—
To tell the truth, out of necessity.

Nothing that I expressed in the last couplet
Intended any breach of amity.

I taunted none—or let my face be blackened!
I am not prone to such insanity!

My fortunes may be ill: not so my nature;
Thank God, I pass my days contentedly

God is my witness, Ghalib is no liar;
I set great store by my integrity.

The poem seems to have satisfied the king and allayed his displeasure, but it is in fact far from being a mere apology. As in so much of Urdu poetry, there are other meanings besides the surface one, and many of them are not complimentary either to the king or to his ustad. They emerge already in the second couplet where he says, in effect, 'I am a noble, whose ancestors have for generations followed the noble profession of arms; and as such I would have my place in society even if I had never written poetry',—and he *implies* that this is a claim that Zauq certainly cannot make. It was common knowledge that Zauq was a man of humble birth, and only his poetry had won him social status. The seventh and eighth couplets imply that a really great poet says what he has to say in Persian, *the* language of Muslim culture, and that which all the really great Mughal emperors had patronized; if their latter-day successors choose instead to patronize Urdu, so that in order to please them a poet must write in this inferior medium, that, of course, is another matter. These two reactions—to vaunt his ancestry, and to exalt Persian at the expense of Urdu—are, as we have seen, typical of Ghalib when he is under attack, and they do not command much sympathy from a modern reader. But the tone of the poem as a whole is admirable; his assertions of his own position in the third, eleventh, and twelfth couplets are sincere and dignified, while the implied irony of the fourth and fifth hit hard at the king and his tutor in a way which delights us because we feel that they are getting what they deserve. In particular the piling up of the words 'wealth' and 'rank' and 'dignity' reminds us forcibly that it was in the king's power to bestow all these things, and that he had chosen to bestow them on much lesser men than Ghalib. Finally, the last couplet, with its emphatic assertion that he is a man of his word, ostensibly rounds off the poem; but it inevitably suggests comparison with the last couplet of the original prothalamion and could well be interpreted as a reassertion that what he had written there was no more than the plain truth. It is difficult to think that the king did not see these possible implications, but there was nothing the poem overtly said to which he could take exception—indeed, it is precisely in the lines that hit hardest that the surface meaning is unexceptionably meek—and he would be forced to accept it at its face value.

Ghalib's high-brow claim that Urdu was not really a fit medium for poetry reflects a feeling which possessed him more strongly at some times than at others. One result of his ties with the king in these last years before the revolt of 1857 was an increase in his output of Urdu verse. Hali comments:

> It is important to emphasize here that Ghalib did not regard Urdu poetry as his field. For him it was a diversion; he would write an occasional ghazal sometimes because he himself felt like it, sometimes at the request of his friends, and sometimes in fulfilment of the commands of the king or the heir-apparent. That is why in his Urdu diwan there is no significant number of poems in any form other than the ghazal. In a letter to Munshi Nabi Bakhsh [Haqir]...he writes, 'My friend, you praise my ghazal, and I am ashamed of it. These are not ghazals, but things I write to earn my bread. The Persian odes that I pride myself upon, nobody enjoys. My sole hope of appreciation now arises when His Majesty the Shadow of God takes it into his head to issue his command, saying, 'My friend, it is some time since you brought me a present'—i.e. a new Urdu poem. So willy-nilly occasion arises when I compose a ghazal and bring it to court.'... He did not look upon the ability to write Urdu poetry as an accomplishment; in fact he thought it beneath him. Thus he writes in lines generally said to have been addressed to Zauq:[30]
>
> > Look at my Persian; there you see the full range of my aritistry
> > And leave aside my Urdu verse, for there is nothing there of me.
> > I tell you truth, for I am one must tell the truth when all is done,
> > The verse on which you pride yourself is verse
> > I should feel shame to own.
>
> Yet since most of his contemporaries were men of cultivated taste and quick to discern poetic merit, in his Urdu poetry too he was concerned to maintain the same pre-eminence as in Persian, and he gave all his attention and all his efforts to writing it.

Hali's estimate is on the whole a sound one. There were indeed some verses which were written simply as a necessary chore, as the letters already quoted make clear. But other letters to Haqir show that during these same years he produced Urdu verse of which he felt proud, even where it was at the king's instance that he wrote.

[30] Ghalib's own words show that what was 'generally said' of these lines was quite correct.

Where he was pleased with the results he praised them with an engaging lack of reserve, and demanded that Haqir praise them equally highly; and, indeed, some of his very best ghazals are the product of these years. Early in 1851—probably between April and June—he writes:

> You should know that when I attend upon the king he usually asks me to bring him Urdu verse. Well, I wouldn't recite any of my old ghazals. I compose a new one and bring that. To-day at midday I wrote a ghazal which I shall take and recite to him tomorrow or the day after. I'm writing it out, and send it to you too. Judge it truly; if Urdu verse can rise to the height where it can cast a spell or work a miracle, will this, or will this not, be its form?

He then appends not one ghazal, but two. The second is still one of his best-loved.

In May or June 1852, he writes enclosing another, now famous, ghazal: 'My friend, in God's name, give my ghazal its due of praise. If this is Urdu poetry, what was it that Mir and Mirza wrote? And if that was Urdu poetry, then what is this?' In other words, 'My verse is in another class from that of Mir and Mirza (the colloquial names for Mir and Sauda, the two greatest Urdu poets of the eighteenth century)—so much so that you cannot call their work and mine by the same name.' He goes on: 'This is how I came to write it. A gentleman—one of the Mughal princes—brought this *zamin* with him from Lucknow [*zamin* is a technical term in Urdu poetics: it is a prescription for a ghazal in which metre, rhyme and end-rhyme are all laid down]. His Majesty himself composed a ghazal on it, and commanded me to write one too; and I fulfilled his command.'

From a letter of somewhat between 10 and 23 April 1853, it appears that the king could, on occasion, issue such commands fairly frequently. Ghalib writes: 'The king has given instructions for a mushaira to be held at the Fort. It is held twice a month, on the 15th and the 29th. His Majesty prescribes one *zamin* for Persian and one for Urdu'. He then states what these were for 'the last mushaira, held on the 30th Jamadi us Sani' and continues: 'I wrote one ghazal in Persian and one in Urdu on the prescribed pattern, and another in Urdu on the same pattern, but incorporating something different. I'm writing out all three for you. Read them, and show them to friend Tufta too.' Once again, one of the three ghazals is one of his very best.

The following year the king's old ustad Zauq died and Ghalib was appointed in his place—an appointment that was probably reluctantly made and reluctantly accepted. In the forties and early fifties Zauq, Momin, and Ghalib were the only poets of outstanding reputation in Delhi, and Momin had died in 1852, two years before Zauq. Thus the king could hardly avoid choosing Ghalib as Zauq's successor. He did so knowing perfectly well the poor opinion of Zauq as a poet which Ghalib held. Hali writes of how Ghalib felt about his new duties:

> In 1271 AH [AD 1854] when Shaikh Ibrahim Zauq died, the duty of correcting the king's verses fell to Ghalib, but it seems that he discharged this duty with an unwilling heart. The late Nazir[31] Husain Mirza used to relate how he and Ghalib were sitting in the Hall of General Audience one day when a footman came to tell Ghalib that His Majesty was asking for his ghazals. Ghalib told him to wait, to turning to his own servant said, 'In the palanquin you'll find some papers wrapped in a cloth, bring them here.' The servant brought them at once, and Ghalib opened the package, and took out eight or nine sheets of paper, each with one or two half-verses written on it. He called for pen and ink and started to write ghazals, each beginning with one of these half-lines. He completed eight or nine as he sat there, and handed them over to the footman. According to Nazir Husain Mirza, it took him no longer to write all these ghazals than it takes a practised ustad to read through a few ghazals and make occasional corrections. When the footman had gone off with them, he turned to Nazir Husain Mirza and said, 'Now I am free; for the first time for ages all His Majesty's occasional commands have been fulfilled.'[32] Whatever Ghalib wrote in his own style— whether in verse or in prose—cost him a great deal of effort and concentration, as he himself tells us more than once in his writings. But whenever he did not need to write in his own style, he could compose with very little effort.

The fact that the kind of poetry which both Zauq and his royal pupil admired could be churned out without effort in this way constituted the whole basis of Ghalib's poor opinion of it, and it was this fundamental difference in their view of poetry which was, in great measure, responsible for the uneasiness of their relationship,

---

[31] Nazir is a title, and indicates that he was Steward to the Royal Household.
[32] The clear implication is that some of Zafar's poems were not in fact his own work but that of his ustad. A similar tradition is current about Zauq.

an uneasiness evidenced, among other things, by the fact that
Ghalib never received the title of Malik ush Shuara (King of
Poets—i.e. Poet Laureate) which he might legitimately have ex-
pected, and that the new appointment was not accompanied by any
increase in his stipend. Much of Zauq's and Zafar's verse is pol-
ished, but much of it lacks depth, and Ghalib was strict in these
matters. He could neither admire nor pretend to admire verses
which he thought mediocre. Hali writes:

> In our society it is the general rule that when a man recites his verse,
> every line—good or bad—is greeted with cries of approval, and no
> one distinguishes between a good line and a bad one. Ghalib's way
> was quite the opposite of this. No matter how revered and respected
> a poet might be, until he heard a line that he really liked he never
> on any account expressed appreciation. Towards the end of his life
> he became completely deaf, but this was not the case in earlier years.
> One had to raise one's voice in speaking or reciting to him, but if
> this was done he could hear perfectly well. Yet until he heard a verse
> that really appealed to him he would remain quite unmoved. Some
> of his contemporaries were offended by this attitude, and that is why
> they found fault with Ghalib's poetry; but although Ghalib was by
> temperament one who did not like to quarrel with anybody, he never
> deviated from his practice in this respect.

Hali goes on to make it clear that there was no motive of jealousy
behind this:

> Yet to any verse that did move him, he gave praise that was almost
> extravagant—not because he wanted to please anyone, but because
> his own love of poetry compelled him to praise it. His rivalry with
> Zauq is well-known. Yet one day when Ghalib was absorbed in a
> game of chess, the late Munshi Ghulam Ali Khan recited this verse
> of Zauq to someone else who was present:

> > Tired of all this, we look to death for our release
> > But what if even after death we find no peace?

> He used to say: The moment Ghalib caught some snatch of this he
> at once left his game and asked me, "What was that verse you
> recited?" I recited it again. "Whose verse is it?" he said. I told him
> it was Zauq's. He was astonished, and made me recite it again and
> again, savouring it every time I did so. You may see in his Urdu letters
> that he speaks of this verse repeatedly, and wherever he quotes
> examples of good verses, this one is always included. In the same
> way, when he heard this verse of Momin's:

> I seem to feel that you are by my side
> When all are gone and I am quite alone,

he praised it highly and said, 'I wish Momin Khan would take
my whole diwan and give me this one verse in exchange.' This verse
too he has quoted in many of his letters....

Hali's evaluation of Ghalib's stand in these matters is borne out
by other evidence. His judgement of a verse was not influenced
one way or another by his opinion of the man who wrote it,
whether as a man or as a poet. For Zauq he seems to have had no
great liking in either capacity. On his death he writes respectfully
enough of him to Haqir: 'The latest news here is that friend Zauq
is dead.... The truth is that the man was unique in his own way
and in this age a poet to be thankful for.' But a well-attested
tradition says that his first reaction to the news of Zauq's death was
to express his satisfaction that 'the man who spoke in the language
of a lodging-house keeper' was no more. It is noticeable that his
opinion of Momin as a poet, expressed also in a letter to Haqir of
21 May 1852 shortly after Momin's death, had been given in
similarly vague and non-committal words: 'He wrote well in his
own way. A man of a fertile and inventive turn of mind.' But this
is preceded by warm praise for Momin as a man:

> You must have heard that Momin Khan is dead. It is ten days since
> he died. Just see, my friend, one after the other our children die;
> one after the other people of our own age die; the caravan moves
> off, and we ourselves are waiting with one foot in the stirrup. Momin
> Khan was of the same age as I, and was a good friend too. We got
> to know each other forty-two or forty-three years ago when we were
> no more than fourteen or fifteen years old, and in all these years there
> was never the slightest bad feeling of any kind between us. And, my
> good sir, you'd be hard put to it to find even an enemy of forty years'
> standing, let alone a friend.

Because he knew that much of the poetry that he would hear
there was worthless, it was with mixed feelings that he went to
mushairas. Some of his Persian letters describe his experiences at
them. Thus he writes to Majruh:

> The King's command came, bringing joy to those that dwelt near
> and good tidings to those who dwelt afar; and the Chamberlain of
> his Court directed the poets to the Hall of the Royal Steward, saying
> that on Friday 25, February they should come to that auspicious

abode and ply one another with the wine cups of poetry. A band of the princes of Babur's line and a few of the capital's men of distinction gathered together, and so great a throng assembled that every space was filled, and you would have said that body merged with body. First of all the Prince of Poets, Shaikh Muhammad Ibrahim Zauq plucked the string and recited a ghazal of the King in a voice so sweet that Venus descended from the sky to listen. Then that prince who possesses Yusuf's beauty... Mirza Khizar Sultan Bahadur, recited... ghazal in such wise that you would think that the Pleiades had sprinkled the carpet with their stars. Then the melody of the verses of Mirza Haidar Shikoh and Mirza Nur ud Din and Mirza Ali Bakht Ali rose on high, and then Ghalib... who was seated at the side of Mirza Ali, recited his ten couplets. Then a stripling named Mahvi, one of those who drink the wine of Sahbai's tavern [i.e. a shagird of Sahbai's] tuned his intoxicated lay. And Mirza Haji Shuhrat presented to the ears of us seated in the assembly a poem of some seventy couplets. [A ghazal should be a *short* poem.] I, on the pretext of easing a physical need, rose from the gathering and took the road to my abode of sorrow. The doors of the shops stood open and the lamps were still burning, and clearly the hour of midnight had not yet passed.... I sat and took wine. As the next morning drew to a close I made my way to the Auspicious Fort. The four princes whose names the tongue of my pen has already spoken revived the melodies of the night, and I again recited my ghazal. Friends told me that the whole night had passed in these diversions and the assembly had dispersed as the white light of morning began to appear. They say that as the gathering drew to a close the Prince of Poets [Zauq] recited two ghazals of his own....

Ghalib's ironical tone, the purely conventional praises, and the absence of any reference to the content of the ghazals recited, including his own, speak for themselves.

On other occasions he found himself pleasantly surprised. He writes to Shefta:

On Friday, as night fell, the poets held their assembly. I had not composed a ghazal, and, ashamed to go empty-handed I sat with head bowed, and the thought of going to the gathering was far from my mind. But... Nawwab Ziya ud Din Khan, whom God preserve, sent two angels to stand over me—Zain ul Abidin Khan Arif and Ghulam Husain Khan Mahv. These two insistent, stubborn men came as evening fell to my lonely cell of solitude riding on an elephant; and loading me on it just as a man loads a tiger he has killed in the hunt, they bore me off to the gathering. There the sight of my exalted master…Maulvi Muhammad Sadr ud Din Bahadur [Azurda] made up for all the sorrow I had suffered on the way…and I too raised my voice in melody and recited….

In other letters to Shefta he speaks slightingly of poets who wrote only in Urdu: 'Those who make verse in Urdu were there in plenty to recite their great long ghazals, and it was past midnight when I got back home and lay myself down to sleep.' And, in another letter:

A man had been sent to ask…Azurda to come. He came late, but come he did, bringing radiance to my heart and voice to my tongue. I had written an ode…but I was thinking to take the manuscript back with me, like a rejected petition, and not to vex the hearts of the poets of Urdu. But…Azurda's coming put me in good heart and gave my tongue leave to sing.

Even those who knew him well did not always understand his attitude in these matters. As a man whose literary reputation now stood very high, many a would-be poet sought the honour of becoming his shagird, while other writers would approach him to write forewords to their works. His generous nature made it difficult for him to refuse these requests, while on the other hand his integrity as a writer would not allow him to express any greater measure of praise than he sincerely felt. This latter trait put his forewords into a class on their own. The standard foreword of his day was an elaborate piece of ornate Persian prose full of exaggerated praise for the book and its author. Hali remarks:

Obviously only a very few books really deserve high praise. Ghalib would not refuse the requests made of him, but he wrote his foreword in a fashion which would please the author without doing violence to the truth. He would begin with describing the author's good qualities, or his character, or the sincerity of his love and affection; or else he would write of other interesting…topics which had some relevance to the book; and these things would occupy the greater part of the foreword. Then he would add a few pertinent sentences about the work in question which contained points of substance, and at the same time would be enough to satisfy the author. But…it did sometimes happen that people complained to him that he had been rather niggardly in his praise.

This happened in the case of Ghalib's friend Hargopal Tufta. Tufta was a devotee of Persian poetry, and had himself been writing it for a number of years, with Ghalib as his ustad. By 1848 he had a volume ready for publication, and Ghalib wrote an introduction to it at his request. A letter from Ghalib to Haqir on 25 May 1855 recalls what Tufta's reaction had been:

> On one occasion I wrote an introduction to please him, and the reward I got was that he got cross with me and wrote to me saying that what I had written 'ridiculed him with seeming praise'. I wrote back, 'My friend, you are not my rival, not my enemy. You are my friend, and you call yourself my shagird. Curses upon that friend who would ridicule his friend with seeming praise, and a thousand curses upon that ustad who feels a rivalry with his shagird and so ridicules him.' That shamed him somewhat, and he calmed down.

Ghalib was quite capable of writing to Tufta in these terms, but if he did, the letter has not survived. We do have another letter, written with more restraint in May 1848:

> I received your letter, and though it did not please me, at any rate it did not displease me either. Anyway, you may continue to think of me—unworthy and despised of men though I am—as your well-wisher. What can I do? I cannot change my ways. I cannot write the way the Indian writers of Persian do, and start talking all sorts of nonsense like a hired panegyrist. Look at my odes and you will see how long the preamble is and how relatively short the panegyric proper. My prose is the same. Look at my foreword to Nawwab Mustafa Khan's [i.e. Shefta's] tazkira to see how much praise you find in it. Look at my introduction to Mirza Rahim ud Din Bahadur Haya's diwan. Take the foreword I wrote, at Mr John Jacob's request, to the Diwan of Hafiz—you will see that apart from one couplet of verse in which I have mentioned his name and praised him, all the rest is taken up with quite different themes. I swear by God that if I had been writing a foreword to the diwan of some prince or nobleman I would not have praised him so highly as I have praised you. If you knew me and my ways you would have counted what I wrote as ample praise. Anyway, in short, I have taken out the sentence I wrote about you and written another in its place, just to please you. It is clear to me that you don't think these things out for yourself, but allow yourself to be misguided by other gentlemen, most of whom, I expect, will regard my verse and prose as worthless. And why? Because their ears are not accustomed to its sound. Well, you can't expect people who rank Qatil as a good writer to appreciate the real worth of prose and poetry.

In at least one famous case Ghalib was to find that in attempting to please an author and to express his own views at the same time, he had bitten off more than he could chew. In the early 1850s he was approached by Sayyid Ahmad Khan, later to become Sir Sayyid Ahmad Khan, and the outstanding leader of the Indian Muslim community in the last three decades of the century. Sayyid Ahmad Khan had just completed the task of editing *Ain i Akbari*, the work in which Abul Fazl, the minister of Akbar, the greatest of the Mughal emperors (1556–1605), describes in detail Akbar's system of administration. Hali writes:

> Prominent men in Delhi had written prose introductions to the work, and Ghalib wrote one in verse.... He was very attached to Sir Sayyid, and was on intimate terms with him and his family. But he was not an admirer of Abul Fazl's style; he thought the system of administration which *Ain i Akbari* describes beneath all comparison with those of modern times; and, as he himself admitted, he felt no interest in history. Hence he regarded the editing of *Ain i Akbari* as a pointless task...and could not restrain himself from saying so in his introduction.

Not surprisingly, Sayyid Ahmad Khan did not include Ghalib's introduction along with the others when the book was published, 'for the introduction found fault with *Ain i Akbari*, and far from praising the excellent work which Sir Sayyid had done, expressed the view that it was valueless.' In consequence relations between the two men remained strained for a number of years.

The same considerations which influenced him in his writing his introductions governed also his conduct as an ustad. He readily accepted requests from poets to correct their verse, and despite the volume of work this involved, he gave it his most careful attention.

From a letter of 18 October 1855 it seems that he was even prepared to correct the verses of poets whom he did not even know, for he writes to his friend Shafaq, who, it seems, had proposed to forward such verses to him, 'I shall be waiting now for the other gentlemen's ghazals to arrive. Would you please be kind enough to write, along with the takhallus of each of them, his name and a few particulars about him?' Tufta, whose output was prolific, apologized on one occasion for sending him so many verses to correct. Ghalib replied on 18 June 1852:

Listen, my good sir. You know that the late Zainul Abidin Khan was my son,[33] and that now both his children, my grandsons, have come to live with me, and that they plague me every minute of the day, and I put up with it. God is my witness that you are a son to me. Hence the products of your inspiration are my spiritual grandsons. When I do not lose patience with these, my physical grandsons, who do not let me have my dinner in peace, who walk with their bare feet all over my bed, upset water here, and raise clouds of dust there—how can my spiritual grandsons, who do none of these things, upset me? Post them off at once for me to look at. I promise you I'll post them back to you at once. May God Almighty grant long life to your children—the children of this external world—and give them wealth and prosperity, and may He preserve you to look after them. And on your spiritual children, the products of your inspiration, may He bestow increase of fame and the gift of men's approval...

At the same time he expected those who accepted him as their ustad to be ready to take his forthright criticism. He writes in an undated letter to Tufta (about mid-1853), quoting a Persian half-line which he had submitted for Ghalib's comment. The line, literally translated, means: 'Whether the rose, or the lily, or the dog-rose, or the eglantine, do not make.' Ghalib comments,

The 'do not make' should complete the meaning. It is not superfluous; the trouble is that whether you leave the half-line in Persian or translate it into Urdu, it has no sense or meaning.... 'Do not make'—'Do not on any account make'. Do not make what? Only when you yourself reply, 'Do not make mention, sir' will anyone *know* what; otherwise no one could ever discover that you mean 'Do not make mention'. And what's more, even if you tell me, 'I mean "do not make mention",' then how does your honour establish a connection between the 'mention' and the 'rose' and 'lily' and 'dog-rose' and 'eglantine'? You'll reply, 'I have not "mention", it's true, but "speech" in the preceding half-line.' But you can drag your 'speech' with ropes and chains, and it still won't connect with these four words. Do what you like... but you won't get your line to make sense. It's absolutely meaningless.

A few months later (13 January 1854) he begins another letter:

Your word '*did-mast*' is a new invention. I understand what you mean, but you may depend on it, no one else will. This is what they

[33] Actually, his wife's nephew. For Ghalib's relationship with him, and his adoption of his two sons after death, see p. 105 below.

mean when they say 'The meaning is in the mind of the speaker'....
In all these verses there is nothing wrong—and nothing of interest.

In Urdu and Persian poetics immense importance was attached
to precedent. An apprentice-poet whose ustad criticized some
expression in his verse would, if he could, justify himself by
producing a precedent from the verse of a classical poet. Ghalib's
attitude in these matters is characteristic of him. He had objected
to Tufta's use of a double plural, and Tufta, in reply, had produced
a precedent from the poet Saib. Ghalib wrote again, quoting a well-
known Persian verse:

> To find fault with our elders is a fault

and continuing:

> My dear friend, in such instances we should not find fault with the
> verse of the classical writers; but we should not follow them either.
> Your humble servant will not tolerate a double plural; nor will he
> say anything against the great Saib.

And on occasion he could be even more emphatic. In a letter of
mid-1853 he writes:

> In this couplet [which he has just quoted] Hazin [a classical Persian
> poet] has written one 'hanoz' too many; it is superfluous and absurd,
> and you cannot regard it as a precedent to be followed. It is a plain
> blunder, a fault, a flaw. Why should we imitate it? Hazin was only
> human, but if the couplet were the angel Gabriel's you are not to
> regard it as an authority, and are not to imitate it.

One of the tasks of the angel Gabriel, in Muslim belief, has been
to convey the words of God to the prophets sent to mankind; he
is therefore associated with divine eloquence.

Ghalib encouraged the same independence of judgement in his
friends and shagirds. Thus he wrote in a Persian letter to Hisam
ud Din Haidar Khan:

> The rhythmic speech which men call poetry finds a different place
> in each man's heart and presents a different aspect to each man's eyes.
> Men who make poetry all pluck the strings with a different touch
> and from each instrument bring forth a different melody. Pay no
> heed to what others see and feel, and bend all your efforts to increase
> your own perception.

At the same time he had definite views as to which poets and
writers repaid attentive study—and he included himself in their

number. In a Persian letter to Nawwab Ali Bahadur he writes of
how the secrets of poetry are to be learned:

> If you seek to find these secrets and desire to know the frets of this
> lute then keep before your eyes, of the Urdu poets, the verse of Mir
> and Mirza [Mir and Sauda] and, of the legion of the poets of Persian,
> the poetry of Saib, Urfi, Naziri and Hazin. Keep them before your
> eyes—but not in such wise that the black lines on the page do not
> travel from your eyes to your heart. Bend all your efforts to this end,
> that you may come to know the essence of each word, and that the
> range of meanings may come beneath your gaze, and that you may
> know true coin from counterfeit.
>
> If *Panj Ahang* had not been my own work I would have said that
> the wise approve it as a model of Persian writing. In it there are deep
> and subtle points expressed, and in its pages is abundance of beautiful
> phrases and sweet and fair words.

Nothing delighted him more than meeting a man whose love
of poetry and discriminating judgement matched his own. This
was above all the basis of his warm feelings for Haqir, as one can
see from the remarkable Persian letter which he wrote to Tufta after
they first met:

> In these days when night descends on the darkling day of my life—
> and how dark must be the night of him whose day has been so
> dark!—I sat in the darkness of sorrow and solitude, at war within
> myself. My tortured heart that burns with grief to look upon my
> solitude, is the one poor lamp that lights the black abode in which
> I dwell. But God's compassion sent a man to me who brought balm
> for my bruises and the comfort of his comradeship to quell my pain,
> and set a thousand stars to shine in the dark night of my soul. Truly
> his eloquence has lighted a candle, a candle by whose shining light
> I see shine out the lustre of the pearls of poetry my lips have spoken,
> when in the thronging darkness of misfortune's night their lustre
> had lain hidden from my eyes. O Tufta, you whose verse roves in
> new realms, singing new melodies, this wise man without peer,
> Munshi Nabi Bakhsh [Haqir] is a gleaming gem of a man in whom
> great God has made the talent of man manifest and given insight of
> the soul in high degree. For though I am poet and know poetry, until
> I met this venerable man I did not understand what understanding
> is or what it means to be well-versed in verse. The tale is told that
> when the Great Creator bestowed beauty upon men He made two
> halves; and one half He bestowed on Yusuf and the other half He
> sprinkled over all mankind. What wonder if when He gave out the
> power to value poetry and know its meaning, in this same way He

took two portions? One He apportioned to this man of many virtues; the other was the portion of the others. Tell the revolving heavens not to turn for me, and leave my destinies to sleep unheeding; for I have found a friend the joy of whose comradeship frees me from all fear of the age's enmity and this is a wealth which leaves me no complaint against the world.

We have seen that he had a similar opinion of, among others, Fazl i Haq and Shefta.

Ghalib sometimes had occasion to make it clear to his shagirds that to accept him as their ustad meant, in his view, to accept his corrections, though he did not mind these being questioned before they were finally adopted.

It is noteworthy that he did not attempt to impose his own style on his shagirds. In a letter to Haqir dated 3 September 1853, he singles out one couplet from a ghazal Haqir had sent him for correction and begins his letter: 'My friend, who wrote this verse? [He then quotes it.] Yes, who else? It could only be one of mine or one of my brother's [i.e. yours]. By God, what a verse! It has a distinctive quality that not everyone is master of.' On 6 October 1853 he speaks of the same ghazal again:

> One of its couplets was in my style, as I wrote to you. And all the rest of the couplets are good, without any fault or unevenness. Had there been room for correction I would not have overlooked it. My relationship with you isn't such that I would flatter you. I look upon your verse as my verse, your skill as my skill, your faults as my faults. Now look at the ghazal. I cancelled one or two couplets, and in the opening couplet and one other, made some verbal changes. The verses that I marked with *swad*[34] are very good, and you're to be congratulated on them. And the ones I have left unmarked are just good.

He goes on to praise a piece of someone's Persian prose which Haqir had sent him to correct, calling it, characteristically, 'the equal of Zuhuri's *Sih Nasar*, and half the equal of [his own] *Panj Ahang*.' He then details some of its good points and goes on,

> I am obliged and grateful to you, because thanks to your kindness I have had the opportunity to see it.... I am one who pays good writing its due, and wishes writers well. Where there is room for correction I do not shirk it. Beyond that, I am not the kind of man

---

[34] The first letter of *sahih* (correct) and the sign regularly used by an ustad to show that a verse needs no correction.

who interferes with writing which has no fault or defect in it. Return
these pages to their owner and give him my greeting; and show him
these lines I have written.

Elsewhere he states his attitude towards criticism. It seems that
some acquaintance of Tufta's had criticized his verse, even after
Ghalib's corrections had been incorporated. Ghalib tells him:

Although his objection is absurd and the question he raises a
pointless one, it would not become us to refuse to reply or to discuss
it. His objection to your verse is really a criticism of me, since I had
seen and approved it. I am not concerned with whether he accepts
this or not. I am satisfied that our verse is essentially sound and true,
and anyone who knows the language will understand it. If out of
ignorance or perversity they don't understand it, well, so be it. It's
not our job to improve and instruct all humanity. Education and
instruction are for our friends, and not for others. I don't need to
remind you how often I have told you: See to it that you aren't in
the wrong, and never mind if other people are. Today your verse is
such that no one can pick holes in it.

The ustad-shagird relationship between Ghalib and the king
was, of course, of a different order. When Tufta and others made
him their ustad they did so freely, and he accepted freely, whereas
in the present case it was because neither could see any other course
open that the king had made, and Ghalib had accepted, the
appointment. In the circumstances he seems to have limited
himself to such corrections as he felt the king would be likely to
accept without reluctance. Each knew perfectly well that the other
did not greatly admire his verse. Ghalib used to complain to Shefta
of the king's inability to appreciate what he wrote. 'One day', writes
Hali, 'he went straight to Shefta's house after leaving the Fort.
"Today His Majesty was pleased to show his appreciation of me",
he said bitterly. "I had presented an ode of congratulation on the
occasion of Id, and when I had recited it to him he graciously said—
Mirza, you recite excellently".' Ghalib did indeed 'recite excel-
lently', but this was hardly the kind of praise the occasion called
for. Moreover the effectiveness of his recitation was generally
acknowledged. Hali describes one occasion when he himself had
heard him:

His style of reciting his verse, especially in mushairas, was most
moving and effective. I myself only heard him once at a mushaira,
a few years before the Mutiny, when mushairas used to be held in

the Hall of General Audience. His turn came at the very end, so that it was already morning when he rose to recite. 'Gentlemen', he said, 'I too must sing my lament'. Then he recited, first an Urdu ghazal, and then one in Persian... in a voice so full of feeling that his voice alone seemed to be saying that in this whole assembly he sought in vain for one who knew his worth....

It was not only because the two men were ill-matched as poets that Ghalib's relationship with the king was a somewhat uneasy one. As a member of the nobility, a great writer, and from 1854, as the king's ustad (and hence in this sphere his formally-acknowledge superior) he took it for granted that he could treat the king with considerable freedom, and he did so, employing only the minimum of formality. For the same reasons he often found his duties as a courtier irksome. We have seen how often he evaded his unwritten moral obligation to present odes on formal occasions, and in this matter it seems that the king, to his credit, did not specifically insist, as he might have done, on his producing them. But where on occasion His Majesty saw fit to command his courtiers, they could hardly disobey, whatever their own inclinations might be. Ghalib wrote of such an occasion to Haqir on 9 December 1856:

His Majesty has for the last twenty days or so been holding court every day. I go between eight and nine and return at twelve, and the call to midday prayer comes either while I am still having my lunch or as I wash my hands after it. All the courtiers are in the same position. I expect that some of them eat before they go, but I can't manage it. All this was bad enough. And the day before yesterday the king in his kindness commanded me, saying, 'There is kite-flying every evening on the sand by the riverside. You must come to Salimgarh [the northern extremity of the Red Fort] too.' In short, I go in the morning, return at noon, have my lunch, rest a couple of hours, go again, and get back as the lamps are lighted. My friend, I swear by your head, I lie down to sleep at night as exhausted as a labourer. It's four days since your letter came, and only today have I been able to get time to write to you. And that too only because instead of resting after lunch I have written this letter to you.

Hali tells a number of stories which show how freely Ghalib behaved with his royal master.

One day...Bahadur Shah, accompanied by Ghalib and a number of other courtiers, was walking in the Hayat Bakhsh or the Mahtab

Garden. The mango trees of every variety were laden with fruit, but
the fruit of these gardens was reserved exclusively for the king and
his queens and members of the royal family. Ghalib looked at the
mangoes repeatedly, and with great concentration. The king asked
him, 'Mirza, what are you looking at so attentively?' Ghalib replied
with joined hands, 'My Lord and Guide, some ancient poet has
written:

> Upon the top of every fruit is written clear and legibly:
> "This is the property of A, the son of B, the son of C"

and I am looking to see whether any of these bears my name and
those of my father and grandfather.' The king smiled and the same
day had a big basket of the finest mangoes sent to him.

Equally characteristic of Ghalib was the freedom with which he
joked about religion both in conversation with the king and in
poems addressed to him, though the king was, in the main,
religiously orthodox. However, we have to distinguish here be-
tween Ghalib writing in his official capacity and Ghalib speaking
his own mind. As a poet and writer in the king's employ it was
the king's religious views which he was sometimes required to
express. Hali writes:

On one occasion the king fell seriously ill. At the time Mirza Haidar
Shikoh [a member of a branch of the Mughal royal family long
settled in Lucknow]...had come to Delhi on a visit from Lucknow
and was staying as the king's guest. He was an Asna Ashari [a Shia
sect], and when nothing seemed to bring the king any relief, healing
dust[35] was administered to him at Mirza Haidar Shikoh's instance,
after which the king recovered. Mirza Haidar Shikoh had made a
vow that if the king recovered he would make an offering of a
standard at the shrine of Hazrat Abbas in Lucknow. [Abbas was the
cousin and standard bearer of Husain, the grandson of the Prophet,
at the fatal battle of Karbala.] When he returned to Lucknow he
wrote to the king to say that the fulfilment of his vow was beyond
his financial means, and requesting the king's help. The king had
money sent to him and the offering of the standard was made with
great pomp and ceremony, in the presence of the whole royal family
of Oudh and and the most prominent nobles and divines....
   This incident gave rise to a general rumour that the king had
become a Shia, a rumour which caused him much pain.... Hakim

[35] Dust brought from Karbala, the scene of the martydom of Husain, and
believed to have miraculously curative properties.

Ahsanullah Khan had a number of pamphlets published to counter the rumour and...proclamations were posted...in the markets and byways. On the king's order Ghalib too wrote a masnavi in Persian...in which the king was cleared of the charge of having turned Shia. Ghalib expressed nothing of his own views in the poem, but simply put into Persian verse whatever Hakim Ahsanullah Khan told him. When the poem reached Lucknow, the leading Shia divine[36] enquired from Ghalib whether the views which it expressed about the Shia religion and Mirza Haidar Shikoh were his own. He wrote in reply, 'I am in the king's employ and carry out whatever order he gives me. You may attribute the contents of the poem to the king and Hakim Ahsanullah Khan and the words to me.'

Ikram adds further details:

In 1853–4, when the rumour went round that Bahadur Shah had become a Shia, the leading Muslim divines in Delhi warned him that if this rumour were correct they would exclude his name from the Friday sermons and the Id address. To refute the rumour, Bahadur Shah had Ghalib write a Persian masnavi. After this the king wrote a book... [in vindication of Sunni beliefs], to which Ghalib wrote an eloquent and forceful foreword....

It is worth noting in passing that this foreword was written in Urdu, and Ghalib, with his usual bluntness, makes clear in the course of it that this medium was not his own choice. 'When this work was completed,' he writes, 'the command came from His Majesty...that the servant of his court Asadullah should show his graceful submission in writing a foreword, contenting himself to adorn his eloquence with the adornment of the Urdu tongue.... The fulfilment of this command is incumbent upon me....'

In point of fact, says Hali,

Ghalib's real religion was 'enmity towards none', but he inclined towards Shia beliefs and held... [Ali], after the Prophet of God, to be pre-eminent. On one occasion...Bahadur Shah said in the presence of his court, 'I hear that Mirza Asadullah Khan Ghalib is of the Shia persuasion.' Ghalib was informed of this and wrote a number of rubais which he presented to the king. I remember one of these... and quote it here. [In prose translation the verse reads:] 'Men who are deeply hostile to me call me "heretic" [i.e. Shia] and "atheist". How can one who is a Sufi be an atheist? And how can

[36] *Mujtahid ul asar*—a title officially conferred by the Lucknow kings on the leading Shia divine.

one who hails from "Beyond the River" be a Shia?' The gulf that
exists between atheism and Sufism is clear: the atheist denies even
the existence of God, while to the Sufi all that exists is God, and
all else is nothing. So how can a Sufi be an atheist? The point of
the fourth line is that the people of 'Beyond the River', i.e. of
Turkestan, are proverbial for their Sunni bigotry... and since Ghalib's
ancestors came from 'Beyond the River' he asks how a man from
'Beyond the River' can be a heretic or a Shia.

Hali continues:

> People who are not well-acquainted with Ghalib's temperament and
> his way of writing may think that Ghalib falsified his religion in order
> to safeguard his access to the king. But the truth is that all these rubais
> were written simply to amuse the king and raise a laugh among his
> courtiers; for there was not a man in the court who did not know
> that Ghalib was a Shia, or at least a tafzili [one who, though not a
> Shia, acknowledges the pre-eminence of Ali]. Ghalib frequently
> recited verses of this kind... for the king's amusement. On one
> occasion when the court was assembled the conversation turned on
> the close relations that had existed between [the medieval Muslim
> saint]... Nizam ud Din and [the Persian poet] Amir Khusrau. Ghalib
> at once composed and recited the following verse:

> > Two holy guides; two suppliants. In this
> >   God's power we see.
> > Nizam ud Din had Khusrau: Siraj ud Din has me.

(Siraj ud Din was the king's real name. He took the name Bahadur
Shah when he came to the throne.) The verse neatly combines a
compliment to the king with a compliment to himself, suggesting
that Bahadur Shah matches the great Nizam ud Din in holiness
and spiritual power while Ghalib matches Amir Khusrau, who was
universally honoured as one of the greatest of the old Persian poets.

Bahadur Shah may indeed have found these incidents as amus-
ing as Hali says he did. Ghalib, for his part, gave him little oppor-
tunity to take him seriously. Whenever the king said anything
which could suggest that he was chiding Ghalib for his religious
shortcomings, Ghalib's rejoinder was generally flippant and irrev-
erent. 'On one occasion,' writes Hali, 'after Ramzan was over the
king asked him, "Mirza, how many days' fasts did you keep?"
Ghalib replied, "My Lord and Guide, I failed to keep one",' and
left it to the king to decide whether this meant he had failed to
keep only one or failed to keep a single one. Colloquially, eating

during the periods when one should fast (between daybreak and sunset) is called 'eating the fasts'. Ikram writes:

> It was perhaps on this same occasion that he read the following verse before the Royal Court:
>
> > The man who has the wherewithal to break
> > the fast when evening comes
> > Must surely keep the fast; it is his
> > bounden duty to.
> > He who has nothing he can eat when it is
> > time to break the fast
> > Can only eat the fasts themselves; what
> > else is he to do?
>
> At the same time he presented a rubai in which he wrote that to keep the fast was an article of faith with him—and he would keep it if only he had the means to do so in comfort. Ghalib wrote to Haqir on 4 June 1854 quoting both these short poems and adding: 'His Majesty was very amused, and laughed heartily.'

Ikram writes:

> In the ghazals of this period there are any number of flippant verses of this kind.... Towards the end of 1851 Bahadur Shah planned to make the Pilgrimage [to Mecca—an act of great religious merit]. Ghalib [who thought that if he could go he would enjoy the journey] included the following couplet in a ghazal which he wrote at this time:
>
> > He goes to Mecca; if the king will take
> > me in his company
> > Gladly will I transfer to him the merit
> > that accrues to me.

One of his ghazals ends with the couplet:

> > Ghalib, you write so well upon these
> > mystic themes of Love Divine
> > We would have counted you a saint, but
> > that we knew your love of wine.

Hali says:

> I have been told that when Ghalib recited this ghazal, the king commented on the final couplet, 'No, my friend; even so we should never have counted you a saint.' Ghalib replied, 'Your Majesty counts me one even now, and only speaks like this lest my sainthood should go to my head.'

More Letters, 1848–56

Hali, after suggesting the reasons for Ghalib's changing from Persian to Urdu as the medium for his correspondence, continues:

> Ghalib probably at first thought it beneath him to adopt Urdu as the medium of his writing. But it sometimes happens that the very achievement which a man regards as trifling and of little weight becomes the basis of his fame and popularity. Wherever one looks, Ghalib's fame throughout India owes more to the publication of his Urdu prose [i.e. his letters] than it does to his Urdu verse or to his Persian verse or prose. True, people generally already regarded him as a very great Persian poet, and thought of his Urdu verse too as poetry of a high order beyond the comprehension of the ordinary reader, but these opinions were based on hearsay, and not on their own reading.

He goes on to say that Ghalib was himself aware of this, and saddened by it.

One may share Ghalib's regret that his verse and his works of Persian prose were not generally appreciated, without belittling the achievement which his Urdu letters represent. In them one finds a vivid picture of the man and of the life he led, and one which, incidentally, assists substantially in the understanding of his avowedly literary work. Even among his Persian letters one occasionally finds one in the homely style and content more characteristic of his Urdu. For example, on 1 December 1848 he writes to Jawahir Singh, the son of his old friend Rae Chajmal Khatri:

> You will remember that I had a cap made of kid-skin. Well, it is moth-eaten now, and I am without a hat. I want a silk turban, the kind they make in Peshawar and Multan, and which distinguished men in those places wear. But it must not be of a bright colour or a youthful style; and it must not have a red border. At the same time it should be something distinctive and elegant, and finely finished. I don't want one with silver or gold thread in it. The silks in the material must include the colours black, green, blue, and yellow. You can probably get something like this quite easily in those parts. See if you can find one, get it for me, and send it me by post. And tell me how much it costs. I shan't accept it until you've told me what it costs. It's not a gift. A gift, a present, is something you send without being asked. You can't give a man something that he's asked for as a present. I don't mean that I wouldn't accept a present from you. Not at all. I only mean that I'm buying the turban, and I'll only accept as a gift

something that I haven't asked for. Anyway, please send the turban without delay, and don't hesitate about telling me what it costs.

In the Urdu letters it is this sort of informal, intimate writing on everyday personal matters that prevails. Most of those given in the last chapter relate either to Ghalib's employment at the Mughal court or to poetry and criticism. But there are many more, and they cover a wide variety of themes.

Some of them express his love of children, a love which he perhaps felt all the more strongly because he had none of his own.

Little is known in detail about his family life, for in Indian Muslim society one did not (and does not) talk about one's wife and children. His marriage was, as far as we know, no more and no less successful than most in his society, but he seems always to have felt that a wife was an encumbrance he could very well have done without. Hali writes:

> Ghalib's wife, the daughter of Ilahi Bakhsh Khan Maruf, was an exceedingly pious and sober lady, meticulous in keeping the fasts and in saying her prayers. She was as strict in her religious observances as Ghalib was lax in these matters—so much so that she even kept her own eating and drinking utensils apart from her husband's. At the same time, she never failed one iota in her duty of serving him and looking to his welfare. Ghalib always spent his time in the men's apartment, but...at an appointed time every day without fail he would go into the zenana, and his treatment of his wife and her relations was always considerate in the extreme....

One wonders whether Ghalib really was so considerate to his wife as Hali makes out, but his description of the wife is entirely convincing. There were and are thousands like her. From a brief reference in one of Ghalib's letters, written many years later, we know that she bore him seven children, but none survived longer than fifteen months. There were times when, hard-pressed by financial worries, he counted this his good fortune, but at other times it grieved him, for he was genuinely fond of children. Having no son of his own, he gave a father's love to Zain ul Abidin Khan Arif, his wife's nephew; his verse includes a Persian poem in Arif's praise. 'He is the flame of the candle that lights my house,' he writes, 'and the pen in my fingers dances for joy as I write his name.' But Arif's health was poor, and in 1851 he fell seriously ill. In a letter to Haqir, written probably between April and July of that year, he describes his sickness:

He has had a sudden attack of *ru'āf*, In this disease there is usually a flow of blood from the nose, but he has been losing blood mainly from the mouth, and only a little from the nose. The blood flowed from his mouth like water from a water-carrier's goat-skin. In the course of a week—may God strike me if I tell a lie—he lost something like ten to fifteen pints of blood—black and foul-smelling. No one thought he would live, and all hope was given up. But in the end God saved him. You may imagine what he looks like now. Even before he was nothing but skin and bone, and now he has shrivelled up until he is as thin as a rake. He is still confined to bed. Not only can he not move about; he cannot even get out of bed. But his life is out of danger.

Ghalib's concern was all the greater because Arif's wife was suffering from a prolonged illness at the same time. In the same letter he writes:

For three months she has been suffering from fever and a persistent cough. God have mercy on her and on her children, and save her life. I cannot tell what will happen, but you may take it that if she lives it will be as though she had returned from the dead.

Ghalib's fears proved only too well-founded. Arif's wife died in January 1852. Arif himself survived her for only three or four months. One of Ghalib's simplest and most moving ghazals was written on his death.

They left two small boys—Baqir Ali, aged five, and Husain Ali, aged two. If the letter to Tufta quoted above (p. 94) is correctly dated, he must have taken both of them into his care; but in that case it must have been a temporary arrangement, and the elder boy soon went to his grandmother, Arif's mother. The younger, Ghalib and his wife adopted as their own child. Hali says: 'Ghalib loved him more than if he had been his own child, and never let him out of his sight'. He often speaks of him in his letters.

He was also very fond of Haqir's children, and there are few letters to Haqir in which he does not ask after them and send them his blessing. The thought of them seemed to bring him some sort of consolation even in his keenest grief. The letter of 9 January 1850 already quoted, in which he wrote of the bitterness of his grief, his desire to leave Delhi and the insuperable obstacles that prevented him doing so, goes straight on:

Today amid this same tumult of grief and sorrow, my thoughts turned to you and your children. It is a long time since I heard how you are faring, and how my dear little niece, i.e. [Haqir's daughter] Zakiya is faring. Nor have I any news of [your sons] Munshi Abdul Latif and Nasir ud Din...

Somewhere between August and October 1850 he wrote:

How is my nephew and my dear little niece? You told me in an earlier letter that she takes her own pen and inkpot and sits down to write letters to me, and that when she quarrels with you she says, 'I'll go off to stay with Mirza Sahib'. Now you must tell her to stop calling me 'Mirza Sahib' and call me 'Uncle'.

On 8 January 1853 he ends a letter with:

My blessing to Munshi Abdul Latif and to Nasir ud Din...and last of all I send my blessing to my dear niece Zakiya Begam: May Exalted God preserve her and grant that I may see her face; otherwise as the days pass by she will grow up and become a lady, a gentleman's daughter. And then I don't suppose she'll appear unveiled before me. She'll hide herself from me, because I'm not really her uncle; I've only laid claim to be her uncle on my own account.

On 27 March 1854 he writes of her again. It seems that Haqir was anxious to give her a good education, but Ghalib urges what was in his time (and, indeed, continued to be long after his time) a more traditional view:

Give my blessing to all the other children, especially Zakiya Begam. My friend, for women it's quite enough if you teach them the letters, so that they can read the Holy Quran at sight. Don't lay too much stress on her education.

It must have been only a few days later that Husain Ali caught the fever too, for on 3 October 1854 Ghalib writes:

Today it is thirteen days since he opened his eyes. He lies there day and night with the fever, unaware and unconscious. Yesterday, the twelfth day, he was purged, and he passed four motions. All he has to live on is medicine three or four times a day and barley-water two or three times. The outlook is not good. His grandmother [Ghalib's wife] is also ill. Every day at midday she gets a fit of shivering. It leaves her at evening. She has to miss the midday prayer, but manages to say the afternoon prayer at the right time.... My friend, I am not too concerned about my wife, but Husain Ali's illness drives me to desperation. I love him dearly. May God preserve him to survive me when I am gone. He has grown thin as a rake. I didn't write to you before, but sickness is spreading here on a huge scale...all kinds of fevers, most of them recurring ones. In other words if in a household of ten persons, six are sick and four well, three of the six will get well and the four well ones will fall ill. So far all ended well, but now people have begun to die.... In short it's a case of

> The seven heavens[37] are turning night and day.
> *Something* will happen: set your mind at rest.

Three days later he had despaired of Husain Ali's recovery:

I told you of Husain Ali's condition in my last letter. Today is the sixteenth day of the fever, and the ninth since he had so much as a grain of solid food. He has grown thin as a rake. Today he is being given an enema. I cannot bear to watch it, and am sitting in the sitting room writing this letter.... Let us see what the result is. I am in despair.

But on writing 15 October he is able to write: 'Husain Ali is better now. That is, the fever has left him. His urine is cloudy and his stomach is hard. He is weak beyond all measure. God grant he may be spared and get completely well.' On 5 November 1854 he writes again:

Husain Ali is better now, except for the hardness in his stomach and his stomach-orifice. And yes, there is still some swelling. Yesterday, for the first time in several days, he again had a fever. It left him as the night ended, and today he is well. Let me see how he is tomorrow. His real grandfather, that is, Zain ul Abidin Khan's [Arif's] father and my wife's sister's husband, Nawwab Ghulam Husain Khan, has died. His death is much to be regretted. He was a very humane and affectionate man.

Less than a year later Arif's mother also died, and Ghalib took Arif's elder boy Baqir Ali into his care. His position caused him some anxiety. He wrote to Haqir on 23 June 1855:

Let me inform you that Zain ul Abidin's [Arif's] mother, that is, Husain Ali Khan's grandmother, died on Wednesday, 28th Ramzan. Zain ul Abidin's elder boy, Baqir Ali Khan has come to live with me too. Do you see, my friend, the tricks that cruel fate plays on me? Load upon load it piles upon me. Wound upon wound it inflicts upon me. There is nothing I can do. My income is the same; my expenses have increased. But I must fear God. I cannot behave callously towards them. And there is no one to whom I can say, 'Look after your own boys. I can't afford it.' Anyway, I hold my peace and am at a loss what to do. May God safeguard my honour.

[37] Whose movement determines men's destinies.

The children are mentioned once or twice more in the letters to Haqir. The first, written during Ramzan, 1856 (4 June 1856) says: 'Both your children, Baqir Ali Khan and Husain Ali Khan, are well. They break the fast three or four times a day, and as the time for breaking the fast [sunset] draws near, stand sentry over the mouths of those that are keeping it.' The second comes just over a year later, on 27 July 1856: 'Both the boys are happy. They wander about the place demanding mangoes, but no one will give them any. Their grandmother [Ghalib's wife] has got into her head that she mustn't let them eat their bellyful of food.'

Several letters throw a sidelight on the marital and other problems of a common acquaintance of theirs. Somewhere between April and July 1851 he writes:

> My friend, for God's sake make Hasan Ali Beg see sense. Is this any way to go on—to leave his wife for a boy? Even your mother takes no interest in what has happened to her. The poor woman is stranded there with her aunt. Write to your mother and tell her to write and persuade the girl to come to her so that she can send her off to you. I mean, give Mirza [Hasan Ali Beg] this piece of advice, and give him a good talking to.

Sooner or later this advice seems to have had some effect, and Hasan Ali Beg returned to his wife.

In the remaining letters of this period, all manner of subjects come up. Like the preceding ones, most of them are letters to Haqir, but there are letters to other correspondents too, notably to Ghalib's and Haqir's common friend Tufta.

On 22 June 1853—corresponding to Ramzan 14th—he writes to Haqir:

> You may well ask about the heat. Scorching winds and burning heat like this hasn't been seen for the past sixty years. On the 6th–7th of Ramzan there was heavy rain. No one had ever seen such rain in the month of Jeth [May–June]. Now the rain has stopped. The sky is overcast all the time. When there is a breeze it is not hot, and when the breeze drops the weather is unbearable. The sun is fierce. I'm keeping the fast—whiling it away, that is. Every now and then I take a drink of water or smoke the hookah, or eat a bite of bread. People here have warped minds and strange ways: here am I whiling away the fast and they inform me that I'm not keeping it. They can't understand that not to keep it is one thing, and to while it away is another.

On 4 June 1854, to Haqir:

My friend, praise to God, everything else is all right, but the heat is intense that we cry to God to protect us. I suffer from heating of the blood as it is, and there's this torture on top of it. I was taking only one meal a day, and now I've discontinued that too. All I have to eat is curd, and how long can I go on eating that? I don't know what to do. To keep the fast is well beyond my powers, but I'm in a worse state than those that do keep it—and it's hard to describe their state. I have four servants, and all of them are keeping the fast. By the end of the day they look like four corpses walking about. And amid all these troubles I've got nothing that would provide some relief from them—no cooled room, and no iced water.

I'm dying of overheating, but I'm on the alert to see when the mango crop is ready. I'm certain they must already have ripened in Bengal. I lived two years in Calcutta, and mangoes are on sale there in June. About three days ago a fruit-seller brought five mangoes, but they had no taste. The hot wind had ripened them.

On 3 June 1855, to Haqir:

You, and I, and his father are all to be congratulated on Abdus Salam's starting his schooling. Your writing Abdur Rashid by mistake was a good omen. It means that he will be *rashid* (dutiful). I was glad to hear about Munshi Abdul Latif. It doesn't matter whether it's a hakim or a doctor who attends him. It's the results you're concerned with.

Good wares we want, from any shop you please. My friend, you're involving the poor boy in the toils of [a second] marriage. [Abdul Latif's first wife had died.] But, God keep them, Abdus Salam and Kulsum are enough to preserve his name. For my part, my friend, I believe in Ibn i Yamin's words:

Wise is that man who in this world refrains
    from just two things:
He who would pass his days in peace must
    steel himself to say,
'I will not wed, though I might have the
    daughter of a king,
I will not borrow, though I get till
    Doomsday to repay.'

I hope it's not the case that he doesn't want to marry and you are pushing him into this misfortune. Find out from men he confides in what is in his mind. If he is willing too, I've nothing more to say. But if he isn't, then in my opinion it would be an imposition.

On 5 July 1855, to Haqir:

> My dear friend, congratulations upon Munshi Abdul Latif's marriage, first to him, then to his parents, and then to his sisters and brothers. I tell you again, God grant that it has been done with his willing consent. Congratulations on Zakiya Begam's engagement.
>
> The air is very pleasant now, and it rains every day.... This time I had to wait a long while for a letter from you, and several days ago I felt like writing to complain. But the rain made it impossible for me to send my man out to the post, and after that your letter came two days ago. Yesterday it still rained, but today it's cleared up, that is, the rain has stopped. I've been to the Fort, and written this letter to you too.

On 26 July 1855, to Haqir:

> It's rained until there's a river wherever you look, and the sun appears as briefly as the lightning flash—that is, it only shows its face very occasionally. Many houses in the city have collapsed. It's still raining as I write this. I'm writing the letter, but let's see when it can be taken to the post office. I'll tell my man to wrap a blanket round him and go.
>
> The mangoes this year have been ruined—so much so that if for the sake of argument, a man climbs a tree and picks one from the bough and sits and eats it there, even then he finds that it's rotted and decayed.

In 1856 he writes to Yusuf Ali Khan Aziz replying to various questions about gender:

> There is no generally agreed rule about gender. See! people in this [part of the] country regard 'lafz' [meaning 'word'] as masculine, while people further east [i.e. in Lucknow and what is now eastern UP] make it feminine. Anyway I write whatever comes to my tongue. In this matter nobody's poetical works can prove anything; one community agrees on one thing, another grouping settles on another. There is no definite rule.

He goes on to give the genders of the letters of the alphabet and to answer queries about particular words. At one point he remarks in passing, 'English has been current in Bengal for the past hundred years, and in Delhi and Agra for the past sixty.'

Among the last letters we have before the momentous year of 1857 are two written to his friend Mir Ahmad Husain Maikash:

> Bravo! a thousand times bravo! I thoroughly enjoyed your

chronogram. God alone knows how good the dates on which it was composed must taste. Look here, my friend!

A darwesh speaks only when he has seen.

I have seen the chronogram, and have praised it. When I've eaten the dates, I'll praise them too. Don't get the idea that this is a polite way of asking for some, and put poor Din Muhammad to further trouble. He has just brought your note; don't make him come again to bring me dates. God forbid! However, if by any impossible chance you do decide to do just that and send me some dates by Din Muhammad, [then they'll be welcome].

Before many more months had passed Maikash was taken and executed by the British for complicity in the 'Mutiny'.

Such are the varied themes of the letters of the years before 1857. Exactly what was going to happen in that year, Ghalib could not have foreseen. But he had seen for years the few remaining powers of the Mughal king being whittled away by the British, and by the early fifties had become fully aware of the threat that this involved to the stability of his own position. Close as he was not only to the Mughal court but to influential British officials, he knew very well how to read the signs of the times, and already in 1852, when the king had been taken ill, he had expressed anxiety about his future in a Persian letter to a friend, Munshi Hira Singh: 'Since the evening of Id the king has been ill. What will happen now? And what will become of me, who sleeps in the shade of his wall?' [i.e. who depends on him for my livelihood.] The year 1854 which brought him the most considerable accessions to his regular income he was ever to receive, also brought him fresh warning, for in that year the British decided that after Bahadur Shah's death, the royal family was to vacate the Red Fort and live outside the city in the area of the Qutub Minar. He received a letter about this time from Junun in which he had apparently been asked about mushairas being held in Delhi. He replies:

Mushairas are not held anywhere in the city. In the Fort the Timurid princes gather to recite ghazals.... Sometimes I go, and sometimes I don't; and this assembly [the court] itself will not last many days more.... It can vanish at any moment....

In 1856 he suffered two serious losses of income, with the death of the Mughal heir-apparent and the British annexation of Oudh. About the former event he wrote to Haqir on 27 July 1856:

> You must bear in mind that the death of the heir-apparent has been
> a great blow to me. It means that my ties with the Empire [i.e. the
> Mughal court] will last now only as long as the king does. God knows
> who the new heir-apparent will be. He who appreciated my worth
> has died. Who will recognize me now? I put my trust in my Creator,
> and resign myself to His will. And there is this immediate loss: he
> used to give me ten rupees a month to buy fruit for Zain ul Abidin
> Khan's [Arif's] two boys. Who will give me that now?

He does not mention the stipend which he had received as the heir-
apparent's ustad.

The whole future of the Mughal court now became even more
uncertain, for the British decided that Bahadur Shah's successor
was to be styled 'Prince' and not 'King', and that the allowance
paid him by the British government was to be reduced. Not
surprisingly, Ghalib thought it prudent to seek other sources of
support. First he decided to try his luck with the all-powerful
British themselves. He wrote a Persian ode in praise of Queen
Victoria, and sent it to the Governor-General, Lord Canning, for
forwarding to London. Along with it went a letter containing a
none too subtle hint of his motives in writing it. He later wrote
of this letter:

> I indicated what my expectations were by saying that the emperors
> of Rum and of Persia, and other conquering kings, had been
> accustomed to bestow all manner of bounties on their poets and
> panegyrists. They would fill a poet's mouth with pearls, or weigh
> him in gold, or grant him villages in fief or open the door of their
> treasuries to shower wealth upon him. And so your poet and
> panegyrist seeks a title bestowed by the imperial tongue, and a robe
> of honour conferred by the imperial command, and a crust of bread
> from the imperial table.

At the end of January 1857 he received a reply from London which
greatly encouraged him, saying that when enquiries had been
made, appropriate orders in the matter of the title and robe would
be issued. About the same time, early in 1857, through his old
friend Fazl i Haq, he established a link with the small princely state
of Rampur. On Fazl i Haq's suggestion, Ghalib addressed a Persian
letter to its ruler, Nawwab Yusuf Ali Khan, and followed this up
by presenting him a copy of his diwan. The Nawwab, who had
once studied Persian under Ghalib in Delhi, now appointed him
his ustad, and sent him occasional gifts of money.

Ghalib did not make these new contacts any too soon. A few months later, in May 1857, the Indian soldiers at Meerut rose in revolt against their British rulers. They entered Delhi on 11 May, and were to hold it for several months. But with the British victory in the struggle that followed, the Mughal power was finally swept away.

The Revolt of 1857

What Ghalib did during the 'Mutiny' we know, for the most part, from his own accounts. In a letter to Sarur written eighteen months later (18 November 1858) he writes:

> On 11 May 1857 the disorders began here. On that same day I shut the doors and gave up going out. One cannot pass the days without something to do, and I began to write my experiences, appending also such news as I heard from time to time. But I made it a binding rule to write it in ancient Persian, the language of *Dasatir*, and except for the proper names, which, of course, cannot be altered, to use no Arabic words.

It was the established tradition in Ghalib's day to choose the title of a work not to indicate its content but rather to assert in poetic metaphor its literary worth; he accordingly entitled this work *Dastambu* ('A Posy of Flowers'). It continued to occupy him on and off for fifteen months.

What else he did besides beginning *Dastambu* in the four months during which the rebels held Delhi we do not know in any detail. *Dastambu* itself treats this period very briefly, and his private letters too are noticeably reticent. But in a letter written much later—on 14 January 1858—to the Nawwab of Rampur he says,

> In those turbulent days I held myself aloof [from the court]. But I feared that if I completely severed all connection with it my house might be destroyed and my very life perhaps endangered. Thus I continued inwardly estranged, but outwardly friendly.

Several weeks earlier—on 5 December 1857, he had told Tufta, 'In this upheaval I have had no part in any matter of policy. I simply carried on with my verse-correcting....'

No such statements are to be found in *Dastambu*, at any rate in the form in which it has come down to us. This qualification is

necessary because, as we shall see later, Ghalib conceived the idea
in 1858 of presenting the work to the British authorities as a means
of winning their favour and patronage. With this in mind Ikram
comments, 'To assume that Ghalib has recorded the whole course
of events plainly and without inhibition would not be correct'. But
if we may safely assume that he may on the one hand have omitted
or toned down passages which could give serious offence to the
British, and on the other may have added emphasis to his horror
at the acts of the rebel sepoys, there is nevertheless no reason to
believe that the book in any way misrepresents his essential
attitudes, and it remains the clearest connected account we possess
of his personal experiences during these months and his reactions
to the momentous events taking place around him; for, as he writes:
'This book from start to finish records what has befallen me and
what I have heard'. (He adds that where he records what he has
heard, he does so in the conviction that it is true.) The book is also
a work of remarkable literary power. For both these reasons we
translate the greater part of it in this and the next chapter.

Because he conceived *Dastambu* primarily as a work of literature,
he does not come immediately to its essential subject matter, but
begins, as a true Muslim should:

> In the name of God, from Whom comes all success, and Who created
> sun and moon, and night and day.
>   A Mighty Ruler is He, who raised the nine heavens aloft and
> endowed the seven planets with light, and great is His knowledge
> Who caused the soul to enter the body and taught reason and justice
> to mankind, and caused these seven and those nine, sustained by no
> foundation and no prop, to endure eternally....

He goes on to argue that if the heavens influence human fortunes,
they do so as the servants of His will: 'The stars are the servants
of a Just Ruler, and the servants of His justice may not pass beyond
the orbit of equity.' If then the stars bring misfortune upon man,
all this is part of the working of God's purpose:

> The Minstrel's plectrum strikes against the strings
> But who does not know what his purpose is?
> Joy lies concealed in grief. 'Tis not in anger
> The washerman beats the clothes against the stone.

> In truth the annihilation of one thing serves only to bring another
> into being. Ease and toil, success and degradation, are all of God's

gift, and whatever He sends tends to man's gain and betterment and happiness and delight.... Is this not gift enough to us, that He exists?...The heavens turn like a millstone, and neither heavens nor millstone move without a mover....

> God sets the skies in motion. Understand then
> Nothing that comes from them can be unjust.

All praise to Him Who confers existence and sets a term to nothingness, Who nurtures equity and stamps out oppression, Whose justice saps the might of the mighty, and Whose kindness gives strength to the weak.

Yes, that God Who can transform nothingness into being, can in the same way annihilate all that is. If He who said 'Be', and in a moment brought the whole universe into being, should in another moment say 'Cease!' and annihilate all, what man would dare to murmur against Him?

In short, God is great, and God is good, and the wise man who knows this, accepts with equanimity and joy all that God sends.

Ghalib then prepares to move towards his subject proper, and a passing reference to 'armies that throw off their allegiance to their commanders' foreshadows what is ultimately to come. Ultimately, but not yet. There follows a long comparison and contrast between the fall of Persia before the invading Arab Muslims and the revolt of the Indian sepoys against their British masters, each presaged, according to astrologers, by the same conjunction of Mars and Saturn in the same mansion.

He then turns abruptly to his own position:

Let the reader of this book understand that I, the motion of whose pen spills pearls upon the page, have from my childhood eaten the salt of the English government. So to say, since I cut my first teeth my bread has come from the table of these conquerors of the world. Some seven or eight years have passed since the king of Delhi summoned me and desired that in return for six hundred rupees a year I should write the history of the Timurid kings. I accepted, and set myself to my task. After some time, when the old ustad of the king passed away, the correction of his verses too fell to me. I was old and infirm, accustomed to ease and solitude. And more than all this, my deafness made me a burden to the hearts of others, as in every assembly I gazed intently at the lips of every speaker. Willy-nilly, I would go once or twice a week to the Fort. If the king came out of his apartments I would stand for some time ready to serve him; if not, I would sit there for a little while writing, and then return home. Whatever I had written I would either take to the king myself or send it to him by another's hand. Such was my occupation when the far-ranging thought of the swift-moving sky planned a fresh revolution, to destroy my insignificant and harmless ease.

> I swear by His name, Whose unheeding sword
> Strikes down impartially both friend and foe.

He then describes how

...this year, at midday on Monday 16th Ramzan, 1273 AH, which corresponds to 11 May 1857...the gates and walls of the Fort and the battlements of Delhi were suddenly shaken. It was not an earthquake: on that inauspicious day a handful of ill-starred soldiers from Meerut, frenzied with malice, invaded the city—every man of them shameless and turbulent, and with murderous hate for his masters, thirsting for British blood.

He relates how they were admitted by the city guards and quickly overran the city, killing every Englishman they found and not resting until they had burnt their houses to ashes.

There were humble, quiet men, who passed their days drawing some modest sum from British bounty and eating their crust of bread, living scattered in different areas of the city. No man among them knew an arrow from an axe.... In truth, such men are made to people the lanes and by-lanes, not to gird up their loins and go out to battle. These men, when they saw that a dam of dust and straw cannot stem the fast-flowing flood, took to their only remedy, and every man of them went to his home and resigned himself to grief. I too am one of these grief-stricken men. I was in my home. When I heard the noise and uproar, I would have made enquiry, but in the twinkling of an eye...every street and every lane was full of galloping horsemen, and the sound of marching men, coming wave upon wave, rose in the air. Then there was not so much as a handful of dust which was not red with the blood of men whose bodies were like the rose; and it seemed that every corner of every garden was stripped of its leaves and fruits, the graveyard of a hundred springtimes. Alas for those wise and just rulers, of good nature and good name! And woe for those fair ladies of delicate form, with faces radiant as the moon and bodies gleaming like new-mined silver! And alas for those children who had barely yet seen the world, whose smiling faces put the flowers to shame and whose dainty steps reproached the partridge's gait! For all of these were dragged down to drown in the vortex of blood. If Death itself, that rains burning coals and issues flames of fire, Death at whose hands men are compelled to lacerate their faces and blacken their clothes, should stand sobbing and lamenting at these victims' graves, and don black raiment in mourning for them, it would be no more than just. And if the heavens should turn to dust and settle on the earth, and the earth in panic move like a whirlwind from its station, it would be no more than fitting.

> Spring, wallow in your own blood, like a stricken bird;
> Age, plunge in blackness, like a night without a moon;
> Sun, beat your head until your face is bruised and black;
> Moon, make yourself the scar upon the age's heart.

At last, when evening fell on that black day, and blacker darkness overspread the earth, then these black-hearted men in their head-strong pride pitched their camps throughout the city and in the Fort, where they made the royal orchards a stable for their horses and the royal abode their sleeping quarters. Little by little, from distant towns the news came in, that in every cantonment sepoys had shed their officers' blood, and as the minstrel draws the melody from his strings, so had these faithless ones, with beating of drums raised the tumult of rebellion. Band upon band of soldiers and peasants had become as one, and far and near, one and all, without even speaking or conferring together, girded their loins to their single aim, and girded them so strongly that the buffetings of a torrent of blood could alone ungird them. It seemed that legions without number and warriors without count were bound in unity as a single thread binds the twigs that make the broom.... And now you will see a thousand armies, marshalled without marshals, and unnumbered bands, led by no commander and yet ready for war. Their guns and shells, their shot and powder are all taken from English arsenals, and are bent to war against the masters of those arsenals. All the ways of war they learned from the English, and now their faces are inflamed with hate and malice against their teachers. My heart is not stone or iron: how should it not burn in sorrow? My eyes are not sightless windows: how should they not shed tears? Yes, a man must both feel anguish at the death of its English rulers, and shed tears for the destruction of Hindustan. City after city lies open, without protectors, filled with men who have none to watch over them, like gardens bereft of their gardeners, studded with trees stripped bare of leaves and fruit. Robbers go freed from the fetters of the law, and merchants released from the burden of levy. House after house lies desolate, and the abodes of grieving men invite despoliation. Nameless men, who lay lost in the oblivion of their obscure homes, have decked themselves out and sallied forth to display their shamelessness. Row upon row, they go with daggers drawn like a line of eyelashes, while peace-loving men of goodwill venture out to the markets bowed down at every step under oppression's weight. The thieves and the light-fingered, in broad daylight, boldly loot and plunder men's silver and gold, and go home at nights to wrap themselves for sleep in silks and brocades; while illustrious families lack even the lamp-oil to illumine their homes. In the dark nights when raging thirst assails them they await the flash of the lightning, that they may see where the pitchers and the goblets lie. See and admire His serene indifference! Men of no rank, who once toiled all day digging earth to sell, have found bricks of gold in that earth; and men of high rank who once in the assemblies of music and wine lit the bright lamps of pleasure and delight with the rose's fire, lie now in dark cells and burn in the flames of misery and degradation. The jewels of the city's fair-faced women...fill the sacks of vile, dishonoured thieves and pilferers. All their remaining wealth was their airs and graces, and these the new-rich, beggars' sons, have stolen from them to swell the stock of their cheap ostentations. Lovers who were to bear the perverse fancies of fair-faced mistresses, must suffer now the whims of these scoundrels. Every worthless fellow, puffed up with pride, perpetrates what he will, like the eddying whirlwind, and every vain, trifling man, who, drunk with vanity, performs the cheap antics of self-display, is like the straw borne swiftly hither and thither on running water. One, once of high resolve and high renown, has seen his honour dragged in the dust of his own lane; and another, who once had nor name nor pedigree nor gold nor jewels, is suddenly become master of rank and status beyond compute. He whose father tramped the streets and by-lanes as though blown by the idle wind, has made the wind his slave; and he whose mother begged fire from her neighbour, has the fire at his command. Shallow men aspire to make fire and wind their servants, and we are of those ruined ones who long for one sigh of contentment and one cry proclaiming justice:

My grievous tale to you is but a story:
The stars weep tears of blood to hear it told.

After a little more in this vein, in which Ghalib laments particularly the complete breakdown of the postal services, so that he no longer has news of his friends, he passes on to speak of the further development of the revolt.

Fate mustered a sepoy from every street corner, a force from every lane and alley, and an army from every point of the compass, and

set them marching on Delhi. The king was powerless to repulse
them; their forces gathered around him, and he fell under their
duress, engulfed by them as the moon is engulfed by eclipse, though
eclipse befalls only the full moon is [i.e. the moon at the height
of its power] and the king was not like that [i.e. his powers were,
already before the revolt, extremely limited].

The prisons had been opened, and freed criminals contributed
their part to the general anarchy and to the pressures on the king.
He goes on to speak of the military situation, and the daily clashes
between the rebels, now 'near enough fifty thousand strong' and
the force of 'the...British rulers, who in all this wide area held
only a hill to the west of the city'.

On Monday, 24th of the lunar month and 14th of September—when
they who lay in the shade of the hill made an assault on Kashmiri
gate with such majestic force that the black forces had no choice
but to flee before them.... And if May drove justice out of Delhi,
September drove out oppression and brought justice back.

In point of fact, the recovery of the city took more than one
day. The attack of 14 September penetrated to the Jama Masjid,
the beautiful mosque built in the reign of Emperor Shahjahan
(1627–58) but it was then thrown back. However, it was renewed,
and although fighting in the streets continued until the 20th, the
city was by then firmly in British hands. It is characteristic of
Ghalib's moral courage that in a work intended for presentation
to the British authorities he makes no attempt to conceal what the
city suffered in the British assault.

Smiting the enemy and driving him before them, the victors overran
the city in all directions. All whom they found in the streets they
cut down. Those distinguished in the city by rank and wisdom one
and all took to their houses and shut the doors, that their honour
might be safe. Of the army of scoundrels still in the city many
determined upon flight, while a few raged to resist the attackers.
These few now grappled with the brave conquerors of the city to
spill, as they thought, the blood of the alien enemy, but as I deem,
the honour of the capital. For two to three days every road in the
city, from the Kashmiri Gate to Chandni Chauk, was a battlefield.
Three gates—the Ajmeri, the Turcoman and the Delhi—were still
held by the rebels. My house...is situated, between the Kashmiri
and the Delhi Gate, in the centre of the city, so that both are

equidistant from my lane. When the raging lion-hearts set foot in the city, they held it lawful to slaughter the helpless and burn the houses, and indeed, in every territory taken by force of arms these are the sufferings that people must endure. At the naked spectacle of this vengeful wrath and malevolent hatred the colour fled from men's faces, and a vast concourse of men and women, past all computing, owning much or owning nothing, took to precipitate flight through these three gates. Seeking the little villages and shrines outside the city, they there drew breath to wait until such time as might favour their return. Or if even there they could not feel at ease, they journeyed on day and night to some other place. As for the writer of these words, his heart did not quake, nor did his step falter. I stayed where I was, saying 'I have committed no crime and need pay no penalty. The English do not slay the innocent, nor is the air of this city uncongenial to me. Why should I fall a prey to groundless fancies and wander stumbling from place to place? Let me sit in some deserted corner blending my voice with my lamenting pen, while the tears fall from my eyelashes to mingle with the words of blood I write.'

He passes on to

... Friday, the twenty-eighth day of the month of Muharram and the eighteenth day of September.... In these five days the black rebels who had strayed from the right path fled like pigs from within and without the city, and the conquerors gained full control of the city and the Fort. The tumult of arrests and killings reached this lane, and the heart of every man was rent with fear. You must know that there is only one means of egress from this lane, and the lane holds no more than ten to twelve houses.... Most of those who lived there, the women with children in their arms and the men with bundles of their possessions on their shoulders, left it and fled away. The few that remained ... closed the gate to the lane from the inside, and piled stones all about it....

From 15 September every house and every room had been shut up, and neither shopkeepers nor shoppers were anywhere to be seen—no grain-dealer to supply our grain, no washerman to wash our clothes, no barber to cut our hair, no sweeper to clear away the refuse. For five days people had gone out, returning always with water, and sometimes, when they could find them, with salt and flour too. But in the end the doors were barricaded with stones and the mirrors of our hearts were rusted over.... With light or heavy hearts, we ate what we could get, and drank water so sparingly that a man might think it came from a well we had dug with our fingernails. And then the water in the jugs and pitchers, and the fortitude in the hearts of men and women, ran out, and there was no more. The stage passed where we could delude ourselves that we could sustain the burden of the day with patience or that food and drink would come, and for two nights and days we went hungry and thirsty.... But on the third day...release from our troubles came. It came about in this way. The ruler of Patiala, Maharaja Narendar Singh Bahadur...was with the victors in this war, and his army had from the outset been ranged at the British army's side. Some of his favoured servants were distinguished noblemen of Delhi, holding high rank at his court, and among them were Hakim Mahmud Khan, Hakim Murtaza Khan, and Hakim Ghulamullah Khan, all sons of that Hakim Sharif Khan who dwells in Paradise: and they lived in our lane. Their houses stretch in a long line, threshold to threshold, roof to roof, on both sides of the lane, and the writer of these words had been for ten years the neighbour of one of these beneficent men. The first of the three, with his wife and children, lived in the capital, in accordance with the tradition of the family, while the other two lived in Patiala, privileged to be companions to the Maharaja. Foreseeing the retaking of the city, the Maharaja in his gracious kindness to his servants, had secured from the mighty warrior-lords [the British] a promise that when the flowing tide of time should bring them victory, protectors should take their stand at the gate of this lane so that the British soldiers...should do it no harm....

On the third day, then, the Maharaja's soldiers came, a guard was posted, and the dwellers in the lane were freed from the fear of looting and attack. They came out of their houses, saying to themselves 'Now come what may', and asked the soldiers' permission to leave the lane. Since the guard was one of friends and not of enemies, their request was granted to this extent: they were told 'You may go as far as Chandni Chauk: to go beyond is to go to the slaughter'. In hardship, misery and fear and trembling they opened the gate. Water-skins and water carriers there were none, and a man from each house, and two of my servants, ventured out. Sweet water was far away, and far they must not go. Of necessity they filled their pots and pitchers with brackish water and brought them back home; and at last that fire whose other name is thirst was quenched. They who had gone out and fetched the water said that in the lane beyond which they were not permitted to go, soldiers had broken down the doors of several houses, but the sacks in them were empty of flour and the vessels empty of oil. I said, 'God's true servant is he who speaks not of vessel or sack, of oil or flour. Our livelihood is in the hands of Him Who forgets us not. To fail in thanksgiving to God for His bounties is Satan's work'.

In these days we thought of ourselves as prisoners, and in truth the life we led was a prisoner's life: none could come to us that we might listen, nor could we go out to see what could be seen; thus our ears were deaf and our eyes were blind. And in this trouble and perplexity, a dearth of bread and water! One day out of the blue, clouds gathered and rain fell. We hung out a sheet and put a pitcher beneath it, and got water. They say the clouds draw water from the oceans and rain it down on earth: this cloud of great price and auspicious shadow brought water from the fountain of life, and that which Sikandar, for all his kingship, vainly sought, I, for all my wretchedness, found....

At this point he breaks off to tell of his present difficulties. The use of the present tense and 'this year' in the sense of 1857, show, the original character of *Dastambu* as a narrative of events written as they happened from day to day:

This year [1857] I enter my sixty-second year, stirring the dust of this ancient world of dust. And for fifty years I have used up my strength in the pursuit of poetry.... [He then gives the history of his pension.] Until the end of April of this year—I write these words in 1857—I drew my pension from the treasury of the Collector of Delhi. But the doors of that treasury have been closed since May, and I am face to face with misfortune, and wild and fearful fancies throng my heart. Formerly I had none to support but my one wife, with neither son nor daughter. But some five years ago, I took to my bosom two orphaned boys from the family of my wife, prime source of all my troubles. They had just learned to talk, and love for these sweetly-speaking children has melted me and made me one with them. Even now in my ruined state they are with me, adorning my life as pearls and flowers adorn my coat. My brother, who is two years younger than I, at thirty years of age gave sense and reason to the winds and trod the ways of madness and unreason. For thirty years he has passed his life unaware, troubling no man and making no commotion. His house is apart from mine, at a distance of about two thousand paces. His wife and daughter, with the younger children and the maid-servants, saw that their best course lay in flight, and went away, leaving the mad master of the house with the house and all it contained, with an aged doorkeeper and an old maid-servant, to fend for himself. Had I had an enchanter's power I could not in those days have sent anyone to bring the three of them and their goods to me. This is another heavy sorrow, another calamity that has descended on me like an avalanche. Two tender children, tenderly reared and cherished, ask for milk and sweets and fruit, and

I cannot give them. Alas! at such a stage the tongue falls silent. We
live in anxious thought for bread and water, and die in anxious
thought for shroud and grave. Constant care for my brother
consumes me. How did he sleep at night? What did he eat by day?
And no news comes, so that I cannot even tell if he be still alive or
if the weight of constant hardship has broken and killed him.

> More than the cry which echoes the heart's strife would leave my
>   lips
> God and my soul the very breath of life would leave my lips!

The things that I have written sap my life; and things I have not
written afflict my soul. I look to men who know of these things to
give ear to my complaint and judge me justly. The end of life draws
near, and I am like the flickering lamp of early dawn or the sun that
sinks to rest behind the roof-tops....

He again breaks off to relate how he had two years earlier composed
an ode in Queen Victoria's honour, and what had been the response
to this, and how the revolt had prevented matters coming to a
conclusion. Then he resumes:

On Wednesday, 30 September, seventeen days after the taking of the
city and the sealing of our lane, news was brought to me that robbers
had attacked my brother's house and looted it, and the whole lane had
been plundered. But they spared... [his] life and those of the old
doorkeeper and old maid-servant. These two old people, helped and
accompanied by two Hindus who in the panic and uproar had fled
there and found refuge with them, had spared no effort to find water
and food. Be it known that in the uproar of tumult and reprisal that
shook the city, just as the modes of violence and oppression varied
from lane to lane, in the same way the ways of the soldiers in killing
and plundering varied, and ruthlessness or mercy was shown accord-
ing to each soldier's mood and temperament. I surmise that in this
assault the orders were to spare the life of him who bows the head of
submission and take only his goods, while he who resists must yield
his life and wealth and property all three.... And this is the general
belief.... And to cut down old people and women and children is not
held lawful.... Ye men who worship God, exalting equity and justice
and condemning violence and oppression...remember first the
Indians and see their character who in enmity without cause and
malice without foundation, in full knowledge that the murder of
one's masters is a sin, drew the sword against their rulers and
murdered helpless women and sent to their long sleep in the dust and

blood children whom their mothers would have lulled to sleep in their cradles; and then behold the English, who when they rose to battle against this enemy, and marshalled their forces to take revenge upon the guilty, might in their just suspicion of Delhi's citizens have left not a dog or cat in the city alive. On fire with an anger whose flames could burn the heart to ashes, they yet restrained it, and harmed not a hair on the head of any woman or child....

Yet a few lines later he continues:

Many of the wretched people of the city have been driven out, and the rest lie here, prisoners of hopes and fears...and there is perhaps no balm to soothe the pain of either those within or those without the city. If only those within and those without could have news of each other's lives and deaths!.... All one can tell with certainty is that every man, wherever he is, is in want. Those...within the city who sigh deeply for their fate and those without, who rejected by fate, and condemned to rove aimlessly, their hearts alike carry a full burden of sorrow and their faces alike are pale with the fear of death.

He then relates an incident which took place

...suddenly at midday, on Monday, 5 October, when a small band of British soldiers came along the wall which runs from the gate to the lane, climbed onto a roof, and thence jumped down into the lane. The Maharaja's soldiers attempted without success to stop them, and disregarding the smaller houses, they came straight to the house of him who writes these words. In the goodness of their hearts they did not touch any of the household effects, but took me, and the two fair-faced boys, and two or three servants and a few good-hearted neighbours with them, using, however, no violence or harshness, and brought us to a point rather more than two furlongs from our lane, to the house of the merchant Qutub ud Din, on the other side of Chandni Chauk, where the wise and capable Colonel Brown[38] had his headquarters. He spoke to me courteously and humanely, asked me my name and the others their occupation, and there and then dismissed me with every kindness. I offered thanks to God, sang in my heart the praises of that gracious man, and returned to my house.

Here he turns again to the wider scene. He is puzzled on 7 October to hear a salute of twenty-one guns, 'for the Lieutenant-Governor's approach is saluted by seventeen, and the Governor-General's by nineteen'; but he ultimately concludes that this must salute some

[38] It appears that, in fact, the Colonel's name was Burn.

further victory over the rebels, 'for be it known that in many places—Bareilly, Farrukhabad, Lucknow—band upon rebel band is still bent upon stirring up evil... their hearts—may God crush them to blood—are set upon war, and their hands—may God strike them useless—are set to their task.' Other disturbances have arisen too,

> ...as though Hindustan has become the arena of the mighty whirlwind and the blazing fire. And if in these grievous days whose beginning none can remember and whose end none can tell, mine eyes have seen aught but weeping, may their windows be blocked with dust. Save the darkness of my fortunes, there is nothing I can claim my eyes have seen.... To leave the house, to set foot on the threshold, to walk the lanes and streets, and see Chandni Chauk in the distance—these, except for that one day when the English soldiers took me—have not fallen to my lot. It is as though the sage of Ganja [the Persian poet Nizami] spoke for me when he said
>
> > I do not know what passes in the world
> > Or what of good or bad befalls men there.
>
> Afflicted by these ills without remedy, these wounds without balm, I must think that I have died, have been called to life to give an account of my deeds, and in punishment of my sins have been suspended head-down in the pit of Hell, thus to live for ever in misery and degradation. Woe upon me if all my todays and tomorrows are to be like this!...
>
> On 19 October, a Monday once again—that day whose name should be struck from the list of the week's days—...in the first watch of the day, my brother's doorkeeper with downcast face and dishevelled hair, brought me the joyous news of my brother's death. I learned that he had taken the road to oblivion and walked with hurrying steps: for five days he had burned in high fever, and then half an hour after midnight, had urged the steed of life to leap from this narrow pass. Think not of water and cloths, seek not for corpse-washers and grave-diggers, ask not for stone or brick, talk not of lime and mortar; but say how can I go to him? Where can I take him? In what graveyard can I consign him to the earth? Cloth, from the dearest and finest to the cheapest and coarsest, is not to be had. Hindus may take their dead to the river and there at the water's edge consign them to the fire. But what of the Muslims? How could a Muslim join with two or three of his fellows and, joining shoulder to shoulder, pass through the streets carrying their dead to burial? My neighbours took pity on my loneliness and at length girded their

loins to the task. One of the Patiala soldiers went in front, and two of my servants followed. They washed the corpse, wrapped it in two or three white sheets they had brought with them, and in a mosque at the side of his house dug a hole in the ground. In this they laid him, filled up the pit with earth once more, and came away. Alas for him who in his life of sixty years passed thirty happily and thirty in sadness...God grant him His mercy—for in his life he knew no comfort—and send some angel for his delight and grant his soul to dwell in Paradise for ever. Alas for this good man of ill fortune...who in the years of sanity never showed anger and in the years of madness troubled no man...but lived his life a stranger to himself...and on the 29th night of the month of Safar, died.

> Bow down your head and ask for God's forgiveness;
> Where'er you do so, there His threshold is.

He turns to speak of what happened to his kinsmen of Loharu.

In the same week in which British army conquered the city, Amin ud Din Ahmad Khan Bahadur and Muhammad Ziya ud Din Khan Bahadur, men renowned for their wisdom and justice, bethought them that their honour might best be safeguarded and their hopes for the future made stronger if they left the city. They set out with their wives and children, with three elephants and about forty fine horses, and took the road to the domain of Loharu, which had always been their estate. They first halted at Mihrauli, where in the radiance of that blessed burying ground[39] they partook of the provisions for their journey and rested for two or three days. While they were there, robber soldiers surrounded them, and robbed them of everything except the clothes they wore. Only the three elephants, whom their loyal and faithful companions had led away the moment the tumult began, survived to remind them of their former state, like three burnt granaries [on a plundered estate]. You may well imagine the plight of these victims of robbery and ruin, and they set out, without provisions and without equipment, for Dujana. They were welcomed by Hasan Ali Khan Bahadur, of noble name and fairest fame, who gave proof of his humanity and courage, telling them 'My home is yours' and escorting them to Dujana. I will not speak at length: this laudable leader of men acted towards his peers with all the gracious generosity that Iran's emperor...showed to Humayun.[40]

[39] Mihrauli is burial place of the saint Qutub ud Din Baktyar.
[40] Humayun, second of the Mughal dynasty, reigned from 1530 to 1556. Early in his reign he was forced to flee for some years to Iran.

When the Commissioner[41] Sahib Bahadur heard the news, he sent for them to come to Delhi. Accordingly they returned to the city and presented themselves before him. For some time he spoke to them with unkind taunts, but they returned soft answers to him, and he fell silent. He directed them to a place in the Fort, next to the hall of the king's steward-in-chief, and commanded them to take up residence there. Regard for the even flow of his writing did not permit the writer of these words to tell the full tale of loss and ruin that befell this family. Know then that while their owners fell a prey to pillage in Mihrauli, their empty houses in Delhi were plundered and laid waste. Of all they had taken with them, they brought only their fainting lives to Dujana, while the rest in its entirety fell to the robbers. While here, of their mansions and palaces nothing remained but bricks and stones and pebbles. They were stripped bare; not a trace of their silver and gold remained, and not a thread of their carpets and their clothing. God grant His mercy to these guiltless men, and an auspicious end to this inauspicious beginning, bringing them comfort out of distress. It was Saturday, the 17 October when these two men, unrivalled in wisdom, returned to the city, and, as I have said, took up their residence in the Fort.

About the princes no more than this can be said, that some fell victims to the rifle bullet and were sent into the jaws of the dragon of death, and the souls of some froze in the noose of the hangman's rope, and some lie in prisons, and some are wanderers on the face of the earth. The old and infirm king, confined in the Fort, is under trial. The lords of Jhajjar and Ballabgarh and he who adorned the throne of Farrukhnagar, have been taken separately, on separate days, and hung on the gallows tree, that none might say that their blood has been shed.'[42]

On this blunt note Ghalib ends his account of 1857, and though there is more in *Dastambu*, it is convenient to break off at this point and see what further light on his experiences is shed by other sources.

We have seen that in *Dastambu* he discreetly ends his account of his connection with the Mughal court at the point when the entry of the sepoys into Delhi 'destroyed his insignificant and

[41] Of Delhi.

[42] Much later, on 13 June 1858, he records that Bahadur Jang Khan had now been released, granted an allowance of Rs 1000 a month, and ordered to take up permanent residence in Lahore.

harmless ease'; whereas in his letter to Tufta and to the Nawwab of Rampur already quoted he says that he continued during the rebel occupation to perform his duties as the king's ustad, and in general to maintain outwardly friendly relations with the court. There are similar differences in the period from 14 September, when the British launched the assaults that recaptured the city. The British soldiers did not behave with quite the restraint which, while not concealing their ruthlessness, he praises in *Dastambu*; and Ghalib knew it. During the fighting many excesses were committed; and, much worse, they continued long after Indian resistance had ceased. All able-bodied men were assumed to be rebels and all who could be found were sought out and killed indiscriminately. Ghalib's feelings are expressed in a poem evidently written at the time, and appended without comment to a short letter on quite another topic written in 1858.

> Now every English soldier that bears arms
> Is sovereign, and free to work his will.
>
> Men dare not venture out into the street
> And terror chills their hearts within them still.
>
> Their homes enclose them as in prison walls
> And in the Chauk[43] the victors hang and kill.
>
> The city is athirst for Muslim blood
> And every grain of dust must drink its fill....

Another thing missing from *Dastambu* is Ghalib's characteristic humour, which he no doubt felt to be inappropriate to such a work. That it did not desert him even in the worst days is evident from two incidents that occurred when he was carried off by the British soldiers to be interrogated by Colonel Burn. The first is related by Hali, and the second by Ghalib himself. Hali writes:

> I have heard that when Ghalib came before Colonel Brown [Burn] he was wearing a tall Turkish-style headdress. The Colonel looked at this strange fashion and asked in broken Urdu, 'Well? You Muslim?' 'Half,' said Ghalib. 'What does that mean?' asked the Colonel. 'I drink wine, but I don't eat pork,' said Ghalib. The Colonel laughed, and Ghalib then showed him the letter which he

---

[43] Mihr notes that after the mutiny the British hanged offenders in Chandni Chauk, in front of the police headquarters.

had received from the Minister for India [*sic*] in acknowledgement of the ode to Her Majesty the Queen which Ghalib had sent.[44] The Colonel said, 'After the victory of the government forces why did you not present yourself at the Ridge?'[45] Ghalib replied, 'My rank required that I should have four palanquin-bearers, but all four of them ran away and left me, so I could not come.' The Colonel then dismissed him and all his companions with every courtesy.

Hali evidently did not know that Ghalib himself had written an account of this incident, and that his own version of his reply to the Colonel's final question is a little more elaborate. He says he told him:

The rebel soldiers were posted outside the gates to prevent people leaving. How could I come? If I had made up some story to deceive the rebel sentry I might have got out of the city, but as soon as I came within range of the English sentry on the Ridge he would have fired at me. And let us suppose that I did get past the rebel guard, and the English sentry did not shoot me—just look at me and consider my condition. I am old and crippled and deaf, and as unfit to confer with as I am to fight. I do pray for your success, and have done all along; but I could do that from here.

Ghalib's remark that he was 'half a Muslim' was not entirely flippant. 'At this point in his book *Dastambu*,' says Hali, 'Ghalib writes, "A free man does not hide the truth; I *am* half a Muslim, free from the bonds of convention and every religion; and in the same way, I have freed myself from grief at the sting of men's tongues".'[46]

In *Dastambu*, Ghalib puts a bold face on it and says of his decision not to flee before the British assault that 'his heart did not quake, nor his step falter', nor did he 'fall a prey to groundless fancies'. It is not to deny his courage to say that his letters tell a rather less confident story. A letter to Tufta written towards the end of the year, on 5 December 1857, looks back on what has passed since the retaking of the city, and its whole tone is very markedly—and very understandably—apprehensive. He explains how the lane in which he lived received the protection of troops from Patiala, and continues:

[44] Cf. p. 113 above.
[45] High ground outside the city, where the English forces were encamped.
[46] The words which Hali quotes do not in fact appear at this point in *Dastambu*, but in another context. See p. 135 below.

But for that I should not have been in Delhi now. Do not think I am exaggerating: everyone, rich and poor alike, has left the city, and those who did not leave of their own accord have been expelled. Nobles, grant-holders, wealthy men, artisans—none are left. I am afraid to write you a detailed account. Those who were in the service of the Fort are being drastically dealt with, and are harassed with interrogations and arrests—but that is only those who entered the service of the court during these months and took part in the revolt. I am a poor poet, attached to the court for the past ten to twelve years for writing chronograms and correcting verses—call it court service if you like, or call it wage-labour. In this upheaval I have had no part in any matter of policy. I simply carried on with my verse-correcting, and considering that I was innocent of any offence, I have not left the city. The authorities know that I am here, but they have found nothing against me either in the royal papers or in the statements of informers, and accordingly I have not been summoned to appear before them. Otherwise, when high-ranking nobles have been summoned or brought in under arrest, of what account am I? In short I stay in the house and cannot as much as step outside the door, much less get into the palanquin and go visiting. As for anyone coming to see me, who is there left in the city? House after house lies deserted, and the punishment of offenders goes on. Martial law was introduced from 11 May, and today, Saturday 5 December 1857, is still in force. No one knows how life goes on in the city. In fact, the authorities have not even turned their attention to such things. Let us see what will come of it all. No one can enter or leave the city without a permit. On no account should you think of coming here. We must still wait and see whether the Muslims are permitted to return to their homes in the city or not. Anyway, give my regards to Munshi Sahib[47] and show him this letter. Your letter has just come, and I have sat down and replied to it right away and given it to the postman.

Well might Ghalib, even so late in the year, feel 'afraid to write', and well might he feel the need to assure Tufta that he was 'not exaggerating'. For the British reign of terror continued for weeks after the retaking of the city, and the measures taken against the people of Delhi were so drastic as to seem almost incredible. As soon as the city was retaken, the British expelled the whole population, and Ghalib, in the same letter to Tufta, vividly describes the uncanny sense of desolation that this produced:

[47] Munshi Nabi Bakhsh Haqir.

Do you understand what has happened, and what is going on? There was a former birth in which you and I were friends, and all the many things that happen between close friends happened between us. We composed our verses and compiled our diwans. In that age there was a gentleman who was our sincere friend—my friend and yours. Munshi Nabi Bakhsh was his name, and Haqir his takhallus. Suddenly that age came to an end, and all the friendly dealings and sincerity and love and joy ended with it. After a while we received another birth. But although to all appearances this birth is exactly like the first—I write a letter to Munshi Nabi Bakhsh Sahib and receive his reply, and today I get a letter from you, and your name is still Munshi Hargopal and your takhallus Tufta, and the city I live in is still called Delhi and this muhalla is still named Ballimaron muhalla—yet not one of the friends of that former birth is to be found. By God, you may search for a Muslim in this city and not find one—rich, poor, and artisans alike are gone. Such as are here are not Delhi people.

The expulsion of the population had taken place in mid-September. By mid-October its sufferings were extreme. Mrs Saunders, wife of the commissioner of Delhi, wrote in a letter on 25 October, 'The inhabitants of this huge place seven miles round are dying daily of starvation and want of shelter,' and accounts by contemporary English observers support Ghalib's statement that in December, when the cold at nights is severe in the Delhi region, the position was still unchanged.

The anxious, defensive tone in which he describes the nature of his connection with the Fort is fully understandable. No reference to his name had been found in the royal papers, but some reference might yet be found, and however harmless its nature, it could in the mood then prevailing have had the direst consequences for him. Similarly, informers were everywhere active, and men were paying off old scores against their enemies by denouncing them to the British as supporters of the rebel cause. Reports like these were being acted upon without any attempt at independent verification, and Ghalib knew from abundant evidence all around him that anyone who felt a strong enough grudge against him could put his life in immediate danger. For weeks together, therefore, fear and uncertainty continued to oppress him, so that even in his private letters he is afraid to speak of what is going on. On 26 December 1857 he writes to Hakim Ghulam Najaf Khan:

I got your letter.... You say that I've never written to you. Be fair! What am I to write? What can I write? What news is there that can be put into writing? What did your letter amount to? And what does this letter of mine amount to? Nothing more than this, that both of us are still alive. And more than this neither you nor I can write.

We shall see in the next chapter that weeks later he is still writing in the same vein.

Not until long after this does he feel that he can safely express his feelings about the heavy toll which the revolt and its aftermath took of his friends. It is in an undated letter to Tufta, written perhaps as late as June or July 1858, that he reveals all that he felt. We give it here in full. Though it speaks of other things besides his grief, the quotation from his own verse with which, without any preamble, he begins his letter, sets the tone of the whole, and the intensity of his emotion rises to its highest pitch as he approaches the end.

> If Ghalib sings in bitter strain, forgive him;
> Today pain stabs more keenly at his heart.

My kind friend, first I have to ask you to convey my greetings to my old friend Mir Mukarram Husain Sahib. Tell him that I am still alive and that more than that even I do not know. Give my regards to Mirza Hatim Ali Mihr Sahib and recite this verse of mine on my behalf:

> Keep strong your faith in the unseen—else you are no believer.
> You who are hidden from my sight, love for you is my faith.[48]

I had already sent off an answer to your first letter. Your second letter came two or three days later. Listen, my friend, when a man has the means to devote all his days free of care to the pursuit of the things he loves, *that* is what luxury means. The abundant time and energy you give to poetry is proof of your noble qualities and your sound disposition; and brother, the fame of your poetic achievement adds lustre to my name too. As for me, I have forgotten how to write poetry, and forgotten all the verses I ever wrote too—or rather, all except a couplet-and-a-half of my Urdu verse—that is, one final couplet of a ghazal, and one line. This is the couplet. Whenever my

---

[48] In the original the verse is all the more apt because the word translated 'love' is 'mihr', which is also the takhallus of the man to whom it is here addressed.

heart sinks within me it comes to my lips and I recite it—five times, ten times—over and over again:

> Ghalib, when *this* is how my life has passed
> How can I call to mind I had a God?

And when I feel at the end of my tether I recite this line to myself:

> O sudden death, why do you still delay?

and relapse into silence. Do not think that it is grief for my own misery or my own ruin that is choking me. I have a deeper sorrow, so deep that I cannot attempt to tell you, and can only hint at it. Among the English whom those infamous black scoundrels slaughtered, some were the focus of my hopes, some my well-wishers, some my friends, some my bosom companions, and some my pupils in poetry. Amongst the Indians some were my kinsmen, some my friends, some men whom I loved. And all of them are laid low in the dust. How grievous it is to mourn one loved *one*. What must his life be like who has to mourn so many? Alas! so many of my friends are dead that now if I should die there will be none to weep for me. 'Verily we are for God, and verily to Him we shall return'.[49]

These letters and the narrative in *Dastambu* afford adequate materials for an assessment of Ghalib's attitude to the revolt, even though the conditions in which he wrote them prevented him from expressing all that he felt. The picture is substantially what one would have expected. When the revolt broke out he was fifty-nine years old, and his attitudes had long been formed. A Mughal aristocrat, steeped in the traditional culture of Mughal India, he was at the same time a highly intelligent, clear-sighted and unsentimental man who had seen Calcutta, the British capital, and had lived for more than forty years in Delhi, where, outside the precincts of the Mughal court, the British were in full control. He knew the material strength and vitality of the civilization to which, in the last resort, the British owed their success in the struggle for supremacy in India, and he had been deeply impressed by it. Equally well he knew how effete were the political representatives of the old Mughal order, and how powerless to resist the new force which confronted them. We have seen how some years before the revolt, he had written that the Mughal court would not survive many days more.

[49] The last words are a verse from the Quran; they are always quoted when someone dies.

At the same time Ghalib resented the encroachments of the British. In a letter of 23 February 1857 written to a friend in Oudh he speaks of his feelings about the British annexation of 1856: 'Although I am a stranger to Oudh and its affairs, the destruction of the state depressed me all the more, and I maintain that no Indian who was not devoid of all sense of justice could have felt otherwise.'

But what moves him most deeply and makes the most lasting impression upon him is the personal tragedy of individual men personally known to him, caught up and destroyed in the play of forces far beyond their control. He had friends in all camps— among the English, among the Hindus, among Muslims who aided the British and Muslims who supported the revolt—and he mourned all of them deeply and sincerely, and felt their death as an irreparable loss. The sense of loss forced into the background all his partial political sympathies, and overshadowed even his sense of personal danger.

1858: The Aftermath

The crushing of the revolt brought changes in the life of Delhi which could never be reversed. Yet with the new year elements of normality were beginning to return. On 5 December 1857 Ghalib had written that while the Muslims were still excluded from Delhi, 'some of the Hindus, it is true, have returned to their homes'. The British held that it was the Muslims who had been mainly responsible for the revolt, and though Hindus and Muslims were penalized indiscriminately in the period immediately following the retaking of the city, the Hindus were later freed from the most drastic of the restrictions which had been imposed. Those to whom Ghalib refers must however have been exceptional, for it was not until January 1858 that a general return of the Hindus to the city was permitted. He himself writes of this in *Dastambu*:

> In the early days of January 1858 the Hindus' freedom was proclaimed, and permission was granted them to return to their homes in the city. From all quarters they hastened back. But on the walls of the homeless 'Muslims' homes the grass grows green, and its tongues whisper every moment that the places of the Muslims are desolate.'

Ghalib had some cause to rejoice that he was a man who formed sincere friendships in all communities. His Hindu friends were now able to send him wine and to help him in other ways. He writes in *Dastambu*:

To tell the truth—for to hide the truth is not the way of a man free in spirit—I am no more than half a Muslim, for I am free from the bonds of convention and religion, and have liberated my soul from the fear of men's tongues. It has always been my habit at night to drink nothing but French [wine], and if I did not get it I could not sleep. But these days in Delhi foreign wine is very dear and my pockets are empty. What would I have done had not my stalwart God-fearing... friend, the generous and bounteous Mahesh Das sent me wine made from sugar-cane,[50] matching French in colour and excelling it in fragrance? Had he not with this water quenched the fire in my heart, life would have left me, and the raging thirst of my soul would have laid low.

> Long had I wandered on from door to door
> Seeking a flask of wine or two—no more.
> Mahesh Das brought me that immortal draught
> Sikandar spent his days in seeking for.

Justice is not to be denied, and what I have seen, I cannot fail to speak. This virtuous man has spared no effort that the Muslims might be allowed to return to their homes. But heaven's decree was against him.... The Hindus' freedom to return, all know to have come from the kindness of kind rulers, though in this too the works of this man, who loves good and does good and wishes the good well, have played their part. In short he is a good man, who does good to his fellow men and leads a good life amid music and wine. Our acquaintance is not of long standing; yet we talk whenever we chance to meet, and from time to time he sends me a gift; and for both these things I am indebted to him; indeed he does all that kindness could demand. Amongst my other friends and shagirds is Hira Singh, a young man of good heart and of good name; he is very kind to me. He comes to see me and beguiles my sorrow. Among others in this half-desolate, half-peopled city, is that wise young man of illustrious birth, Shiv Ji Ram Brahman. He is like a son to me. He knows my stricken heart, and seldom leaves me all alone, but serves me with all the resources at his command and prospers all my works. His son too, Balmukand, is at one with his father, ever ready in service and

[50] Presumbly rum.

unequalled in sympathy. Among the friends who are far from me is that full moon in the sky of love and kindness, that sweetly-speaking poet Hargopal Tufta, my old friend, a man of one spirit and one voice with me. Since he calls me his master in poetry, his verse and all its God-given excellence is a source of pride to me. In short, he is a man free in spirit, love embodied, and kindness incarnate. Poetry is the source of his fame and he the source of poetry's flourishing. In my abundant love for him I have taken him into my heart and soul and dubbed him 'Mirza Tufta'.[51] He has sent me money from Meerut, and is always sending me letters and ghazals.

I had no need to record these things, but I have been at pains to do so, for I wished to render thanks to God for my friends' love and human kindness....

The other source of comfort to him during the first six months of the year was the steady successes of the British in crushing the revolt in its remaining centres. He records his satisfaction at every fresh victory—on 20 February, when a salute of twenty-one guns 'roaring like the giants of the land and the monsters of the deep', celebrated the success of a major attack on the rebels at Lucknow; on Wednesday, 24 February, when the chief commissioner, '...up-right cypress of the garden of justice, bright moon of the skies of splendour...commander of forces bright and innumerable as the stars, rode into Delhi...while the voice of thirteen guns brought to men's grieving hearts the news of coming balm of mercy and kindness, and the universal rejoicing made one think that the days of Shahjahan had returned;' on Thursday, 18 March, when 'the azure vault of the sky rang with the voice of the guns, bringing the glad news of the expected recovery of Lucknow'; in early May, when Muradabad was taken and handed over to Nawwab Yusuf Ali Khan [of Rampur]; and with special satisfaction on 22 June, when Gwalior was taken from the rebels.

Ghalib seems to have seen this as sealing the fate of the revolt.

It seems that all signs now proclaim the evident end of these lost men, who had fled from all directions to gather in Gwalior, and have now suffered such patent defeat. For some days more, broken and desperate, they will range the land, raiding and robbing on the roads, to meet in the end at every point, degradation and destruction. You

[51] Mirza is strictly speaking the form of address appropriate to men of Mughal (Turkish) stock, such as Ghalib himself. It was also conferred as a title by the Mughal emperors.

will see their horses coursing the grassless deserts until they stumble and their breasts scrape the ground as they breathe their last. You will find their equipment weltering in the mud of flowing watercourses. Then Hindustan will be swept clear of thorns and straw, and every corner of the waste will bloom with luxuriant verdure, and every by-lane shine with the radiance of prosperity.

But the overall tone of *Dastambu*, and of most of his letters of this period, is not one of rejoicing. The passage of *Dastambu* quoted above, in which he says that he has written about the kindness of his Hindu friends because 'I wished to render thanks to God for my friends' love and human kindness' continues without a break,

...and because I desired that when this tale reached my friends they should know that the city is empty of Muslims. No light burns in their homes at night, and no smoke rises from them by day. Ghalib, who knows this city, who had a thousand friends, who had a friend in every home and an acquaintance in every house, now dwells in loneliness with none but the voice of his pen to speak with him and none but his shadow to bear him company.

My face is pale; only the tears of blood
Bring colour to the cheeks whence colour fled.
My soul and heart are grief and fear entire
And briars and thorns the texture of my bed.

Had not these four men [i.e. the Hindu friends mentioned earlier] been in the city there would have been none even to witness my helplessness.

His letters express his feelings more fully—his grief for the loss of his dead friends, the loneliness which oppresses him in his enforced isolation from those who still survive, and (what receives little or no emphasis in *Dastambu*) his continuing fear for his own position. But now Tufta was able to send him money from time to time. In a letter written only four days later he acknowledges a gift of a hundred rupees:

Late in the afternoon of Wednesday, 3 February the postman brought me a registered letter. I opened it and found your draft or bill, or whatever you call it, for Rs 100 inside. I sent off the servant with the receipt with my seal on it, and in little more than the time it takes to get there and back, he was back with a hundred rupees in coin. I had borrowed twenty-four...so I repaid that, gave fifty to my wife, and put the remaining twenty-six in my box; and as I had to open the box to do so, I wrote this letter at the same time. Kalian [Ghalib's servant] has gone to the shops. If he is back soon I will send him to post this letter today. Otherwise it will be tomorrow. May God reward you and keep you. These are evil days, my friend, and I cannot see them ending well. In short, everything is finished.

All the same, not all the letters, even in this period, reflect anxiety and dejection. While some were clearly written under emotional strain, others show that there were times when Ghalib's troubles weighed less heavily upon him. The letters themselves show his varying moods, and little or no comment is called for. On 5 March 1858 he writes to Mihr:

Complaint itself bears witness that the pain has passed.
The heart's pain comes out through the tongue, and finds release.

My friend, your humble servant does not take your complaint ill. But complaint is an art which no one knows but I. The excellence of a complaint consists in this: not to turn one's face from the truth, and not to leave the other person any scope for a rejoinder. Can I not make rejoinder to you that I had been told that you were going to Farrukhabad and so did not write? Can I not say that I wrote you several letters during this period, and all of them were returned to me? What you write is no complaint against me; you are simply laying your own sins at my door. When you left you sent me no word of where you were going, and when you got there you sent no word of where you were staying. Yesterday your kind letter arrived, and today I am sending you one in reply. Do I not then live up to my claims? It is not well to harass the afflicted too much. You are displeased with Mirza Tufta simply because he has not written to you. I do not even know where he is these days, but I have today put my trust in God and written to him at Sikandarabad. Let us see what we shall see.

Somewhere about the same time he writes to Hakim Ghulam Najaf Khan:

Wake up, brother? When did I ever enclose a letter? And when did I ever write that I was forwarding a letter from Sher Zaman? It was just a joke. Sher Zaman in his letter to me had asked me to pay his respects and I said I was enclosing them in my letter. That was all. You have received his respects, wrapped up, so to speak, in my letter to you. So put your mind at rest.

About the same time, he writes to his young friends Shihab ud
Din Khan and Ghulam Najaf Khan; it seems they had been
planning to bring out a fresh edition of his diwan, and had sent
specimen verses for him to see. It produced an explosion:

Brother Shihab ud Din Khan, what in God's name have you and
Hakim Ghulam Najaf Khan done to my diwan? God knows what
child of adultery has inserted the verses you have sent me. After all,
the diwan is printed. If these verses are in the text they are mine,
and if they are entered in the margin they are not mine. And if they
do occur in the text the explanation is that some pimp has scratched
out the original verses and written in this trash. In short, curses upon
the scoundrel who wrote these verses, and on his father, and on his
grandfather and on all his bastard ancestors back to the seventieth
generation. What more than that can I say? What with you, and the
boy Miyan Ghulam Najaf, misfortune has come upon me in my old
age that my verse has fallen into your hands.

Tell your calligrapher not to include that trash in his text, and if
he has already written these two pages, make him take them out and
substitute new pages, written out afresh. You had better send someone
to me with the diwan that your calligrapher has written, so that I can
look through it and send it back. Well, that's all. I am sorry, but today
I haven't got either a stamp or the money to buy one....

The same month he writes to Hakim Ghulam Najaf Khan:

I expect you have heard about Mustafa Khan [Shefta]. God grant
he may be released when the sentence comes up for review; for
how can one who has lived in luxury stand a seven-year prison-
sentence? Have you heard the news about Ahmad Husain Maikash?
He has been hanged—as though there was no one else of that name
in Delhi.

The implication of the last sentence is, perhaps, that someone
named Ahmad Husain (which is a common name) had been
wanted for a capital offence, and that because this was Maikash's
name, the authorities had assumed it was he. Ghalib continues in
the same despondent tone:

I have applied for my pension to be renewed. But even if it is, how
far will it go? True, there are two points about it—first, it will mean
I am cleared of suspicion, and secondly, as the people say, 'I shan't
starve'.... I get some pleasure from Bedil's lines:

Our evenings bring no tidings of a coming morn;
Our mornings show no glimmer of the dawn's white grace;

When all our strivings end in nothing but despair
Take the earth's dust and fling it into heaven's face.

I felt like talking to you, and I have told you what I was feeling. I have nothing more to write now.

In April 1858 he fell ill. On 24 May he writes to Tufta:

After I had sent you my last letter I fell ill, so ill in fact that I thought I should die. It was the colic, and so bad an attack that it had me writhing in pain the whole day long. In the end I took gamboge and castor oil. For the moment I am better, but this is not the end of the story. I will put it briefly. You know the sort of meal I eat when I am in good health? Well, in ten days, on two occasions only, I ate half that amount—in other words, I regaled myself on one full meal in ten days. Mainly I lived on rose-water and essence of tamarind and juice of Persian plums. Yesterday I no longer felt that I should die, and it began to look as though I might survive. This morning I have taken my medicine and written you this letter, and I am sure that today I shall be able to eat my fill....

We may note in passing that he speaks later of the care he takes with verse sent to him for correction: 'I have, as usual, noted by each correction the reason I have made it.'
On 19 June 1858 he writes to Tufta:

Well, what is it, Sahib? Why are you angry with me? It must be a month since I heard from you—or it will be in a day or two. Work it out for yourself. You know how many friends I had, and how I was never without two or three of them around me. And now there are only two—Shiv Ji Ram Brahman and his son Balmukand, who visit me from time to time. Then I would always be getting letters—from Lucknow, and Kalpi, and Farrukhabad and I don't know where else. And now I don't even know what has happened to all the friends who used to write them; I neither know where they are nor how they are faring. The old stream of letters has dried up. There are only you three[52] that I can expect to write, and two of you only occasionally. You, it is true, usually favour me once or twice a month. Listen Sahib, make it a binding rule to write to me once a month. If you have occasion to, write twice or three times. Otherwise just post off a line to tell me how you are.... If you are not cross with me, answer this letter the day after it reaches you. Let me know how you are, and how Munshi Sahib [Nabi Bakhsh Haqir] is, and how

[52] Ghalib means Tufta, Nabi Bakhsh Haqir, and Maulvi Qamar ud Din Khan.

Maulvi Sahib [Qamar ud Din Khan] is. Also be sure to tell me, in words suited to the needs of the times, whatever you know about the disturbances at Gwalior... and what the situation is in Agra. Are the people there afraid at all, or not?

At the end of June—immediately after an entry for 22 June—comes an entry in *Dastambu* recording his feelings as he enters his sixty-fourth year reckoned by the Muslim calendar:

Sixty-three years of my life have passed, and the infinite woes which ceaselessly beset me proclaim the impertinence of looking to fate to grant me many more years of life; and involuntarily I hear the pleasing voice of the poet of Shiraz [Sadi], on whose shining spirit be all my blessings, singing the lines of his enchanting verse; and as one mourner draws consolation from another, his melody brings me, not happiness to be sure, but a moment's release from the bonds of grief:

Alas for all those springs and all those flowers
The world will look upon when we are gone!
Springs, summers, winters—all will come and go
When we are mingled in the dust and stone.

His last entry in *Dastambu*, made at the end of July, shows to what straits he was reduced. Not only had every regular source of income ceased, but his wife's jewellery—traditionally the very last reserve of an Indian family—was gone. He writes:

I marvel at the varied wonders of Fate. In the days of killing and looting, when it seemed that every house in the city was emptied even of its dust, my house escaped the looters' grasping hands. Yet I swear even so that nothing but clothes to wear and bedding to sleep upon was left to me. The answer to this riddle and the key to this false-seeming truth is this: that at the time when the black rebels seized the city, my wife, without telling me, gathered her jewels and valuables and sent them secretly to the house of Kale Sahib.[53] There they were stored in the cellar, and the door of the cellar blocked up with clay and smoothed over. When the British soldiers took the city and were given leave to loot and kill, my wife revealed this secret to me. Now there was nothing to be done; to go there and bring them back was impossible. I said nothing and comforted myself with the thought that we were destined to lose these things and that it was well that they had not been taken from our own home. And now

[53] Cf. p. 72 above.

it is July—the fifteenth month—and I see no sign that I shall again receive the pension which the British government formerly granted me. And so I sell the clothes and bedding to keep body and soul together, and a man might say that where others eat bread, I eat cloth. I go in fear that when all the cloth is eaten I shall die naked and hungry. Of the servants who had long been with me there are some few who even in this tumult did not desert me. These too I must feed, for in truth, man may not turn his back on man, and I too need them to serve my needs. Besides these are those suppliants who in former days laid claim to a share in the gleanings of my harvest. Even in these bad times they cry to me, and their cry, more unwelcome than the cock's untimely crow, pierces my heart and adds to my distress. And now that these raging sicknesses and sorrows which oppress my body and soul have sapped all my strength and spirit, the thought comes suddenly to my mind, 'How long can I occupy myself adorning this toy I call a book?' For this distress must end either in death or in beggary. In the first case, this tale must needs for ever more lack an ending... and so sadden its readers' hearts. And in the second case, the one clear outcome is that I must raise the beggar's cry from door to door, here gathering a crumb, there driven with abuse from the lane and humiliated in the open street. And for how long should I tell such a tale, myself spreading the fame of my disgrace? Now even if my pension is restored it cannot wipe clean the mirror of my heart, and if it is not, that mirror will itself be shattered, as by a stone. And... whichever may befall, the air of this city will be noxious to such ruined ones as I, and I must go and live in some strange land. From May of last year to July of this I have written what has befallen, and from 1 August I stay my pen.

He then expresses the hopes which even now he entertains, of a title, a robe of honour, and a pension granted by Queen Victoria's grace, and adds thirty-four lines of verse in her praise. The final paragraph reads:

After completing this book I named it *Dastambu* (A Posy of Flowers), and sent it from hand to hand and from place to place to sustain the souls of the learned and steal the hearts of the eloquent. And it is my hope that this handful of the flowers of learning may be a posy of colour and fragrance in the hands of the God-fearing, and a globe of flame in the sight of them that are of Satanic nature....

The arrangements which Tufta and his friends were making on his behalf brought him into contact with Munshi Shiv Narayan Aram, an enterprising young man in his twenties who published a newspaper from Agra and owned a press. It appears that Aram's first letter to Ghalib was a request to see what he could do to get subscribers to his paper in Delhi; he also asks Ghalib to write an ode which he wants to present to an English official, and says that, hearing that Ghalib makes his own envelopes, he is sending off a packet to him to save him the trouble. Ghalib replies:

> I received your letter, and the newspaper, and the news of the envelopes you are sending me. You should not have troubled. Making envelopes keeps me amused. What else has an idle man to do? But, anyway, when they arrive you shall receive my grateful acknowledgements. For:
>
> Whatever comes to us from friends, is good.
>
> Where would I find anyone here to subscribe to your paper? The moneylenders and merchants who inhabit this city go around finding out where they can buy grain most cheaply. If they're exceptionally generous men, they'll weigh you out full measure. What do they want with a paper at a rupee a month?
>
> Your letter reached me yesterday. All last night I sweated blood to compose your ode, and managed one of twenty-one lines in fulfilment of your order. My friends—Mirza Tufta especially—know that I can't compose chronograms. But in this ode I have found a way of expressing '1858'. I hope you will like it. You yourself appreciate poetry, and you have three friends [Tufta, Haqir, and Mihr] who are masters of the art. So my efforts will receive their due meet of praise.

Even the harassed weeks and months which had preceded this satisfactory result had yielded their moments of pleasure. Ghalib enjoyed even the sheer volume of the correspondence involved. He writes to Nabi Bakhsh Haqir on 22 September 1858:

> Amidst all these troubles, how I laugh to think that you and I and Mirza Tufta have turned correspondence into conversation.[54] We talk together everyday. By God above! these will be days to remember. What letters upon letters we have written! I spend half my time making envelopes. I am either doing that or writing a letter. It's a good thing that postage is only half an anna. Otherwise we'd have seen what this conversation cost us!

[54] The idea and the turn of phrase clearly appealed to him. He repeats it in a letter of about this time to Mihr.

But there were deeper satisfactions than this. In 1857 Hatim Ali Mihr, with his uncle's help, had saved the lives of seven of the English by giving them shelter in his house. He was now rewarded by the British authorities with an estate of two villages and with other honours. It was probably in this period that Ghalib heard the news and wrote to express his sincere pleasure:

> You showed real courage, and staked your life on it. It is your manly and resolute conduct which has brought you this reward. What more can the world give than wealth with good repute?...How well I remember the time when Mughal[55] spoke to me about you, and how she showed me the verses in praise of her beauty which you had written with your own hand. Now a time has come when letters pass between us. But if God Almighty wills it, the day will come when we shall sit and talk together and lay our pens side.

In October he discovered that there had been a long-standing connection between his family and Shiv Narayan Aram's. On 19 October 1858 he writes to him:

> Munshi Shiv Narayan, my son, I had no idea who you were. When I discovered that you were the grandson of Nazir Bansi Dhar I felt I had discovered a beloved son. From now on if I address you formally I'll count it a sin. You won't know about the relations between my family and yours. Let me tell you.
> Your [paternal] grandfather's father and my [maternal] grandfather Khwaja Ghulam Husain Khan were companions in the days of Najaf Khan[56].... When my grandfather retired from active service and returned home your great-grandfather also retired. This was further back than I can remember. But I can remember when I was a young man seeing my grandfather and yours, Munshi Bansi Dhar, together, and when my grandfather laid his claim for his estate... before the government, Munshi Bansi Dhar acted as his agent and managed the whole thing on his behalf. He and I were about the same age— there may have been a year or two's difference one way or the other. Anyway I was about nineteen or twenty and he was about the same. We were close friends and used to play chess together; we would often sit together until late into the night. His house was quite near mine and he used to come and see me whenever he liked. There was only Machia the courtesan's house and the two by-lanes between us. Our big mansion is the one that now belongs to Lakhmi Chand

---

[55] A courtesan whom Ghalib and Mihr had both known, cf. pp. 185–6 below.
[56] The last imperial minister of any distinction. He died in 1782.

Seth. I used to spend most of my time in the stone summer-house near the main entrance. I used to fly my kite from the roof of a house in one of the lanes nearby and match it against Raja Balwan Singh's. There was a big house called Ghatia Wali, and beyond that another near Salim Shah's takiya[57] and then another adjoining Kale Mahal and beyond that a lane which used to be called Gadariyon Wala and then another lane called Kashmiran Wala—that was the lane where the house was. Your grandfather had a man named Wasil Khan who used to collect the rents for him.

And listen! Your grandfather had made a lot of money. He had bought land and acquired a big estate which paid something like ten or twelve thousand rupees in land revenue to the government. Have you inherited all that? Write to me soon and tell me all about it.

The publication of *Dastambu* seems to have suggested to Shiv Narayan Aram and Tufta the idea of collecting and publishing Ghalib's Urdu letters too. It is interesting to note his reaction. He writes to Aram on 18 November 1858.

As for your wish to publish the Urdu letters, that too is unnecessary. Hardly any of them were written with proper thought and care, and apart from these few the rest are just what came on the spur of the moment. Their publication would diminish my stature as a writer. And leaving that aside, why should we let others read what only concerns us? In short, I do not want them to be published.

Tufta must have tried to persuade him, for two days later, on 20 November 1858, he writes again both to him and to Aram. He tells Tufta: 'I don't want the letters to be published. Don't keep on about it like a child. And if nothing else will satisfy you, why ask me? Do as you like. *I* am against it.' And to Aram, a little more politely: 'I have already forbidden you to publish the letters, and you and Mirza Tufta must respect my wishes in the matter.' It is interesting that the reason which Ghalib puts first is that his letters are not good formal prose—which still meant, in his day, the elaborately contrived, rhythmical and rhyming prose based on Persian literary models. This, as we have seen, he could write extremely well; but it never seems to have occurred to him to have attempted anything similar in Urdu, and now he thinks about it, he wonders whether Urdu is capable of producing really good prose at all. In another letter to Aram on 11 December 1858 he refers to a request

[57] The abode of a faqir.

made to him by Mr Henry Stuart Read to write a book in Urdu prose for use in the schools. (Read was Director of Education in what was later to become United Provinces.)

> But, friend, you can imagine for yourself—if I write in Urdu how can my pen wield its full power, and how can I express the niceties of meaning? I am still wondering what to write.... If you have any ideas, write and tell me.

Later on he was to be persuaded of the literary value of his Urdu letters, and helped to collect copies of them for the collections published in 1868 (the year before his death) and 1869. And there is no doubt that these collections helped to win the battle to make the colloquial Urdu of educated speakers the standard literary language also.

It was the loss of his Urdu verse, which he had once belittled as not really worthy of him, which seems to have grieved him most. A month or two earlier he had written to Mihr:

> I have never kept any of my verse by me. Nawwab Ziya ud Din Khan and Nawwab Husain Mirza used to write down everything I composed and keep it. Both of their houses were looted, and libraries worth thousands of rupees destroyed. And now I long for my own verse. A few days ago a faqir who has a good voice and sings well discovered a ghazal of mine somewhere and got it written down. When he showed me it, I tell you truly, the tears came to my eyes. I am sending the ghazal to you, and ask in reward a reply to this letter.

Ghalib's bald statements about the libraries in these two letters conceal a shocking story of the senseless vandalism of the British troops. These libraries and that of the Royal Fort which they destroyed really were of inestimable value.

In general, from the time *Dastambu* was printed to the end of 1858, Ghalib was in buoyant mood. But a letter to the Nawwab of Rampur sharply reminds us of his continuing financial distress. Still without any source of regular income, Ghalib had sought to develop the relationship with Rampur which he had initiated early in 1857, but which had been cut short by the revolt. The Nawwab seems to have shown no great alacrity in providing the regular support which a noble was expected to extend to a man of letters, and for which it should not have been necessary to ask in so many words. But desperation forced Ghalib to write in a tone which he must have felt it painful and humiliating to adopt, and on 17 November he tells the Nawwab bluntly: 'Whatever you send unasked, I do not refuse. Nor do I feel shame in asking when I am in need. The heavy burden of grief has crushed me. Once I had little in hand, and now I have nothing. Please hasten to help me....' This blunt appeal brought him a gift of Rs 250.

Two letters to Mihr well illustrate his prevailing mood. Early in December 1858 he writes:

> First I want to ask you a question. For several letters past I have noticed you lamenting your grief and sorrow. Why? If you have fallen in love with some fair cruel one, what room for complaint have you there? Rather should you wish your friends the same good fortune and seek increase of this pain. In the words of Ghalib (God's mercy be upon him!)[58]

> You gave your heart away; why then lament
>   your loss in plaintive song?
> You have a breast without a heart; why not
>   a mouth without a tongue?

And what a fine second couplet!—

> Is one misfortune not enough to drive
>   a man to beggary?
> When you become his friend why should
>   the sky[59] become his enemy?

And if—which God forbid—it is more mundane griefs that beset you, then my friend, you and I have the same sorrows to bear. I bear this burden like a man, and if you are a man, so must you. As the late Ghalib says:

> My heart, this grief and sorrow too is
>   precious; for the day will come
> You will not heave the midnight sigh, nor
>   shed your tears at early morn.

With Aram he is by this time on sufficiently informal terms to tell him something which in his first letter to him a few months earlier he had politely kept to himself:

> Your letter with the package of envelopes has just come. Friend, I can't help it, but I don't like these envelopes with 'From...' and

[58] Words always used of a saint after his death!
[59] I.e. fate.

'To...' and 'Date...' and 'Month...' printed on them. The lot you sent me before I also gave away to friends. I'm sending back this package of envelopes so that you can send me plain ones instead— without 'To...' and 'From...' printed on them—(like the ones you send your own letters in)—and take these in exchange. And if you haven't got plain envelopes, it doesn't matter. I don't really need them.

Ghalib had promised to get a seal engraved for him, and Aram must have asked if it could be done on an emerald. Ghalib's letter continues:

As for the seal, where in this desolate city can you get an emerald?— and that too the size of chick-pea, and eight-sided. The seal will be of cornelian, and of a good colour—black or red, as you wrote in your earlier letter, and eight-sides. *I* shall be sending you this seal— what concern of yours is it whether it cost four annas a letter or six annas? If you want to get a seal engraved yourself, do—on an emerald or a diamond or what you like. *I'm* giving you one on cornelian....

When I wrote to Tufta that he was cross with me I did it in the same spirit as I once wrote the same thing to you. Good heavens, he is like a son to me: I know very well he wouldn't be cross with me. I have had two or three letters from him since then, and am posting one to him by the same post as I send this letter to you.

Tufta was indeed 'like a son' to him, and he had the satisfaction of knowing that Ghalib relied on him more than any other to help him feel that life was worth living. On 27 December 1858 he writes:

Well, Sahib, are you still angry? And are you going to keep it up? Or will you cool down? And if you won't cool down, then at least tell me what has upset you. In this solitude it is letters that keep me alive. Someone writes to me and I feel he has come to see me. By God's favour not a day passes but three or four letters come from this side and that; in fact there are days when I get letters by both posts—one or two in the morning and one or two in the afternoon. I spend the day reading them and answering them, and it keeps me happy. Why is it that for ten and twelve days together you haven't written— i.e. haven't been to see me? Write to me, Sahib. Write why you haven't written. Don't grudge the half-anna postage. And if you're *so* hard up, send the letter unstamped.

At the end of the year (19 December 1858) in a letter full of rather grim humour, he writes to Tufta:

Your letter has come and told me all I wanted to know. I feel sorry for Umrao Singh, and envy him too! Wonderful are God's ways! There is he, who has twice had the fetters struck from his feet,[60] and here am I hanging for the last fifty-one years with my neck in the hangman's noose—and the rope doesn't break, and I don't die. Tell him, 'I'll look after your children; why do you let your troubles get the better of you?'[61] The line you quoted is one of Hakim Sanai's and the story is in his *Hadiqa*: 'A son came weeping to his father and said, "Please arrange my marriage". The father replied, "My dear son, live in sin with some woman, but do not talk of marriage. Learn sense, not just from me, but from all the world. If you are caught in fornication you will still be released in the end. But if you marry you are bound for life, and if you leave your wife you are disgraced."' [The original is in Persian verse.]

Look at me—neither bond nor free, neither well nor ill, neither glad nor sad, neither dead nor alive. I go on living. I go on talking. I eat my daily bread and drink my occasional cup of wine. When death comes I will die and that will be an end of it. I neither give thanks nor make complaint, and all my words are no more than a tale. But, after all, wherever you are and however you fare, write me a letter once a week.

Not all of his troubles were so serious. On 18 November 1858 he writes to Sarur:

My kind friend, your kind letter of 15 November reached me today, Thursday, 18 November. If a letter from Marahra [Sarur's town] reaches Delhi in four days, how is it that a letter from Delhi to Marahra takes longer? See, to please you I am sending this letter unstamped. ['From this,' notes Mihr, 'it seems that Sarur had himself asked Ghalib to send his letters unstamped.'] But let me know what day it reaches you.

He then goes on to explain the circumstances in which he wrote *Dastambu*, and continues:

So I am sending you a copy. As a matter of fact I am presenting it to my most revered and respected master, Sahib i Alam. Since he is your elder I could not have the temerity to present it to you, telling you to give it to him to read too.

[60] I.e. he had twice been married, and both wives had died.

[61] Hali, in a note on this letter, says that Umrao Singh had argued that for the sake of his children he should marry a third time.

What I write next is addressed to my master, Sahib i Alam. Though we are of the same age, I am his disciple; though we practise the same art, he is my master; and I trust he will forgive my shortcoming. I am sixty-three years old; I have gone deaf; but there is no defect in my sight, nor do I wish to resort to spectacles. But if my sight is keen, my understanding is dim, and I cannot read your handwriting. In my two previous replies I had gone by guess-work; I had not been able to read your letters properly. After all, Chaudhri Sahib [Sarur] is your devoted admirer, and as close to you as any of your kin. Let *him* write down faithfully whatever you command him. I will reply to everything as soon as I hear from you that you have received the book and when I receive your letter, rewritten in Chaudhri Sahib's hand.

This was not the first time that he had had to complain of Sahib i Alam's hand, and it was not to be the last. In an earlier letter (undated) he had written to Sarur, 'I am forced, in my complete perplexity, to return the enclosed letter to you. For God's sake copy out the revered words of my spiritual lord and master on another sheet and send it back to me, so that a miserable wretch can see what he wrote.' From another letter to Sarur dated 1 December 1858, it seems that Sahib i Alam had ignored the request he had so politely expressed in his letter of 18 November:

I had requested [Sahib i Alam] to get you to write whatever he had to communicate. He has ignored this and has again written me something in his own special hand. I swear to God that neither I nor anyone else could read it. Don't say a word to him, but copy it out in your own hand and have it sent to me. Be sure to do this, and do it quickly.

Burdened as he was by personal troubles, he was still alert to note what was going on in the wider world around him. On 21 September 1858 he writes to ask Mihr whether it is true what people are saying, viz. that 'in Agra proclamation has been made, and it has been announced at the beat of the drum, that the [East India] Company's contract has been ended and India brought under the British Crown.' If so, he says, it is good news. About a month later he writes to Aram:

Let me tell you the news from this city. An order has been issued that on the night of Monday, 1 November all well-wishers of the English are to illuminate their houses, and there are also to be illuminations in the bazaars and on the Deputy Commissioner Sahib's bungalow. Your humble servant, even in this state of penury, not having received his appointed pension for the last eighteen months, will illuminate his house, and has sent a poem of fifteen couplets to the Commissioner of the city.

The purpose of this, which, it seems, was not revealed until the night in question, was to proclaim the end of the Company's rule and the bringing of India directly under the Crown.

On 20 November 1858 he tells Tufta of 'the general amnesty now proclaimed'. And finally, in a letter of 22 December to Majruh, he surveys the Delhi scene, and calmly and humorously, if without much hope, speculates on what the new year will bring:

Bravo, Sayyid Sahib! What distinguished prose you've started writing; and what a distinguished pose you've started striking! For several days I've been intending to answer your letter, but the cold has put me out of action, and today, now that it's cloudy and the cold less intense, and I've decided to write to you, I'm at a loss to match the enchantment of your style. You've lived so long by the watercourse in Urdu Bazaar that you've yourself become a river of eloquence— Urdu's Mirza Qatil,[62] in fact! But never mind all that. I'm only laughing at you. Come, let me tell you what's happening in your beloved Delhi.

The well near the pool in front of the Begam Bagh gate in [Chandni] Chauk has been filled up with stones and bricks and rubbish. Several shops near the entrance to Ballimaron have been demolished, and the road widened. There is still no order permitting anyone, rich or poor, to return to his home in the city, and as for pension-holders, the authorities are not concerned with them. Taj Mahal, Mirza Qaisar, the wife of Mirza Jawan Bakht's brother-in-law Mirza Wilayat Ali Beg Jaipuri—all of these have been released in Allahabad. The King, Mirza Jawan Bakht, Mirza Abbas Shah and Zinat Mahal have all reached Calcutta and will be embarked aboard ship. Let us see whether they will be kept at the Cape or sent to London. People here have hazarded a guess—you know what Delhi's inventors of news are like—and spread a rumour which has now spread throughout the city that in January 1859 there will be general permission for people to return to their homes in the city, and bags and bags of money will be given to pension-holders. Well, today is Wednesday, 22 December. Saturday will be Christmas Day and the Saturday following 1 January. If we live we shall see what happens. Let me have a reply to this letter, and soon....

---

[62] A very left-handed compliment! Qatil, to Ghalib, typified all that was objectionable in Indian 'authorities' on Persian.

1859

The experiences that were to befall him during 1859 were to justify his scepticism. The one substantial gain he could register when it ended was the establishment of a regular contact with the Nawwab of Rampur which eased to some extent his financial distress. His correspondence with Rampur shows that he was already receiving occasional gifts before July 1859, and that as from that month the Nawwab granted him a regular monthly allowance of Rs 100. But this was not enough for his needs, and he continued to seek for other means of supplementing it—without success. Until June, he had rising hopes of the restoration of his pension from the British, but these were dashed—at any rate temporarily—by an adverse report about him made by the commissioner of Delhi, and the reception of *Dastambu* similarly failed to justify the hopes he had placed in it. He hoped also to receive something from Wajid Ali Shah, the ex-king of Oudh, whom the British had removed to Calcutta when they annexed his kingdom in 1856, but whose resources still permitted of the exercise of a measure of patronage. But here too his hopes were disappointed, and by the end of the year he had ceased to expect anything from that quarter.

Meanwhile, in Delhi, conditions continued far from normal, with British policies alternating unpredictably between leniency and severity. Not until August was the regulation withdrawn whereby entry into and exit from the city required a permit; and even then a residence permit was still needed for a stay of even one night in the city. It was November before Muslims were finally allowed to enter and take up permanent residence, more than two years after their original expulsion. The very face of Delhi was changing, and large scale demolition of historic buildings was making way for open expanses and new roads.

News from outside was also often bad enough. Ghalib's old friend Fazl i Haq was sentenced to transportation for life, and his appeal was rejected. His friend Husain Mirza and his family, for whom Ghalib held a sort of watching brief in Delhi, tried in vain to make some progress in their negotiations with the Delhi authorities over their extensive properties there, and by the end of the year were at a loss where to go and to whom to turn for help in securing their future.

In these circumstances it is hardly surprising that the letters for 1859 are often anxious, despondent, and occasionally written in great distress and bitterness, though even in the deepest dejection Ghalib's humour will unexpectedly assert itself in a sudden flash. But with this short introduction the letters may be left to speak for themselves.

On 3 January 1859 he writes to Tufta:

See here, sir. I don't like your ways. I write to you in 1858 and you reply in 1859; and if I speak to you about it you will reply that you answered my letter on the very next day. And the best of it is that both of us are right!

The same day he writes to Bekhabar:

Today is Monday, 3 January 1859. It must be about nine in the morning. The sky is overcast, and a fine drizzle is falling. A cold wind is blowing. I have nothing to drink, so I have had to eat instead.

> The clouds of spring are spread across the sky
> But in my cup of clay there is no wine.

I was sitting here feeling depressed and despondent when the postman came with your letter. I saw that it was addressed in your own hand, and felt very pleased. I read it, and found that it did not bring me the news I wanted; and again felt sad:

> Oppression's force has driven us from home.
> How should good tidings come from lands like ours?

And in this sadness I felt like talking to you. So although your letter did not call for a reply I began to write you one.

So first let me tell you that your letter has been delivered to your friend; but he has twice written to me to say that he has already posted off a reply to the address given on the envelope, and now awaits a reply to his reply.

You know that when despair reaches its lowest depths there is nothing left but to resign oneself to God's will. Well, what lower depths can there be than this that it is the hope of death that keeps me alive? And my resignation gains strength from day to day because I have only another two to two-and-a-half years to live; and somehow the time will pass. I know you will laugh and think to yourself I am talking nonsense. But call it divine revelation or call it superstition, I have had this verse kept by for the past twenty years:

Who am I to expect eternal life,
When Naziri has gone, and Talib died?
If they ask you the year of Ghalib's death
Simply tell them in answer, 'Ghalib died'.

[In the original 'Ghalib died' is *'Ghalib murd'*, and is a chronogram.]
It is now 1275, and *'Ghalib murd'* gives 1277. Let me experience
whatever happiness may come to me in this short space; and then
I shall be gone.

The next day he again laments to Aram that he is called upon
to write a work of Urdu prose.

My friend, how can I write in Urdu? Is my standing so low that this
should be expected of me? Still, it *is* expected of me. But where am
I to turn, hunting for tales and stories? I haven't a book to my name.
Let my pension be restored and I'll get the peace of mind to think
of something.

Give me food and drink
Then see how I can think!

(It is interesting that this jingle which he quotes is in Panjabi.)
On 26 January 1859, he writes to Tufta: 'I got your letter...I am
late in replying because I had gone by the mail to Meerut to
see Mustafa Khan [Shefta]. I stayed three days, and came back
yesterday.' A letter of 2 February 1859 to Majruh gives more
details:

Now let me tell you what I have been doing. Nawwab Mustafa Khan
Shefta had been sentenced to seven years' imprisonment. Now he
has been pardoned and released. So far that is all. No orders have
yet been issued regarding his Jahangirabad estate or his properties
in Delhi or his pension. So he is obliged to stay where he is in Meerut
as the guest of a friend. As soon as I heard the news I took the mail
and went to Meerut to see him. I stayed four days and then returned
home, also by the mail. I can't remember the dates, but I went
on a Saturday and returned on a Tuesday. Today is Wednesday,
2 February, and I have been back nine days. I was waiting for a letter
from you so that I could answer it when I wrote. Your letter came
this morning, and I am writing this reply at midday.

He goes on to describe conditions in Delhi:

The city gets fresh orders every day—
But what is going on, no one can say.

When I got back from Meerut I saw how strict they are here. Not content with the guard of British soldiers, the police officer at Lahori Gate sits on a chair overlooking the street, seizes anyone who has slipped past the British sentries and sends him to the cells, where he receives five strokes of the cane by the commissioner's orders or pays a fine of two rupees. After that he is kept in prison for eight days. Also, orders have been issued to all police stations to find out who in the city has a permit and who is living here without one. Lists are being drawn up at the police stations. An inspector from our district came to see me too about this. I told him, 'My friend, don't enter my name on your list. Write a separate statement about my position, to the effect that the pensioner Asadullah Khan has been living since 1850 in the residence of the brother of the Patiala hakim. He did not move during the days when the blacks held the city, nor did he leave it (nor was compelled to leave) when the whites came. His residence there was authorized by the verbal order of Colonel Brown Sahib Bahadur, and no one in authority has hitherto modified that order. Now it is for the authorities to decide.' The day before yesterday the inspector forwarded this statement, with his list for the muhalla, to the office of the Chief of Police. Yesterday an order was issued stating that people were building themselves houses outside the city without authority. All such houses are to be demolished, and proclamation made that for the future such building is prohibited. It is also rumoured that five thousand permits have been printed; any Muslim who wishes to take up residence in the city will have to make a contribution according to his means— of which the commissioner will be the judge—and will then receive a permit. In other words, 'Pull your houses down and settle in the town.'

Tufta had apparently sent a letter containing a message for Raja Umid Singh asking him to send him his full address. Ghalib replies on 19 February 1859:

My friend, you are a man of intuition, and your knowledge of the unseen is accurate. I was expecting a letter from you so that I could reply when I next wrote, and yesterday evening I got one. I am replying this morning.

The point is that a letter addressed to anyone who is well-known doesn't require to be addressed to any muhalla. I am only a poor man, yet letters addressed in Persian and in English reach me safely. Some of the Persian letters do not give the name of the muhalla, and the English letters carry no address at all other than 'Delhi'. I have had three or four letters from England. Do you think anyone there knows or cares what 'Ballimaron Muhalla' is? And he [Raja Umid Singh] is a much more important man than I am. He gets hundreds of letters in English every day. But, in short, I again sent a man to him to show him your letter to me. He told my servant, 'Give the Nawwab Sahib [Ghalib] my respects and ask him if he would himself kindly send the necessary information'. Well, I've told you the position about this, but in accordance with your wish I now inform you that his house is in Dason ka kucha, muhalla Ballimaron.

Some time in April he writes again to Majruh:

Friend your incessant demands for answers to your letters will be the death of me!

A curse upon the heavens, that move so perversely! What harm had I done to them? I had no wealth or goods or rank or majesty— only a few possessions and a corner where a handful of poor beggars would gather together to laugh and talk. But

> That too you could not bear to look upon,
>   o cruel sky,
> Although to look upon each other was
>   our only wealth.

Remember, this couplet is Khwaja Mir Dard's.[63] 'Since yesterday I keep thinking of Maikash,' [you write]. So? You tell me, what am I to write? When the memories of all the times we and our friends used to sit and talk come back to you, all you can think of doing is making me write you letter upon letter. But a man cannot quench his thirst with tears. And my writing is no substitute for their talking. Anyway, I'll write you something. Let's see what I can think of to write.

Well, my friend, *you* can sit here or not as you like, but *I'm* going off for my lunch. Everyone here, in the zenana and outside it, is keeping the fast—even the elder boy, Baqir Ali Khan. Only I and my son Husain Ali Khan are eating—the same Husain Ali Khan whose daily cry is, 'Get me some toys' and 'I want to go to the shops.' Give my blessing to Mir Sarfaraz Husain and mind you read him this letter. And my blessing to my boy Mir Nasir ud Din.

The letter illustrates a very lovable side of Ghalib's character. No one could have felt more deeply than he the loss of Maikash and all his other friends, but is ready to respond to Majruh with a letter to cheer him up.

---

[63] A famous Urdu poet of the eighteenth century.

In March or April he writes to Hatim Ali Beg Mihr:

Keep strong your faith in the unseen—
else you are no believer.
You who are hidden from my sight, love
for you is my faith.

Your auspicious portrait has gladdened my sight. Do you know what Mirza Yusuf Ali Khan Aziz meant by what he said to you? I must have said some time in the company of friends, 'I should like to see Mirza Hatim Ali. I hear he's a man of very striking appearance.' And, my friend, I had often heard this from Mughal Jan.[64] In the days when she was in Nawwab Hamid Ali Khan's service I used to know her extremely well, and I often used to spend hours together in her company. She also showed me the verse you wrote in praise of her beauty.

Anyway, when I saw your portrait and saw how tall you were, I didn't feel jealous because I too am noticeably tall. And I didn't feel jealous of your wheaten complexion, because mine, in the days when I was in the land of the living, used to be even fairer, and people of discrimination used to praise it. Now when I remember what my complexion once was, the memory is simple torture to me. The thing that *did* make me jealous—and that is no small degree—was that you are clean-shaven. I remembered the pleasant days of my youth, and I cannot tell you what I felt. But as Shaikh Ali Hazin says:

I rent my clothes when I was young
and felt a lover's frenzy.
Now I may wear my woollen cloak and feel
no sense of shame.

When white hairs began to appear in my beard and moustaches, and on the third day they began to look as though ants had laid their white eggs in them—and, worse than that, I broke my two front teeth—there was nothing for it but to...let my beard grow long. But remember that in this uncouth city [Delhi] everybody wears a sort of uniform. Mullahs, junk-dealers, hookah-menders, washerman, water-carriers, innkeepers, weavers, greengrocers—all of them wear their hair long and grow a beard. The day your humble servant grew a beard he had *his* hair shaved off—But God save us! what am I prattling about?

[64] The style of name shows that she was a courtesan.

An undated letter to Sahib i Alam clearly belongs to about this time, as internal evidence shows:

> I spend my days and nights thinking to myself, 'This is what life was like; now let me see what death will be like.'
>
>> I lived my life waiting for death to some
>> And dead, I still must see what else I face.
>
> The couplet is my own, and it aptly describes my state of mind.
> ... The story is told that Abul Hasan Khirqani (God's mercy be upon him) was asked, 'How are you faring?' He replied, 'How will that man be faring of whom his God demands the fulfilment of his religious duty, and his Prophet the observance of his own standards, and his wife his wealth, and the angel of death his life?'
> In short, I live on in hope of death....

On 15 July 1859 he writes to Yusuf Mirza:

> I'm not going to correct your masnavi until I have the whole of it. You can put forward as many plausible arguments as you like, or appeal to my sense of shame, but until I get a complete ghazal, or a complete masnavi, how am I to correct it? Give your uncle [Husain Mirza] my regards (because I love him) and my humble submission (because he is a Sayyid) and my blessing (because he is my intimate friend and I am his ustad) and ask him what else he expects me to write.

In an undated letter of about this time he writes to Majruh:

> My devoted son, did you see the poem? It's a faithful reflection of my state; there's no poetry left in me. I had meant when I sent it off to write a letter too, but the children were pestering me, 'Come on, grand-dad, dinner's ready. We're hungry.' I had already got three letters written and I thought to myself, 'Why should I write any more now?' So I just put the paper in the envelope, stamped it, addressd it, gave it to Kalian [Ghalib's servant] to post, and went to dinner. I did it to provoke you too. 'This will annoy Mir Mahdi [Majruh]. Let's see what he says,' I thought to myself. And that's just what happened. A real outburst of indignation! Well, here I am sitting down to write to you. Tell me, what shall I write? Miran Sahib will have told you all about what's going on here. But don't believe what he's told you. The question of my pension is now before the governor-general in Calcutta. The commissioner here left a minute when he went, but what harm can that do me?
> I had written this much when two friends came to see me. It was not long before sunset. I shut up my box and went out to sit with

them. It got dark, and and the lamp was lighted. I was lying on the bed, with Munshi Sayyid Ahmad Husain sitting at the head on a rush-chair, when all of a sudden that Eye and Lamp of the family of Faith and Learning, Sayyid Nasir ud Din arrived, riding-whip in hand, and accompanied by a servant carrying on his head a basket covered over with green grass. I said to myself, 'Aha! Good! Good! The King of Divines, Maulana Sarfaraz Husain of Delhi has sent me a fresh supply [of wine].' But it turned out not to be that, but something else—not special bounty, but general largesse; not wine, but mangoes. Well, no harm in such a gift either; in fact it's better than the other. I thought of each mango as a sealed glass, filled with the liquor of the grape. And filled with such superb skill that not so much as a single drop spilled from any of the sixty-five glasses. The man said there had been eighty, but fifteen went bad—rotten, in fact—and he threw them out in case they should affect the others. I said, 'There are plenty left, my friend'. I was not pleased, though, that you had put yourself to such trouble. You haven't enough money to go spending it on mangoes. God grant you prosperity and increase of wealth.

There's a kind of English drink called 'likur' [liqueur]—an exquisite liquor with a fine colour, and as sweet to the taste as a thin syrup of sugar. Let me tell you, you won't find its meaning in any dictionary, except perhaps in Sarwari.

Give my blessing to the Authority of the Age [Mir Sarfaraz Husain], and to Hakim Mir Ashraf Ali, who is the key to his learning, and has gathered half penny pamphlets to the value of forty to fifty rupees.

It was perhaps in the same period that he wrote an undated letter to Tufta:

My friend, the way your mind works beats me! When did I say that your poetry was not good? When did I say that you will find none in the world to understand it and appreciate its worth? But it's true that you are intent on poetry, while all my faculties are intent on attaining oblivion. To me the learning of Avicenna and the poetry of Naziri are alike wasted, and pointless and illusory. To pass one's life one needs a little ease—and all the learning and power and poetry and magic are nothing. What of it if an avatar comes to the Hindus? And what of it if a prophet arises amongst the Muslims? What of it if a man wins fame in the world? And what of it if he lives out his life unknown? Let a man have something to live on, and physical health, and the rest is nothing, my dear friend. As a matter of fact these too are nothing, but I have not yet reached the stage where

I realise it. Perhaps in due course this veil too will fall from my eyes, and I shall pass beyond the stage where getting a living, and enjoying health and pleasure mean anything to me, and pass into a world where sensation ceases.

In the desolation in which I live I am lost to the whole world, indeed to both worlds. I go on giving my answers to suit the questions I am asked, and behave with every man as our relationship warrants; but it is all illusion in my sight—not a river, but a mirage; not reality, but fantasy. You and I are not bad poets. Suppose I grant we win the same fame as Sadi and Hafiz. What did their fame bring them? And what would ours bring us?....

On 29 October 1859 he writes to Husain Mirza:

What can I do? I could say that my very life is yours to command, but that would be mere formal politeness. No one gives his life for another, or asks another to give his life for him. But the Lord my God knows the thought I take for you and what resources I possess. My resources you too know....

I write these few lines to tell you that your creditor Chunni Lal came a little while ago. He was asking me about you. I told him a mixture of truth and lies and got him to consider sending you another hundred to two hundred rupees. I talked to him like a *baniya*.[65] 'Lala', I said, 'when a man wants the fruit of a tree, he first waters it. Husain Mirza is your farm. Water it, and it will give you grain'. My friend, that softened him a little. He got me to write down your address and took it away with him saying that he would discuss the matter with his son Ramji Das and would come and let me know what they decided. If he sends you money, what more do you want? And if he writes to you first, be sure to tell him in your reply that what Asadullah told him was quite true and that the matter will shortly be coming to fruition....

On 8 November 1859 he writes to Majruh:

Friend, I have neither paper nor stamps, and only one unstamped envelope left. I've torn this paper out of a book to write you and I'll post it off in the unstamped envelope. Don't worry. Last night some booty came in, and today I'll send out for paper and stamps. It is the morning of Tuesday, 8 November—what the people call 'high morning'. I got your letter two days ago and today I felt like writing to you; so I'm writing these few lines....

[65] A caste of Hindus who deal in grain and in money-lending. 'Lala' is the title by which they are addressed.

How should *I* know what's going on in the city? There's a thing called 'Pown Tuty' been introduced. ['Town Duty'—i.e. a tax levied on all commodities entering the city.] Except grain and cow-dung cakes[66] every single thing is liable for it. All round the Jama Masjid to a radius of twenty-five feet there's to be an open space. Shops and houses will be pulled down. The Dar ul Baqa[67] will vanish. [There is a play on words here: Dar ul Baqa means literally 'House of Eternity'.] Nothing but the name of God abides. From Khan Chand's lane to Shah Bula's banyan tree everything will be demolished. The picks and shovels are plying from both sides. Otherwise all is well. We hear that the Highest Ruler [the governor-general] is coming this way. Let's see whether he visits Delhi, and, if he does, whether he holds a durbar, and if he does, whether this sinner will be invited, and if he is, whether he will get a robe of honour. I've heard nothing about the pension, and no one knows anything about it.

He gives further news in a letter of 9 November 1859 to Husain Mirza:

General resettlement is now permitted,[68] and people are pouring in. Formerly only owner-occupiers were allowed in, and no one was allowed to rent a house; but since the day before yesterday this too has been permitted. But don't get the idea that you or I or anyone else can let any part of his house to a tenant. People who never owned a house and always lived in rented accommodation are taking up residence, but the rent they pay goes to the government.

On 13 November 1859 he writes to Aram:

I have had two letters from you, and today the newspaper arrived. My cousin Ziya ud Din Khan gets this 'Avadh Akhbar' and sends it on to me. So I don't need it. Why waste my postage and your own on it? All I wanted was that since you are not far from Farrukhabad and news from there must be reaching you all the time, you should write and tell me whatever you hear. And when the... [governor-general] comes to Agra you should write and tell me what you yourself observe. That's all. I'm putting the newspaper you sent me in a fresh envelope and sending it off today....

[66] Used for fuel.
[67] The seminar for the teaching of literature, medicine and the religious sciences, established by Azurda. The students were maintained free of charge and provided with books.
[68] More than two years after the population of the city had been expelled.

I am very concerned about your father. I pray for him. May God
grant my prayer and send him a complete recovery.... I got your
news of Mirza Yusuf Ali Khan Aziz. He is a man of distinguished
family, brought up in every luxury. God will reward you for anything
you can do to serve him....

On 28 November 1859 he writes to Yusuf Mirza in an outburst
of bitterness:

Yusuf Mirza, none but Lord and God knows my plight. Men go mad
from excess of cares and sorrows; their reason deserts them. And if
amid the griefs that beset me my reflective power is failing, that is no
ground for surprise; indeed, not to believe it is monstrous. Grief and
cares for what? you may ask. For death; for separation; for my
livelihood; for my honour. Whose deaths? Leave aside the Inauspicious
Fort,[69] and count up only the men of Delhi: Muzaffar ud Daula;[70]
Mir Nasir ud Din; Mirza Ashur Beg; my nephew's[71] son Ahmad
Mirza, a mere child of nineteen; Mustafa Khan, son of Azam ud
Daula; his two sons Irtiza Khan and Murtaza Khan; Qazi Faizullah.
Did I not love these as much as my own kin? Yes, and two more names
that I forgot: Hakim Razi ud Din Khan and Mir Ahmad Husain
Maikash. O God, O God! What can replace these men? Separation
from whom? From Husain Mirza, and Mir Mahdi [Majruh] and
Mir Sarfaraz Husain and Miran Sahib—may God preserve them! If
only they could have been happy where they are! But their homes
are sunk in darkness and they are condemned to wander. When I
think of the state in which Sajjad and Akbar are living my heart
breaks within me. These are words that any man can say, but I swear
to you as Ali is my witness that, grieving for the dead and parted
from the living, the world is plunged in darkness in my sight.

I had one brother, and he died insane. His daughter, his four boys
and their mother, my sister-in-law are stranded in Jaipur. In these
three years I could not send them a penny. What will my niece be
thinking? She must wonder whether she *has* an uncle. Here the
wives and children of men who were once wealthy nobles are
begging in the streets, and I watch them helplessly. To bear such
affliction needs a stout heart.

Now listen to my own tale of woe. I must support my family—
a wife and two children; then there are the servants—Kallu, Kalian

---

[69] The Red Fort had been called the Auspicious Fort in the days when it
was the seat of the Mughal court.

[70] Husain Mirza's elder brother and Yusuf Mirza's own uncle.

[71] Sister's son.

and Ayaz. Madari's wife and children are still here as usual; in short, it's as though Madari were still here. Miyan Ghamman had only left me a month when he came back. 'I've nothing to eat.' 'Very well, my friend, you too can stay.' Not a penny comes in, and there are twenty mouths to feed. The allowance I get from you know where [Rampur] is just enough to keep body and soul together. And I have so much to do that during the twenty-four hours I get practically no time to myself. There is always something to worry about. I am a man; not a giant, and not a ghost. How am I to sustain such a heavy load of care? I am old and feeble. If you could see me, you would know what a state I am in. I can sit for an hour or two, but I spend the rest of the time lying down—practically confined to my bed. I can neither go out visiting regularly, nor does anyone come to see me. That liquid which sustained me, I can no longer get. And more than all this, is all the bustle because of the governor-general's coming visit. I used to attend the durbar, and receive a robe of honour. I cannot see that happening now. I am neither one of the accepted nor one of the rejected, nor a culprit, nor an informer, nor a conspirator. Well, tell me yourself: if a durbar is held here and I am summoned, where am I to get an offering to present?[72]

I have sweated blood day and night for the past two months to write an ode of sixty-four couplets. I have given it to Muhammad Afzal the painter, and he will let me have it on 1 December.... I set myself the task of recording the events of my life in it. I will send you a copy.... See how I can write, even though my heart lacks fire,—indeed, lacks life.

I could not manage a new ode to the Refuge of the World [Wajid Ali Shah, the deposed king of Oudh]. This one [i.e. the one I have already sent] was never presented; so I have put Wajid Ali Shah in Amjad Ali Shah's[73] place. After all, God himself did the same. Anwari[74] repeatedly did this, altering an ode in one man's praise for presentation to another. So if I alter the father's ode to suit the son, that's nothing so terrible, especially amid all the afflictions which I have briefly related to you. And I wrote it not to show my prowess in poetry, but to beg.

Anyway, tell me, did the ode arrive safely? I had a letter from your uncle two days ago, but he didn't say whether the ode had reached him. Put me out of my uncertainty and write plainly whether it

[72] It was considered obligatory for a man granted audience at court to bring a present suited to his status.

[73] Father and predecessor of Wajid Ali Shah on the throne of Oudh.

[74] The great Persian poet.

arrived or not. And if it did, has it been presented to His Majesty? And if it was, by whom was it presented? And what orders were given? Write to me quickly about all this....

I'm waiting for a final decision about my pension; then I shall go to Rampur. Jamadi ul Awal to Zil Hij[75] is eight months. Then with Muharram, the year 1277 will begin. I have to live through perhaps two, perhaps four, perhaps at the most ten or eleven months of it—nineteen to twenty months in all. For that space I shall face whatever grief or joy, whatever humiliation or whatever honour is fated for me, and then repeating Ali's name I shall depart for the land of oblivion—my body to the realm of Rampur, my soul to the realms of light. O Ali, O Ali, O Ali!

Let me give you another piece of news, my friend. Brahma's son fell ill; he lay ill for two days, and on the third day died. Ah me, what a nice, inoffensive boy he was! His father Shivji Ram is distraught with grief. Thus I have lost two more companions, for one is dead and one is sick at heart....

On 2 December 1859 he writes again. Majruh must have asked him what Delhi was like these days. He replies:

My friend, what a question to ask! Five things kept Delhi alive— the Fort, the daily crowds at the Jama Masjid, the weekly walk to the Jumna bridge, and the yearly fair of the flower-men.[76] None of these survives, so how could Delhi survive? Yes, there was once a city of that name in the realm of India.

The governor-general will be here on 15 December. We shall have to see where he stays and what arrangements are made about the durbar. In former durbars the lords of seven principalities used to be in attendance, and each was received separately—Jhajjar, Bahadurgarh, Ballabgarh, Farrukhnagar, Dujana, Pataudi and Loharu. Four of these have gone. [The British abolished the four first-named after the Mutiny.] Two of the others—Dujana and Loharu— come under the Hansi-Hissar authorities. That leaves Pataudi. If the Hissar commissioner brings his two here, that will make three nobles. Otherwise only one. In the general durbar all the Hindu notables and so on will be there. Only three [prominent] Muslims are left—Mustafa Khan [Shefta] in Meerut, Maulvi Sadr ud Din Khan in Sultan Ji, and that slave to the things of this world Asad [Ghalib] in Ballimaron. And all three are despised and rejected, destitute and distressed.

[75] Months of the Muslim calendar.
[76] Cf. p. 221 below.

We smashed the wine-cup and the flask;
  what is it now to us
If all the rain that falls from heaven
  should turn to rose-red wine?

If you're coming, come along. Come and see the new road
through Nisar Khan's Chatta, and the new road through Khan
Chand's Lane. Come and hear how Bulaqi Begam's Lane is to be
demolished and an open expanse cleared to a radius of seventy yards
from the Jama Masjid. Come and see Ghalib in all his despondency.
And then go back....

On 13 December 1859 he writes again:

I have no wine:
  the pen I hold will not move on.
The wind is cold. O smokeless fire,
  where are you?

Mir Mahdi Sahib, it is morning, and freezing cold. The brazier is
before me. I write a word or two, then warm my hands. True, there
is warmth in the fire, but alas! where is that liquid fire, two sips of
which run coursing through your body the moment you swallow
them, bringing strength to the heart, and illumination to the mind
and ecstasy to the power of speech? O cruel fate that the lips of one
who serves the saki of Kausar,[77] should be parched!

On 23 December 1859 he writes to Tufta. It seems that someone
named Abdur Rahman, a distant kinsman of Ghalib's, had behaved
badly towards Tufta, who had asked Ghalib to remonstrate with
him. He writes in reply:

My dearest friend, what are you thinking of? Can every created
mortal be a Tufta or a Ghalib?
  Each man was made to fill his proper role. 'Last thoughts are
best'.[78] Sugar is sweet, salt savoury; and nothing can change a thing's
inherent taste. If I write and remonstrate with this man, can't you
see what he will think? He will think to himself, 'How would Ghalib
know who Abdur Rahman is? And what have I got to do with him?'
And he's sure to realize that you must have written to me. I shall
make myself cheap in his eyes and he'll be even more cross with you.
As for what you write about my numbering him among my kinsmen,

[77] Ali, the son-in-law of the Prophet, whom Ghalib specially revered, will
pour the wine of purity for the blessed in Paradise. Kausar is the name of a
spring in Paradise.
[78] I.e. one must think a thing out to the end before deciding how to act.

my gracious friend, I hold all mankind to be my kin and look upon
all men—Muslim, Hindu, Christian—as my brothers, no matter
what others may think. And as for that kinship which the world calls
affinity, in that, community and caste and religion and way of life
all have their place, and there are grades and degrees of affinity.
Viewed by these standards, you will find that this man isn't related
to me in the smallest degree. If I was polite enough to write of him
as kinsman, or speak of him as kinsman, what of that? Zain ul Abidin
Arif was the son of my wife's sister, and this man is the son of *his*
wife's sister. Make what you can of that! In short, when *he* can't
behave with ordinary decency, to write to him is pointless, useless,
and even harmful.

I had already heard of your journey to Meerut and your meeting
Mustafa Khan [Shefta] there. Now your letter tells me of your arrival
at Sikandarabad via Muradabad. May Almighty God in His glory
keep you well and happy.

On 29 December 1859 he writes to Husain Mirza:

I hear that it is proposed to establish in Lahore a department to award
compensation, to ten per cent of its value, to citizens whose property
was looted by the blacks [the rebel sepoys]. That is, a man who asks
a thousand rupees will be given a hundred. As for the plundering
which the whites did, that's all pardoned; there will be no compensa-
tion for that....

Why do you speak of 'Hamid Ali Khan's houses'? They were
confiscated long ago, and became government property. The grounds
look quite different now. There were British soldiers occupying the
zenana and the big house. Now the main gate and a whole row of
shops have been pulled down, the brick and stone sold by auction,
and the proceeds sent to the treasury. Don't get the idea that the
rubble sold was Hamid Ali Khan's. It was its own seized property
that the government demolished. Well, when the king of Oudh's
properties are treated as they are, who is going to care about the
properties of ordinary citizens? You haven't yet got it into your head
what the authorities intend, and you never will. Your Navind Rae,
and copies of orders, and appeals mean nothing. The orders issued
here in Delhi are the decrees of fate and destiny, against which there
is no appeal. Say to yourself, 'We never were nobles; rank and wealth
were never ours; we had no property, and never drew a pension.'

Rampur shall be my dwelling-place in life and my resting-place
when I am dead. It makes me laugh when you write pressing me
to go there. I am certain that I shall see the new moon of the month
of Rajab...in Rampur....

How much life is left to me? Seven months of this year and twelve of next year. Then in this very month I shall go to my Master, where hunger and thirst and piercing cold and raging heat will be no more. No ruler to be dreaded, no informer to be feared, no rent to be paid, no clothes to be bought, no meat to be sent for, no bread to be baked. A world of light, a state of pure delight.

O Lord, how dear to me is this my wish:
Grant Thou that to this wish I may attain!

The slave of Ali, son of Abi Talib,
Who longs for death's release,

> Your servant,
> Ghalib.

On this despondent note the letters for 1859 end.

1860

He begins 1860 on a more cheerful note, writing to Majruh, on 1 January:

Where are you, my boy? Where are you roving? Come here and listen to the news.

Orders have been issued for the general return of the Muslims' properties. Those who had been paying rent for them have now been exempted from paying it.... If you think fit, come and take possession of your property. Then stay on here or return [to Panipat] just as you like.... Give my blessing to Hakim Mir Ashraf Ali and tell him to write out the prescription for those pills he gave me and send it to me quickly....

What he was planning in relation to his pension does not become clear until March, when in a letter to Bekhabar (dated only 'March 1860') he explains what he did after being told that the Chief Secretary would not receive him because he had been a well-wisher of the rebels.

The next day I wrote a letter[79] in English to the effect that it was sheer conjecture to think that I had been a well-wisher of the rebels, and requesting an investigation so that my name could be cleared and my innocence established.

[79] I.e., presumably, had a letter written.

Then, either because he decided after all that his hopes were futile, or because he saw no need to stay on in Delhi waiting for the British to reply, he decided to carry out his intention to go to Rampur.

The Nawwab had long been pressing him to come—ever since early 1858, in fact—and letters from him in November 1858 and April 1859 had repeated the invitation. Ghalib had replied that he wished to wait until the British restored his pension, as he was generally confident that they ultimately would. Thus he had written to the Nawwab on 18 April 1859: 'The day after I receive the [pension] money I shall ask you for money to pay for conveyance and porterage; and the day after I receive it I shall start out for Rampur.'

But, as we have seen, 1859 passed by, and the restoration of his pension was not yet in sight. On 8 December 1859 he had had to ask the Nawwab bluntly for extra money:

> Your draft of Rs 100 for...November 1859 reached me. I drew the money and spent it, and was again hungry and naked. Whom should I tell if not you? If you will send me Rs 200 over and above my regular allowance, I shall be able to breathe again—provided that it is not reckoned against my allowance, and that you send it very soon.

The Nawwab sent him the money, and at the same time repeated his invitation to him to come to Rampur. Ghalib had in any case intended to accept the invitation in due course, and in the circumstances probably felt that he could not reasonably delay much longer.

On the way to Rampur, on 21 January 1860 he wrote to Tufta:

> My friend, I have left Delhi for Rampur. I reached Muradnagar on Thursday 19th and Meerut on Friday 20th. Today, Saturday 21st, I am staying on at the insistence of our friend Mustafa Khan [Shefta], and I'm posting off this letter to you from here. Tomorrow I shall stay at Shahjahanpur and the day after at Garhmukteshar, and then go on to Rampur via Muradabad. So send your next letter to me to Rampur. All the address you need write is my name, and Rampur. This is enough for now. I will write to you again from Rampur.

He also wrote from Meerut on the same day to Hakim Ghulam Najaf Khan giving him the same information adding:

> It's nine o'clock [a.m.], and I'm sitting here writing to you. I am getting my food free, and shall stuff myself to my heart's content....

I've got the two boys to write to their grandmother [Ghalib's wife] and am sending their letters off. Go to my house with this letter and read it out to your teacher [Ghalib's wife] and tell her that I am safe and sound.... I've thought it best to tell you the stages of my proposed journey, but now if anyone asks you, tell him plainly that I am in Rampur. Don't make a secret of it. I want every one to know the position plainly.

Tufta, as usual, was not content to address his letters [in his view] in the inadequate style Ghalib had suggested. Ghalib's next letter (undated) rebukes him:

You say that your son doesn't know the world, but you're no better yourself. Tell me first, who in Rampur doesn't know me? Do you think they know Maulvi Wajih uz Zaman Sahib better [Tufta had presumably addressed Ghalib in his care.] His house is a long way from mine. And I'm not at the Nawwab's court. He entertained me in his own mansion for four days, and then I asked for separate accommodation.... It so happens that the post-office is near where I am living, and the post-office clerk has got to know me. Letters reach me from Delhi all the time addressed with my name and 'Rampur', and that's all.... In fact if you address me c/o the Maulvi Sahib and the court your letters may go astray....

He was very well satisfied with the treatment he received at Rampur. He writes to Hakim Ghulam Najaf Khan on 3 February 1860:

Write and tell me in detail any fresh news of what is going on in Delhi. And now let me tell you my news: I am treated with great honour. I have met the Nawwab three times, and have been given a house which is three or four houses in one. There is no stone here...and only a handful of the houses are brick-built. Mud walls and tiled roofs—the whole population lives in this kind of house, and my houses too are of the same kind. So far we have not discussed anything together. I shall not make the first move, and he too will not speak to me directly, but through his officials. Let me see what he has to say and what allowance he will make me. I had thought that once I arrived here, things would be settled very quickly, but so far—and today is Friday, my eighth day here—nothing has been said. The Nawwab has both meals sent to me every day, and there is enough food for all of us. It's not unacceptable to my taste either. As for the water, I cannot find words to express my thanks to God for it. There's a river here called the Kosi. God be praised! Its water is so sweet that you would think it was diluted sherbet—clear, light, refreshing and quickly assimilated. For these eight days I have been safe from attacks of constipation. I develop a really good appetite in the mornings. The boys are thriving and my servant [unnamed] well and strong. True, Inayat [another servant, says Mihr] has been out of sorts for the last two days, but he'll soon be well....

On 14 February 1860 he writes again to Hakim Ghulam Najaf Khan:

What is this that you write, telling me to write home[80] more often? The letters I write to you are in effect written to her too. Is it too much to ask of you to go and read them to her? Now she will be wondering what was in the English letter. Take this letter of mine with you and go and read it to her word for word.

The boys are both well. Sometimes they amuse me, and sometimes they plague me. Their goats, and pigeons, and quails, and their kites—small and big—are all in good order. I gave them their two rupees apiece for February, and they spent it all in the first ten days. Then two days ago the younger gentleman came to me and said, 'Grand-dad, give me something on indefinite loan.' So I gave him something. Today is the 14th, and the end of the month is a long way off. Let's see how many times he comes back to borrow more....

Ask at home whether Kidar Nath has paid all the servants. I have sent the pay for all of them—even the sweeper....

However, he did not stay on in Rampur. In a letter to Aram dated 14 March 1860 he says, 'I am leaving for Delhi on Saturday, March 17th'—without, however, giving any explanation of his departure. There is a hint in a letter to Yusuf Mirza written on 2 April 1860, which tells us that he arrived back in Delhi on 25 March, the first day of Ramzan, the Muslim month of fasting, and adds: 'The children made my life a misery: otherwise I would have stayed a few days more.'

But a letter of 6 April 1860, to Majruh is more explicit. Majruh had apparently been surprised to learn of Ghalib's return to Delhi. Ghalib rebukes him with mock solemnity:

Mir Mahdi, have you forgotten my accustomed ways? Have I ever once missed listening to the recitation of the Quran at the Jama Masjid during the blessed month of Ramzan? How could I stay in Rampur during this month? The Nawwab tried to detain me, and tried very hard, in fact, tempting me all the time with the prospect

[80] I.e. to his wife.

of the mangoes I would get there during the rains. But, my friend, I would have none of it, and moved to such purpose that I reached here on the night of the new moon [from which Ramzan begins]. The holy month began on the Sunday. And from that day to this I have been present every morning at Hamid Ali Khan's mosque to hear the reverend Maulvi Jafar Ali Sahib's reading of the Quran. Every night I go to the Jama Masjid to say the *tarawih* prayer.[81] Sometimes, when I feel so inclined, I go into the Mahtab Garden at sunset and break my fast there and take a draught of cold water. And, oh, how happily the days pass by!

And now let me tell you the facts. I took the boys with me to Rampur and they made my life there a misery. I didn't like to send back on their own. If anything should happen to them on the way, I thought, I should never live it down. So I came away sooner than I had intended; otherwise I should have passed the hot season and the rains there. Now, if I live, and if I can go there alone, I shall return after the rains,[82] and not come back here for a long, long time. The position is that ever since July 1859—that is, for the last ten months—the Nawwab has been sending me a hundred rupees a month. When I got to Rampur he paid me an additional hundred rupees a month, calling it 'hospitality allowance'. This meant that as long I stayed in Rampur I should get two hundred a month, whereas in Delhi I should get only a hundred. Well, my friend, the point is not whether I get two hundred or a hundred. The point is that the Nawwab treats me as his friend and his ustad, and gives me my allowance in that spirit, and not as though I were his employee. It was as a friend too that he always met me, with the deference and warmth which friends observe in their intercourse with one another. I had the boys offer presents when we were received, and that was all. Anyway, I'm fortunate; I must be thankful that my daily bread is well provided for. Why should I complain that it is not enough?

And so, my dear friend, things are back to where they were. I sit in my little room with the *khas* screen in place.[83] A breeze is blowing; and full pitcher of water is beside me, and I am smoking the hookah and writing you this letter. I felt like talking to you, so I did....

---

[81] A special prayer of twenty genuflexions performed at night during Ramzan.

[82] I.e., late in October or early in November.

[83] In the hot season screens of a particular fragrant grass called *khas*, drenched in water, are placed at the doors so that the air is cooled as it passes into the rooms.

Ghalib's return to Delhi gave rise to a good deal of speculation, some of which he reports in a letter to Tufta dated 30 March 1860:

You know that I went to Rampur at the end of January and returned at the end of March. Do you know what the people here are saying about me? One lot says, 'This man was the ustad of the Nawwab of Rampur and has been to visit him there. If nothing else, the Nawwab must have given him at least five thousand rupees'. Another group says, 'He went there to look for a job, but he couldn't get one'. Another says, 'The Nawwab gave him a job, and fixed his salary at two hundred rupees a month. But the lieutenant-governor came to Rampur from Allahabad, and when he found out that Ghalib was employed there he told the Nawwab that if he wanted to continue in his favour he must dimiss him; and so the Nawwab gave him the sack. And now you've heard all that, let me tell you the facts, Nawwab Yusuf Ali Khan has been my friend for thirty-one years and my shagird for five or six years. He used to send me money from time to time and now regularly sends me a hundred rupees a month—since July 1859. He had often invited me to Rampur, and now I have been there. I stayed two months, and then came back. If I live, I shall go again after the rains. But by God's grace I shall get my hundred rupees a month whether I am here or there.

There has been much speculation about what led the British authorities to restore Ghalib's pension. Ghalib himself had hoped that the Nawwab of Rampur could influence them in this direction, and his efforts may indeed have played a part, for Ghalib's statement in one of his letters that the restoration of the pension was not the Nawwab's doing, but God's, does not necessarily contradict this. Ikram argues that the efforts of Sir Sayyid Ahmad Khan probably played a decisive part. He writes:

Maulana Abul Kalam Azad says that Sir Sayyid exerted every effort to get Ghalib's pension restored... and there are signs which support this statement.... On his return journey [from Rampur] he stopped at Muradabad, and Sir Sayyid, who was at that time Sadr us Sudur[84] there, went to the inn where he was staying and brought him to his own house. It is reasonable to assume that during his stay he told all his troubles to Sir Sayyid, and that Sir Sayyid used the influence which he had acquired after the Mutiny to remedy them. Possibly because Sir Sayyid was a government employee, or perhaps from some other consideration, it was not considered advisable to speak

[84] A judicial post of some importance.

of these efforts. Maulana Abul Kalam Azad's statement also seems plausible because it was in March 1860 that Ghalib stayed with Sir Sayyid and the restoration of the pension was made only a month or two later, in May 1860.

However that may be, Hali's account (in his life of Sir Sayyid) of Ghalib's stay at Muradabad on this occasion is interesting. It shows amongst other things that any sense of estrangement that may have arisen over the *Ain i Akbari* incident some years earlier was now ended. He writes:

> Sir Sayyid used to say that when he was in Muradabad, Ghalib had gone to visit...Nawwab Yusuf Ali Khan at Rampur. 'I did not know he had gone there, but during his return journey to Delhi I heard that he had stopped at Muradabad and was staying at an inn. I at once went there and brought him and his luggage and all his companions to my house.' It would seem that when Sir Sayyid had refused to print Ghalib's introduction [to *Ain i Akbari*], the two men had kept at a distance and felt a certain reserve towards each other, and that this was why Ghalib had not informed him of his coming to Muradabad. Anyway, when Ghalib arrived at Sir Sayyid's house from the inn and got out of the palanquin, he had a bottle [of wine] in his hand. He took it into the house and put it down in a place where anyone who passed could see it. Sir Sayyid later picked it up and put it in a storeroom. When Ghalib found the bottle missing he got very upset. Sir Sayyid said, 'Don't worry, I've put it in a safe place'. Ghalib replied, 'Show me where, my friend'. Sir Sayyid then took him to the storeroom and produced the bottle. Ghalib took the bottle from him and held it up to look at it, and then said with a smile, 'There's some missing, my friend. Tell me truly, who's had it? Perhaps that's why you took it away to the storeroom. Hafiz was right:
>
> > These preachers show their majesty in mosque and pulpit
> > But once at home it is for other things they do.'
>
> Sir Sayyid laughed and made no reply, and in this way the sense of strain between them that had lasted for several years was removed. Ghalib stayed on for a day or two and then returned to Delhi.

When the arrears of his pension were swallowed up in paying off his accumulated debts, Sarur suggested that he should write an ode in praise of the Nizam of Hyderabad and allow him to have it presented on Ghalib's behalf by an intermediary at the Nizam's court. The proposal depressed him, and he replied in an undated letter showing how fate had always frowned on him in these matters:

> First let me write of some matters which you will at first sight think irrelevant. I was five years old when my father died, and nine when my uncle died. In place of the income from his estate, I and my blood relations were to be granted ten thousand rupees a year from the estate of Nawwab Ahmad Bakhsh. He refused to give more than three thousand a year, of which my own personal share amounted to seven hundred and fifty. I pointed out this misappropriation to the British government. Colebrooke Sahib Bahadur (the resident of Delhi) and Stirling Sahib Bahadur, secretary to the government at Calcutta, were in agreement with me that my right must be restored. But the resident was dismissed and the secretary met an untimely death.
>
> After a lapse of many years the king of Delhi appointed me to a pension of fifty rupees a month, and the heir-apparent to one of four hundred rupees a year. Two years later, the heir-apparent died.
>
> Wajid Ali Shah, king of Oudh's court, appointed a sum of five hundred rupees a year to be paid to me in reward for my odes of praise. He too did not survive more than two years, by which I mean that though he still survives, his kingdom was destroyed, and destroyed within those two years. The kingdom of Delhi was a little more tenacious of life. I drew my daily bread from it for seven years before it was destroyed. There are no stars so baneful as those that kill my patrons and destroy my benefactors. Now if I turn to the ruler of the Deccan [the Nizam's dominions, Hyderabad], mark my words, my intermediary will die, or fall from office, or if neither of these things happens, then his efforts on my behalf will be fruitless and the ruler will give me nothing. And if by any chance he does, then his state will be levelled in the dust and put under the asses' plough.
>
> And suppose I put all that aside and make up my mind to write a panegyric. Well, I can make up my mind to it, but not carry it through. Fifty to fifty-five years of practice have given me a certain talent, but I have no strength left in me. I sometimes look at the prose and verse which I wrote in former days; I know that it is mine, but I am lost in wonderment that I could write such prose and compose such verse. Abdul Qadir Bedil spoke as though with my tongue when he wrote:
>
> My story echoes round the world—and I am nothing.
>
> My life is ending, and my heart and mind are spent. My hundred rupees from Rampur and my sixty rupees' pension suffice amply for my maintenance. Fluctuations of prices are always with us. For better or for worse, the work of this world goes on. Caravan upon caravan

is ready to depart. See, Munshi Nabi Bakhsh [Haqir] was younger
than I, but he died last month. Where shall I find the strength to write
a panegyric? And if I make up my mind to it, how shall I find the
leisure? And if I write it, and send it to you, and you send it to the
Deccan, when will our intermediary find an opportunity of present-
ing it? And if he does, what will be the response? Do you think I shall
live to see all these stages passed? 'Verily we are for God, and verily
to Him we shall return. There is no god but God, and none who
may be worshipped but He, and nothing exists but God, and God
was when no other thing was, and God is now just as He was'.

All the same, the restoration of his pension and of his standing
with the British must have been a source of much satisfaction to
him. Another welcome event of the same time was a move to re-
issue his Urdu diwan. Here he inadvertently landed himself in
difficulties. He explains in a letter to Aram dated April 1860:

Let me tell you the facts about my diwan being printed at Meerut.
Then you can have your say. I was still in Rampur when I received
a letter headed 'Petition of Azim ud Din Ahmad, of Meerut'. May
God strike me if I know who this Azim ud Din is or what profession
he follows. Anyway, I read the letter and learned that he wanted to
print my Urdu diwan as a business venture, and expected to make
a profit out of it. Well, I made no reply. When I got to Meerut from
Rampur, I stopped off at friend Mustafa Khan's [Shefta's]. There my
old friend Munshi Mumtaz Ali came to see me. He said, 'Send me
your Urdu diwan. A bookseller named Azim ud Din wants to print
it.' Now listen to this: where was I to find a fully complete copy of
the diwan? True, before the Mutiny I had a copy made and sent to
Nawwab Yusuf Ali Khan Bahadur at Rampur. When I was about to
leave Delhi for Rampur, brother Ziya ud Din urged me strongly to
get the diwan from the Nawwab, get it copied by a scribe, and send
it to him. Accordingly, during my stay there I got it copied by a scribe
and posted it to Ziya ud Din at Delhi. Now let me return to what
I was saying. When Munshi Mumtaz Ali said that to me, all I could
say was, 'Very well, I'll get the diwan from Ziya ud Din and send
it you. But who will be responsible for correcting the proofs?'
Nawwab Mustafa Khan [Shefta] said, 'I will'. Now, tell me, what
could I do? When I got to Delhi I got the diwan from Ziya ud Din
and sent a man with it to Nawwab Mustafa Khan. If I had been in
a position to make what arrangements I pleased for printing it, do
you think I'd have ignored our own press [i.e. Aram's] and sent it
to someone else's? I am writing this letter to you and at the same
time writing off to our friend Nawwab Mustafa Khan to tell him

that if printing has not already started, he is not to give it for printing, but is to send it back to me as soon as possible. If it comes, I'll send it on immediately to you; if the scribe there has already started it, then there's nothing I can do. I am not at fault; and if, now you've heard what happened, you think I am to blame, well, my friend, then please forgive me. People will be involved with Ramzan and Id; I feel sure that the copying won't have begun; my diwan will be sent back to me, and shall then be sent on to you....

Some good-humoured sarcasm in a letter to Yusuf Mirza on 9 May 1860 shows that the situation was unchanged up to then:

As for our friend Fazlu, Mir Kazim Ali, how could he know what 'book' means and what weapon is called 'Agra' and what tree bears the fruit called 'Sikandar'? My Urdu diwan went to Meerut; Sikandar Shah took it for me and delivered it to Nawwab Mustafa Khan....

It transpired that Azim ud Din, having once got his hands on the diwan, was not prepared to give it up. Ghalib writes to Sayyah on 11 June 1860:

What can I say about the printing of my diwan? That unknown stranger known as Azim ud Din, who got me to send him the diwan, is not a man but an apparition, a horror, a ghoul—in short, a very uncouth sort of person—and I don't want to put the printing of my diwan into his hands. I am asking him to return it, but he won't. God grant that I get it back. You too must pray for it.

But in the end all turned out well. He was able to write to Aram on 25 June 1860:

Friend, I have sinned against you, and kept your book [i.e. the diwan] to myself. It cost me a lot of effort and labour to stop it being printed there and to get it back. Today, Monday, 25 June, I have sent it off by parcel post. So now forgive me my sin and restore me to your pleasure and write and tell me you have done so. The book—my Urdu diwan—I give over to you entirely. Now it belongs to you. I don't say, 'Print it' and I don't say 'Don't print it'. Do whatever it pleases you to do. If you print it, put me down for twenty copies. And, yes, my son, do please take great care to see that it is printed correctly.

He writes again on 3 July 1860:

My son, you make me laugh. The diwan I sent you is comprehensive and complete. What are these 'two or three ghazals in Mirza Yusuf

Ali Khan Aziz's possession, which are not in the diwan'? On this score you can set your mind completely at rest. I have not written a single line which is not in this diwan. However, I'll speak to him too and get him to send these ghazals for me to look at. What do you want with a picture of me? And how can Aziz, poor fellow, get my portrait done? If it's all that important, write to me about it. I'll get a portrait done and send it to you. You don't need to present anything, not even your respects. I love you like a son, and I give thanks to God that you are a dutiful son. God grant you long life and give you all that you desire.

Ghulam Rasul Mihr thinks that an undated letter to Nawwab Ziya ud Din Ahmad Khan relates to this same period—or at any rate to the same year. 'Diwan', he writes, 'here means the collected Persian verse….' The letter would seem to be one of 1860, when he contemplated getting his collected Persian verse printed at Munshi Newal Kishor's press. The letter reads:

Reverend sir, why are you so reluctant to give me the diwan? It's not as though you studied it every day. Nor is it so dear to you that you can't digest your dinner until you see it. So why won't you let me have it? There'll be a thousand copies instead of just one. My verse will win fame. My heart will rejoice. The whole world will see my ode in your praise. Everyone will be able to read the prose encomium on your brother. Are not these advantages enough? As for fear that the book may be lost, that is just a baseless feeling. Why should it? And if by any chance it *is* lost, if the mail is robbed between Delhi and Lucknow, then I'll travel at once by the mail to Rampur, and bring you the copy transcribed by the late Nawwab Fakhr ud Din Khan. Perhaps you'll tell me, 'Go to Rampur and send it off from there.' But don't you think they would ask me why I don't send the Delhi copy? And if I write and tell them that Nawwab Ziya ud Din Sahib won't give it to me, don't you think I'll be told, 'When your own relation and neighbour won't give it to you, why should I, who am so far away, give you my copy?' And if you tell me to borrow Tafazzul's copy and send that, what am I to do if he refuses to part with it? And if he does part with it, what use is it to me? In the first place it's incomplete, and then it's defective in other ways. There are some panegyrics in it in which I've altered the names for presentation elsewhere, and which in his edition still bear the earlier names. Shihab ud Din's copy too, which Yusuf Mirza has taken, has both these defects, and moreover is full of mistakes. Not a couplet, not a line is free of them. This thing can't be done without your help; and you lose nothing by it. You may *think* you do, but that's just a baseless fear, a bogy. And if you do, I'll guarantee to make good your loss, as I have already said. So make up your mind to grant my request and write to me accordingly so that I can inform the man who has asked me for it, and when he asks again, can send it to him.

For the rest of 1860 there is no further mention of either the Urdu or the Persian verse. We find him in the middle of the year preoccupied with the weather, with the Delhi scene, and with the problems of moving house—and on occasion with other themes, some more weighty, and some less so.

He was conscious that the year in which he had predicted he would die—1277 AH, due to begin on 20 July 1860—was now approaching. On 6 June 1860 he writes to Majruh:

Dear friend, I have just been so ill that I myself felt sorry for myself. For four days I couldn't eat. Now I am fit and well again. To the end of Zil Hij [the last month of the Muslim year], 1276, I have nothing to fear. From the Ist Muharram [the first month of the Muslim year] God knows.

On 11 June 1860 he writes to Sayyah:

It grieves me to hear of the desolation of Lucknow, but remember that there this destruction will give way to creation—that is, the roads will be widened and the bazaars improved, so that everyone who sees it will approve what has been done. In Delhi destruction is not followed by creation, and the work of destruction goes on all the time. The whole appearance of the city, except for the street of shops that runs from the Lahore Gate of the Fort to the Lahore Gate of the city ['i.e.,' says Mihr, 'Chandni Chauk and Khari Baoli'] has been spoiled, and will go on being spoiled....'

But he laments the fall of Lucknow all the same. On 30 June 1860 he writes again to Sayyah:

What praise was too high for Lucknow? It was the Baghdad of India, and its court—may God be praised!—a mint of rich men. A man could come there penniless and become wealthy. Alas that autumn should come to such a garden!

On 8 July 1860 he writes to Ala ud Din Khan Alai:

For the last ten to twelve years I have lived in Hakim Muhammad Hasan Khan's mansion. Now Ghulamullah Khan has bought the house, and at the end of June he asked me to move out. I've been trying to find two adjacent houses somewhere, so that I can make one the zenana and have the other for my own use. I couldn't find any, so I had to content myself with looking for a house in Ballimaron to which I could move. But I couldn't get one. Your aunt came to my rescue, and gave me Karorawali mansion to live in. It wasn't what I wanted, in that it wasn't near the zenana, but anyway, it's not all that far away. I shall move in tomorrow or the next day; so I have one foot on the ground and one in the stirrup....

To Tufta he describes his house-moving difficulties in more detail, writing on 20 July 1860:

I had been living in these narrow confines for the last ten to twelve years. For seven years I had paid four rupees every month. Now I paid three years' rent—something over a hundred rupees—in a lump. The owner sold the house, and the new owner told me—insisted, rather—that I must move out. That's all right if you can find another house. But he had no consideration and began to pester me by starting on the repairs. He put up scaffolding by the balcony (about two yards deep and ten yards long) overlooking the courtyard. That's where I slept at nights. What with the oppressiveness of the heat and the closeness of the scaffolding I felt as though it was the scaffold nearby, and, come morning, I should be hanged. I passed three nights in this state, and then on Monday, 9 July at midday, I got a house. I moved in, and felt as though my life had been saved. This house is a paradise as compared to the other, and the best of it is that it's in the same muhalla, Ballimaron....

Letters of the same period to Shafaq review the whole Delhi scene. He writes in a letter dated only '1860', but evidently belonging to early July:

Lord and Master, it was twelve o'clock, and I was lying on my bed practically naked smoking the hookah when the servant brought your letter to me. As luck would have it, I was wearing neither shirt nor coat, otherwise I'd have rent my clothes in frenzy. (Not that your lordship would have lost anything by that—*I* would have been the one to suffer by it.) Let's begin at the beginning. I corrected your ode and sent it off. I received an acknowledgement. Some of the cancelled verses were sent back to me with a request to be told what was wrong with them. I explained what was wrong with them, wrote in words that were acceptable in place of those to which I had objected, and said that you might now include these verses too in the ode. To this day I have had no reply to this letter. I handed over to Shah Asrar ul Haq the paper addressed to him and wrote to you the verbal message he gave in reply. This letter too your Lordship has not answered.

My heart is vibrant with complaint as
   is the harp with music.
Give it the slightest touch and hear the
   strains it will pour forth.

I think to myself, 'I sent both letters unstamped. I cannot conceive that they should have been lost.' Anyway, it was a long time ago. No point in complaining now. You don't re-heat stale food, and 'service means servitude'

Five invading armies have fallen upon this city one after another: the first was that of the rebel soldiers, who robbed the city of its good name. The second was that of the British, when life and property and honour and dwellings and those who dwelt in them and heaven and earth and all the visible signs of existence were stripped from it. The third was that of famine, when thousands of people died of hunger. The fourth was that of cholera, in which many whose bellies were full lost their lives. The fifth was the fever, which took general plunder of men's strength and powers of resistance. There were not many deaths, but a man who has had fever feels that all the strength has been drained from his limbs. And this invading army has not yet left the city. Two members of my own household are down with fever, the elder boy and my steward. May God restore both of them speedily to health.

The rains have been plentiful here too, but not as plentiful as in Kalpi and Banaras. The farmers are happy, and the fields ready for harvest. Anxiety about the autumn harvest is at an end. For the spring harvest they need rain in the month of Pus [December–January].

There is more about the weather in a letter of 19 July 1860:

What is the weather like? The hot season, the cold season and the rains have all come together, not to speak of the hailstorms.... I always find this season hard to bear. In the hot weather I feel the heat as badly as an animal that pants for water, especially now when I have to bear not only the heat but the innumerable griefs and anxieties that beset me.

   The flames of Hell cannot give out such heat—
   For hidden griefs burn with a different fire.

And in the next letter too:

It rained last night and the wind was cold enough to be dangerous. Now it's morning, and a cool, harmless breeze is blowing. The sky is covered with light cloud. The sun is up, but you can't see it....

In July 1860 he writes:

I have a story which will amuse you. The postman who delivers
letters to Ballimaron these days is some baniya—somebody Nath or
something Das—and he can just about read and write. I live on the
upper storey. He came into the house, handed a letter to my steward
and said, 'Say that the postman presents his respects and his
congratulations. The king of Delhi made him a Nawwab, and now
there's a letter from Kalpi giving him the title of Captain.' I wondered
what on earth he was talking about. When I looked carefully at the
address I found that my name was preceded by the words 'makhdum
i niyaz keshan' [Master of his humble servants'—an honorific term
of address]. The poor pimp had ignored the other words and read
'keshan' as 'kaptan'. [In the Urdu script the two words resemble one
another more closely.]

On 24 August 1860 he writes:

The dearness of grain is a calamity from heaven, and disorders of
the blood make life a misery. Swellings everywhere, and huge boils—
and no remedy avails, and no effort counts for anything. Was it the
rebel army from Meerut that descended on Delhi that morning of
11 May, or was it the onset of repeated visitations of divine wrath?
From end to end of the realm of India the doors of disorder and
disaster are opened wide—and Delhi, distinguished before, is just
as distinguished now in this too. 'Verily we are for God, and verily
to Him we shall return.'

In September 1860 he writes to Sarur:

Here it seems as though the whole city is being demolished. Some
of the biggest and most famous bazars—Khas Bazar, Urdu Bazar, and
Khanam ka Bazar, each of which was practically a small town, have
gone without a trace. You cannot even tell where they were. House-
holders and shopkeepers cannot point out to you where their houses
and shops used to stand. It is the rainy season, but there has been
practically no rain, and it is under the rain of picks and shovels that
houses are collapsing. Food is dear, and death is cheap, and grain sells
so dear that you would think that each grain was a fruit.

In another, undated letter he had in fact hinted at a visit to Sarur
in the cold season:

You invite me to Marahra and remind me that I had planned to come.
In the days when my spirits were high and my strength intact, I once
said to the late Shaikh Muhsin ud Din how I wished I could go to
Marahra during the rains and eat mangoes to my heart's content and

my belly's capacity. But where shall I find that spirit today, and from where recover the strength I once had? I neither have the same appetite for mangoes nor the same capacity to hold so many. I never ate them first thing in the morning, nor immediately after the midday meal; and I cannot say that I ate them between lunch and dinner because I never took an evening meal. I would sit down to eat them towards evening, when my food was fully digested, and I tell you bluntly, I would eat them until my belly was bloated and I could hardly breathe. Even now I eat them at the same time of day, but not more than ten to twelve, or, if they are of the large...kind, only six or seven.

> Alas! how the days of our youth have departed!
> Nay, rather the days of our life have departed!

Now I would make the journey only to see you; and I can stand the troubles of travelling only in the winter, not in the rains....

When it came to the point he seems to have felt unable to face the physical strain which travel involved. Thus he had written to Ala ud Din Khan Alai on 2 July 1860:

I should very much like to see you, but that can happen only if you come here. I wish you could have come with your father and visited me....

> Meet with my rival if you like:
> I leave that to your whim.
> But what is wrong with asking after me
> as well as him?'

It was certainly not lack of interest which held him back. On 31 December 1860, he replies to a letter which his friend Sayyah had written him from Banaras:

My friend, I like Banaras: it is a fine city. I have written a poem in praise of it called 'The Lamp of the Temple'. It is in my volume of Persian verse. Have a look at it.... You have written an account of your journey from Lucknow to Banaras, and I'm expecting you to go on with it. I am very fond of travelling and sightseeing.... Oh well, if I cannot travel, never mind. I will content myself with the thought that 'To hear of pleasure is to experience half of it', and will think of Sayyah's account as itself a journey.

Among his other preoccupations during the latter half of the year was the correcting of the verses which his friends sent him.

He writes to Ala ud Din Alai on 2 July 1860 that this is the most that his remaining poetic powers enable him to do:

> You ask me for recent verses. Where from? Verses on themes of love are as far from my taste as faith is from unbelief. I was the government's hired bard. I wrote my panegyrics and got my robes in reward. But the robes stopped coming, and I stopped writing. No ghazals, no odes. Lampoon and satire is not in my line. So, tell me, what am I to write? I am like an old wrestler, who can only explain the holds. Verses keep coming in from all directions, and I correct them. Believe me, I am telling the literal truth.

On more than one occasion he had to protest, not for the first time, his inability to write chronograms. He writes to Sayyah on 31 July 1860:

> My friend, I swear to you by your life and by my faith that I am a complete stranger to the art of the chronogram and the riddle. You won't have heard of any chronogram by me in Urdu. I have composed a few in Persian, but the position there is that while the verses are mine the words giving the date were supplied by others. Do you understand me? Calculation is a headache to me, and I can't even add up. Whenever I work out a chronogram I always find that I've calculated it wrongly. There were one or two of my friends who, if the need arose, could work out for me the words which gave the required date, and I would fit them into a verse.

He goes on to say that whenever he has attempted a chronogram himself he has had to make provision for additions and subtractions to such an extent that the whole thing becomes laughable: 'In Calcutta a mosque was built at the tomb of the late...Siraj ud Din Ali Khan. His nephew...asked me for a chronogram, and I wrote one which you will find in my volume of Persian verse.' He then quotes it, and shows by what tortuous methods he gets the right date, by selecting a key word which gives far too large a total and then finding ways of indicating that from this must be deducted numbers yielded by two other words. He concludes, 'I ask you, can you call this a chronogram?' This lead him on to quote two other examples which he likes better, because they incorporate a method which he had himself invented. He goes on:

> You write that 'Sayyid Ghulam Baba' doesn't fit into any metre. How do you make that out? [He then writes two four-line verses, each in a different metre, and each incorporating this name, and goes on:]

Produce some indicating word which fits into this metre and you'll have your chronogram. The friends who used to produce the key words for me have all departed for Paradise. And I, as I wrote above, am helpless in the matter.

Perhaps the best chronogram which Ghalib composed himself was that on the Mutiny—*rustkhez i beja*—which he worked out and included in *Dastambu*; and since it well illustrates some of the points which his letters of this time discuss, it is convenient to analyse it here. The phrase is indeed an apt one, for it both fixes the date of the Mutiny and expresses Ghalib's view of it. It is not easy to translate. 'Unseasonable tumult' is an approximate equivalent, but 'unseasonable' does not convey the sense of outrage which *beja* here carries. The other word, *rustkhez*, means 'Judgement Day', but is also used to describe any great tumult or upheaval, including emotional tumult such as the stunning impact of a woman's beauty, or the sudden news of a friend's death, might cause. If one adds up the numerical values of the letters of the word *rustkhez* as written in the Urdu script, they give a total of 1277. From these must be deducted the combined values of the two letters '*ja*'—for *beja* may read as a single world (and, indeed, must be so read to give the meaning required), or alternatively as two words '*be ja*', meaning 'without (or, minus) *ja*'. The total of '*ja*' is 4, and 1277 minus 4 comes to 1273, which gives the date of the Mutiny in the Muslim era.

Sometime during 1860—the letters are undated—he wrote to Mihr the last two letters to him which we possess. They are of exceptional interest. Mihr had written to tell him of the death of his mistress, a courtesan named Chunna Jan. Ghalib replies:

> Mirza Sahib, I received your letter with its grievous news. When I had read it I gave it to Yusuf Ali Khan Aziz to read, and he told me of your relationship with her—how devoted to you she was and how much you loved her. I felt extremely sorry, and deeply grieved. Listen, my friend: in poetry Firdausi, in ascetic devotion Hasan of Basra, and in love Majnun—these three are the pre-eminent leaders in these three arts. The height of a poet's attainment is to become a second Firdausi, the limit of an ascetic's achievement to rival Hasan of Basra, and the ideal of a lover is to match Majnun. His Laila died before him, and your mistress died before you; in fact you excel him, for Laila died in her own home, while your beloved died in yours. Friend, we 'Mughal lads' are terrors; we are the death of those for whom we ourselves would die. Once in my life I was the death of a fair, cruel dancing girl. God grant both of them His forgiveness,

and both of us, who bear the wounds of our beloveds' death, His mercy. It is forty years or more since it happened, and although I long ago abandoned such things and left the field once and for all, there are times even now when the memory of her charming ways comes back to me, and I shall not forget her death as long as I live. I know what you must be feeling. Be patient, and turn your back on the turmoil of earthly love.... God is all-sufficient: the rest is vanity.

We have no means of knowing how long an interval elapsed between this letter and the next, but it seems that Mihr could not overcome the grief he felt at his mistress's death, and Ghalib adopts quite another tone in an effort to rally him:

Mirza Sahib, I don't like the way you're going on. I have lived sixty-five years, and for fifty of them have seen all that this transient world of colour and fragrance has to show. In the days of my lusty youth, a man of perfect wisdom counselled me, 'Abstinence I do not approve: dissoluteness I do not forbid. Eat, drink and be merry. But remember that the wise fly settles on the sugar, and not on the honey.' Well, I have always acted on his counsel. You cannot mourn another's death unless you live yourself. And why all these tears and lamentations? Give thanks to God for your freedom, and do not grieve. And if you love your chains so much, then a Munna Jan is as good as a Chunna Jan. When I think of paradise and consider how if my sins are forgiven me and I am installed in a palace with a houri, to live for ever in the worthy woman's company, I am filled with dismay and fear brings my heart into my mouth. How wearisome to find her always there!—a greater burden than a man could bear. The same old palace, all of emerald made, the same fruit-laden tree to cast its shade. And—God preserve her from all harm—the same old houri on my arm! Come to your senses, brother, and get yourself another.

Take a new woman each returning spring,
For last year's almanac's a useless thing.

After which he drops the subject completely and goes on to talk of other things.

Although Mihr lived for another nineteen years, no letters written to him after this survive.

As the year draws to a close he again falls despondent. On 18 December 1860 he writes to Majruh:

You tell me that I'm not to invite Miran Sahib to Delhi until you say so—as though *you* are the only one that really loves him, and I don't. My friend, come to your senses and just think. I haven't got the means to invite him here and fix him up with a separate house to stay in and, if nothing more, give him thirty rupees a month, and say, 'Here you are, take this and tour the ruins of Dariba and Chawri Bazar and Ajmeri Gate Bazar and Bulaqi Begam's lane and Khan Dauran Khan's mansion'.

As the Christian year ended, nearly half of AH 1277 had already elapsed and Ghalib still believed in his own prediction that he had at the most another six to seven months to live. He perhaps has this in mind when he writes to Sayyah on 31 December 1860:

My weakness is at its height, and old age has made me useless. I am weak, slothful, lethargic, depressed, and weary of life. My foot is in the stirrup and my hand on the bridle. I have a long, long journey to travel and no provision for the road, for I go empty-handed. If I am forgiven without being questioned, well and good. If I am called to account then I shall dwell in hell and damnation will be my station. Alone to face eternal torment. How well some poet[85] has said:

Tired of all this, we look to death for our release
But what if even after death we find no peace?

1861

Ghalib's first letter of 1861 is addressed to Majruh. In further letters to Majruh he returns again to conditions in Delhi. In one dated only '1861' but perhaps written in April or May, a verse which Majruh had sent him for correction starts him off. He quotes the verse,

My friend, this is the language
Delhi people speak.

and comments:

Oh, Mir Mahdi, aren't you ashamed of yourself? My good sir, 'Delhi people' now means Hindus, or artisans, or soldiers, or Panjabis or Englishmen. Which of these speak the language which you are praising? [It's not like Lucknow.] The population of Lucknow hasn't changed. The state has gone [the British annexed Oudh, of which Lucknow was the capital, in 1856], but the city still has its masters of every art.

In short, the city has become a desert, and now that the wells are gone and water is something rare and precious, it will be a desert like

[85] Zauq—cf. p. 81 above.

that of Karbala.[86] My God! Delhi people still pride themselves on Delhi language! What pathetic faith! My dear man, when Urdu Bazar is no more, where is Urdu? By God, Delhi is no more a city, but a camp, a cantonment. No Fort, no city, no bazaars, no watercourses. ...

Other things depressed him too. He had written to Tufta on 20 January 1861, evidently replying to a letter in which Tufta had told him that he was having his collection of Persian verse printed; he had entitled it *Sumbulistan* (The Hyacinth Garden). Ghalib replies gloomily:

I got your letter from Meerut...God prosper you in publishing *Sumbulistan*. He alone guards your honour. Most of my life has passed, and only a little more remains; and I have no complaints either about the past or the future. I ask myself, 'What good did the fame of Urfi's ode do Urfi, that the renown of mine should profit me? What fruit did Sadi reap from his *Bostan* that you should reap from your *Sumbulistan*?' Apart from God, all that exists is unreal, a fantasy—no poetry, no poets, no odes, no desire to write. Nothing exists but God.

He wrote again on 19 April 1861, when *Sumbulistan* had appeared and Tufta had sent him two copies:

Mirza Tufta, my dear sir, you've thrown your money away, and shamed both your own poetic power and my corrections. Alas! What a wretched production the book is! Had you been here you would have seen the true parallel to your verse and its printed form; you would have seen the ladies of the Fort moving about the city, their faces fair as the moon and their clothes dirty, their trouser-legs torn, and their shoes falling to pieces. This is no exaggeration. Your *Sumbulistan* is like a lovely woman meanly clad. Anyway, I've given the two copies to the two boys and told their teacher to set their lessons from it. And they've started on it today.

On 22 February 1861 he had complained to Junun of his deteriorating physical and mental powers:

My memory is as good as gone, my sense of smell diminished, and my hearing defective. There is nothing wrong with my sight, though it is not so sharp as it was:

Old age, a hundred ailments, as they say.

[86] The place where Husain and his companions were martyred, after their access to water had been cut off.

But, in general he is not in bad humour during these months, and even where he has something distasteful to say he handles it with a light touch. A letter of 4 April 1861 to Ala ud Din Ahmad Khan Alai, is typical:

The lion feeds its cubs on the prey it has hunted, and teaches them to hunt their prey. When they grow up they hunt for themselves. You have become a competent poet, and you have a natural talent. Why should *you* not compose a chronogram on the birth of your child? Why should *you* not work out a name that yields the date? Why trouble me, an old man grieved at heart? Ala ud Din Khan, I swear by your life: I worked out a chronogram-name for your first son and put it into a verse; and the child did not live. The fancy haunts me that this was the effect of my inauspicious stars. No one whom I praise survives it. One ode apiece was enough to dispatch Nasir ud Din Haidar and Amjad Ali Shah [kings of Oudh]. Wajid Ali Shah [the last king] stood up to three, and then collapsed. A man to whom I addressed ten to twenty odes would end up on the far side of oblivion. No, my friend, may God protect me, I will neither write a chronogram on his birth nor work out a chronogram-name. May Exalted God preserve you and your children and confer long life and wealth and prosperity on you all.

Listen to me, my friend. It's a rule with men who worship beauty that when they fall in love with a youngster they deceive themselves that he's three or four years younger than he really is. They know he's grown up, but they think of him as a child. Your tribe is no better. On my faith I swear: here is a man whose honour and fame are known and established among men; and you too know it, my friend. But you can't feel happy until you shut your eyes to all that and think of the poor fool as a nobody, whom no one has ever heard of. I have lived fifty years in Delhi. Thousands of letters come in from every quarter. Some who write don't even give the name of the muhalla. Some address me at the muhalla where I formerly lived. Letters from the authorities, in Persian and in English—even letters from England—come addressed simply with my name and 'Delhi'. You know all these things. You have seen such letters. And then you ask me for my address! If you don't class me as a noble, well and good. But at any rate I'm not an artisan, that the postman can't find me unless you write the muhalla and the police station. Address me by name at 'Delhi'. I'll stand guarantee that your letters reach me.

He concludes an undated letter (probably of May or June 1861) to Majruh:

These days Maulana Ghalib (God's mercy be upon him) is in clover.
A volume of the *Tale of Amir Hamza* has come—about 600 pages of
it—and a volume of the same size of *Bostan i Khayal* (The Garden
of Fancy).[87] And there are seventeen bottles of good wine in the
pantry. So I read all day and drink all night.

> The man who wins such bliss can only wonder
> What more had Jamshed? What more Alexander?'

In June 1861 he writes to Nawwab Amin ud Din Ahmad Khan's
son Ala ud Din Khan Alai that he loves him as any man would love
the son of one who has been a friend to him:

You are the fresh fruit of that tree which came to maturity before
my eyes, and in whose cool shade I have rested, blessing his name.
How could you be otherwise than dear to me? As for our seeing each
other, there are only two possibilities: you should come to Delhi,
or I to Loharu. But you cannot come, and I must be excused. Do
not listen to my excuse—I tell you this myself— until you have heard
from me who I am and what my story is:

Listen: there are two worlds, the world of spirits, and this world
of earth and water. The Ruler of both these worlds is one who has
Himself proclaimed the question: 'Whose shall be the kingdom this
day [Judgement Day]?' and has Himself given the answer: 'That of
the one God, the All-Powerful'. Though it is the general rule that
those who sin in this world of earth and water receive their pun-
ishment in the world of the spirits, it has sometimes happened that
those who have sinned in the world of the spirits are sent to undergo
punishment in this world. Thus I, on the 8th Rajab 1212 AH[88] was
sent here to stand trial. I was kept waiting in the cells for thirteen
years, and then on the 7th Rajab 1225 AH[89] I was sentenced to life-
imprisonment. A chain[90] was fastened on my feet, and the city of
Delhi having been designated my prison, I was committed there, and
condemned to the hard labour of composing prose and verse. After
some years I escaped from prison and ran away to the east [Calcutta]
where I roamed at liberty for three years. In the end I was appre-
hended in Calcutta and brought back and thrown into the same
jail. Seeing that I would try to escape again, they fettered my hands

[87] Enormously long medieval-style romances. The *Tale of Amir Hamza* runs
into eighteen bulky volumes.
[88] The date of Ghalib's birth.
[89] The date of Ghalib's marriage.
[90] Ghalib's wife.

as well.[91] The fetters chafed my ankles, and the handcuffs wounded my wrists. My prescribed hard labour became a greater burden to me, and my strength departed from me entirely. But I am a man without shame. Last year I got my feet free, and, still handcuffed, ran off, leaving my fetters in a corner of my cell. By way of Meerut and Muradabad, I made my way to Rampur. A few days short of two months had passed when I was apprehended and brought back again. Now I have promised not to run away again. And how can I? I no longer have the strength. I await now the order for my release. When will it come? There is just a faint possibility that I may get out this very month—Zil Hij, 1277.[92] But, be that as it may, a man released from jail makes straight for home, and I too, when my deliverance comes, will go straight to the world of spirits.

> Happy that day when I shall leave this prison house of earth,
> Forsake this barren vale, and reach the city of my birth.

His words make it clear that he now felt it unlikely that his prophecy that he would die in 1277 was going to be fulfilled.

A letter of this same month of June 1861 to Junun suggests that he has deliberately changed his mind about it:

> Why have you written like that about the mangoes? Gifts do not have to be repeated for evenmore, especially when the gift is itself something that does not last. My dear sir, this year mangoes are scarce everywhere, and what few there are, are dry and tasteless. And it is not to be wondered at. There was no rain in the winter months and none in the rainy season. You can ford the rivers on foot, and the wells are dried up. How can one expect the fruit to be juicy? Please do not think anything of it. I shall prove my own revelation false, and live on till next year's rains to eat your...mangoes.

And 1277 did indeed elapse with Ghalib still surviving. In due course, as we shall see, he thought up an ingenious explanation, but for the moment he had other things to occupy his mind. His patron, the Nawwab of Rampur, had just celebrated with great pomp the marriage of his second son. Arshi describes the occasion:

> Preparations had been started months beforehand. Robes of honour had been distributed to the courtiers, and food sent to every citizen of the capital; and throughout the city gatherings were held where

[91] The two boys whom Ghalib adopted as 'grandsons'.

[92] Because Zil Hij is the last month of the Muslim year, and Ghalib had prophesied that he would die in 1277.

dancing girls and musicians entertained the people. Dependents of the court outside the state were sent invitations to come to the wedding. Ghalib too received one, but he was not well enough to come....

The Nawwab then sent him a gift of Rs 125 in lieu of the tray of choice food and the robe of honour traditionally conferred on such occasions. Ghalib was either exceptionally short of money at the time or else he felt that where the Nawwab had spent so much, he might be persuaded to spend a little more. Accordingly he writes on 11 July 1861:

> I am not writing to you but conversing with you, and, seeking your pardon for my impertinence and your permission to speak my mind, what I have to say (and I say it by way of a joke) is this: You have presented me with Rs 125 to provide myself with a feast and a robe of honour. I am starving. If I spend it all on feeding myself, and don't use any of it for getting the robe made, will your highness still owe me money for a robe or will you not?
>
> May you live on another thousand years
> And every year have fifty thousand days.

At the same time he composed and sent the Nawwab some poems in honour of the occasion, of which the Nawwab expressed his appreciation. However, an incident now occurred which aroused his displeasure. Ghalib's friends, Miran Sahib and Mir Sarfaraz Husain, had with Ghalib's approval, gone to try their fortunes at Rampur, and Ghalib had given them a letter of introduction to the Nawwab's Chief Steward. This perfectly reasonable action seems to have upset the Nawwab, who presumably thought that Ghalib ought to have approached him direct, and Miran Sahib and Mir Sarfaraz Husain had to come away empty-handed. Ghalib's distress is evident from the letter he wrote the Nawwab on 22 July 1861:

> It is seven or eight years since I entered your service and began to share in your bounty. I have made it a binding rule never to make an improper request of you or recommend anyone to your favour.... I did not send Mir Sarfaraz Husain or Miran Sahib—I swear by God I did not. They went looking for employment. That is Mir Sarfaraz Husain's profession; and Miran Sahib recites elegies [on the martyrdom of Husain], and is outstanding amongst his fellows here in this art. When I wrote to your Chief Steward that they had such-and-such qualifications, what I had in mind was that during Muharram

when half a dozen or more reciters are retained for the occasion, Miran Sahib might make one of them; and since, after all, there are numerous officials needed to take charge of your police stations and of the administrative sub-districts, Mir Sarfaraz Husain, who is an intelligent and able man, might be appointed to some such post in some district. Had both or either of these things been done, well and good. They have not been done; well and good. What I wrote was indeed not a recommendation; my aim was simply to introduce them. Had I wished to recommend them, could I not have written to you? Where I am concerned, you may set your mind at rest.

> For years and years no breath has passed my lips
> But such as tended to your happiness.

To Majruh he wrote, understandably, in different terms. In a letter dated simply 'July 1861' he writes:

Your letter came yesterday in the middle of the afternoon. I feel sure that Mir Sarfaraz Husain must have reached you at much the same time, or at any rate that same evening. You will hear from his own mouth how he fared on his journey. I don't know what *I* can write. Whatever I have heard, I too have heard from him. His coming back empty-handed was not what I had wished and not what I had intended; but it accords with what I had believed and expected. I knew that he would get nothing there. He has spent a hundred rupees for nothing, and since he spent it trusting in my suggestion, I feel ashamed. In my sixty-six years I have often been shamed and disgraced in this way, and when a man bears a thousand such scars, well, he can bear one more. But my heart feels keenly the pain of his loss.

Why bother to ask about the epidemic?[93] This was the one arrow left in the quiver of Fate, the unerring marksman. Where killing has been so general, and looting so merciless, and famine on so great a scale, why not an epidemic too? 'The Voice of the Unseen'[94] had proclaimed ten years ago:

> Ghalib, all other woes have come to pass
> And only unexpected death remains.

My friend, I was not mistaken about 1277, but I thought it beneath me to die in a general epidemic. Really, it would have been an action most unworthy of me. Once this trouble is over we shall see about it.

[93] There was a severe epidemic of cholera in Delhi at the time.
[94] A title by which the Persian poet Hafiz is often known. Here Ghalib applies it to himself.

The printing of my collected Urdu verse is finished. Most probably you'll be receiving a copy through the post this week—or at the latest by the end of the month.

There are plans for printing the collected Persian verse too. If everything works out, that too will be printed....

The epidemic has died down somewhat. For six or even days it raged everywhere. Two days ago Khwaja Mirza (son of Khwaja Aman) came to Delhi with his wife and children. Yesterday night his nine-year-old boy contracted cholera and died. 'Verily we are for God and verily to Him we shall return.'

The epidemic affects Alwar too. Alexander Heatherly, known as Alec Sahib, has died. I tell you truly and sincerely, he was very dear to me, a man who wished to advance my interests and served as a link between me and the Raj. And it was for this crime that death has taken him. Well, this is the world of causes and effects. What are its workings to us?

Mihr notes of Alexander Heatherly:

His father was French,[95] and he had married an Indian woman. He was a very good Urdu poet, one of the disciples of Zain ul Abidin Arif [the 'nephew' of Ghalib who died young and whose two children Ghalib adopted as his 'grandsons']. His usual pen-name was Azad, but he sometimes used Alec, the shortened form of Alexander. He died at the age of thirty. His younger brother Thomas had his collection of Urdu verse printed at Agra in 1863.

In his next letter, dated 8 August 1861, he returns to the Rampur fiasco:

My friend, you are right when you say

Nothing befalls the sons of man but passes by.

But what pains me is that they went there on the strength of my letter, and suffered by it....

But after a few lines he returns to other themes.

The volume of my Urdu verse is printed. Alas! When the Lucknow press prints a man's diwan it raises him to heaven. The calligraphy is so good that every word shines radiant! May Delhi and its water and its press be accursed! They call for the poet of the diwan as a man calls for his dog. I looked at every proof as it was brought to me. But the copyist was not the man who brought the pages to me,

[95] This is incorrect. His father was English, and his mother an Indian Muslim lady.

but someone else. Now that the copies are printed and I have received my author's copy I find that not a word has been corrected. The copyist has left them just as they were. All I could do was make a list of errata, and this has been printed. Anyway, no matter whether I like it or not, I'll buy several copies, and, God willing, a copy each will reach the trinity of you this very week. But I got no pleasure from it, and you won't either.

And what's this you write—'There are customers here: write and tell me the price?' I'm not an agent, nor a merchant, nor the manager of the press. The Ahmadi Press is owned by Muhammad Husain Khan, and managed by Mirza Amu Jan. The press is in Shahdara— Muhammad Husain Khan, near Painters' Mansion, Rae Man Lane, Delhi. Price of the book: six annas [about sixpence]. Postage to be paid by the customer. Give this information to anyone who wants the book. Anyone who wants to order copies—two, or four, or ten, or five—should write to Muhammad Husain Khan, Painters' Mansion, Rae Man Lane, Delhi, and ask him to send them off by post. The books will come by post, and payment can be sent off in cash or in stamps, as you like. What's it got to do with me and you? You know what to tell anyone who asks.

I can't tell you whether an epidemic's mounting or subsiding unless there is an epidemic. There is a man of sixty-six here [Ghalib] and a woman of sixty-four [his wife]. If either of them had died we would have known that there was an epidemic. A fig for such an epidemic! It's Thursday, 5 August, but there's no sign of the lunar month. Last night we put one stool on top of another, and several people kept climbing on them to look. But the new moon was not to be seen. (The Muslim month begins when the new moon is actually seen.)

This letter makes it unmistakably clear that the Urdu diwan had not been printed in Agra after all. Not until 10 January 1862 do we find any indication why. But on that date he writes to Aram:

It seems to me that Maulvi Mir Niyaz Ali Sahib has not presented my case to you properly. What I wanted him to make clear to you was that the printing of the Urdu diwan in Delhi had already begun before Hakim Ahsanullah Khan could bring me the proof-sheet you had sent him, and that I had authorized the press here to print the diwan because I thought you no longer proposed to do so. Just consider: remember how Muhammad Azim, the owner of the press at Meerut, implored me to let him have the diwan, and how in order not to incur your displeasure I compelled him to return it to me. How could I then give anyone else permission to print it? You had

left off writing to me, and I thought you must be cross with me.
I told Maulvi Niyaz Ali Sahib, 'You must please persuade my son
Shiv Narayan to forgive me!' My friend, I swear to God, I regard
you as a dear son. Why speak of the diwan and the picture? It was
for you alone that I got the diwan copied out and brought it from
Rampur. It took me a lot of searching to find the portrait in Delhi,
but I found it, and brought it, and sent both things to you. They
are yours. You may do as you like with them—keep them, give them
away, or tear them up and throw them out. You had a fine edition
of *Dastambu* prepared and made me a present of it: I sent you my
portrait and my Urdu diwan. You are the living memorial of my
cherished friend Nazir Bansi Dhar:

O fragrant flower, your fragrance pleases me
Because it holds another's fragrance too.

On 22 September 1861 he writes again to Majruh. He had
corrected some verse of Mir Sarfaraz Husain and returned it,
apparently with only a brief covering note. Majruh seems to have
objected, for Ghalib now writes:

Yes sir? What do you want of me? I corrected the manuscript…and
returned it. What more did you want me to write?…. You prefer the
ways of Muhammad Shah's reign [he was emperor from 1719 to
1748]: 'Here all is well, and I desire to know of your welfare also.
I had received no letter from you for many days. I was pleased to
hear from you. The manuscript, duly corrected, is returned here-
with. Please give it to my dear son Mir Sarfaraz Husain, and give
him my blessing also. And further, give my blessing to Hakim Mir
Ashraf Ali and to Mir Afzal Ali. It behoves you as a dutiful son always
to continue writing to me in this way.'
What do you say? Isn't it a fact that this is the way they used
to write letters in those days? Good heavens, what an attitude—
that unless it's written like that, a letter's not a letter but a well
without water, a cloud without rain, a tree without fruit, a house
without light, a lamp without radiance! I know that you are alive:
you know that I am alive. I wrote what was necessary, leaving it
to another time to write the superfluities. And if I can't please
you without writing like this, well, my friend, I've written you
a line or two in that style now—and when a man makes up for a
prayer he has missed, his atonement is accepted.[96]…So forgive me,
and don't be cross.

[96] A Muslim unable to say one of the five prayers at the prescribed time
is permitted to make good the omission later.

Two days later, on 24 September 1861, he sends a letter of recommendation to Shihab ud Din Khan:

> Light of my eyes Shihab ud Din Khan, my blessing upon you! This is to tell you that the man who has come with my note is named Hasan Ali, and is a Sayyid. His skill in making medicines is unmatched, and in making pickles and preserves, unparalleled. His father Jan Muhammad was employed at the king's court, and his uncle [father's brother] Mir Fatah Ali now holds a post at Alwar at a salary of Rs 15 a month. Anyway, I have told him that he will get Rs 5 a month and will have to go to Loharu. He refused, saying that on an income of five rupees he could neither keep himself nor send anything to his wife and children here. I replied, 'It's a big establishment. If your work pleases them, they will raise your salary.' He said, 'Very well, on the strength of that I'll accept the small salary; but I must be provided with two meals a day. Otherwise I can't possibly manage.'
>
> Listen, my son. The poor fellow is quite right. Unless he gets his keep he can't manage. I'm sure that when you report the facts, you can get this authorized. So much for that. Now he says, 'Let me have two months' salary in advance so that I can get some clothes made and leave them something at home to be going on with. And let me have money to cover the expenses of food and conveyance for the journey.' Here too I think he's in the right, but I'm not in a position to say anything on this point. Anyway, you can send on this note I've written you to our lord and master [Ala ud Din Khan] Alai.

He writes to Alai himself the next day. Alai must have asked him how it was that he could go to Rampur (as he had done the previous year), but could not come to Loharu. He replies on 25 September 1861:

> Lord and master Alai, I've just received your letter, and sat down to answer it the moment I finished reading it. Here's a fine thing! I am to be your ox, and my ties with Rampur your goad—or I your horse and taunts about Rampur your whip. Why should my ties and commitments to Rampur hinder and prevent my coming to Loharu? I'm not the Nawwab's representative, posted to a certain area. Just as nobles provide for the upkeep of faqirs, so does the court of Rampur provide for mine. The only difference is that a faqir is expected to call down God's blessings on his patron while I am expected to correct his verse. If I like, I can stay in Delhi, or in Agra, or in Lahore, or in Loharu—just as I like. I have only to hire a conveyance for my clothing, pack a dozen bottles of wine in my trunk, contract for the services of eight palanquin-bearers, leave two

of my four servants here, take two along with me, and set off. Any letter from Rampur can be sent on by the boys' tutor. I can arrange for the conveyance; I can get the wine; I can find the palanquin-bearers. But where shall I get the strength? When I go for my meals from my own quarters to the zenana (which is quite near) it takes me almost half an hour to get my breath back, and the same when I get back to my drawing room. And after all, the Nawwab of Rampur too invited me to his son's wedding and I told him the same thing, 'I hardly exist any more. Your auspicious influence sustains me to correct your verse, but expect no service from me beyond that.'

I would love to see both my brother [your father] and you. But what can I do? I can hope to come when the sun is in Scorpio or Sagittarius, that is, in November or December, but I wish it were only Gurgaon or Badshahpur I had to get to instead of Loharu. You'll say, 'Is Rampur any nearer, then?' But it's two years since I went there, and my strength fails and declines with every day that passes. You can't come here, and I have not the strength to go there. So if in November or December my final assault succeeds, well and good. Otherwise

I grieve because I cannot see my friends
And for no other thing....

Alai evidently responded by sending him a present of Bikaner sugar-crystal, for he writes again on 12 November 1861:

Today at the time I usually go to the zenana for lunch Shihab ud Din Khan arrived with your letter and a bag of sugar-crystal. I had it taken along with me and had the crystal weighed in my presence. It came to about four ounces over the four pounds. God prosper your dwelling-place! That is enough and more than enough, and I don't need any more. When I came out again after having my lunch, your cousin's [Shihab ud Din Khan's] servant was waiting to ask me for an answer to your letter, saying that the camel-man was about to leave. I usually lie down after lunch, so I've written this acknowledgement lying here. I'll answer the other things in your letter tomorrow.

A letter from Shafaq, in which he had apparently complained of ill-treatment by his relations, provokes an outburst of bitterness on Ghalib's part against his. He writes on 22 October 1861:

Most reverend sir,... In matters of feeling, the union of two opposites is beyond the bounds of possibility. How can it be that at one particular time one particular matter can be at once the cause of joy and the grounds of grief? Yet in reading your letter I found just that, for I felt both pleasure and pain. Glory to God! I find that in so many things you and I have shared the same fate—ill-treatment from our relatives, grievance against our kin. Throughout the realm of India I have no fellow-countryman. One or two in Samarkand and a hundred or two among the nomads of the deserts of the Khifchaq [Central Asia] there may be. But relations by marriage I have; and I fell into their toils when I was only five, and for sixty-one years have borne their tyranny.

> Ghalib, were I to tell the tale of all my
>   kin have done to me
> Then hope—that custom men observe—would
>   leave the world for evermore.

You cannot come to my support, nor I to your aid. Oh God! I have swum the river, the further shore is near, and two more strokes will bring me to the land.

> I lived my life waiting for death to come
> And dead, I still must see what else I face.

...You are a prey to grief and sorrow, but...to be the target of the world's afflictions is proof of an inherent nobility—proof clear, and argument conclusive....

His depression must have been enhanced by the fact that he was ill at the time, as a later letter shows.

The same good humour pervades an undated letter to Sahib i Alam:

> Lord and Master, to what can I compare the couplets you write in my praise and how can I thank God sufficiently for them? It is God's goodness to His servants that makes His chosen favourites speak well of such a disgrace to creation as I am. It seems that this great good fortune was written in my fate that I should come through this general epidemic alive. O God, my God, praise to Thee that Thou hast saved one who deserved death by sword or fire, and then raised him to high estate! I sometimes feel that the throne of heaven is my lodging and Paradise my back garden. In God's name, compose no more verses in my praise, or I shall not shrink from claiming Godhead myself!

1862

Ghalib's first letter of 1862 was that to Aram already quoted in the previous section—the only one to Aram in this year. A second, dated 19 January 1862, to Maududi tells the welcome news of the release of Ghalib's old friend Azurda:

> Our revered Maulvi Sadr ud Din [Azurda] had been in detention for a long time, but he was brought before the court for trial, and at the end of the proceedings the court ordered that his life be spared. He lost his employment, and his property was confiscated. Willy-nilly, in his penury he made his way to Lahore. There the financial commissioner and lieutenant-governor, as an act of clemency, returned half his property, and he now has possession of it. He lives in his own mansion and lives on the rent which he receives [from his other property]. He can manage on it, for he has thirty to forty rupees a month coming in, and there is only himself and his wife. But Imam Bakhsh's children are closely related to him, and there are about ten to twelve of them. So he doesn't live very comfortably. He is old, and very infirm, and getting on for ninety years old. May God preserve him. We must be grateful for such as he these days.

Most of February and early March are taken up with letters to Alai. A remark in a letter from Alai evokes a more serious theme:

> At two separate points in your letter yesterday I see that you have written that Delhi is a big city and there must be plenty of people with all sorts of qualifications there. Alas, my dear boy, this is not the Delhi in which you were born, not the Delhi in which you got your schooling, not the Delhi in which you used to come to your lessons with me to Shaban Beg's mansion, not the Delhi in which I have passed fifty-one years of my life. It is a camp. The only Muslims here are artisans or servants of the British authorities. All the rest are Hindus. The male descendants of the deposed King—such as survived the sword—draw allowances of five rupees a month. The female descendants, if old, are bawds, and if young, prostitutes.

He ends his next letter of 17 July 1862: 'Stopped drinking wine on 22 June: started again on 10 July:

> Thanks be to God! The tavern door is open
> once again!'

He was asked to explain what this was all about, and in his next letter (of 28 July 1862) he does so. But he has something more remarkable to write of first:

> Listen, my dear boy: Thursday to Thursday makes eight days; Friday nine, Saturday ten, Sunday eleven. And not for a single moment has

it stopped raining. At this very moment it is pouring down. I have had a charcoal brazier lit beside me, and after every two lines I write, I hold the paper to the fire to dry it out. What else can I do? Your letter demands an answer. So listen....

Fifty years ago the late Ilahi Bakhsh Khan produced a new metre and rhyme scheme, and at his command I wrote a ghazal in it. [He then quotes what he regards as its best couplet, and its concluding couplet, and continues:] Now I find that someone has added an opening couplet and four more, included these two couplets of mine, and made a ghazal out of them which is being sung all over the place. The last couplet and one other are mine, and the other five some idiot's....

Pay my respects to your father and tell him that the days are past when I could take one loan from Mathura Das, and touch Darbari Mal for another, and come away with loot from Khub Chand Chain Sukh's house. They all had my notes of hand, sealed with my seal and carefully preserved. Not that it did them any good, for they got neither principal nor interest. More than that, my aunt paid my living expenses, and the Khan [Ahmad Bakhsh Khan?] would occasionally give me something besides, or would manage something from Alwar, or my mother would send me money from Agra. But these days all I have is the sixty-two rupees eight annas of my pension from the authorities and my hundred rupees from Rampur, and only the one agent from whom I can borrow and to whom I must pay interest and an instalment of the principal month by month. There is income tax to pay, the night-watchman to pay, interest to pay, principal to pay, the upkeep of my wife, the upkeep of the children, the upkeep of the servants—and just the Rs 162 coming in. I was in difficulties, and could hardly make my way. I found I could not even meet my day to day needs. I thought to myself, 'What shall I do? How can I solve the problem?' Well, a beggar's anger harms no one but himself. I cut out my morning cool drink, halved the meat for my midday meal, and stopped my wine and rose-water at night. That saved me twenty rupees or so a month, and I could meet my day to day expenses. My friends would ask me, 'How long can you go on without your morning and evening drinks?' I said, 'Until He lets me drink again.' 'And how can you live without them?' they asked. 'As He vouchsafes me to live,' I replied. At length, before the month was out I was sent money from Rampur, over and above my stipend. I paid off the accumulated instalments on my regular debt. That left the miscellaneous ones—well, be it so. My morning drink and wine at night were restored, and I again began to eat my full quota of meat.

Since your father asked why I had stopped drinking and then started again, read this part of my letter to him....

He then turns upon one Hamza Khan, a maulvi who had once been tutor to Alai in his childhood and had now been ill-advised enough to have Alai write to Ghalib that it was time to act on the words of Hafiz:

> Hafiz, old age besets you: leave the tavern now.
> Debauchery and drinking go along with youth.

Without even breaking the sentence Ghalib goes straight on:

> ...and give my respects to Hamza Khan and tell him:

> You who have never known the taste of wine
> We drink unceasingly

You see how He vouchsafes me drink? To make a name as a maulvi by teaching the baniyas and brats of Dariba, and to wallow in the problems[97] of menstruation and post-natal bleeding is one thing: and to study the works of the mystics and take into one's heart the essential truth of God's reality and His expression in all things, is another. Hell is for those who deny the oneness of God, who hold that His existence partakes of the order of the eternal and the possible, believe that Musailma shares with the Prophet the rank of the Seal of the Prophets, and rank newly-converted Muslims with the Father of the Imams. My belief in God's oneness is untainted, and my faith is perfect. My tongue repeats, 'There is no god but God', and my heart believes, 'Nothing exists but God, and God alone works manifest in all things.' All prophets were to be honoured, and submission to each in his own time was the duty of man. With Muhammad (peace be upon him) prophethood came to an end. He is the Seal of the Prophets and God's Blessing to the Worlds.... Then came the office of Imam, conferred not by the consensus of men, but by God: and the Imam ordained by God is Ali (peace be upon him), then Hasan, then Husain, and thus onwards until the promised Mahdi (peace be upon him):

> In this belief I live, in this I die.

Yes, and there is this more to be said, that I hold free-thinking and atheism to be abhorrent, and wine-drinking to be forbidden, and myself to be a sinner. And if God casts me into Hell, it will not be to burn me, but that I may become added fuel to the flames, making them flare more fiercely to burn those who deny God's oneness and

[97] In Islamic observances.

reject the prophethood of Muhammad and the Imamate of Ali. Listen to me, Maulvi sahib. Perhaps you will be stubborn and think it no sin to hide the truth; but if not, you will remember, and confess that you remember, how once in the days when you taught the *Gulistan* and *Bostan*[98] to Ala ud Din Khan [Alai] you slapped the poor boy two or three times. [His father] Nawwab Amin ud Din Khan was in Loharu at the time, but Ala ud Din's mother turned you out of the house. You came to me with tears in your eyes, and I told you, 'My friend, the sons of nobles and of gentlemen may be scolded, but not struck. You were at fault. Never do such a thing again.' And you repented your folly. And now you graduate from school-mastering and take up preaching to seventy-year-olds. By dint of repeated fasting you memorize one verse of Hafiz:

Hafiz, old age besets you, etc.

and recite it—and that before one who has written twice and three times as much verse as Hafiz did, to say nothing of prose. And you do not observe that, as against this one verse, Hafiz has thousands which contradict it:

Come, mystic, for the cup is clear as crystal
That you may see the ruby-red, pure wine.

Drink the pure wine and look upon the faces of fair women
A fig for *their* religion! Gaze upon the beauties here.

He quotes two other couplets of Hafiz in the same sense and then drops the subject and turns again to address Alai:

My son, I'm in great trouble. The walls of the zenana have collapsed [because of the continuous rain]. The lavatory is in ruins. The roofs are leaking. Your aunt [Ghalib's wife] keeps saying, 'We'll be buried! We'll be killed!' My own apartments are in an even worse state. I am not afraid of death, but I can't stand discomfort. The roof is like a sieve. Where the sky rains for two hours, the roof rains for four. The landlord can't do any repairs even if he wants to. If only the rain would stop he could attend to everything, but even then how can I sit here while the repairs are going on? If you can manage it, get your father, for as long as the rains last, to let me have the mansion where Mir Hasan used to live for your aunt [Ghalib' wife] and the upper apartment and the downstairs sitting-room of the house where the late Ilahi Bakhsh Khan used to live, for myself. Once the rains

---

[98] Works of the classical Persian writer Sadi, commonly used as elementary Persian texts.

are over and the repairs are done, then the sahib and memsahib and the babas will go back to their old house. Where your father has so often made sacrifices to help me, let him show his kindness once more and do me this favour in my closing days.

The next day, 29 July 1862, he writes to Majruh:

...Speaking of the rains, let me first give the overall picture. First came the mutiny of the blacks, then the wrath of the whites, then the disturbance of the demolitions, then the disaster of the epidemics, then the calamity of the famine; and now the rains have come like all these things rolled into one. This is the twenty-first day. The sun appears as briefly as the lightning flash, and when occasionally the stars appear at night people think they are fireflies. The dark nights are a boon to the thieves, and not a day passes but what two or three burglaries are reported. Do not think I am exaggerating: thousands of buildings have collapsed, and hundreds of people have been buried beneath the ruins. Every lane is like a river. The earlier famine was caused by lack of water. There was no rain, and so no grain. This one is caused by excess of water. The rain has fallen in such torrents that the sown seed has been washed away, and those who have not yet sown their fields cannot do so. So that's how things are in Delhi. Apart from that there's nothing new.

Ghalib's appeal to Alai had the desired effect. On 6 August 1862 he writes:

I do not fear death, nor do I lay claim to patience. And I believe not in freewill but in predestination. You played the role of my go-between and my brother [your father] helped me like a brother. Long may you live, and long may God preserve him! And may we lodge till Judgement Day in this same mansion!

To clarify the obscure and add detail to the general picture, the position was that the rain fell in torrents. The younger boy was afraid and his grandmother too [Ghalib's wife] was disturbed. I remembered the door of the private apartment that faces west, and, opposite it, a room with three doors. When you hurt your foot I used that door when I came to see you. With this in mind I planned to make that room the zenana, thinking that carriages and palanquins could come there and the various maid-servants, and the tribes of women who come to sell vegetables, and oil, and betel, and what not...could use that door, while the children and I could come and go through the drawing room. God protect us if all of them were to come trooping through the drawing room, and we and the visitors were to have the spectacle of these witches forever before our eyes!

Bi Wafadar[99]—you know her a little, and your father knows her well—has had the title of Wafadar Beg conferred upon her by your aunt [Ghalib's wife]. She goes out to do the shopping. At least, she doesn't do much shopping, but she's an affable soul, and sociable, and trots around talking to the people she meets in the street. Once she's out of the house it's unthinkable that she shouldn't take a walk along the canal and talk to the sentries at the gate and pick flowers and bring them back to show to her mistress, with 'These flowers are from your nephew's garden.'[100] Alas, alas, that so fine a drawing room should suffer such a fate and that a crazy, sensitive man like me should be so plagued! On top of that, I could not contemplate the idea that the small room would suffice for my servants and for the children to have their lessons in. For could the [children's] peacocks and pigeons and sheep and goat be kept outside with the horses? I muttered the verse 'God is recognized in the failure of man's plans',[101] and said nothing more. But let your refined mind be at rest: all cause for uneasiness and fear has gone. The rain has stopped; the landlords have had repairs put in hand; the boy is no longer afraid; the mistress is no longer disturbed; I no longer suffer discomfort. I have the open roof, the moonlit night, the cool breeze. All night long Mars can be seen in the sky, and an hour before first light shining Venus comes into view. As the moon sinks in the west, Venus rises in the east: and I enjoy my morning draught of wine amid this radiance.

Letters to Majruh and Tufta dominate the remainder of the year. Majruh had had fever, and it seems that on his recovery he had written about himself in what Ghalib felt to be quite unnecessary detail. Ghalib replies on 16 September 1862:

> Bravo, your lordship! What a letter! What's the point of writing all that nonsense? All it amounts to is that you're back in your own bed, back in your own bedclothes, and again have your own barber and your own lavatory, that you no longer disturb the night with, 'Come quickly! Come quickly!' That your life is saved and your servants too no longer plagued to death.
>
> And now my nights are nights and days are days.

[99] 'Old Faithful'—nickname of an old maidservant.

[100] In the original, these words are quoted in the old woman's own peculiar speech.

[101] The equivalent of 'Man proposes, God disposes.'

But you haven't said whether Miran Sahib got my letter or not. I suspect that he didn't. Because if he had, you would certainly have seen it too, and he would have asked you for the facts of the matter, and in that case you would surely not have filled your letter with all that trash but would have told me instead what passed between you. So if, as I suspect, the letter never reached him, never mind. But if it did—well, you kept pestering me to answer Miran Sahib's letter: why don't you keep on at him to answer mine?....

You have seen for yourself what things are like here. The water is warm; the breeze is warm; there is fever everywhere; and grain is dear.... Don't ask me to describe the rains. God's wrath has descended on us. Qasim Jan's Lane is like Saadat Khan's Canal. The gate of the house I'm living in which opens on to Alam Beg Khan's Katra has collapsed. The stairs are on the point of collapse. The walls of the small room where I sit in the morning are leaning. The roofs are like sieves. If it rains for half an hour, they rain for an hour. My books and writing materials have all been stored in the storeroom. Here and there on the floor are bowls and basins [to catch the water that leaks from the roof]. Where can I sit to write a letter? Still, for the last four or five days things have been better. The landlord is seeing about getting repairs done. Today I had the chance of a few minutes' peace and decided to answer your letter.

Alwar's displeasure, the hardships of your journey, the burning of the fever, the ill effects of the heat, your dejected mood, your overwhelming troubles, your present worries, your concern for the future, your grief at your fallen fortunes...nothing you can say exaggerates them. These days everyone is in the same boat. I hear that in November the Maharaja of Alwar's powers are to be restored, but it will be the same sort of power as God has given to His creatures—all power is in His mighty hand, and we mortals are disgraced.

Tell me more of how you have got over your illness. God grant that your fever has gone for good and that you are quite well again. Mir[102] says:

It is a thousand blessings to be well.

Mirza Qurban Ali Beg Salik has supplied another line to precede it. It's a good one, and I like it very much:

Salik, if you are free from poverty
It is a thousand blessing to be well.

[102] The great eighteenth-century Urdu poet.

On 20 November 1862, he writes again:

> Where would I have a copy of it...[the Nawwab of Rampur's
> diwan]? The Nawwab Sahib didn't present me with a single page
> of it. There are some copies that were sent here for sale. I bought
> one to send to Mustafa Khan [Shefta] at Jahangirabad. Now I'll speak
> to Muhammad Bakhsh and Pirji about it. If one of them can get me
> a copy I'll send it off...at once.
>
> I know very well exactly what your expectations of employment
> are. It's a case of 'the king's salary'. You buy a job—i.e. you present
> your offering of money [which convention demanded of a man
> presented at court] on the understanding that you will be given
> employment. Then you serve without pay for six months or a year
> until the pay due to you equals your offering.

Mihr explains:

> In the last days of the Exalted Fort, the court officials instituted a
> practice of taking sums of money by way of 'offerings' and giving
> employment in return. The employee would have to serve without
> pay until his arrears equalled the sum of the offering. Moreover, men
> whose salary was several months in arrears would be given a part of
> the arrears in a lump sum on condition that they signed a receipt
> for the whole.

Ghalib goes on to answer various questions on Urdu usage and
then talks about various items of news.

> 'News of the king's death appeared in *Avadh Akhbar*, but I've not seen
> it confirmed anywhere.... They say that the Jama Masjid is to be
> given back. I shouldn't be surprised if it's true. It's also rumoured
> that the king of Oudh's property has been restored to him.
>
> Well, what more can I write? I'm writing this sitting in the sun
> by the parapet of the balcony overlooking the road....

He writes again a month later, on 16 December 1862:

> You who seek news of Delhi and Alwar, accept my greetings. The
> Jama Masjid has been returned. On the steps on the Chitli Qabar
> side, the kabab-sellers have set up shops, and eggs and hens and
> pigeons are on sale. It has been put in charge of a committee of ten—
> Mirza Ilahi Bakhsh, Maulvi Sadr ud Din [Azurda], Tafazzul Husain
> Khan, and seven more.
>
> On Friday, 7 November and the 14th of Jamadi ul Awwal of the
> present year (1279 AH and AD 1862) Abu Zafar Siraj ud Din Bahadur
> Shah was freed from the bonds of the foreigner and the bonds of
> the flesh. 'Verily we are for God, and verily to Him we shall return.'

It's getting cold, and I have only enough wine left to last me for today: from tomorrow night only the brazier's heat will support me, and the glass and bottle will be put aside.

I'm sitting in the sun, and Yusuf Khan and Lala Hira Singh are with me. Food is ready, and when I've written this letter and sealed it I shall give it to my man to post and go to the house. There is a room there that gets the sun. I shall sit there. I shall wash my hands and face, soak a light chapati in the curry and eat it, wash my hands with gram-flour, and return here. After that God knows who will come to keep me company....

Letters to others are mainly on literary themes. On 19 June 1862 he writes to Shafaq:

The target of the arrows of oppression, the old dotard—i.e. Ghalib— presents his respects. When I read your kind letter I realized that I had crossed out your line.... I had intended to write 'svad' [the first letter of the word 'sahih', meaning 'correct'] against the verse. God knows how my pen came to cross it out. I am no longer in full possession of my senses. I have lost my memory. I often write words which I do not mean to write. I am in my seventieth year, and must expect such stupidities now. I have sinned against your verse and am put to shame before you. Please forgive me.

In an undated letter of about the same time he writes to Tufta: 'Don't think that everything men wrote in former ages is correct. There were fools born in those days too....' And on 27 August 1862 he writes at some length on his own qualifications as a Persian scholar and a poet:

Persian as we know it is a compound of two languages—Persian and Arabic. In the colloquial, Turkish words are also used, but only to a small extent. I am no scholar of Arabic, but I am not completely ignorant of it either. All I mean is that I have not studied the language deeply. There are points on which I have to consult the scholars, and I have to ask them to quote authorities for various words. In Persian, from the Bounteous Source I received such proficiency that the laws and structure of the language are as deeply imbedded in me as the temper is in steel. Between me and the Persian masters there are two differences: first, that their birthplace was Iran and mine India; and second, that they were born a hundred, two, four, eight hundred, years before me....

It makes me laugh when I see how you think that I am like other poets, who set some master's ghazal or ode before them, or copy out its rhymes and then fit other words to them. God preserve me from such things! Even in my childhood when I began to write Urdu verse, may I be accursed if I ever set an Urdu poem or its rhyme-scheme before me. All I did was look at the metre, the rhyme and the end-rhyme, and then set to write a ghazal or ode on the same pattern. You write that I must have had Naziri's diwan open before me when I wrote my ode…I swear to God that until I got your letter I never even knew that Naziri had written an ode in this scheme…. My friend, poetry is the creating of meaning, not the matching of rhymes.…

On 27 November 1862 he writes:

What you have written is unkind and suspicious! Could I be cross with you? May God forbid! I pride myself that I have one friend in India who truly loves me; his name is Hargopal, and his pen-name Tufta. What could you write which would upset me? And as for what someone else may whisper, let me tell you how matters stand there. I had but one brother, who died after thirty years of madness. Suppose he had lived and had been sane and had said anything against you: I would have rebuked him and been angry with him.

My friend, there is no strength left in me now. The hardships of the rains are past, but I feel increasingly the full effects of old age. I lie about all day. I can't sit up, and generally write lying down. Besides, I feel now that you're a mature and practised poet, and I feel confident that I shall find nothing in your verse that calls for corrections. More important than that, all your odes are on themes of love, not written to serve any material purpose.[103] Anyway, I'll look at them some time. There's no hurry. There are three things involved: my slothfulness, the fact that your verse stands in no need of correction, and the fact that no particular gain is to be expected from any of your odes. And in view of these things I have left them on one side. A parcel from Lala Bal Mukand Besabr came ages ago, and I have not even opened it. And ten to fifteen of the Nawwab Sahib's [of Rampur] ghazals are also laid aside.

> Ghalib, old age has left you fit for nothing,
> Else you were once man to reckon with.

This ode of yours came yesterday. Today I've already gone through it, before the sun is really up, corrected it, and given it to my man to take to the post.

---

[103] E.g. not to a patron, in expectation of reward.

1863

The physical weakness of which he complained to Tufta was to grow worse in 1863, so that in August he had to write to Sayyah: 'For the last year I have been a prey to ailments caused by disorders of the blood....' But it is not until the end of March that he begins to show acute distress. Meanwhile his troubles are lighter ones, and there is even one great piece of good news.

On 11 January 1863 he writes to Ghulam Najaf Khan:

...And now tell me, when are you coming? How many more years or months or days will you keep me waiting? Things here are the same as ever—you saw how it was when you were here:

The earth is hard, the sky is far above.

It's really cold now; the mighty are stiff with pride, and the poor are stiff with cold. The new excise regulations have struck me a heavy blow, and so has the restriction on distilling. On the one hand, the prohibitions of the excise authorities, and on the other the high price of foreign wine. 'Verily we are for God, and verily to Him we shall return.'

...Well, Zahir ud Din [Ghulam Najaf Khan's son], don't you think I deserve a separate letter from you, or a separate note on your father's letter sending me your respects in your own hand? Hakim Ghulam Najaf Khan sat down to write to me, and while he was about it sent your respects to me too. And even your guardian angels knew nothing of it! What pleasure can such 'respects' bring me?

About the same time, in a letter to Majruh he writes:

We've had several showers of winter rain. There'll be a good crop of wheat and gram, and the spring harvest looks hopeful.

The clouds of spring are spread across the sky,
But in my cup of clay there is no wine.

I have a wound on my right hand, a sore on my left arm and a boil on my right thigh. That's how it is with me. Otherwise everything's all right.

In March 1863 he received a quite unexpected piece of good news. The fullest account is in a letter to Bekhabar dated only 'March 1863':

In hopelessness hope still sends forth a ray—
The black night's end brings in the white of day.

Reverend sir, today for your pleasure and happiness I write you the record of what has befallen me. Preamble: In 1860 the Lord Sahib [Governor-General] came...to Delhi. I went...and sent in my name to his Secretary.... The reply came, 'During the Mutiny you spent your time flattering the rebel king; now the Government cannot agree to receive you'. I am a persistent beggar, and was not to be put off by this prohibition. When the [Governor-General] returned to Calcutta I sent him an ode, in accordance with my old custom. It was returned to me with instructions that in future I was not to send these things. I gave up hope and stopped calling upon the Delhi authorities.

Event: At the end of last month, February 1863, the Lieutenant-Governor of the Punjab [Sir Robert Montgomery] came to Delhi. People here ran to the Deputy Commissioner and the Commissioner to get their names on the list. I was outside all this, a man under a cloud in the eyes of the authorities. I stayed in my corner and called upon no one. The durbar was held, and all attained their wishes. On Saturday 8 February I went on my own account to visit Munshi Man Phul Singh in his tent. I sent in my card to the Secretary and was called in. Finding him well disposed towards me, I asked if I might meet Lieutenant-Governor. This request too was granted, and these two distinguished officials showed me more kindness than I could ever have contemplated.

Digression: I had had no previous dealings with the Lieutenant-Governor's chief clerk, on the strength of which I could hope to meet him. But he indicated, without saying it in so many words, that he would like to see me; so I went. When the two high officials had immediately acceded to my request to see them, I can well imagine that it was on their prompting that he indicated his wish to see me. 'God sends his blessings by stealth.'

Conclusion of the record: On Monday 2 March the Governor encamped on the outskirts of the city. Towards evening I went to see my old friend Maulvi Izhar Husain Khan Bahadur. In the course of conversation he said, 'Your attendance at durbars and robe of honour have been restored.' I was astonished, and asked him, 'How can that be, my good sir?' He replied, 'The present Governor-General [Lord Elgin] on his arrival from England examined all the papers in your case, both in English and Persian, and gave orders in council that Asadullah Khan's [Ghalib's] attendance at durbars, and order of precedence, and robe of honour were to be restored in accordance with previous practice'. I asked him, 'Sir, what gave rise to this decision?' He said, 'I do not know. All I know is that fourteen to fifteen days after the order was minuted, it was sent on here.' I replied, 'Glory to God'.

> He who achieves our ends devises means to them
> While *our* devisings for our ends increase our pains.

On 27 March 1863, he writes to Mir Sarfaraz Husain:

> I shall probably not be able to write again for some days.... During the month of Rajab I got a spot on my right hand, which developed into a boil, which burst and formed a wound, which got worse and became a great cavity. Now the flesh has putrefied over an area as big as the palm of my hand. For the last two weeks I've been under English treatment. A black[104] doctor comes every day, and he's decided that today he'll cut away all the putrefied flesh. He'll be here any time now. So I've written this in a hurry and sent it off before I get to work on my hand and send the pieces flying.

A letter to Aram—the last to him which we possess—dated 3 May 1863, shows how long his hand continued to trouble him:

> It is six months now since a spot on my right hand turned into a boil...Indian surgeons treated me, but things got worse and worse. A black doctor has been treating me for the last two months. He has been cauterizing the wound and cutting the flesh away with a razor; and for the last twenty days it looks as though it has begun to mend....

In this year we find for the first time evidence that Ghalib had now revised his earlier opinion about his Urdu letters. In 1858 he had strongly opposed suggestions from Tufta and Aram that they should be collected and published. But now he writes to Alai in a letter dated only '1863' but placed by Mihr between March and May:

> I write to tell you that some of my friends want to get together my Urdu letters and publish them. They have asked me to send such letters to them, and have collected others from various quarters. I don't keep copies of what I write. I just write the letter and send it off to its destination. I am sure you must have a lot of my letters. If you will parcel them up and send them by post or by anyone who may be coming here during the next few days I shall be grateful to you. And I think you too will be pleased to have them printed...'

[104] I.e. an Indian practitioner of modern medicine.

Alai, however, raised objections, and Ghalib's next letter reproaches him very bluntly:

What you wrote about sending my Urdu letters was something I could not have expected from a man of your good nature. I am very upset about it, and if I were to write and tell you all the reasons why, it would probably cover a whole sheet of paper. So let me say just this, in the fewest possible words: Listen, my friend. If you want to keep the letters to yourself and the idea of their becoming generally known goes against the grain, then don't send them—not on any account. That will be an end of the matter. And if you are afraid they may be lost, then keep the originals by you, get some clerk to copy them, and either send the copies off by post or give them to someone to bring by hand. But for God's sake don't get angry and send the originals in the spirit of 'I throw your gift back in your face'. That's not at all what I want. I tell you, my friend, I'm afraid of what you might do.

It seems that Alai did not respond immediately, but that in spite of this Ghalib did not raise the matter again. At this Alai seems to have felt concerned, thinking that Ghalib might be cross with him. Ghalib's next letter, of 30 May 1863, reassures him:

Nothing exists but God, and in the name of that God Whom I think of in these terms and in Whom I believe, and besides Whom I hold all else to be non-existent, I swear that it was not because I was cross with you that I didn't press you again to send me the letters. I dropped the matter for the time being because I found that the man who wanted them had cooled off somewhat. His intermediary was a man of high rank, while he himself is only a dealer in books, concerned with estimating what he'll gain or lose, what he'll have to pay out and what he can save. I'd been under the impression that his intermediary was the man who was going to manage the whole affair, and thought it was he who was going to have them printed. I collected thirty letters from one source and sent them off to him. When he wrote to acknowledge them he as good as said that he had asked for them at the instance of a bookseller, and that the bookseller had now disappeared. Presumably he's gone off somewhere to sell his books or to get fresh supplies. The twenty-three envelopes and the thirty-four letters you sent me are still safe in my box. If the intermediary starts pressing me for them, I'll send copies of them to him and the originals back to you. And if not, then all the papers will go back to you.

On 11 June 1863 he writes to Alai again:

> To lose one's life is bad, but just as bad
> Is to fall prey to your suspicious mind.

I have twice written to you that I never kept a copy of the ode. I have twice written that I can't remember which quatrains you want. And again you write, 'Send the quatrains; send the ode'. My friend, I swear by the Quran and by the Gospel and by the Pentateuch and by the Psalms and by the Hindus' Four Vedas and by the [holy books of the Zoroastrians], and by the Guru Granth [of the Sikhs] I haven't got the ode, and I can't remember the quatrains.

On 19 June 1863 he writes to Junun:

Both your letters reached me. I am alive, but half-dead. I lie here for twenty-four hours of the day, confined to my bed in the full sense of the words. For the last twenty days my foot has been swollen. It began with the sole and the instep, but the swelling has gone beyond that now and reached the calf. I can't get my foot into my shoe, and it's difficult for me to get up and go to the lavatory. But leave all that aside: the pain is torture to me. I was not allowed to die in 1277 [the year in which he had foretold he would die] so that I should be proved a liar; but for these last three years I have tasted death anew every day, and I am at a loss to know why I live on when I lack all the requisites of life.

My soul dwells in my body these days as restless as a bird in a cage. I find no joy in any man's company, nor in any gathering or assembly. Books I hate, poetry I hate, my body I hate, my soul I hate. There is no exaggeration in these words: I state a fact:

> Happy that day when I set out
> to leave this barren wilderness.

If in this distracted state I fail to answer your letters I must be forgiven.

About the same time he writes to Tufta:

Two days ago, in the morning, I put all your papers [presumably, corrected verses] in an envelope and sent them off to the post office. 'Now I shall have some peace for a day or two', I thought; but the same evening I got another letter from you. Well, I'm sending that off too. I told you all about myself in my letter of two days ago. It's enough to say that now I do all my writing lying down. And it's diverting to see that you don't believe my own account of myself and *do* believe what somebody else tells you about me: 'The swelling on Ghalib's leg has gone now; and he drinks wine in the day time too'. And your lordship believes it! Twenty years ago the position was that during the rains I used to drink three glasses either before lunch or towards evening, and that without making any reduction in the amount I drank every night. In these last twenty years, twenty rainy seasons have passed by, and torrents of rain have fallen; but let alone drinking [during the day], the very thought of it has never crossed my mind; and in fact I've reduced the quantity I drink at night. The swelling on my leg has increased beyond all measure. It turned out that it had not reached the stage where the matter can be drawn off, and inflammation set in. Two or three hakims are attending me, and on their advice a poultice of neem leaves will be applied from tomorrow. When that brings things to a head they will think about lancing it. So I have open wounds in the sole of my foot and in my calf too. If the hard-hearted eunuch who gave you that news [that I was better] is a liar, then curses upon him; and if *I* am lying then a hundred thousand curses upon me.

On 3 July 1863 he tells Alai the history of the trouble:

More than a month ago my left foot began to swell, and the swelling spread from the sole to the instep and from there to the calf. If I stand up it feels as though the veins in the calf are going to burst. Anyway I would get up; but instead of going to the zenana for my food I had it sent here. I *had* to get up to make water, but I had a chamberpot kept here. I can't manage without squatting down. I pass a motion only every second or third day, but, anyway, the time comes when I do have to go. Imagine all these different occasions and think for yourself what I must be going through. And over and above all this it looks as though a hernia is developing:

Old age, a hundred ailments, as they say.

I repeat my own line to myself again and again:

O sudden death, why do you still delay?

And it's not 'sudden death' any more. For all the signs and accompaniments of death are there. Ah, what a wonderful line the late Ilahi Bakhsh Khan wrote:

Let me once die, and I can breathe again!

No point in writing any more.

A number of undated letters to Sarur—the last to him which we possess—clearly belong to this time, for there are references to his illness in words almost identical to those of dated letters to other correspondents. These need not be repeated here. Their main subject-matter, as usual in his letters to Sarur, is Persian, and poetry, and other literary themes. In one of them he responds to praise of his poetry with the remark that he must regard it as appreciation higher than it deserves.

> There is a verse of Naziri (God's mercy be upon him) which you may write on a piece of paper, and tie round my neck, and then expel me from the company of poets. This is the verse:
>
> > The brightness of my vision is all rusted over now.
> > Alas! that He who made my mirror did not cherish it!

In former times, mirrors were made of polished steel. The metaphor recalls the passage which Ghalib wrote about himself... 'The love of poetry which I had brought with me from eternity assailed me and won my soul, saying, "To polish the mirror and show in it the face of meaning—this too is a mighty work."'

And the complaint is the familiar, deeply felt one that God, who granted him his poetic powers, did not also grant him to live in an age where true appreciation of his verse would have acted as a constant stimulus to them, so that they would not fail. The letter continues:

> Pretension is one thing, and accomplishment is another.... Jalalae Tabatabai (God's mercy be upon him) wrote a letter to Sedaya Hindi. I forget his exact words, but the gist is that one day Maulana Urfi (God's mercy be upon him) and Abul Fazl[105] were disputing together. The Shaikh [Abul Fazl] said to Urfi, 'I have prosecuted my studies to the furthest limit and brought my knowledge of Persian to perfection'. Urfi replied, 'How can you match my experience? Ever since I was old enough to understand, every word that I have heard from the old men and old women of my house was spoken in Persian.' The Shaikh replied, 'I acquired my Persian from Anwari and Khaqani;[106] and you learnt it from old women.' Urfi replied, 'And Anwari and Khaqani too learnt it from old women'.

[105] The great minister of Emperor Akbar, 1556–1605.
[106] Two celebrated classical Persian poets.

Another letter discusses the wording of a sentence in a preface written for a collection of Ghalib's letters to him which Sarur proposed to publish. It ends on a despondent note:

> Today I got another letter from my lord and master. I have not read it yet, but Shah Alam Sahib has written on the back of it, 'You have not replied to my letter'—although...I have already written to say that I no longer have the strength to write or the quickness of mind to correct verses. Why should I repeat the same thing a dozen times? I conceive two possible ends to my present state: recovery, or death. In the first case I will inform you myself; in the second, all my friends will know of it from others. I write these lines as I lie in bed.

In the same despondent, even bitter mood, he writes to Tufta on 23 July 1863:

> I wrote to you that I was well, and you believe it and offer thanks to God. I wrote what I had said about the severity of my illness was poetic exaggeration, and I expect you believe that too, although both these things were said ironically. I am sick of lies, and heartily curse all liars. I never tell a lie. But when all my attempts to persuade you I was telling the truth had no effect, then I wrote and told you I was well. And I did so after I had sworn to myself that so long as there was breath in my body, so long as my hand could hold a pen, and so long as I could contemplate correcting your verse, I would send back the very next day every sheaf of papers you sent to me. Briefly, I am near to death. I have boils on both my hands and my leg is swollen. The boils don't heal and the swelling doesn't subside. I can't sit up. I write lying down. Your double page arrived yesterday and today I have corrected it lying here and sent it back. Take care that you go on thinking of me as in good health, and send sheet upon sheet to me. I shall never keep it more than a day. If I am near to death, well, what of that?

On 1 September 1863 he writes to Maududi:

> Why does my revered Sayyid Sahib put himself to such trouble? If he really wants to send me something, let him not think in formal terms of gifts and presents. I am a beggar who does not beg: if he sends me something I shall not reject it. Let him not bother about how little or how much, but enclose whatever note he pleases and sends it in his letter.

The next letter bluntly corrects one of Tufta's recurring misapprehensions:

God save us! what cursed fool agreed to correct your verses 'out of love for poetry'? I tell you I am sick of poetry—or may my God be sick of me!... But a good wife determines to stand by her worthless husband through thick and thin; and that is how things are between me and you.

1864

On 15 February 1864 he writes to Shafaq:

The past year has been a trying one for me. I was confined to my bed for twelve to thirteen months. I found it difficult to get up, let alone to move about. For nine to ten months I could neither eat nor sleep, and was in pain both day and night. If I did fall asleep at night, before I had slept an hour the pain in some of my boils would wake me up. I would keep tossing and turning, fall asleep once more, and be awakened once more. Three-quarters of the year passed in this way; then things began to improve, and over two to three months I made some sort of recovery. I felt as though my soul had entered my body anew and the angel of death had given up in disgust at my toughness. Now I am well, but weak and lethargic. I haven't got my wits about me, and my memory is gone. It takes me as long to stand up as it does to build a wall the height of a man. I'm filled with gratitude at your enquiry after me: only when you heard I was dead did you ask after me. The oral statement of the man who told you I was dead and my written statements (for example, this one) are half true and half false. If I'm dead, then I'm only half-dead; and if I'm alive, I am only half alive.

My soul strives feebly on to break the body's bonds.
I live: it lacks the strength to struggle free.

On 22 June 1864 he writes to Amin ud Din Ahmad Khan:

Allow me to tell you that your being in Delhi was a source of moral strength to me. Even though we did not meet, at any rate we were in the same city.

Brother, when I survey the scene I see a number of people, like birds who have lost their nests, flying about here and there. One or two of them occasionally come this way even. Now, sir, tell me when are you going to keep your promise? When are you going to send Alai to see me? These days one can still travel by night and rest by day. [Mihr explains: 'In those days there was no railway [from Delhi] to Loharu. In the hot season it was customary to travel by night and not by day.'] Once the rains start, your permission will be of no avail. The traveller will think, 'I'm a walker, not a swimmer. How can I get from Loharu to Delhi without a boat? Where will I get a steamship from?'

> O you who do not know what leisure is
> Do what you have to do without delay.

On 28 June 1864, he writes to Junun:

> A hundred and twenty mangoes have reached me. May God preserve you! I have handed over ten pens and two ounces of ink to your servant. God grant they reach you safely. I am not ill, but I am old and weak and so to speak, only half alive. I have passed sixty-nine years in this world, and performed not one religious act. Alas! A thousand times alas!

On 2 July 1864, he writes to Miran:

> My dear boy, I got your letter, but it doesn't explain why Mir Sarfaraz Husain was off to Jaipur. Anyway, give my blessings to Mir Mahdi [Majruh] and tell Mir Sarfaraz Husain from me: 'You went to Jaipur, and I entrusted you to God's keeping: whose keeping did you entrust *me* to?'

On 10 July 1864, he writes to Alai. It appears that Alai had contemplated writing an ode directed against someone whom he disliked and incorporating a chronogram of some incident in this connection. Ghalib tells him not to:

> Understand this, my friend: Granted that 'to curse Yazid[107] is to worship God'; yet one *speaks* the words, 'A curse on Yazid!' No true Muslim yet has written an ode to curse him. Among your natural talents is one for composing chronograms; you have earned merit in heaven by it, and, God willing, will get your reward. Don't now bring censure upon yourself and distress to others. Don't manifest your enmity, and if it is manifest already, don't add permanence to it.

He goes on:

> The late Ali Bakhsh [he had died six months earlier] was four years younger than me. I was born in 1212 AH, and in Rajab of this year shall be entering my sixty-ninth year. He lived to be sixty-six. He

---

[107] The man responsible for the martyrdom of Husain and his companions at Karbala.

had a novel way of speaking and writing. Once he met Muir Sahib[108] in Agra. In the course of conversation he said, 'I served with my uncle in Lord Lake's army [in 1803], and took part in the battles against Holkar [the commander of the Maratha forces]. I should be offending against propriety if I were to take off my clothes; otherwise I could show you that my body is a mass of scars from sword- and lance-wounds'. He [Muir] was an alert and intelligent man; he looked at him and said, 'Nawwab Sahib, I should guess that in General Lake's time you would be about four or five years old.' He replied, 'Quite so, your honour'.

May God forgive him and not call him to account for his harmless lies.

An undated letter to Salik belongs perhaps to this time:

My dear friend, what foolish thoughts beset you? You have mourned a father: now lament an uncle too. God grant you long life, and bring to realization all your plans and fancies. For my part I no longer look even to God to help me, much less to His creation. Nothing goes right for me. I watch myself from the sidelines and rejoice at my own distress and degradation. In other words I see myself through the eyes of my enemy. At every blow that falls I say, 'Look! Ghalib's taken another beating! Such airs he used to give himself! "I am a great poet, a great Persian scholar. Today for miles around there is none to match me!" Let us see *now* what he has to say to his creditors. Ghalib's finished; and call him Ghalib if you like; I call him atheist and infidel, and that's the truth! I have made up titles to confer upon him. When kings die they write after their names, 'Whose abode is in Heaven', or 'Who rests in Paradise'. Well, he thought himself King of the Realm of Poetry, and I've devised the forms 'Who dwells in Hell', and 'Whose Station is Damnation' to follow his name.

'Come along, Star of the Realm!'—one creditor has him by the scruff while another reviles him. And I say to him, 'Come, come, My Lord Nawwab Sahib! How is it that you—yes, you a Seljuk, and an Afrasiyabi—are put to such indignity? Well, where is your tongue? Say something! Wine from the shop, and rose-water from the druggist's, and cloth from the drapers', and mangoes from the fruiterer's, and loans from the banker's—and all on credit all the time. He might have stopped to ask himself where he'd get the money to pay it back'.

[108] Sir William Muir, who later became Lieutenant-Governor of United Provinces.

Another letter to Salik dated 11 July 1864 (and these are the only letters to Salik we possess) is in a similar tone:

'God sends His blessings by stealth.' I hear that you are fit and well. We must be thankful that we are alive. 'If you have your life, you have everything.' They say that to despair of God's help is to be an infidel. Well, I have despaired of Him and am an infidel through and through. Muslims believe that when a man turns infidel, he cannot expect God's forgiveness. So there you are, my friend: I'm lost to this world and the next. But you must do your best to stay a Muslim and not to despair of God. Make the text [of the Quran] your watchword: 'Where there is difficulty, there is ease also'.

All that befalls the traveller[109] in the path of God
Befalls him for his good.

All's well at your home.... Yusuf Ali Khan Aziz sends his regards and Baqir and Husain Ali [Ghalib's adopted 'grandchildren'] their respectful service. My steward Kallu presents his obeisance. The others lack the status even to do that. Keep on writing to me. Farewell, from him who longs for death, Ghalib.

On 24 August 1864, he writes to Junun:

Exalted sir, the ghazal your servant brought has gone where I am going—to oblivion. That is, I have lost it....

About the same time—the letter is dated only '1864'—he writes to Bekhabar:

I have heard from an outside source that you are writing a pamphlet refuting my work...*Qate i Burhan*.[110] I didn't believe it, but I was certainly surprised....

In this city there is a festival called the Flower-men's Festival. It takes place in the month of Bhadon [August–September], and everyone in the city, from the nobles to the artisans, goes off to the Qutub [Minar]. There they stay for two to three weeks. All the shops in the city—Muslim and Hindu alike—stay closed throughout this time. Our friend Ziya ud din Khan, and [his son] Shihab ud Din Khan and my two boys have all gone to the Qutub. In the men's quarters these days there's no one but me, and my steward, and one servant who is ill. When our friend [Ziya ud Din Khan] comes back

[109] In the original, 'salik', which, in a letter to Salik is particularly appropriate.
[110] See p. 249 below.

he'll write to you again. He's come down the big hills[111] and gone up the little hills.[112] That's why he hasn't written.

Bekhabar evidently replied with indignation to the suggestion that he could write a polemic against Ghalib, for Ghalib's next letter begins:

Master and guide! One does not get cross at such things! 'I heard...but I didn't believe it.' So far I provide no target for wrath. So what we quarrel about is my surprise. Well the occasion for surprise is that your friend says that...you...who are my shagird, are writing a reply to my *Qate i Burhan*. If saints behave like this, then alas for the state of us sinners! What I wrote to you was a report, not a complaint. I wear the dress of a worldly man, but I am a faqir, and a faqir of independent spirit, not one who cries loudly of his need or cheats his fellow men. I am seventy years old, and I tell you without exaggeration that seventy thousand men must have passed before my eyes—and that too counting only the gentlemen; how many of the common people I have seen I cannot compute. I have seen two sincere men, men whose love is true: one, Maulvi Siraj ud Din (God's mercy be upon him), and the other [yourself], Munshi Ghulam Ghaus [Bekhabar] (may Exalted God preserve him). My lamented friend did not possess beauty of form, and his sincere and unfeigned friendship was something specially for me. Praise be to God! my second friend is all mankind's well-wisher, a man (may no evil befall him) of handsome form, and one perfect in love and loyalty, and utterly sincere. In fact, radiance upon radiance. I am not a mere man, but a man who knows men:

My glance is like a burglar that breaks through
Into the inmost chamber of the heart.

Rejoice, you pillars of hypocrisy!
Rejoice! for I have left these fields behind.

I have held you to be a man who possesses in the fullest measure the qualities of kindness and love, and of this much I am certain: Once I looked to two men to mourn for me when I am gone. One I have myself had to weep for, and now—may God preserve him— one friend is left. I pray to Him, 'O God, let that day never come when I must bear the wound of parting from him. May I die while he yet lives!' My friend, I love you truly.

[111] The foothills of the Himalayas, where those who can afford to, go to escape the worst of the hot season.
[112] The Qutub Minar stands on slightly higher ground than Delhi.

Our friend [Ziya ud Din Khan] is not back from the Qutub yet....

His next letter (also dated only '1864') tells him:

> There is a gentleman in Calcutta, a deputy-collector[113] named
> Maulvi Abdul Ghafur, pen-name Nassakh. We have never met, but
> he has sent me his published diwan...I have written him a letter of
> acknowledgement, and since this is suitable for inclusion in my
> collection of Urdu prose,[114] I am sending it to you. And tell me, my
> good sir, is the collection going to be printed or not?[115] If it's already
> printed, then please send your humble servant as many copies as
> Munshi Mumtaz Ali Khan Sahib's magnanimity impels him to grant
> as the author's right.

The letter to Nassakh is interesting as an example of what he now
thought fit to write in Urdu with publication in mind, but more
interesting still for the brief review of his own poetic experience
which it contains. It begins with a paragraph of elaborate (and, one
cannot help feeling, exaggerated) praise of Nassakh and his verse,
ending with the words: 'You are wise in the secrets of the Urdu
tongue, and the pride of the whole realm of India.' He then turns
to himself:

> Your humble servant turned to the practice of Urdu poetry when
> he first entered the years of discretion, and again in middle age, as
> the servant of the king [Bahadur Shah], for some days plied his pen
> in this same style. My love and inclination are for Persian verse and
> prose. I dwell in India, but bear the wound of the sword of Isfahan.[116]
> And as far as my powers allowed I prated much in the Persian tongue.
> But now I no longer think of Persian, no longer speak of Urdu,
> expecting nothing of this world, and hoping for nothing from the
> next. I, and the unending sorrow of disappointment; as I myself say
> in...one of my odes:

> > My eyes are opened now to see what I have done:
> > The future holds no hope, the past fills me with shame.

[113] The second administrative officer of an Indian district.

[114] Bekhabar was collecting Ghalib's Urdu letters for publication.

[115] Literally, 'will it be printed or will it be hidden?'—in the original,
'chapega' (with 'a') or 'chupega' (with 'u')? In the Urdu script the short vowels
are generally not written.

[116] I.e. I love Persian poetry. The city of Isfahan is the symbol of his beloved
[Persian poetry], the sword of whose glance wounds her lover's heart.

I have lived nine and sixty years in the world. And how much longer can I hope to live? One Urdu diwan of some thousand to twelve hundred couplets, one Persian diwan of ten thousand and some hundred couplets, and three small books of prose—these five things are the outcome of my work. And now what more should I write? My odes earned no reward, my lyrics no due of praise. I have consumed my life in idle versifying, and now, as Talib Amuli (God's mercy be upon him) says:

> I closed my lips from speaking: you would think
> My mouth was once a wound, now long since healed...

On 6 September 1864 he writes to Tufta:

Yesterday I sent off a parcel of your verses. I put a one-anna stamp on it and wrote on it, 'This is a parcel, not a letter'. The post-office clerk told my servant to post it in the box for letters. He can't read, and did as the clerk told him. The words, 'This is a parcel, not a letter' constitute an acceptable certificate: so if the postman there demands the letter-post fee you can refer him to that.

In November he had news that the Nawwab of Rampur had fallen ill. Despite occasional differences, he had helped Ghalib a great deal, and Ghalib had a genuine regard for him. He writes on 8 November 1864 in some distress:

Ever since I heard from elsewhere of Your Highness's indisposition, He Who knows the unseen is witness to the distress which I and my wife and my son Husain Ali have experienced. For a whole day no food was cooked in my house, and all of us fasted through both the morning and the evening meal. In the end this alarming news proved to be false, and we recovered our composure. But we shall not feel fully at ease until I hear the good tidings that you have recovered and bathed, and I have sent you a chronogram to celebrate the occasion.[117] For the moment all I ask is a reply to this letter, telling me the true position about your ailment....

> May you live on another thousand years
> And every year have fifty thousand days.

This letter brought a reply on 12 November, and on 13 November 1864 Ghalib wrote again:

[117] Muslim usage prescribes bathing after recovery from illness, and the occasion is one for celebration.

I cannot tell you how I passed the days and nights between 1 and the 11 November. It is a long way to Rampur, and I am ill, and my resources are inadequate; but if there had been mail-coach leaving Delhi for Rampur I would not have hesitated a moment, but would have come to attend upon you. There is no electric telegraph to bring me speedy news of your health. So all I could do in my agitation was send off a letter to you on the 8th of this month. God's kindness and my perfect spiritual guide's (Your Highness's) missive brought me out of the vortex of distress before there was time for a reply to my letter to come. Your kind letter came yesterday, 12 November and I felt that life had returned to me....

On 27 November 1864 he wrote again:

My tongue cannot express and my pen cannot write of the anxiety and care in which I have passed the last week to ten days. Every day until evening my eyes were on the door, watching for the postman to come with a letter from Your Highness. At length God showed his kindness, and my life began anew; for last night, some two hours after dark the postman brought your kind letter. When I read it, a new spirit entered me and my blood coursed through all my veins. To sleep, to go to bed, was out of the question. I sat down by the light and began to write verses of congratulation. Only after I had written seven couplets, including the chronogram of your restoration to health, did I sleep. Now I have written it out in fair and am despatching it.

The Nawwab seems to have been genuinely appreciative. On 25 January 1865 he writes to Ghalib:

I received the poem of congratulation on my restoration to health which you sent me, and the joy of recovery increased twofold. What other man can write such verse and such chronograms? It is the truth that Almighty God made you without peer or equal; no matter to what field one turns one's gaze, you are the one, unsurpassed master.... Truly such men as you are not to be found. The skies revolve for thousands of years to produce a man of such perfection. May God grant you long life and health and prosperity, and long may the world draw benefit from your presence....

On 9 December 1864 he writes to Tufta:

Last year I was ill, but I was not found wanting in serving my friends. Now I am dead, and a dead man cannot do anything. I've given up calling upon the Delhi authorities—the commissioner, the deputy commissioner and so on—but I *have* to meet the deputy commissioner once a month because he has charge of the treasury, and if I didn't meet him he wouldn't issue my pay to my agent. Now the deputy commissioner, Mr Decrowther (?) has taken six months' leave and gone to the hills. Mr Rattigan has been appointed in his place. Of course, I had to meet him. He is writing an account of the poets of India in English, and he asked my help. I've borrowed seven books from brother Ziya ud Din Khan and sent them to him. Then he asked me to write out and send him accounts of poets whom I knew well. I sent him accounts of sixteen, limiting myself to men who are still living.

He then names three of the list—Ziya ud Din Ahmad Khan, Shefta, and Tufta himself. Five days later, on 14 December 1864 he writes again:

Come along, Mirza Tufta, and give me a hug. Then sit down and hear what I have to tell you.

My hearing had already given up the ghost, and now my eyesight has grown very weak. All my powers, all that a man possesses, are declining. I can't keep my wits about me at all. My memory's so poor you'd think I'd never had one, and I'm as though I'd never had any aptitude for the art of poetry. The Nawwab of Rampur gives me a hundred rupees a month. Last year I sent word to him to say, 'A man must have his wits about him to correct verse, and I do not find that I have. I ask you to excuse me from performing this service, and to reckon what I receive from your court as a return for past services. If you will, count me as your "sick number",[118] or, if you will, a beggar who lives on your crumbs. And if your bounty is conditional upon my performance of service, then my fate depends upon your will.' For a whole year he has sent no verse, but I have received my usual monthly grant up to November. Let's see what happens as time goes on. So far the Nawwab Sahib in his magnanimity keeps sending me my allowance. As for you, my friend, practice—touch wood—has made you perfect. There is nothing that needs correction in your verse. And if you insist willy-nilly on believing that your verse still needs correction, then, my dear friend, what will you do when I am gone? I am like the lamp dying at morning, the sun setting behind the mountain's crest. 'Verily we are for God, and verily to Him we shall return.'

[118] Ghalib uses the English words—in a somewhat adapted form. He means that the Nawwab should continue his allowance, regarding it, if he so chooses, as sick pay.

1865

But if Ghalib felt that he was 'the lamp dying at morning, the sun setting behind the mountain's crest', the letters for 1865 are none the less as varied and lively as ever. He seems to have kept in moderately good health throughout the year, despite the inevitable weakness of old age. His friend Alai at last visited him in Delhi. His old patron, the Nawwab of Rampur, died in April, and for a while he was uncertain how much he could expect from his successor. But to his satisfaction, the new Nawwab treated him as well as the old. In October he was well enough to travel to Rampur, staying there for the celebrations of the Nawwab's accession and returning only a few days before the end of December.

On 5 January 1865 he writes to Alai. He begins with a complaint that neither the last days of the Muslim month of Rajab nor the first days of Shaban have brought him a visit:

> Well, sir, Mirza Rajab Beg has died, and you did not mourn him. Shaban Beg has been born, the ceremonies of the sixth day have been held, and you did not come to them....
>
> My son I don't know how I manage to write you these few lines. Shihab ud Din Khan's illness has taken away the zest of life. I tell you, I wish I could die in his place. May God grant him life, and let me not see the day when I must mourn his loss. O God, grant him health! O God, grant him long life! Three children, and another yet unborn—O God, preserve him to watch over them!

Fortunately, Shihab ud Din survived his illness. In the same month Ghalib writes again:

> God has had mercy on Ziya ud Din's[119] old age and on my help-lessness. My dear Shihab ud Din is safe. Piles and dysentery, and fever and migraine—what varied ills beset him! But now at last he is restored to health in all respects. His weakness will leave him in its own good time. And who could call him strong before, that he should think him weak now? An old man was passing along a lane when he stumbled and fell. 'Alas for old age!' he said. He looked around, and when he saw that there was no one about he muttered as he went on his way 'and youth was no better, either.'

The next day, 13 February 1865, he writes to Alai:

[119] Shihab ud Din's father.

My dear boy, congratulations on the auspicious arrival of your new guest! May Exalted God grant you and the child and its brothers increase of life and wealth! From what you write it is not clear whether the blessed newcomer is a boy or a girl. Saqib[120] thinks it is a boy, and Ghalib thinks it is a girl. Write plainly, remove our uncertainty. Your letter was addressed to Saqib. But fie upon me! Why do I say letter? It was a long screed and I read it from end to end....

My friend, this is a field in which I share your inauspicious stars and feel your pain. I am a man devoted to one art. Yet by my faith I swear to you, my verse and prose has not won the praise it merited. I wrote it, and I alone appreciated it. Of all the aspirations my Creator placed in me—to roam in happy poverty and independence, or to give freely from my ample bounty—not even a thousand part of them was realized. I lacked the bodily strength; else I would have taken a staff in my hand, and hung from it a checkered mat and a tin drinking-vessel and a rope, and taken to the road on foot; now to Shiraz, now sojourning in Egypt, now making my way to Najaf[121] I would have roamed. I lacked the means; else I would have played host to a world of men; or if I could not feast a world of men, no matter; at least within the city where I lived none would have gone hungry and unclad....

The target of God's wrath, rejected of men, old, weak and ailing, poor and afflicted...a man who cannot bear to see another beg, and must himself beg his bread from door to door—that man am I.

Ten days later he is in a happier frame of mind. On 23 February 1865, he writes to Alai again:

I got your letter yesterday and am sending off a reply to it today. Rajab Beg, Shaban Beg, and Ramzan Beg—these famous months have passed without your coming. I haven't heard of Shawwal Beg as a man's name, but Idi Beg is a possibility. So as the auspicious day of Id approaches, what wonder if...you find that you can come?...

Congratulations on the arrival of a daughter. Saqib disputed with me. 'I have a nephew,' he said. 'No,' I said, 'I have a granddaughter.' Well, I've won, and he's lost....

On 1 April 1865, he writes to Hakim Ghulam Najaf Khan, who had apparently complained that Ghalib had not written to him:

My friend, I received your complaint with the utmost respect, but listen to my account and don't go by your own imaginary

---

[120] Shihab ud Din, Alai's cousin.
[121] The site of the tomb of Ali.

calculations. First, I had a letter from my dear Zahir [Hakim Ghulam Najaf Khan's son]. I answered it as soon as I had read it and sent it to the post the next day. The gist of it was this: 'You are always getting boils and pimples. The reason is that your blood and mine are as one, and I am the special favourite of heating of the blood.' Then your letter came. I answered it three days later, to this effect: 'My dear grandson Zahir ud Din is a better man than you. He came to see me before he left and wrote to me as soon as he arrived.' The post office doesn't issue receipts for letters posted. Both letters were stamped. It's out of the question that my two letters are stranded at the post office here. If the Shaikhupur postmen didn't deliver them, is that my fault? I grant you I wrote only your name and 'Shaikhupur' as the address. I didn't write the muhalla, and perhaps that's why the letters didn't reach you. Your letter has just this moment come, and I am writing these lines lying down. Now I'll send Inayatullah to your [Delhi] house and get him to find out and bring me the details of your Shaikhupur address.

Well, sir, Inayatullah is back with a note. I'm addressing the envelope accordingly, but I shan't have time to catch the post, so I'll send it off tomorrow morning.

Hakim Zahir ud Din Khan, my blessings on you. Sonny, I haven't the energy to write more at present. You must be content with my blessings. I've already sent off an answer to your letter, as I've written above. A curse on all liars. You say: 'And yet more curses.'

Nawwab Mustafa Khan [Shefta] arrived here yesterday. He's brought his family with him. The little boys are to be circumcised in the month of Zi Qad and Muhammad Ali Khan married in Zil Hij.

Five days ago we had hail in Delhi as big as hen's eggs—in some cases even bigger. The new lieutenant-governor came and held a durbar. I was honoured and treated with a kindness more than I could have expected. When you come I'll tell you all about it.

In the collection of letters to Hakim Ghulam Najaf Khan this is followed by an undated note clearly written after he was back in Delhi:

The rice was poor stuff—it doesn't swell up, and hasn't got long, thin grains. Don't go into a long argument about it, but see that I get old, thin-grained rice. Buy and send me one rupee's worth. And remember, my experience is that new rice gives you constipation, while old rice doesn't.

On 13 April 1865, he writes to Sayyah to thank him for a photograph:

...Look here, Munshi Sahib. I know that everyone else approves the invention of photography, but your humble servant doesn't subscribe to this. Just look at the gentleman's picture! It goes as far as his elbows, but his forearms and the rest of him are missing. Let alone talking to him, I can't even shake hands with him!...

On 21 April 1865, he writes again to Safir Bilgrami:

Light of my eyes and joy of my heart (because I love you), master (because you are a Sayyid), Maulvi Sayyid Farzand Ahmad Safir [Bilgrami], God grant long life to you! I was delighted with your pearls of verse. All your verses are good, but these I write down here went straight to my heart. [He then quotes three couplets.]

May you live on and on till Judgement Day
And every day your health and grace increase.

About the same time—Mihr places the letter, which is undated, between February and May 1865—he writes to Tufta in terms which belie his earlier certificate that Tufta's verse no longer needed correction:

I'm greatly surprised that after I'd written objecting to the rhymes [of an earlier poem] you've written a ghazal based on those same rhymes.... This ghazal's a write-off. Write another and send it to me to correct.

A letter of 14 May 1865, begins on a similar note: 'Grow old, and learn! I grant that you write good verse and without effort, but what you call enquiry is nothing but whims and fancies. You go by guesswork, and sometimes your guess corresponds to the facts, and sometimes it doesn't....' It ends with the laconic sentence: 'My money for April, and acknowledgement of my letters of condolence and congratulation, have come from Rampur; for the future, what God wills.' Ghalib might well wonder what the future held in store for him. Nawwab Yusuf Ali Khan had died in April, to be succeeded on the 21st of that month by his son Kalb i Ali Khan. Ghalib's relations with the old Nawwab were of long standing, and apart from exhibiting displeasure when Ghalib ventured to make what could be interpreted as an attempt to recommend others to his bounty, the Nawwab seems always to have treated him with consideration. His successor was largely an unknown quantity, and Ghalib's early letters to him, as we shall see, suggest that he felt some apprehension on this account.

Other undated letters to Tufta are placed by Mihr after this one. In one he evidently appologizes for some lapse—perhaps for not returning promptly verses which Tufta had sent for correction:

> My dear friend, the shame I shall feel on the Last Day before God, because I did not worship Him, and before the Prophet, because I offended against the Holy Law, is perhaps less strong than the shame I feel before you.

In a second he speaks scathingly of some highly-placed person unnamed to whom Tufta had addressed an ode:

> Listen to me, my friend. The man to whom you addressed your ode is as much a stranger to the art of poetry as you and I are to the problems of our respective religions. In fact, you and I, in spite of our ignorance of religious matters, at any rate have no aversion for them, while this is a fellow whom poetry makes sick.... These people aren't fit to be spoken of, much less to be praised. Ah, Anwari!

> Alas, there is no patron who deserves my praise!
> Alas, there is no mistress who inspires my verse!

On 26 May 1865, he writes to Alai's father, Amin ud din Ahmad Khan:

> For your entertainment I am sending you a new ghazal I have written. God grant that it please you and you have it taught to a singer.
> Let me tell you the Delhi news.... Yesterday, Thursday, 25 May early in the day there was a really fierce duststorm. Then rain fell heavily, and it turned so cold that Delhi was like a frozen world. The gate to Bara Dariba has been demolished. The rest of Qabil Attar Lane has been destroyed. The mosque in Kashmiri Katra has been levelled to the ground. The width of the street has been doubled. God, God! The domes of the mosques are being demolished, while on the thresholds of the Hindus' temples the flags and banners flutter in the wind. A great monkey,[122] strong as a lion and huge as an elephant has been born. He roves the city, demolishing buildings as he goes. He has seized the little domes on Faizullah Khan Bangash's mansion and shaken them one by one until he destroyed them to their foundations and brick rang against brick. Monkey, the deeds you do! And in the city too!

---

[122] This suggests the Hindu monkey-god Hanuman.

The next words presumably refer to Amin ud Din's son Alai:

> From the land of the desert [Loharu] the son of a noble, rich in
> children and poor in wealth, a master of three languages, Arabic,
> Persian and English, has come to Delhi. He is staying in Ballimaron
> muhalla and, as need arises, visits the Delhi authorities. For the rest,
> his doors are kept closed. From time to time—not every morning
> and every evening—he comes to the humble abode of the faqir
> Ghalib.... The citizens of Delhi are at a loss to know what he lives
> on. Some say, 'He has turned against his father' but I believe that
> his father has unreasonably withdrawn his favour from him. Let us
> see how it will end. Ghalib's...watchword is, 'Wish well to all'.

By mid-June 1865 he was in the awkward position of having to
suggest to the new Nawwab of Rampur that there were occasions
when money might appropriately be sent him from time to time
over and above his monthly allowance. He had recently sent an ode
of congratulation, but this had not produced quite the expected
response, and he has to write on 14 June 1865:

> Lord and Master, it was the custom of his late Highness whenever
> I sent him an ode, to acknowledge it with a letter of praise and
> appreciation, and—I feel ashamed to say this, but there is no other
> way—to enclose in the envelope as a gift a draft of Rs 250. The
> panegyric odes are included in the volume of my collected Persian
> verse in Your Highness's library, and you may confirm what I have
> said about the letters from your files. The practice was not a bad one,
> and if it could be continued that would be good.

There is no indication in subsequent letters that the Nawwab
responded as desired.

The Nawwab had asked him to come to Rampur. On 18 June
1865, he replies:

> I will certainly come to attend upon Your Highness...[but] the heat
> beats down so fiercely that the very wings of the birds are burning.
> And after fire will come water [the rains]. In both these conditions
> a man may be excused the toils of travel, especially when he is old
> and sick. Let the sun once move into Libra, and the seasons of fire
> and of water be passed, and I will put on the robes of pilgrimage
> for the journey to the splendid city of Rampur.

He was evidently pleased with the new Nawwab's initial treatment
of him. On 7 July 1865, he writes to Bekhabar:

> May God preserve the ruler of Rampur! I received my money for
> both April and May as of old, and, God willing, the money for

June…will come too. Today is Friday, 7th July. As a rule the Nawwab's letter with the draft comes about the 10th or 12th. I have sent off the ode in celebration of his accession, and received the acknowledgement. I no longer keep copies of my verse and prose. My heart is sick of this art. It is so hot that I do not know where to turn. And on top of that are my physical ills and spiritual sorrows.

On 17 July 1865, he writes again to Majruh and Mir Sarfaraz Husain:

The delight of my eyes Mir Mahdi [Majruh] and Mir Sarfaraz Husain must be cross with me. They will be grumbling at me and saying to themselves, 'Just see, he hasn't written to us.' Well,

I too possess a tongue; if only you
Would ask me, I would hasten to explain.[123]

So let me explain that you too have not written, so there was no letter to reply to. When Miran Sahib came I asked after you and told him to send you my blessings when he wrote. And that is the most I can manage. He came yesterday. I asked him, 'Have you heard from Alwar?' He said, 'No, not this week'. How shall I describe to you the state I am in? I used to chant this verse of mine to myself:

Back! thronging hosts of black despair,
  lest you reduce to dust as well
The one joy left to me—the joy that
  unavailing struggle brings.

But now this is a song I can no longer sing, because the joy of unavailing struggle has turned to dust. 'Verily we are for God and verily to Him we shall return'.

This is the last letter which we possess to Majruh or to any of his circle.

A week later, on 23 July 1865, he writes again to the Nawwab of Rampur:

Here we need rain, and the wind seems to rain sparks of fire. In the scorching sun men's faces and the rocks of the hills burn…. Wherever you turn are hosts of varied sicknesses, and only on men's limbs, which run with sweat, is any trace of moisture…to be found. Either the hot wind blows, or the air is completely still. I write these lines because I wonder all the time how Your Highness is faring. The sooner you favour your well-wisher with a reply, the greater will be the boon that you confer on him.

[123] Ghalib is here adapting one of his own couplets.

On 26 July 1865, he writes to Amin ud Din Ahmad Khan:

> I learned from your kind letter that two Persian ghazals I sent had
> reached you. Did the third one [he here gives the rhyming words]
> not reach you?—the one I sent at your request. Surely it must have
> been done, and you must have forgotten. Your representative in
> constant attendance at the court of Asadullah [Ghalib], i.e. Maulana
> Alai, has, with a view to the pleasure of him who sent him there,
> kept on at me until I wrote an Urdu ghazal. If you like it, get it taught
> to a singer. It should go well in the higher ranges of the *jhinjoti* mode.
> If I live that long I will come in the winter and hear it too.

His appreciation led him when he heard a few days later that the
Nawwab was ill, to offer his friendly advice as to the treatment he
should adopt:

> I am not a physician, but I am a man of much experience, with the
> understanding that seventy years of life brings to a man. I would not
> speak in these terms to others, but I cannot help expressing my
> opinion to Your Highness. God knows what it was, or what your
> physicians thought it was, that caused your illness, but in my opinion
> disorders of the stomach and of the heart both contributed to it. Now
> in order to safeguard your health it is important that you should take
> coconut-water from time to time. To strengthen the heart you
> should take the gold-and-ambergris electuary made up according to
> the prescription of the late Hakim Babar Ali Khan. Its ingredients
> are gold leaf, white ambergris, essence of *kewra* [a strong-scented
> flower], and white crystallized sugar—made to a special recipe in
> which the use of too many ingredients was deemed inappropriate.
> (Other electuaries have many more ingredients.) Avicenna's stimu-
> lant, conserve of pearls, conserve of ox-tongue and ambergris,
> essence of meats prepared without intoxicating ingredients, com-
> pounded with stimulants and tonics which are neither too heating
> nor too cooling.... [a word or two is evidently missing here]. From
> time to time you should drink oxymel[124] and rose-water. Your diet
> should include plenty of fowl, and lightly-done eggs, but you should
> exercise care not to eat fowl and eggs at the same sitting. With goat's
> meat, eggs are permissible, and, indeed, delicious and good to eat.
> Essence of mint and essence of the small cardamom should always
> be in your medicine-chest. Increase the use of perfumes. Refrain
> from sexual intercourse after meals. Sheep's foot gravy should always
> be on your dinner-table, for you to partake of whenever you feel the
> inclination.

[124] Vinegar, lime-juice or other acid, mixed with sugar or honey.

May you live on and on till Judgement Day
And every day your honour and wealth increase.

He writes again on 18 September 1865 to condole with the
Nawwab on the death of his wife:

> I want to write something, but I do not know what to write. I ought
> to have written a poem of condolence in the Persian language and
> in eloquent style. But I swear by your feet, I could not bring myself
> to do so. An ornate style, in verse or prose, is for occasions of
> rejoicing, when the heart, in the exuberance of its joy, blooms like
> a flower and the mind expands and words are sought for and themes
> created. But now I am half-dead, and my heart is despondent and
> my spirit dejected.... How fair is my fortune, that before I had done
> justice to themes of praise and congratulation I should be called upon
> to write an elegy!... At the very outset of Your Highness's reign you
> have had to suffer the greatest blow that could be imagined. When
> the outset of your reign brought you such extreme of pain, it is surely
> demanded now that for ever and ever, as long as you live no sorrow
> should befall Your Highness....

He enclosed a four-line chronogram on the lady's death.

Within a month he was himself on the way to Rampur, to be
present at the celebrations of the Nawwab's accession. He writes
of his impending departure in a letter to Alai of 1 October 1865.

> The occasion of my going is to mourn the late Nawwab and
> congratulate the present one. I shall have to stay there two or three
> months, so from now on address any letters to Rampur. No need
> to write the address of the house. My name and 'Rampur' is enough.

By 11 October 1865, he was well on his way to Rampur, for he
wrote on that date from Muradabad to Hakim Ghulam Najaf
Khan:

> It's Wednesday, and it must have been about nine in the morning
> when I got to Muradabad, travelling alone in a palanquin.... The
> two boys, the two carts, the carriage, and the servants are following
> on behind. They'll be here any time now. If the night passes
> uneventfully, and if I live, I shall reach Rampur tomorrow. I'm ill
> at ease. It's three days since I passed a motion. The boys are well.
> Tell your teacher [Ghalib's wife]. Give Mirza Shihab ud Din Khan
> my blessing and Nawwab Ziya ud Din my regards. Read out my
> letter to both of them—mind you do! Zahir ud Din won't be pleased
> if I send him my blessing, so tell him I send my respectful service.

From a letter to another correspondent we know that he reached
Rampur on 13 October. Eight days later, on 21st, he wrote again
to Hakim Ghulam Najaf Khan:

> I learned from your letter that you are worried about my diet. Well,
> I swear by God that here I am happy and well. I get my morning
> meal so early in the day that by about nine o'clock my servants have
> eaten too. [The servants would not eat until after their master had
> finished his meal.] The evening meal too comes early. Several kinds
> of meat and vegetable dishes, pulao, mutanjan [meat boiled in rice
> with spices and sugar]...and at both meals both leavened bread and
> chapaties, with chutneys and preserves. I am happy, and the boys
> are happy. Kallu is better again. A water-carrier, a scullion and a
> sweeper are provided from the Nawwab's establishment, and I have
> engaged a barber and a washerman. So far I have met the Nawwab
> twice. The honour he shows me and his consideration and courtesy
> leave nothing to be desired.
>
> Zahir ud Din Khan Bahadur, my blessings upon you. Take this
> letter to your grandmother [Ghalib's wife] and read it to her, and
> tell her that that thing I told her is not correct. There's nothing in
> it. All is well with us here.

The next letter, dated 2 November 1865, is not to Hakim
Ghulam Najaf Khan but to his son Zahir ud Din:

> ...Tell me, my son, how are you? And how is your brother Mirza
> Tafazzul Husain? If you see him, give him my blessing and ask
> after his health. And give your respected father my blessing and tell
> him that his letter was in answer to mine, so there was nothing in
> it that demanded an answer from me. And listen, Zahir ud Din my
> son, go at once to your grandmother [Ghalib's wife] and tell her that
> both the boys and I are well, and ask her whether Shihab ud Din
> Khan sent her allowance of fifty rupees for October or not. [Mihr
> says that Ghalib's wife received a regular monthly allowance from
> Loharu.] And has Kidar Nath been to the house to issue their pay
> to Jafar Beg, Wafadar and the others, or not? Well, my son, ask your
> grandmother these two things and then write to me at once. Mind
> you don't put it off.

Two days later, on 4 November 1865, he writes to Rizwan:

> Today is...4 November. The day before yesterday the Nawwab
> Sahib went off on tour. He said when he left that he would return
> in two weeks, spend four days here, and then go to see the exhibition
> ground at Bareilly.

Hali says that 'as the Nawwab left, he entrusted Ghalib, in the usual phrase, "to God's keeping". Ghalib replied, "Your Highness, God entrusted me to *your* keeping. And here are you handing me back into His".' Ghalib's letter continues:

> When he gets back from there he will await the arrival of the Commissioner of Bareilly. He will be here by 5 December. Then there will be the celebrations, lasting for three days. Two or three days after that Ghalib will leave Rampur. God grant that he gets to you alive.

The day after the Rampur celebrations ended, on 6 December 1865, he wrote to Alai to describe them:

> The celebrations here are of a magnificence which would have astonished Jamshed. There is a place called Aghapur about three miles outside the city. For eight to ten days there were tents pitched there. The day before yesterday the Commissioner of Bareilly, accompanied by a few other Britishers and their wives, arrived and occupied the tents. There must have been nearly a hundred people gathered there, and all were the state guests of Rampur. Yesterday, Tuesday, 5 December, his illustrious highness journeyed there with great pomp. He reached there at two in the afternoon and returned at evening, clad in his ceremonial robe. Wazir Ali Khan, his Steward, threw money from the elephant's howdah as he passed along the route. Over the three miles it can't have been less than two thousand [rupees] that was distributed. Today the exalted sahibs [the British guests] are to be feasted. They will have their lunch and dinner here in Rampur. The illuminations and the firework display will be on a scale that will turn night into day. There will be hosts of dancing-girls and a great assemblage of British officials.... Some say that the Commissioner and the other exalted sahibs will be leaving tomorrow, some say the day after. Now let me draw you a portrait of the Nawwab. In stature, complexion, appearance, and good qualities he is just like [your uncle] Ziya ud Din Khan. There is a difference in age, and some diversity of features and the style of beard. He is kind, considerate, mild, generous, courteous, religious and abstemious. He is a man of good poetic taste, and knows hundreds of couplets by heart. He does not himself write verse, but he writes [Persian] prose, and writes it well, in the style of Jalalae Tabatabai. He has such an open, pleasant face that the very sight of him banishes all sadness. He speaks so well that to listen to him speaking is to feel that a new soul has entered your body. God grant him eternal prosperity and increase his glory. When all these gatherings are over, I shall seek leave to depart, and when leave is given, shall return to Delhi. Give

your father my regards—provided you are permitted to enter his
presence and say what you have to say—and write and tell me such
news as you have of how the children are faring. It's just before eight,
on Wednesday, 6 December 1865. The writer's name is probably [in
Urdu, Ghalib] known to you.

Ghalib writes again to Alai on 22 December 1865:

Mirza, it's better to sit face to face than side by side. Come and sit
down facing me. At seven this morning Baqir Ali Khan and Husain
Ali Khan, with fourteen cocks—six large and eight small—left for
Delhi. Two of my servants went with them. One and a half—that
is, Kallu and the boy Niyaz Ali—are here with me. When they left,
the Nawwab presented each of them with a shawl. Mirza Naim Beg,
son of Mirza Karim Beg, has been here for the last two weeks. He's
staying with his sister. He says, 'I'll come with you to Delhi, and go
on to Loharu from there.' As for my departure, God willing, I shall
be off before the week is out.

You've made a wrong move. You were writing a letter in Urdu
on a single theme and suddenly switched into Persian—and that too
the Persian of an office clerk.... Anyway, I won't produce the letter,
but just convey its contents, and that will serve the purpose....

I've already written the date above. My name I've changed to
Maghlub. [Ghalib means 'vanquisher', maghlub, 'vanquished'.]

On 26 December 1865, he writes again: 'Your two nephews [i.e.
Ghalib's 'grandsons'] left [today] for Delhi. I shall take the
road...the day after tomorrow.'

He then makes a laconic comment in an adapted verse to the
effect that where honour and kindness were concerned, they were
shown to him in such degree that what was the peak for others
was only the starting point for him—and that where wealth and
money were concerned he came away empty-handed.

1866

The tone of a letter of 13 January 1866 to Alai also suggests that
he was again in good form:

When I was about to leave [for Rampur] your uncle [Ziya ud Din
Ahmad Khan] asked me to get him a pellet-bow, and when I got to
Rampur I was able to get one without any effort.... I put it aside.
I told the boys, the servants and everyone else that it was for Nawwab
Ziya ud Din. A week before I left, you asked for one. My friend,

I can't tell you how I searched, but I couldn't get one—not even though I was willing to pay up to ten rupees. I asked the Nawwab Sahib [of Rampur] for one, but even he had not got one in his stores. Then I heard of a noble who had one, and hastened to him. I found that he had the bamboo for the bow—and what a bamboo!—as outstanding among its fellows as men of our [fresh Turanian] stock among Najaf Khan's [degenerate] Turanians. I had no time to get the whole thing made, for the next day I left Rampur. Mind you treat this bamboo with proper respect, and have it prepared with care.

About the same time he writes to Tufta, who had apparently been so upset by some recent experience that he was contemplating abandoning the world and becoming a faqir. Ghalib's reply plays on the conventional phrase for such an action, which literally means 'unclothing oneself'.

Why do you want to 'unclothe yourself'? What have you got to wear anyway, that you should take it off and throw it away? You can abandon clothing, but that won't release you from the bonds of existence, and you won't get by without eating and drinking. Take hard times and good and trouble and ease as they come. Let things come and go as they will:

Resolution alone will serve you, Ghalib;
Troubles press hard on you—and life is dear.

On 23 April 1866, he writes indignantly to Sayyah. He had already objected in a letter of 21 February to Sayyah's sending him Rs 5 to pay for books which Ghalib had expected him to accept as a gift: 'My friend, what are these five rupees' worth of stamps you've sent me? I'm not a bookseller or an agent. Your action offended me, and you shouldn't have done it.' He now returns to the same theme:

Maulana Saif ul Haq [Sayyah], nowadays every letter you send has a note or a draft or stamps in it. I ask you, *you* tell me, what are these two and a half rupees for? What are they to pay for? That five rupees you sent me before upset me, and now these two and a half crown it all. Anyway, write and tell me about it. Why have you sent it? What is it for? I want an answer to this note quickly. I'll send off the hats after Id.

On 17 June 1866 he again writes to Sayyah:

Friend, my greetings to you. Your letter came, and I read both your ghazals and rejoiced. Flattery is not your humble servant's way, and if flattery be allowed to enter into matters where the craft of poetry is concerned, then a man's shagird cannot perfect himself. Remember, you've never yet sent me a ghazal in which I have not made corrections, especially of Urdu usage. These two ghazals are, in word and content, without blemish. No correction was called for anywhere. A hundred thousand praises upon you!

Mir Ghulam Baba Sahib really is just as you say he is. In your travels you must have seen ten thousand men pass before your gaze. And when out of this great legion you single out one for your praise, he must indeed be one in thousands. 'That is beyond all doubt.'[125] [From the next words it seems that either Sayyah or Mir Ghulam Baba Khan had expressed a wish to send Ghalib a gift and had wanted Ghalib to suggest one.] I don't know what I should ask for. What shall I ask you to send? I'm very fond of mangoes—I like them as much as I like grapes. But how are they to get to me from Surat and Bombay?... You would be paying four rupees postage on one rupee's worth of mangoes; and then too it's quite likely that not more than ten in every hundred would get here. No, you really mustn't think of it. There are plenty of good *desi* mangoes of all kinds and varieties to be had here—select and fresh and delicious and fragrant. Plenty of *paiwandi* mangoes too. The Nawwab Sahib often sends me presents of mangoes from his orchards in Rampur. Just see! Today two baskets arrived from a friend at Bareilly—two baskets, each holding a hundred mangoes. Kallu my steward opened them in my presence. Out of two hundred mangoes only eighty-three were sound, and a hundred and seventeen were completely rotten.

Early this month—June—we had rain for a week. Ever since then it's again been raining fire, and the hot wind is blowing.

A number of other letters which bear only the date '1866' or, in some cases, no date at all, may be taken here. One is to Hakim Ghulam Najaf Khan—the last to him which we possess:

If you have been making a fool of me and calling me your ustad and your father by way of a joke, well and good. But if you sincerely respect and love me, then do what I ask you and forgive Hira Singh his transgression.

From what follows it appears that Hira Singh had been under Hakim Ghulam Najaf Khan's treatment, but had, without his knowledge, gone to consult other hakims instead. Ghalib continues:

Be fair, my friend. If he went to Hakim Ahsanullah Khan, he went to a man who is your cousin and from whom you yourself have

---

[125] A quotation from the Quran.

learned. And if in his anxiety he went to Hakim Mahmud Khan, well, you served your own apprenticeship under his father, beginning your studies under his direction. In short, if the poor fellow consulted others besides you, it was precisely because of your connection with them that he did so—and that too in a state of anxiety, driven to it by his hysterical fears. Now when he comes to see you it is incumbent on you to be even more attentive to him than before and concentrate all your attention on giving him the treatment that his condition needs.

Most of the other letters are to Bekhabar. Some make reference to the volume of Ghalib's Urdu letters which Bekhabar was preparing for publication at this time, though it did not ultimately appear until October 1868. Most are concerned with the correction of verses and discussion of the points that arise from them. But mingled with them are more personal themes.

In one letter he writes, apparently in reply to a request for a preface to the forthcoming volume of his letters: 'I have already told you before that I am confined to bed and cannot get up or sit up. I write my letters lying down. How can I write you a preface in this state?' And in the next letter:

> If an old servant who has obeyed your commands all his life fails to carry out an order in his old age, that is no crime. If the collection of my Urdu prose [letters] cannot be printed without a preface by me, then I opt not for impression but for suppression. Sadi—God's mercy by upon him—says
>
> > It is the way of men with freedom in their gift
> > To free their slaves when once old age has come to them.
>
> You come in that category. You are a 'man with freedom in your gift'. So why don't you act upon this verse?

Two more very short, undated letters are the only others to Tufta which we possess. They form a fitting conclusion to the record of Ghalib's friendship for a man who could clearly be stupid, obstinate and insensitive, and yet who, equally clearly, sincerely loved Ghalib and was loved by him in return. Both letters acknowledge odes which Tufta had written in Ghalib's praise. The first reads:

> I cannot praise your ode too highly. What ingenuity your verses show! But alas! it is untimely and misplaced. Your praise and the object of your praise are respectively like an apple-tree or a

quince-tree that springs up on a rubbish-dump. May god preserve you! You bring your custom to a shop that is failing.

The second is even shorter: 'I cannot find words to praise you.... A hundred thousand praises are the praiser's due: a hundred loathings are the due of him you praise.'

Thus, many of the letters of 1866 show a mental liveliness, a range of interest, and a capacity to react sensitively to all the varied experiences of life which persisted to the end of his days. But his health was declining, and with it—what grieved him no less than this—his capacity to be of service to his friends. Already perhaps at the end of March 1866—the letter is dated only '1866'—he had written to Bekhabar:

> I am counting the months of my seventh decade. I used to have recurrent bouts of colic; now it is with me all the time.... I eat less and less, and now my diet, if not non-existent, is something approaching it.... I also feel a strange burning in my liver, and though I take only a mouthful at a time, God knows how much water I drink from morning to the time I go to bed.

On 8 April 1866 he writes to Maududi:

> Do you know the state I am in now? I am extremely weak and feeble. [My hands] have begun to tremble, my eyesight has got much worse, and my senses are not with me. I have done what I could to serve my friends, reading their pages of verse as I lie here and making corrections. But now my eyes cannot see properly and my hands cannot write properly. They say of Shah Sharaf Ali Bu Qalandar that when he reached advanced old age God exempted him from his religious duties and the Prophet excused him the prescribed observances. I expect of my friends that they will exempt me from the service of correcting their verses. The letters they write out of love for me I shall continue to answer to the best of my ability.

Later letters show that this did not stop his friends from continuing to send verses for correction. Ghalib did not rebuke them, and to the extent that his health allowed, continued to perform this service for them.

By August increased financial worries add to the burdens he has to bear. On 10 August 1866 he writes to the Nawwab of Rampur:

> Today is Saturday, 10 August 1866. Your humble servant was watching and waiting for the postman to come bringing a kind letter from you with your draft enclosed. Unexpectedly, he brought

instead a letter from my young friend Munshi Sil Chand,[126] asking me why I had not sent a receipt for my allowance for the month of June. After that there was a sentence saying that letters to accompany the July remittances were being prepared and that my own allowance would be sent after a day or two. I was completely puzzled. 'Good God,' I thought to myself, 'I sent off the receipt for June as usual. Why am I being asked for it again?' Then the announcement that the July allowance would be despatched shortly was a virtual sentence of death to me. Good God! On the 10th it is promised, on the 13th or 14th it is despatched; by the 20th it will reach me. And my position is that my English pension goes to my wife, and towards paying off an instalment on my debts, and it is on Your Highness's bounty that I and my servants and Husain Ali[127] live. My remaining debts amount to something like four hundred or four hundred and fifty rupees, and no one is willing to loan me money any more. In short, I have two submissions to make: first, that I have already sent the receipt for the allowance for June; if it was lost in the post, I could send another; secondly, no matter if this month's (July's) allowance does not reach me until 20 August but for the future orders may please be given that your humble servant's allowance, which is no more than a gift of alms, be despatched on the 1st or 2nd of the month.

> May you live on and on till Judgement Day
> And every day your honour and wealth increase.

The Nawwab's response was as Ghalib had hoped, if perhaps a little tardy. He wrote on 25 August that there was no need for Ghalib to send another receipt for the June allowance, and that orders had been issued that for the future his allowance should be despatched in time to reach him by the first or second of the month. On 25 September 1866 he writes to Maududi:

> When you send me a currency note, do not do what Calcutta people do and send half the note at a time. A letter addressed to me may get stranded at the post-office of the city it is sent from, but once it reaches the post-office in Delhi it is out of the question that it should be lost.

On 6 October 1866, he writes to Maulvi Numan Ahmad. He had written to him previously on 5 September praising him highly

[126] One of the Nawwab's staff.

[127] The elder boy, Baqir Ali, was by now, it seems, no longer a liability to Ghalib. He ultimately got employment in Alwar.

for the skill with which he writes Persian prose in Ghalib's own style. Numan Ahmad must have replied in terms which suggested that he thought Ghalib was flattering him, and Ghalib now responds with some indignation:

> Your humble servant has many faults, and one of them is that he does not tell lies. Because I am a man of noble family that has had ties with the [British] authorities, I often have occasion to meet persons in authority and to have dealings with them from time to time. I have never flattered any of them. I ask you why should I lie to you, respected sir? Why should I flatter you?

No wonder that two months earlier, on 6 October 1866, he had written appealing for financial help to the Nawwab of Rampur:

> I am afraid that my young friend Nawwab Mirza Khan[128] has not informed you...of my position. Your highness can bestow wealth and property as much as he pleases on whomever he pleases. I ask from you only relief, and relief means only that I should be able to pay off my remaining debts and should not have any need to borrow again.

It was some months before the Nawab responded.

1867

Money matters again preoccupy him as 1867 opens. He writes on 8 January 1867 to the Nawwab of Rampur:

> My lord and guide, thanks to your charity my debts have now been paid, freeing my pension from deduction and myself from distress. Alike with heart and tongue I sing the praises of your bounty and generosity and pray that your wealth and prosperity may endure for ever. Half of my debt was cleared by your earlier gift, and half by the present one. Now I have to say something which I cannot say and yet cannot help saying. If an allowance of fifty rupees a month each for the two boys be made with effect from January 1867, that is the present month of the present year, and sent month by month along with your humble servant's stipend, then your loyal retainer will never need to incur debt again.

This request was not to be granted during his lifetime. He writes to Zaka on 15 February 1867:

[128] The young poet Dagh.

My brother, I do not know why I feel such faith in you and such love for you. Clearly it has to do with the world of the spirit, for evident causes do not enter into it.... I am in my seventy-third year.... My memory has gone so completely that one would think I never had one. My hearing had long been defective; now, like my memory, it is gone altogether. For the last month now my state has been such that when friends come to see me, all our conversation, beyond the formal polite enquiries after each other's health, is done by their writing down what they have to say. My diet is practically non-existent. In the morning, crystallized sugar, and the juice of peeled almonds; at midday, meat broth; towards evening four fried meat kababs; and before I sleep, five tolas[129] of wine mixed with an equal quantity of rose-water. I am old and useless, and a sinner and a profligate and a disgrace. Mir Taqi's verse describes me aptly:

> The whole world knows me, but my tale is done.
> In short, do not pursue me; I am gone.

Today I was feeling somewhat better. I had another letter to write, and when I opened my box, the first thing I saw was your letter lying there. I read it again and found that there were some points to which I had not replied.

He then turns abruptly to another theme. He has received an anonymous letter from Hyderabad in which the writer attempts to estrange him from Zaka. His response is characteristic:

I am not a man who thinks perversely or whose understanding is at fault; my judgement is sound and not followed by misgivings. When I have once assessed a man, I never need to revise my assessment. I do not keep secrets from my friends. Someone has sent me an anonymous letter through the post from Hyderabad. He had not sealed it well, and in opening it one line got cut off from the rest. But the purport is clear all the same. The sender's object was to create bad feeling between us, to make me displeased with you; but by God's power my love for you increased and so did my certainty of your heartfelt love for me. I am enclosing the letter exactly as it is and sending it off to you. On no account, if you recognize the writing, are you to quarrel with the man who wrote it. I send it you so you will know that thanks to it, I am aware of your advancement and increased salary.

On 25 August 1867, he writes to Sayyah. He explains to him, as he had to others, why he could not write his own letters, and continues:

---

[129] About an ounce.

I don't employ a clerk. If a friend or acquaintance calls, I get him to write the replies to letters. My friend, I have only a few more days to sojourn in this world.... I have had a detailed account of my condition printed in the newspapers, and asked to be excused answering letters and correcting verses. But no one has acted accordingly. Letters still come in from all sides demanding answers to previous letters and enclosing verses for correction; and I am put to shame. Old, crippled, completely deaf and half blind, I lie here day and night, a chamber-pot under the bed and a commode near it. I don't have occasion to use the commode more than once in every three or four days; and I need the chamber-pot...five or six times in every hour.

I was very sorry to hear how a son had been born to you and had died. My friend, I know exactly what such a loss means. In my seventy-one years I have had seven children, both boys and girls, and none lived to be more than fifteen months. You are still young. May Exalted God give you patience, and another son in his place.

An undated letter—the last of his letters to Qadr Bilgrami—perhaps belongs to this time:

Sir, your humble servant has given up writing verse and given up correcting it. The sound of it he can no longer hear, and the sight of it he cannot bear. I am seventy-five [sic] years old. I began writing verse at fifteen and babbled on for sixty years. My odes have gone unrewarded and my ghazals unpraised. As Anwari says:

Alas! there is no patron who deserves my praise.
Alas! there is no mistress who inspires my verse.

I look to all poets and to all my friends not to write my name in the roll of poets and never to ask my guidance in this art.

Asadullah Khan poetically named Ghalib, entitled Najm ud Daula [Star of the Realm]—God grant him His forgiveness.

A little earlier, in a letter of 19 August 1867 to the Nawwab of Rampur, comes the first mention of a matter that was to bring him much distress in the months to come:

That slave bought by your gold, Husain Ali Khan, is now engaged to be married, to a girl of his own family—that is, to the grand-daughter of the full-brother of the late Nawwab Ahmad Bakhsh Khan. The month of Rajab has been fixed for the marriage. And it is in your hands, in my old age and penury, to preserve my honour.

Whom should I tell my need if not to you?
For I must speak; there is no other way.
May you live on another thousand years,
And every year have fifty thousand days.

On 5 September 1867, he writes again to the Nawwab of Rampur:

I was honoured by the receipt of your kind letter. I found that it
contained your command in connection with the marriage of
Husain Ali Khan to submit, in brief what it was I desired. I obey
your command and submit. In brief, I am a beggar that sits in the
dust at your palace door, and he is your slave. In more detail, I have
neither cash, nor goods, nor possessions, nor property, and my wife
has not a single, small item of gold or silver jewellery. None is
prepared to give me an advance or a loan. I ask you to grant me
money, so that this task may be accomplished and a poor old man
not put to shame among his fellows.

The second matter is, that I receive as alms from your court a
hundred rupees a month, and as a pension (in lieu of an estate) from
the British government sixty-two rupees, eight annas a month. He
Who knows the unseen knows that I live with great difficulty on this
income. How am I to support my boy's bride?[130] Let Husain Ali
Khan be granted an allowance, but let it be issued not in his name,
but in that of this wife, Husn Jahan Begam, daughter of Akbar Ali
Khan. And let the receipt for it be sealed with her seal. The amount
of the grant for the expenses of the wedding and the amount of the
allowance must be left to my lord and master's magnanimity and to
this wretched cripple's fortunes.

The Nawwab replied in a somewhat pompous, half-Persian style
on 18 September 1867:

Since your kind self did not commit to writing the amount of the
expenses of the marriage which he proposes, I therefore impel my
pen to write in this missive of love, asking that first you inform me
of the expenses of the marriage; when these are once ascertained,
then an appropriate dispensation for this special occasion will be put
into effect, because, as is demanded by our mutual affection and
ancient amity, the writer keeps always in view that in matters that
are fitting, he act for his kind friend's pleasure.

Ghalib wrote again on 23 September 1867:

---

[130] When a young man is married he genrally brings his bride home to live
under his parents' roof.

I was honoured by the receipt of your kind letter. Great is God! Your Highness's sympathy and affection and graciousness to his humble servant have reached such heights that none before him save Sultan Sanjar among the kings of Persia and Shahjahan among the kings of Hindustan can have shown such care and solicitude for his servants. Baqir Ali Khan was married to a girl of Nawwab Ziya ud Din's family. He [Ziya ud Din] spent two thousand rupees on food and clothing [to celebrate the wedding] and my wife spent two thousand five hundred rupees, including five hundred in jewellery. The father of Husain Ali Khan's bride, Akbar Ali Khan, is a man of our family, but he is not rich; he is in employment. How can I bring myself to say what you should give? I am a beggar, and it is not customary for a beggar to name the sum he begs. I have stated the position about what was spent on the [earlier] marriage in our family. Two thousand or two thousand five hundred rupees would enable us to celebrate the wedding very well. But let me add at the same time that I have not served you well enough to feel that I have the right to ask so much. I will manage the wedding on whatever you see fit to give.

A note entered by the Nawwab's chief clerk on the back of the envelope in which Ghalib's letter was received reads: 'Presented. No instructions for a reply yet issued. 28 September 1867.' Nor does Ghalib again refer to the matter until December. But on 29 December 1867, he writes again:

Today is Saturday, the first of the blessed month of Ramzan.... In the month of fasting kings and nobles distribute alms, and if the marriage of the orphan Husain Ali Khan can fall within this dispensation, and money be sent to this poor old cripple, then preparations can be put in hand this month and the marriage ceremony performed in the month of Shawwal. And since in this blessed month the doors of bounty are opened and the beginning of the English year also falls, the twenty-five rupees' monthly allowance of which you have made auspicious mention can be issued to the said Husain Ali Khan as from January 1868, and I would feel that I have won both worlds.

The Last Years, 1868–9

If Ghalib hoped that the Nawwab of Rampur would enable him to enter 1868 feeling that he had 'won both worlds', the Nawwab, on the other hand, apparently did not feel any compulsion to put him in this happy position. Arshi notes that he replied to Ghalib's letter of 29 December 1867, on 6 January 1868, making no reference of Ghalib's request.

The year therefore opened on a gloomy note, and had Ghalib but known it, there was worse in store. In December 1867 he had brought an action for defamation against one Miyan Amin ud Din of Patiala, and the outcome was a painful one. But this was the end result of developments which had begun some years previously, and must now be explained. Hali writes:

> When Ghalib had completed *Dastambu* [in August 1858], in the loneliness and desolation that still prevailed what could he do but make his pen and inkwell his friend and companion, and forget his sorrow...by occupying himself in reading and writing? The only two books he had by him at the time were [the Persian dictionary] *Burhan i Qate* and *Dasatir*. He took up *Burhan i Qate* and began to glance through it. At first glance he noticed inconsistencies in it, and when he then began to read it more attentively, he found numbers of words which had been wrongly explained...and [numerous other] offences against the principles of lexicography.... He began to note down the points which were open to objection, and they gradually accumulated to make up a book, which he entitled *Qate i Burhan*. This he printed and published in 1276 AH. Then, in 1277 AH,[131] he published a second, augmented...edition, to which he gave the name of *Dirafsh i Kawiani*.'

Hali then gives a number of examples of Ghalib's objections to the entries in *Burhan i Qate*, and continues:

> At the time he wrote *Qate i Burhan* he had no other dictionary...by him, and no other materials on which to base his researches into various words. He relied on his memory in all that he wrote, or on his good taste and intuition. Despite this, except for a few places where he has indeed been guilty of lapses, all his charges appear to be sound....
>
> The book was no sooner published than every Tom, Dick, and Harry girded up his loins to do battle with Ghalib, and against this one book a number of pamphlets...were written. The reason for this opposition is clear. Blind acceptance of tradition has become so essential a part of us—not only in religious matters, but in everything else—in every field, in every branch of learning, in every art—that

---

[131] These dates are not correct. *Qate i Burhan* was published in March 1862 (1278 AH) and *Dirafsh i Kawiani* in 1865 (1282 AH). *Qate i Burhan* had been written in 1859, as Ghalib's letters show.

it never occurs to a man that he should enquire into things for himself, nor does he think anyone else fit to utter a word against what men of past generations have said. Any book written a century or two centuries ago is regarded as a work of divine revelation, which is to be accepted as such. So no matter how sound and reasonable Ghalib's objections to *Burhan i Qate* might have been, it was out of the question that they should not arouse fierce opposition. Some think that this opposition arose mainly because Ghalib's mischievous sense of humour frequently leads him to make fun of the compiler of *Buharn i Qate*, and because he occasionally gets angry and allows himself to use harsh words of him. But this view is not correct. Even if he had not written such words..., he still would certainly have aroused opposition, because Indian scholars of the old school, whom nobody pays the slightest attention to these days, no longer get the chance to emerge from their obscure holes and corners except when some eminent and distinguished man writes a book, and they can write a refutation, and so show the world that they too are men to reckon with...

Hali's sarcastic words reflect Ghalib's own attitude in the matter, and whatever the rights and wrongs in specific points of the controversy, there is no doubt that Ghalib's essential position is sound. He asserts his own exceptional proficiency in Persian and claims that this gives him every right to dispute the dogmatic (and, not infrequently, ignorant) assertions of Indian lexicographers of Persian, whether of his own day or of the past, and not accept their findings unquestioningly simply because everyone else does. As we have seen, what he now asserted did not represent any new development. In the Calcutta controversy of nearly forty years earlier he had already made his standpoint clear, and his letters to his shagirds over the years had again and again restated the salient points. Their reactions alone must have shown him that he would often be fighting a lone battle, but this did not deter him. In his letters to his friends he expresses himself bluntly and unequivocally. Thus he writes to Sarur in a letter dated only '1859':

And let me impress this upon you: you will find that what I have to say about the construction of Persian words and the flights of meaning in Persian verse is usually at variance with what the general run of people say; and *I* am in the right.

He knows that there will be few who share his stand. He writes to Majruh (July 1859) promising to lend him his own authentic text of *Qate i Burhan*, but goes on,

But let me tell you, you can be sure that those who read it won't understand it. They'll swear by *Burhan i Qate* alone. Only a man who has a number of qualifications will take his stand with me. First he must be a man of learning; next, one who knows the art of lexicography; thirdly, a man well-versed in Persian—one who has a real love of the language and who has not only read a great deal of the great poets of the past, but who also knows some of their verse by heart; fourthly, he must be a fair-minded man, not pig-headed; and fifthly, he must be a man of sound taste and intellect, not one of crooked wit and perverse understanding. No man who lacks these five things will pay me the tribute due to my labour.

He does not expect to find many such men in an age where universal, almost religious, veneration is accorded to the Indian scholars of Persian whom he attacks.

There are passages in his letters in which he explains in, for him, relatively measured terms what in his view is the weakness in their position and in the attitudes of those who support them. Thus he writes to Sarur, in another letter dated only '1859':

Nizami[132] is now reduced to the state that until the khatri of Faridabad Dilwali Singh, known also by his pen-name Qatil[133] ...confirms it, his verse cannot serve as an authority. To Qatil the works of the classical poets are a closed book. His knowledge of Persian derives from the speech of people who migrated to Lucknow from further west in the time of Sa'adat Ali Khan [ruler of Oudh, 1798–1814].

Most of these, he continues, though Persian-speaking, were not Persians from Iran; and in any case, the language of speech is one thing and the literary language another—otherwise why would the great writers of Persian prose have sweated blood to write as they did? As for the attitude of their supporters towards them, he writes to Sarur in the letter first quoted:

First I ask your honour: these gentlemen who write commentaries— are they all angels of God? Is all they write divinely inspired? The meanings they extract are based on conjecture. I do not say that in every case their conjecture is wrong. But neither can anyone say that their every pronouncement is correct.

[132] The classical Persian poet.
[133] Cf. p. 56.

It grieves him that even his own friends and admirers are inclined
to reject his opinion automatically if it goes against that of Qatil or
of the later Rampur lexicographer Ghayas ud Din; for even if, for
the sake of argument, one accords them a fairly favourable estimate,
they have no greater claim than he to be considered authorities.
He feels so strongly on this point that he allows himself to speak
with some sarcasm even to one whom he normally addresses with
great respect. He writes to Sahib i Alam in an undated letter:

> I do not say that you must willy-nilly accept what I write, but do
> not rate me below that son of a khatri [Qatil] and this schoolmaster
> [Ghayas ud Din].... Use your intelligence! Think! Abdul Wase was
> not a prophet. Qatil was not Brahma. Waqif was not a great saint.
> And I am not Yazid or Shimar.[134] If you accept this, well and good.
> If not, that's your concern.

He laments that what he lacks is not their qualifications but their
good fortune. He writes to Sarur in February 1859: 'Where shall
I get the good fortune of Qatil of Lucknow and Ghayas ud Din,
the mullah schoolmaster of Rampur, that a man like you should
hold me in high regard and depend upon my word?'

Ghalib's argument that his judgement and learning are at least
as worthy of respect as theirs, was one designed to make his friends
pause to reconsider their position. It implies, merely for the sake
of this argument, an estimate of Qatil and others far more favour-
able than he personally was prepared to grant them. In letters where
he gives his own estimate he leaves absolutely no room for ambi-
guity. He tells Tufta in a letter dated 14 May 1865, that in venerating
men like Qatil people are repeating the error of the children of
Israel: 'By the power of enchantment the calf began to speak with
a human voice, and the children of Israel worshipped it as God'—
an apt hit when one remembers that Qatil was originally a Hindu,
and that to the Hindus the cow is sacred. Where he had told Sarur
that of the conjectured meanings given by the lexicographers 'no
one could say that their every pronouncement was correct', he tells
Rahim Beg that they are 'rarely correct, and mostly incorrect'. He
sums up his general view of Qatil and Ghayas ud Din in the letter
to Sahib i Alam already quoted: 'Pure Persian was ruined by that
son of a khatri Qatil..., and Ghayas ud Din finished the job.'

---

[134] The men responsible for the death of Husain, the grandson of the
Prophet.

He is no less scathing about his own contemporaries. He writes to Shakir towards the end of 1865 about Rahim Beg, who had written a pamphlet against him:

> He is a Meerut man. For the last ten years he has been blind; he cannot read a book, he has to have it read to him; he cannot write, he has to dictate. In fact, people from Meerut say that he is not a man of substantial learning, but has to be helped by others. Delhi people say that he never studied under Maulvi Imam Bakhsh Sahbai, but gives it out that he did so as to increase his standing. What *I* say is, alas for the poor good-for-nothing who thinks that to have studied under Sahbai is a matter of pride and honour.

In moments of indignation he can be much more virulent. He tells Tufta in a letter of 4 October 1861 that in his eye dictionaries like Ghayas ud Din's are on a par with 'the rag a woman wears when she is menstruating', and choice insults like these are not confined to his private letters, for Ghalib replied to his critics in a series of pamphlets, and the controversy was a fierce one, conducted in terms which mid-twentieth-century man too easily forgets were the norm until quite recent times, even if today they seem lacking in decorum and decent restraint. Reasoned, if vehement, argument of the real points at issue formed a part of it, but the participants attacked one another along a much wider front, and name-calling and downright abuse were among the weapons employed on both sides. Ghalib does indeed at one point find an ingenious argument for asserting that, where his opponents are concerned, name-calling is not permissible. In a reply to one of his critics he writes:

> He has used all the choicest epithets of abuse to describe me, not stopping to think that even if Ghalib is no scholar and no poet, yet he has a certain standing as one of noble birth and noble degree, that he is a man to whom honour and distinction are shown, a man of distinguished family, a man known to the nobility and gentry and maharajas of India and numbered by the British government among the nobly-born, one on whom the king [Bahadur Shah] conferred the title of Star of the Realm, one who is addressed in official correspondence as 'Khan Sahib, our most kind friend'. Is he whom the government addresses as Khan Sahib to be called 'madman' and 'ass'? In point of fact such abuse is an insult to the government....

All the same Ghalib was not to wilt under vigorous attack, no matter how indecorous, and, in general, he cheerfully withstood such blows and repaid them in kind.

However, a stage was reached where one of his adversaries over-stepped the mark. Miyan Amin ud Din of Patiala, published in 1866 a pamphlet against Ghalib which, Ikram writes, was 'full of obscene abuse and filthy insinuations'. Hali uses similar words of it, but adds that Ghalib's first reaction was to ignore it:

Somebody pointed out to Ghalib that he had made no rejoinder. Ghalib replied, 'If you are kicked by a donkey, do you kick it back?' But on further reflection he evidently decided that the terms in which Amin ud Din had attacked him were intolerable, and he brought an action against him. Ikram describes what happened. 'The case came before the British assistant commissioner's court in December 1867. Appearing as witnesses for Ghalib were Lala Pyare Lal Ashob, Hakim Latif Husain, Maulvi Nasir ud Din and Lala Hukm Chand, while on the other side were...Maulvi Ziya ud Din (professor of Arabic at Delhi College), Maulvi Sadid ud Din, and some other scholars. The whole point at issue was whether the sentence which Miyan Amin ud Din had written about Ghalib in his book and the...insinuations he had employed, could properly be called obscene and abusive. Maulvi Ziya ud Din and the other witnesses for the defence, in order to save the accused, testified that these sentences bore meanings which made the charges against the accused impossible to sustain. When Ghalib saw that, thanks to these interpretations, it would be difficult for him to win his case, at the instance of a few of the noblemen of Delhi, he entered on 23 March 1868, a statement that he was satisfied, and withdrew his charge; but it is clear that the whole experience must have been deeply painful to him, not only because of Miyan Amin ud Din's abusive words about him, but also because of the testimony of eminent gentlemen like Maulana Maulvi Ziya ud Din, who not only interpreted Miyan Amin ud Din's filthy insinuations without the slightest regard for truth and justice, but in open court spoke of Ghalib as a 'chronic drunkard' and on these grounds contended that such...phrases as 'the kalal[135] of Agra' could legitimately be used to describe him....

Hali writes in this connection: 'Some of these maulvis were on visiting terms with Ghalib. Somebody asked him why they had testified against him. Ghalib quoted a couplet of his Persian verse in reply.' Hali then quotes it. The gist of it is 'I am a noble born and bred, and a man who acts nobly in this world finds himself abandoned by all his fellow-men.' Hali's account continues:

[135] A low-class community of men who make and sell wine.

When Ghalib brought his action some little time elapsed, and then people began to send him anonymous letters...cursing him for a wine-drinker and an irreligious man, and so on, and expressing the fiercest hatred and contempt and condemnation. They had a powerful effect on Ghalib. In those days he was all the time extremely depressed and dispirited, and whenever the postman came with the mail his whole expression would change, from apprehension that there would be some such letter in it. It so happened that in those days I had occasion to go to Delhi with the late Mustafa Khan [Shefta]. I did not know about these contemptible anonymous letters, and in my ignorance I one day committed a blunder, the very thought of which always fills me with shame. Those were the days when I was drunk with religious self-satisfaction. I thought that in all God's creation only the Muslims, and of the seventy-three Muslim sects only the Sunnis, and of the Sunnis only the Hanafis, and of the Hanafis only those who performed absolutely meticulously the fasts and prayers and other outward observances, would be found worthy of salvation and forgiveness—as though the scope of God's mercy were more confined and restricted than Queen Victoria's empire, where men of every religion and creed live peacefully together. The greater the love and affection I felt for a man, the more strongly I desired that he should meet his end in the state in which alone, as I thought, he could attain salvation and forgiveness; and since the love and affection I felt for Ghalib were intense, I always lamented his fallen state, thinking, so to say, that in the garden of Rizwan [in Paradise] we should no more be together and that after death we should never see each other again. One day, throwing to the winds all regard for Ghalib's eminence and talent and advanced years, I began to read him a dry-as-dust lecture like an arid preacher. His deafness was by now complete, and one could only converse with him by writing what one had to say. So I wrote a long-winded lecture all about how the five prayers were obligatory and how he must perform them, and laid it before him. It requested him to start saying the five prayers regularly—standing, sitting, by token gestures, in any way at all he found possible; if he could not perform ablution with water before them, then he should use dust [to cleanse himself], but he should in no case fail to perform the prayers. Ghalib deeply resented this initiative on my part, and indeed, with every justification—and the more so because in those days anonymous letter-writers were attacking him in the most unseemly terms for his way of life, expressing their hatred and contempt for him in the sort of downright abuse one hears in the market-place. What Ghalib said in reply to my stupid note is worthy of attention. He said, 'I have spent my life in sin and wrong-doing. I have never said a prayer or kept a fast or done any other good deed. Soon I shall breathe no more. Now if in my few remaining days I say my prayers—sitting, or by token gestures—how will that make up for a lifetime of sin? I deserve that when I die my friends and kinsmen should blacken my face and tie a rope round my feet and exhibit me in all the streets and by-lanes and markets of Delhi, and then take me outside the city and leave me there for the dogs and kites and crows to eat—if they can bring themselves to eat such a thing. Though my sins are such that I deserve even worse than that, yet without doubt I believe in the oneness of God, and in the moments of quiet and solitude the words "There is no god but God" and "Nothing exists but God" and "God alone works manifest in all things" are ever on my lips.' It was perhaps on that same day when this exchange was over and Ghalib was taking his food, that the postman came with a letter... Ghalib concluded that it was another anonymous letter..., and handed it to me, telling me to open it and read it. When I looked at it I found that... it contained nothing but obscene abuse. He asked me, 'Who is it from? And what does he say?' I hesitated to tell him, and he snatched it out of my hand saying, 'Perhaps it is from one of your spiritual disciples.' Then he read it from start to finish. At one point the writer had even abused Ghalib's mother. [Coarse abuse in Urdu concentrates its fire not directly on the man under attack but on the honour of his women-folk, accusing him (in less polite words) of incest with his mother or sister or daughter, according to his age, or accusing his wife of some similar immoral behaviour.] Ghalib smiled and said, 'This idiot doesn't even know how to abuse a man. If your man is elderly or middle-aged you abuse his daughter.... If he's young, you abuse his wife...and if he's only a boy you abuse his mother. This pimp abuses the mother of a man of seventy-two. Who could be a bigger fool than that?'

Hali goes on to relate how a three-way exchange of poems between Ghalib, Shefta and himself restored friendly relations.

Ghalib's letters of this period are understandably fewer in number than those of earlier years. Many of them show an awareness that death was not far off, but even in these an occasional flash shows that his old qualities did not desert him.

On 21 June 1868, he writes to provide Alai with written proof that he has designated him as his successor, entitled to guide others in matters of literature as Ghalib himself had done before him:

I have given you a statement in writing—you will remember in what year I wrote it—designating you my successor, my caliph, where

Persian is concerned. Now I am only four[136] years short of eighty, and I estimate that the span of life left to me is not to be measured in years, and perhaps not even in months. I may perhaps live another twelve months, that is a year; but it may be a matter of two to three months, six to seven weeks, ten to twenty days. Now being in my right mind, I give it you in writing in my own hand over my own seal that in the craft of Urdu verse and prose you are my successor. Those who acknowledge me are to acknowledge you as they did me, and accept your authority as they accepted mine.

Meanwhile his financial problems had been growing more pressing, causing him more and more anxiety. As early as 9 March 1868, he had written again to the Nawwab of Rampur about Husain Ali Khan:

I render you due thanks for my allowance for February 1868. Glory be to God! What miraculous increase this Rs 100 holds! It feeds a hundred mouths and meets a hundred other of your humble servant's needs.

Mirza Husain Ali Khan's wedding had been fixed for the month of Rajab. But because Your Highness's bounty did not come, it had to be postponed. Today is the 15th Zi Qad. Thus fifteen days of this month remain and the whole month of Zil Hij. If in this very month of Zi Qad Your Highness be pleased to bestow your bounty, the wedding can be arranged before Zil Hij is over. God grant that my lord and master may bear in mind too that when Ghalib brings the bride to his house, he must have the means to feed her. By which I mean that payment of Husain Ali Khan's allowance should commence. Your Highness, I have no one who can present my requests to you from time to time, and I am ashamed to write again and again like this.

He must have felt as time went on that he should have someone in Rampur to speak for him if he was to get his requests granted. From a letter to the Nawwab dated 27 July 1868, it is clear that he chose the young Nawwab Mirza Khan [Dagh] for this role,[137] while one of 13 August 1868 indicates that he also approached one Muzaffar Husain Khan. In the first of the two letters he writes:

It is being said in Delhi today that Your Highness has sent Rs 500 from Rampur to the widow of the late Mufti Sadr ud Din [Azurda] for his funeral expenses. This leads me, your humble servant, to

[136] Mihr regards this as a miscopying for 'seven'.
[137] As he had done once before. Cf. p. 244 above.

think that when I die my corpse too shall not want for a shroud and a grave. As Jalal Asir says:

I still shall drink your bounty's
draughts when I am gone.

I have yesterday sent off a letter to Nawwab Mirza Khan [Dagh]. God knows whether he will show it to Your Highness or not. In it I gave details of the position of Mufti's [Azurda's] widow, saying that she was childless and draws Rs 60 [a month] in rent from house-property. Amin ur Rahman is her sister's son, not related to the Mufti Ji.

Now I submit my own position to you. In my last years I have three requests to make of you. First, I have debts of ten to twelve hundred rupees, and I wish them to be paid before I die. My second request is this, that a special grant of your bounty enable me to go through with the marriage of Husain Ali Khan. And the third is that the hundred rupees' allowance which I receive be granted to him for the duration of his life. These two (that is, the last two) wishes may be granted either during my lifetime or after my death.

The second letter (13 August 1868) indicates that letters from his two intermediaries had assured him that his 'three requests' had been accepted:

If Merciful God wills, then, in accordance with Your Highness's commands, by the coming of winter—that is, in November or December of the present year of '68, my debts will be cleared and Husain Ali Khan's marriage too will take place.

In fact, as we shall see, either his intermediaries had misled Ghalib, or the Nawwab had misled them. On 7 September 1868, Ghalib feels obliged to write again:

My lord and master, the parents of Husain Ali Khan's betrothed bride are pressing me hard, and life is a misery to me. My brief request is this, that just to win favour in God's sight, Your Highness bestow on me whatever you think fit, and in addition fix an allowance for Husain Ali Khan. But let both these things be done quickly.

At last, on 17 November 1868, he writes in desperation:

My affairs have gone from bad to worse, until now they have reached such a pass that I have only Rs 54 of the hundred rupees left.... Altogether I need Rs 800 to save my honour. Willy-nilly, I have given up all thought of Husain Ali Khan's wedding and allowance. I will never mention it to you again, I promise you. Just give me another Rs 800. How can I think of the marriage? If my honour is saved, it is enough to be thankful for. I have sent a letter to my young friend Nawwab Mirza Khan [Dagh] giving him full details, and he will acquaint you with them. In brief, my life and my honour are in your hands; but let what you grant me be sent quickly.

To die in debt was a terrible disgrace to a Muslim of noble family, but more than a month later the Nawwab had still sent nothing, though he had apparently promised Dagh that he would do so. Meanwhile Ghalib had made a move to win the sympathy of the Raja of Alwar. His elder 'grandson' Baqir Ali Khan, was at the Alwar court, and Ghalib wrote to him on 7 December 1868:

> Your letter in answer to mine reached me, but there was nothing in it that called for a reply. I write now to tell you of a new development, namely that last month I had a copy of *Sabad i Chin* [a volume of Ghalib's Persian poems written after the publication of his collected Persian verse], along with a petition, sent to Alwar through...Mir Tafazzul Husain Khan. Accordingly, this week I received through him a letter from...His Highness...the Raja, in which he...has addressed me with titles of great honour and written many kind and gracious things about me. You are on the spot. Did you know of this, or not? And if you did, why didn't you write to me? Now I want to ask you whether anyone ever speaks of me in the durbar or not, and if they do, in what forms; and when I am mentioned, what does His Highness say?

Whether this produced any worthwhile result, we do not know. To the Nawwab of Rampur he wrote again on 17 December 1868:

> Many days have passed since my young friend Nawwab Mirza Khan [Dagh] wrote to congratulate me upon the good news that Your Highness had agreed to meet my debts and had asked their amount. I sent word to him that Rs 800 would meet them all. I write now simply to remind you.

Arshi notes that the back of the envelope bears a note: 'Presented; no orders issued.' On 10 January 1869, he wrote his last letter to the Nawwab: 'Your highness, my creditors have reduced me to desperation. All I can do is to remind you; beyond that, it is for Your Highness to decide.' Even then it seems that the Nawwab issued no instructions. The next letter to Ghalib was simply the regular monthly remittance of Rs 100. It arrived an hour before

Ghalib died. Thus he died with his debts unpaid, and knowing that no provision had been made for his wife[138] or for Husain Ali Khan, much less for Husain Ali Khan's marriage. Husain Ali Khan acknowledged the receipt of the last hundred rupees with dignity:

> On the 15th February of this year, 1869, corresponding to the 2nd of Zi Qad, on Monday at the time of the afternoon prayer, my revered and honoured grandfather, Nawwab Asadullah Khan Ghalib known as Mirza Nosha Sahib, departed from this transient world. Your loyal servant cannot express the grief and sorrow into which this heartrending loss has plunged him. And my honoured and respected grandmother has in her old age been reduced by grief to a state which no words can describe. Your Highness's kind letter, with a draft for a hundred rupees on account of the allowance for January, '69 brought honour to our house one hour before my grandfather's death. I submit a receipt for the draft for Your Highness's information.

Hali has described his last days:

> A few days before his death he became unconscious. He would remain unconscious for hours at a time, coming to for only a few minutes before relapsing again. It was perhaps the day before he died that I went to visit him. He had come to after being unconscious many hours, and was dictating a reply to a letter from... Nawwab Ala ud Din Ahmad Khan [Alai], who had written from Loharu asking how he was. He replied with a sentence of his own and a Persian couplet, probably of Sadi's. The sentence was: 'Why ask me how I am? Wait a day or two and then ask my neighbours.' And the second line of the couplet—I cannot remember the first line—was:

> You could not come to see me. Well, God keep you!

Before he died he often used to recite the verse:

> My dying breath is ready to depart,
> And now, my friends, God, only God, exists.

At last, on the 2nd of Zi Qad, 1285 and 15 February 1869, at the age of seventy-three years and four months, he departed this world and was buried at the foot of his father-in-law's tomb in the precincts of the shrine of Hazrat Sultan Nizam ud Din.... I was present at

---

[138] Mihr notes: 'The Nawwab... granted [Azurda's] widow an allowance of Rs 200 a month while to Ghalib's widow he granted nothing.'

the funeral, when the funeral prayer was said outside Delhi Gate. Most of the nobles and eminent men of Delhi were there—such as Nawwab Ziya ud Din Ahmad Khan, Nawwab Muhammad Mustafa Khan [Shefta], Hakim Ahsanullah Khan and others. Large numbers of people, both Sunnis and Shias, were present to take part in the funeral procession. Sayyid Safdar Sultan...approached...Nawwab Ziya ud Din Ahmad Khan and said, 'Mirza Sahib [Ghalib] was a Shia. If you permit us we will conduct his funeral in our own style.' But the Nawwab Sahib would not agree, and all rites were conducted in accordance with Sunni ritual. No doubt, none was in a better position than the Nawwab Sahib to know exactly what Ghalib's religious beliefs really were, but in my view it would have been better if Shias and Sunnis had both said the funeral prayer—either together or separately—and as Ghalib had during his lifetime treated Sunnis and Shias alike, so after his death too both alike should have paid their last tribute to him.

Hali says that

...chronograms of his death without number continued for a long time to appear in the Urdu newspapers,...and elegies on his death were written, in Urdu by Mirza Qurban Ali Beg Salik, Mir Mahdi Husain Majruh and the writer of the present book, and in Persian by Munshi Hargopal Tufta.

2

Ghalib's Delhi

Percival Spear

THE TITLE 'GHALIB'S DELHI' MIGHT seem to call for a straight description of Delhi and district between 1800 and 1870. But with whose eyes are we to view the Delhi scene? The same objects may convey different impressions to the minds of different individuals, according to the quality of their consciousness. The Delhi scene, for example, presented very different pictures to the landholder and retired adventurer like James Skinner, to the administrator like Fortescue, to the traveller like Jacquemment or Bishop Heber, to the Orientalist like Garcin de Tassy, and to the worried soldier like Archdale Wilson. Within the Mughal court of Akbar II, what to some was a scene of dignified resignation and graceful simplicity, appeared to others as tawdry finery against a background of squalor. The sturdy independence of the villagers in the eyes of some observers was anarchic turbulence in the view of the administrative martinet. Before, therefore, we describe Ghalib's Delhi, we have to consider the sort of things which Ghalib would have noticed out of the sum total of Delhi phenomena. Our observation glass of the Delhi stage must also be a separating glass to remove from our vision what Ghalib would not have seen. Ghalib's Delhi is the Delhi that Ghalib saw; the Delhi that impinged on his consciousness.

Mirza Muhammad Asadullah Beg Khan, Ghalib, was born at Agra in 1797.[1] His parentage on both sides was aristocratic by birth, Turkish in race and military in tradition. Ghalib's paternal grandfather was the first member of the family to come to India; he spoke Turkish, and took service under Shah Alam's chief minister, Mirza Najaf Khan. Thus Turkish family pride and Persian skill and polish came within Ghalib's experience. His maternal grandfather, Khwaja Ghulam Husain Khan, was a well-known soldier, receiving lands near Agra for his services and adding the sobriquet Kamin Dan (?commander) to his name. His uncle Nasrullah, to whose care Ghalib fell on his father's death in 1802, was also a soldier and at the time the governor or *subadar* of Agra. The next thing one notices is that these men, in the long tradition of Indian military adventurers, were ready to serve anyone without nice distinction of race or religion. Both Ghalib's grandfathers served the Mughals or their officers. His father, after serving in Shia Lucknow and Sunni Hyderabad, ended up as an officer of the Rajput Rao Raja Bakhtawar Singh of Alwar. His uncle, whose household he entered in 1802, was then holding Agra for the Maratha chief Daulat Rao Sindia, not far from Sindia's French general Perron's headquarters of Aligarh. On the capture of Agra by the British in 1803, Nasrullah Khan was given a command of 400 men and lands worth one and a half *lakhs* of rupees by the British general, Lord Lake. The family thus, at this early stage of Ghalib's life, had added Persian, Rajput, Maratha and British contacts to their Turkish lineage and military traditions. Like so many immigrants before them, these transmontane arrivals had within two generations become accredited members of the cosmopolitan north Indian aristocracy. It is wrong to suppose, as the late Sir Jadunath Sarkar did, that the stream of northern immigrants dried up in the eighteenth century, depriving the empire of its military sap. They continued to come; what was needed was a firm hand to hold the imperial umbrella over them, or, one might say, an administrative irrigation engineer to direct these energies and potential loyalties into fruitful channels. Not immigrant soldiers were lacking, but immigrant emperors.

With these circumstances it is clear that Ghalib was brought up in an atmosphere of Persian culture and north Indian high politics.

---

[1] For the family details which follow I am indebted mainly to A. C. S. Gilani, *Ghalib*, Karachi, n.d.

Ghalib's stay with his uncle Nasrullah brought a further involvement with local politics which was to run through the rest of his life. Nasrullah had married the sister of Ahmad Baksh Khan, another adventurer of Turkish origin, the son of an emigré from Bokhara. Ahmad Baksh was a diplomatic agent of the Alwar chief, who represented his interests with the British during the Maratha war of 1803–6. In the words of Sleeman, he was in attendance on Lord Lake during the whole war. 'He was a great favourite; and his Lordship's personal regard for him was thought by those chiefs to have been so favourable to their cause, that they conferred upon him the Pergunnah of Loharu in hereditary rent-free tenure.'[2] Ahmad Baksh came to the rescue of Nasrullah when the British took Agra, securing for him much the same esteem from Lord Lake as he enjoyed himself. In the Cornwallis-Barlow settlement in 1805–6, Ahmad Baksh was given the estate or principality of Firozpur Jhirka in the Punjab. He thus held Firozpur from the British and Loharu from the Alwar raja. All seemed well until Nasrullah fell off his elephant and died in 1806. Lord Lake rose to the occasion; he transferred Nasrullah's *jagir* to Ahmad Baksh in return for an annual pension of Rs 10,000 to Nasrullah's dependants. But Ahmad Baksh thought that this was too much and managed to whittle it down to Rs 3000. Here was an abiding source of friction between the two families, to be complicated by the vicissitudes of Ahmad Baksh's descendants. It would be best to follow this complication to its tragic end.[3]

Nawwab Ahmad Baksh had three sons. In 1822 he declared his eldest son, Shamshuddin, his heir in both his principalities, but in 1825 he prevailed on Shamshuddin to assign by deed Loharu as provision for his two younger brothers, who were thus cousins of Ghalib. Soon after Shamshuddin succeeded in 1825, disputes arose stemming from Shamshuddin's desire to recover Loharu. Ghalib was involved because the dispute over the family pension with Shamshuddin made him espouse the cause of the two younger brothers in their efforts to get their own allowance from the eldest. Appeals went to and fro until William Fraser, now Agent to the

---

[2] W. H. Sleeman, *Rambles and Recollections*, London, 1844, vol. II, p. 211.

[3] The Shamshuddin case is described by W. H. Sleeman (op. cit., pp. 209–31) who had it from the magistrate Gubbins, and in my *Twilight of the Mughuls*, ch. 9.

government of India, severely rebuffed Shamshuddin. There followed Fraser's murder on 22 March 1835, the tracing of the crime to the Nawwab and his execution by hanging outside the Kashmir gate on 3 October. Along with the bringing of the canal water to Delhi in 1820 and the Colebrooke case in 1829, it was one of the three great sensations of the pre-Mutiny British occupation of Delhi. Firozpur Jhirka was resumed by the British government, but Loharu remained with the brothers and the family continues there to the present. It was the quest for an increase in his pension from this source that led Ghalib on his journey to Lucknow, Benaras and Calcutta in 1827–9 and proved so fruitful to his muse. A further effect of Ghalib's share in these controversies was suspicion of his part in the Nawwab's exposure because of his known animosity and his contacts with British officials.[4]

Ghalib moved to Delhi at the impressionable age of fifteen or sixteen and remained there for the rest of his life, with breaks for his visit to Calcutta in 1827–9 and for two brief visits to Rampur. He lived in a number of houses in the neighbourhood of Bazar Ballimaran and Gali Qasim Jan, just off the Chandni Chowk and not far from the Fatehpuri Masjid. There are houses here whose gateway inscriptions were composed by him.[5] He thus became intimately bound up with the life of the city in most of its aspects. His irregular or even wild life during his early years must have brought him into contact with that underworld which was as active, though on a reduced scale, as in the heyday of the empire. His literary and intellectual tastes naturally brought him into close touch with the learned and literary world. His aristocratic connections gave him the entrée to that world of Muslim notables striving to keep up appearances on pensions, making titles do duty for estates. Both these circles led him towards the Mughal court, still maintained in the Qila-i-mu'alla or the Red Fort by the pensionary Mughal emperors. Akbar II and after him Bahadur Shah were the natural heads of both circles, the latter being a poet in his own right with the pen-name of Zafar. It naturally became Ghalib's ambition to become the latter's court poet or laureate. Here he had to contend with the reigning laureate, Shaikh Muhammad Ibrahim,

[4] A. C. S. Gilani, *Ghalib*, Karachi, n.d.

[5] E.g. that of Hakim Ahsanullah Khan, *List of Hindu and Muhommedan Monuments in Delhi Province*, Delhi, 1912, vol. I.

whose pen-name was Zauq. He had been Bahadur Shah's tutor before he became his laureate. Ghalib unfortunately first paid his addresses to Mirza Salim, Akbar II's candidate for the succession and thus Bahadur Shah's rival. It took thirteen years[6] and fifteen *qasidas* to live this down, so that it was not until 1850 that he received the titles of Najm-ud-daula, Dabir-ul-mulk and Nizam Jang, a commission to write a history of the House of Taimur, and a salary of Rs 50 per month. There followed patronage by the heir-apparent, Mirza Fakhr-uddin, of Rs 400 per annum and succession to the laureateship on Zauq's death. These successes were short-lived, for the Mirza died in 1856 and the Mutiny followed a year later. But his efforts taken with his achievement lasted over twenty years and this makes the Delhi court one of the interests of his life.

Lastly we come to the British. His family and that of Nawwab Ahmad Baksh Khan had their first and very satisfactory contacts with the British in the persons of Lord Lake and his officers. Ahmad Baksh was held in high regard by Charles Metcalfe, the resident, nicknamed the King of Delhi, from 1811 to 1819. Ghalib was in touch with successive residents and agents, including Sir Edward Colebrooke and William Fraser. James Thomason, later lieutenant-governor of the North-Western Provinces, thought highly enough of him to consider him for a post in the Delhi College. After his fruitless Calcutta journey, he developed the habit of composing *qasidas* for each visiting dignitary. His European contacts survived the curious episode of his imprisonment in 1847 on a charge of gambling, as they did the far greater strain of the Mutiny upheaval.[7]

We can therefore say that Ghalib's range of conscious interest included not merely the literary and intellectual circle of Delhi; it extended to the whole aristocratic circle in the city and on to the imperial court itself. It went beyond the court to the new British rulers, and it burrowed below the dignified upper classes to the raffish and spendthrift Delhi underworld. What it did not do, as far as can be seen, was to extend to the commercial concerns of the city or the rural concerns of the countryside. Ghalib was concerned with pensions rather than commerce, with pay offices rather than estates. It is on this basis that we must look at Ghalib's Delhi.

[6] Gilani, op. cit., p. 61.
[7] Ibid.

The Delhi of Ghalib's youth was the centre of a district torn by anarchy and strife. After the death of Mirza Najaf Khan, Zulfiqar-ud-daula, the last Mughal minister of any authority, in 1782, the region had been ridden, marched and fought over by Mughal and Rohilla chiefs, by Marathas, Rajputs and Jats, by French-led disciplined troops and by the British and their allies. To the north, Sikh bands made plundering raids from self-acquired strongholds. Even the *sannyasis* organized themselves for war, so that Himmat Bahadur and his Gosains were a recognized mercenary force.[8] Allegiances changed with startling rapidity, mercenary officers generally being willing to defect to the winning side and the soldiers glad to follow wherever their pay was secure. There were some islands of stability, such as the Begam Samru's *jagir* at Sardhana, where her well-organized force gave steady support to the emperor and repelled all attempts at interference. So also did General de Boigne at Aligarh, Sindia's officer with two brigades of disciplined troops—until he left for France with his fortune. These cases and that of the sailor George Thomas, who for two years maintained a principality at Hansi, show the bizarre nature of the times. George was a sailor who collected some followers, seized Hansi, built a fort which he called Georgegarh, and was overthrown only after a siege by a regular Maratha force. The Begam was the widow of the German adventurer Walter Reinhardt, nicknamed Sombre or dark, wanted by the British for his share in the Patna murders of 1763. She became a Christian, succeeded to the *jagir*, built a cathedral and a palace, had a special bishop named Julius Caesar, and lived till 1836.[9]

Behind these picturesque figures and their plottings we must note two sinister facts. The first is the great Delhi famine of 1781–2 when, it is thought, a third to a half of the population died. When the British arrived in 1803, 600 villages were still abandoned, and Fortescue reported in 1820 that 200 had still not been reoccupied.[10] The second is that the victims of the campaigns,

---

[8] See, e.g., H. G. Keene, *Fall of the Moghul Empire*, London, 1887, pp. 142 and 168.

[9] For G. Thomas, see H. G. Keene, op. cit., pp. 215–43. For the Begam Samru, see Brajendranath Bannerjee, *Begam Samru*, Calcutta, 1925. For the situation generally, see J. Sarkar, *Fall of the Mughal Empire*, Calcutta, 1950, vol. IV, especially chs 41, 46, 47.

[10] *Punjab Govt. Records, Delhi Residency and Agency Lahore*, 1911, p. iii, Report on the Revenue System of the Delhi Territory, 1820, par. 162, by I. Fortescue.

whoever won, were the villagers. It was they who paid the revenue which supplied the pay to the troops who would mutiny if it was withheld too long—say more than a year. It was they who were the objects of as many campaigns as avowed enemies in order to raise money for the next campaign. It was they whose lands were marched over, crops destroyed and houses looted if the fighting moved that way.

The area concerned was large and the particular forces involved usually small, but such conditions produced a general sense of insecurity along with detailed cases of oppression and disaster. This is how Charles Metcalfe described the state of affairs when the British took control in 1803, while defending his rule in 1811–18:[11]

> When the force at Dihlee was not sufficient to keep in awe the neighbouring villages; when the Resident's authority was openly defied within a few miles of that city; when it was necessary to draw a force from another district, and employ a battalion of infantry with guns, and a squadron of cavalry, to establish the authority of government in the immediate vicinity; when the detachment was kept on the alert by bodies of armed villagers menacing the pickets, and when sepoys who strayed were cut to pieces, when it was necessary to disarm villages; and when swords were literally turned into ploughshares; when every village was a den of thieves, and the city of Dihlee was parcelled out into shares to the neighbouring villages, of which each co-partnership monopolized the plunder of its allotted portion; when a company of infantry was necessary to attend the officer making the revenue settlement, and even that force was threatened with destruction, and taunted with the menace of having its muskets taken as playthings for the villagers' children; when to realize a single rupee of the settlement then concluded, purposely concluded on the lightest terms, it was necessary to employ a battalion of infantry with guns; when to subdue a single unfortified village a force of five battalions with cavalry and artillery, was decreed necessary, and when the villagers, instead of awaiting the assault, sallied forth against this force, and for an instant staggered the advancing columns by the briskness of their attitude—if that gentleman had been at Dihlee in those days he would probably have been more indulgent towards a system which had brought the Dihlee territory into the state in which it was at the end of 1818.

[11] J. W. Kaye, *Papers of Ld Metcalfe*, London, 1855, p. 55.

This description may be somewhat overdrawn, though all the incidents described undoubtedly occurred. What happened was that the villagers, being a vigorous and militant people when roused, fortified themselves and defied all comers, showing an independence which earned them from Metcalfe the epithet 'little republics'. They seized old *serais*, garden enclosures, or enclosed themselves with mud walls and thorn hedges. They were so enterprising that they sometimes mulcted the government *amils* or Agents instead of being fleeced by them. Nevertheless trade and cultivation went on, the condition being that merchants and travellers needed armed escorts, and had to bargain with the larger villages for safe conduct as formerly they had to bargain with officials at octroi posts. The traveller Twining journeyed to Delhi in 1794 without mishap. Everyone, he said, between Delhi and Agra was armed with a scimitar and a round, black shield.[12] Sir J. Malcolm's evidence from Malwa, an equally disturbed region, about insurance rates witnessed both to the insecurity by the inflation of the rates, and to the existence of trade by the fact of there being rates at all.[13] Much trade continued to move with the tribal carriers, the Banjaras, who were their own guards and equal to anything less than a large-scale premeditated attack. A material mark of these years was decay rather than destruction. There was in fact little to destroy in the countryside, such as railways, bridges or mansions. There were mosques and temples, but these were respected; there were the typical Muslim domed tombs, but these were already in ruins. There was a lack of new construction and a failure to maintain, through lack of means, so that the country must have had a very run-down appearance. A minor inconvenience, which Ghalib may have felt as a boy, was that you could not visit nor picnic at any of the monuments around either city without an escort for fear of being picked off by some lurking sharpshooter. In 1827, young Charles Trevelyan reported that lions still roamed to the north of Delhi in Hariana: 'Hurriana is famous for being the only part of India where lions are to be found.' (He evidently did not know about the Gujarat ones.) 'They are not perhaps quite so large or fierce as the African lion and their colour approaches

[12] T. Twining, *Travels in India a Hundred Years Ago*, London, 1893, p. 219.
[13] Sir J. Malcolm, *Memoir of Central India*, 3rd edition, London, 1832, vol. II, pp. 366–9.

nearer to a black than a red. Still they are formidable animals. Having intelligence of several, I hope with the assistance of my cavalry guard to do some execution among them.'[14]

The first thing which the British did was to restore order. The revenue was at first collected from resistant villagers by detachments of troops with the collector riding on an elephant. But they soon realized that the government pressure was steady as well as occasionally overpowering. Charles Metcalfe's discovery of the local village communities and his willingness to do business with their leaders, the *muqaddams* or village proprietors, greatly helped the process of pacification. One evidence of its success was the restoration of Ali Mardan's canal from the upper Jumna to Delhi. It was said that when the water flowed down the Chandni Chowk 'the people went out to meet it, and threw flowers into the stream'.[15] This canal transformed the country to the north of Delhi, so that John Lawrence in 1842 could write of riding 'for miles as through a highly cultivated garden'.[16] A second evidence was the gradual extension of houses beyond the city walls. At first the British built bungalows along the city wall from the Kashmir Gate southwards. The British deputy commissioner had his, with its classical portico and coat of arms, in Daryaganj.[17] Later they spread on the plain to the north of the city as far as the Ridge. Mahrauli became a country retreat for the Delhi gentry, with a palace for the Mughal, *dargahs* for the pious, a feast of *punkahs* in the rains for the people and abandoned Mughal tombs for conversion into European summer-houses.[18] Suburbs extended to Sabzimandi and Kishenganj and a new quarter was planned by Trevelyan, long known as Deputy *ganj*.

Metcalfe largely used Indian agency in his administration. He had rarely more than three European revenue officers, and on one occasion when reduced to one, wrote cheerfully that he could spare him too if government had need of him elsewhere.[19] He abolished

[14] Charles Trevelyan Papers. Letter of May 1827.

[15] Lord Ellenborough's Political Diary, 2 vols, London, 1881, vol. II, p. 157.

[16] *Selected Reports on the Revenue Settlements under Reg. IX, 1833, in Delhi Territory*, 2 vols, 1846. Report of J. Lawrence on the Sonepat district.

[17] Still to be seen in 1930.

[18] E.g. Mohd Quli Khan's and Adham Khan's.

[19] C. T. Metcalfe's *Report on Delhi Territory*, par. 88. See P. Spear, *Twilight of the Mughuls*, Cambridge, 1951, p. 88.

capital punishment and *suttee* within the Territory by executive decree; though he had the odd notion that you could discourage escapes from prison by doubling the sentences for each attempt, his administration was in general humane as well as firm. Some of his officers were original as well as independent. The French botanist Jacquemment wrote of William Fraser: '... he is half Asiatic in his habits, but in other respects a Scotch Highlander and an excellent man, with great originality of thought, a metaphysician to boot, and enjoying the best possible reputation of being a country bear.'[20] Land settlements it is true, were at first haphazard, and Fraser, who preferred Persian *ghazals* to measurements, was noted for over-assessments and a trail of deserted villages in his wake. Nevertheless there was order, if not to everyone's satisfaction, and growing prosperity.

In achieving this result Metcalfe, and indeed the inhabitants generally, knew that there was a strong reserve of military force. There was the cantonment at Meerut, forty miles from Delhi, with a British brigade, and there was the frontier station of Karnal, seventy miles to the north, later moved to Ambala. This faced Ranjit Singh's Sikhs but was also an effective reserve for dealing with civil disturbance. Reserve of military power made villagers amenable and police action effective. In Delhi itself there were no British troops, partly in deference to the feelings of the Mughal, still the implied though unacknowledged head of the Territory. But the Indian regiments in the cantonments beyond the Ridge (the present university site) had British officers, and these, with a gradually growing group of civil officers and subordinate Europeans and Eurasians, made up the European element. They had developed a miniature metropolitan life of their own, with the resident (later commissioner and agent) as its centre, Ludlow Castle as its Buckingham Palace, Metcalfe House as its Windsor, the Dilkusha at Mahrauli as its Sandringham, and St James' Church in Kashmir Gate for its cathedral. There were enough people in later years to support a local newspaper, the *Delhi Gazette*.[21] It was chiefly filled with local gossip and reprints from down country. Christmas was a time for coming in from the districts for special

[20] V. Jacquemment, *Letters from India*, 2 vols, London, 1834. To V. de Tracey, 11 January 1832, vol. II, p. 254.
[21] Files of this paper are to be seen in the Delhi Fort Museum.

celebration. 'Delhi', said Jacquemment, 'is the most hospitable place in India.'[22] By 1857 the British society consisted of the civil officers such as the collectors, magistrates and their assistants, the military officers, technical officers such as those dealing with roads, canals and medicine, and a group outside the charmed circle who mostly lived in Daryaganj, between the Red Fort and the Delhi Gate. It contained a few business people such as bank managers and merchants, and many subordinates, both European and Eurasians, who served the public offices and the new branches of the administration such as posts and telegraphs. On the fringe were people such as the descendants of adventurers like the Skinners and some Portuguese. For the most part this group lived a life apart from the city. They were connected by two rather frail bridges; one was the ex-adventuring families just mentioned, who had Persian tastes and some branches of whom became Muslim, and a few officials at the top who had Persian tastes whether of duty or inclination, and an interest in recent Indian history. The magistrate Prescott, with whom Ghalib consorted, was one of these, and so was Fraser, and so was the historian Henry Elliot. The group had its hardworking ornaments like Charles Trevelyan and John Lawrence, and its oddities like William Fraser and the German head of the Delhi College whose trousers were removed by his wife every night to prevent his wandering in the city.[23] The head of this society for eighteen years (1835–53) was Thomas Metcalfe, the lesser brother of Charles. He built Metcalfe House and presided with static dignity, periodically lamenting that he had been overlooked and passed over, particularly in the sending of John Lawrence (his junior) to the Punjab. He had a passion for Napoleon and collected his relics including a bust by Canova. All these disappeared into the hands of the Gujars, and it was said that a bust of the radical Lord Brougham was later found doing duty as a god at a local shrine. He adopted Napoleon's habit of pinching the ears, in his case of offenders, with mock indignation, first donning a pair of kid-gloves presented to him on a silver salver.[24] He thought oranges and mangoes messy, so that his daughter used

[22] V. Jacquemment, op. cit., vol. I, p. 189.

[23] P. Spear, op. cit., p. 165. Hardcastle Papers.

[24] Hardcastle Papers, *In Great Grandmother's Days*, Autobiography of Lady Clive Bayley, pp. 20 and 33.

to eat them at the top of the Qutab Minar with Richard Lawrence, in order that the traces could be removed in time when his buggy appeared on the dusty road from the city. His daughter Emily thus described him:[25]

> He was not a tall man, I should think about five feet eight inches, but well-made.... His hair was gray and he was bald on the top of his head; his eyes were blue, a straight nose, well-formed mouth, with often a whimsical expression on it.... He was very sprightly in all his movements and had a very pleasant voice.... His clothes...were made by a first-class London tailor, Pulford in St James' Street, and were sent out regularly every year....
>
> Everything was ordered with the greatest punctuality.... After he had had his breakfast, his Hookah was brought in and placed behind his chair. It stood on an embroidered carpet worked for him by some lady friends and was a beautiful erection in itself. The stand was of solid silver about eighteen inches in diameter at the bottom, and the cup for the sweet-smelling tobacco mixture which he smoked, of beautifully embossed silver, with silver chains hanging from it. The snake-like pipe was from about six to eight feet long and the mouth piece at the end of it was exquisitely wrought in silver.... The gurgle of the Hookah still rings in my ears.
>
> His carriage always appeared punctually at ten o'clock, under the Portico. He passed through a row of servants on his way to the carriage, one holding his hat, another his gloves, another his hand-kerchief, another his gold-headed cane, and another his despatch-box. These were put in the carriage, his Jemada mounted beside the coachman and he drove away with two *syces* (or grooms) standing up behind.

More important than the loan of the *hookah* was the cult of the Mughal dignitary or *omrah*. The up-country Europeans seem to have fallen into this insensibly and certainly without acknowledge-ment. Indeed, a few exceptions apart, they became more aggres-sively British as time went on. The omrah had his town house and his country retreat in the form of a walled garden within which a family tomb might be built. He lived in state with many retainers. Some of the British may have fancied themselves as country gentlemen; but what they actually produced was the air of the omrah. Sir David Ochterloney, twice resident of Delhi, built classical mansions wherever he went of which that of Karnal later in the possession of the Liaqat Ali Khan branch of the Karnal family,

[25] Ibid., p. 20.

survives. He had one in Delhi near Azadpur which has disappeared.[26] The resident used Dara Shikoh's palace in Kashmir Gate. Charles Metcalfe built a garden house in the overgrown Shalimar gardens with a smaller villa for his private work which was still standing a few years ago.[27] Colebrooke built the house later known as Hindu Rao's. Skinner of Hansi had his classical town house in Kashmir Gate complete with marble bathroom in the Mughal style and Bengali-style apartments for the ladies.[28] Indeed, he went one better than the rest by building St James' Church opposite his house, as nawwabs would build mosques.

In 1829 Delhi was convulsed by the suspension and ultimate dismissal of the resident, Sir Edward Colebrooke. It was a David and Goliath contest for his accuser was a young civilian only two years in service, by name Charles Trevelyan.[29] Within the service the event was a confrontation of the old outlook and the new. But it shook the city as well for Sir Edward had many connections with the gentry and, with his son, others less defensible with the city financiers, including the leading banker, Joti Prasad. However necessary it may have been to put a stop to Sir Edward's methods of administration, the result of the crisis was to draw the British further apart from Indian society. The utilitarian query, on surveying the old world of Mughal Delhi, of to what purpose is this waste, became louder and more widespread. The distinction between 'them' and 'us' became sharper.

The city itself was prosperous, being the distributing centre for the northern trade to the east and south. By 1852 it had about 160,000 inhabitants.[30] Within it there lived the merchants, the financiers, the learned and the dependants of the court. Of the 2104 *salatin* or descendants of the emperors listed in 1852, a considerable proportion lived outside the Fort walls.[31] The neighbouring nawwabs

[26] A picture of this house exists in a book compiled by Sir T. T. Metcalfe in 1844 for his daughters, entitled *Reminiscences of Imperial Delhi*. This is in the J. M. Ricketts collection in the India Office Library.

[27] For a sketch of the remains of this villa, see P. Spear, op. cit., p. 164.

[28] For many years used by the Hindu College in Delhi.

[29] For an account of this incident, see my *Twilight of the Mughuls*, Cambridge, 1951, ch. 8.

[30] *Punjab Government Records, Delhi Residency and Agency*, Lahore, 1911, p. 431. Statement by Sir T. T. Metcalfe based on a Mughal statement, 1848.

[31] Ibid.

and rajas had town houses for their occasional visits. Since political power was denied them, the well-born turned their attention to where the last Mughal emperors held full sway within the Red Fort. Looked at with hindsight the pre-Mutiny pageantry has a dreamlike quality as though it never actually existed. It was the product of a group pretending that a dead past still existed because they had nothing to look forward to. And if the dream ended in a nightmare of violence, at least, while it lasted, it provided amusement, diversion and some mental refreshment to the people. The court held its regular *durbars* in the Diwan-i Khas, but what struck the imagination of the people at large were the frequent public ceremonies and processions. On the great festivals the emperor would parade the streets on his elephant, the ministers, the heir-apparent and the Mirzas in their places. A straggle of foot soldiers went in front and behind; musicians sounded trumpets and rhapsodists recited the imperial praises—a slightly tarnished and tawdry assembly perhaps, and raucous to the ear, but cheerful and colourful and much appreciated.[32] The royal elephants moved constantly about, one frightening the horse of a buggy which threw out two British officers on the road to the Qutab. No injuries were received, but, said the report: 'The gentlemen were very angry.'[33] The emperor would march to the Jama Masjid on important occasions and usually sacrificed a camel at Id. Hindu festivals, including Holi, were also observed, as Mughal miniatures testify, and there was the Persian custom of ceremonial weighing against seven kinds of grain, gold and coral (in the heyday of the empire it had been gold, silver and precious stones) on the Persian Nauroz or New Year's Day. Communal relations, though they hardly reached the height of fraternity suggested by C. F. Andrews in his book on Zaka-ullah,[34] seem to have been generally good. The city was about equally divided between Hindus and Muslims. Each had an extremist wing and each its action groups. The Muslims had the butchers at hand and the Hindus the Jats with their *lathis* who would readily come in from the countryside at call. But the court in general favoured peace; Bahadur Shah employed the Christian

[32] The details can be seen in contemporary Mughal paintings and drawings.

[33] National Archives of India, Foreign Dept. Misc. Political, vol. 361. *Palace Intelligence, Delhi 1851–54*, 22 August 1851.

[34] C. F. Andrews. *Zaka ullah of Delhi*, Cambridge, 1929. pp. 15–17.

doctor Chiman Lal as one of his physicians. Then there was the influential Kayastha community, the hereditary servants of the empire, who acted as a bridge between the two faiths. Over fifty years I have found no record of a communal riot, and only one of a dispute which reached the lieutenant-governor. The running dialogue concerned the desired extension of the right to sacrifice cows on the part of some Muslims and Hindu resistance.

The court was not merely a show, if only a tawdry one. Firstly, it exercised a positive influence in three directions. It was a school of manners and etiquette, Bahadur Shah himself being noted for his punctiliousness in this respect. The 'old-world dignity and courtesy' often praised by travellers and visitors as one of India's virtues, stemmed from this centre and affected Muslims and Hindus alike. Long after Delhi had ceased to be the Paris of power it continued as the Versailles of good manners. Secondly, it continued the royal tradition of patronizing the arts. Not much could be done for architecture from lack of money, though both Akbar and Bahadur Shah erected some modest buildings. Bahadur Shah was fond of gardens, the Roshanara and Qudsia in particular, and laid out one of his own at Shahdara. But with fine arts the case was different. Calligraphy, that most distinctive of Islamic arts, flourished, and so did painting, whose patronage extended from royalty through the nobles to the British. Jivan Ram was a leading painter,[35] and the school has left a legacy of miniature portrait paintings on paper and ivory, of court scenes and royal processions. It was a dying art perhaps, but attractive in a subdued and rather plaintive way. The most favoured, however, was poetry. It was the major intellectual occupation of the Delhi classes, both in the Persian and Urdu idioms. The poetical contests at the literary assemblies or *mushairas*, at which the emperor himself would sometimes preside, were major social events, and the spectators would experience something of the euphoria of a cup-tie. Literary controversies were a substitute for political ones and their factions for political parties. It was unfortunate that Bahadur Shah was too involved himself under the pen-name Zafar, to be an impartial judge. The irreverent whispered that his own poems owed much to the polishing of Zauq; hence that poet's firm hold on the laureateship.

[35] W. H. Sleeman, *Rambles and Recollections of an Indian Official*, London, 1844, ch. 2, p. 285.

The world of Islamic learning had the Delhi College for a centre, and here, after an English department had been added to the existing Oriental, something of a Muslim renaissance began in the late forties and fifties. There was a sudden enthusiasm for western knowledge, especially scientific, and the first sign of recognition of, and interest in, a new world beyond that of Islam among the Indian Muslims. Munshi Zaka-ullah[36] is the best-known product of this period but it was perhaps no accident that Sayyid Ahmad Khan, then a young man, was in Delhi compiling his *Asar-us-Sanadid*.[37] Other members of the school like Nazir Ahmad, joined the Sayyid later in his Aligarh movement.

Behind this show and mild intellectualism there was a background of decay and corruption. Beyond the solemn decorum of the Diwan-i Khas, hundreds of *salatin* or imperial descendants lived in squalor. They had pensions of Rs 5 or less per month and they spent their time in gambling on cockfights or bemoaning their lot. In the city there was an underworld of vice stimulated by idleness and frustration. This same consuming frustration, with its urge to make the most of what little there was, produced an atmosphere of intrigue, of faction and of bitterness. Munshi Zaka-ullah in his old age declared: 'People speak of "the good old times"; but those times, as a whole, were not good, when they are compared with the days in which we are now living. They were full of corruption and decay.'[38]

This world of mediatized sovereignty, of Weimar-like elegance against a back-cloth of squalor and despair, a Mughal sunset glow, might have faded imperceptibly into the night of oblivion. It had already been arranged to move the court to Mahrauli while modern influences were increasingly playing upon the city. But the after-glow was extinguished by a thunderstorm of violence; the Mughal dream ended in nightmare. With it the world of Ghalib and his contemporaries crashed around them, never to be the same again. The crisis came on the morning of 11 May 1857, when the mutineers from Meerut took over the city and were joined by the regiments in the Delhi cantonment. Bahadur Shah was unwillingly made the titular head of the movement and Delhi was held for a

[36] See C. F. Andrews, op. cit.
[37] First published 1847.
[38] C. F. Andrews, op. cit.

little more than four months, until the storm of 14–20 September. It was a time of acute discomfort and great suffering for most of the citizens. No one except some discontented Mirzas, for whom anything was a relief from the tedium of life, and the more fanatical of the *maulvis*, really wanted a rebellion. The king's adviser, Hakim Ahsanullah Khan, was scandalized; the gentry lost their rents and peaceful *durbars*, the literati their audiences and personal contests. A wave of terror swept the city; anyone being suspected of sympathy with the British or tainted with Christianity was in danger of his life. Ghalib was one of these and he lived in great danger both during the siege and after the city's capture. The mercantile community fared no better for it was subject to looting by the soldiery and exactions by the royal government. As the situation worsened, suspicion, panic and disorder increased. It should be remembered that the *gardi* or calamity which followed the recapture of the city was preceded by the *gardi* of the actual mutineer occupation. In both cases it was the citizen who received the blame and who suffered the blows. If the British could have controlled their troops after the storm they would have found a grateful populace ready to welcome them. If they had been content to blockade the city a little longer, it must have surrendered for want of food.[39] In either case the disaster of Delhi's desolation and the feelings that went with it would have been avoided.

As it was, the horror of the rebel occupation was eclipsed by the greater horror of the British restoration. During the siege the city was short of food and at the end threatened with famine; many went in fear of their lives from denunciation as friends of the British; and all suffered from looting as each new batch of distraught soldiery arrived in the city. But afterwards the storm of seven days passed into a sack, accentuated by the troops' discovery of large stocks of liquor in the 'Europe' shops. It was at this time that Ghalib's mentally sick brother, Yusuf, was shot by a British soldier.[40] The whole population was driven out and was still in the open on the brink of the cold weather in December. Then the

[39] P. Spear, op. cit., pp. 209–10. Most of the evidence comes from the *Mutiny Papers* in the India Office Library and Indian accounts of the siege.

[40] *Two Native Narratives of the Mutiny in Delhi*, London, p. 72. Ghalib's own account, however, differs from this. See Russell and Islam, *Ghalib, Life and Letters*, London, 1969, pp. 123ff.

Hindus were allowed to return. Nothing like normality returned until well into 1858. Next, there were the penal measures. For months there were five or six hangings a day. A special commission with summary power sentenced 372 to death and fifty-seven to life imprisonment. The victims of irregular action were far greater— stray figures shot by officers on the prowl, like the twenty-one villagers because their village had handed a servant of Sir J. Metcalfe to the mutineers, and those who were mistaken for someone else, or not mistaken at all and just shot. After this violence came the demolitions and the violations of the palace and mosques. The whole built-up area between the Fort and the Jama Masjid was destroyed to give the Fort a field of fire. A complex system of tickets for compensation did not prevent much hardship, or touch the extensive confiscations of property throughout the city.[41] In the palace the Diwan-i Am was turned into a hospital and the Diwan-i Khas into an officers' mess. The Zinat-ul Masjid became a bakery until Lord Curzon's time. Both the Jama and the Fatehpuri mosques were seized, and there were loud cries for the former's destruction.

During the last years of Ghalib's life the city slowly recovered from this hammer-blow. It was not till 1872 that the population approached the pre-Mutiny figure. Culturally the Mutiny was a mortal thrust. The Mughal family, with Mirza Illahi Baksh at its head, survived, but there was no pageantry, no *durbars*, no patronage of the arts. Delhi was a depressed provincial city still numb with communal shock. Only the merchants and those linked with the British prospered. Can it be wondered that Ghalib retreated more and more within himself, that his gaze was fixed on eternity rather than on earth and that his themes were disillusioned and tragic? The citizens could neither enjoy the present nor look back with pleasure on the past. A generation was to pass before they really began to look forward with confidence into a new world.

---

[41] P. Spear, op. cit., pp. 221–2 and ch. 9 for the whole paragraph.

GHALIB'S

Poetry

PART II

Getting to Know Ghalib

Ralph Russell

GHALIB (1797–1869) IS ONE of the greatest poets South Asia ever produced and, in my view, the greatest poet of two of its greatest literary languages, Persian and Urdu. Persian is, of course, not a South Asian language but it was for centuries the administrative and literary language not only of its homeland, Iran, but also of a much wider area, including most of South Asia where Muslim dynasties ruled, just as Latin was the literary language of medieval Europe. About a century before Ghalib began to write, it had yielded place to Urdu as the accepted medium of poetry, but Ghalib was one of those who regretted this change and continued to write in Persian as well as in the new medium. If his language had been English, he would long ago have been recognized all over the world as a great poet, and this book is an attempt to present some of his poetry in English dress so that English speakers may be able to judge his work for themselves. This means that its intended audience is primarily those who have English as their mother tongue—in Britain, the USA and all the other countries where this is the case. But it is aimed also at those speakers of other languages who know English well. These include many who live in South Asia, Ghalib's homeland, but have languages other than Urdu as their mother tongue. It is also for those numerous people

who come from Urdu-speaking families in India and Pakistan who
saw fit to send their children to English-medium schools or from
families which settled in English-speaking countries and whose
children and grandchildren have grown up in circumstances which
have made English their first language and denied them the
opportunity to master the language of their cultural identity.

I hope the book will appeal also to many who know Urdu well.
Because it presents Ghalib's Persian verse as well as those in Urdu,
it should be of value to the many Urdu speakers who do not know
Persian or, when they do, do not know it well enough to read and
appreciate Persian poetry in the original. Addressing so wide an
audience gives rise to some problems, for some readers will need
information that others do not. For this reason, I have compiled
a very detailed Explanatory Index and shall explain below how I
hope readers will use it.

The fact that Ghalib wrote in Urdu and Persian is not the only
thing that stands in the way of the modern English-speaking reader
who is interested in making the acquaintance of his poetry. Like
poets of other ages and other countries, he shared with his readers
a fund of knowledge and tradition which English readers one
hundred and fifty years later do not possess. For instance, the same
is true of Milton. His contemporaries who read *Paradise Lost,* with
its frequent references to the Bible and the legends of Greece and
Rome, were familiar with these stories to a far greater extent than
modern readers are. Modern readers of both poets therefore need
to be told things which no one in their contemporary audience
needed to be told.

Of course, as is the case with all great poets, there is much in
Ghalib that needs no such explanations. Some of the best of his
verse deals with themes that are universal, themes that have been,
and probably always will be, intelligible everywhere. He expresses
them in a form called the ghazal, in which a simple thought or
feeling is encapsulated in a single couplet of the poem.

Sleep is for him, and pride for him, and nights for him
Upon whose arm your tresses all dishevelled lay

Parting and meeting—each of them has its distinctive joy
Leave me a thousand times: come back a hundred thousand times

Not one created atom here but what is destined to decay
The sun on high a lamp that flutters in the windy street

Desires in thousands—each so strong it takes away my breath anew
And many longings were fulfilled—many, but even so, too few

The steed of life runs on. None knows where it will stay its course
The reins have fallen from our hands, the stirrups from our feet

Other verses are no less effective, provided that the reader understands the allusions that occur in them, and this understand- ing is what the Explanatory Index is intended to supply. Ghalib wrote within a Muslim tradition, for an audience who had grown up in that tradition, and his verse is therefore full of Muslim concepts, stories, references to aspects of the Muslim way of life, etc. As will become clear, he was far from orthodox both in his practice and in his own understanding of religion, and the thoughts he expresses through such verses are challenging and relevant to people of any religion or none. But to appreciate them, the reader needs to understand what his Muslim readers would understand by the people and situations he refers to.

Some of these are not too difficult for people familiar with stories that occur in the Bible, for many biblical characters also occur in the Quran, and in many respects what the Quran relates of them corresponds with the biblical accounts. But there are important differences too. In the first place, Islam classifies many of them, from Adam onwards, as prophets. Then there are often additional stories about these characters in the Quran. For instance, Adam has an importance which the Bible does not give him. Islam teaches that God decided to create Adam to be his 'vicegerent' on Earth. (This rather unusual word has connotations which includes those of 'deputy', 'representative' or 'agent' but which none of these words fully conveys.) He told the angels of his intention, said that Adam (and by implication, his descendants) would rank above the angels, and that they must therefore prostrate themselves before him. A leading angel, Iblis (also called Shaitan, a word akin to our 'Satan') refused to do this and was banished forever from God's presence.

Ghalib, like many other ghazal poets, uses Adam as a symbol for humankind as a whole and asks God why He treats so badly those to whom He himself gave so exalted a status. He does so more boldly than most. It is a reference to the story of Adam and Iblis when he writes:

Today we are abased. Why so? For yesterday you would not brook
The insolence the angel showed towards our majesty

Other prophets who came after Adam include Ibrahim (recognizable as the biblical Abraham) and Musa (known in the Bible as Moses). In both cases, many things in the Islamic tradition related of them will be unfamiliar to many readers, but in the Explanatory Index will be found all the information needed to understand all such references in Ghalib's verse.

There are references too to other figures whose names do not occur either in the Bible or the Quran. For instance, Ghalib writes:

I am not bound to take the path that Khizar indicates
I'll think an old man comes to bear me company on my way

The couplet means nothing until one knows who Khizar was; once this is known, it becomes a very significant one. It is related of Khizar that he was able to explain to a perplexed Musa some of God's inscrutable deeds. It is said of him that he accompanied Sikandar (the Muslim name for Alexander the Great) on a search for a spring, hidden in deep darkness, of the 'water of life'. He found it (Sikandar did not) and drank of it and thus has eternal life. He wanders in the wilderness and guides travellers who have lost their way back onto the correct path. Khizar is thus a figure greatly revered by Muslims and one whose guidance is infallible. I don't think it infallible, says Ghalib. I have to find my own way in life, and I have the resources to do that.

Khizar is one of a number of names which figure in Ghalib's allusions. Wherever they do appear, the Explanatory Index will provide all that the reader needs to know about them and so should always be referred to whenever an unfamiliar reference arises.

This book is about Ghalib's poetry. Some readers may want to know more about the man and his times. *Ghalib: Life and Letters*, by myself and Khurshidul Islam (Oxford University Press India, 1994), gives the full story of his life, told largely in his own words. A good shorter book is Pavan K. Varma's *Ghalib: The Man, the Times* (Penguin India, 1989). Those who wish to know more about Urdu literature as a whole can read two books by myself: *Hidden in the Lute* (Carcanet and Penguin India, 1995), an anthology of two centuries of Urdu literature in English translation; and *The Pursuit of Urdu Literature: A Select History* (Zed Books, London and Oxford University Press India, 1992). *Hidden in the Lute* was republished in 1999 as *An Anthology of Urdu Literature*.

Ghalib and the Ghazal

This book deals with the poetry which Ghalib wrote in the ghazal form. This is one of a number of traditional genres which came originally from Arabic and was then adopted in Persian and, later still, in Urdu. The ghazal was the most important of these. It was in this form that Ghalib wrote almost all of his Urdu and a substantial part of his Persian verse. It is still by far the most popular of the traditional genres. The ghazal consists of a series of couplets, every one of which encapsulates a complete theme. Sometimes the theme is continued in other couplets, as for example, in these seven couplets (from a ghazal of thirteen) in which Ghalib warns those who would dedicate their lives to the pleasures of wine and music.

> Newcomers to the assembly of the heart's desires
> Beware, if it is wine and music that you seek!
> Look well at me, if only you have eyes to see
> Listen to me, if you have ears to hear me speak
> The saki's charm will steal away your faith, your wits
> The minstrel's song will rob you of your sense, your powers
> At night you see the carpet laden all with bloom
> A gardener's apron, filled with fresh, sweet-scented flowers
> The saki walks, the flute plays on enchantingly
> Heaven to the eyes, paradise to the ears of all
> Come in the morning; look at the assembly then
> Life, joy, wine, music—all are gone beyond recall
> Bearing the scar of parting from its erstwhile friends
> One silent candle, burnt out, shows you how it ends

In the typical case, however, the ghazal is a poem in which a close unity of form (which I shall explain later) stands, to the English reader, in startling contrast with a complete disunity of content. Every couplet is normally a completely independent, self-contained entity, and the poet's mood may change completely from couplet to couplet. Only exceptionally is a couplet linked in a connected statement to one or more of those immediately following.

There are solid reasons for this switching from mood to mood which are not obvious to readers whose normal mode of encountering poetry is reading it. That was not, and still is not, the way in which the Urdu lover of poetry (and almost every Urdu speaker was, and is, one) encounters the ghazal. It is significant that in Urdu idiom you don't *write* verse; you *say* verse; and the poet who 'says' it presents it to his audience by reciting it to them. Only later does it appear in print. The verse has always been presented in a *musha'ira*, that is, a gathering, sometimes small, sometimes quite large, at which numbers of poets assemble to recite their verse. An element of competition among them has always been present (especially when, as was often the case in Ghalib's day, the host of the gathering prescribed beforehand a half-line of verse which had to be incorporated in their own poems by all the poets attending, with both metre and rhyme prescribed for them). Each couplet is assessed by its hearers as the poet recites it, and approval, indifference or disapproval is politely but unmistakably expressed. Clearly, poets who compose in this tradition need qualities which those who compose for a tradition of written transmission do not need at all. Besides the essential qualities of a poet they need, if they are to make their mark, something of the talents of an orator, a debater and an actor. They must be able to hold their audience, and hold it, moreover, in competition with their fellow poets; and they must be able to react swiftly and sensitively to the audience's changing moods. The *musha'ira* is a long-drawn-out affair and the poets' main enemy is monotony. If they are to participate effectively in a *musha'ira* which will perhaps last for hours together, they cannot hope to do so without resort to variety. The audience knows as soon as the first couplet has been recited what the metre and the rhyme scheme are. Unless the ghazal is one of quite exceptional force, uniformity of tone and emotional pitch is likely to pall.

The ghazal is a short poem, but though it rarely comprises less than five couplets or more than twelve, its length is not strictly prescribed. But almost everything else is. Its rhyme scheme is AA, BA, CA, DA and so on. That is, the first couplet is a rhyming one but the others are not. However, the same rhyme as that of the first couplet recurs in the second line of all the others. The rhyme normally has two parts, called respectively, in the usual English translation of the Urdu terms, 'rhyme' and 'end rhyme'—the rhyme being the actual rhyming word and the end rhyme the words, identical in the second lines of each couplet, which follow it. The end rhyme may sometimes be quite long. Thus Mir, Ghalib's great eighteenth-century predecessor, has a couplet:

Perhaps the flower in spring compares with you
Yet what created thing compares with you?

in which 'spring' and 'thing' is rhyme and 'compares with you' is end rhyme. This feature of end rhyme, particularly when, as in the above example, it is a long one, makes an enormous appeal to the audience at a *musha'ira*, for quite often they can see what the ending of the second line of the couplet will be and will recite it along with the poet. Everyone who has seen it happening knows how much they enjoy this.

A ghazal may be written in any metre, but once the poet has chosen a metre it must be followed without variation throughout. In the last couplet of the ghazal, the poet has to include his *takhallus*, his pen-name. Ghalib is such a pen-name. (His actual name was Asadullah Khan.) The *takhallus* is used in a number of ways. It can be the third person subject of a sentence ('Ghalib goes...' or 'Ghalib says...', etc.). Sometimes someone else is addressing Ghalib ('Ghalib, you must not...'). But one also often finds 'Ghalib, I...' or 'Ghalib...me...' where the 'Ghalib' and the 'I' or the 'me' are one and the same person. For instance, this is the case in the following couplet, which the poet recited to his royal patron:

Ghalib, if he will take me with him on the Pilgrimage
His Majesty may have my share of heavenly reward

It is not often possible to reproduce all these features of the ghazal in English translation, and there are special difficulties where rhyme is concerned, for where Urdu has rhyming words in great abundance, English notoriously does not. But a few examples in which something like end rhyme has been achieved can perhaps convey to the English reader something of the effect which the form of the original ghazal exercises upon its Urdu hearers. It should be remembered that, as each couplet is read, it is expected to be completely independent in meaning.

The world is but a game that children play before my eyes
A spectacle that passes night and day before my eyes

True, I am lost in self-esteem, in self-display. Why not?
In all her radiant beauty she sits there before my eyes

My faith restrains me while the lure of unbelief attracts me
That way, the Kaba: and, this way, the Church before by eyes

In the last couplet, the Kaba, the building in Mecca where Muslims go for pilgrimage, stands for Islam. The church symbolizes unbelief because 'unbelief' to a Muslim includes not only irreligiousness but also adherence to religions other than Islam.

> You stand away, and purse your lips, and show their rose-bud form
> I said, 'How do you kiss?' Come, kiss my lips and say, 'Like this!'

> How should I not sit silent facing her in her assembly?
> Her silence is itself enough to tell me, 'Sit like this!'

> If people say, 'Can Urdu then put Persian verse to shame?'
> Recite a line of Ghalib's verse and tell them, 'Yes! Like this!'

> At least you have the thorns of grief and yearning to behold her
> Love cannot pluck the flowers of heart's desire? Then be it so!

> You who seek wine, if need be put your lips straight to the cask
> Today there is no saki there to pour it? Be it so

> I do not long for people's praise; I seek no one's reward
> And if they say my verses have no meaning, be it so

> Treasure the joy of life spent in the company of fair women
> Ghalib, though you may not live life's full span. Well, be it so!

This last example illustrates a feature that is sometimes found in the ghazal; namely, a unity of mood. Each couplet stands on its own but the 'be it so' of the end rhyme conveys that *all* the couplets speak of the need to come to terms with situations which fall short of what one would like but with which one must nevertheless be content.

The Major Theme of the Ghazal: Love

As has been shown, the range of possible themes in the ghazal is almost infinite, for any thought which can be encapsulated in a simple couplet is, so to speak, eligible for inclusion in it. Nonetheless, its major theme is love. (The word 'ghazal' itself originally meant something like 'conversation between lovers'.)

In the ghazal, the poet-lover expresses his passionate, all-consuming love for his beloved.[1] In couplets throughout his

[1] The ghazal poet speaks in the person of a male lover, but the poetry is more concerned with the passion than with the sex of the person who feels it, and can make as great an appeal to a woman as to a man. (By contrast, in much of Hindu love poetry, the poet speaks in the person of a woman

ghazals, Ghalib writes of being overwhelmed by love, of power-lessness in the face of love, of the joy of loving even if one's love is not returned, the even greater joy if it is returned; he also speaks of the compulsion to love, even if she whom he loves spurns him, violates all the religious commands of the community in which he and she live or, having once loved him, is not true to him.

> No one can govern love, Ghalib. This is a kind of fire
> No one can kindle; and, once kindled, no one can put out
>
> All that she is puts Ghalib's soul in turmoil
> All that she says, and hints, and looks, and does
>
> With only half your charm you lay the base of a new world
> A new earth is created and new heavens start to turn
>
> He who sits in the shade of his beloved's wall
> Is lord and king of all the realm of Hindustan
>
> I shall write to you even without cause
> Simply to write your name fills me with love
>
> Without you, just as wine within the glass is parted from it
> My soul is in my body, but is not a part of it
>
> No, she does not bow down to God
>   Yes, she is faithless too. Now go!
> If I had prized my heart and faith
>   Would I have gone into her lane?

At the same time he can treat the experience of love in all its aspects, including his own experience of it, as though he was outside it all, looking at it with the humorous detachment of a sympathetic but somewhat sceptical non-participant observer. In this respect, he is breaking with the tradition of the ghazal poets, and this sceptical eye is seen by Urdu speakers as something characteristically Ghalib.

For instance, he uses in a new way the traditional image of the nightingale, the symbol of the passionate lover, and of the rose, the symbol of his indifferent beloved.

---

expressing her passionate love for a man. In both traditions the poet may in fact be either a man or a woman, and in neither tradition do poets, listeners or readers of either sex feel that the poetry is alien to them.)

All that the nightingale can do provokes the rose's laughter
What we call love is really a derangement of the mind

On occasion, Ghalib ridicules the idea—standard in the ghazal—
that love is synonymous with adoration of the beloved:

To think desire is adoration is to be a fool
How should I *worship* her who treats me with such tyranny?

He tells lovers, himself included:

You gave your heart away. Why then lament your loss
    in plaintive song?
You have a breast without a heart. Why not a mouth
    without a tongue?

His love for his mistress is unshakeable, and is proof against
indifference, contempt and cruelty alike. But this does not mean
that he cannot put her in her place and claim his own rights from
her.

To every word that I utter you answer, 'What are you?'
You tell me: is this the way then I should be spoken to?

'It is not love, but madness.' Be it so
My madness is your reputation, though

In other words, it is because I am your lover that people so admire
you.

One as beautiful as she is bound to have many suitors for her
love and she has a right to test them all. But this is a right she can
no longer claim once she has made her choice.

If this is testing, can you tell me what would persecution be?
It is to him you show your favour. Why then are you testing *me?*

Much of this contrasts strikingly with other expressions of love
which are standard in the ghazal poets, including Ghalib, and which
are baffling to modern readers who do not know the background
to them. Two essential features of this need spelling out at greater
length. First, the love which the ghazal portrays is all illicit love. The
poet's beloved may be someone else's fiancée or wife or a courtesan
or a boy, and in South Asian society, such lovers have faced drastic
penalties. Secondly, and perhaps even more unexpected to western

readers, she (or he) may not be a human beloved at all. The poet may be expressing his love for God or for any ideal in life to which he commits himself absolutely and for which he is prepared, if necessary, to sacrifice his life. The poet needs a language and a symbolism which enables him to speak on all these levels of meaning at the same time. It is also necessary to understand the setting of love in the society in which the ghazal poet lived.

Love in South Asian Society

Passionate love, in all societies, may entail suffering and distress. In the kind of society that produced the Persian and the Urdu ghazal, it invariably and inevitably did. The very much more fortunate twentieth-century lover who was born and brought up in one of the countries of the modern West can best envisage the situation of the lover in the ghazal if we compare it with what a black lover of a white beloved or a white lover of a black beloved can face in societies such as South Africa or the southern states of the USA. These must live in the knowledge that their love will bring pain, shame and anger to almost all around them, and not least to those whom they themselves hold most dear—their parents and their family. This anger may be so intense as to drive those who feel it to murder; the lovers know this to be the case and feel that they live their lives in constant danger.

In the social setting of the ghazal, it is not considerations of race or colour that give rise to these intense, bitter, distressful and distressing feelings, but the fear, no less strong and all-pervading, of a love which is seen, in just the same way, as subversive of the very foundations of ordered society and of all the traditions upon which its whole way of life is based. For the ghazal is the poetry of what may loosely be called a medieval society, that is, a society of static ideals; its structure is hierarchical, its ideal 'a place for everyone and everyone in his place', its norms of conduct strictly prescribed, sanctioned by centuries of unquestioned tradition, explicitly founded upon a final, eternally valid religious revelation and enforced by the overwhelming pressure of public opinion.

In such a society, whether European or Asian, marriage has nothing to do with passionate, romantic love. Marriage is an alliance between families and its aim is to maintain the social status, the purity of lineage and the standards of social and economic security

which the families of the boy and girl who are to be married have
been accustomed to. The arrangement of such a marriage is con-
sidered to be far too important a matter to be left to youngsters and
requires maturity, experience and skills which they cannot possibly
possess. What they do possess—and this may have unfortunate
consequences—is the sexual appetite and the desire to be in love
which develop in every girl and boy, and all responsible parents
feel it to be their duty to arrange a suitable marriage for them
before their emotions lead them astray. Early marriage, and even
earlier betrothal, of a kind so binding that it can be broken only at
the cost of great scandal, have always been favoured. Society has
reckoned (and with more justification than those who are the
products of western society tend to think) that provision for the
satisfaction of sexual desire within marriage is enough to keep
most couples reasonably happy and forestall the possibility of
major upheavals in the family's emotional life. It has also reckoned
(again with considerable justification) that courtship after marriage
can result in just as satisfactory an outcome as courtship before
marriage. It won't generally produce in the married couple the
passionate, all-consuming love that the ghazal celebrates, but no-
body wants it to, and if in exceptional cases it does, everyone
would much rather not know about it, because such love is by
definition dangerous, and, normally, a menace to the foundations
of ordered social life.

Unfortunately for medieval society, arrangements that work well
enough for most people do not work well for everybody. In the
first place, parents do not always manage to arrange their sons' and
daughters' marriages in time to forestall their falling in love. And
even when they do, marriage does not always obviate the danger
of one or other of the partners seeking and finding love elsewhere.
Even at the level of sheer sexual desire, the attraction of someone
else may prevail over that which you feel for your partner, and
sexual desire itself, however closely it is allied to love, is not the
same as love and cannot satisfy fully the desire to love. So marriage
is not always an adequate safeguard against love.

In a society where early marriage was the norm, it followed that
in the typical case, any girl who was physically capable of love was
either married or betrothed by a binding agreement between two
families. And in South Asian Muslim society, she was in any case
kept in the strictest seclusion by the institution of *parda* (purdah)

so that no male outside her closest kin could so much as see her face. If another male did see her, fell in love with her and acted accordingly, he provoked a degree of anger and outrage which could well endanger his life. The girl herself, who knew the danger to her reputation and honour which his love necessarily brought, would often hate him for loving her, and even if she returned his love, would feel that she must put him to the severest of tests before she could trust herself to him.

Opportunities for the lovers' meeting were rare, and, in the typical case, the prospect of permanent union non-existent. And since the lovers themselves in the last resort accepted the social code that condemned them, love was a tragedy for all concerned. It is this intense, stressful love that provides the dominant themes of the ghazal.

In real life, the poet may well have not dared to allow himself to love a woman betrothed or married to someone else, for the deterrents against love which purdah society had at its disposal were generally quite effective enough to make most of its members hold back from so dangerous a love. In such a case, he used his poetry to create a beautiful fantasy beloved for himself and his readers. But this is not to say that most poets had nothing more than a fantasy experience of love. Other possibilities existed.

First, as in any other society where the sexes are strictly segregated, love found one outlet in homosexuality, and one of the 'beloveds' of the Urdu ghazal is a beautiful boy. Most Urdu poets must have had at least some emotional experience of homosexual love and this experience will have been part of the raw material of their poetry. In the cultured society of Ghalib's day, such love, strongly condemned though it was in orthodox Islam, was commonplace and in practice evoked no hostile reaction. Two of Ghalib's letters bear striking testimony to this fact. In one he speaks with strong disapproval of a man who, for love of a boy, has left his wife ('Is this any way to go on—to leave his wife for a boy?'). But it is not because he loves a boy that he is rebuked but because he has left his wife.[2] In the second letter, a passing reference to homosexual love is even more matter-of-fact. 'It's a rule with men who worship beauty', he writes, 'that when they fall in love with a youngster they deceive themselves that he's three or four years

[2] *Ghalib, Life and Letters*, p. 111.

younger than he really is. They know he's grown up, but they think of him as a child.'[3]

Second—and this is again true of other societies in history besides that of Mughal India—sexual segregation, and along with it, the low cultural level of the respectable women of society, produced the courtesan, the woman who learned all the skills of love-making as a professional accomplishment and added the cultural attainments which are also necessary to the satisfaction of a cultured man. Like homosexual love, resort to courtesans was formally frowned upon, but in the polite society in which the poets and their patrons moved, courtesans were a normal part of the social scene and many poets experienced some sort of relationship with them. Ghalib makes no bones about the fact that *he* did and found it normal and unremarkable that his friends did too. Two of his most famous letters are to his friend and fellow-poet Hatim Ali Beg Mihr, condoling with him on the death of his courtesan mistress and telling him of his own deep love for a *domni*, a singing and dancing girl. And an anecdote related of him tells how on one occasion when Ghalib visited his friend Fazle Haq, 'they had barely sat down when the maulvi sahib's [i.e. Fazle Haq's] courtesan came in from the other room and sat down with them'. In the original, the word used for courtesan is the blunt word *randi*, which one normally translates as 'prostitute', but to translate it so here would convey to most English readers a strongly pejorative sense which in this context it certainly does not bear. Fazle Haq was one of the most famous and respected Muslim divines in Delhi, and it is clear that his keeping a courtesan as a mistress caused no scandal.

These experiences of homosexual love and of relationships with courtesans find direct reflection in the verses of the ghazal, and to the ghazal poet all these loves are to be treated with the same acceptance and respect.

Since the love situations with which the ghazal deals are stressful ones, it is worth noting that the three situations of love described have one feature in common—the lover knows that his love must in the last resort be hopeless. A girl married or betrothed to another man could, in South Asian society, never be his; a boy grows up; and a courtesan by the very nature of her calling cannot give herself

[3] Ibid., p. 254.

to one lover alone. The desperation of the lover portrayed in the ghazal is, therefore, a desperation founded upon the real life experience of love.

Mystic Love

The Urdu ghazal bears a striking resemblance to the love poetry of medieval Western Europe. The situations of earthly love portrayed in both are broadly similar, and these situations of passionate, illicit love between two human beings are used as symbols of the similar love of the mystic lover for his God, his Divine Beloved, or, to put it in broader terms, for those high ideals in life which medieval people, unlike many of their modern descendants, could conceive of only in religious terms, as ideals embraced in obedience to the Divine Beloved's commands. The mystic lover's love for God necessarily led him into the same dangers as his love for a human beloved did. The logic of his situation is this: his starting point is his soul's longing for God, a longing which owes as little to reason as does a lover's involuntary, powerful attraction to a human beloved. It is this direct, deeply emotional relationship with God on which the whole structure of mystic love is built. This in itself means that it is potentially a doctrine subversive of medieval society and therefore deeply suspect to it. If your one overriding aim in life is to draw ever closer to your God, then the great ones of this world are unimportant in your eyes. And you rely on your love of God to guide you, you do not need the advice of learned divines or accept their pretensions to be in some special sense the guardians of true religion.

In the ghazal, the radical, potentially subversive trend in mysticism is made quite explicit, and indeed, like almost everything else in the ghazal, carried to an extreme. The hero of the ghazal poet, in his mystic role, is Mansur al Hallaj, who was crucified by the orthodox in AD 922, centuries before the great masters of the ghazal composed their verse, for crying out *ana'l haq! ana'l haq!* ('I am God! I am God!'), words which to the mystic express the complete merging of the individual soul in the Divine Beloved, but which to the orthodox are unspeakable blasphemy. In the convention of the ghazal, the poet's position is Mansur's position, and it is taken for granted that this means exposure to the same persecution from the pillars of society and of orthodox religion as Mansur himself had to face. Thus the mystic lover shares at the hands of society the same prospect as the earthly lover of a human beloved.

As in the poetry of earthly love, it is often the case that the poet's identification with the kind of mystic of which Mansur is the exemplar, and indeed, with less extreme mystics, is in great measure a fantasy one. We know of no Urdu poet who was in real life the same kind of mystic as Mansur and only a few—the eighteenth-century poet Mir Dard is the most famous—were mystics at all in any very meaningful sense of the term. But the best of them, including Ghalib, share with the mystics many of the values that guide them in their conduct toward their fellows; all the really worthwhile Urdu poets have in common with the mystics a sense of dedication to ideals which they feel to be greater than themselves and for which they are prepared, in at least some measure, to sacrifice themselves, knowing that this dedication will bring them into varying degrees of conflict with most of their contemporaries.

It has already been stated that there are many verses in the ghazal which can equally well be taken as expressions of earthly love and as expressions of mystic love, and the two themes blend inextricably. There are in almost any ghazal some couplets which one naturally takes in the earthly sense and others which one takes in the divine sense, but many of them could be taken in either sense or in both senses at the same time. And though there is no certain means of knowing the sense that was uppermost in the poet's mind in composing a particular verse—earthly, divine or both together— we do know that ghazal poets are fully aware of the whole range of possible interpretations and are quite content with the knowledge that different readers may understand a verse in different ways.

It is for this reason also that the poet needs a symbolism which makes it possible for him to move simultaneously on the two planes of earthly and divine love. This is one of the reasons why in the ghazal tradition, the beloved is portrayed as unrelentingly cruel to her lover. No doubt his earthly beloved sometimes was, when his love was not only unwelcome to her but also put her in a very dangerous position. But in the ghazal she nearly always is and there is a logic in this portrayal. The lover-hero of the ghazal is portrayed as one who accepts without hesitation all the misfortunes, up to and including death, which his devotion to his love will inevitably bring upon him. Indeed, he does more than accept all this; he welcomes it and rejoices in it all, for this enables him to prove his complete and utter devotion to his beloved. The supreme test comes when she too persecutes him, and since the lover needs to be shown as passing this test, his mistress needs to be shown in this light.

The moment one looks at all this in the context of the Divine Beloved, one sees the appropriateness of this symbolism. This lover loves Her[4] regardless, though She inflicts upon him distress which, in his human frailty, he finds it very hard to conceive of as justified. The standard metaphors used to describe the human beloved are appropriate metaphors for the Divine Beloved too. She seeks to bind him for ever in his love for her. She is a fowler, out to snare her lover and imprison him. The long tresses of her hair are the bonds with which she binds him; her glances are arrows, her eyelashes daggers that pierce the lover's heart. At her most cruel, she is her lover's executioner and he gladly bows his neck to receive the blow of her sword. The ghazal poets, Ghalib included, work within these conventions and Ghalib has many verses on this theme.

The lover too is portrayed as one who is not always, to the western reader, a very sympathetic character. He is under extreme stress and his reactions are correspondingly extreme and find expression in ways that may not strike a chord with us. But we need to remember that, as Dorothy Sayers once put it, 'there are fashions in sensibility as in everything else'.[5] In the ghazal, the lover suffers, and he sees no reason why he should not tell the world how intense his suffering is. (It may be useful to remember that neither did Shakespeare's Romeo.)[6] This self-pity is perhaps more acceptable now than it was a generation ago when, to quote Dorothy Sayers again, a man was expected to 'react to great personal and national calamities by a slight compression of the lips and by silently throwing his cigarette into the fireplace' (a convention, she adds wryly, 'of very recent origin'). The lover's self-praise is equally uninhibited.

---

[4] The ghazal's readiness to identify God with a beautiful woman should be a salutary jolt to the preconceptions of societies which have always imagined God as a male. All the same, in what follows, I shall generally use the more familiar 'He' for God.

[5] In the introduction to her translation of *The Song of Roland* (Penguin, 1957), p. 15. The quotation below is from the same page.

[6] See *Romeo and Juliet*, Act III, Scene 3.

Neither the lover's self-praise and his self-pity nor the beloved's unremitting cruelty were distasteful to the ghazal's audience. These are the conventions with which they grew up and they saw nothing strange in them. If they seem strange to us, we would do well to think of our attitude to many of our own conventions and reflect that conventions, whether in literature or in personal and social life, very commonly lack any discernible rational basis and perhaps have the power they do for that very reason. What John Stuart Mill wrote of 'rules of conduct' is equally applicable to literary conventions, and is worth quoting at some length. He asks 'what these rules should be' and remarks:

> No two ages, and scarcely any two countries, have decided it alike: and the decision of one age or country is a wonder to another. Yet the people of any given age and country no more suspect any difficulty in it than if it were a subject on which mankind had always been agreed. The rules which obtain among themselves appear to them self-evident and self-justifying...the subject is one on which it is not generally considered necessary that reasons should be given, either by one person to others or by each to himself. People are accustomed to believe...that their feelings on subjects of this nature are better than reasons and render reasons unnecessary.

So where in this selection you meet a couplet that seems a bit outlandish, pause to think why it seems so. The chances are that it has been included because I felt that only the unfamiliarity of the convention in which it is expressed will stand between you and the appreciation of a worthwhile verse, and that in such cases it will do you no harm to get used to accepting the unfamiliar convention.

To sum up, the ghazal's audience was accustomed to a poem in which, so to speak, everything also means everything else. Take for example Ghalib's verse:

> Though I have passed my life in pledge to all the age's cruelties
> Yet never was the thought of you once absent from my mind

By the 'you' of this couplet, Ghalib may mean a woman or God or any ideal to which he was passionately committed or *all* of these things.

The ghazal's 'beloved' is thus any person or any ideal to whom or to which the poet-lover, whether in real life or in fantasy, is prepared to dedicate himself, sacrificing himself for its/her/his sake and willingly accepting the hostility of his fellow men as an inevitable consequence of his love.

The intensity of the emotions typically conveyed in ghazal poetry is enhanced by being necessarily condensed into two lines. This in turn has led poets to use a range of conventional similes, metaphors and symbols. Only a small sample of these has been given above. For a western reader to appreciate the full power of a ghazal couplet, it is necessary to get a sense of the range of allusions and connotations such symbols can have. For example, let us see what Ghalib's readers see when they read this couplet. The literal picture is one of a lover watching his beloved combing her hair.

> You, combing out the tresses of your hair
> I, and my endless dark imaginings

Take the literal picture first. What are the lover's 'endless dark imaginings'? First, they are endless and dark because her long black tresses themselves suggest this. The long black tresses of the beloved's hair are regularly compared with the long dark night which her lover has to spend in enforced separation from her. Then they are a metaphor for the bonds in which she binds him. But is it him she wants to subdue? Or is it some rival of his of whom he has not yet learnt?

But the literal picture may be serving simply as a symbol. The 'you' of the first line may be God, who in his inscrutable ways may be planning a future of misery for you. Or it may be a cause to which you have irrevocably committed yourself with a commitment which may demand of you sacrifices which you may not have the strength to make. All of these things suggest themselves to readers who are familiar with the ghazal, and to those who have, so to speak, grown up with it, this great diversity of the possible meanings of the poet's verses presents no problem. To the modern western reader it often does.

In fact, to the ghazal's traditional audience, it is this very universality that gives it its strongest appeal. Every verse can serve (to apply Olive Schreiner's words to this context) as 'a little door that opens into an infinite hall where you may find what you please'[7] and the poets who come to a *musha'ira* know that they will be

[7] Olive Schreiner, *The Story of an African Farm* (London, 1896), p. 172.

speaking to an audience of considerable diversity. Some will have come to be entertained simply by a display of a mastery of poetic techniques; others will be entering for some hours into a world of pure fantasy; others—those with the greatest sensitivity and strength of spirit dedicated to a high ideal in life—will be responding to the message of a poetic tradition, enhanced by the great poet's own individual contribution, which sustains and glorifies anyone who strives to serve a beloved to the end no matter what suffering this may entail. They know also that people's ideals vary and, indeed, clash. And they speak in words and symbols which enable all of those present in this varied audience to find in them what they are seeking, uninhibited by any feeling that a particular comparison restricts their range of identification to a particular context.

Poets against Fundamentalists

I said earlier that the ghazal poet, in his role as the mystic lover of God, shares with the real mystics a great many values. He lives his life by principles radically different from those of the orthodox, personified in the ghazal as the shaikh, a word which originally meant an older man but subsequently acquired the connotations of an elder, a presbyter, a religious leader. Thus he rejects with contempt their doctrine of a conduct of life motivated by hope of reward and fear of punishment in the life to come. Ghalib speaks for all ghazal poets when he says:

> Abstinence wins no praise from me. What though it be sincere?
> Behind it lies raw greed to win reward for virtuous deeds
>
> God's will be done; but not from greed for heaven's wine and honey
> Take hold of paradise, someone, and cast it into hell!
>
> The shaikh sings loud the praises of the gardens of Rizvan. To us
> They lie, a bunch of faded flowers, upon oblivion's shelf[8]

Ghalib adds to these traditional mystic sentiments his own distinctive views. God's promises of heavenly reward for virtuous conduct in this life are no doubt valid, he says. But not only are these not the motive for good conduct for the true lover of God; they are also

---

[8] Rizvan is the guardian of the gardens of paradise.

rewards that don't amount to much, and, in any case, are to be valued less than the pleasures already available here on earth. At best, he thinks:

> I know the truth regarding paradise but all the same
> Since it gives happiness, Ghalib, the thought of it is good

In Islamic tradition, the promised joys of paradise include wine (prohibited to Muslims on earth). Ghalib enjoyed wine and while cheerfully admitting that it was sinful to drink it, made no secret of the fact that he didn't propose to stop drinking it. He writes:

> One thing alone gives paradise some value in my eyes
> What else, if not the wine, red as the rose, fragrant as musk?

And he has another comment on this topic, which is very typical of him:

> I'll drink pure wine, but where will be the dread of being caught?
> And where in paradise the spice of fear it will not last?

Unless paradise provides again those joys he had already experienced on earth, it will be a grave disappointment to him:

> They offer paradise to make up for our life below
> It needs a stronger wine than this to cure our hangover

> All that they say in praise of paradise is true. I know
> God grant though that it be illumined by *your* radiance

> He who drinks wine unceasingly alone with his beloved
> Knows well the worth of *houris* and of streams of paradise[9]

Not surprisingly, he says of himself:

> The meek ascetic wins rewards in heaven
> I know, but I cannot incline that way

Ghalib shares most of the mystics' beliefs as expressed in the ghazal. One can piece together from the lines of the ghazal what these were, and one can readily understand why the orthodox abhorred and hated the mystics and why this hatred was most

[9] *Houris* are the beautiful women provided for the pleasure of the inhabitants of paradise.

cordially returned. Some of the leading ideas are these. The worship of God means the love of God, and love as all-consuming as that between human lovers. Rituals of worship are of no significance as compared with this. Of the Five Pillars of Islam, the five fundamental duties of faith, prayer, fasting, alms giving and pilgrimage, only the first is essential, for except for faith—belief in the one God and in Muhammad as His last and final prophet—all the others involve observance of strictly defined rituals.[10] Performance of them *may* conceivably help you to draw closer to God but mostly they are harmful to true religion, for they lead you to see religion as the hollow performance of the external rituals, and if you perform them, may lead to an arrogant self-satisfaction that you are 'not as other men are'.

Ghalib thinks that for many who observe the Ramzan fast, abstinence during the day is no more than hunger used as a sauce to enhance their enjoyment of the food they can eat once the sun has set and again before dawn comes.

> Abstinence only heightens their concern to fill their bellies
> The bustle of the meals is all; Ramzan's of no account

He attaches little importance to the pilgrimage to Mecca. No doubt it brings heavenly reward; but he once had the prospect of making it in the company of his patron, the last Mughal king, and this excited Ghalib because he loved to travel and for no other reason. When the king told him of his intention to make the pilgrimage, Ghalib recited this verse to him:

> Ghalib, if he will take me with him on the pilgrimage
> His Majesty may have my share of heavenly reward

Ghalib mocks the conventionally pious as well:

> To put it briefly, my heart too inclines to piety—but then
> I saw the way the 'good' behaved and fell in with the infidels

Far better than Muslims who see the performance of ritual observances as the essence of religion are Hindu idolators who love God with all their heart, though they call Him by another name. For God reveals Himself in many forms, and the worship of His

---

[10] For notes on each of these, see the Explanatory Index.

true lovers is acceptable to Him, no matter in what form they worship Him. In Ghalib's words:

> One must be constant to the end; this is the essence of the faith
> The priest dies in his temple—let the Kaba be his burial place[11]

In short, says Ghalib:

> Our creed is oneness, and our cry, Abandon rituals
> So that communities dissolve to constitute one faith

Along with most ghazal poets, Ghalib also uses the common mystic concept of God revealing Herself (or Himself) in the beauty of the universe and therefore equates the worship of beauty with the worship of God, whether it be the beauty of nature or of a beautiful woman or of a handsome boy. And this leads to the symbolic use of Hinduism, the religion with which Indian Muslims were in closest contact, as the embodiment of the worship of beauty. The orthodox abhor the Hindus because they worship idols. To the mystics, this is not important. For them the issue is not whether they worship idols but whether in doing so, they are expressing in their own way a true love of God. All the practices of their religion afford a vivid symbol of the worship of God through the worship of beauty. The idol is the symbol of the irresistibly beautiful mistress you 'idolize' and adore. And she, in turn, besides being herself, is also the symbol of your Divine Beloved.

All these concepts make 'Hinduism'—that is, Hinduism as a symbol rather than actual Hinduism—the expression of one of the mystics' key beliefs. Ghalib writes, conveying a serious message in a characteristically humorous form:

> Put on the sacred thread and break the hundred-beaded rosary
> The traveller takes the path he sees to be the even one

The rosary symbolizes narrow, orthodox Islam, the sacred thread Hinduism. It is easy to travel that smooth path—as the fingers run easily along the thread. The other path is hilly—the fingers go up and down over each bead. At the same time the mystic has just as

---

[11] In the original, 'priest' is 'Brahmin', a member of the highest Hindu caste. The Kaba is the 'house of God', the building in Mecca which is the Muslim holy of holies and the focus of Muslim pilgrimage.

cordial a dislike for the arrogant, bigoted Hindu, symbolized by the Brahmin, as he does for his Muslim counterpart, the shaikh.

The Humanism of the Ghazal

The essential sense of brotherhood with the true worshippers of God, whatever their formal religious affiliation, is one aspect of the ghazal's emphasis on humanism. To love God means also, to use the Biblical phrase, 'to love your neighbour as yourself'. The great fourteenth-century Persian poet Hafiz wrote:

> Do not distress your fellow-men, and do what else you will
> For in my Holy Law there is no other sin but this

And the ghazal is permeated by the same spirit. As Ghalib put it:

> The object of creation was mankind and nothing else
> We are the point round which the seven compasses revolve

By the 'seven compasses' he means the seven skies whose revolution determines one's fate.

To the ghazal poet, humankind is the finest of God's creations, 'the noblest of created things', as the common Muslim phrase goes, and is higher than the angels. God's treatment of his 'noblest of created things' seems incomprehensible. Ghalib says:

> Those whom You frown upon toil on with neither bread nor water
> Those whom You favour, sated, are still plied with heavenly food

Like others before and after him, he is puzzled by the problems that arise from a belief that God predestined everything that people do and at the same time gave them free will.

> Good conduct is from You; we do not ask to be rewarded
> And if we sin, that is Your doing. Why then take revenge?

But he has a more sophisticated complaint, too:

> He hid in this handful of dust two lightnings poised to strike
> One the harsh law of fate and one the sorrow of free will

By 'this handful of dust', he means himself or any other human being. 'The sorrow of free will' may mean either regret that God did not give us the gift of free will, or regret that it is so restricted, or that we exercise it and find that it has involved us in disaster. He speaks up quite impudently on behalf of humankind:

> The angels write and we are seized. Where is the justice there?
> Did we have no one present when they wrote their record down?

In Islamic belief, everyone's every action in life is recorded by the recording angels, and their record determines his or her fate on Judgement Day. Ghalib, making a joke of this, wants to know why evidence for the prosecution is heard and no evidence for the defence is called.

Ghalib is never overawed by God. His friend and first biographer Hali tells us:

> He was lying on his bed at night looking up at the sky. He was struck by the apparent chaos in the distribution of the stars and said, 'There is no rhyme or reason in anything the self-willed do. Just look at the stars—scattered in complete disorder. No proportion, no system, no sense, no pattern. But their King has absolute power and no one can breathe a word against Him!'

In many verses Ghalib speaks bluntly and even mockingly of God's incomprehensible ways, criticizes Him for His inconsistent and unjust treatment of humankind and, most characteristically of all, notes with a mixture of mockery and pity God's inability to recognize the potential of one particular man and to treat him accordingly. This particular man is Ghalib himself. He asks why God created him:

> When nothing was, then God was there
>   Had nothing been, God would have been
> My being has defeated me
>   Had I not been, what would have been?

In fact, why did He create anything at all?

> When all is You, and nought exists but You
> Tell me, O Lord, why all this turmoil too?
> These fair-faced women, with their coquetries
> Their glances, airs and graces, what are these?
> Why the sweet perfume of their coiling tresses?
> Why the collyrium that adorns their eyes?
> Where does the grass, where do the flowers come from?
> What is the cloud made of? What is the breeze?

And why, having created Ghalib, does He not recognize his potential?

> He gave me both the worlds and told Himself, 'He is content'
> And I, tongue-tied with shame, had not the heart to ask for more

> Would that I could have looked out from an even greater height
> Would that I had my dwelling place above the throne of God

It is said that Musa (Moses) asked God to show Himself to him. God took him to the Mount of Tur and when he got there, told him that He would show His radiance to the mountain and if the mountain remained in place, Musa might look upon Him. But God's radiance reduced the mountain to dust and Musa fell down in a swoon. Ghalib writes:

> You should have let Your radiance fall on *me*,
>   not on the Mount of Tur
> One pours wine in the measure that the
>   drinker can contain

In other words, unlike the Mount of Tur, I, Ghalib, could have sustained Your full revelation. It is no good giving a man more liquor than he can hold.

He does not know the answers to questions such as these but if God appears to behave stupidly or unjustly or is miserly in what He offers, He is nevertheless to be loved:

> We, ignorant and powerless, maintain our love for you
> Intoxicated always with a wine that does not fail

Which does not, however, absolve Him of the duty to treat Ghalib with proper respect. Ghalib tells him:

> I serve You, but my independent self-respect is such
> I should at once turn back if I should find the Kaba closed

Wine and Music

Because the impulses of the heart are the mystic's chief guide, the poet, as mystic, assumes the role of a man to whom wine and music and romantic love—the first prohibited by Islam and the others disapproved of by orthodox Muslims—are not forbidden. On the contrary, they are, so to speak, his allies, for they banish the

cowardly inhibitions of worldly wisdom and the austere attitudes
of pharisaical pride and stimulate all that is free and generous in
him. The wine may be wine in the literal sense or it may be simply
a symbol of divine inspiration and of that truly religious under-
standing which only the true lover of God can attain to.

The symbols of wine, wine drinkers and the tavern pervade the
whole of Urdu ghazal poetry and are used alike by those relatively
few poets (like Ghalib himself) who did indeed drink and the much
more numerous ones who, as far as we know, did not. Ghalib
writes:

> The pious bow in prayer to God; no radiance lights their forehead
> See how the wine lights up the faces of the wine drinkers!

By wine, Ghalib may mean literal wine or symbolic wine or both.

He commonly addresses the conventionally pious in a tone of
good humoured mockery.

> Beneath the shade of every mosque should be a tavern
> Just as the eye, your reverence, is near the brow

The mosque, with its arch, is compared to the eyebrow, and the
tavern to the eye—and it is obvious which is to be valued the more!
'Mosque' and 'tavern' could be taken literally but are more
probably used as symbols of formal and mystic religion respectively.

In the ghazal metaphor, wine is served to the drinkers by the
saqi, a beautiful youth who often rouses the amorous feelings of
those whom he serves. He is sometimes the symbol of God himself
as the source of mystic intoxication and sometimes the medium
of God's message to His lovers.

The wine drinker is often called the *rind*, a word of which
'profligate' or 'rake' is a not very satisfactory English translation.
He is one who cares nothing for the conventions of the sober
citizens of the society in which he lives and for whom wealth and
social status are unimportant. He is content to be a *faqir* or a *darvesh*,
words in which the sense of beggar and holy-man are still closely
associated.

Ghalib's statements on all these themes strike us the more force-
fully because we know that his verses are not simply exercises in
the conventions of the ghazal but the expressions of his own beliefs
and practice. We know that he never said the five daily prayers,

never kept the Ramzan fast and never went on the pilgrimage. We know also that he had friends in all communities. He writes in one of his letters: 'I hold all mankind to be my kin and look upon all men—Muslim, Hindu, Christian—as my brothers, no matter what others may think.' In short, his life and his poetry are in complete harmony.

The Ghazal Drama

As we have seen, the lover-hero in the ghazal is the lover of both an earthly beloved and a divine one, a lover who will be true to the end, knowing full well that this will bring down upon him unending persecution. This means that the world of the ghazal is one in which the conflict between the lover, as the representative of the best and bravest of humankind, and the shaikh, as the representative of their irreconcilable enemies, is at its sharpest point. It is important to understand that the ghazal is concerned only with this aspect of human experience and that the ghazal poet surveys humankind from this viewpoint, judging his fellows by the way they react—or fail to react—to this central conflict. He sees that between himself and the shaikh stand the millions who constitute the rest of humankind. He notes the typical reaction of different sections and encapsulates each in a stock character, which represents this behaviour in its purest form. It is not necessary to detail here the full range of the types he describes since, wherever explanations are necessary, these are given at the point when these types are introduced in this selection and also in the Explanatory Index. But two points should be made about them.

The first is that they are types. In the ghazal context, shaikh always means a contemptible, vicious hypocrite; outside that context the ghazal poet knows as well as anyone else that the shaikh does not necessarily mean that—just as the English reader knows that 'Pharisee' in one context means one who thanks God that he is 'not as other men are', and in other contexts is a purely neutral term describing a member of a particular sect. Similarly, in the ghazal context, another standard character, the *raqib*, the rival, is always an insincere lover; outside that context, the poet knows as well as anyone else that two rivals for a woman's love may both be equally sincere.

The second point is that the categories into which the ghazal divides humankind are, in my opinion, entirely relevant for the modern reader. The lover-hero of the ghazal is one in whom all the finest human potentialities have reached their full development and who has the capacity to remain true to chosen ideals and to practise them in every aspect of life, no matter what the personal cost. All human societies have needed, and are long likely to need, such people, and poetry which sustains and inspires them will have the power to appeal as long as this need exists. It is true that some of the situations which the ghazal portrays—or, more often, of which it assumes a knowledge and understanding—are now quite unfamiliar to the modern reader in the West, and some of the lover-poet's reactions to these situations are correspondingly difficult to comprehend and assimilate. Even there, the sustained, imaginative effort to discover what they were all about, and in the course of this to understand and sympathize with the lover-poet's reaction to them, is one that is well worth making. Besides, the situations of love and life which the ghazal portrays are, in their essence, not so unknown in the contemporary world as one might at first think. In many modern societies, the contexts of loving have changed, but the contexts of the world of the ghazal, though no longer universal or typical, are still to be found even in modern societies. In all those countries where racial or communal tension prevails (and their number has greatly increased since the end of the Second World War) lovers from different racial or religious groups are likely to experience all the hostility which all lovers experienced in the society that produced the ghazal, and millions who will never experience this hostility in the course of their own loves, have, one hopes, the imaginative sympathy to identify with what such lovers must feel. The experience of unrequited love is still both universal and common. Even more common is the experience of two people who fall so deeply in love that their love informs and guides their whole life, and yet have to live their lives physically apart because the fulfilment of their love for each other which they would otherwise desire would violate their obligations to others—partners, husbands, wives, children—voluntarily entered into and voluntarily maintained to the end. Homosexual lovers—gay men and lesbian women—still face deep prejudice and hostility. It is relevant to recall in passing that the ghazal is absolutely free of this. The great twentieth-century ghazal poet Hasrat Mohani wrote:

All love is unconditionally good
Be it for God, be it for human beauty

To all such lovers and to all who have the humanity to identify with
them, the ghazal still has a great deal to say.

In the wider areas of life, the ghazal's contemporary relevance
is perhaps even greater. Today there are millions of people whose
ideals are as strongly and passionately held as were the religious
ideals of their medieval forebears. The best and bravest of human
beings dedicate themselves to their ideals without counting the
cost, and anyone who strives to be such a person can read the
expression of this dedication in the symbols of the ghazal and can
identify with its lover-hero and with the poet who speaks for him.

Other characters also have a contemporary relevance. For in-
stance, the 'rival', the self-styled 'lover' whose real motive is mere
self-interest, has a familiar modern counterpart in politicians who
profess high ideals of service of 'the people' and see this as no more
than a means to attain their own selfish ends and all too often
succeed where the honest fail because they can use all the
demagogic tricks which honest people cannot. In Ghalib's words:

My rival's honeyed words have worked
   the spell that he intended
And I am dumb; the thought 'He loves me'
   does not cross her mind

Anyone who, in any society and any country in the world, takes
a stand for principles which the establishment disapproves of will
soon find how accurately the ghazal categories portray the most
common reactions of his or her fellow citizens. It soon becomes
evident that few people are prepared, for the sake of what they like
to call an 'abstract principle', to do anything whatever that incurs
even the mildest disapproval of those in authority over them. And
when taking a stand for the principles they profess would mean
putting their livelihood, or even their life, at risk, one knows very
well what most people do. What was the attitude of most Germans
during the Hitler years when the Jews were being exterminated?
What was the attitude of most Americans when McCarthy and
his lieutenants were slandering and persecuting those who upheld
the principles set out in the Constitution of the USA and so
found themselves accused of 'un-American activities'? Hitler and

the much less terrible McCarthy were the shaikhs of their respect-
ive societies. The vast majority of their fellow citizens fitted the
other categories which the ghazal describes. And those small
numbers of people who put their lives or their livelihoods at risk
and actively resisted evil acted as the *ashiq*, the lover-hero of the
ghazal, acts, and one hopes that both they and he command respect
and admiration.

What Ghalib has to Say

We possess exceptionally abundant information about Ghalib's life.
His frankness about himself in his letters to and conversations with
his friends is the main source of this. His poetry would still have
exercised its appeal even if this had not been the case, but the
knowledge of how closely it reflected his own life nevertheless adds
something to our appreciation of it.

Thus he himself tells us of his sexual relationships with women
other than his wife and of his attachment to a young singing and
dancing girl; his letters suggest that there may have been more than
one such attachment.

Similarly, we have seen that when his verses express mystic and
quasi-mystic themes, they express things in which he really be-
lieved. His first biographer tells us that: 'From all the duties of
worship and the enjoined practices of Islam he took only two—a
belief that God is one and is immanent in all things, and a love for
the Prophet and his family. And this alone he considered sufficient
for salvation.'

We should now look at how he avails himself of the freedom
the ghazal gives him to speak of all the other things which were
significant in his life experience. To understand these fully, one
needs to know something of the times in which he lived and of
his reaction to them.

The first great age of Urdu poetry was the eighteenth century.
The poets of that age saw themselves as, and prided themselves on
being, members of a predominandy Muslim elite which had ruled
the greater part of India for centuries. The last and greatest Muslim
dynasty had been that of the Mughals, who ruled over an empire
of great splendour. T. G. P. Spear has described its capital, Delhi,
as having been in its heyday: '...a great and imperial city...with

anything between one and two million inhabitants...the largest and most renowned city, not only of India, but of all the East from Constantinople to Canton. Its Court was brilliant, its mosques and colleges numerous, and its literary and artistic fame as high as its political renown.'[12]

But after the death of its last great emperor Aurangzeb in 1707, the empire had gone into rapid and catastrophic decline. For most of the eighteenth century, bitter awareness of this decline and a nostalgic yearning for the return of former glory dominated the thought and feeling of Muslims and of their great poets Mir and Sauda, and their poetry gives powerful expression to this. By the time Ghalib came to manhood, it was clear to realistic minds, Ghalib's among them, that this was a yearning for the impossible. In 1803, the British had occupied Delhi and they now controlled the emperor, from whom, in purely formal terms, their power derived its legitimacy. Ghalib was fully aware of this and prepared to come to terms with it; he no longer felt as keenly as his eighteenth-century forebears the sense of loss which the collapse of the Mughal power had induced in them. This was partly because he was fascinated, as his forebears had not been, by the material achievements on which British power was based and by the possibilities for the future which these achievements opened up. He was also on terms of close friendship with important British administrators. Most of these in those days felt a respect—a very proper respect, as Ghalib would have thought—for the traditional Muslim elite and its culture. (Many of them were proficient in Persian and Urdu and not a few of them wrote poetry in both of these languages.) Moreover, although they came from a country where medieval institutions had, in the main, long since been superseded, they maintained in India all the medieval modes, merely injecting into them or grafting onto them some of the more modern social and political institutions that prevailed in contemporary Britain. It is not surprising, therefore, that Ghalib, with all his awareness of what was new in the world around him, saw it from within the framework of medieval ways of thought and shared many of the attitudes of his eighteenth-century predecessors in poetry. Like them, he prided himself on his membership of the old ruling elite and regretted (though much less keenly than they)

---

[12] *Twilight of the Mughuls* (1951), p. 1.

the loss of its former power. More significantly, he shared their firm dedication to its traditional ideals of personal conduct which, as they and he both believed, were more and more rarely observed in practice. It is equally unsurprising that he expressed his reactions in poetry. For him and his contemporaries, poetry was the natural medium of expression, as it had been for his forebears. Prose literature had never commanded the same esteem as poetry did; and indeed, in South Asian society to this day poetry is in general more popular and more highly regarded. Writing poetry meant, as we have seen, writing it in the traditional genres. And so while Ghalib expresses many things which go well beyond traditional medieval concepts, he does so within the medieval ghazal form.

Ghalib on His Contemporaries and Himself

Ghalib's verse often comments on the society in which he lived. He was a warm-hearted, generous, sociable man and a popular one too. But with all this he felt, and had good reason to feel, that many of his contemporaries neither understood nor appreciated him, and that, in particular, his friends among the wealthier and more influential sections of the nobility did not meet the obligations of true friendship and true nobility. He himself was meticulous in meeting his obligations towards both his friends and his dependants, and this enhanced his sense of bitterness. He sometimes felt that it was his own observance of the traditional high standards which incurred the hostility of those who professed these standards but did not practise them. Late in life he wrote to his friend Shafaq: 'You are a prey to grief and sorrow, but...to be the target of the world's afflictions is proof of an inherent nobility—proof clear, and argument conclusive.'[13] This was a judgement he was to repeat little more than a year before his death, when he was involved in a court case and had to witness the spectacle of respectable gentlemen who had been on visiting terms with him taking the stand in court and testifying against his character in the most insulting and humiliating terms. When his friend Hali asked him about this, he quoted in reply one of his own Persian verses:

> Like draws to like; and all men draw to others of like quality
> The measure of my friendlessness is my inborn nobility

[13] *Ghalib, Life and Letters*, p. 264.

Not a few of his verses make the same point.

> I may be good, I may be bad—I live in ill-matched company
> A flower thrown on the bonfire or a weed among the flowers
>
> How can I tell the virtues of the men to whom this age gave birth?
> They do me harm to whom I have done good repeatedly
>
> Were I to tell the tale of all my friends have done to me
> The custom men call hope would vanish utterly from earth

This disgust with them sometimes makes him tell himself:

> Now let me go away and live somewhere where no
>   one else will be
> Where there is none that knows my tongue,
>   where there is none to speak with me
> There let me build myself a house with, so to say,
>   no doors, no walls
> And live there without neighbours and with no one
>   to keep watch for me
> If I fall ill, then there should be no one to come
>   and visit me
> And if I die let none be there to weep and wail
>   and mourn for me[14]

His bitterness against many of his fellows did not prevent him observing himself with humour and detachment. In a letter of 1864, he writes of the difficulties and humiliation he is having to face at the time and says: 'I watch myself from the sidelines and rejoice at my own distress and degradation. In other words, I see myself through the eyes of my enemy. At every blow that falls I say, "Look! Ghalib's taken another beating! Such airs he used to give himself!"' He goes on to paint the picture of himself from an uninhibitedly hostile point of view. In one ghazal he writes:

> I, and myself reflected in imagination's mirror
> Are one, and one who constantly confronts another one

He reflects wryly:

> I sought my own delight and found abundant misery
> Good news for any enemy that I may seek to harm

---

[14] 'So to say, no doors, no walls'—he means a house to which access is impossible.

He knows that he nourishes within him the elements of his own destruction:

> In my construction lies concealed the stuff that is to ruin me
> The hot blood of the peasant holds the lightning for his crops

For he is a lover—in all senses of the word—and he knows that all lovers ultimately have to choose between their desire to live a carefree life and their love:

> I pledge myself entire to love—and love of life possesses me
> I worship lightning—and lament the lightning's handiwork

Ghalib's Philosophy of Life

His awareness that in many fundamental respects he stood alone, his lack of strong sentimental attachment to the old political order, his interest in British achievements and his own lively intelligence and inquiring mind all went to form a distinctive philosophy of life.

He is acutely aware of unceasing change. At every moment something new is coming into being and something is decaying. Reality is infinitely rich, and one who is alive to this can already see things that have not yet come into existence.

> A new creation comes each time you close your eyelashes
> The eye thinks, 'This is just the same'—it is not just the same
>
> The roses surge within the branch, driven by the force of spring
> Like wine still held within the flask—concealed yet not concealed
>
> He who has eyes to see counts up the beauties spread before him
> And sees all Azar's idols dancing locked within the rock[15]

He wants to see everything, good and bad, beautiful and ugly alike, not to flinch from confronting anything he sees nor to miss the largest significance of even the smallest thing:

> Ghalib, it is the rose's beauty teaches us to gaze
> No matter what the scene, no one should ever close his eyes
>
> Unless the sea within the drop, the whole within the part
> Appear, you play like children; you still lack the seeing eye

[15] Azar carved statues of unparalleled beauty.

Given the desire to see and the skill in seeing, you *can* see:

> You are the one that does not know the music of His secrets
> Hidden no more than melody lies hidden in the lute

He has a hatred of stagnation and a desire to see constant change, even though change brings misfortune to him:

> Let the sky's ancient dome collapse and fall—I shall be glad
> Even though it be on my own head that it collapse and fall

He wants to experience fully and deeply all that life brings, including all its sorrows:

> Home is not home unless it holds the turmoil of strong feeling
> If there are cries of grief, not songs of joy, then be it so

> My heart, this pain and sorrow too is precious,
>   for the time will come
> You will not heave the midnight sigh nor shed your tears
>   as morning dawns

> Though it play only strains of grief, my heart,
>   yet you must treasure them
> The music of this lute of life will all be stilled one day

It is the substance of experience that matters, not the form in which it comes:

> If you dislike me, saki, pour the wine in my cupped hand
> I may not have the cup? So be it. Let me have the wine

If the joys of life are transient and if they are for others and not for you, rejoice in them and celebrate them nonetheless:

> Spring is soon fled? What of it? It is spring
> Sing of its breezes, of its greenery

> The fair are cruel? What of it? They are fair
> Sing of their grace, their swaying symmetry

If you are to experience life to the full, you must not confine yourself to actions approved by the virtuous. You must sin. Here he is in the tradition of his predecessors. There are two aspects to this: first, that many of what the orthodox regard as sins are not sins at all, and secondly, that even when they are, those who love God will be forgiven their sins because, as every Muslim notes before he undertakes any task, even so everyday a task as writing a letter, God is 'the Compassionate, the Merciful'. Thus Mir wrote:

> It is God's mercy that we sinners speak of
> Fasting and prayer are never mentioned here

Ghalib, as usual, goes beyond this. He doesn't bother to consider whether his sins are real sins or not. His one regret is that he cannot commit more of them, and he explicitly tells God not to overlook them:

> Sin's ocean was not vast enough; it dried right up
> And still my garment's hem was barely damp with it

> Note too how I regret the sins that I could not commit
> O Lord, if you would punish me for these committed sins

For Ghalib, life is an unending search. Neither the holy of holies in Mecca nor even the attainment of paradise is the end of it.

> The object of my worship lies beyond perception's reach
> To those who see, the Kaba is a compass, nothing more

> Lost to themselves, they doze, reclining there in Tuba's shade
> Is *this* the high resolve of men who set out before dawn?

Tuba is the name of a tree in paradise.

It is a search in which you may accept the help of anyone who seems competent to give it but in which, ultimately, you are on your own and you must not surrender yourself to anyone else's judgement. You can never reach the final truth but you must never give up either.

> I go some way with everyone I see advancing swiftly
> So far I see no one whom I can take to be my guide

> Lost to myself, I strive and strive unstinting on—and fate
> Gives every goal I reach the aspect of a starting point

> My heart insists that I maintain the struggle, for as yet
> My fingernails still owe a debt to this half-loosened knot

You must be content to know that you are searching; never despair; the fact that you never cease to work for what you desire is enough for you even when you have no other source of joy.

I too gaze on the wonders that my longing can perform
It matters nothing to me whether I attain my wish

Back! thronging hosts of black despair, lest you reduce to dust as well
The one joy left to me—the joy that unavailing struggle brings

And don't assume that your struggle will always be unavailing;
prepare for success as well as failure, even when the odds against
success seem overwhelming.

I have not ceased to struggle; I am like the captive bird
Who in the cage still gathers straws with which to build his nest

Many things will happen which are out of your control, but what-
ever happens, face the prospect calmly.

All night, all day the seven heavens are turning
Something will happen; set your mind at ease

Rely on yourself. It is no use praying to God to help you.

If you would solve your problems, prayer's enchantment
    does not work
O Lord, accept my supplication: Long may Khizar live!

In other words, to pray for something you want is as pointless
as to pray for something that has already been granted. God has
already granted Khizar eternal life.

Take it for granted that grief will be your lot, but be like all true
lovers:

Grief nourishes us lovers in the bosom of adversity
Our lamp shines through the tempest like the coral through
    the stormy sea

Ghalib on His Poetry

One of Ghalib's most heartfelt complaints about his contemporar-
ies is that they do not recognize his greatness as a poet. Some of
them assumed that he could not rank with the ancient poets simply
because he was a modern poet and their own contemporary. He
appealed to them not to hold so arbitrary an opinion:

You who are lost in wonder at the poets of the past
Do not deny my claims because I live in your own time

Relatively few of them understood the verses into which he put most of himself and this saddened him.

> O Lord, they do not understand nor *will* they understand my words
> Give them another heart or else give me another tongue

In his sixty-eighth year, Ghalib wrote to his friend Alai: '...I share your inauspicious stars and feel your pain. I am a man devoted to one art. Yet by my faith I swear to you, my verse and prose has not won the praise it merited. I wrote it, and I alone appreciated it.'

Of the great value of his poetry, he himself never had the slightest doubt, and he felt an immense and justified pride in it. He tells us, in effect, that to be a poet was his destiny:

> Ghalib, it was not by your wish that you attained this rank
> Poetry came itself and asked if it might be your craft

He does not claim that his poetry ranks with the Quran, the word of God, and yet:

> Who says my verse is so inspired it brings
>   God's message to mankind?
> Yet you and God can surely say my verse is
>   nonetheless inspired

He regrets that he cannot bring before his hearers all the thoughts that throng his mind:

> I cannot bring onto the page all that is in my heart
> In the assembly flowers are few—and in the garden, many

but:

> I speak to tell you something worth your hearing
> What of it if my verses are but few?

And, he tells them, if he is sparing in what he writes, it is because he does not write poetry merely to display his skills, because poetry is not poetry unless it comes from the heart and that too a heart that has experienced all the suffering of life, and then has something deeply significant to say, something that banishes complacency and threatens the accustomed order of things.

What of it you write a hundred thousand novel verses?
Speak *one,* a cry that comes to us all blood-soaked from your heart

The words 1 hide within my breast are not those of a preacher
Words to be spoken at the stake, not spoken from the pulpit

There is something to be said about Ghalib's choice of the ghazal as the medium of most of his verse. The fundamental reason for his choice is that, for him, the ghazal is not just an exercise in conventional themes but the expression of thoughts and feelings which really do accord with his own. But there is more than this to be said. All the ghazal's traditional themes occur in his verse, including that of passionate, all-consuming love of a man for his mistress. We know that Ghalib himself did not experience—more accurately, perhaps, did not allow himself to experience—such love, taking care to be, as he expressed it in one of his letters, 'the wise fly that settles not on the honey but on the sugar'. But that is not to say that he never wished he could have experienced it. In a letter written perhaps only a year or two before his death, he looks back on his life and quotes a verse of the Persian poet Anwari as describing his own position:

Alas! there is no patron who deserves my praise
Alas! there is no mistress who inspires my verse

and one of his own verses says:

Ghalib, don't ask again why I wander so restlessly
I said, my forehead seeks a threshold to bow down upon

It is not too fanciful to think that in some of his verses he is creating in fantasy the beloved which real life denied him and expressing for her all the feeling which he would have wished to experience but which no real woman in his life ever inspired in him. And as we have seen, the ghazal form does not inhibit him from adding to the traditional themes his own humorous, detached comments on love and on the lover's situation.

The mystic themes too he handles with equal ease—and allowing himself equal freedom. And since, as we have seen, the ghazal accommodates verses on any theme that can be expressed within the compass of a single couplet, he takes full advantage of the scope which this gives him.

But his choice of this form has a deeper relevance to his needs. If we look at the essential character of the ghazal's lover-hero, we can soon see why it appeals to Ghalib so powerfully. The lover is someone whom the experience of an all-consuming love has completely transformed. Few people in the society in which he lives have ever undergone such an experience, and to one who has not undergone it, it is something that thought and emotion alike can hardly ever begin to comprehend. Yet it is this experience which alone gives meaning to the lover's life. All other values, all other standards of conduct, are either discarded or are absorbed into, and given new meaning by the way of life which is learnt from love, and which love alone can teach. The lover thus lives out among others a life dedicated to, and directed by, ideals which even the most sensitive and sympathetic among them cannot comprehend. That great majority, which is neither particularly sensitive nor particularly sympathetic, because it cannot comprehend his values, shuns him, fears him and resents him. If you condense this description and express it in more general terms, you can say that in the ghazal the lover-hero, and the ghazal poet taking on that role, is someone to whom all the things that are most precious in life are the product of a unique, nearly incommunicable experience which is all-important, but which isolates him from his fellows and condemns him to live his life among people who cannot understand him, let alone appreciate him, and who cannot really accept him as one of their own community. But if this is true, anyone who is a poet and who feels himself to be in this position, can express what he feels by using the ghazal's portrayal of the situations of the lover as the symbols of his own experience. Ghalib, both as a poet and as a man, felt himself to be in this position, and used the ghazal in this way. When therefore he depicts himself in his ghazals as the true lover of a beautiful woman, gladly suffering all her cruelties, what he is often doing is asserting in traditional symbolism his unshakeable conviction of the soundness of his values and/or of the high quality of his poetry and declaring that so long as he has breath, he will continue to affirm them. For he has an unshakeable conviction of the originality and of the value to humankind of what he has to say and a determination to say it, upholding his beliefs to the end, no matter what other men may think of them.

> I filled the bloodstained pages with the story of my love
> And went on writing, even though my hands were smitten off

And in the last resort, he doesn't mind if his contemporaries lack the qualities which would enable them to value his poetry as it should be valued.

> I do not long for people's praise; I seek no one's reward
> And if they say my verses have no meaning, be it so

He was confident that it would win the esteem it deserved after his death and compared it to wine, which would be valued most once it had grown old. He too would then be 'a poet of the past':

> Today none buys my verse's wine, that it may grow in age
> To make the senses reel in many a drinker yet to come
> My star rose highest in the firmament before my birth
> My poetry will win the world's acclaim when I am gone

His confidence was justified. His 'world' was the world of Urdu-speakers, and since the beginning of the twentieth century these have come to understand and value him as his contemporaries could not. So too has that diminishing number of readers that can understand his beloved Persian. This book has been written in the hope that the boundaries of his 'world' can be extended and that English-speaking people too will be enabled to see something of his greatness.

4

Selections from Ghalib's Verse
Introductory Note

Ralph Russell

NOW THAT YOU ARE ABOUT to read a selection of Ghalib's coup-
lets, it may be useful to be reminded of some things I told you
earlier.

First, the division into Urdu and Persian is a purely conventional
one and has no other significance.

Remember that each couplet is, in the typical case, a completely
independent entity, unconnected in content with neighbouring
couplets. When couplets are connected, they are sometimes printed
accordingly, without a space between couplet and couplet.

I have printed the couplets in the order in which they occur in
the ghazals to which they belong, so that you can get some idea
of the impact they make in the original on an Urdu reader. The
abundance in Urdu, and no less striking lack in English, of
rhyming words makes it impossible in most cases to reproduce in
English one of the clearest indications of the formal unity of the
ghazal. I have, however, tried wherever possible, to use metres
resembling those of the original and have in all cases maintained
uniformity of metre throughout this ghazal.

I have used notes and explanations as sparingly as possible. Sometimes a little thought (and sometimes quite strenuous thought) will make the meaning clear to you. Where it doesn't, you should use the Explanatory Index, where I hope you will find all the help you need.

I have included in this selection only couplets which I think are worth your reading and have discarded those which are not of much worth or which defy adequate translation. In some cases, this has meant presenting only one couplet of a ghazal. Some I have included may at first sight be disconcerting and seem to offer you very little; if I am right, this will not be because they have nothing significant to say but because what they have to say is expressed in modes which the conventions of Urdu poetry sanction and those of English poetry do not. I have not thought this a sufficient reason to exclude them. See if you can learn to accept some of the conventions which, to Urdu readers, are entirely familiar.

The figures in the left-hand margin of the translations are there to help you in using the Explanatory Index. For example, if you will need to look up Tur in the index, you may well want to look at all the verses in which it is mentioned. You will find there (e.g.) U.63 (7), which means couplet 7 of Urdu ghazal no. 63. Similarly, P. stands for Persian. These number references are also for the benefit of readers who know Urdu and/or Persian and wish to compare my translations with the original. Readers who use Arshi's edition of the Urdu and Abidi's of the Persian should remember that I have omitted some couplets and that (e.g.) P.17 (7), which means the seventh couplet in my selection, will not necessarily be the seventh in the original Persian ghazal. But readers should not have any difficulty in identifying the couplets translated.

Ghalib's Urdu Verse

Ralph Russell

⌁ 5 ⌁

1   Love taught my nature what it is to know the zest of
      life
    I found a cure for sorrow in a sorrow without cure

2   Simplicity so full of wiles! Such unaware awareness!
    When beauty shows indifference, then comes the
       testing time

1   'zest'—this translates the dominant sense of the Urdu *maza* (taste) in this
context, but the more general sense, which would comprehend the
bitterness as well as the sweetness of life, is also relevant here. The
first 'sorrow' is the restlessness and dissatisfaction of life. The second
'sorrow' is the sorrow of love, love which gives meaning to life, and which
no one who has known it will ever abandon, though it brings lifelong
pain.

2   Beautiful women use their seeming simplicity, their seeming unaware-
ness of the impression they make, as a means of testing the resolve of
their admirers, of seeing whether their love can survive their indiffer-
ence.

❧ 6 ❧

1   Love, in whatever colour, is at enmity with worldly things
      Qais, even in the painting, stands naked and destitute

2   The rose's scent, the heart's complaint, smoke rising
        from the lamp—
      None comes from your assembly but distraught, in
        disarray

3   I hear again the clamour of lament arising in my heart
      Alas, the tear that I forbore to shed is now a flood!

1 The true lover can never hope for worldly affluence. Qais (see Explanatory Index) lost all for love. Even in the pictures of him, which cannot capture more than a part of the reality, this essential characteristic of him is depicted.

2 If I, your lover, am distressed when I leave you, that is only to be expected. *Everything* that leaves you is in disarray.

3 Love, despite all efforts to suppress it, will inevitably manifest itself.

❧ 11 ❧

The two are one: the words I breathe, the fragrance
    spreading from the rose
The garden blooms: and from it comes the flowering
    of my song

❧ 13 ❧

Why did I give my heart to her, thinking she would be true?
What a mistake to think an infidel a Musalman!

'infidel'—see Explanatory Index.

❧ 14 ❧

1   Love cries: Even the heart cannot contain me
      The pearl contains the ocean's restlessnes

2   Spring is the henna on the feet of autumn—nothing
        more:
      In this world, lasting sorrow follows transient delight

3   Parted from her I grieve. How then could I enjoy
        the garden?
      I could not bear to see the pointless laughter
        everywhere

1   All the ocean's restlessness seems to reside in a small pearl. The lover's
     heart is infinitely more capacious, but still it cannot contain all the restless
     striving of love.

2   Women stain their feet with henna to celebrate occasions of rejoicing, but
     it soon wears off.

3   The flower is said to laugh when it blooms. The sight of flowers in bloom
     is appropriate to a mood of joy, not of sorrow.

➤ 15 ↝

1   For every single drop my heart must render an
        account
      It held its blood in trust for my beloved's eyelashes

2   Now I must mourn the sacking of a city of desires
      You broke the mirror that reflected all I looked
        to find

1   My heart was wholly hers, as though I held it in trust for her. The grief
     I suffered in love for her crushed it to blood and I wept *tears* of blood,
     and every one of these tears was something which I owed as a debt to
     her. The beloved's eyelashes are often compared to daggers which wound
     the lover.

➤ 16 ↝

1   I pledge myself entire to love—and love of life
        possesses me
      I worship lightning—and lament the lightning's
        handiwork

2   Saki, the thirst the drinker feels is matched to his capacity
      And if you are a sea of wine, I am the thirsty shore

1   My dearest wish is to love, and yet I also want to live, and I know that
     love will destroy me.

2   It is no reflection on the beloved to feel that nothing she can give me
     can satisfy my thirst for more.

❧ 19 ❧

1   Beauty cannot shine forth unless it have the aid of darkness
     The garden is the mirror's verdure to the breeze of spring

2   The self-possession of the shore can never match the
               raging sea
     Where you are saki 'I am sober' is a spurious claim

1   Mirrors were made of burnished steel. 'verdure'—the green coating that
     develops when it is not kept burnished.

2   The appeal of beauty and love is irresistible.

❧ 20 ❧

1   What wonder if His mercy should accept in expiation
     The shame that will not let me ask forgiveness for my sins

2   What joy I feel as I go to the place of execution!
     My coming wounds are roses in the apron of my gaze

2   One of many extreme statements of the lover's willing acceptance
     of suffering, whether inflicted by a human or a divine beloved.
     Even death ('execution') must be welcomed if his death is what the
     beloved desires. He contemplates his coming wounds with the same joy
     as the gardener looks at the roses he has picked and carries in his apron.

❧ 21 ❧

1   Jealousy says, Alas! Alas! Her love is for my rival!
     Reason says, One cold as she cannot love any man

2   Love furnishes the pride of those whose hearts are
       truly humble
     Makes every grain of sand a desert, every drop a sea

3   I grapple with that fragment of ill fate that is my
       untamed heart
     The enemy of ease, the friend of reckless wandering

✎ 22 ✎

1   All that the nightingale can do provokes the rose's laughter
     What we call love is really a derangement of the mind

2   A hundred times I slipped the bonds of love, and I was free
     But what am I to do? My heart is foe to liberty

✎ 23 ✎

1   Exceeding difficult an easy task can prove to be
     Not every man can manage to achieve humanity

2   The place of slaughter offers lovers joys unspeakable
     The moon of Id appears for them each time she bares
       her sword

3   She took my life, and then repented of her cruelty
     Alas for the repentance of her who repents so soon!

2   Cf. ghazal 20.2. Muslims look forward eagerly to Id, which begins when
the new moon is sighted, after the month-long fast of Ramzan. Her
curved scimitar too resembles the new moon.

3   'so soon' —ironical. She repents because she no longer has a lover able
to meet all the demands which love will make of him.

✎ 26 ✎

1   My heart no longer holds desire; her very memory is gone
     Fire so consumed this house that all it held was burnt
       to ash

2   Ghalib I stand alone; my heart seeks only for despond-
        ency
    The warmth of worldly men was such it burnt
        my heart to ash

2   Ghalib, as often in the last couplet of a ghazal, is addressing himself.
Experience of the ostensible, but empty, friendliness of man for man is
so bitter that Ghalib no longer wants to feel anything but the constant
despondency which such bitterness should inspire. Cf. ghazal 88.2.

⤜ 27 ⤛

1   How simple is my yearning heart! Just see!
    How I recall again that sorceress!

2   I could have passed my life somehow without it
    Why then recall the lane in which you lived?

3   How endless is the desolation here!
    The desert scene recalls my home to me

4   How fiercely I shall quarrel with Rizvan
    If I recall your house in paradise!

1, 2 A 'wiser' man would forget a mistress who had caused him such sorrow,
and not call to mind the places where he had seen her.

4   Because, compared with your house, paradise will be a disappointment.

⤜ 28 ⤛

1   From all time God has given grace to those of high resolve
    The drops that did not turn to pearls dwell in the eyes

2   Sin's ocean was not vast enough; it dried right up
    And still my garment's hem was barely damp with it

1   A tear is a drop of water, and so, originally, is a pearl (see Explanatory
Index). God shows His special grace to lovers whose tears, the mark of
a sensitive heart, are more precious than pearls.

2   I committed all the sins there were to commit, and would have committed
many, many more. Cf. ghazal 79.2.

~✖ 29 ✖~

1   I have no more the strength to offer love's
     submissiveness
  I have no more the heart on which I used to pride myself

2   I go, bearing upon my heart the scar of all my yearning
  I am that burnt-out candle the assembly needs no more

3   My heart, think now of other ways to die; I am no
     more
  A worthy target for the blow of my beloved's knife

4   East, west, north, south, above, below are mirrors on
     all sides
  The world no more distinguishes the 'perfect' from the
     'flawed'

5   Now love has loosed the fastenings of all that veiled
     her beauty
  Now nothing but my gaze remains, a barrier between

6   Though I have passed my life in pledge to all the age's
     cruelties
  Yet never was the thought of you once absent from my
     mind

7   I no more long to reap a harvest from my love for her
  All that was gained by it was grief that nothing could
     be gained

8   Asad, I do not fear the pain of love's injustice, but
  I have no more the heart on which I used to pride
     myself

---

4   The mirror reflects the 'perfect' and the 'imperfect' impartially. When one
grows wise one realizes that the 'perfect' and the 'flawed' are alike mani-
festations of God.

5   The radiance of her beauty is such that the eye cannot dwell on it.

6   'in pledge to'—in pawn to—i.e. at the mercy of.

8   Asad = Ghalib. See Explanatory Index.

⤳ 30 ↩

I am collyrium freely given for the eyes of men
My price the recognition of what I confer on them

⤳ 33 ↩

1   Desire and fortitude alike are now a sea of blood
    That used to be a road more lovely than a rose in
        bloom

2   This corpse without a shroud is Asad's. Life has
        broken him
    God grant him His forgiveness! He was truly a free man

1   The grief of love crushes the heart to blood. The force of love moves
    it with all the power of a raging sea. Before love afflicted it, my heart was
    joyous and carefree, like a garden in bloom.

2   Like all true lovers he was indifferent to worldly possessions, and lacked
    even the means to provide properly for his burial.

⤳ 34 ↩

1   You are the one that does not know the music of
        His secrets
    Hidden no more than melody lies hidden in the lute

2   My heart insists that I maintain the struggle, for as yet
    My fingernails still owe a debt to this half-loosened knot

2   That is, it is my task to go on trying to solve the problems of life.

⤳ 35 ↩

1   Does your independence know no bounds, my
        gracious love? How long
    Shall I pour my heart out to you, just to hear you
        answer 'What?'

2   If it please his grace the preacher, let him come, with
         all my heart!
     Only let someone persuade me: What will he persuade
         me of?

3   If the preacher would confine me, very well then; be it so
     Does he really fancy that the ways of frenzied love will go?

4   I was born her tresses' slave, and fetters cannot frighten me
     Imprisoned in the bonds of love, the prison holds no
         dread for me

⤛ 36 ⤜

1   Now she deprives me even of her cruelty. Oh God!
     That she whom I so love should go so far in enmity

2   Ghalib, it is the rose's beauty teaches us to gaze
     No matter what the scene, no one should ever close
         his eyes

⤛ 37 ⤜

1   The shaikh sings loud the praises of the gardens of
         Rizvan; to us
     They lie, a bunch of faded flowers, upon oblivion's shelf

2   What words can tell the piercing pain her eyelashes
         inflict on me?
     My drops of blood are beads to make a coral rosary

3   In my construction lies concealed the stuff that is to
         ruin me
     The hot blood of the peasant holds the lightning for
         his crops

4   My silence hides a hundred thousand longings
         drowned in their own blood
     I am a burnt-out, tongueless lamp upon a stranger's grave

5   Some gleam still reaches to my heart, some traces of
        the thought of her
    It is a cell in Yusuf's jail where light comes filtering
        through

1   The pillars of orthodoxy seek to tempt their flock to do God's will with
the pleasures of paradise. The truly religious serve God because they are
lost to self in the love of God, and do not even remember the promises
of heavenly reward.

2   Cf. ghazal 15.1.

4   Those who can afford it keep a lamp burning on the graves of their loved
ones. Strangers have no one to light a lamp on their grave, and keep it
burning; 'tongueless' means both 'silent' and 'without the tongue of
flame' which burns in a lamp.

～✗ 38 ✗～

1   What urges to achieve, desire has brought us!
    And but for death where would be all life's joys?

2   What will this heedlessness achieve, my proud one?
    How long these 'What?'s to my petitionings?

3   I want your gaze to turn full force upon me
    Why try me so with constant heedlessness?

4   A straw on fire burns only for a moment
    Can lust be equal to the tasks of love?

5   Each breath a wave of self-oblivion's ocean
    Why should we blame the saki's heedlessness?

6   Each drop sings from the heart, 'I am the ocean!'
    'We are all His!' What greater praise than this?

7   1 will stand guarantee; look here, and fear not
    Who pays blood-price for those slain by your glance?

8   All that she is puts Ghalib's soul in turmoil
    All that she says, and hints, and looks, and does

5   Here, the saki stands for the beloved. If he does not pour us wine, it does
not matter. We are lost to self, sunk in self-oblivion's ocean, so that we

are that ocean, and its waves are the breaths we draw. True love demands nothing of the beloved.

6 The soul can reach no higher development than to merge in God, and can ask and receive no higher praise than the recognition that it is now indistinguishable from Him.

7 A beautiful beloved has every right to slay her lover, so the question of blood-price does not arise. So have no fear. Look at me, and slay me with your glance.

⤳ 39 ↝

Alas that I of all men should come thirsty from the tavern!
I had sworn not to drink—but what had happened to the
    saki?

It was the saki's duty to press me to drink, and he failed in his duty. The fact that I had determined not to drink does not absolve him from his duties.

⤳ 40 ↝

1 My home would have been ruins had I never shed a tear
Had the sea not been sea, it would have been a desert waste

2 You must not blame your straitened heart. The heart
    makes its own laws
Were it not straitened it would then have been in disarray

3 After a lifetime's abstinence he would have let me in
Alas that it was not Rizvan stood sentry at her door!

1 My house had been destroyed in a flood of weeping. But the true lover's house is fated to be destroyed anyway.

2 Two interpretations are possible. 'Straitened' translates the Urdu word *tang*, which can mean either distressed or narrow; 'heart' translates *dil*, which can also mean mind; 'in disarray' translates *pareshan*, which can mean either worried or scattered. One interpretation would be that the heart *wants* to experience the grief of love, and is anxious if it does not experience it. The other would be that it is the most narrow-minded men who experience the greatest peace of mind. The power of imagination that makes you think that you may be mistaken can also disorient you, and leave you in anxious uncertainly about how you should live.

3   The picture is of a lover who has never been allowed access to his beloved. Her doorkeeper has always barred his way. To get into her house is more difficult than to get into paradise.

❧ 41 ❧

1   If you were late, there must have been some reason
      for your lateness
     Left to yourself, you would have come; but someone
      held you back

2   I am at fault if I call you the cause of my undoing
     Some hint of my good fortune was a factor in it too

3   In prison, your distracted lover still thinks of your
      tresses
     True, he has also felt the burden of his heavy chains

4   You came and went before my eyes like lightning
      flashing. Why?
     Could you not speak to me? My ears were thirsting
      for your words

5   The angels write, and we are seized. Where is the
      justice there?
     Did we have no one present when they wrote their
      record down?

6   Ghalib, you aren't the only one supreme in Urdu verse
     They tell me that in former times there lived a certain
      Mir

1   'someone'—i.e. my rival. There is thus an implied reproach to her.

2   'good fortune'—*apparently* ironical, but really not so. To love her was indeed good fortune, besides which his inevitable ruin is nothing.

3   Imprisonment in chains brings *some* distress, but my constant awareness of my love for you all but banishes it. 'tresses'—the beloved's tresses, which hold the lover captive, are regularly compared to the chains which are put on a prisoner.

5   'The angels'—i.e. the *kiramun katibin*. The verse is a humorous assertion of *man's* rights—even against God.

6 'Mir'—the greatest Urdu poet of the eighteenth century, and one of the supreme exponents of the ghazal. See Ralph Russell and Khurshidul Islam, *Three Mughal Poets* (1968)—republished by Oxford University Press, Delhi, 1991; paperback edition, 1993.

～✲ 42 ✒～

1 It was her beauty I described, and my words that described it
   And he is now my rival who was once my confidant

2 Would that I could have looked out from an even greater height
   Would that I had my dwelling place above the throne of God

3 What special wisdom did I have? What unique skill was mine?
   Heaven had no reason, Ghalib, to become my enemy

2 Ghalib seems to be saying 'I stand level with the throne of God, in the highest heaven, from where I can survey the whole universe. Would that there were an even higher point from which I could see even more, including heaven and hell.'

3 'Heaven'—the sky, the stars, fate. It is the most talented men that fate ruins. Why does it ruin *me*? Ironical.

～✲ 43 ✒～

1 This was not to be my fate that all should end in lover's meeting
   Even had I gone on living, I should still be waiting, waiting

2 Did your promise save my life? Yes!—for I knew you would not keep it
   Would I not have died of joy if I had thought you would fulfil it?

3 Am I still to call it friendship when my friends start preaching at me?
   Someone should have brought me comfort, someone should have shared my sorrows

4   From the flint blood would come flooding—such a
     flow that none could staunch it
     Had what you see as my sorrow been the fire that
     hides within it

5   Grief wastes our life away, and yet—how shall we flee
     the heart within us?
     Had we not known the grief of love, we would have
     known the grief of living

6   With what style you handle, Ghalib, all these themes of
     mystic teaching!
     What a saint we would have thought you if you had
     not been a drinker!

4   The sorrow that I endure is far greater than you can conceive of. Had
     the hard, unfeeling flint had to bear such sorrow, not sparks, but blood,
     would have flowed from it in a stream that none would have been able
     to staunch. I, the lover, the true man, am stronger than stone. I can bear
     a sorrow that nothing else in creation can.

6   It is said that Ghalib recited this verse in the presence of Bahadur Shah
     Zafar. The King said, 'No, my friend; even so we should never have
     thought you a saint.' Ghalib replied, 'Your Majesty thinks me one even
     now, and only speaks like this lest my sainthood should go to my head.'

～✗ 44 ✗～

When nothing was, then God was there; had nothing been,
     God would have been
My being has defeated me. Had I not been, what would
     have been?

What was God's purpose in creating me?

～✗ 45 ✗～

1   Night has fallen; once again the shining stars come
     into view
     In such majesty as if the temple doors were opened
     wide

2   Though I do not understand her words, and may not
know her heart
Is it not enough that one so beautiful now speaks to me?

3   In the thought of beauty dwells a sort of thought of
goodness too
Here within my grave a door has opened onto paradise

1   'temple'—see Explanatory Index.

3   To think of your beloved, and of beauty, is itself a sort of good deed—
and in the grave, a door opens for those who have lived a good life, and
through it blow the cooling breezes of paradise.

～✖ 46 ✖～

1   She has foresworn her cruelty—but can she?
She says, 'How can I show my face to you?'

2   All night, all day, the seven heavens are turning
Something will happen; set your mind at ease

3   She fights me, and I tell myself she loves me:
When she feels nothing, what can I dream then?

4   See, I keep pace with him who bears my letter
Am I then to deliver it myself?

5   What though a wave of blood should overwhelm me?
How can I leave the threshold of my love?

6   I passed my life waiting for death to take me
And dead, I still must see what I must see

7   She is perplexed. She asks me, 'Who is Ghalib?'
Tell me, someone, What answer can I give?

1   Shame at the thought of her past cruelties makes her hide her face—and
that is cruel!

4   'keep pace'—so impatient am I to have her reply.

5   What though every conceivable misfortune should befall me?

6   'what I must see'—what God has in store for me.

✄ 47 ✄

1 My pain would not accept salve's healing favours
Well, if I am not well, that is not ill

2 Where shall I go to try my fortunes then?
You would not try your dagger on my breast

3 How sweet your lips must be! Even my rival
Relished the insults they bestowed on him

4 The news comes hot that she is on her way
Just on the day my house is empty, bare

5 Was it a case of Namrud's godhead then?
Submission to Your will brought me no gain

6 I gave my life; I gave her what was hers
It would be right to say right was not done

7 The wound was bound; blood did not cease to flow
A plan was thwarted; no more came of it

8 Ghalib, recite some verse, for people say
Today we still await one of your ghazals

1 That malady of love which consents to be cured deserves no respect.

5 Perhaps You whom I worship are not really God at all. Otherwise, what has become of Your all-powerful beneficence?

7 When my wounds were bandaged, the flow of blood should have stopped—but it did not. When my plans were thwarted, there should have been some other way forward—but there was not. In short, both in love and in life I was doomed to failure.

✄ 48 ✄

1 We serve You; yet our independent self-regard is such
We shall at once turn back if we should find the Kaba
closed

2 Lament that cannot reach the lips will scar the heart within
The drop that cannot be the sea is swallowed by the dust

3 Such grief fell to my lot as has befallen no one else
   Such trials beset my path as never yet faced anyone

4 Unless, when you are telling it, blood drips from every
      hair
   You tell the Tale of Hamza, not the story of your love

5 Unless the sea within the drop, the whole within the part
   Appear, you play like children; you still lack the seeing eye

6 The word went round that Ghalib would be hacked in
      little pieces
   We went to see the sight, but there was nothing there
      to see

2 Everything worthwhile should find expression; to suppress it, and so
   make it worthless, is a matter for shame.

4 The reference is to the voluminous medieval romance of Islamic chivalry,
   in which the exploits of Amir Hamza, the Prophet's uncle, are recounted.
   It was enjoyed by men of all classes (including Ghalib), but not regarded
   as serious literature. If your love is real love, its story will be a classic.

5 You are not mature unless you can see the part as a microcosm of the
   whole.

6 Ghalib's beloved had sworn to hack him to pieces, and his enemies went
   to exult in the spectacle. But she did not appear—either because she was
   too indifferent to his love to bother to put him to the supreme test, or
   because she knew he would pass that test, and there was therefore no point
   in subjecting him to it.

～✗ 56 ✗～

Draw not a single breath outside desire's assembly
No wine yet comes? Wait for the goblet to come round

Never cease to desire, and to hope.

～✗ 57 ✗～

1 Beauty will rest, its war of glances cease, now I am gone
   Fair cruel mistresses will live at peace now I am gone

2 Love's throne will seek in vain a lover worthy of my place
   And beauty's airs, and beauty's graces fail now I am gone

3 The candle is put out; smoke from it rises in the air
   Love's flame dons black to mourn my memory now I
   am gone

4 Laid in the dust, my heart is crushed to blood, because
   I know
   The fair will not need henna for their hands now I am gone

5 Love's frenzy clasps its lovers in a last farewell embrace
   And lovers' garments will no more be rent now that I
   am gone

6 Who now takes up the challenge of love's wine? Who
   drains the cup?
   This is a cry the saki must repeat now I am gone

7 I die of grief, for now the world will not bring forth a man
   To mourn the death of love and loyalty now I am gone

8 Ghalib, I see love's helplessness, and weep to see it so
   Whose home will its destroying flood turn to now I
   am gone?

The whole poem is the poet's proud assertion of his uniqueness as a lover.
Only one couplet has been omitted in translation. Love and fair women,
he says, will alike find no scope for their work when I am dead. The theme
is repeated in all the standard metaphors of Urdu love poetry.

1 Fair women do not use the dagger of their glance against men unworthy
   of their steel.

4 Women adorn their hands with henna to please their lovers. Now that
   there are no lovers worthy of their attention, they do not need it.

5 The frenzied lover rends his garments. Now there will be no true lovers,
   and the rending will cease.

6 Hali, Ghalib's friend and biographer, has commented on this couplet in
   a way which illustrates very well how the Urdu reader scans the ghazal
   to extract every nuance of every verse. The saki offering wine is the
   beautiful woman inviting men to fall in love with her—men who have
   the courage and steadfastness to bear the trials of love even at the cost
   of life itself. After I am gone, says Ghalib, no one will take up that
   challenge. But, says Hali, Ghalib himself used to say that there is a subtle

point in the reference to the repetition of the saki's cry. He cries it first
as a challenge, in a bold and defiant tone, and the second time he repeats
it sadly to himself, knowing that the answer is, 'No one!'

➤ 59 ✦

1   It makes my heart quail when I see the effort of the
       blazing sun
    I, a mere drop of dew that hangs upon the desert thorn

2   I see the sunset-reddened cloud and find myself
       remembering
    How, parted from you, fire would rain upon the
       rose-garden

3   Don't quarrel with him, Ghalib, if the counsellor is
       harsh with you
    Think of yourself—how violently your own hands
       rend your clothes

1   He compares his heart with a drop of dew, and the dew's shimmering
with his heart's trembling. Both are delicate and beautiful, and all the
immense forces of nature and of the world expend their strength to crush
delicate and beautiful things.

3   It's his nature; he's no more at fault than you are when you rend your
clothes in love's frenzy.

➤ 60 ✦

The staring mirror's brightness is discoloured in the end
The standing water grows its own green surface in the end

No matter how pure your heart, it will itself become impure unless it is active
for good.

➤ 62 ✦

We cry to fate, 'Restore to us the life of ease that once was ours!'
We think our looted wealth a debt the robber owes to us

⤳ 63 ⟿

1   To practise general cruelty denies the honour due to love
     I hold back when I see that you are cruel without cause

2   I give my poetry away, and give myself along with it
     But first I look for people who can value what I give

3   Put on the sacred thread, and break the hundred-
        beaded rosary
     The traveller takes the path he sees to be the even one

4   You should have let Your radiance fall on me, not on
        the Mount of Tur
     One pours wine in the measure that the drinker can
        contain

1   One wants a *discriminating* beloved, who practises her cruelty only on those who truly love her.

3   The rosary symbolizes narrow, orthodox Islam. The sacred thread symbolizes Hinduism, which itself symbolizes the worship of beauty (beautiful women, 'idols') as an aspect of the true worship of God. It is easy to travel that smooth path—as the fingers run easily along the thread. The other path is hilly—the fingers go up and down over each bead.

4   Unlike the mountain, I could have sustained Your full revelation. It's no good giving a man more wine than he can hold.

⤳ 64 ⟿

1   Since I have made my home, without your leave, right
        by your door
     Will you say, even now, you need directing to my house?

2   She says, when I no longer even have the power of
        speech
     'How should I know a man's heart if he does not
        speak to me?'

3   I have to do with her of whom no man in all the world
     Has ever spoken yet without calling her 'cruel one'

4   I have nothing to say to you; else I am not the man
To hold my tongue; I would speak out though it cost
     me my head

5   I will not cease to worship her, that infidel, my idol
Though all creation never cease to call me infidel

6   I mean her airs and graces, but I cannot talk of them
Unless I speak in terms of knives and daggers that
     she wields

7   I talk of contemplating God but cannot make my point
Unless I speak of wine-cup and intoxicating wine

8   Since I am deaf I make a claim to double kindness
     from you
I cannot hear what you have said unless you say it twice

9   Ghalib, you must not lay your plea repeatedly before her
All that you feel, she knows; you need not speak a
     single word

1   I've constantly asked you to visit me and your excuse has always been 'I
don't know the way'. But now....

6, 7   An acceptance of the conventional metaphors of the ghazal.

8   Humorous. He wants her to repeat her words of kindness, and makes
the excuse that he is deaf. And Ghalib became deaf as he got older!

9   The 'her' and 'she' could be taken to refer to God.

～✗ 65 ✗～

1   Because her every gesture seems to hint at something
     different
When she shows love for me I think, 'She must mean
     something else'

2   O Lord, they do not understand, nor *will* they
     understand my words
Give them another heart, or else give me another
     tongue

3   For all the expertise I have acquired in breaking idols
     So long as *I* exist a heavy stone still blocks my path

4   The world holds other poets too who write good poetry
     But Ghalib's way of saying things, they say, is
       something else

3   'idols'—false beliefs and conventions. Love, whether for woman, or God, or one's ideals, has not reached its full development until one's ego has been destroyed.

⤙ 68 ⤚

If you would solve your problems, prayer's enchantment
     does not work
O Lord, accept my supplication: Long may Khizar live!

It is useless to *pray* for what you want. Prayers are never granted—unless, of course, you pray *this* kind of prayer! (Khizar had already been granted eternal life!)

⤙ 69 ⤚

1   I am no melody, I am no lute
     I am the sound that my own breaking makes

2   You, and the coiling tresses of your hair
     I, and my endless, dark imaginings

3   Love of my captor holds me in her snare
     It is not that I lack the power of flight

4   Now Asadullah Khan is dead! Alas!
     That zest for wine and beauty is no more!

2   A play on words too; 'coiling' suggests perplexity and anguish. The long black hair of the beloved is regularly compared to the endless dark nights of separation.

⤙ 78 ⤚

1   My sighs will need a lifetime to touch your unfeeling heart
     Who lives so long a life that he can hope to conquer you?

2   Within the coil of every wave a hundred monsters lurk
    See what the drop endures before it can become a pearl

3   Love demands patience; longing and desire brook no delay
    How shall I rule my heart till resolution takes control?

4   I grant you that you will not be indifferent—but then
    I shall be dust before you realize that I am there

5   The radiance of the sun teaches the dew to lose itself
    I too live till I win the favour of a glance from you

6   O heedless one, your lifespan lasts no longer than a glance
    Our life here is as transient as is the dancing spark's

7   Asad, the grief of life can find no other cure than death
    The candle, come what may, burns on until the
        morning dawns

This is a complete ghazal, characteristic in the discreteness of its constituent verses, but with an overall tone of humorous irony in those that are addressed to his beloved.

5   The word translated 'lose itself' is that regularly used in Urdu to signify complete merging of, or death of, the individual soul in God.

～✗ 79 ✗～

1   If you are sure that God will grant your prayer, then
        do not ask
    That is, ask only for a heart that has nothing to ask

2   It calls to mind the number of the scars of thwarted
        yearnings
    So do not ask me, God, to count the number of my sins

2   Cf. ghazal 28.2.

～✗ 80 ✗～

They make me feel ashamed to face the breezes of the spring
My empty wine-cup and my heart that takes no joy in flowers

❧ 82 ❦

1 We who are free grieve only for a moment
And use the lightning's flash to light our homes

2 Asad, a hundred thousand longings live their life
confined in it
To me, my heart, crushed all to blood, is just a
prison-house

❧ 83 ❦

1 He took my life in foreign lands, far from my own country
Thanks be to God, who saved me from the shame of
friendlessness

2 Her coiling tresses lie in wait for me. I pray to God
I claimed that I am free: God grant I am not put to shame!

1 Most people prefer to die among friends. But if one dies friendless in a
strange country, and receives a pauper's funeral, at any rate he is unknown.
To die thus in your own country, where everyone knows you, and *still*
to die uncared for would be a great disgrace. Ostensibly an expression
of thanks to God; in fact a bitter complaint against his fellow-countrymen.

❧ 85 ❦

1 You stand away, and purse your lips, and show their
rose-bud form
I said, 'How do you kiss?' Come, kiss my lips and say,
'Like this!'

2 How does she steal your heart? Why ask? She does not
speak a word
But every gesture, every grace, is telling you 'Like this!'

3 At night, and flushed with wine, and in my rival's
company—
God grant that she may come to me, but not, O God,
like this

4 How should I not sit silent facing her in her assembly?
   Her silence is itself enough to tell me, 'Sit like this!'

5 I said, 'From love's assembly every rival should be
      banished'
   What irony! She heard me, sent me out, and said,
      'Like this!'

6 If people say, 'Can Urdu then put Persian verse to
      shame?'
   Recite a line of Ghalib's verse and tell them, 'Yes! Like
   this!'

~ 87 ~

Though it play only strains of grief, my heart, yet you
   must treasure them
The music of this lute of life will all be stilled one day

Cf. ghazal 139.

~ 88 ~

1 You who gaze in the mirror, look at *me*
   And see the longing gaze I turn on you

2 Ghalib, I dress myself in beggar's clothing
   And watch the way the bountiful behave

1 The mirror is said to gaze spellbound at the beloved's beauty. But the
   impact on me is even greater.

2 Cf. ghazal 26.2.

~ 90 ~

What greater trial than this, that when she heard how
      Laila came to Qais
She asked in wonderment, 'Do people *really* act like this?'

❧ 91 ❧

1 I may be good, I may be bad—I live in ill-matched
    company
   A flower thrown on the bonfire, or a weed among the
    flowers

2 Asad, I am prisoner, enslaved by beauty's kindnesses
   Her loving arm's embrace is like a collar for my neck

2 'collar'—the collar fastened on a slave's neck.

❧ 93 ❧

Love for the rose binds all. All claims to liberty are false
The garden's prison holds the 'independent' cypress fast

The rose is the beloved of not only its traditional lover, the nightingale, but
of the whole garden. The tall, proud cypress (itself often used as a symbol of
independence) claims to be independent, but love for the rose in fact roots
it where it is.

❧ 95 ❧

1 She gave her heart, and now she too knows what it is
    to sit alone
   At last she knows my helplessness for what it really is

2 Not one created atom here but what is destined to decay
   The sun on high a lamp that gutters in the windy street

❧ 96 ❧

1 Now meeting's joys and parting's tears have fled away
   Those nights and days and months and years have fled
    away

2 Who now has time for all the many tasks of love?
   The urge to gaze on beauty now has fled away

3   I have no heart, no fancy even, to seek such things
     The frenzy that fair faces roused has fled away

4   One person's image was the source from which it
         sprang
     Now all imagination's grace has fled away

5   What now can make the tears of blood flow from my
         eyes?
     That fortitude, that firm resolve, has fled away

6   The gaming house of love will know me now
         no more
     All that I had to wager there is fled away

7   Cares of the world beset me now, and now the
         strength
     To bear all life's calamities has fled away

8   All Ghalib's powers are wasted now, and in decline
     That elemental harmony has fled away

⟳ 98 ⟲

1   True love does not despair of its effect
     Life-sacrifice is not a willow tree

2   Your radiance gives being to the world
     The sun's light shines in every particle

3   If I should die it could betray her secret
     I have no other hidden fear of death

4   Fear that a change may come in your good fortune
     Eternal deprivation brings no grief

5   They say that it is hope that we all live by
     I do not even hope that I shall live

---

1   The willow tree bears no fruit.

4   If you have known no other state, you do not grieve at its continuance.
   It is reversals of good fortune that bring distress.

～ 99 ⋉

My rival's honeyed words have worked the spell that he
　　intended
And I am dumb; the thought, 'He loves me' does not cross
　　her mind

～ 100 ⋉

1　Were it not easy to gain access to you, all were easy
　　The difficulty is just this: it is not difficult

2　Unless you love, you cannot live; but, for myself, I know
　　I lack the strength to bear the joy of all love's cruelties

3　I have seen Asad many times, in private and in public
　　If he is not demented, then he also is not sane

1　Because access to you is not difficult, I am in difficulties, for I fear I may
have rivals.

～ 101 ⋉

1　Love has laid waste my home, and I am overcome by
　　shame
　　All that I have to offer is the longing to rebuild

2　Asad, they hear my verses now merely for their
　　amusement
　　I know now, nothing comes of showing skill in poetry

1　. I am ashamed because I have nothing more for love to destroy. I would
have liked its destruction of all I possess to continue forever.

～ 102 ⋉

1　It is the sun that sends its gaze in particles to gather there
　　No particles of dust are these that throng the windows
　　　of her home

2   All that gives radiance to life comes from the love that
      ruins your home
    Only the lightning that destroys the crops lights up
      this gathering

3   Slain by the pride of her who came with all the beauty
      of the spring
    Only the rose's radiance—no dust—is found within
      my grave

4   Ghalib, who honoured you at home, that other lands
      should value you?
    Be frank: you are the straw that does not feed the
      bonfire's flame

❧ 104 ☙

1   My sighs are an implied request, ingenious torturer
    Asking for—not complaining of—your cruel tyranny

2   They call this love?—to labour amid Khusrau's luxury?
    A 'good name' like Farhad's is one that I would not accept!

3   Its desolation matches this, but where this vast expanse?
    The desert brings me ease that banishes all thought of
      home

4   The radiance that lights your lane lights paradise as well
    The scene is just the same, but where's the joy in
      living there?

5   Ghalib, what right have you to make complaint of
      other lands?
    Do you forget the callousness of all your friends at home?

❧ 105 ☙

Once you are kind to me you can send for me when you will
I am not like time past, that I can never come again

✤ 106 ✤

At last she came into my home—such is the
    power of God!
Sometimes I turn my gaze on her, sometimes
    upon my home

✤ 107 ✤

1   If she is true to me my rival calls it cruelty
    To speak ill of the good has ever been the
        common way

2   Today I go to tell her of the turmoil of my heart
    I go, but when I see her let us see what will be said

3   They are survivors of a former age; do not
        condemn them
    They think that wine and music can make sorrow
        flee away

4   The object of my worship lies beyond perception's
        reach
    To those who see, the Kaba is a compass, nothing
        more

✤ 108 ✤

1   Her cruelty does not mean that she doubts my loyalty
    She means to tease me, not to put my true love to
        the test

2   What words can tell my gratitude for such especial
        kindness?
    She asks how I am faring—and yet does not speak
        a word

3   Her cruelty is dear to me, and I am dear to her
    What if she is not kind to me? She is not then unkind

4 No kisses? Very well then; but at least you can
     revile me
   You may not have a mouth, but after all you have
     a tongue

5, 6 Although the violence of your wrath dissolves my
     life to nothing
   Although I lack the strength I need to bear it all,
     and win
   My soul still sings the melody of 'Strike me
     yet again!'
   My lips are strangers to the lilting song of
     'I give in!'

7 Love's madness brings no loss. What if my home
     goes all to ruin?
   A desert for a plot of land is not a bad exchange!

8 You want to know what has been written in my des-
     tiny
   —As though the mark of idol-worship were not on
     my brow

9 He gives me something of the meed of praise my
     verse deserves
   What if the angel Gabriel speaks in another tongue?

4 In poetic hyperbole, the mistress's mouth is represented as being so small
   as to be non-existent.

7 The desert in which the frenzied lover roams is, so to speak, his domain.

8 Which *shows* that my destiny is to worship beauty. Those who are
   assiduous in their prostrations acquire a callous on their forehead. In
   poetic legend, and in popular proverb, your fate is inscribed upon your
   forehead.

9 The angel Jibril (Gabriel) conveyed the Quran, the word of God, to the
   Prophet, and is himself renowned for his eloquence. 'In another tongue'
   has more than one meaning: angels do not speak the same language as
   men; he does not speak my language and therefore can't appreciate it
   properly, and that's why he gives me only something of the praise I
   deserve; his eloquence is no match for mine, so how could he be expected
   to appreciate the full excellence of mine?

⤙ 109 ⤚

1   He never sent the wine-cup yet my way in her assembly
I wonder if the saki has mixed something with the wine?

2   When she rejects all love, how can she fall into his snare?
Why these misgivings that my friend has dealings
with my foe?

3   When I am with you, fear of *him* makes me feel ill
at ease
What baseless fancy troubles *you* and agitates you so?

4   Thousands of signs of love cannot match one averted gaze
Thousands of self-adornings cannot match one flare
of wrath

5   Ghalib takes wine no more, but even now from time
to time
He drinks, when skies are cloudy, or on nights the
moon shines bright

1   In her assembly, the saki has never yet poured me wine, and yet today
he does. Why? Maybe because he too loves her, and sees me as a rival,
so he has put something in the wine to poison me.

2   'my friend'—my beloved; 'foe'—i.e. rival.

3   *I'm* uneasy for fear that my rival may break in upon us. What's troubling
you? Some baseless fancy that I too have a liaison with someone else?

5   The rainy season and the moonlit nights traditionally provide the
inspiration for drinking. Cf. ghazal 115.1.

⤙ 110 ⤚

1   Forget tomorrow! Pour the wine today, and do not stint
Such care reflects on him who pours the wine in paradise

2   Today we are abased. Why so? For yesterday You would
not brook
The insolence the angel showed towards our majesty

3   The steed of life runs on. None knows where it will
        stay its course
    The reins have fallen from our hands, the stirrups
        from our feet

1   The saki is reluctant to pour the wine in the full measure Ghalib asks
    for because he is afraid that he will not have enough left to pour tomorrow.
    Ghalib takes 'tomorrow' in a sense common in Urdu poetry—that of life
    after death. On that tomorrow, he says, there will be wine in abundance,
    and to think that there will not is reflection upon Ali, the saki in paradise.

2   'You' is God; 'the angel' is Iblis; 'we' means humankind, the descendants
    of Adam.

➤ 111 ⮜

1   See! She too says, 'He is of no repute, of no renown'
    If I had known, I would not thus have given all I had

2   I go some way with every one I see advancing swiftly
    So far I see no one whom I can take to be my guide

3   To think desire is adoration is to be a fool
    How should I *worship* her who treats me with
        such tyranny?

4   I thought that others too, like me, appreciated art
    I thought a man's accomplishments were pleasing
        to them too

1   It was for her that I sacrificed my good name, my everything. When *others*
    despised me for it, I could bear it....

4   One of Ghalib's many complaints that his contemporaries do not
    appreciate true talent.

➤ 113 ⮜

1   He gave me both the worlds and told Himself,
        'He is content'
    And I, tongue-tied with shame, had not the heart
        to ask for more

2 At every stage there are a few too tired to journey on
There They cannot find the way to You; what else are they
to do?

2 All who maintain the search for God (or for truth) as far as their varying
powers allow them deserve our (and His) sympathy and respect.

✼ 114 ✼

1 Where are they all? Some bloom again as tulips
or as roses
There in the dust how many forms forever lie
concealed!

2 I too remembered gatherings rich in all kinds
of beauty
Now they are only forms and patterns on
oblivion's shelf

3 Sleep is for him, and pride for him, and night for him
Upon whose arm your lovely tresses all dishevelled lay

4 I went into the garden, and it seemed a school
assembled
The nightingales heard my laments, then sang their
songs of love

5 How ill my fate! her lowered eyes show only
eyelashes
Why then, O God, is it that they can pierce right
through my heart?

6 How, even if I reached her, could I answer her
revilings?
All my fair words were spent in gaining access to
her house

7 Wine gives such life to man that on the hand that
takes the goblet
Every line seems like a vein through which the life-
blood runs

⁸ Our creed is 'God is one', our cry, 'Abandon rituals!'
So that communities dissolve to constitute one faith

⁹ When one becomes inured to sorrow, sorrow vanishes
Such hardships have befallen me that life is easy now.

¹ Beauty that mingles in the dust reappears—sometimes—in new shapes
of beauty. *Sometimes....*

⁵ Her eyes are lowered in modesty and he can see only her eyelashes. Yet
these pierce his heart through, as though they were the arrows of her full
gaze upon him.

⁸ The cardinal doctrine of Islam is that God is one; the concept is here used
not in the usual sense of the orthodox, who point to it as the expression
of the superiority of Islam to most other religions, but in the mystic sense
of the essential oneness of *all* true religions, the oneness of all who love
their god, under whatever name they know him.

⤜ 115 ⤐

¹ Let someone tell me, What is wrong then with the
    moonlit night?
What of it if the day was cloudless and the air
    was still?

² When I present myself she has no word of greeting
    for me
When I depart to go elsewhere she does not say
    farewell

³ If joy and sorrow go together, what is that to me?
The heart that God bestowed on me is one that
    knows no joy

⁴ Ghalib, why keep reminding her of promises
    she made?
What use is it to tell her if she answers
    'I forgot'?

¹ If the *day* was not the kind of day on which you like to drink, never mind;
the *night* is. Cf. 109.5.

❧ 116 ✐

No, she does not bow down to God
  Yes, she is faithless too. Now go!
If I had prized my heart and faith
  Would I have gone into her lane?

Ghalib was broken, and is dead.
  Nothing has ceased since he has gone
Why do they weep so copiously?
  Why do they beat their breast and mourn?

❧ 117 ✐

1   Your heart is sick with envy? Fire it with the zeal
      to see
    Keep gazing on; your narrowed eyes may yet be
      opened wide

2   The urge to sin should match the scale of yearning
      in my heart
    The seven seas would do no more than wet my
      garment's hem

1   The more you see of the world, the less reason you find to envy any man.

2   'urge to sin' is obscure. The point is the same as that of 179.1. The supply
    of sin is far short of what I need to satisfy my urge to sin. The metaphor
    in the second line is a common one in Urdu. You plunge into sin as
    you plunge into water. Alas! there is not enough water in all the seven
    seas.

❧ 118 ✐

1   I feel no such constraint, I do not tell you 'You must
      love me'
    Feel what you feel for *me*, though it be only enmity

2   The grievance that I feel is that you talk about my rival
    I feel it even though you do it to complain of him

3   Each of us is a world in which all kinds of fancies
        throng
    I sit in an assembly even though I am alone

4   To live in freedom does not mean to hold yourself
        aloof from men
    Flee from yourself, and not from others, if you want
        to flee

5   Nothing can take away the grief that life is all too short
    Though every precious hour be spent in bowing
        down to God

⤝ 119 ⤞

1   Be knowingly indifferent, that I may have some hope
    This wayward glance that does not know me is like
        poison to me

2   So sensitive are you, you take my silence for complaint
    So vulnerable I, your mere indifference tortures me

⤝ 121 ⤞

1-3 Now let me go away and live somewhere where no
        one else will be
    Where there is none that knows my tongue, where
        there is none to speak with me

    There let me build myself a house with, so to say, no
        doors, no walls
    And live there without neighbours and with no one to
        keep watch for me

    If I fall ill, then there should be no one to come and
        visit me
    And if I die let none be there to weep and wail and
        mourn for me

2   I.e. to which access is impossible.

❧ 123 ❦

1   Meet with my rival if you like; I leave that to your whim
    But what is wrong with asking after me as well as him?

2   None will escape the retribution due on Judgement Day
    And if my rival murdered me, he did so in your sight

3   The tavern is no more. What does it matter where I drink?
    Be it the mosque, the seminary, or the hermitage

4   All that they say in praise of paradise is true, I know
    God grant, though, that it be illumined by *your*
    radiance!

❧ 124 ❦

1   If I rest in the Kaba, do not taunt me. Do I then
    Forget the claims the people of the temple have on me?

2   God's will be done; but not from greed for heaven's
    wine and honey
    Take hold of paradise, someone, and cast it into hell!

3   How can I tread the beaten path to heavenly reward?
    The knife that nibbed the pen that wrote my fate cut
    it askew

4   Ghalib, no matter how I toil, my labour bears no fruit
    Lightning will strike my granaries if locusts spare my
    fields

1   If I have become a true Muslim, that does not mean that I do not
    remember with gratitude all that idol-worshippers gave me.

❧ 126 ❦

1   Here in my cage I mourn; and even if my plaint
    displeases them
    Yet does my being harm the birds that fill the garden
    with their song?

2   The rumour spread abroad they would be making
        fetters for my feet
    And deep within the mine the iron in the ore
        stirred restlessly

3   I feel no joy though clouds should mass a hundred
        times above my fields
    To me it means that lightning seeks already to find
        out my crop

4   One must be constant to the end; this is the essence
        of the faith
    The priest dies in his temple—let the Kaba be his
        burial-place

5   My destiny was martyrdom, for God had made my
        nature so
    That every time I saw the sword I bowed my neck to
        take its blow

6   Had he not robbed me in the day, could I have slept
        so sound at night?
    I feel no more the fear of theft. My blessings on the
        highwayman!

7   Can I not then write poetry, that I should go in quest
        of jewels?
    Have I not then a heart within, that I should go and
        dig in mines?

---

4   Addressed to the orthodox Muslim. He should hold the priest ('Brahman'
in the original) who has lived true to his beliefs worthy of burial in the
Islamic holy of holies.

⤳ 127 ↢

1   You gave your heart away. Why then lament your loss
        in plaintive song?
    You have a breast without a heart. Why not a mouth
        without a tongue?

2   She will not change her nature and I have my
        standards to maintain
    How can I stoop to ask of her the reason for her
        high disdain?

3   My confidant has brought me shame. A love like this
        is an offence!
    He lacked the strength to bear my grief. Why then
        accept my confidence?

4   Here in my cage fear not, my friend, to tell me all;
        that would be best
    When yesterday the lightning struck, why should I
        think it struck my nest?

5   You have no cause to blame my love. Who is to
        blame? Do you not see?
    We should no longer be at odds. Did you not struggle
        to be free?

6   Is this affliction not enough to work one's ruin utterly?
    When you become a friend why should the sky
        become an enemy?

7   If this is testing, can you tell me what would
        persecution be?
    It is to him you show your favour. Why then are you
        testing me?

8   You said, 'Why should I be ashamed if he too comes
        to visit me?'
    A wise remark! A just remark! Yes, ask yourself,
        'Why should I be?'

9   Ghalib, what do you hope to gain, that you should
        taunt her as you do?
    You tell her that she is unkind. Will that, then, make
        her kind to you?

---

3   It is a matter of honour that nothing in the conduct of either the lover
or his confidant must betray the identity of the beloved. My confidant
is so grieved at *my* grief that he cannot keep my secrets.

✺ 129 ✺

Green grass grows lush from every wall and doorway
of my house of grief
This is my spring. No words can tell what will my
autumn be

✺ 132 ✺

1   The thought that beauty would be kind possessed me.
What simplicity!
Your coming was no more than just the prelude to
your going

2   How can I tell the virtues of the men to whom this
age gave birth?
They do me harm to whom I have done good
repeatedly

✺ 133 ✺

1   Would that I had not voiced my grief! But how was I
to know, my friend
That this itself would only make the pain I feel more
keen?

2   How should the saki of the skies pour you the wine
of happiness?
He sits there with his—one, two, four—his seven
cups upturned

3   Ghalib, I long to be with her, and grieve that fate
keeps us apart
God grant I may tell her one day this longing and
that grief

2   I.e. the seven heavens, whose revolving determines your fate.

⤙ 135 ⤚

1   It is the love of Thee that moves the universe
    The radiant sun gives life to every speck of dust

2   He who sits in the shade of his beloved's wall
    Is lord and king of all the realm of Hindustan

3   Does it not show how well she knows I will be true?
    Ghalib, my heart rejoices that she is unkind!

⤙ 139 ⤚

My heart, this pain and sorrow too is precious, for the
    time will come
You will not heave the midnight sigh nor shed your
    tears as morning dawns

Cf. ghazal 87.

⤙ 140 ⤚

1   We pass our lives in journeying in constant
    restlessness
    This year it is the lightning, not the sun, that marks
    time's course

2   Struck in the heel, I can no more stand firm and
    battle on
    Lacking in strength to flee away, too weak to
    make a stand

3   We reckless drinkers hold the whole wide world as
    our domain
    The thoughtless think this world a thing of no account

4   What consolation can I bring to my despairing heart?
    Granted, my eyes have won the joy of gazing on
    your face

ᵂᐟ 141 ᵂᐟ

None would have ever known all that was passing in
    my heart
It was my choice of verses that disgraced me in their eyes

The world saw what kind of poetry Ghalib liked, and this betrayed his secret
nature and told the strait-laced what kind of man he was.

ᵂᐟ 144 ᵂᐟ

1   What can I now expect of her when she is fully grown?
    She who would not hear my story even when she was
        a child

2   Thus to wish distress on someone is not good. Were
        that not so
    I would have prayed, 'O Lord, give my life to my enemy!'

1   'my story'—the story of my love for her.

ᵂᐟ 145 ᵂᐟ

They offer paradise to make up for our life below
It needs a stronger wine than this to cure our hangover

ᵂᐟ 149 ᵂᐟ

1   If even after killing me you are not satisfied
    And want to test me further, I am ready. Be it so!

2   At least you have the thorns of grief and yearning
        to behold her
    Love cannot pluck the flowers of heart's desire?
        Then be it so!

3   You who seek wine, if need be put your lips straight
        to the cask
    Today there is no saki there to pour it? Be it so

4　The fire of Qais's sighs brings light and radiance to
　　the desert
　　It cannot reach the dark of Laila's dwelling? Be it so

5　Home is not home unless it holds the turmoil of
　　strong feeling
　　If there are cries of grief, not songs of joy, then be it so

6　I do not long for people's praise; I seek no one's reward
　　And if they say my verses have no meaning, be it so

7　Treasure the joy of life spent in the company of fair
　　women
　　Ghalib, though you may not live life's full span, well,
　　be it so!

～ 152 ～

Such pleasure does the garden feel when you come into it
Each rose-bud flowers wide to gather you in its embrace

～ 153 ～

The rose has opened wide her arms for the farewell
　embrace
Come, nightingale, it's time to go! The days of spring are
　gone

～ 154 ～

Grief nourishes us lovers in the bosom of adversity
Our lamp shines through the tempest like the coral
　through the stormy sea

～ 155 ～

1　Union is separation where pride and restraint persist
　　She must be gay and spirited, and he in ecstasy

2   Yes, one day you'll win kisses from those lips, but you
           will need
      To summon boundless love and reckless courage to your aid

~ 164 ~

1   O Lord, where shall I turn to find one to admire
           my madness?
      I envy now the easy life of those who lie in chains

2   Ghalib's in love. Now he is in no better case than me
      This Mirza Sahib who counselled me never to fall in love

2   'Mirza'—a deferential form of address for nobles of Turkish stock. Here
      ironical.

~ 170 ~

The garden knows my apprehension, and it frightens me
To me the shade of every rose's branch looks like a snake

~ 171 ~

My corner of the cage is like an egg that cramps my wings
Once I am out of it I can begin my life anew

~ 176 ~

1   The dew has sprinkled water on the mirror of the
           rose-petal
      See, nightingale, the spring is getting ready to depart

2   Now she has promised me to come I cling fast to
           that promise
      Whether she comes to me or not, I still shall wait for her

1   Heavy dews begin to fall when spring is in its last days, and the air becomes
      cooler. In Iran it was the custom to sprinkle water on a mirror when a
      traveller set out on a journey, in the belief that this would ensure a safe
      return.

✖ 178 ✖

Ghalib, do not take umbrage if preachers speak ill of you
I ask you, Is there any man of whom all men speak well?

✖ 179 ✖

1   Note too how I regret the sins that I could not commit
     O Lord, if you would punish me for these committed
          sins

2   When all men turn away from you, Ghalib, do not
          despair
     When all abandon you, my friend, God is still on
          your side

✖ 180 ✖

1   Beneath the shade of every mosque should be a tavern
     Just as the eye, your reverence, is near the brow

2   It was for fair-faced women that I learnt to paint
     One needs some pretext, after all, for meeting them

3   What idiot takes to wine in hope of finding joy?
     Each day, each night, I seek a refuge from myself

4   Tulip and rose and eglantine wear different hues
     With every hue let us affirm the joy of spring

1   The mosque, with its arch, is compared to the eyebrow, and the tavern
     to the eye—and it is obvious which is to be valued the more!

✖ 181 ✖

1, 2 What is the autumn? What the season
      They call spring? Throughout the year
      We live on, caged, lamenting still
      That once we had the power to fly

❧ 182 ❧

1 'It is not love, but madness!' Be it so
   My madness is your reputation though

2 Do not break off the bond uniting us
   If nothing else, grant me your enmity

3 Why should my meeting you put you to shame?
   Alright, meet privately, not publicly!

4 I will not be my own worst enemy
   My rival loves you. What is that to me?

5 Get from *yourself* whatever you can get
   If not awareness, then obliviousness

6 Life passes quick as lightning. Even so
   It gives you time to turn your heart to blood

7 I am not one to fail in loyalty
   Whether you call it love, or misery

8 Grant me *something* at least, O cruel sky
   If only leave to sigh and make lament

9 Well, I will learn the trait of calm acceptance
   Given *your* habit is indifference

10 Asad, lay constant siege to your beloved
    If you can't win her you can yearn for her

3 An ingenious excuse for a more enjoyable meeting with her!

4 If I deprived myself of the joy of loving you, I should be my own worst
   enemy. It does not matter to me that someone else is also in love with you.

5 In the last resort, rely only upon yourself. If you never really get to know
   yourself, you can at least learn to be indifferent to the promptings of your
   ego.

6 I.e. to love.

❧ 185 ❧

The cash-in-hand of this world and my draft upon the next
Are nothing, for my high resolve removes me from myself

Even the thought of longing for the rose no longer
    troubles me
Now that I am not free to fly I feel a strange content

1   My dedication to a high ideal has made me indifferent to both worldly
and otherworldly reward.

➤ 186 ↩

1   Love lovely women to your heart's content
    If *they* love *you*, then what more could you want?

2, 3   Asad would win the love of lovely women
    He should look in the mirror. Tell him that!
    Does he not know? To love these radiant beauties
    You too must be someone worth looking at

➤ 187 ↩

1   Let her come to me in my dreams, and soothe my
        restlessness
    But first the turmoil of my heart must cease and *let*
        me dream

2   If you dislike me, saki, pour the wine in my cupped hand
    I may not have the cup? So be it. Let me have the wine

➤ 189 ↩

1   When by some chance she feels inclined to think she
        should be kind to me
    The thought of all her cruelties makes her hold back
        in shame

2   Lord, how the passion of my heart recoils upon me!
        Why is it
    The more I strive to draw her close, the more she
        draws away?

3   Give me respite, despondency, lest I should have to
       face the day
    You wrest out of my grasp the memory of my love for
       her

4   Ghalib, how can I bear the thought she journeys with
       my rival?
    She whom I would not willingly trust even to God's
       care

⤳ 190 ⤶

1   An age has passed since last I brought my loved one
       to my house
    Lighting the whole assembly with the wine-cups'
       radiance

2   I seek to gather up once more the pieces of my heart
    As in time past to be the target of her eyelashes

3   Once more I feel the ways of circumspection choking
       me
    Long years have passed since lover's frenzy made me
       tear my clothes

4   Once more my spirit burns to loose the sparks of
       hot complaint
    An age has passed since I have looked upon their
       shining lights

5   Once more my heart goes pilgrim to her lane,
       courting disgrace
    Leaving the shrine of self-esteem empty and desolate

6   Once more I seek a purchaser willing to take my love
    And offer wit and heart and soul to her if she will buy

7   I long once more to see one standing there upon
       the roof
    Black tresses loosed to play dishevelled all about
       her face

8   My yearning stirs once more to see someone
         confronting me
     The daggers of her eyelashes sharp with collyrium

9   My spirit seeks once more the leisure I once had to sit
     Lost night and day in memories of loves that won
         my heart

2   Shattered by the trials of love, he lost the courage to love again. Now he
     wants to regain that courage; 'her eyelashes' are regularly described in
     metaphor as arrows, or (as in 8) daggers.

✦ 191 ✦

1   A strong snare lay in wait for me, concealed close
         to my nest
     I had not even taken wing when it imprisoned me

2   I filled the blood-stained pages with the story of my love
     And went on writing even when they had cut off my hands

3   To flee the field of love is to give victory to lust
     Where you withdraw, lust will advance and plant its
         standard there

4   Asad, I took to begging, but I kept my sense of humour
     And am the suppliant lover now of the munificent

2   The original has a characteristic, but untranslatable, play on words. *hath
     qalam hue* means, 'My hands were cut off'—but the words could mean
     'My hands became pens'.

4   'munificent' is ironical.

✦ 193 ✦

How can your lovers' weakness bring disgrace to you?
Here no man hears another man's complaint

True lovers should not complain of their mistresses, but if some of your lovers
are weak enough to do so, you have nothing to fear. No one in this world
is prepared to take any notice of another's distress.

⤙ 194 ⤚

Abstemious one, why do you push the cup away?
It's wine! It's not the vomit of the bee!

The pious Muslim thinks *honey* a great delicacy. Wine, Ghalib tells him, is much better!

⤙ 195 ⤚

You ask what balm will soothe the wounded heart?
Its main ingredient is diamond dust

⤙ 197 ⤚

I too gaze on the wonders that my longing can perform
It matters nothing to me whether I attain my wish

⤙ 199 ⤚

1   My house of darkness holds the tumult of the night
       of grief
    A single silent candle argues that the day has dawned

2   No news that she will come, no chance to gaze upon
       her beauty
    The rivalry of eye and ear has ended long ago

3   Wine has worked on her beauty's pride and banished
       her reserve
    Yes! Now love gives me leave to say farewell to self-
       control

4   Look at the jewels set in the collar that adorns her neck
    To what a zenith has the jeweller's star ascended now!

5   Wine? To see *her*. Saki? Our courage. Drinkers?
       Shining eyes
    The tavern of our fantasy is silent, undisturbed

6–12 Newcomers to the assembly of the heart's desires
Beware, if it is wine and music that you seek!
Look well at me, if only you have eyes to see
Listen to me, if you have ears to hear me speak
The saki's charm will steal away your faith, your wits
The minstrel's song will rob you of your sense, your powers
At night you see the carpet laden all with bloom
A gardener's apron, filled with fresh, sweet-scented flowers
The saki walks, the flute plays on enchantingly
Heaven to the eyes, paradise to the ears of all
Come in the morning: Look at the assembly then
Life, joy, wine, music—all are gone beyond recall
Bearing the scar of parting from its erstwhile friends
One silent candle, burnt out, shows you how it ends

13 These themes I write of come into my mind from
the unseen
Ghalib, the sound my moving pen makes is an
angel's voice

1 Ghalib himself commented on this couplet: 'The tumult of the night of grief' means pitch darkness, with such total absence of any sign of the morning that one would think God had never even created morning. Only one feature of the scene argues that it must be morning—the silent (i.e. extinguished) candle, because it is when morning comes that you put out the candle. When the one argument of morning is itself something that contributes to the darkness, how utter that darkness must be!' The darkness symbolizes the very depths of despair and sorrow.

2 Eye and ear used to be in rivalry, each vying with the other to be first to receive what it hoped for. But now, for a long time there has been neither sight nor sound of her.

5 The sight of her is like wine to her lovers. The boldness which we summon to enable us to look at her is our saki. Our shining eyes drink in the wine of her beauty. And all this happens in silence, unlike the noise and bustle of a tavern.

❀ 200 ❀

1 What will my friends mourn for when I am gone?
The verse that spoke of my distracted love

2   Opposite me I find my opposite
She sees me in full flood, and freezes up

✦ 201 ✦

1   Just see the sweetness of his speech! At everything I
        hear him say
I feel as if that very thought is there in my heart too

2   Back! thronging hosts of black despair, lest you reduce
        to dust as well
The one joy left to me—the joy that unavailing
        struggle brings

✦ 204 ✦

Ghalib, the grass is growing green on every wall
I roam the desert, and the spring comes to my home

I left my home, and, left deserted, it has become a wilderness, and grass is growing on its walls. Yet grass is a sign of the coming of spring. Why then have I left the springtime of my home to wander in the wilderness?

✦ 205 ✦

Ah! Asadullah Khan, the age has settled scores with you
Where now is all that zest for life? Where now that vibrant
    youth?

✦ 207 ✦

Ghalib, when *this* is how my life has passed
How can I think that I too had a God?

✦ 211 ✦

1   Khizar, we are alive, for we are known to everyone
Not you, who slunk away unseen to steal eternal life

2   I have not ceased to struggle; I am like the captive bird
    Who in the cage still gathers straws with which to
        build his nest

3   The universe strives in his era to attain fresh beauty
    New stars will be created now to deck the firmament

3 A verse in praise of a nobleman who was one of Ghalib's friends.

✸ 212 ✸

1   I will not cry for more if I may only look at you
    But there among the houris let me look upon your face

2   I am not bound to take the path that Khizar indicates
    I'll think an old man comes to bear me company on
        my way

1 In this world I will be content with being able to do no more than look
at you. And in the next world let me only hope that one of the houris
will look like you.

✸ 213 ✸

1   If some days more of life are left to me
    I am resolved to take another path

2   The flames of hell cannot give out such heat
    For hidden griefs burn with another fire

3   Ghalib, all other ills have come to pass
    And only unexpected death remains

✸ 214 ✸

1   None of my hopes can ever be fulfilled
    Seek as I may, I see no way ahead

2   Death surely comes on its appointed day
    Why then does sleep not come the whole night through?

3 Once I would contemplate my wounded heart
   And laugh. Now laughter never comes to me

4 The meek ascetic wins reward in heaven
   I know, but I cannot incline that way

5 If I keep silent, it is for a reason
   You surely know I have the power to speak?

6 I am so far away that even I
   Have not the least awareness where I am

7 Ghalib, you have the face to go to Mecca?
   But then you never feel a sense of shame

✎ 215 ✍

1 O foolish heart, what has befallen you?
   Do you not know this sickness has no cure?

2 I long for her, and she is weary of me
   O Lord above, tell me, what does this mean?

3 I too possess a tongue like other men
   If only you would ask me what I seek!

4–7 When all is You, and nought exists but You
   Tell me, O Lord, why all this turmoil too?
   These fair-faced women, with their coquetries
   Their glances, airs and graces, what are these?
   Why the sweet perfume of their coiling tresses?
   Why the collyrium that adorns their eyes?
   Where does the grass, where do the flowers come
       from?
   What is the cloud made of? What is the breeze?

8 See how I look to her for loyalty
   Who does not even know what loyalty is

9 'Do good to others: good will come to you'
   This, this alone, is the dervish's cry

10 I would lay down my very life for you
    I do not know what *praying* for you means

11 I grant that you are right: Ghalib is nothing
    But if you get him free, then what's the harm?

➳ 216 ☞

Clearly, the *nakirain* will not take fright and run away
—Unless there is the smell of last night's wine upon my
    breath

The *nakirain* are two angels that come into the grave to question the dead man
about the kind of life he has led. Ghalib proposes to escape this cross-
examination by drinking wine on the night before he dies.

➳ 217 ☞

1 I go and get another from the shop if it should break
   No goblet of Jamshed for me! This cup of clay is
       good!

2 Only the things that come to one unsought taste
       really good
   The beggar who excels is he who has not learned to ask

3 It was thanks to his pick Farhad held converse with
       Shirin
   Whatever be your talent, to excel in it is good

4 I know the truth regarding Paradise, but all the same
   Since it gives happiness, Ghalib, the thought of it is good

1 To the conventional way of thinking, no cup could be better than Jamshed's.

➳ 218 ☞

1 'That cruel one gets angry at the mention of
       complaint'
   Do not say even this to her! This too is a complaint!

2 My heart is vibrant with complaint as is the harp
    with music
  Give it the slightest touch and you will see what
    happens then

3 If Ghalib sings in strains of bitterness you must
    forgive him
  Today he feels a pain that stabs more keenly at his heart

⮜ 219 ⮞

1 To every word that I utter you answer, 'What are you?'
  You tell me; is this the way, then, I should be spoken to?

2 What grieves my heart is that he is allowed to speak
    with you
  It is not that I fear the ill my rival speaks of me

3 I set no store by that which merely courses through
    the veins
  Only the blood that comes in tears of blood has any worth

4 One thing alone gives Paradise some value in my eyes
  What else, if not the wine, red as the rose, fragrant as
    musk?

5 He is the King's companion now. See how he struts
    about!
  But what the city thinks of Ghalib everybody knows

5 Actually a thinly-veiled hit at Zauq, the King's companion and poet
laureate. Zauq was a man of humble birth and in Ghalib's view a facile
versifier but not a poet. It is said that Ghalib composed the first line with
direct reference to Zauq. The King heard of it and called him to account,
whereupon Ghalib completed the couplet so as to make the whole thing
refer humorously to himself.

⮜ 220 ⮞

1 There if you speak, your voice at once is stifled
  She speaks and other mortals listen on

2   Who knows what I am raving in my madness?
     God grant that nobody can understand

3   You know how Khizar treated Alexander
     How then can one make anyone one's guide?

4   Ghalib, when expectations have all crumbled
     Why would a man complain of anyone?

✗ 221 ✗

1   Life passes by unused, although it be as long as Khizar's
     He too will ask himself tomorrow, 'What have I
     achieved?'

2   Had I the power, I would demand an answer from
     the earth
     'What have you done, vile miser, with the treasures
     that you hold?'

3   When she is obstinate, that's it! But this at least is good:
     When she forgets, she can keep scores of promises
     she made

4   Ghalib, you know yourself what sort of answer you
     will get
     No matter how you talk, and how she goes on
     listening

2 The treasures mean the great ones who have died and been lost to the world.

✗ 222 ✗

1   All wrath? All cruelty? Be what you may
     I wish that all you are had been for me

2   When, Lord, you fated me to bear such grief
     You should have given me more hearts than one

3   Ghalib, she surely would have come to you
     Why could you not live on a few days more?

⤳ 223 ✍

1   This is the mode God's light desired to show its radiance
     Its fortunes prospered when your face and form came
       into being

2   Preacher, you cannot drink it, nor can you give *us* to
     drink
     What then is all this talk about your 'wine of purity'?

3   My slayer rails at me on Judgement Day, 'Why have
     you risen?'
     It seems as though her ears have not yet heard the
      trumpet sound

4   Is spring then on its way? I hear the nightingale's
     sweet song
     There is a rumour in the air; the birds all speak of it

5   Although they are not there, yet they were once
     expelled from there
     The Kaba and these idols share remote affinity

6   Why should we think that all who go will get the
     same reply?
     Come on, let us too make the trip to see the
      Mount of Tur

7   Say what you have to say with force—but not so
     forcefully
     That he to whom you speak is sure to feel aggrieved
     at you

8   Ghalib, if he will take me with him on the Pilgrimage
     His Majesty may have my share of heavenly reward

---

1   God wanted to show His radiance to Musa on the Mount of Tur. You
were the perfect form in which He could reveal it.

3   My mistress is so preoccupied with her own beauty and her own absolute
command over me that she does not even hear the last trumpet, which
summons all men to rise from the dead. She thinks it an impertinence
on my part to rise until *she* commands me to.

5   An ironical rejoinder to those who reproach his unorthodoxy. Before the advent of the Prophet, the Kaba, originally the House of God, had become a place in which idols were worshipped. The Prophet expelled them, and restored the Kaba to its original function.

8   Ghalib recited this to Bahadur Shah Zafar when he was contemplating performing the pilgrimage to Mecca. He always declared that he liked to travel.

✖ 224 ✖

1   Qais faced the test of Laila's form, Farhad, of Shirin's tress
From where I stand it is the stake and gallows that I face

2   There is no grip in nooses like their rosary and
      sacred thread
The Brahmin and the shaikh alike must face the test
      of constancy

3   When sorrow's poison seeps into your every vein,
      then you will see!
So far you feel its bitterness upon your mouth and
      tongue

1   The great lovers faced hardship and death for the sake of a woman. It was Laila's tall stature that attracted Qais and Shirin's long hair, Farhad. They suggest respectively the impaling stake and the gallows rope. My love is wider in its scope and faces more drastic penalties.

2   The noose of the rosary and the noose of the sacred thread are contrasted with the noose of the hangman's rope. Convention regards the shaikh who tells his beads and the Brahmin who wears his sacred thread as pillars of their respective faiths. But they will prove their faith only if for the sake of it they can face the hangman's noose without shrinking.

✖ 225 ✖

1   I would feel shame to tell the saki, but the truth is this
Let all the wine be poured: I will be happy with the
      dregs

2   No hunter draws his bow, no fowler lies in wait for me
Here in the corner of the cage I live a life of ease

3 Abstinence wins no praise from me. What though it
      be sincere?
   Behind it lies raw greed to win reward for virtuous deeds

4 What makes the wise so proud? Where is the special
      road they take?
   Common convention marks the path in which they
      set their feet

5 Leave me by Zamzam; why would I go walking
      round the Kaba?
   See how my robes of pilgrimage all bear the stains
      of wine

6 My heart is not yet blood that issues from my eyes.
      Wait, death!
   Let me stay here a while; I have abundant work to do

～ 226 ～

1 Shall I not wait for death? For death one day will
      surely come
   Shall I love you? *You* will not come. Nor can I
      summon you

2 No one can govern love, Ghalib. This is a kind of fire
   No one can kindle, and, once kindled, no one can put out

～ 227 ～

1 He gave his heart to her. Well, he is human. What is
      there to say?
   He was my messenger, and is my rival. What is there
      to say?

2 Envy's the punishment you're sure to get for writing
      poetry
   Hostility's what you get paid for talent. What is there
      to say?

❧ 228 ❧

1   Do not say, mocking, 'I am cruel to you'
     I greet your every word with 'Very true!'

2   She takes your life! Blood price is due to her!
     It cuts your tongue out? Speak the dagger's praise!

3   The fair are cruel? What of it? They are fair
     Sing of their grace, their swaying symmetry

4   Spring is soon fled? What of it? It is spring
     Sing of its breezes, of its greenery

5   Your ship has reached the shore. Why cry to God
     Against your captain's cruel tyranny?

❧ 229 ❧

1   The world is but a game that children play before my
       eyes
     A spectacle that passes night and day before my eyes

2   The throne of Sulaiman is but a toy in my esteem
     The miracles that Isa worked, a trifle in my eyes

3   You need not ask how I feel when I am away from you
     See for yourself how you feel when you are before my
       eyes

4   True, I am lost in self-esteem, in self-display. Why not?
     In all her radiant beauty she sits there before my eyes

5   My faith restrains me while the lure of unbelief
       attracts me
     That way, the Kaba: and, this way, the Church
       before my eyes

3   I feel in your absence all the agitation you feel in my presence.

5   The key words are to be taken in a much more general sense than the literal one. They express the clash between the traditional ways of thought and the new ideas inspired by the experience of British rule.

⤳ 230 ↜

1   Desires in thousands—each so strong it takes away
        my breath anew
    And many longings were fulfilled—many, but even
        so, too few

⤳ 231 ↜

1   I shall write to you even without cause
    Simply to write your name fills me with love

2   At night I drank by Zamzam, and as morning dawned
    I washed the wine-stains from the robes of pilgrimage

3   Love has left Ghalib fit for nothing at the last
    Or else he too was once a man to reckon with

⤳ 232 ↜

1   The spring has come again, and in such wise
    The sun and moon look on with shining eyes

2   From end to end the earth is clad in green
    Matching the blue expanses of the skies

3   And now the earth is clothed, its mantle spreads
    In the green weed that on the water lies

4   To gaze upon the green grass and the flowers
    God opens up the blind narcissus' eyes

5   The air has wine's intoxicating power
    To breathe is to take wine in other guise

---

4   In Urdu and Persian legend, the narcissus is blind.

Ghalib's Persian Poetry

A. Bausani

THE AIM OF THIS PAPER is chiefly stylistic. I shall therefore not
dwell upon the relations between Ghalib's Persian poetry and his
social environment, nor on the contribution that the study of
Ghalib's Persian poems might give to a better understanding of his
age.[1] A word should be said also on the type of my stylistic approach.
All agree now in admitting that Persian, or, generally speaking,
eastern poetry, cannot be studied successfully by applying to it
sic et simpliciter the canons of our western stylistics. For this reason
some of those western scholars (very limited in number) who have
devoted themselves to the aesthetic study of Persian poetry have re-
studied the eastern approach (Persian classical treatises on rhetoric,
ars poetica, etc.). This, I think, is a very meritorious and rewarding
study; but they have often applied the oriental canons of aesthetic
judgement too mechanically to the object of their study. To mention
only one example, this seems to me to be the case in certain recent

---

[1] This is not the place for a Ghalib bibliography. Very much has been written
on him in India and Pakistan, but too often these essays are of a purely
'belletristic' character. Westerners have contributed very little to a scientific
study of Ghalib. See J. Rypka, *History of Iranian Literature*, Doordrecht, 1968,
pp. 731, 734, 836–7, and my article 'Ghalib' in the new edition of the
Encyclopaedia of Islam.

articles by the greatest scholar in this field, Professor J. Rypka of Prague,[2] on Nizami.

My personal system is a middle course between the two: neither a belletristic tattling of a pseudo-historical or pseudo-psychological character, nor a pure copy of the technical descriptive stylistic of eastern criticism, with its sharp distinction between *lafz* (word) and *ma'nā* (meaning). (One typical instance is the study of Ghalib by Hali, in spite of all the new and modern aspects of Hali's aesthetic doctrine.)[3] I have tried to follow this middle course in my studies of Persian poetry[4] and, *insha allah*, this is also the course I intend to follow here.

A summary description of the Persian poetical works of Ghalib is obviously indispensable as an introduction. In spite of their great fame, no really critical and scholarly edition of Ghalib's works has yet been published; in this he is in good company, because the same is true of many of the greatest geniuses of Persian literature. I shall therefore follow the Nawalkishor edition of 1925, comparing it here and there with the more recent (but not always better) Lahore edition of the *Kulliyat*.[5]

[2] For instance, J. Rypka; 'Der vierte Gesang von Nizami's Haft Paikar neu übersetat', *Oriens*, 15, 1967, pp. 234 ff.

[3] A. H. Hali, *Yadgar-i Ghalib*, 1897 and various lithographed editions. For an appreciation of Hali's literary criticism and of his peculiar ideas on 'natural' (*nechural*) poetry, see my article 'Hali's Ideas on Ghazal', in *Charisteria Orientalia*, Prague, 1956.

[4] See especially, A. Bausani, 'Contributo a una definizione dello "stile indiano" nella poesia persiana', *Annali dell'Ist. Or. di Nepoli*, N. S., vol. VII, 1958, pp. 167 ff., and A. Bausani, *Storia della Literature Persiana*, Milan, 1960, 2nd edition, 1968.

[5] *Kulliyat-i Ghalib*, Nawalkishor edn, 1925. The latest edition I know is that of Lahore, 1965, publisher Shaikh Mubarak 'Ali, with an introduction by the well-known Urdu contemporary writer Mihr. An attempt at a chronological arrangement of Ghalib's verses has been made by S. M. Ikram, *Armughan-i Ghalib*, n.d. Mihr too laments the lack of really scientific studies on Ghalib and expresses the wish that somebody may accomplish what he calls 'two important tasks', first, a real 'Kulliyat' edition, i.e. a fully comprehensive collection of all his Persian poetry, including even those scattered verses that are excluded from the traditional *Kulliyat*, first published during the life of Ghalib himself in 1863 by Nawalkishor and then successively reprinted without variations. Also the 'prison verses' (*habsiyat*) of Ghalib, the so-called *Sabad-chin*, should be included. The *Sabad-chin* contains verses written by Ghalib during his imprisonment in

The Persian *Kulliyat* of Ghalib opens (pp. 11–53), with a section comprising sixty-six *qit'as*, or fragments, on various subjects: *fakhr*, poetical criticism, satire, *madh*, descriptions (including one of his cat), occasional and celebrative verses including a qit'a congratulating Nawwab Yusuf 'Ali Khan of Rampur, upon the grant of new territory by the British government (*sarkar-i Angrezi*), one celebrating the British victory in the Punjab in 1846, etc., chronograms, elegies, etc.

The section following is devoted to strophical poems (pp. 53–68), very limited in number: one *mukhammas* in praise of 'Ali (our poet was a Shi'a and often praises the Shi'a *imams* in his poems), three *tarkib-band* (chiefly elegiac: on 'Ali, the Shi'a martyrs, and a young prince, son of the Mughal sovereign Abu Zafar) and one *tarji'-band* in praise of the Mughal Emperor Abu Zafar (deposed by the British in 1858). Though these few strophical poems are of a simple beauty, the small number of them shows that the 'architectonic' structure of the strophe poem was rather foreign to Ghalib's poetic taste.

Narrative art, too, seems to have been rather uncongenial to him. The section devoted to the *masnavis*, the *instrumentum princeps* of poetic narrative and of description in Persian (pp. 69–160), does not contain a single 'epic-narrative' masnavi, and Ghalib's attempts at narrative style seem rather poor (e.g. in the second masnavi). The masnavis number eleven in all.

The *Surma-e binish* (50 couplets, metre *ramal*) is of a basically mystical character and opens with the first verse of Maulana Rumi's *Masnavi-i Ma'navi*. Like some other short masnavis of Ghalib it looks structurally rather like a *qasida*, with an exordium, a *madih* (in this case a panegyric of Siraj-ud-Din Bahadur Shah) and a central part, ending with the *takhallus* of the poet.

1847 under the accusation of having kept a gaming-house and, 'for reasons of expediency', not included in the ordinary editions of the *Kulliyat*. The second task, says Mihr, should be the publication of a historical commentary on Ghalib's Persian verses, showing the occasions on which they were composed, identifying the personalities and events mentioned, etc. We hope that the celebrations of the centenary of the death of the poet may have as one result the fulfilment of these hopes of Mihr. This study of mine is based on the generally available edition of the *Kulliyat* and excludes the *Sabad-chin* to which unfortunately I have had no access. The numbers of pages refer to the above-mentioned Nawalkishor re-edition of 1925.

The *Dard-u-dagh* (188 couplets, metre *sari'*) is of a didactic-narrative character. A very poor peasant leaves his home together with his old parents. In the desert they almost die of thirst. They meet a *darvish* in a hermitage. He offers them water, and after having prayed to God for them, informs them that God will grant one and only one wish to each of them. 'The sweetness of these words washed their ears with waves of pearls.' So the old mother asks to become a young girl, the old father expresses the desire to become rich, and the young peasant asks for success and fortune in life. After various events (told in a style that seems to me rather shallow) the conclusion is that there is nothing that can be done against destiny (*bakht*), and everyone returns to his former state. The narration lacks any sort of realistic detail; no names of places or of persons are given, and the characters of the tale seem abstract allegorical figures.[6] Here too the lyrical form is preserved, with the name of the poet being mentioned towards the end.

The *Chiragh-i dair* ('The Lamp of the Temple': 108 couplets, metre *hazaj*) is in praise of Benares/Kashi, and apart from the famous description of that town (reproduced also in 'anthologies'; see for instance that of Ikram),[7] is also chiefly lyrical (including the *takhallus* towards the end). Ghalib invites himself to go back to his country (Delhi) from that idolatrous place, which is however very favourably described in the first part of the poem, in the typical mystico-lyrical way. It is interesting to remark that when he speaks of Hindu objects his style is strongly 'Indian' and reminds one of Ghanimat Kunjahi.[8] The beauties of Benares are described: 'their coquetry is a rose garden intoxicated and brim-full

[6] In this Ghalib is quite different from Bedil, who used his peculiarly difficult (and for Ghalib incorrect) style to obtain sometimes results of a proto-realistic type. See my article 'Bedil as a Narrator', in *Jadname-ye J. Ripka*, Prague, 1967.

[7] Shaikh M. Ikram, *Armughan-i Pak*, Karachi, 1953. It is a good anthology, with a critical introduction in Urdu, of the Persian poetry of India. For Ghalib, see pp. 72–4 and 299–315. An excellent anthology of Ghalib's Persian and Urdu poems is the *Intikhab-i Ghalib* by Imtiyaz 'Ali 'Arshi (Rampur, Bombay, 1942). This selection was prepared by Ghalib himself in 1866. The notes are exclusively taken from Ghalib's own explanations scattered here and there in his 'Letters'.

[8] Perhaps one of the most Indian of the Persian poets of the subcontinent. He died in 1107AH/1695. His *masnavi Nirang-i 'isbq* is particularly interesting for its descriptive and narrative techniques which utilize the 'twistedness' of

of blandishments; their graceful walking embraces the hundred turmoils of Judgment Day!'

The *Rang-u-bu* ('Colours and Scents': 154 couplets, metre *sari'*) is again of a narrative character, and allegorical. Its chief characters are wealth and power (*daulat*), fortune (*iqbal*), magnanimity (*himmat*) a generous king, and a proud beggar. The gist of the story is that himmat is superior to daulat and iqbal. In spite of Ghalib's repeated assertion that he is more Iranian than Indian (to quote only one example, he says in a *ghazal:* '(Ghalib was a nightingale of the rose garden of Persia, only by mistake I called him a song-bird of India'). In one of the verses of this *masnavi* there is a *tajnis* (play on words) understandable only to a speaker of Hindi/Urdu. It is when the proud beggar says to the king: 'I am not begging, it is rather I that have something to sell to you. 'I am a comber of the waving ringlets of passion [*sauda*, also "melancholy", "blackness", and "trade"]; it is I that sell goods [*kala*, which in Hindi/Urdu means also "black", like *sauda*] to you.'

The *Bad-i mukhalif* ('The Contrary Wind': 154 couplets, metre *khafif*) is addressed to the literary critics (*sukhanparvaran*) of Calcutta. (The only important journey that Ghalib ever made was that to Calcutta; he was away nearly three years, from mid-1827 to November 1829.) It contains interesting material for a better understanding of his ideas on Persian poetry. He calls himself an uninvited guest (*na-khvanda mihman*) and protests against the unjust criticism of his Persian poetry by the representatives of the new 'Indian style', who especially praised Qatil (d. 1817). Bedil, though not Persian, is not so ignorant (*nadan*) as Qatil.

This *nadani* is an interesting aspect of his criticism of the poetry of his enemies: their ignorance of Persian is such that they cannot even use it grammatically (p. 94 contains hints at the grammatical rules of 'real' Persian).

'Those who really know Persian all agree in saying that Qatil is not a native speaker of that language [*ahl-i zaban*]; he certainly is not from Isfahan, and therefore one cannot rely on him or follow his example. This language is the specific tongue of the Iranians, difficult for us but easy and natural for them: Delhi and Lucknow

---

the Indian style to express details of action and events in a way totally different from the neo-platonic staticity of Persian classical poetry. Some of its extremely heavy compound words seem even an echo of late Sanskrit style.

are not in Persia.... Why should I follow Qatil, abandoning Asir. Hazin, Talib, Urfi, Naziri and Zuhuri?' (pp. 96–7). 'But if my friends insist, let us make peace, I'll praise Qatil!' The *masnavi* ends in a bitterly ironic, hyperbolic panegyric of Qatil!

The *Bayan-i numudari-yi shan-i nubuvvat u vilayat ki dar haqiqat partav-i nuru'l-anvar-i hazrat-i uluhiyat ast* ('Declaration of the Appearance of the Glory of Prophecy and Sanctity, that is in Reality the Ray of the Supreme Light of the Godhead': 129 couplets, metre *ramal*) is of a religious, or, more specifically, of a Shi'a character, and provides very interesting materials for the study of Ghalib's religious attitudes. (The importance of this aspect of him is somewhat underestimated by some of his students.) Ghalib sets out to prove that the great Saints, and 'Ali in particular, must be venerated. Both Muhammad (more directly) and 'Ali and the Saints derive from the Divine Light. Jacob venerated the shirt of Joseph and Majnun the dog of Laila, not in themselves, but because they were symbols of their beloved. The fact that one loves Laila is not a good reason to despise the *mahmil* (camel-litter) of Laila. In this way Ghalib even arrives—if I am not mistaken—at a patriotic revaluation of the cult of local Indian saints:

'Every country has its own special customs [*rasm-i khass*]. Why do you want to destroy such customs? Yes, we too reject the customs of infidelity [*rasm-i kufr*] and unite justice [*dad*] and wisdom [*danish*]; to reject infidelity is the manner [*a'in*] of the pure [*arbab-i safa*], but, oh foolish one [*tira-dil*], to reject the Divine Bounty is the manner of which place?... Negation without affirmation is nothing but error [*zalal*].... One cannot affirm God and deny the signs [*ayat*] of God...' (pp. 101 ff.).

This is typically Shi'a and anti-modernistic reasoning. But this is not the place for a further study of the religious ideas of Ghalib, though this would be, I think, a rewarding subject.[9]

---

[9] He was a spiritual pupil of the mystical school of Maulana Fakhr ad-Din.

In a letter to 'Ala ud-Din 'Alai, a rebuke to a mulla in 'Alai's household who had urged Ghalib to give up drinking wine leads him on to an account of his religious position. 'Tell him...[he writes] that there is a great difference between studying the problems of the books of Abu Hanifa, plunging oneself into hair-splitting discussions on menstruation and impurity periods of women after childbirth (*nifas*), and assimilating in one's heart the words of the gnostics ('*urafa*') on the reality of the Absolute and the unity of Being (*haqiqat-i haqq wa wahdat-i wujud*). Infidels are those who confuse necessary and contingent

The seventh, *Tahniyat-i 'id-i shavval* ('Congratulations for the Feast of Shavval': 42 couplets, metre *sari'*), and the eighth, *Dar tahniyat-i 'id ha-vali-'ahd* ('Wishes for a Happy Feast to the Crown Prince'; 39 couplets, metre *sari'*), are panegryrical short *masnavis* of no great importance; and so also are the ninth and tenth, respectively *Dibacha-e nasr mausum ba bist-u-haft afsar tasnif-i hazrat-i falak-rif'at Shah-i Avadh* ('Preface [in verse] to the Prose Work "Twenty-seven Crowns" by H.H. the King of Oudh': 33 couplets, metre *hazaj*) and *Taqriz-i A'in-i Akbari musahhaha-e Sayyid Ahmad Khan sadru's-sudur-i Muradabad* ('Afterword to the Edition of the *A'in-i Akbari* made by the *sadru's-sudur* of Muradabad, Sayyid Ahmad Khan': 38 couplets, metre *ramal*).[10]

The eleventh and last *masnavi* is the *Abr-i guhar-bar* ('The Cloud that Rains Pearls': 1098 couplets, metre *mutaqarib*). Being the best and the longest of Ghalib's *masnavis* it deserves a more detailed

---

Being. Infidels are those who want us to believe that Musailima the Liar shared the gift of prophecy with the Seal of the Prophets. Infidels are those who consider a band of newly converted Muslims [the first three 'caliphs'] as peers of the Father of the Imams [= 'Ali]. Hell is the final destiny of such people. But I am a pure monotheist [*muwahhid*] and a perfect believer. I say with my tongue: "There is no god but God," meaning in my heart: "There is no being [*maujud*] but God," i.e. there is no mover of beings but God [*la mu'assir fi'l-wujud illa 'llah*]. I believe that the prophets, all of them, are worthy of veneration and that each of them was the unique legislator of his age and all had to obey him. With Muhammad prophecy ended, for Muhammad is the Seal of the Prophets and a Mercy to all Nations; and I believe that the sunset of prophecy was at the same time the dawn of imamate, and that the imamate is not elective [*ijma'i*] but by appointment from God [*min Allab*] and that the *imams* appointed by God are, first 'Ali, then Hasan, then Husain and so on until the promised Madhi' (letter dated 28 July 1862).

It is interesting to notice, in this profession of faith, the blend of Shi'a and Sufi ideas, typical not so much of early Shi'ism but rather of later post-Safavid Iranian Shi'ism. It is this sort of Sufi reinterpretation of Shi'ism that gives Ghalib his typical and remarkable 'freedom of expression' in religious subjects (e.g. in the twelfth *masnavi*). Works like that of the late Khalifa 'Abdul-Hakim, *Afkar-I Ghalib* ('The Thought of Ghalib') in Urdu (Lahore, 1954), though useful, do not seem to me worthy of too serious consideration.

[10] The editor of *A'in-i Akbari* was the famous Sir Sayyid Ahmad Khan. In its *taqriz* Ghalib praises 'British technical progress' (including steamships) and considers it a useless task to publish such an old collection of laws!

analysis, though it is no more than the introduction to a *masnavi* on the Holy Wars of the Prophet Muhammad that Ghalib never finished. Ghalib wrote the *Abr-i guhar-bar* in his old age, as is shown by some verses (e.g. p. 145: 'Now that the time has arrived for me to pass away and to return to God...', or p. 157 where the poet complains of the disappearance of the blackness of his hair). It is divided into various chapters. The usual praises to God are powerful and majestic. The holy name of God 'is so sweet that holy men engrave it on their hearts as on a seal-ring. Every one who imprints His mark on his own heart feels such a burning pleasure that he sacrifices everything to His beauty'—free translation of the Persian.

A description of the firmament and of the marvels of nature is another remarkable feature of this introduction. A *munajat* ('prayer' or, better, 'intimate dialogue' with God) then follows: everything in this world comes from the double set of divine attributes, those of *jamal* (grace) and *jalal* (power) as an immense fresco in black and white. Poetry (*sukhan*, 'the Word', artistic Word) too comes only from God. The form of Ghalib's expression is here almost pantheistic:

'Thou art in the innermost of ourselves such as the humidity in the ocean, the warp in the brocade.' In contrast to this absoluteness, is the abjectness and servitude of man, but 'Though we are base and unworthy, yet we are the blades of grass in Thy garden.' This concept is more graphically expressed by means of an allegorical *hikayat* (story). A king goes to war and comes back after winning a brilliant victory. But together with those who spread flowers under the feet of his horse and bring congratulatory gifts to the sovereign, there are those, the poor and miserable, who not only do not bring anything, but are like a black spot on the beautiful picture of that glorious day. A minister wants to chase them away, but the king says: '[They too are mine;] being consumed by fever from my burning light they are the atoms of dust dancing in the rays of my sun.'

'Do the same with us, O Lord, at the Day of Judgment [adds Ghalib] because, ultimately, our sins and our sorrows too derive from Thee. My sins are not many; perhaps the only one is wine-drinking. But I am full of sorrows, and wine is the dispeller of sorrows. Wine-drinking could have been a sin for King Bahram or King Parviz, but not for me, who am poor and constantly tormented by preoccupations and anxieties' (p. 124). An interesting passage follows, in which, after his usual complaints about his unhappy circumstances, he says that his heart will not be able to find rest even in the traditional 'Paradise'. The classical 'other world' is criticized in verses, the first origin of which can be retraced in a typical leitmotif of Sufism. These verses of Ghalib seem, however, to possess a certain 'modernity' and originality of expression:

> How canst Thou burn with a fire-mark in Hell a heart that finds no rest even in a garden? And, in Paradise, it is true that I shall drink at dawn the pure wine mentioned in the Quran, but where shall I find again the star of dawn I used to see on earth, and my crystal cup? Where in Paradise are the long walks of intoxicated friends in the night, or the drunken crowds shouting merrily? In that holy tavern, silent and still, how canst Thou introduce the sounds of the flute and the gay bustle of the taverns of this earth? Where shall I find, there, the intoxication of raining clouds? Where there is no autumn, how can spring exist? If the beautiful houries are eternally in one's heart, what of the sweet thought of them? Where will be the sadness of separation and the joy of union? How could we be thankful to an unknown beauty? What will be the pleasure of a sure fruition of love, without waiting? Where shall we find, there, a girl who flees away when we would kiss her? Where will be, there, one who betrays us with false oaths of love? The beauties of Paradise will obey us and their lips will never say anything bitter; they will give us pleasure, but with a heart forever closed to the desire for pleasure. Will there be in Paradise oglings, the pleasure of coquettish glances from afar? Where will it be, in Paradise, the dear window in a well-known wall?

The eulogy of the Prophet (na't) then follows, and after that a beautiful description of the Prophet's ascension to Heaven (mi'raj). Its various elements are: the blackness of that night (actually more shining than day); the angel, which is the First Intellect; his dialogue with the Prophet; the extreme speed and lightness of the miraculous flight; the various celestial spheres and the zodiacal signs (each one hinted at with appropriate metaphors); the throne of God ('arsh) that, though more sublime than the angels, 'can tremble for the lament of the inhabitants of this dusty earth; if the heart of an afflicted one aches, a veil of dust is deposited on those immaculate steps; the noise of the broken spine of an ant here on earth is nothing; in those holy precincts it is a roar!' Then Ghalib attempts a description of the indescribable (curiously enough, chiefly with cabbalistic means); then comes the return from *Haq* (God) to *haq* (reality).

The eulogies of the Prophet are followed by those of 'Ali (*manqabat*), so hyperbolic that Ghalib himself adds: 'Do not take this, however, for *ghuluww*. In my youth too I always loved 'Ali, but now that I am old I should like to go on pilgrimage to his holy tomb at Najaf; may my body be buried there, where my soul already is' (p. 145). He then expresses a sense of envy of the great poet 'Urfi, who was buried there.

The extant part of the poem is closed by a *Mughanni-nama* ('Book of the Minstrel') and a *Saqi-nama* ('Book of the Cup-bearer'). They contain poetical concepts already well known in other compositions of this type, but these by Ghalib seem to me characterized by a sort of conscious reflection on the ideas and poetical expressions found in the older classical ones (e.g. Hafiz or Nizami). In the *Mughanni-nama* there is what we could call a powerful hymn to sorrow (*gham*) considered as a purifying, an exciting, a creating element:

In the path followed by my Thought,[11] the guiding Khizr of my poetical journey has been Sorrow. I am not a Nizami, who learnt the rules of the 'legitimate enchantment' of poetry from the phantom of Khizr, nor a Zulali, who was led by Nizami in a dream to bedew with the crystalline rivulet of Art the garden of Wisdom...I have been influenced only by Sorrow; Sorrow made me a mourner weeping and singing at the death-bed of joy. Nizami spoke directly with the inspiring angel Surush, Zulali was inspired by Nizami, but I, alone, from my aching heart, raised the sweet lament of the *ghazal*. And, in the *ghazal*, my melody reached such a stage that you should not marvel if this Royal Hymn become a Revelation and be sent to descend—as on its Prophet—upon me!... In the dark treasure chamber of my life, in that frightful night, I requested my pure soul to give me a Lamp, a Lamp not accessible to flying moths, a Lamp far away from any house, a Lamp in which you would not see a trace of oil, and whose flame would silently weep over itself; that Lamp, that I lighted without oil, was my heart burnt by the fire of Sorrow! God gave me Sorrow as the heart-enlightening Lamp of my nights and the brilliant star of my days!

[11] *Andisha*, as a *terminus technicus*, seems to me of Bedilian origin. See my article, 'Note su Mirza 'Abdu'l Qadir Bedil', *Annali dell'Ist. Univ. Orientale di Napoli*, NS VI, 1957, pp. 163 ff.

This passage is interesting also for the study of what Ghalib thought of his own poetry. In the *Saqi-nama* he says further that he does not want to be led by Nizami out of his way, that is, of lyrical poetry and not mystical epos. (Note that Ghalib shared the opinion of some later Persian critics according to whom Nizami was to be interpreted *mystically*.) He states that his lyrics are based on a sort of humanistic immanentism: *tasawwuf* is not an indispensable constituent of lyrics (as many of his contemporaries thought) nor is the ghazal-form the only possible channel to express this kind of lyrical emotion. At the end he declares the aim of his poem: that of singing the epic exploits of, not ancient kings like Khusrav or Rustam, but those of the Prophet Muhammad.

Ghalib's *qasidas* are rather numerous and occupy 170 pages out of a total of 340 pages of qasidas plus ghazals; in other words, their verses equal in quantity those of the ghazals, in sharp contrast with the Urdu *divan* in which the ghazals and the 'fragment' are sovereign. The *Kulliyat* contains sixty-four qasidas. The first is of a religious character, on *tauhid;* nos 3 and 4 comprise praises of the Prophet (*na't*); and the fourth includes also eulogies of 'Ali. To the praise (*manqabat*) of 'Ali are devoted also the four following qasidas (nos 5–8). The ninth is in praise of the martyred grandson of the Prophet, Husain; the tenth is devoted to the *manqabat* of the second Shi'a *imam*; the eleventh sings the praise of another Shi'a, a martyr, 'Abbas son of 'Ali; whereas the twelfth sings the praise of the twelfth *imam*, who is, according to Shi'a beliefs, 'in occultation' and will come back at the end of the world. Of the following sixteen qasidas, one is dedicated to the Mughal Muhammad Akbar Shah (this qasida is dated 1250/1835) and fifteen to the last Mughal Emperor, Abu Zafar Bahadur Shah (exiled in 1858). Three qasidas (nos 29, 30 and 31) are in praise of Queen Victoria, and another fourteen extol various British personalities in India: Lord Auckland (the qasida is dated 1837), Lord Ellenborough, and judges, governors, etc. The last nineteen qasidas of the collection are directed to various dignitaries of the Mughal court, to the Nawwab of Oudh, Vajid 'Ali Shah and other Indian personalities (including two non-Muslims, Shiv Dhyan Singh Bahadur and Raja Narendar Singh). The last one is directed to Ghalib himself. In spite of the enthusiastic judgement of Hali[12]

---

[12] I translate from the text reproduced as an Introduction to the above-mentioned Lahore edition (1965) of Ghalib's *Kulliyat*, p. 104.

('The qasidas of Ghalib, both from the point of view of quantity and quality, are the literary *genre* in which he excels most.... In them he sometimes follows Khaqani, sometimes Salman and Zahir, or 'Urfi and Naziri, and always with success: the best part of Ghalib's qasidas is their *tashbib* rather than the actually panegyrical section...'), I think that Ghalib is great above all as a lyric poet, which is in a way confirmed by Hali himself when he speaks of the especial excellence of Ghalib in precisely the most lyrical part of the qasida, namely the tashbib. Here are—as a specimen—some rather original verses of the tashbib of the twenty-sixth qasida in praise of the Mughal Emperor Abu Zafar Bahadur Shah. In it Ghalib emphasizes one of his typical motifs, that of the 'penetrating glance' (*nazar, nigah*) of the 'seer' (*didavar, durbin*):

'When the Wayfarers consider the pearls of the blister of their sore feet, they attribute to them a station higher than the Pleiads.' This is the beginning of the ode, rather uncongenial, I am afraid, to western literary taste, and almost untranslatable. The general idea, or to put it better, '*Stimmung*', underlying the entire poem, is that of the positiveness of active life, expressed by means of extremely varied symbols and metaphors centred on the idea of the Way, the Wayfarer, the blisters on the sore feet, the paths of the desert compared to eternally pulsating veins:

'They see the Way as a pulsating vein in the body of the Desert,' united with the active and almost alchemic effect of the 'glance', which not only sees things, but also transforms them. But these *didavaran*, these 'active seers', are at the same time detached from that world through which they incessantly wander, and from the things that they continuously transform with their piercing glances:

'They do not attach their heart to the magic spell of the world, and everything they look at, is, for them, a mere show and entertainment.' The entire passage is the best expression of the double position of Ghalib, at the end of the Indo-Muslim mystical Middle Ages, and at the beginning of the new 'modern' world.

This ideal Ghalibian Man, half old *darvish*, half modern scientist tinged with virile sadness, is at the base of all of his verses, and is the real protagonist of his work.

Speaking of Ghalib's Persian ghazals, one is naturally led to a comparison with his Urdu ghazals. But I shall only say here that Ghalib's Persian ghazals are more 'regular' according to the rules of the classical ghazal, whereas his Urdu poems, as he himself declared, are purely an *intikhab*, a selection, more similar to qit'as than to the classical ghazal (and this, by the way, is just what makes them more agreeable to our taste).

Since it is not possible to 'describe' or summarize a collection of ghazals, I think it useful to attempt an experiment: that of making a list of the 'characters' of two ghazals selected at random. The characters of ghazal are—obviously—not persons, but rather the substantive nouns included in them, a sort of pale and fading gallery of ideas 'at random strung'.

First ghazal (eleven couplets):

ba-khud rasidan: coming back to one's self
naz: feigned disdain
tamanna: desire
dam: net
jism: body
pirahan: shirt
khar: thorn
qatl: killing
jib: pocket
dastar: turban
namus: honour
fasana: legend
iadda: way
qamat: stature
bahar: spring
★gul: rose
★chaman: meadow, garden
shahid: beautiful ephebe
bazar: market
gham: sorrow
parkar: pair of compasses
kamar: waist
fana: annihilation, or non-being
hasti: being
pud-u-tar: woof and warp
fitna: tumult
avaragi: wandering
naghma: melody
tar: string
Adam: Adam
nuqta: point
haft parkar: seven compasses = the skies
afarinish: creation
★nigah: glance
partau: ray

**rukh:* cheek
a'ina: mirror
sarab: mirage

Second *ghazal:*

dagh (twice): fire mark, wound, scar
parkala: patch
shaqa'iq: anemone
jigar: liver
nala: lament
atishkada: fire, temple
*gul (twice): rose
lala: tulip
khuy: manner
vafa: loyalty
sharar: spark
bidad: injustice
*rukh (twice): cheek
ab (twice): water, purity
dallala: bawd
saqi: cupbearer
qadah: cup
bada: wine
**nigah:* glance
chashm: eye
khun: blood
masti (twice): intoxication
mashshata: bride-dresser, tiring-maid
husn: beauty
**chaman:* meadow, garden
qand: sugar
Bangala: Bengal
mauj: wave
khiram: graceful walking
jauhar: pearl
anjum: stars
khurshid: sun
barq: lightning
dam: breath
shiraza: stitch
butkhana: an idol temple
khatt: down on the cheek
ru: face
rang: colour
mah: moon
hala: halo
mulla: mulla
qalib: mould

khak: dust
qaza: destiny
gusala: calf
rag: vein
abr: cloud
qalam: pen
zhala: dew

(N.B.: The words present in both poems are marked with an asterisk. The poems are selected at random, and these repeated words seem rather numerous; we can be sure that 'rose', 'meadow', 'cheek' and 'glance' will recur thousands of times in this sort of poetry.)

One is tempted to say: put everything into the small pot of the ghazal, add some verbs and adjectives as spices, mix together, and you'll have the poem!

A comparative statistical inventory of such and similar key words from different poets of different areas and periods would be, I think, a rewarding, though a rather laborious, task.[13] Here, for instance, we find some typically Indian-style 'characters' not very frequent in the classical Persian ghazal (e.g. the _shiraza_ or 'stitching of books', the _gusala_ or 'calf', etc.). They are, however, only the first stratum of the different layers of which a ghazal is composed. On a higher level we could recognize the conceptual 'motifs' whose basic ingredients are those key words. At this point a second type of inventory is needed, that of the motifs. Synchronical and diachronical comparisons among various of these inventories of different poets will be the only basis of a serious investigation of Persian styles. For the time being, let us limit ourselves to a purely empirical tentative hint at the chief general trends of the contents of Ghalib's ghazals.

(1) One is the general trend exemplified by the famous Urdu verse:

'God being absolutely beyond every limit of human perception, what people call _qibla_ [the object of our prayers, our earthly

---

[13] A first purely terminological list of the key words of the motifs of Hafiz is being published by Amir Muqaddam in the _Nashriye-Daneshkade-ye Adabiyat_ of Tabriz (first instalment no. 4, XVII, 1344/1965). It is a useful work that should be supplemented by deeper typological and historical studies.

'Absolute'] is really no more than a *qibla-numa,* i.e. the needle of the compass, pointing at the Absolute, not the Absolute itself'. The same concept we have already seen in some of the Persian verses already quoted, and, to quote a further instance, in this *ruba'i:*

'There is a path from the worshipper to the presence of God, whether you take the long one or the short one. This Kausar and Tuba are signs, are a spring and a shade halfway along the path.' I would call this motif: poetically expressed consequences of the Absolute transcendancy of God. This includes relativism, the idea of the endless way, activity, etc. But these truths are recognized only by the *ahl-i nazar.*

(2) A second general trend is therefore that of the alchemical value of the *nazar/nigah,* a motif which has an ancient tradition in the Persian lyric, but is particularly emphasized by Ghalib. A good example of it is provided by the verses on the *didavaran,* already quoted.

(3) A third general trend is cerebralism: personal experiences are not expressed directly (as in modern western poetry), nor through socially translatable symbols (as in the classical Persian lyric, e.g. Hafiz's) but rather by means of a bookish rethinking of the traditional symbols, a sort of second-degree intellectual meditation on the classical Persian poetical elaboration of reality, rather than on reality. Instances can be taken almost at random from Ghalib's ghazals. Let us take the first verse of the ghazal with *radif...khuftast* utilized by Hali in his comparison between Ghalib and Naziri.

Here a first layer (the deepest) is the simple expression of an emotion: 'So full of difficulties and dangers is the path of my life, that I must travel on it with my inner strength or "on my breast", rather than with my feet'.

The second layer is the symbolic filter: the sequence of the (seven or more) Valleys of the Pilgrimage, the miraculous guide Khizr with his rod (*'asa*), the sore foot of the Wanderer. But these symbols are not directly used to express the first emotional layer; they are considered as already well-known motifs of a given imagery.

A third layer is superadded, in which Ghalib reshapes those already-known motifs in a personal but purely cerebral, intellectual way. The result is an expression more or less of this kind:

'In a valley in which even the rod of Khizr is sleeping [impotent], I travel in myself [or I travel on my breast, creeping] even if my feet are asleep [tired, impotent].' It is from this point of view that we should interpret some, at first sight, proto-realistic elements of Ghalib's style, e.g. the verse, at p. 10, *ba-Firdaus rauzan ba-divar ku?* The *rauzan ba-divar* is not something invented by the poet, it is a well-known element in the given set of images, or symbols, of Indo-Persian poetry. Nor is (perhaps) the way in which Ghalib uses it as an element for a further construction.

(4) A consequence of all this, which we may also call a fourth general trend, is introspection: neither nature, nor *tasawwuf,* nor philosophy, nor God nor even a more-or-less clearly imagined 'Beloved' are the subjects of Ghalib's ghazals, i.e. neither a *masjud* nor a *mamduh* nor a *ma'shuq.* Its real subjects are the psychological movements of his self (mostly dissatisfaction, sadness and related sensations) analysed in detail and expressed by means of the above-mentioned poetical instruments.

But this is also, at least partly, a characteristic of the 'Indian style' in Persian poetry. In what sense and to what extent is Ghalib 'original', not in Persian poetry in general, but in the particular background of the Indian style?

Before giving a tentative answer to this question—in the next paragraph—some words should be said on Ghalib's *rubaiyat* (quatrains) that form—as customary—the last section of the *Kulliyat.* They are comparatively few in number (104) and almost all show an interesting characteristic: that of being—if compared with other verses of Ghalib—very simple. This derives partly from the fact that the *ruba'i* form cannot physically contain a too complicated imagery; but probably also from the fact that Ghalib (like other classical poets) did not use them as a too 'serious' form of poetry, confining to them, therefore, those more direct and immediate expressions of feeling that for us are just the most interesting matter of poetry. Here is an instance, a simple cry of pain:

'In the garden of my desire, by the iniquity of hail not a palm remained alive, nor a branch nor a leaf; since the house is ruined, why should I complain of floods? If life itself is a plague, why should I fear death?'[14]

In the terms of a tentative typology of the *ruba'i* form that I have sketched in my *Literary History of Persia,*[15] the majority of Ghalib's

[14] Another, stylistically very simple, *ruba'i,* has been already quoted above.
[15] See the chapter on *ruba'is,* pp. 319 ff.

ruba'is are of the type that I called 'triangular', the most common perhaps, and most generic amongst the types of *ruba'is*.

Reading Ghalib's work as a whole, one is struck at first sight by a curious double stylistic 'contradiction'. One horizontal, between his Urdu and Persian works, the other vertical, between his prose and his poetry. To put it in a very simple or rather oversimplified way, his Urdu verse is more Bedilian and complicated than his Persian poetry; on the other hand his Persian prose is very much more Bedilian and complicated than his Urdu prose (noted as a model of simplicity). Before attempting an explanation or justification of these contradictions, let us say a word on the famous subject of Ghalib's Bedilism. In another article of mine,[16] I tried to demonstrate that, where Ghalib's Urdu poetry is concerned, the idea of a passing from an initial Bedilism to a progressive rejection of Bedilian style is not accurate. This succession is more true of his Persian poetry; but here also the idea should be taken *cum grano salis*. The 'salt' consists chiefly in recognizing that this generally-accepted interpretation of Ghalib's style is based on judgements given by himself and by eastern critics, who used as a *mizan* (balance, scales) of aesthetic judgement their own system of stylistics, and measured and defined 'Bedilism' and 'non-Bedilism' on scales quite different from ours, bearing in mind especially purely *lafzi* and even lexical, syntactic or grammatical characteristics.[17] A re-reading of the famous letter of Ghalib to Chaudhri 'Abd al-Ghafur,[18] the starting-point of this generally accepted interpretation, may be useful. The letter refers to a long discussion between Ghalib and his master (*pir-u-murshid*), Sahib 'Alam, about the new style of such Persian poets of India as Qatil and Vaqif against whom Ghalib makes his strongest protests, accusing them even (an

[16] A. Bausani, 'The Position of Ghalib in the History of Urdu and Indo-Persian Poetry: I. Ghalib's Urdu Poetry', *Der Islam*, vol. 34, 1958, pp. 99 ff.

[17] Ghalib, who, as is known, had in his youth an Iranian teacher for Persian, a former Zoroastrian, converted to Islam, Mulla 'Abd as-Samad Hormuzd, was always keenly interested in grammatical and lexicological problems, as is shown by his famous *Qati'-i Burban*, with connected polemics, and by the numerous grammatical observations strewn here and there in his Urdu letters. He felt that he knew Persian grammar and syntax like a Persian, not like an Indian. This feeling led him to the imitation of 'good Persian' models rather than to the continuation of the un-Persian, but 'new' style of a Bedil or a Ghanimat.

[18] *Ud-i Hindi*, Lucknow, 1941, pp. 64–6.

interesting point that confirms what I have said before) of 'not knowing Persian'.

My master Sahib 'Alam [Ghalib says] is angry with me because I have said that the poetry of Mumtaz and Akhtar is defective [*naqis*]. In this letter I shall take the liberty of expounding a standard [lit. 'scales', *mizan*] of poetry, and Hazrat Sahib is kindly requested to weigh the poetry of those gentlemen, i.e. the verses of the Indian poets from Qatil and Vaqif up to Bedil and Nasir 'Ali, on these scales. Here is the standard. A group of poets is that which goes from Rudaki and Firdausi up to Khaqani, Sana'i, Anvari, etc. The poetry of these personalities, notwithstanding differences of small account, is based on the same style [*vaz'*]. Then Sa'di was the founder of a special style [*tarz-i khass*]. Sa'di, Jami, Hilali: such personalities are not numerous. Fighani is then the inventor of another special art [*shiva-e khass*] bringing delicate images [*khayalha-e nazuk*] and sublime meanings [*ma'ani-e buland*]. Perfection in this kind of art was achieved by Zuhuri, Naziri, 'Urfi and Nau'i. God be praised! It was as if life itself were poured into the mould of speech. This style was then given the unction of a fluent simplicity by other poetical natures: Sa'ib, Kalim, Salim, Qudsi and Hakim Shifa'i are of this circle. The style of Rudaki and Firdausi was abandoned at the time of Sa'di. On the other hand, Sa'di's art being of an 'inaccessible simplicity' [*sahl-i mumtana'*], it never found wide diffusion. It was then Fighani's style which spread widely and, in it, new and original refinements emerged. Summing up, there are three styles [*tarzen*] in existence: that of Khaqani and his peers, that of Zuhuri and his followers, that of Sa'ib and those like him. Now tell me truly, in which of these styles is the poetry of Mumtaz, Akhtar, etc., composed? You no doubt will answer me that they write in another style, and that we have to consider it as a fourth one. Well, it may be a style, perhaps even a good one; but it is not a Persian style, it is Indian. It is a coin, but not one coined in the Royal Mint; it is a false coin. Be just!

Another important statement by Ghalib himself is that contained in his own *taqriz* to the Persian *Kulliyat*.[19] He mentions there his continuous self-correction, applying to this 'literary dissatisfaction' his own couplet (again exemplifying one of the general trends of his poetry mentioned above): 'On the Way, I passed beyond everything I had in front of me: I saw the Ka'ba, but I called it the footstep of an eternal Wanderer!'

[19] Pp. 515–17 of the 1925 Nawalkishor edn, and pp. 661–3 of the Lahore edn (1965).

And then he goes on to say:

Though the Mind, that is a divine angel, was at the beginning too, speaking accepted words and looking for chosen expressions, at first, due to my wanderings here and there, it followed the way of unknown people and took their crooked gait for the stumbling of poetical intoxication, until a moment when, in this running to and fro, my forerunners, finding me worthy of being their colleague were moved to compassion and, saddened by my literary straying, looked at me with a teaching eye. Shaikh 'Ali Hazin, with a smile, showed to me my errors, and the wrathful glances of Talib Amuli and the blazing eyes of 'Urfi Shirazi burnt and destroyed those unworthy and frivolous absurdities in front of my walking feet. Zuhuri, with kind interest, bound an amulet around my arm and supplied me with provisions for travel and Naziri in his carefree way encouraged me in my own typical style. Now, as a result of the prosperous and glorious protection of those angelical souls, my dancing pen walks like a cock pheasant, plays melodies like Pan pipes, shines like a peacock, flies like a Phoenix!

In spite of these solemn affirmations, this 'great change' should be taken, I think, to indicate a syntactic and linguistic change rather than a real stylistic change. Ghalib himself seems to confirm this when, for example, he writes to Chaudhri 'Abd al-Ghafur Sarur (*Ud-i Hindi*, Lucknow edition, 1941, pp. 22–3): '...anyhow it is known to you...that unless I see an expression [*lafz*] or a compound [*tarkib*] in the works [*kalam*] of the great classical [*qudama*] or the good later [*muta'khkhirin*] poets such as Sa'ib, Kalim, Asir and Hazin [all Persians of Iran!] I do not use it in prose or verse...'. Fortunately this extreme *taqlid* and traditionalism remained only syntactic and lexical.

Actually if we compare poems of some of Ghalib's masters with similar ones of his own we shall notice, apart from obvious exceptions, that the most 'Bedilian' and 'Indian' of the two is Ghalib. Let us take, for instance, some couplets of a *javab* by Ghalib to a ghazal of Naziri of Nishapur with the *radif khuftast*, of which we have already quoted one verse, In the interpretation—not always easy for a westerner—of these couplets, we have the guidance of Hali in his study of Ghalib's Persian poetry.[20] The first couplet corresponds to this verse by Naziri.

[20] Hali compares the two poems in -*khuftast* of Naziri and Ghalib, and also that of Zuhuri *ba-'ishq qabil-i divanagi khiradmand-ast* with Ghalib's *ghazal: chu*

The idea is that love is born at first sight: a hunter is 'sleeping' in (or concealed inside) the glance of the beloved; the poor lover—like a man near to death—does not know when the sudden end will come. It is—compared with the elaborate verse of Ghalib—a comparatively simple, and—as Hali says—'natural' (*nechural*) expression of more or less real love.

Naziri says further: 'How could I be saved from the coquetry of the glances of a half-asleep beauty? Temptation is rising from sleep, and my foot is asleep!'

The corresponding verse of Ghalib portrays—it is true—a more general feeling, but at the same time it uses 'secondary' intellectualized images: 'Which joy can I have from the fact that the way is sure and the Ka'ba [the final station] is near, when my camel is lame and my foot asleep?'

Another instance from the same poem:

Naziri expresses a very common feeling of lovers in this rather simple way: 'Only he who for several nights has slept separated from his partner finds a real pleasure in the embrace of the day of union!'

Ghalib does not express the psychology of personal love, but a more general feeling of unhappiness: 'The length of nights, my lying awake, all this is nothing; tell me rather where has my Good Luck gone to sleep?'

In the traditional symbolism, *bakht-i bidar* (waking luck) is good luck, and *bakht-i khufta* (sleeping luck) is bad luck. Here these symbols are re-employed in a 'secondary', reflected way.

Further examples would render this paper too long. It is now time to say something on the historical position of Ghalib's Persian poetry in Ghalib's India, i.e. in the India of the first half of the nineteenth century.

Attempts have been made to compare Ghalib's poetry to the metaphysical poetry of English literature, or to Euphuism; I have also suggested certain stylistic resemblances between Ghalib and Gongora.[21] Though all comparisons of this kind are open to obvious criticism, they can nevertheless be useful for a better

---

subb-i man zi siyabi ba-sham manand-ast. The considerations stated by Hali are especially interesting for a study of his own ideas on style and poetry. See pp. 89 ff. of the Introduction to the Lahore edn of the *Kulliyat.*

[21] In my above-quoted article on Ghalib's Urdu poetry, p. 121.

understanding of certain aspects of Ghalib's art. But those who make them seem to forget that the literary situation of India at the period of Ghalib was perhaps more similar to that of our Middle Ages than to more modern periods of European literary history.

Persian held, in Mughal India, a position somewhat similar to that of Latin in our early Middle Ages. It was not the mother tongue of anybody, and vernaculars like Urdu (to speak only of the Muslim environment) were already alive. 'Indian-style' poets are in a position, *mutatis mutandis*, comparable to that of certain authors of the early Middle Ages studied by Auerbach in his stimulating essays. In his 'Latin Prose of the Early Middle Ages',[22] trying to explain the twistedness and difficulty of the style of writers like Cesarius of Aries, Gregory of Tours, and Raterius, he says that they used those specific stylistic forms not because of their inability to write in classical Latin, but simply because 'the objects and the thoughts that had to be expressed, could not be expressed in the stylistic forms of the high classical culture' (p. 98 Italian edn). The 'mannerism of Raterius' language is certainly not erudite ornamentation but the peculiar form assumed by his new content' (p. 133). 'He thinks that his obscurity aims at a superior clarity, which, however, reveals itself only to those who make an effort to understand him' (p. 134), speaking *a la* Ghalib, to a *zabandan* (p. 412):

'If there is one here who knows the language, bring him to me. This stranger in the city has something to say.' (Similar expressions can be found in Bedil.) Some sentences of Auerbach, in that same essay, could be almost literally applied to the situation of the 'Indian style' of a Bedil, only changing 'Latin' into 'Persian': 'His [he still speaks of Raterius] peculiar quality is due not only to his temperament, but also to the linguistic materials he uses. It is a Latin [read: Persian] that had for a long time no more been enlivened by everyday usage.... In order to express his own peculiar quality he had no other means than that of adding a sort of expressionistic ornamentation, operating through the disposition of words, etc.' (p. 135). This is why a Bedil, a Qatil and a Vaqif wrote in what for Ghalib was such a 'bad' Persian. Ghalib felt it

[22] Included in his collection of essays, *Literatursprache und Publikum in der lateinischen Spatantikeund in Mittelalter*, Bern, 1958. I quote from the Italian translation, E. Auerbach, *Lingua letteraria e pubblico nella tarda antichitd latinae nel Medioevo*, Milan, 1960.

412 ✖ A. BAUSANI

his duty to 'reconstruct' the real 'Iranian' Persian, if not that of Firdausi or Sa'di, at least that of Zuhuri and Naziri. But the sixteenth century and the social, spiritual and linguistic conditions of Mughal India of that age were forever gone; this is the reason why the 'better' and simpler Persian of Ghalib seems to us not much more than a literary exercise. His public—still to use Auerbachian concepts—was the extremely restricted literary aristocracy of Delhi, and even they were not always in agreement with him, as is shown by their criticisms.

Just as he had nothing poetically new to say in Persian poetry— and therefore he could exercise himself in writing in the comparatively simple style of the ancient tradition—so too he could exercise himself in difficult Persian prose; he had no urgent need of being understood by people. Conversely, in Urdu verse he felt he had something new to say, and this new element, stylistically, in the conditions of the Mughal India of his time, could not but be the historical continuation on more modern lines of Bedil's novelty and, therefore—at first sight—difficult. But in Urdu prose he had a practical need to be understood; hence his famous clarity and simplicity. Of course he was not himself conscious of all this and, as everybody knows, he preferred his Persian verses. What is *rang*? It is colour, ornament, conscious effort of style, exercise. In the *'intikhab'* (selection) of 'pearls at random strung', without too much conscious exercise of style (that is his Urdu *divan*), he wrote not for the public but for himself, and therefore he followed his own secret taste. Paradoxically the result was that in the last resort he identified himself with historical reality, whereas the 'public' for which he studied his *rangs* in Persian poetry was the only possible public for Persian in India, the idealized public of the century of Zuhuri and Naziri.

This, I think, is a fairly satisfactory explanation of the contradictions of Ghalib's styles. Ghalib, seen from this point of view, is the last Persian poet of India, and the first 'modern' Urdu poet. But, being a really poetical genius, it is obvious that even in his more artificial Persian 'exercises' he achieves remarkable results of 'pure poetry'.

Ghalib himself felt a clear conscience about being a 'last' representative of classical Mughal India; the outward power and glory of the Mughals was transformed in him into a poetical, spiritual glory:

The pearl has been taken away from the royal standard of Persia and in exchange a pearl-strewing pen was given to me. The crown has been torn away from the head of the Turks of Pashang, and the flaming Glory of the Kais was transformed, in me, into poetry!

The pearl was taken from the crown and was set in wisdom: what they outwardly took away, was given to me in secret.

And in a *ruba'i* he says that 'the broken arrow of my ancestors was transformed into my pen'.

His was not therefore a social or political poetry, but rather an intimate, 'hidden' one. Ghalib was what would be called now a 'formalistic poet'. In his form, in spite of his repeated claims of 'Iranism' he was typically Indian, and it is not an accident that he is presently more celebrated in India than in Pakistan. The subtlety of his poetical analysis of reality is characteristic of Indian style:

The real seer is the one that, when he analyses the psychological details of love, is able to see in the heart of the stone, the dance of the fire-idols of Azar!

To see what is potentially hidden in the given stony reality is the task of the poet; not that of giving more or less social messages. The woof and warp of Ghalib's poetry is a sort of dialectical monism, transposed into poetical forms (and in this too, his Bedilian heritage is evident). It would be a fascinating subject of study—though an extremely difficult one—to retrace possible Indian sources in the stylistic trends of Indian style, of which Ghalib is one of the last examples in Persian. But since my task is to speak of Ghalib's Persian poetry, I can do no more here than mention this possibility. It is certain, however, that some verses of Ghalib seem to call to mind Sankara's monism or even certain aspects of modern dialectic idealism. With one of them I close my rather haphazard considerations of him. It is particularly appropriate because it seems to invite to silence, after so many, perhaps useless, words: 'Do not spoil thought with words: let thy heart bleed in thought and cease speaking!'

Ghalib's Persian Verse

Ralph Russell

~*~ 1 ~*~

1   Hidden and Manifest, Your way is ever to raise turmoil
    Discoursing all the time with all, yet acting far
        beyond all

2   Sikandar's power, Sikandar's very life could not
        win water
    Khizar would give his life—to You, his coin is counter-
        feit

3   Ali's defeat is light and roses gracing Your assembly
    Karbala's tragedy a tune that issues from Your lute

4   Those whom You frown upon toil on with neither
        bread nor water
    Those whom You favour, sated, are still plied with
        heavenly food

5   Do not discount my tears; eternal wisdom has decreed
    That in this flowing stream the seven millstones all
        revolve

⁶ We, ignorant and powerless, maintain our love for You
   Intoxicated always, with a wine that does not fail

Nearly all the verses are addressed to God. They stress His apparent
indifference to the sufferings of even the best of mankind, like Ali and
Husain, and praise His true lovers, who gladly submit to His inscrutable
will with utter faith in His beneficence.

1 God is ever active in working His purpose out, and was so even before
   He created man. He speaks with all His creation, of which man is only
   a part, and He is still engaged in work to which the existence or non-
   existence of man is irrelevant.

2 Not all the power of Sikandar, ruler of the world, could avail him to get
   the water of life, and God withheld it from him to the last. Khizar, having
   gained eternal life, grew weary of it, and would gladly have surrendered
   it to God, but God rejects it as though it were counterfeit coin.

3 'Ali's defeat'—all his misfortunes from the death of the Prophet until his
   eventual murder.

4 'heavenly food'—in the original, *maida*, one meaning of which is the table
   which God let down from heaven, laden with manna and salva—food and
   drink to sustain His chosen people as they journeyed through the
   wilderness towards the promised land.

5 The seven millstones are the seven heavens, the revolution of which
   determines the fate of man. But it is the force of the stream of tears man
   sheds in his suffering that causes the millstones to revolve. So man himself
   contributes to the making of his own fate.

6 The wine is the wine of love of God. We are powerless and ignorant, but
   we love You utterly and steadfastly. Compare this ghazal with ghazal 182.

⌒⋆ 3 ⋆⌒

I owe much to the impact of my loyalty: at least
My way made plain the standards by which others
     live their lives

That is, how far short they fall of the standards of conduct which true love
demands and which I satisfy.

⌒⋆ 4 ⋆⌒

1 I am a free man; joy and pain pass through my
      heart and do not stay
   Wine and pure blood are one to me; my heart is
      like a sieve to both

2   I am a *huma*, but a boon to no man; for I fly
      so fast
    The shadow of my wings goes upwards, rising in
      the air like smoke

1   Neither great joy nor great suffering deflect me from pursuing calmly my
    chosen course in life.

2   Like the *huma*, I too am an auspicious being. But people who want worldly
    advancement need not look to me. I am far above such things.

✖ 5 ✖

1   I can bear every blow; my nature is of the
      most delicate
    I am a rock; think of me as a workshop of
      fine glass

2   I feel depressed in loyalty, embarrassed by
      your cruelty
    You try to torture me, alas!, so ineffectively!

1   I combine extreme fortitude with extreme sensitivity, and each quality
    supports the other. The second line suggests this. Glass is made from
    rock, and the rock is thus, in a sense, a workshop in which glass is
    made.

2   I must be true to you, but it saddens me that you are so lacking in the
    skills of a true beloved that I feel ashamed for you.

✖ 6 ✖

1   I solace my despondent heart by holding out
      the hope of death
    But what hope can sustain Khizar, and Isa,
      and Idris?

2   I blotted out the world entire when once I closed my
      eyelashes
    Lost to myself I bore away the world with me as well

1   All of these had been granted eternal life.

⚡ 7 ⚡

My eyes and heart are yours; don't ask me how you
    should adorn yourself
Does he who longs to pluck the flowers know anything of
    gardening?

Your beauty holds my eyes and heart enthralled. I neither know nor care how
such beauty is produced.

⚡ 10 ⚡

1   Without you, just as wine within the glass is parted
        from it
    My soul is in my body, but is not a part of it

2   Ghalib, it was not by your wish that you attained this
        rank
    Poetry came itself and asked if it might be your craft

⚡ 11 ⚡

One does not treat one's slave with *this* degree of cruelty
And did I ever force you to accept me as your slave?

⚡ 12 ⚡

1   My longing for the roses' beauty was so dear to me
    I turned to blood to show myself the beauties of the
        spring

2   All my concern is with myself; my heart is full of me
    I am a host of keen regrets for all I could not do

3   In loving one like you it is myself that I oblige
    Complaint to you expresses all the thanks I give to me

4   I, and myself reflected in imagination's mirror
    Are one, and one who constantly confronts another one

❧ 13 ❧

Hail wine! and flowing Zindarud, and this fine life we live!
Would you die thirsty-lipped among religions' mirages?

mashrab, translated here in the sense of 'way of life', can also mean 'sweet water'.

❧ 14 ❧

1   Each time my gourd is filled with wine such ecstasy
      possesses me
    I think an end has come to all the helplessness of life

2   To put it briefly, my heart too inclines to piety:
      but then
    I saw the way the 'good' behaved, and fell in with
      the infidels

3   I do not grieve if in men's eyes I seem to be a beggar
    Within the realms of meaning it is Ghalib's writ that runs

❧ 15 ❧

My home became a desert, and the desert more enchanting
For walls and doors do not agree with prisoners of love

❧ 16 ❧

1   Such is my love that she alone can cast a spell on me
    I make her think that someone else can cast a spell
      on me

2   Speak of the joy of gazing, and I am at once your friend
    Hint at a supple waist, and you can cast a spell on me

3   Just speak of wine; you can at once plunge me in fantasy
    I see the fruit; the branch's flower can cast a spell on
      me

⁴ I tell a tale; my own heart's pain is evident in it
The merest motion of her head can cast a spell on me

⁵ My heart is sore; complaint will come unbidden to
my lips
Two words from her rebuking me can cast a spell on me

⁶ Her arrow flies unerringly; say that it was my heart
That it was loosed to wound: your words will cast a
spell on me

⁷ The night of parting knows no dawn; yet for a little
while
Talk of the dawn; maybe your words will cast a spell
on me

⁸ True love is in my nature, Ghalib. Even so, no claim
That true love melts a fair one's heart can cast its spell
on me

1   I do so to arouse her jealousy, and make her more attentive to me.
3   I already experience the joy that is yet to come.
4   I can interpret that as a sign that my story moves her.
5   I.e. at once charm me into silence.
6   I *know* that it was not at me that she loosed her arrow because I know
that her arrow never misses its mark. But I can deceive myself into
thinking that it was aimed at me.

➤ 17 ✐

¹ You cannot think my life is spent in waiting? Well
then, come!
Seek no excuses; arm yourself for battle and then come!

² These meagre modes of cruelty bring me no joy. By
God!
Bring all the age's armoury to use on me, and come!

³ Why seek to slay your lovers by your awesome majesty?
Be even more unbridled than the breeze of spring,
and come!

4 You broke with me; and now you pledge yourself
      to other men
   But come! The pledge of loyalty is never kept.
      So come!

5 Parting and meeting—each of them has its distinctive
      joy
   Leave me a hundred times; turn back a thousand
      times, and come!

6 The mosque is all awareness. Mind you never go
      that way
   The tavern is all ecstasy. So be aware, and come!

7 If you desire a refuge, Ghalib, there to dwell secure
   Find it within the circle of us reckless ones,
      and come!

1 The lover tells her to come, and see for herself—and this of course ensures
that he no longer has to wait!

2 The lover's sufferings are inflicted partly by his mistress and partly by
the hard times in which he lives. He says, add these too to your own
armoury. Only if you inflict upon me all the suffering you can shall I know
the joy of bearing it.

6 Awareness of the demands of conventional life contrasted with awareness
of the things that matter.

⚡ 18 ⚡

1 Give me a wine that, poured into the cup
   Is strong enough to make the cup go round

2 All that these cruel times inflict upon me
   I think of as proceeding from your heart

3 She full of rage—and Ghalib asking kisses
   Love never knows what is the proper time

2 My sufferings are caused by the age I live in, but I think of them as
cruelties inflicted on me by you because I love you. And this thought
enables me to bear them gladly.

⤳ 19 ⤶

1   The lute, the cup, the melody, the wine—all kindle fire
The salamander knows; ask him the way to my
      assembly

2   Without the joy your cruel wrath brings to me I
      should die
Think, then! Why is it I complain against you
     without cause?

3   Ghalib, the love of wine is in your nature, for the cup
From which you drink it takes your pedigree back to
     Jamshed

1 It was believed that the salamander lived in fire.
2 That is why! My baseless complaints make you angry, and your anger is
a joy to me.

⤳ 20 ⤶

Thirsty, there on the river's bank I will give up my life
If I suspect its ripples are the creases on its brow

I would rather die than accept anything given unwillingly.

⤳ 21 ⤶

Hid in the universe, we are the universe's essence
Lost as the drop is lost within the river's flowing stream

'Hid'—because the world does not see and recognize our value.

⤳ 22 ⤶

There on the road, lost to the world, I sit and find
    another world
For every man, lost to himself, that goes that way encoun-
    ters me

Every selfless person is the kin of every other such person.

~✶ 25 ✶~

I think they may stay here and rest, where there is shade
    and water
My valued friends are travellers that I have left behind

I go ever forward to new goals. *They* have no such compelling urge to go on
and on.

~✶ 28 ✶~

1   You are soon drunk, and I am one who knows your
      secret well
    Take but a draught, and hand the measure over to
      my care

2   The night of parting stretches on beyond endurance.
      Come!
    For one glimpse of your face I'll give a thousand
      years of life

1   The implication is, 'I'll prove a better saki than you—aware and able to
serve the wine in accordance with the capacity of the drinker'.

~✶ 30 ✶~

1   You are the sum of all the graces of the spring,
      unending
    Your fragrance comes to me from every flower that
      I smell

2   Ghalib, enough! You cannot be a burden to your
      friends
    So let the poetry you write be written for yourself

~✶ 31 ✶~

From love I graduated to become a king's companion
I marvel at the skill with which the world has cheated me

'graduated' is ironic.

✣ 32 ✣

She wears a dress of *katan*, and in her simplicity
With every breath condemns the moonlight for
    exposing her

Moonlight *does* that to *katan* and there is no sense in upbraiding it for doing
what it cannot help doing. Also 'moon' is a standard metaphor for a beautiful
woman. It is she herself, her own beauty, that has this effect. The picture is
that of a beauty so great that nothing can adequately conceal it.

✣ 33 ✣

Let me be blunt; my lips thirst for your kiss and your embrace
Clear from my path the net of all your subtle kindnesses

✣ 34 ✣

The world holds wine and beauty in such measure,
    you would think
God sent into the world first Adam, and then paradise

✣ 35 ✣

If wine is banned, the Holy Law does not prohibit wit
No praise when I excel? Well then, no censure when I sin

✣ 36 ✣

Ghalib has cut all ties with life. Henceforth his one desire
Is to retire into his niche and there to worship God

✣ 37 ✣

[1] My heart is never still—and I am free from every fear
     A sense of peace pervades me all the while this cradle
        rocks

2   Your cruelty brings me such joy that, dead and in
      my grave
      My soul is steeped in longing to return to life again

❧ 38 ❧

1   The night is dark, the goal is far, I cannot see the
      path ahead
      I die with joy to see wine's radiant lightning flash
      from time to time

2   Locked in the structure of my deep humility there
      dwells a pride
      You cannot separate the drop from the drop's power
      to raise a storm

2   It is the drops of which the sea is comprised that hold within them the
     power to raise the whole sea in a storm. The apparently insignificant are
     not to be underestimated.

❧ 39 ❧

To measure out the wine has been declared unlawful,
    saki. Come!
And dash your flask to pieces on the wine-cup in my
    hand

Wine should be poured, and no account taken of *how much* the drinker
asks.

❧ 41 ❧

The world holds rich and poor—and those are proud
    and these are helpless
So, Ghalib, shun the company of rich and poor alike

Do not be proud, and do not resign yourself, either, to what life brings you.
Exert yourself to the full, and do whatever little you can do to change your
fate.

⇥ 45 ↦

1 Go out and find some wanderer, strayed from the
    beaten track
    You may find one whose high resolve stirs tumult
    in the world

2 In the world's glass, see, manifest and hidden both
    are mirrored
    Your thought cannot embrace them? Be content to
    gaze on them

3 Meaning eludes you? Be content with what your
    eyes can see!
    Look for fair women's coiling tresses and exulting pride

4 How long must we be mirrors longing for the sight
    of you?
    Come forth in all your radiance. Enslave us with a
    glance

5 Look in the scar of yearning and see bliss reflected
    there
    You seek the brightest night? Then go and find the
    darkest day

6 Hold fast the little time you have and learn to
    treasure it
    Spring mornings are not in your grasp? Then seek
    the moonlit night

2, 3 What cannot be fully understood may nevertheless be enjoyed. And
increased understanding may come with enjoyment.

5 You cannot appreciate the full extent of joy unless you have also
experienced the full extent of sorrow.

⇥ 46 ↦

1 Her qualities are many, and my love is pledged to
    every one
    What wonder if her anger only strengthens my desire?

2   The lightning cannot be content to occupy a single
place
What wonder if harsh thoughts of her cannot dwell
in my heart?

✎ 47 ✐

I slept; she came into my dreams, her tunic open,
drunk with wine
I cannot tell what spell my love had cast on her
last night

She is so shy that she does not normally appear before me even in a dream.

✎ 49 ✐

1   See how the morning breaks; the flowers are
opening. Awake!
Beauty, like worlds of flowers in bloom, awaits
your eyes. Awake!

2   Awake! Breathe in the bounty of the fragrance of the
flowers
The breeze of morning, perfume-laden, is astir.
Awake!

3   See how it silently invites you! Go and fetch the cup
The wine you drank last night is wet upon your lips.
Awake!

4   The morning star is greeting you, calling on you
to gaze
See how the twinkling eye of heaven is beckoning
you. Awake!

5   Your ears await the gurgle of the wine poured from
the flask
The wine-cup, with expectant eye, would have you
drink. Awake!

6 The mark of every living heart is movement.
      Do not stay!
   The lustre of the eye is born of watching.
      Do not sleep!

7 Your eyes are there to look for ways to serve friends.
      Open them!
   Your heart is there to feel the pain of other men.
      Awake!

3 'it'—the wine.

➤ 51 ✖

1 This garden does not match the one that blooms
      within my breast
   No heart can flower that has not been laid open
      by your sword

2 My life is ending; she is still intent on cruelty
   They say the fair cannot be constant; how can
      that be so?

3 Paradise is no salve to heal the sadness of my heart
   It was not made to match the desolation that is me

2 She is constant—constant in cruelty.

➤ 55 ✖

1 I die for her—and fear that she (such are her doubts
      of me)
   May think I wash my hands of life because I yearn
      for peace

2 I gaze at her; she thinks it is because I have no shame
   She turns away; I think it is because she feels too shy.

2 She assumes that my motives are bad; I assume that her motives are good.
   (And probably we are both wrong!)

❧ 57 ❧

1　In love you've lost your colour, and your autumn
　　　is a spectacle
　　That all the colours of the world in springtime
　　　cannot match

2　Counsellor, I would die for you! For when you
　　　speak her name
　　That word can cast a spell which all your eloquence
　　　cannot

❧ 58 ❧

1　Those words are true—and never have they issued
　　　from my lips
　　You said, Fair women's hearts are made of stone;
　　　and that is true

2　Ask of my love, and ask of my desire; that is no sin
　　You said, Desire should have no place in love—
　　　and that is true

❧ 59 ❧

Better go boldly forward, and not fear what you must face
The river's depths are Salsabil, the river's surface, fire

❧ 60 ❧

1　Come out! The spring has come! See how the
　　　flowers all in bloom
　　Reveal their forms more boldly than the city's
　　　courtesans

2　She hears my grief, and for a while retires into herself
　　What captivating sympathy! What artless mastery!

3 The object of creation was mankind, and nothing else
   We are the point round which the seven compasses
      revolve

2 She presents a picture of compassion for me, but this is really a means
   of captivating me all the more.

3 I.e. the seven skies, whose revolution determines the course of events.

~✕ 63 ✘~

1 Each atom gazes on the radiant beauty of the One
   East, west, south, north, above, below—mirrors on
      every side

2 What can I do? I must accept the fowler's callousness
   I'll think the circle of the snare the circle of my nest

3 Your feet are trapped in snares your fancy lays for
      them. In truth
   Each world tells you the story of another world beyond

4 The springtime comes, and breaks the bridle of
      your self-possession
   —The rose's every vein a whip to lash the steed of love

5 Ghalib, don't ask again why I wander so restlessly
   I said, My forehead seeks a threshold to bow down upon

2 Be content with what you cannot change.

3 Addressed to those who have not developed the power to see things as
   they are, and so see beyond things as they are.

5 There is no one, and no cause, to evoke the love and commitment of
   which I am capable, and which I yearn to give.

~✕ 64 ✘~

1 What fate's decree denied a man, no man would ask
      from fate
   The shaikh's cup did not look for wine: we asked for
      wine—no more

2   One, struggling, drowns; another slakes his thirst in
Dajla's stream
Neither one harmed the other; neither sought the
other's aid

3   High rank does not know learning: learning does not
need high rank
Your touchstone never knew our gold: nor our gold
your touchstone

4   That which he seizes openly no governor returns
That which fate's scribe writes secretly can never
be erased

5   Drunk with heart's blood, not wine, our drunkenness
requires no cup
Our heart's lament's a melody—a song that needs
no lute

6   Abandon disputations: seek the tavern; for in there
No one will want to waste his breath on Fadak or Jamal

7   To dissolutes like us to worship God would be no burden
But she, our idol, will not share the tribute due to her

8   I bore it all, and easily: it was not helplessness
If I did not ask fate for compensation due to me

1 We asked for wine—knowing that those who drink wine can expect this and nothing more than this.

2 Every man encounters his own fate, and goes to it alone.

3 The learned and the cultured do not seek the approval of the powerful, knowing that the powerful have no idea what true learning and culture are.

4 It is pointless to hope for what experience shows to be impossible.

6 Go to the tavern, where you drink the wine of true religion, and turn your back on pointless disputation. Fadak and Jamal refer to disputes between eminent personalities in the early history of Islam. In each of these, members of the Shia sect support one party and members of the Sunni sect the other.

8 'it'—i.e. the sufferings inflicted by the beloved. The ordinary man would demand redress on Judgement Day; for the lover this is out of the question. It is his pride and joy in the strength of his love, not cowardice and timidity, that keeps him silent.

⤳ 65 ⤶

1 I have a heart more delicately structured than the blister
I set my foot down softly, for the thorn is delicate

2 When I lament, don't pride yourself upon your heart
of stone
Think how the mountain's strength derives from
stuff most delicate

3 It grieves her that I bear so patiently her cruelty
So now I will complain, because her heart is delicate

1 I do not fear the pain it will cause me as it pierces my blistered feet. I
put my foot down so softly that the thorn does not pierce it, because I
fancy that it pains the thorn to do so.

2 Cf. 5.1. The mountain provides the raw material from which glass in
made. So your heart too may one day be transformed into something
delicate enough to be affected by my grief.

⤳ 66 ⤶

1 The beauty of her form was captured in the river's water
Now, mirror-like, the river has forgotten how to flow

2 My heart has slain me! Those it loved were ever cruel
to it
It saw their sweet deceptions and said, 'These are
kindnesses!'

3 You give me now good tidings of the coming of the *huma*
But I am free—its shade will be a burden on my head

3 Once I would have rejoiced in my good fortune. Now I value much more
highly my freedom from all such ambitions.

⤳ 67 ⤶

1 What comfort is there in complaint that does not
reach your ears?
Alas for all those hopes I had—they are no longer there

2   I can beguile my heart if you will promise to be cruel
The pride I felt that you were true—that is no
longer there

3   In love of you, fair robber, my heart gave you all it had
The fear of loss, the hope of gain—these are no
longer there

⤙ 68 ⤚

1   Lost to themselves, they doze, reclining there in Tuba's
shade
Is *this* the high resolve of men who set out before dawn?

2   Turmoil attracts me; what it this good news of
paradise?
I see things clearly; pious sermons are no use to me

1   No one who wants to attain all that a human being is capable of is content
to accept paradise as the end of the road.

2   'Turmoil'—all that goes on in this world. I see clearly all that goes on in
this world, am engrossed in it all, and desire nothing else. I need no
alluring promises of paradise to keep me happy. The key word in the
second line of the Persian, translated as 'clearly', is *be-ghash*, which can
mean both 'without illusion' and 'without desire'. Cf. U.149.5.

⤙ 69 ⤚

1   Nothing disturbed its tenor; on and on, and to no end
Khizar's long life? An item on a list, and nothing more

2   The liveliness of my own thought is me, from top
to toe
My being's warp and woof is constant movement—
nothing more

3   Shine forth!—and I will not be in your debt.
I am the atom
And you, with all your beauty, are the sun,
and nothing more

⁴   Yes, colour, charm, significance it has—but I must say
     That Ghalib's verse is only a selection—nothing more

¹ A life without struggle is no life at all, not even if, like Khizar's, it never ends.

³ True, you are the sun, and I am only a particle of dust. But if the particle shines in the sun's light, it owes no debt to the sun. The sun is only doing what it is there to do.

⁴ 'only a selection'—implies a complaint that he has not produced all that he was capable of. But *intikhab*, besides 'selection', can also mean 'the choicest, the cream, the best, the most outstanding', and Ghalib is implying, 'Yes, it's an *intikhab*—in this sense too'.

⌁ 71 ⌁

¹   You promise it, and no one may dispense it—where's
         the sense in that?
     It is not life that, given once, cannot be given again—
         it's wine!

²   Glad tidings! There'll be streams of honey, palaces of
         emerald
     The thing that will fulfil my heart's desire is this—
         there will be wine!

³   Lahrasp, where has your glory gone? And Parvez,
         where are you?
     The fire-temples are empty, and the taverns desolate

¹ The 'it' throughout refers to wine. Man will have wine in paradise, but may not drink it here in this world.

³ Alas that the coming of orthodox Islam destroyed so much of the beauty and the joy of life in pre-Islamic Iran.

⌁ 73 ⌁

¹   Spring comes; my eyes accept your beauty as the
         gift it brings
     It tells the majesty of her from whose fields it was
         gleaned

2   How gracefully spring's clouds bring all its strivings
      to fulfilment
  All that the breeze's heart desires is manifest on earth

3   Measure by us the quality of those who went before us
  Our dregs have settled in the cup which held their
      purest wine

1   I rejoice in the beauty of spring. But I know that it is a reflection of your
beauty, a mere gleaning from your abundant store of beauty.

2   The spring breeze moves the clouds, urging them to rain down on the
earth so that all the flowers of spring may bloom.

3   Poets like us cannot match the achievements of those who went before
us, but we are recognizably of their line, practising their craft and
upholding their values.

❧ 74 ❧

1   My aching heart has pleased me; it implanted in my
      patience
  A hopelessness that brings to me a calm that never dies

2   The passing of my days brings me all manner of regrets
  They are the dregs of wine that settled in the cup of hope

1   Hope makes you restless and agitated. When you cease to hope, you are
calm.

2   If I had not hoped, I would have had no regrets for hopes that went
unfulfilled. So I myself am to blame for my present sadness.

❧ 75 ❧

1   All pleasures and all griefs that come, come linked to
      one another
  The bright day sends dark night away, and then itself
      departs

2   Don't hurry on; stay, raise and kiss the dust of those
      who knew the way
  A thousand such as you have passed along the path of
      poetry

～ 76 ～

1 A star more bright than this should light my fortunes
   in the world
   My ripened wisdom needs the driving force of fate in
   flower

2 I cannot bear to bring the wine in vessels from afar
   My house must head the lane where dwell those who
   dispense the wine

1 In the original, 'old' (i.e. ripe, mature) wisdom is said to require 'young'
fortunes. 'Young fortune' regularly means 'good fortune'.

～ 77 ～

1 Brought to the city from the west, it is abundant here
   Your faith will buy a draught of it; wine is no longer
   dear

2 The lamp holds only dregs of oil, the wine-cup only
   lees
   None of the joys of night remain—and *now* my guest
   has come!

3 Beauty and wine have left me, and, content with
   poetry
   I've planted willows in a garden that is desolate

1 Give up formal religion and drink the wine of true religion.

3 Poetry is now my only source of joy. Beautiful women and wine are like
a garden in flower, but these I no longer have. Poetry is compared to the
willow—a tree that bears no fruit.

～ 78 ～

1 You've heard the story—flames of fire could not burn
   Ibrahim
   See here a man who burns when there is neither spark
   nor flame

2　Today the blooming of the flowers filled me with
　　　　apprehension
　　My nest built on the flowering branch may once
　　　　more be in flames

3　I do not blame the flower-seller; he plies his trade.
　　　　I burn
　　To see the garden's guardian fired with ardour to
　　　　despoil it

2　Spring brings joy to others, but to me each time it has come it has brought
　me the frenzy of love and the sharp pain of separation. I fear that this
　spring too will do the same. The red flowers on the branches suggest the
　red flame that destroys the nest.

3　How outrageous, that those who profess to cherish and uphold higher
　values in fact pander to those whose only concern is with material gain
　and worldly advancement.

～ 79 ～

1　I cannot bring onto the page all that is in my heart
　　In the assembly flowers are few—and in the garden,
　　　　many

2　She does not feel her lovers' pain? Yet she must
　　　　be forgiven
　　She steals hearts without knowing it—and that
　　　　excuses her

3　We did not know the full force of the strong wine
　　　　of her beauty
　　We were misled by seeing how the Brahman was
　　　　unmoved

4　All know the power of sighs and lamentation; but
　　　　don't fear
　　My struggle with myself still keeps me fully occupied

3　The beloved is the lover's idol, and the Brahman worships idols. We saw
　that he was unaffected by the idol's beauty, and thought that we too could
　withstand the influence of her beauty. Alas that we forget that the Hindu

Brahman, like the Muslim shaikh, does not *love* the god he worships. *We* have the capacity to love—and should have known that our idol's beauty was bound to enslave us in love's bonds.

4   The lover tells his beloved: 'Don't fear that my sighs and laments will melt your heart. I have no *power* to sigh. All my strength is engaged in the struggle I wage within myself.'

⤙ 80 ⤚

1   I think you said, 'Good counsel is strong medicine;
          but take it!'
     Away with you! Our wine is stronger medicine than
          that!

2   I know, I see, all that my love's capriciousness can
          do to me
     In this domain I neither know nor care what fate
          will do

3   If not for my sake, for your own you would do well
          to prize me
     The value of the slave adds to the value of his master

1   Formal religion contrasted with the wine of the religion of love.

2   There are several shades of meaning. My beloved, like fate, is capricious.
     I see clearly all that she can inflict on me, and gladly accept it. I do not know,
     and do not care to know, what fate can do to me. Maybe it is fate that decrees
     that she be cruel to me, but that is of no significance to me. As for fate's
     own, direct afflictions, these are insignificant compared with hers.

⤙ 82 ⤚

1   You manifestly steal my heart—and yet not manifestly
     You know that I suspect you—and that you are not
          suspect

2   Though I would speak my love, the body of my
          thought is dumb
     From top to toe I speak to you—and yet I do not
          speak

3   All you command I do, and all I do proceeds from you
      Seen and unseen my work moves on—and yet does
         not move on

4   The flowering garden grieves me—spring has come,
         and will not last
      The furnace pleases me: autumn is here—and is not here

5   The value of each drop that merges in the ocean's stream
      Accumulates—for it is lost; and yet it is not lost

6   A new creation comes each time you close your
         eyelashes
      The eye thinks, 'This is just the same'—It is not
         just the same

7   The roses surge within the branch, driven by the force
         of spring
      Like wine still held within the flask—concealed, yet
         not concealed

1   ...not manifestly,...not suspect. That is, *I* know, with absolute certainty, but there is nothing to show to the world at large.

3   You inspire all I do, and yet in my *main* effort—the effort to win your love—I make no headway at all.

4   The withered leaves and flowers burn constantly in the flames of the furnace—and the furnace burns constantly, whatever the season. I rejoice, therefore, that at least *something* in this changing world is constant. The bright flames of the furnace display an eternal autumn.

5   Every individual is part of humanity at large and contributes to its greatness. The drop merged in the ocean in a sense *becomes* the ocean.

6   At every moment something new comes to birth. The eye may not see it, but it is so.

7   You know that the wine is there in the flask even though you cannot see it. You know that roses will flower on the branch even though there is as yet nothing to be seen.

✗ 83 ✗

1   Her battleground is one on which you cannot carry
         weapons
      And her assembly one in which you cannot speak of wine

2   Your courage will not aid you here; the lightning
flashes fast
Here you must be a moth, not seek to be a salamander

3   The trials of life are over—why complain of cruelty?
What if you suffered? Can you speak of it on
Judgement Day?

4   We travel fast and do not seek the water and the shade
Don't speak to us of Tuba's tree and Kausar's flowing
stream

5   The words I hide within my breast are not those of a
preacher
Words to be spoken at the stake, not spoken from the pulpit

6   How strange it felt to be involved in dealings with this
madman!
Ghalib is not a Muslim, nor is he an infidel

1   The arena of love has its own rules. She is not to be resisted, and not
to be cajoled.

2   The lightning flame of love strikes fast, and you have not time to resist
it. In any case the lover gives his all for love as the moth immolates himself
in the candle's flame. It was believed that the salamander lives and thrives
in fire, but he is no model for the true lover.

3   The trials of life are pre-eminently the trials of love. It is the beloved's
nature, and her proper role in life, to inflict suffering, so she has nothing
to answer for on Judgement Day. In any case no true lover complains of
his beloved's cruelty. In a more general sense, the trials of love afflict you
by God's will, and you do not complain against God.

4   Ours is a never-ending quest.

5   My unspoken message to humankind is one which, if I spoke it, would
send me to the gallows.

6   Ghalib is possessed by the madness of love, and lovers are unique. They
cannot be fitted into any of the recognized categories.

～✤ 84 ✤～

1   I said, Where shall I go to learn the secrets of days past?
The saki took his mellow wine and poured it in my cup

2   Her handmaid would enhance the beauty God has
     given her
     Bring roses to the garden, carry sugar to Bengal

1   I think, 'What has my life amounted to?' The saki's silent response suggests several answers: 'Drink, and you'll lose all awareness of life around you. And *that* is how you've spent your days—in unawareness of all that was passing.' Or, 'Drink, and wine will cause the scales to fall from your eyes, and you will see all clearly'. Or, 'Drink, and be merry, and don't ask yourself unanswerable questions'.

2   Her perfect natural beauty cannot *be* enhanced. To attempt it is to carry coals to Newcastle.

❧ 85 ❧

1   If friends are false, meeting is pain: if true,
     parting is bitter
     My eyes grieve me: they cannot bear to look
     upon my friends

2   Adam took up the heavy trust the sky could not
     sustain
     God poured into the dust the wine the cup
     could not contain

1   I am afraid to meet people. If they are false, it is torture to be with them; if they are true, I cannot contemplate the pain I shall feel when I must part from them.

2   Adam, who was made from dust; the sky, which is like an upturned cup. Adam's acceptance of the trust and the sky's refusal of it is as startling as would be the saki's choosing to pour wine on the ground and not into the cup.

❧ 86 ❧

1   You offer no complaint: you are immune to every
     charm
     Tell me, good sir, Whose friend are you? And who
     will be your friend?

2   The universe flows over with Your radiance—but
      where
    Is he can drink this wine of Yours that tests the
      drinker's powers?

1   One who really loves is bound to complain sometimes. One who is capable of love is bound to respond to beauty. But you can relate to no one, and no one to you. What use are you, for all your pretensions?

2   I.e. there are very few who are capable of seeing, and feeling, and assimilating all that God's creation has to offer.

⟿ 87 ⟾

1   Here in this vale where even Khizar has no power to
      guide me
    My legs fail; yet I drag myself along and will not sleep

2   Because I love you utterly, the pride I feel is
      boundless
    A beggar, in the shadow of a palace wall, asleep

3   On doomsday these will rise disgraced who passed
      their lives complaining
    Of pain that has no cure, and, still lamenting,
      fell asleep

4   The wind blows hard, the night is dark, the stormy
      waves are rising
    The anchor's chain is broken, and the captain is asleep

5   His rosary, his prayer mat and his cloak—my heart
      fears for them
    The robber lies awake here, and the holy one asleep

6   Look from afar, and do not seek the company of
      monarchs
    The door is open—at the gate a dragon lies asleep

7   Look at me sleeping—all who have the power to see
      can see it
    I lead the caravan, though in the inn I lie asleep

8   What if the road is safe now, and the Kaba lies before me?
      My mount can go no further, and my legs have
         gone to sleep

3   The true love does *not* complain.

5   Sarcasm at the holy one's expense. The thief knows what he is doing, but the holy one cannot even summon the alertness to safeguard his property, and do what *he* has to do.

6   'The door'—the Persian word means the small door at the side of a main gate. This may be open, but don't fail to notice that right beside it a dragon guards the main gate.

~✖ 88 ✖~

1   The elements of time flee one another
      Day chases night, and night too chases day

2   In drunkenness your feet must surely stumble
      What if they stumble when your head is clear?

3   My wit and faith and life and soul—you took these
      But did not take from me my sense of loss

4   That will shed leaves, and this will scatter flowers
      Autumn and spring alike will pass away

1   The time is out of joint. Nothing moves in harmony with anything else.

2   Your head must not only be clear; you must have the degree of perceptiveness you need to guide you unfailingly through life.

3   Alas that you did not steal also my bitter awareness of what you had done.

~✖ 89 ✖~

1   In India, drunk and little-known, lives one whose
        craft is poetry
      Within this ancient temple there is one who drinks
        unceasingly

2   They say of you, you grant your favour to the
        simple-minded
      It is maturity that fills me with this foolish hope

3   I passed my life without you: gauge the keenness of
     my suffering
     Ignore my death—that is a thing that comes when it
     will come

4   There in the Kaba who will fill my cup with purest
     wine?
     If he asks payment, I can pawn the robes of
     pilgrimage

5   Pure wine comes from the west, and beauties come
     from Tartary
     Baghdad and Bastam? These are the names that
     do not signify

6   Who says my verse is so inspired it brings God's
     message to mankind?
     Yet you and God can surely say my verse is
     nonetheless inspired

2 I am naïve enough to think that you will be kind to me. But that shows
   my maturity. People tell me that it is to the naïve that you are kind. I have
   the maturity to grasp this, and so make myself naïve. But it is a naïve and
   foolish hope I entertain!

3 People lament a friend's death—which comes naturally and inevitably.
   They ought to feel more keenly for the lifelong sufferings he has endured,
   which were in no way inevitable and were deliberately inflicted.

5 I know that the great mystics Junaid and Bayazid came from Baghdad and
   Bastam, but what are these to me? My concern is with good wine and
   with beautiful women.

➤ 90 ✈

1   I am one of the city's poor, one of the world's
     non-entities
     If you have killed me, have no fear. Long may
     you live in peace!

2   Your love reproaches me because my longings are
     unnumbered
     My longing cries, Whose unimagined cruelty is this?

3   Within its walls the garden blooms, like joy in your
          assembly
    With whose awareness has the breeze of morning
          formed a bond?

1   'you' means the beloved.

2   You complain that I expect kindness more than any lover has a right to
    expect. I complain that I never imagined one like you could be capable
    of such cruelty. So, with all our love for each other, there is unending
    conflict between us.

3   When we look at your courtyard, full of flowers, it reminds us of your
    assembly. These flowers bloom under the influence of the morning
    breeze. And what makes the morning breeze blow? We lovers do. It is
    love that gives birth to beauty and movement. Cf. ghazal 92.3.

⤙ 91 ⤚

1   No spark flew up, no residue of ash was left
          behind
    I burned, and yet I do not know the manner
          of my burning

2   Such is the gloom, I need a lamp to light my
          house by day
    My heart burns with the lustrelessness of the
          shining sun

⤙ 92 ⤚

1   My words transform my thought into the garden
          of Khalil
    Your face transforms the mirror to the palm of
          Kalim's hand

2   Men's eyes seek everywhere to find your like,
          and are defeated
    Thought labours to produce my peer, and shows
          its barrenness

3   To find you, all the elements of spring stir into motion
    The words I breathe have force to make the morning
        breeze to blow

1   My thought is like the blazing fire into which Namrud cast Khahil
    (Ibrahim). My words transform this fire into poetry as beautiful as the
    roses which Namrud's fire turned into as Ibrahim entered it. Musa's
    (Kalim's) hand made radiant everything that he held in it. Your beauty,
    reflected in the mirror, transforms it from something quite ordinary into
    something amazingly beautiful.

3   Beauty and love are the motive forces of all creation.

⤳ 94 ↩

1   I am a lover; what have name and fame to do with me?
    The case is special; what have general rules to do
        with me?

2   He who drinks wine unceasingly, alone with his
        beloved
    Knows well the worth of houris and of streams
        of paradise

3   We who are crushed by grief drink wine to heal the
        pain of grief
    What have 'permitted' and 'forbidden' things to do
        with us?

4   The darkness of the day has banished all the fear
        of night
    Dawn never comes; how then should I know when
        the night has come?

5   You say 'The cage is welcome. I can spread my
        wings in it'
    But what can cure the hurt you suffered held fast
        in the snare?

6   Good conduct is from You; we do not ask to be
        rewarded
    And if we sin, that is Your doing. Why then take revenge?

7   If Ghalib has not sold his cloak and his Quran together
    Why is he asking us, What is the price of ruby wine?

2   This present joy is at least as good as the promised future joys of
    paradise—even if one accepts that there *will* be such joys.

3   In any case the use of things normally 'haram' (forbidden) is permitted
    in the treatment of sickness.

5   Do not forget the experience, and the lessons of past suffering in present
    relative comfort. The suggestion is also here that security bought at the
    price of loss of freedom is bought too dearly.

⤙ 95 ⤚

1   She seized the guilty rose when it laid claim to
        scent and colour
    And stopped her lover's mouth that would have
        reconciled the two

2   God's kindness does not move my heart to seek
        enjoyment in it
    It is an infidel addicted to love's cruelties

3   How rapt she has become in contemplation of her charms!
    Stealing my heart with all its thousand longings from
        my breast

4   Our wine comes from one cask—and yet our fates are
        different
    Jamshed was given his cup; the beggar got his begging
        bowl

5   Its every affliction brings ecstatic joy to me
    It seems the sky has learned from her the way to
        torture me

6   Rizvan brought milk and honey and presented
        them to Ghalib
    Poor fellow, he rejected them and took the fragrant wine

1   To the lover, the rose and the beloved are both beautiful. But such is her
    pride that she rebukes the rose for claiming fragrance and beauty in any
    way comparable to hers, and makes it impossible for her lover to express
    any such comparison.

2   'It' in line 2—my heart.

5   He reconciles himself to—indeed enjoys—the hardships of life by picturing them to himself as inflicted by his beloved.

6   Milk, honey, and wine are all among the joys that await the true Muslim in paradise.

⤞ 103 ↩

1   The joy of true philosophy is wine drawn from
         Your cask
      The sorceries of Babylon a chapter from Your book

2   Speak of the cup and mirror, not Sikandar and
         Jamshed
      All that has come to every age is here in our own time

3   You, who are lost in wonder at the poets of the past
      Do not deny my claims because I live in your own
         time

1   Those who seek the truth about the universe and those who practise magic are both Your servants, acting in accordance with Your will.

2   Jamshed is said to have invented the wine cup and Sikandar the mirror. Don't romanticize the past or overrate the importance of particular figures in it. Rejoice that all that the past has achieved has been inherited by the present.

⤞ 107 ↩

1   Clad as she is my mistress makes her way right to
         my heart
      What need is there to loose the ties and let her robe
         fall from her?

2   Dreams are to hearten those whose gaze wanders
         from face to face
      What need has he to dream who gazes spellbound
         upon yours?

2   Men who are still in search of the ideal beloved may at any rate catch a glimpse of it in their dreams. I do not *need* to dream.

❧ 109 ❧

1   Abstinence only heightens their concern to fill their bellies
The bustle of the meals is all; Ramzan's of no account

2   You who seek worldly ends, rejoice! Your struggles
      count for nothing
Our freedom, and your bondage are alike of no
      account

3   The cup that gives the zest to life goes ever round
      and round
Riot of spring is everywhere; autumn's of no account

4   Come Ghalib, break free from illusions' bonds.
      I swear by God
This world, and this world's good and bad—
      all are of no account

2   I.e. of no account to God. Cf. 4 below.

2, 4 Both couplets have a similar theme. God—the only true reality—is
immune to the effects of anything men do.

❧ 112 ❧

1   How long will you be deaf to me while I tell of myself
In story after story in which nothing is said twice?

2   Do not despise me if I stumble as I journey on
Don't think me strange if I go headlong making my
      own way

3–5 From lamentation's warp and woof I weave myself a veil
From smoke that rises from my heart I make a fragrant
      tress
From wounds and scars I make a scene of tulips and of roses
From hills, her canopy; from wastes her hall of audience
Through pain and passion friend and minstrel come to
      comfort me
From thorns and rock I make myself a pillow and bed

⁶   I took the Brahmin's path and have pursued it to the limit
Come Ghalib, open up again the path that Azar trod

¹   The lover tells his mistress stories of love; each story is of a different experience, and yet each experience is his. He hopes that she will soon realise that it is himself he is speaking of.

²   The important thing is that, inspired by love, I make my own way in life, undeterred by any obstacle.

³⁻⁵ There is a single mood pervading these three verses, with Ghalib asserting in various ways that the things which life ought to give him, but which it denies him, he can create out of his own internal resources.

³   'a veil'—i.e. the beloved's veil—alluring because her beauty lies behind it. The black, coiling, pungent smoke that rises from his distressed and burning heart is transformed in his imagination into the black coiling fragrant tresses of his beloved.

⁴   The gaping wound is regularly compared with rose in bloom, and the black scar of separation with the black markings in the centre of the tulip.

⁶   The Brahmin worships idols as the lover worships his beloved. I have loved and worshipped to the limit, says Ghalib. Now I will revive Azar's art and make an idol representing my beloved more beautiful than anyone has ever made before.

⇝ 116 ↜

¹   To battle with calamity intoxicates my soul; perhaps
The wine the saki pours me will be blood wrung
        from my heart

²   You can yourself be paradise if you possess a heart
That grief has crushed and turned to blood and
        drained of all desire

³   The day you come to me, hold me so fast in your embrace
That words that tell my pain will flow unbidden from
        my lips

⁴   Young and abstemious?—when life has got so much to
        offer!
To hell with all abstemious youths! Calamity befall them!

¹   The battle with calamity crushes my heart to blood. Let me hope that the saki will realise that *this* is the finest wine and pour me my own heart's blood to drink.

2 'grief'—the grief that love brings. And to love truly, even though your love is not returned, is to experience the greatest possible joy.

➤ 118 ❧

You bring the tears into my eyes; *you* bring the grief
    into my breast
Pride in that grief—this too *you* bring—gives this content-
    ment to my heart

➤ 120 ❧

Just as in drunkenness the secret issues from the heart
In springtime all your fragrance comes, borne on the
    morning breeze

➤ 121 ❧

1   Happy are they who have nothing but grief
    Happier they who have not even that

2   Better mirages shining in the desert
    Than eyes that lack the radiance of tears

3   Lips that are music, eyes that are flowers that see
    You have a spring the world has never had

1   To love is wonderful. Perhaps to be immune to love would be more wonderful still!

3   Literally, 'Your rose (*gul*) is music, and your narcissus sees all around you.' *Gul* is a metaphor for her rose-bud mouth. The narcissus is always conceived of as a beautiful, but unseeing eye. But *her* eyes see!

➤ 122 ❧

1   In my dark nights they brought me the good tidings
    of the morning
    Put out the candles, turning me towards the rising
    sun

2   They showed their faces, and at once my babbling
        tongue was silenced
    They took my heart away from me, and gave me
        eyes to see

3–7 They burnt the fire-temples, and breathed their fire
        into my spirit
    Cast idols down, and let the conches sound in my lament
    They plucked the pearls that once had decked the
        banner of Iran's kings
    And gave me them to scatter from the treasury of my pen
    Prized from their crown, they set the jewels in my
        crown of wisdom
    All that men saw them take away, they secretly gave back
    The wine they took as tribute from the worshippers of fire
    They gave to me one Friday in the month of Ramazan
    From all they took in booty from the treasures of Iran
    They gave to me a tongue in which to utter my lament

2   Their faces—i.e. the beautiful faces of those one loves, once seen, show
    how utterly inadequate words are to describe them. And to fall in love
    is to become able to perceive all reality clearly for the first time.

        The remaining verses lament the passing of the glory and the beauty
    of ancient, pre-Islamic Iran, where fire was worshipped, wine was drunk,
    there were idols in the temples, and the blowing of conches accompanied
    worship. Ghalib claims he is the heir to all this, and that his poetry has
    the power to re-create it. In 7 'tongue' implies a tongue able to speak
    the pure Persian of pre-Islamic times. Ghalib prided himself on this
    ability. Cf. Ralph Russell and Khurshidul Islam, *Ghalib: Life and Letters*,
    pp. 84–5, 114.

6   Defiant contravention of the requirements of orthodox Islam. Friday, the
    day of congregational prayer, is the most important day in the week.
    Ramzan (pronounced here 'Ramazan' to fit the metre) with its month-
    long fasting is the most important month of the year.

                        ⋙ 123 ⋘

1   Compared to you, the cypress is like one who
        suddenly
    Beside himself leaps to his feet in frenzied agitation

2   How then would men distinguish what is lust and
        what is love?
    God grant the rule of tyranny continue in the world

3   Age upon age the sky revolves; then one who burns
        with grief
    Like me, springs from the family of those whose
        breath is fire

4   Were I to tell the tale of all my friends have done to me
    The custom men call hope would vanish utterly from earth

1   The beloved is regularly compared to the cypress—upright, perfectly
    proportioned, and serene. But you are so much beyond the cypress in
    all these things that the comparison is quite inappropriate. Compared to
    you, the cypress is less like you than it is like one who may be tall and
    upright, but is far from serene.

2   'tyranny'—i.e. the cruelty of the beloved towards her lover. Only this can
    bring out the difference between one who simply desires her and loses
    interest when she is cruel, and the true lover, who loves her come what
    may.

3   Only once in ages does the world produce poets like me, whose breath
    is fire—because their hearts burn with the grief of love. Also, whose
    verses, spoken from the heart, have the effect of fire.

❧ 124 ❧

1   Your message brings us all the joy that seeing you
        could give
    To see? To hear?—your lovers cannot tell the difference

2   I see what trouble lies in store for pocket and for shroud
    A hand that knows no skill but that which teaches it to tear

3   My strong desire will bring the wine into the cup tonight
    And will not know the need to ask the cup-bearer to
        pour it

2   The true lover rends his garments in the frenzy of love, and since love
    is all in all to him, his hand knows no other skill. The 'pocket' holds
    wealth, and the proper ceremonies of burial call for a shroud. But the
    lover is indifferent to both, and cares nothing for respectability either in
    this life or after death.

⤳ 125 ↩

1   The morning breeze ruffles the treetops' leaves
    To wreck my plans is easier than that

2   The lightning and the cloud move to my will
    The dagger flashes in my mistress' hand

3   I choke with envy, and I dance with joy
    To see the pick that leaps in Kohkan's grasp

4   With every breath my free heart leaps for joy
    Who makes the veil move when the air is still?

2   The dagger flashes like lightning in a white hand that moves like the white
    cloud. I love her dagger and her hand so much that I feel them to be
    a part of me, strong enough to direct the forces of nature.

3   I.e. I envy him his strength and resolution, and rejoice that love is able
    to inspire such feats and make them possible.

4   God keeps the universe in motion even when there is, to all appearances,
    nothing causing it to move, and my heart rejoices in the knowledge that
    this is so.

⤳ 126 ↩

I am not so far gone that if the news of her return to me
Should reach me, even from the sky, I would believe it so

'from the sky'—i.e. as a decree of fate.

⤳ 127 ↩

1   I sit content among the preacher's flock; there is no
       music here
    But after all he speaks of lute and viol and aloes'
       fragrance

2   Would that I too could be appeased by such fair words
       of favour!
    How light at heart the fool is as he comes from her
       assembly!

^{3–4} See how men vie with one another, seeking His approval
See in what ways they set themselves to realise their aim
The father goes unhesitating into Namrud's fire
The son lies down and bares his throat beneath his
father's knife

⁵ Ghalib, rejoice! These baseless hopes, these thoughts
of coming pleasures
Are non-existent threads that weave the tapestry of life.

¹ He speaks to condemn them!

^{3, 4} 'The father'—Ibrahim. 'The son'—Ismail.

⁵ The ability to live in fantasy is an essential part of the ability to live.

⤙ 129 ⤚

¹ My soul, rejoice! The barrier of shame no longer
parts us
Summon delight! The time has come to bid
restraint goodbye

² Your sleeve must scatter it, your sword at one blow
sever it
My soul—my body's dust; my head—a burden on
my shoulders

³ Just see His boundless mercy! He comes in the
garb of spring
To justify the ways of those who drink the ruby
wine

⁴ Kohkan let fall the reins of courage, and so lost his life
How weak when he departed, and how resolute
when he came!

² The first 'it' is the soul and the second, the head. The picture is of a wide
sleeve fanning dust away. The idea is, 'Let me fall *properly* in love. Life
without all-consuming love is a burden.'

³ The spring (with moonlit nights and the rainy season) is the time
considered to be especially appropriate to drinking.

⤜ 130 ↝

1 In love you must be free of all dependence on both worlds
Burn that of symbols, and melt down that of reality

2 Put all the wealth of joy into the purse of resolution
Make your indifference a threat to lamentation's life

3 You must not be like lips impelled by love to babble
   nonsense
Be like the heart, whose strings hold all its secret melodies

4 Be radiant and full of joy, like men in mirth's assembly
Be soft at heart, like candles burning in a hermit's cell

5 Conceal your strength, and use it to destroy all
   self-awareness
Join with her in her planning to subdue you by her pride

6 Love spreads its wings; rejoice in all the strength
   that it will give you
Pride shows its majesty: you must be all humility

7 Here in the tavern's yard rejoice in sheer intoxication
There in the corner of the mosque devote yourself
   to prayer

8 You cannot live all restless with desire to gaze upon her
Give up your life, a martyr to her long black eyelashes

1 Love is love. The distinction between 'symbolic' love (between two human beings) and 'real' love (love of God and one's ideals) is absurd.
2 Your resoluteness is fuelled by your joy in life. And when you are in distress, learn to be indifferent to it.
3 The original, in the second line, uses the word *parda*, which means both a screen or veil, and also the fret on a musical instrument.
4 A true man has both these qualities.
5 Destroy all self-seeking, but don't make a show of it.
6 *Your* love, and *her* pride.
7 Act as the situation demands.
8 Don't spend your life in useless longing. Do something about it, and do not count the cost.

❧ 132 ☙

1   Saki, one glance!—that I may recognize which cup it was
From which I drank the wine that broke the bonds
of my reserve

2   I am a ship wrecked by the waves and destined to
destruction
Taken out of the water to be thrown into the fire

1   Was it the wine in the cup? Or was it the wine of your glance?

❧ 133 ☙

1   Better the man that knows that he will starve to
death, and trembles
Than him who sees a guest approaching on the road,
and trembles

2   I am with her, and, like the thief that finds at last
the treasure
And fears its guardian, my heart misgives me, and I tremble

3   When flushed with wine, she looks my way, and her
eyelashes flutter
I feel the shaft loosed unintended from her bow,
and tremble

4   Your shaikh will not permit himself ecstatic joy
in music
But should the thought of sudden death come to
him he will tremble

4   We who love wine and music trust in God's mercy and do not fear
Judgement Day. The shaikh fears God's wrath, and trembles so much at
the thought that those who see him think *he* is dancing too!

❧ 134 ☙

1   The blood of many thousand simple souls is on the head
Of those who said, 'The fair of face are also fair in deed'

2   Ghalib, you must not wear a cloak soiled with hypocrisy
     That cloak alone is clean that has been washed
          in purest wine

～ 135 ～

1   Love is indifferent—it has destroyed us
     The ocean's waves break up the ship. What of it?

2   The seven skies revolve, with us between them
     Ghalib, don't ask what is our fate. What of it?

Fate and love do what they exist to do. Be serene about what you cannot change.

～ 136 ～

1   Swear that you will strike with your sword, and lay
          my heart wide open
     My heart is sore; the arrow's wound cannot fulfil its need

2   Look not for comfort if you are a man; for on this journey
     Pluck the thorns from your feet—your feet will
          tangle with your cloak

～ 137 ～

I am a writer, poet, drinker, friend—and much besides
So be it if my sad lament can never touch your heart

If my poetry doesn't move you, reflect that I am much more than just a poet, and find at any rate something to admire in me! There is a hint that if she can learn to appreciate and respond to a part of him, she may one day come to respond to him and him for *all* he is.

～ 138 ～

1   You walk upon the earth, and so the earth becomes a heaven
     Happy the heaven-dwellers who sit down here, in your
          lane!

2   A hundred doomsdays melted down and fused in
       one another
    Became the essence of the tumult stored up in your heart

3   I summon strength to bear my pain, and say 'Alas! Alas!'
    What shall I do to make you feel my grief, parted from you?

4   Faith? Unbelief? The grime of the illusion of existence
    Cleanse yourself!—and your unbelief will then become
       your faith

2 'stored up'—to emerge and shake your lover to the depths of his being, as Doomsday will never be able to.

4 You think of yourself as separate from the rest of God's creation, and pride yourself on being a follower of the true religion. But God is in everything. God *is* everything. He created 'infidels' and 'believers' alike, and values them alike. And 'infidels' who love Him are as one with 'believers' who love him. Realise this. Cease to regard yourself as essentially different from them, and your 'unbelief'—i.e. what you think of as unbelief—will become faith.

～ 142 ～

They barred Sikandar's road; he could not get a
    draught of water
The beggar at the tavern door has filled his gourd
    with wine

'water'—the water of life. See Explanatory Index.

'his'—the beggar's.

So who is better off? Put reasonable limits to your ambition, and fate will reward you.

～ 143 ～

I talk to her about my grief; she thinks I talk of joy
My day is dark; she thinks it is the shadow of her wall

I feel my sorrows keenly. She thinks that lovers are supposed to find joy in the sorrows of love, and thinks I *do* find it. I feel like one deprived of the light of the sun. She thinks I do not *want* the sunlight, preferring to sit in the shade of her wall.

⇜ 144 ⇝

Let the sky's ancient dome collapse and fall—I shall
    be glad
Even though it be on my own head that it collapse
    and fall

Life must change, no matter what the cost. Cf. Urdu ghazal 149.5.

⇜ 145 ⇝

1   If only all I see before me did not pierce my heart
    How well I could have passed my days in constant
      journeying

2   The spark is not a match for the bright flames of
      my lament
    It leaps out from within the rock: they enter into it

2   The keenness of my lament pierces even to the heart of the rock.

⇜ 147 ⇝

1   My lord desires to enter on his heritage of paradise
    Alas, if he cannot trace back his ancestry to Adam!

2   Hail to the joy her cruelty brings to us! You who
      tread this path
    Will find good company before you even find yourself

⇜ 148 ⇝

Offer your life in love for her, and death cannot pursue
    you
Plunge into love's distress, and you will cease to feel
    distress

Love releases you from fear of death and fear of affliction.

✎ 149 ✎

1   The stream of milk, the luxury of Khusrau left no
    trace
    Farhad has still to bear the shame of honour taunting
    him

2   The bird born in the cage laments—but where is that
    keen pain
    That cries out in the sad lament of one who once was
    free?

3   This caravan of colour has no longer life than this
    The flower drains a cup of wine there in the box-tree's
    shade

3   Spring passes as quickly as if it had only a moment to stay.

✎ 150 ✎

1   'You should on no account drink wine', they said
    That was a lie told in a worthy cause

2   You reign with effort: I submit with ease
    They speak of you: they also speak of me

1   The second line is a direct quotation from the first story of the *Gulistan*
    of Sadi, where two ministers—one good and one bad—accompany the
    king on a visit to a prison. A man condemned to death rails at the king
    in a language he does not understand. He asks the good minister what
    the man has said. The minister says, 'He said that the Quran declares that
    God will be merciful to the merciful.' The other minister tells the king
    what the man really said, whereupon the king praises the first minister
    for his 'lie told in a worthy cause'. The words have become proverbial.

2   My fame and renown are no less than yours—and I am even more
    deserving of fame than you.

✎ 154 ✎

Lost to myself, I strive and strive unstinting on—and fate
Gives every goal I reach the aspect of a starting point

❧ 155 ❦

1   Do not believe that fate is kind—this is the trickster
      who
      Took Yusuf from the well to sell him in the market-
      place

2   They go to her lane, take its dust, and pour it on
      their head
      To banish from their hearts the wish their head
      should wear a turban

2   To be a lover is far better than to achieve fame and honour in this world.
    Special turbans were conferred as marks of distinction.

❧ 157 ❦

1   My deep despair knows nothing of successive nights
      and days
      The day is passed in darkness; it has neither dawn
      nor dusk

2   You make my every particle of dust dance with desire
      The frenzy of true love goes on forever, without end

3   Nightingales in the garden; moths drawn into her
      assembly
      See! Lovers have no peace of mind even with their
      beloved

3   'nightingales', 'moths'—see Explanatory Index.

❧ 158 ❦

1   Poetry has no worth unless it wells up from within
      That tongue that does not drip with blood—seize it
      and tear it out

2   Wise is the saki, strong the wine—and I so hard to please
      I curse the heavy cup if it comes to me less than full

3   I never said God is the source of all our suffering—
yet
God, in this age in which you live, is not kind to
mankind

✕ 161 ✕

1   You walked to keep your tryst with me; I am in tears
Come, stay with me! My love feels shame to make
you roam

2   She always finds a pretext to be cruel to me
Resenting that complaint which I have never made

✕ 162 ✕

1   What joy unless you tread a path beset with thorns?
Don't set out for the Kaba if the way is safe

2   I am a poet, not a theologian
And wine-stained clothes are no disgrace to poetry

3   Bring him, if there be any here that knows my tongue
A stranger to your city has something to say

✕ 163 ✕

My friends, true to themselves no more, opted for peace.
I am still there
Where thorns already pierce my feet though still lodged
in my garment's hem

I move ever forward no matter how difficult the way, and even though my
sensitive nature experiences already the suffering that has not yet befallen me.

✕ 171 ✕

1   I am a beggar at a house I cannot find
Its door, forever closed to me, is like its wall

2   One way she has that steals my heart—she teases me
    Hiding her thoughts and thus, it seems, expressing
    them

1   The door to his beloved's house, or, perhaps, to his own heart.

❧ 172 ❧

What love did to the wielder of the pick was not from
    cruelty
This happens when a hardy lover meets a proud beloved

'the wielder of the pick'—Farhad.
The very logic of love is that you lose your life for it, no matter how strong
you are.

❧ 173 ❧

Despair of You is unbelief: that is not pleasing to You
So my despair brings me again to fix my hope on You

❧ 175 ❧

Father, do not dispute with me. Just look at Azar's son
None who has eyes to see can follow in his father's path

❧ 178 ❧

1   Here in the Kaba I am cramped. Someone should
    come and tell me of
    The spacious temples he has seen in India and China

2   Her anger makes her speak harsh words—and I delight
    so in her speech
    I cherish in my heart the thought, 'Now she will
    speak sweet words'

3   Why have they banished Ghalib? There should be
        somebody in the street
    To tell the secrets of the king to beggars who
        sit there

3   Ghalib has been banished from the king's court because he reveals to
    everyone what goes on there. But a good king should *want* his subjects
    to know this.

✖ 179 ✖

Music and wine I fashion out of them
The wayward acts of a capricious world

I enjoy the spectacle of all that happens in the world—whether good or bad.

✖ 180 ✖

How unbecoming in a man to go begging for joy!
Happy that heart that looks for grief, and so exalts itself

✖ 182 ✖

1   He enters wine's assembly and plays saki—
        it would not be strange
    If He should make the hermit dance attendance
        on the revellers

2   You cry with pain because the thorn has pierced
        your foot? See how the sky
    Struck off the head of Ali's son Husain and set it
        on the lance

3   Go out for joy! Allow no grief a place within your
        heart—for fate
    Takes you for dice and rolls you on the cloth, the
        testing-ground of life

4   Yazid it seats upon the throne to rule as Caliph over all
Kalim it puts in shepherd's dress and sends him out to
roam the wastes

Compare this ghazal with Persian ghazal 1.
1   'He' means God.
2   'the sky'—i.e. fate.
4   'it'—i.e. fate, God's will.

⊰ 183 ⊱

1   Who has just left the prison gate? The agitation that
I feel
Surges so strong it shakes the key the prison guard
holds in his hand

2   Possessed by love, I sit here on the road my love will
pass along
God grant no one will come along to shake me into
wakefulness

3   I know the state of those who fall a prey to him.
How should I not?
The moment he takes up his net I feel my nest begin
to shake

1, 3 Others' sorrow is my sorrow too.

⊰ 184 ⊱

1   Fate burnt his home to ashes: now he wants the gale
to blow
I said, Let breezes blow. He said, Their place is with
the flowers

2   My joy is all in my lament. I feel no jealousy
I want the thorns along the way to pierce my dear
friends' feet

1   The true lover wants all attachment to worldly things to be severed, and

even when his home is burnt to ashes, he is not satisfied, but hopes that a whirlwind will come to sweep away every last trace of it. He prefers a life of unrelieved hardship in love to a life of ease without it.

2 'My dear friends' is ironical. 'I want my well-meaning, insensitive friends to experience what love means.'

~✖ 185 ✖~

Beauty is like a flood of treasure—and my heart grieves
    sore
Why could it never fill the emptiness of our embrace?

'flood of treasure'—in the Persian, 'flowing treasures'—words applied to the treasure of Qarun. Alas that there should be so many beautiful, lovable people and that they do not respond to the love which they inspire.

~✖ 187 ✖~

1 You think the heavens revolve because they have
    no other choice
But He has other choices who has set them
    to revolve

2 I know a secret I should like to tell to all my friends:
If you would look on beauty, find the strength to look
    on it

3 One ranged across the desert, and one cleft the
    mountain's heart
Love set each one of them to work in his own
    special style

4 No word, no sound he utters but what celebrates
    his love
Ghalib must surely have a love that draws forth
    speech from him

2 To look on beauty means to fall in love—and to persist in love demands strength.
3 Majnun and Farhad respectively.

ﮩﺨ 191 ﮥ

1 She is capricious as the age; her beauty makes the
    spring to bloom
  In drunkenness, with full control, she steals the wits
    of sober men

2 Send me a cask of wine, and then in any quantity
    You please
  Make streams of milk to flow to win the hearts of
    the abstemious

3 You tell me, 'Practise piety'. Well, I would die for
    you; but go
  Direct your steps to walk into the house in which
    the pious dwell

3   ...and see whether even those whose way of life is piety can practise piety
in *your* presence!

ﮩﺨ 192 ﮥ

1 Autumn obeys the laws which your capriciousness
    lays down
  And spring holds up a mirror to the beauty of your face

2 Love's ecstasy brings colour to the face of full
    awareness
  Spring comes to beautify the dust that rises as you pass

ﮩﺨ 193 ﮥ

1 Come, see with what intensity I long to look upon you
  See how, transformed to tears, my soul drips from my
    eyelashes

2 My restlessness offended you; you held yourself aloof
    from me
  Come to my dust and see me now. How peacefully
    I lie!

3   I've heard you will not look at me—and I am not
           despondent
     I've heard you will not see me. Come and see how
           I have heard!

4   The seed has sprouted—grown so high that birds can
           build their nests here
     See how my snare waits, hoping that the *huma* will alight

5   Become my spring, and you will see how all my
           being flowers
     Come to my home, and see how I shall drain cup
           after cup

6   Ghalib will never honour those who do not honour
           Ghalib
     See how he bows beneath the shadow of her curving
           sword

3   That is, see what effect this statement has had upon me—no effect at all!
     My hope is undiminished.

4   The same force as that of verse 3. The *huma* is no more than a legend,
     but I hope to ensnare it. I scattered seed to attract it into my snare. The
     seed took root, sprouted and grew into a bush strong enough for birds
     to build their nests in it—and I am still waiting and hoping.

6   Because her scimitar curves, as though bowing before Ghalib, he in turn
     bows beneath it.

✖ 194 ✖

1   When I am dead, I conjure you, remember how I died
     Remember how my corpse lay all unshrouded in your
           lane

2   I was not one of those whose death made no stir in
           the world
     Remember how the pious wept and Brahmins made
           lament

3   Ask how the men of feeling mourned me in
           harmonious song
     Remember how the men of culture wrote their elegies

4   Ask any man the sum of all my loyalties to you
    Remember all the cruelties you practised upon me

5   Say what my soul saw, seeing your intoxicated eyes
    Remember what passed in my head, seeing your
      coiling tress

2   I was mourned by the guardians of both mosque and temple—not presented here in an unfavourable light.

4   Ask—because *anyone* can tell you.

⤙ 195 ⤚

My friend, what have your heaven and hell to give?
    I have within me
The joy of my imaginings, the wound that scars my heart

'joy…wound'—i.e. heaven and hell.

⤙ 196 ⤚

1   My heart, bring me some sign plucked from the
      roses of hope's garden
    You cannot bring a flower in bloom? Bring me an
      autumn leaf

2   Companion of my begging days, get up and go out
      quickly
    Pawn anything—your life, your clothes—and bring
      abundant wine

3   O God, You have brought forth all this from what
      was non-existent
    Bring me a kiss or two, brought from the corner of
      her mouth

3   In poetic convention the beloved's mouth is so dainty as to be almost non-existent, but at any rate it *does* exist. When You could bring forth all the universe out of nothing, can You not produce even a couple of kisses from her mouth?

197

My life has passed, more bitter than destruction
Come, bring me now a death more sweet than life

198

1 Yes, my wise friend, you know the road that takes you to the desert
Bring me the candle that the desert wind cannot put out

2 The water of this vale is salt and bitter: show your bounty
Go to the town and bring me the sweet water that flows there

3 I know that you have gold, that you have access to high places
If the king will not give me wine, go buy it from the shop

4 The wine shop gives it in a gourd? Then take it and get going
The king bestows a jar of it? Then hoist it on your back

5 Sweet basil springs from the green flask; the wine sings as you pour it
Let your eyes feast on it, listen intently to its song

6 Ply me assiduously with wine, that I may lose awareness
Play music to me, that I may return to consciousness

7 If Ghalib, God grant him long life, cannot himself come with you
Bring me at least a ghazal or a verse he has composed

All seven couplets are to be taken together. Someone—not Ghalib (as the last couplet shows)—is asking a friend to bring the wine, and (in the last couplet) the poetry that makes life worth living, and not to stint whatever effort it may cost to supply these things.

1   'the desert'—i.e. my ruined home. 'the candle'—wine, which, like the candle, gives brightness and warmth.

2   'Sweet water...' The original can also mean: 1) an antidote to poison 2) the water of life.

3   Sweet basil, which is fragrant as well as beautiful.

✎ 199 ✐

1   That lightning that burnt lovers' hearts is cold; her heart is wounded
Those hands, once red with blood, lack even henna's redness now

2   She who in solitude would not ask even God to hear her
Goes now to everyone to tell the harshness of her fate

3   That breast, once hidden from men's eyes as life hides in the body
Shines now through tattered garments she has rent in love's despair

4   Her eyes still shine, she burns still with the fire that is her nature
Her weeping eyes shed pearls, and fire is in the sighs she breathes

5   Each day, in hope to move him, she reads Ghalib's verses to him
Do not find fault with her: just see what wisdom she displays!

This whole ghazal portrays a beloved who has now herself fallen in love, and experiences for the first time the kind of pain which she herself has been accustomed to inflict.

1   Women stain their hands with henna when there are joyful occasions (such as weddings) to celebrate.

2   She was once so proud and self-sufficient that she felt she needed nothing, even from God.

4   The brightness of her eyes once struck her lovers down; now their brightness comes from the tears in them. Her fire was once that of power and anger; now it comes from a heart burning with anguish.

5   When Ghalib's verses were addressed to *her*, she dismissed them. Now she realises how powerful they are and uses them in the hope that they will move her beloved as they never moved *her*!

⤳ 200 ⤶

1   O Lord, let frenzy bring new modes into my power
   of seeing
   And make a hundred deserts form the fabric of my
   home

2   The sun that lights the world brings me no hope of
   radiant vision
   Take up this bowl of burning fire and pour it on my
   head

3   Rescue my grieving heart from futile weeping, and
   inspire it
   Dissolve my silent fortitude: bring tears into my eyes

4   Each lightning flash that has the power to melt the
   power of seeing
   Melt it, and pour it in the cup of my desire to see

5   I am drunk with the wine of joy in pain: rouse me
   to action
   Break my heart's flask; scatter its fragments on the
   path I tread

6   Hot blood that courses uselessly, divert into my
   heart
   Lightning that flashes pointlessly, bring to enhance
   my powers

7   Give water brought from everywhere to wet my
   eyelashes
   Take dust from seas and streams run dry and pour it
   on my head

8   The wine-flask cannot come to me to grace my night
with beauty?

Then let my morning bring the fragments of the cup
to me

9   This natural fire is not enough to melt the soul
within me

Squeeze essence from a hundred flames and pour
it into me

10   Poor counsellor, he does not know the joy that
comes from torment

Make me a thorn and set me in the path by which
he comes

The drift of the whole ghazal is 'Make my poetry the powerful expression
of the most intense emotion.'

➼ 201 ↩

1   Seek courage from the keen edge of the pick that
Farhad wielded

Don't be Majnun; don't learn from him to die in agony

2   In drunkenness still hold fast to the tasks that lie
before you

Don't imitate the shifting of the turban's dancing
plume

3   Ghalib, beware! The doers of good deeds lie there
in ambush

I've told you. Do not follow them. Go on your own
way, free

➼ 202 ↩

1   Plucked out of joy's assembly, fate has cast me into
strange hands

I am still drunk; I do not know my head yet from
my heels

2   Doomsday has come; the memory of the night we
        spent together
    Still holds me in its spell with all its joy and fear of dawn

3   O rock, you vaunt your strength; your claim is every-
        where acknowledged
    As yet you have not seen yourself in the glass-maker's
        hands

1   ...but no matter what my condition, I shall never cease to go forward.

2   Even the uproar of Judgement Day cannot awake me from the dream into
which love has plunged me.

3   It is the rock's fate to be melted down and made into glass.

✗ 203 ✗

1   Trust in my love and banish from your head all your
        misgivings
    Sit lovingly with me—or rise and put me to the test

2   You came to visit, not to quarrel. Why this bitterness?
    Sit down and sympathise, and show your grief as you
        depart

3   I'll bring a jug of wine and give it to you every
        morning
    By God I swear it; dwell no more in the wine-seller's
        lane

2   The picture is one of the beloved, moved by the state of her lover, laid
prostrate by the suffering she has caused him, coming to show her
concern for him—but at once relapsing into her habitual hostility to him.

3   He who gives this advice has not grasped that the attraction is not only
the wine but the beauty of those who dispense it.

✗ 204 ✗

1   Lost though I am to consciousness, my empty place
        awaits me
    From time to time I come back to awareness of myself

2 I died and turned to dust—that dust is caught up in
      the whirlwind
   And restlessness possesses me just as it ever has

3 The tumult of a hundred doomsdays breathes in every
      breath I breathe
   And I, fool that I am, live on in fear of Judgement
      Day

3 I already suffer all the agonies of Judgement Day. So let me at least banish
my fear of what will befall me then.

✻ 205 ✻

1 Half sunk in sleep, where will you find the power to
      spread your wings?
   Come out of non-existence; learn from me what men
      can do

2 Give me your kisses: ask for Khizar's life-time in
      return
   Bring me a cup of wine: ask all the pleasures of
      Jamshed

3 Heaven is in my essence: savour Kausar's joys in me
   I hold the Kaba in me; learn of Zamzam's power
      from me

✻ 206 ✻

1 What can you do with one who hides herself in her
      own home?
   What can you do with loves in which nothing is
      happening?

2 She takes your heart and soul when you insist on
      giving it
   What can you do then, when she thinks you owe a
      debt to her?

3   Drink, preacher, if you want the joy that drinking
       wine can bring
     What can you do—for God's sake!—with reports that
       it brings joy?

4   It is not true you cannot find the pathway through
       the waste
     What can you do with those who turn away and will
       not see?

5   Ghalib, the task of kings is to ensure that justice rules
     What can you do with one whose rule ensures the
       opposite?

1   Beauty exists to inspire love and turmoil in the world. A love to which
     nothing is happening means one in which the beloved never appears.

2   Why be content to wait for the wine which you are told you will have
     in paradise when you can have it here and now?

ᴥ 207 ᴧ

He made injustice serve the need of men's desire for
  beauty
Shed blood that it might be the rouge adorning the
  world's face

The blood of the martyrs adorns the pages of history.

ᴥ 208 ᴧ

O God, why waste the gift of paradise upon the pious?
They never felt love's cruelty. *Their* hearts were never
  crushed

ᴥ 210 ᴧ

1   Last night when I prepared to pray there came into
       my ears
     A warning spoken from the cloak I wore upon my back

2 'You, a mere straw burnt in the fire of the muezzin's
    voice
  Pause! Do not give your eager heart to these activities

3 You cannot put your trust in scholars or in worshippers
  One vainly prattles on, the other labours vainly on

4 Words, words are all the stock in trade of this
    censorious tribe
  Mere colour is the way of those who wear the
    dark blue cloak

5 So leave the highway, roam the wastes, and as you
    journey on
  Shun all the hidden snares of wine and love; remain
    aware

6 Rapt beauty offers easy kisses? Mind you do not take
    them
  Wine-sellers offer their wine cheap? Then do not buy
    from them

7 The song, 'Do not obey the law, and do not live
    austerely'
  The warning voice, 'Do not disgrace yourself. Do not
    drink wine'

8 All these 'Do nots' amount to only this, 'Forego your
    being
  We have no tale to tell you, you no tale to listen to'

9 I, empty-handed (for I had not earned the wage of
    worship)
  Said (heart rich with the wealth bestowed on me from
    the unseen)

10 'How shall I turn my face from colour to transparency?
   Where must I go?' The voice said, 'Hide yourself from
     your own gaze'

11 I leapt up, but with wit and wisdom going on before me
   I left myself, but knowledge, action, kept me company

12 I came to an assembly where I saw, both in one moment
Today's wine being poured, the blood-drenched
sleep of yesterday

13 A hermitage all radiance, whence abstinence was
banished
A hall all sweet spring water, full of kisses, full of wine

14 That hall the secret dwelling place of her who gave it
beauty
Who welcomes turmoil, looks up to the sky with open
arms

15 A sun, imparting radiance to every glittering atom
A saki drunk with wine, intoxicating all the world

16 Colours sprung from transparency, such that no eye
can see them
Secrets that only silence speaks, such as no ear can hear

17 No drop falls from the vat that holds a thousand
colours in it
One vat all filled with surging colours, mouth securely
sealed

18 God can be felt entire; the mind can comprehend the
world
Ghalib be silent now. This is a song no voice can sing

This poem is a connected whole and is a sort of manifesto of Ghalib's
beliefs. The full meaning of some of the couplets is not entirely clear, but
taken as a whole, it is forceful and unambiguous. The first four couplets
stress the inadequacy, if not the actual harmfulness, of looking to theology
or the conventional religious life for an adequate code of living.

The remaining couplets say, in effect: Turn your back on orthodox
religion. Forget yourself completely, but use all your resources to assimi-
late what is valuable in every deep experience, neither giving yourself up
to the easy, thoughtless enjoyment of love and wine nor rejecting what
is to be learnt from those who sincerely, and not hypocritically, obey the
letter of the religious law. There is a creative power at work in the universe
which will help you to reach a stage when all significant human experi-
ence, both of pleasure and of pain, appears to you, not in different hues,
but as a single clear, transparent reality—a reality which you can assimilate
within yourself, but which cannot be described in words.

✤ 211 ✦

1 The gurgling of the wine poured from the flask defeats
   your counsel
   Halting it in its passage from my ears into my heart

2 She acts to test her powers, not to harass us unjustly
   Moving mankind to raise lament that pierces to the
   heart

3 Time after time I hold my tongue. You think that that
   is easy?
   Strength more than you can tell preserves her secret in
   my heart

2 'She' may be either a human or a divine beloved.

✤ 213 ✦

1 The peace of paradise is cold—and I want
   To kindle fire on every side of Kausar

2 Hail to that joy that lives immersed in hell fire
   The wine is fire, the glass is fire, the flask fire

3 The stormy waves rise high, and I rise with them
   The fire bums fierce and I dance in the flame

4, 5 We number four, and every one of us four
   Is given fire where we had hope for water
   Scorpio holds the moon; Delhi holds Ghalib
   Fire holds the fish, water the salamander

4 Fire for water, or vice versa, as the last line shows.

✤ 214 ✦

1 My hot sighs raised a canopy: I said, This is the sky
   My eyes beheld a troubled dream: I said, This is the
   world

2   My fancies threw dust in my eyes: I said, This is the
      desert
  The drop of water spread: I said, This is the boundless
      sea

3   I saw flames leaping in the wind: I cried out, Spring is
      coming
  They danced themselves to ashes, and I said, Autumn
      has come

4   The drop of blood became a clot: I knew it as my heart
  A wave of bitter water rolled: I said, This is my speech

5   In exile I felt lost: I said, This country is my country
  I felt the snare's noose tightening: I said, This is my
      nest

6   She sat in pride close to my side: I said, She is my heart
  Capriciously she rose and left: I said, There goes my soul

7   All that I lost in ecstasy accrued to me as gain
  All that remained of consciousness I designated loss

8   For years she held aloof from me: I said, She
      favours me
  She came close for a while: I said, She has her
      doubts of me

9   She was intent on slaying me. Alas for me, that I
  Declared she was indifferent, said that she was unkind

10   To make her feel obliged to me for all I did for her
  She was my host, and yet I told myself, She is my guest

11   I journeyed on beyond each stage I set myself to cover
  I saw the Kaba as the tracks of those who had gone on

12   My hopes told me, She likes to try my powers of
      endurance
  You severed all our ties: I said, She is just testing me

The general tenour of the ghazal is, 'I accept every experience and turn
it into something positive.'

～✖ 216 ✖～

1 Come, climb the skies; above their blue vault make
your resting place
Seek the beloved of both worlds to hold in your embrace

2 Who told you you must ask for favours from the
azure sky?
Be stem; confront the stars, and wrest from them
your heart's desire

1 Go up to where you can encompass both worlds in your range of vision.
See what was the purpose of the creation of both worlds. Make that the
aim to which you dedicate yourself and go forward boldly to attain that
aim.

～✖ 219 ✖～

1 Joy in the raging flood and, like the bridge's image,
dance
Know where you are, but move beyond the bounds of
self, and dance

2 She will not keep her word—treasure the moment that
she gives it
When lovely women pledge their word, rejoice in it,
and dance

3 Delight in moving on. Why think about your
destination?
Don't measure progress; hear the summons of the bell,
and dance

4 Once we were young and flourished like the flowers in
the gardens
Come, flames; now we are straw and thorns, devour
us, and dance

5 The owl's cry too is music; hear, and dance in ecstasy
Hope too to see the movement of the *huma's* wings,
and dance

6 In love you have not yet attained the limit of delight
Be like the whirlwind's dust and rise into the air, and
dance

7 Abandon all the outworn norms so dear to our
good friends
When they are celebrating, wail; when they are
mourning, dance

8 The good are 'angry'. Hypocrites 'love' you. Don't be
like them
Don't hide within yourself. Come out into the open.
Dance!

9 Don't look for grief in burning or for joy in flowering
In the hot wind's embrace, and with the breeze of
morning, dance!

10 Ghalib, rejoice that there is one in whose bonds you
are tied
Flourish; welcome distress; and in the ties of bondage,
dance

1   The bridge stands firm, and so must you. But it rejoices in the force of
the river in flood and in its power to change all around it, and can see
itself apart from itself, with its joy expressed in its reflection that dances
on the surface of the swirling water. You too must develop the same
power.

2   'The bell'—the bell that signals that the caravan is about to move off As
in many other verses, Ghalib is saying that one should know that there
is no final goal to man's spiritual and intellectual journey and that the man
who would develop his potentialities to the full must always journey on.

4   Our usefulness does not end when our youthful vigour ends. Even at the
last there is something we can do to help forward the beauty and the
movement of life.

5, 9   The owl, which haunts desolate places, is a bird of ill omen and here
stands for all the distressing experiences of life, while the legendary *huma*
typifies the highest good fortune that a man can hope to attain. Ghalib
says, 'Welcome and rejoice in *all* human experience.' Verse 9 has the same
message.

6   Only if you reduce yourself to dust, that is, humble yourself completely
before the object of your love, can you hope to experience love's full
ecstasy.

7, 8 Don't live by convention. Establish your own values and live by them, and never mind if the conventional are shocked. The self-consciously good express an anger, and the hypocrites, love, which they don't really feel. Don't be like them; *show* what you really are, and rejoice in doing so.

ᵈ 220 ᵉ

1   Pay frenzy all your stock of wisdom, for that generous
         one
     For every gain you pay it pays you loss a thousand fold

2   Hail to the hand that counts the prayer-beads! For the
         day may come
     When love gives it instead a grasp that closes on the cup

3   Now cruelty rewards your every act of love for her
     See, Ghalib, what she gives in recompense for all *you*
         give

1   Wisdom, gain, loss—i.e. what the conventional world regards as such, but what the lover knows in fact to be the exact opposite of all these things.

2   Value commitment. The man who can commit himself, even though it be to false ideals, may one day learn to transfer the commitment to true ones.

ᵈ 221 ᵉ

1   To put my lips to yours and die—this is my whole
         desire
     To tell one's love, the telling must possess a certain
         charm

2   Unless I pass the Kaba, I see nothing. I set out
     To journey from the temple looking backwards all
         the way

1   The charm of novelty. No one has yet managed to attain to *this* way of telling his love.

2   Neither the temple nor the Kaba is the end of man's spiritual search. Both are stages on an unending journey. But it is a journey on which you must never lose sight of what you have learned at every stage of it.

❧ 222 ☙

1   To trust your promise was mistaken. Yes, that was
     mistaken
   To hope for kisses from your lips was wrong. Yes,
     that was wrong

2   All know you have a tongue that does not speak.
     But have you also
   A heart that does not know? No, that is wrong.
     Yes, that is wrong

2 You know in your heart that I love you. That is enough for me. Whether you say that you know it, and whether you respond to my love, does not matter.

❧ 223 ☙

1   I live my life, but can't get wine. So where's the joy?
   You can, but you don't drink. It's spring. But where's
     the joy?

2   Kausar is fine, and so's the wine that flows in it
   The holy wine is there. I'm here. So where's the joy?

3   The garden blooms; there's no one there to steal
     your heart
   The swirling dust heralds no rider. Where's the joy?

4   Lost in desire to see her coming through the door
   Promises? Nothing! Waiting? Nothing! Where's the
     joy?

5   Why go with care about a task I can't perform?
   I can; she doesn't want me to. So where's the joy?

6   The tree is high, and I can't find a stone to throw
   Until the fruit falls at my feet, then where's the joy?

7   Fettered to wife and children, You are killing me
   I didn't ask to have them; and so where's the joy?

8   You have the power to set me up in Rizvan's place
    I'm lost in dreams; I don't want work. So where's
    the joy?

3   Life without a beloved is pointless. She (or God, or it) alone gives you the capacity to enjoy life's beauty to the full. And she (He, it) alone, like a brigand who plunders all your wealth, destroys your attachment to material things, and provides the joy of life. Rising dust in the desert *could* have signalled the approach of a fast-riding brigand.

4   The desire to see her is an all-sufficient source of joy.

5   If she doesn't want me to do it, I can't do it.

6   A stone to throw at the fruit and bring it down.

7   For Ghalib's attitude to his wife and children, see *Ghalib: Life and letters.* He fulfilled all his obligations to them, but often felt that they were an encumbrance he could well have done without.

8   The fact that Rizvan is the guardian of Paradise doesn't alter the fact that he is a servant, with a task to perform. I don't want to be anyone's servant.

~✖ 224 ✖~

1   How can dead hearts feel a delight in living, breathing life?
    How can plucked flowers feel the joy the breeze of morning brings?

2   Unless your eyes see turmoil, what use are your eyes to you?
    Unless the dagger pierce your heart, what joy can your heart feel?

~✖ 226 ✖~

1   What joy! Since I reject them both, Brahmin and shaikh are now at one
    Belief and unbelief unite—and this has brought me peace of mind

2   Alas! How happy I would be in winter, sitting by the fire
    With wine and meat and witty friends gathered together in one place

3   Morning has come with all its charm. Ghalib, awake
         from heedless sleep!
     The good have gathered in the mosque, the revellers
         among the flowers

1   Since I reject the formalised religion of both mosque and temple, shaikh
     and Brahmin are united in their hostility to me. That is good! The
     'religions' they represent are equally bad, just as the Muslim who truly
     loves his God and the 'infidel' who truly loves his are equally good.

3   Whatever role you have decided upon in life, rouse yourself, and perform
     it.

⤙ 228 ⤚

They made me swift of gait and put a sharp pick in my
    hands
My power makes me take pity on the mountain and the
    waste

Like Majnun and Farhad, respectively. But my regard for the things that I shall
injure if I act as they did holds me back.

⤙ 229 ⤚

1   Colour and fragrance graced you once, and I had all
         I needed
     Your colour and your fragrance faded; all I had is
         gone

2   I need the power of wings, and in these heavy bonds
         I die
     Fast in the snare of suffering, my power and strength
         are gone

3   Would that the sky had tired of turning, Ghalib;
         all my days
     Are past and gone to no effect. Why are they passed
         and gone?

➤ 230 ✶

1 I turned my gaze upon the world; now I am helpless,
   struggling
   Grief that I have so little time; longing to gaze on
   everything

2 You enter into beauty's hall. Make up your mind:
   good sense is gone
   Here is the saki pouring wine; there is the minstrel's
   lilting song

3 Here are my eyes, there is my heart—my misery finds
   no relief
   This holds a hidden suffering: those shed the tears of
   open grief

➤ 231 ✶

1 She lost her way, and found herself at my cell
   Love's guidance had the power to deceive her

2 Take and destroy false lovers' debased coinage
   Now you are governor of love's dominion

3 Do not be proud; accept the truths I teach you
   I have loved to the end: *you* are beginning

1 My love drew her involuntarily to my house, which is like a hermit's cell,
   without her even being aware that this was happening.

2 Now you know what true love is, act accordingly.

➤ 233 ✶

1 *He* is a man who goes to meet the onrush of desires,
   and dies
   Who emulates the thirsty man who wades into the
   stream and dies

2   I die with joy when I behold the glory of the traveller
     Who journeys on and on in hope to find the *anqa's*
          nest, and dies

3   No man is he whom cool restoratives bring back to
          consciousness
     He is a man who goes into the scorching desert wind,
          and dies

4   Grief brings a special happiness, and he who seeks it eagerly
     Experiences a joy, unseen by those who watch him as
          he dies

✖ 234 ✖

1   The waves are rising high and wreckage floats on
          them. Why be afraid?
     With you, I have no fear of fear—I'm not afraid I'll
          feel afraid

2   In that house where a lamp burns bright a man feels
          no uneasiness
     In this dark corner of the earth I have my heart. Why
          be afraid?

3   When you are happy with me, if the times are out of
          joint, why fear?
     When you are true to me, what if the heavens are
          cruel? Why be afraid?

✖ 235 ✖

1   I speak to tell you something worth your hearing
     What of it if my verses are but few?

✖ 236 ✖

1   Yes, minstrel, yes! Now that the wine is flowing
     Sing ghazals to the music of the harp

2   Yes, expert saki, go about your duties
    God's soldier, put to rout the hosts of grief

3   Shatter the flask and dash the glass to pieces
    That we may drink the wine without delay

4   Complaint and gratitude alike are pointless
    I am a glass; my mistress is a stone

4   We each do what our nature, and the nature of our relationship, compels
    us to do.

～✖ 237 ✖～

1   I have no worldly wealth, nor shall I win reward in
        heaven
    I lack both Namrud's power and Ibrahim's fortitude

2   For other men the saki's hand pours pure wine gener-
        ously
    While we stand by the stream and are denied a draught
        of water

3   With you, I feel the joy that Moses felt upon
        Mount Tur
    Alone, I drown, like Pharoah's army entering the
        Nile

4   Your own perfection can alone encompass Your
        perfection
    Your own existence is the only proof that You exist

5   Why is it You bring nothing to the parched lips of
        the Muslims
    When you bestow abundant wine on those who
        worship fire?

6   Why have you made despondent Ghalib poet in a
        land
    Where none knows what distinguishes Naziri from
        Qatil?

❧ 239 ❧

1   I thought, 'I shall expand with joy beyond the grasp
of her embrace'
She simply took me in her arms and held me fast in
her embrace

2   I joy in her anxiety, the pointless fluttering of her heart
Her creased brow as she plays with me, hugging
herself in my embrace

3   The scanty clothes that cover her, more scanty still as,
moist with shame
Sweat soaks them to transparency and she lies bare in
my embrace

4   Discretion washed away by wine, no more aware of
hers and mine
Holding her face against my breast she hides herself in
my embrace

5   Now sleeping, happy, at my side, no sound, no word
comes from her lips
Now with her head laid on my arm, rubbing her chin
in my embrace

6   She came unbidden with the dawn, the tie-strings of
her robe undone
Bearing her letter from the king unopened still in her
embrace

7   Among the flowers, flushed with wine, she roams
around on every side
Her very shadow seems to hold thousands of flowers
in its embrace

8   Yes, Ghalib, locked within your home, those are your
fears, these are your joys
The king's spies lie in wait for you, the king's beloved
in your embrace

6   See verse 8. The letter would have been a summons to her to come.

✽ 240 ✽

Here lying on the carpet it is exiled and at home
The rose-bed is its country and the rose's branch its lane

The rose, plucked to bring beauty to the assembly, is fulfilling an appropriate function, but it is not in its natural setting.

✽ 242 ✽

1 I went to banish staleness from the scene that lies
   before us
   And bring new modes into the scents and colours of
   the world

2 I strike into men's hearts the rage of madness to
   inspire them
   I fill the head of reason with the spells of sorcery

3 I teach our *ghazis* what it means to fight the evil in them
   Their sharp sword sheds its mettle as it trembles in
   their hand

4 My weakness earned for me a special closeness to the
   Kaba
   You spread your prayer mat there, and I have laid my
   bed down there

5 I make a road to take me from the temple into heaven
   I draw wine from the cask and pour it into Kausar's
   stream

6 So that the wine gains strength to lacerate the breast
   more fiercely
   I melt the flask and pour the molten glass into the cup

3 '*ghazi*'—one who wages holy war.
   The really heroic holy war is war against all that is evil in oneself. The
   difficulties of war against infidels are nothing by comparison.

4 Weakness resulting from unceasing, strenuous effort to seek the truth.

5 My wine will enhance the quality of the wine of paradise.

~ 243 ~

1   The flame is flickering, and who cares? The flowers
    are blooming, and who buys?
    I am the candle in the dark. I am the breeze that
    blows at dawn

2   Her body shines like silver ore; her beauty thrills my
    every sense
    My soul melts in the fire of love. See what I gain in
    recompense

3   Ghalib am I, of high renown; no need to ask my name
    and fame
    Yes, I am Asadullah, and Yes, I am Asadullah's man

1   I lighten men's darkness even at the cost of my own life. I bring men
    happiness as the morning breeze causes the flower to bloom. But no one
    recognises what he owes me.

2   If love for her ultimately destroys me, the joy I experience in looking at
    her is more than adequate recompense for what I suffer.

3   Asadullah was Ghalib's name, and also a title of Ali, for whom Ghalib
    felt a special reverence.

~ 244 ~

1   On lips that call on Ali's name we've made the wine
    to flow
    Practising true religion, tasting irreligious joys

2   We got our wine on credit, wasted all our wealth on
    dice
    We did improper things—and did not do them properly

3   We checked our lament on our lips, hid in our hearts
    love's wounds
    We wealthy misers kept our gold safe in our treasury

4   We showed the world a carefree face. How could we
    then lament?
    Such breath as we possessed we used to sing a melody

5 Ghalib, since good and bad alike proceed from fate
  alone
  I put my heart into my task, regardless of all else

ᵜ 245 ᵏ

Forgetfulness, hear my appeal—it is high time, high time!
Lost to myself, from time to time I still recall myself

ᵜ 246 ᵏ

1 Those were the days, days when I could command all
  men's esteem
  My sighs were fire; my tears flowed never-ending from
  my eyes

2 The press of ecstasy has crushed to blood all that
  I lived for
  Gone are the days I knew what past and present
  signified

3 I tell you true, all I remember of myself is this
  That long ago I had a friend, and Ghalib was his name

ᵜ 247 ᵏ

1 I saw its tumult—saw my fear of doomsday had been
  vain
  This was the uproar that in life I carried in my head

2 What do I want with hell and heaven? I am myself
  like them
  With fire that rages in my breast, and pure wine in
  my cup

3 He laid before me yesterday all the two worlds
  contained
  From all their varied riches I took up the heart alone

4 Since I was blind, they drove me from the Kaba
        towards the temple
     Men praised the idol's beauty. I accepted it as true

5 What do you know of all that Ghalib suffered in his
        life?
     His temperament the nightingale's, his task the
        salamander's

4 They drove me from the Kaba because I was blind, and probably they
   were right, because while *they* could see the truth there, I could not. I
   went towards the temple to see the reported beauty of the idol. Perhaps
   I should not have believed these reports. Perhaps the truth is neither in
   mosque nor in temple.

❧ 248 ❧

1 Why is it one rejoices? Why is it another grieves?
     I laugh to see the ignorance of rich and poor alike

2 The sun's bright rays can never pierce the blackness
        I wrap round me
     I am all shadow; night and day are both the same to me

3 My heart, without you, burnt; your coming cannot
        now restore it
     Regrets abound in it; desire to see you finds no place

4 I know Your secrets—and I blame the turning of the
        heavens
     I offer thanks to You—and lay complaint against the stars

1 Both wealth and poverty are God-given and both are transient.
4 I blame fate, not You, for my misfortunes, although I know really that
   fate is the expression of Your will.

❧ 249 ❧

1 My pious friend, come join me. Do not fear
        contamination
     The cloak I wear is regularly washed in purest wine

2   I used my blood to cleanse my cup of every trace
          of wine
     I brought the flood to cleanse my house of all its
          furnishings

⟶ 250 ⟵

1   I sought my own delight, and found abundant misery
     —Good news for any enemy that I may seek to harm

2   I passed my life in love for her; it is no shame to
          say so
     How shall I find occasion to acquaint her with my
          love?

3   I know what happens when the dewdrop meets the
          burning sun
     Give me the strength to tell her how I long to gaze
          on her

⟶ 252 ⟵

1   I copied out the dictionaries of yearning
     There was not one that told me what 'hope' means

2   The past is all regrets, the future yearnings
     'Would that...' are words I wrote a hundred times

3   I fed each thorn my blood, and wrote a manual
     To tell men how to cultivate the waste

⟶ 255 ⟵

1   I saw the wine lacked power to bring awareness of
          life's secrets
     I rose, and crushed my heart, and went and poured it
          in the cup

2   Why are there in this whole wide world no men of
      character?
    The ocean has its foam, and waves, and bubbles—and
      pearls too

✒ 256 ✒

1   Where are the drinkers? Who will taste the joys
      I freely offer?
    I am impatient. Though my wine grows old I sell
      it cheap

2   My pious friend, do not despise the bunch of grapes
      I give you
    Do you not know it means that I have lost a cup of
      wine?

3   The saki's eyes poured wine for every drinker in one
      cup
    I made it serve the needs of faith and unbelief alike

1, 3   'wine'—my message, my poetry.

✒ 257 ✒

1   Here in the world, I am not with the people of the
      world
    Like the *imam* that is not counted when men tell their
      beads

2   I spread my wings, and am not captive in the bonds
      of freedom
    A bird of love, caught in the snare of waiting for its
      love

3   You learnt from me to be acquainted with the ways of
      lovers
    I learnt from you to know the ways of ruthless
      mistresses

4   I am a ship without a pilot. None can know my
      sorrows
      Wrecked out at sea, I am the wreckage cast up on
        the shore

The *imam* is the name given to the large bead in the rosary which marks
the beginning and the end of the circle.

➤ 258 ✍

1   Come, let us in our ecstasy wear roses in our turban
      And pay the rose-red wine the wages of the the joy
        it brings

2   Follow in Kohkan's footsteps; let us utter a lament
      To move the mountain's heart with the desire to
        break in two

3   My own submissiveness demands a matching courtesy
      Beneath the curving scimitar I bend my body low

4   Come, let us breathe our inner secrets into the
        flute's heart
      Then let us pay due tribute to the sound of our
        complaint

3   'matching courtesy'—from you, beloved.

➤ 259 ✍

1   I see her glance at me as I sit there in love's assembly
      Long may I live like this, inspiring her with doubts of
        me

2   I see that she suspects me, carps at me, finds fault with me
      And so devise a number of fresh tests to test her with

3   So that she cannot pick on things I did when I was drunk
      When she would speak, my kisses set a seal upon her lips

➤ 260 ✍

1   I take a kiss, and then say I am sorry. Thus I make
     Some innovations in the rules of social intercourse

2   The mosque is ruined; so I bring its stones into the city
     And build myself a house there in the unbeliever's lane

3   I fashion my own faith and make my faith my own
         reward
     I carve the stone to make an idol, and then worship it

2   A mosque that is empty is no use. Better to destroy it and the lifeless kind
     of religion that it represents and use the materials to serve the needs of
     men who are truly alive. 'Unbelievers' translates the original Persian
     tarsayan, which usually means fire-worshippers. These are associated with
     wine-drinking.

3   I do not accept a faith prescribed for me by others. I work out my own
     faith and am true to it, even if others equate it with unbelief.

➤ 262 ✍

1   How long must I devote my days to bringing joy to
         others?
     Now give me time in which I may live wholly for
         myself

2   From time to time pass by my way happy, and singing
         ghazals
     My role in life is something more than living in disgrace

2   The disgrace which love inevitably brings is acceptable to me—but I am
     not obliged to be content with that alone. Sometimes you should respond
     happily to my love.

➤ 265 ✍

1   Come change the laws that have governed the turning
         of the skies
     Seize heavy fate like a goblet, and pass it round as we
         please

2 Store up the hoard of the gain that the heart and
        eye can amass
    Play host to soul and to body; drive out their fear
        of loss

3 The world goes by; let us leave it. Come in, and shut
        the door
    And post a guard in the lane so that none may come
        any more

4 The governor sends to reprove us? Let us not feel
        any fear
    The king sends gifts? We shall tell him, 'They are not
        wanted here'

5 Let's speak with none—not if even Kalim himself
        should come
    Make none our guest—not if even Khalil himself
        would be one

6 Let's scatter roses and sprinkle rose-water on the
        ground
    Bring wine to pour in abundance and let the cup
        go round

7 No guests, no minstrel, no saki—let's tell them all to
        be gone
    Let there be only a handmaid who knows what is to
        be done

8 Now pleasing you with the sweetness of conversation's
        grace
    Now savouring with our tongues all the passion of our
        kiss

9 Put shame aside; let us grapple in such a bold embrace
    The stars above in the heavens will try to hide their
        face

10 Our hearts afire, we will hold up the coming of the
        dawn
    And banish out of existence hot day before it is born

11   Create in all the illusion night has not yielded to
        day
    Turn back the sheep and the shepherd before they're
        on their way

12   With words of war we will challenge the flower-
        gatherers' bands
    'You come to plunder the garden? Go back with
        empty hands!'

13   With words of peace as the dawn comes we'll lull
        the wakening birds
    Luring them back to their nests with the sweetness
        of our words

14   Is Ghalib, then, destined never to look into your
        eyes?
    Come, change the laws that have governed the turning
        of the skies

❧ 268 ❧

1   The wound I have not suffered yet must not become
        my rival's
    I hold to it to beautify the vista of my gaze

2   My cry must find its way out to my lips through
        sorrow's darkness
    And so I made my life a lamp and set it in the way

2   A lamp set down on the open road is likely to be extinguished, blown
out by a gust of wind. Never mind; I must put my life similarly at risk.

❧ 269 ❧

1   An age has passed: fate has locked fast my arms around
        my neck
    When can I put these arms around the neck of her I
        love?

2   God give me power to bend to my command my lust
       and anger
    Power to banish pleasure and to live at one with grief

1   The convention was that, in despair, a man bowed his head and clasped
    his hands behind his neck.
2   Power to accept that my love will never evoke a response and the strength
    to live serenely with this grief as a permanent feature of my life—in other
    words, strength to be a true lover.

✎ 271 ✍

Leave me; let me be one of those whose station is your
    lane
I lack the strength that bears men on through endless
    journeyings

✎ 272 ✍

1   It is not well to sneer; I know not death from separa-
       tion
    Jealousy cannot strike; for, to me, she and I are one

2   She asks me in her kindness, 'Why so lost?'—and I,
       from fear
    Wallow in blood, and do not know how I should
       answer her

3   I am my wounded heart, displeased at all attempts to
       heal it
    My water is that of the pearl, that neither moves nor
       flows

4   The gold of my intelligence accepts no monarch's stamp
    My capital is art; it does not know the market place

5   Ghalib, he gives unstintingly, and gives in such a way
    That most of what he gives is given unbeknown to me

3   i.e. I am constant in love.
5   'he' or 'He'—i.e. a good patron or God.

❧ 273 ❧

I shun the company of men in striving to perfect myself
My soul a melody that seeks a dwelling in a lute

❧ 276 ❧

1 You fetter me in chains of love to hear their melody
If you like chains so much then make them somewhat
heavier

2 Because my lips can never tell the pain that tears my
heart
Now give me leave to tell it, or know what it is,
untold

3 Place blocks at every step along the road on which I
travel
Launch danger after danger in the stream I navigate

4 I dig and dig within my heart—and I have found no
jewel
You set my task for me; now fix the wage I must be
paid

5 If You would match Your gifts divine to my capacity
Give me an even clearer head and more abundant wine

Most of the couplets assert, either to the earthly or the divine beloved,
the lover's ability, and indeed eagerness, to face even more formidable
obstacles in love's path than he has yet been called upon to encounter.
In the last two he demands a fair recompense for his strivings.

❧ 277 ❧

1 I envy him who, lone and thirsty, travels through
the vale of love
Not them who rest content by Zamzam in the
sanctuary

2   Pass by those broken-hearted ones you do not know,
        but be aware
     That there are broken ones you know, whose grief
        you do not share

3–5 O you who sing the praises of the poets of Iran
     Why do you rate our debt so high to them who gave
        so little?
     In India are men, the fragrance of whose poetry
     Is borne away and spread abroad like musk upon the
        breeze
     Grief-stricken Ghalib does not rank with them; and
        yet he too
     Sits there with them and shares their friendship and
        their poetry

2   You cannot help everyone whom you see to be in distress, but don't make
     that an excuse for not helping those that are close to you.
     Verses 3–5 form a single whole.

～ 278 ～

1   When I am drunk, in early spring, drunk with love's
        frenzy, kill me then
     The wine jar in my hand, and beauty in my grasp—
        yes, kill me then

2   My crime is this: right to the last I passed my days in
        drunkenness
     While I still languish in the land of the wine-sellers,
        kill me then

3   Abate your cruelty to me. If you must murder one like me
     Promise to take me in your arms. The joy I feel will
        kill me then

4   If you feel shame to soil your hands and dagger with
        your lover's blood
     Just send me word that you will come. Waiting for you
        will kill me then

⁵   O God, how could I bear the thought of all my dear
        friends mourning me?
  Away from home, far from my country, strike me
        down and kill me then

⁵ 'Dear friends' is ironical. For the thought behind his prayer, cf. the
couplets listed in the Explanatory Index under 'country, one's own, and
foreign lands',

⤙ 280 ⤚

¹   My strength all spent in love for you, now I shall give
        up love
  Show kindness to me; else I shall show kindness to myself

²   Inured to your indifference, I cannot bear your love
  If I find favour in your eyes I shall fall fast asleep

³   I think that I excel; and I excel in love for you
  How long must I be tortured in the fire of this ordeal?

⁴   Beauty responds to lust and does not recognise true
        love
  Decrease your kindness to me, lest I start to doubt
        myself

⁵   Like blood, the joy my wounds bring me runs
        coursing through my veins
  If this be grief, I will stand surety this is delight

⤙ 281 ⤚

¹   In paradise I wonder what my joy will do to me
  Where wine is inexhaustible no matter how you drink

²   To set my heart at ease in life I ask for nothing else:
  Life is soon passed—God grant that I may live it as
        I should

³   An unbeliever in the king's protection, I can stand
  And drink my wine in Ramazan out in the open street

4 I tell you the reward for writing poetry is this
   To write with your heart's blood, drawn from the
      vein of eloquence

～ 284 ～

He wins the crown of happiness in this world and the
   world to come
Who dies out in the desert, having lived in palaces

He, i.e. the man who can enjoy to the full all the luxuries life can give him,
and be equally happy and serene if he loses all and passes his last days in the
wilderness.

～ 286 ～

1 What makes love thrive? To lay the firm foundation
      of delight
   Weep tears of blood, as lovely as roses of paradise

2 In all this suffering, stay calm, breathing with even
      breath
   In all this sorrow, bear the pain of cruelty till death

3 Caught in the snare's coil, exercise your wings
      unceasingly
   Take in your hands her plaited tress; caress it playfully

4 The footprints of men gone before mark out a path
      for you
   If you would make your way through life you must
      revere them too

～ 287 ～

You, held fast in my embrace, will smooth the creases from
   your brow
I'll close the windows of my heart and shut out both the
   worlds

᷷ 291 ᷷

1   We would drink seas of wine. Where is the pleasure
    When he who serves it, serves it by the measure?

2   You thirst for blood more than our hearts can offer
    We are your hosts, ashamed of what we proffer

᷷ 295 ᷷

1   That disrespect to you may make your anger flare the
        more
    I tune the lute of my complaint so that prayer flows
        from it

2   Eternal hell is, in my eyes, paradise, paradise!
    And long may that realm flourish, for steadfastness
        flows from it

3   Your silent suppliants will make no claims to trouble
        you
    Break every lute of love if supplication flows from it

1   To complain against you shows a lack of respect, and this angers you. But
    implied in my complaint is the prayer, 'Long may you live to continue
    your cruelty!'

2   To continue steadfast in even the most extreme adversity is the true lover's
    supreme virtue. Hell has that virtue too; it continues unchanging forever.
    Moreover hell on earth, and hell after death, is the fate of true lovers.

᷷ 298 ᷷

1   We have become presumptuous; where is your pride
        of beauty?
    We have abandoned loyalty; where is your punishment?

2   Why this pretence of clemency, for God's sake?
        You aren't God
    Where is that grave displeasure and that former
        wrathfulness?

3   Sometimes we broke our ties, sometimes drew closer
        to each other
    But now I feel no sorrow, and you feel no diffidence

4   I'll drink pure wine, but where will be the dread of
        being caught?
    And where in paradise the spice of fear it will not last?

1, 2, and 3 regret the cooling of love.

⁓✗ 299 ✗⁓

1   Divine grace does not falter; give up your useless
        strivings
    You could not be an infidel? Then settle for Islam

2   To rove around is pointless; you cannot be an ocean
    A stream? Go to the garden. A flood? Make for the
        wastes

3   It's good to live in comfort; good too is light
        abounding
    Lodge then, within the Kaba; and be the temple's
        guest

4   Are you the sky revolving? Then bow to fate's com-
        mandments
    Are you the earth's ball? Then you must await the
        mallet's blow

5   Bound in the bonds of patience, I eat away my being
    Now, resolution, fail me! Sorrow flood over me!

6   First grant to me a harvest, and then come and
        destroy it
    Be lightning on my harvest and rain upon my fields

---

1   It is God who decrees which you shall be, but to be an 'infidel', who
    worships beauty and love, would have been better than to be an orthodox
    Muslim.

3   Both conventional religion and unorthodoxy have something to offer you.

4   The metaphors in the second line are taken from polo.

5   I feel the urge to express myself without restraint, but so long as I can control myself, I shall never be able to do so. So I hope for the day when the force of my feeling will overwhelm me and so loosen my tongue.

6   At present I receive only your anger. At least give me some kindness first!

⌁ 305 ⌁

1   I quarrel with my friends—I am so innocent!
     About a friend whose friendship I have never tried

2   Just see my shame! They counted my good deeds and
          found
     None but a single fast I kept—and broke with wine.

⌁ 306 ⌁

1   When you feel shame the seven hells are all encom-
          passed in it
     To pardon one who sins against you is to take revenge

2   You made the grain of sand familiar with a hundred deserts
     You gave the drop of water knowledge of the seven seas

3   Their remedies in stones and herbs, ailments in living
          creatures
     Before You sent these here You had provided all of those

4   My eyes can weep, my tongue lament, my heart can
          feel distress
     All obstacles in Ghalib's path You swept out of the way

1   The first couplet can be taken as addressed to a human beloved, though it applies with even greater force to God. The 'You' of 2, 3, and 4 can only be God. The seven hells describe the lover's feelings.

2   Each element of creation contains the whole within it—and all of us have the capacity to see ourselves as an integral part of the whole scheme of things.

3, 4   Perhaps these couplets have a certain irony in them. It is true (3) that God provided in stones and herbs the remedies for human ills—but why did He ordain sickness to human beings? Similarly (4), in love one needs all the things detailed in the first line—but why did God ordain the distress that love brings?

⤜ 307 ⤛

1   My presence and my absence are, it seems, all one to
    you
    You sit beside me and, it seems, are not displeased
    with me

2   You count your cruelties, and I am in accord with you
    You tell my rivals' deeds of love, and there we disagree

3   You know I am your hapless lover, not a mendicant
    I know that you are my beloved, not a conquering king

4   I prize your great variety—see my fate and my rival's
    With him you were not as you are, with me not as
    you were

⤜ 308 ⤛

1   Wounds are adornments for the breast; yield up your
    heart to cruelty
    Wine is more precious than the spark, let the glass-
    maker take the rock

2   O lovely rose, your colour and scent need not inspire
    such pride in you
    You know the debt you owe the cloud; now give the
    gardener his due

1   The best that a rock can produce is the spark that flies when you strike
    it. So give the rock to one who will transform it into glass—glass destined
    to hold precious wine.

2   'the gardener'—i.e. the lover.

⤜ 315 ⤛

1   With all her virtues, wisdom says, 'Don't seek your
    heart's desire from her!'
    For she has good looks, and good deeds, and good
    repute—alas for her!

2 We have made peace with Ghalib now, but justice
   still has not been done
   For we revile him all the time, and he drinks only
   now and then

✵ 316 ✵

1 Line up a hundred thousand *houris*; I would not
   choose one
   For me it is enough to have a fair one of *this* world

2 What can I tell you of the heart and soul God gave
   to me?
   One is a prey to cruelty, the other in despair

3 He hid in this handful of dust two lightnings poised
   to strike
   One the harsh law of fate, and one the sorrow of
   free will

4 What of it if you write a hundred thousand novel verses?
   Speak one, a cry that comes to us all blood-soaked
   from your heart

5 Ghalib, I do not claim a place among the city's nobles
   I am among those humble ones who dwell in Delhi's
   dust

3 The sorrow of free will—Ghalib may mean either regret that God did
   not give us the gift of free will, or regret that is so restricted, or that we
   exercise it and find that it has involved us in disaster.

✵ 318 ✵

1 Proud in her beauty's graces, tall, in her clinging tunic
   She breaks into my loving heart and steals away its
   strength

2 Venting her wrath upon me like sudden death, most
   bitter
   Giving a loyalty to me fickle as precious life

3 As loath to grant my wishes as any wealthy miser
 Begging my heart from me like one who will not be
 refused

4 Encouraging my boldness, and ready with forgiveness
 Turning my strength to water, trying my fortitude

❧ 319 ❧

1 Into my breast, into my heart, you made your way
 and still
 The glance that stirs men's love for you stirred mine
 and stirs it still

2 Your wrath, your kindness—I no more can tell one
 from the other
 The charm that kills men's intellect killed mine and
 kills it still

3 Still drunk with last night's wine, my love—and I
 would die for you
 The sight of your unsteady gait charmed me and
 charms me still

4 You have not turned to God, and that sarcastic wit of
 yours
 That used to mock at Judgement Day is mocking at it
 still

❧ 320 ❧

1 If you begin to speak your mind about God's holy
 law
 The caravan bound for the Kaba hears, and changes
 course

2 With only half your charm you lay the base of a new
 world
 A new earth is created, and new heavens start to turn

3   You come into my thoughts, and fill them with
        your radiance
     The darkness of the the fear of death is banished
        from my soul

4   I fear your wrath; it makes me seek the long sleep
        of oblivion
     I seek your face; it makes me journey on through
        all the world

5   Your playful wit strikes home and brings distress
        to Muslim hearts
     Your radiance draws fire-worshippers to turn to
        worship you

1   Because the message that you proclaim is more convincing.
5   Because the radiance of your face is brighter than that of the fire they
    worship.

￫ 321 ￩

1   Your sweetness, still unuttered, can pervade my heart
        and soul
     O words, steeped in the sweetness of whose lips are
        you held fast?

2   No infidel will ever have to bear such punishment
     Night, I adjure you: Say, whose day of reckoning are you?

1   The picture is of lips sealed by their own sweetness so that they cannot
    part to utter any words.
2   The night of separation. The beloved's 'day of reckoning' is one which
    makes God's day of reckoning seem much less threatening.

￫ 323 ￩

1   Those days are gone when I would smell your fragrance
        on the wind
     When I would see a flower, and your face would come
        to mind

2   Those days are gone when if your lips had ceased
      reviling me
   I would get angry and prepare to quarrel heatedly

3   Now when I see you true to me it brings not joy
      but pain
   Those days are gone when you would wound me,
      and I would complain

4   Don't bind me in your tresses now; that strength is
      no more there
   Those days are gone when I rejoiced to struggle in
      your snare

5   Now at the last I sue for justice in another place
   Those days are gone when it was you I went to for
      redress

6   Now Ghalib seeks the Kaba; all his aim is centred
      there
   Those days are gone when he would seek the cities
      of the fair

⚓ 327 ⚓

1   The distance from my heart to yours is not a little one
   You are excused if you are slow to understand my words

2   Among us do not think to find desire for paradise
   In this assembly none of us is favoured by the stars

3   The pure wine of our thought is one in which there
      are no lees
   The fire of all our turmoil one from which no smoke
      goes up

⚓ 329 ⚓

1   The pious, and their mosques and pulpits—who needs
      them today?

Today is Id, and dawn has come. Pure wine, where
have you gone?

2   The fragrance of the rose, the dew—these do not suit
my cell
Cold wind, where do you rage? Destroying flood,
where have you gone?

3   I stand on doomsday's plain, and God is judge, and
all is quiet
O my complaint against my callous friends, where
have you gone?

3   Forget about past injustices.

✖ 330 ✖

1   She flirts with you, but if you ask a kiss she writhes
in anger
Though lost in drunkenness, she finds all manner of
excuse

2   He who would look for shame in you or hope for
kindness from you
Seeks piety in taverns, thinks the British will be just

✖ 331 ✖

1   He who has eyes to see counts up the beauties spread
before him
And sees all Azar's idols dancing, locked within the
rock

2   That she may have no ground, either for kindness or
for anger
She says my thanks fall short, and my complaints are
trivial

3 Why should we envy angels? What for? They cannot come to You
Foolish, they want to come to You, but fly around in vain

4 Alas that I should writhe in blood, when it is said of You that You
Count tears as yet unshed and hear lament as yet unuttered

5 If Kausar flows my way, it will dry up before it reaches me
If Tuba bends for me, its boughs be dry, and stripped of fruit

6 There you would see a melting heart, melting in seas of fire
Ghalib, if when I speak a verse, you could look deep within me

332

The pain my enemies inflict is not worth speaking of
My grief is for the wounds made by the unjust deeds of friends

333

1 My caravan is such, its dust is wave on wave of radiant flowers
My rising drunkenness the sun that rises in the East

2 Gaze on these two: my heart in which all seven hells are mirrored
Your beauty, culled from all the eight gardens of paradise

3   My throat is parched; the fire of heart and soul no
       longer burns. Come, then
    Pour the sweet wine that brings both fire and water
       to my aid

4   I do not call you tyrant, but you dwelt within my
       heart—and now
    I have a heart in ruins like a tyrant's ruined house

5   Do not bewail past grief; prepare for joy; see how the
       breeze of spring
    Brings to the garden all the radiant gaiety of your
       youth

4   The belief is that, in the long run, the tyrant is always ruined.

On Translating Ghalib

Ralph Russell

IN ONE OF HIS VERSES Ghalib said of himself that he was 'collyrium for men's eyes' freely offered to them to make their vision more clear. In the century and more since he spoke this verse many thousands of his fellow-countrymen have accepted this collyrium from him, and given him in return the only recompense that he asked, the knowledge that his gift had indeed sharpened their vision and enabled them to see things they had not been able to see before. It is understandable that from the time of his death more than a century ago men who have known him and loved him should have sought for ways to make the wealth that he offers more widely accessible.

Their task has not been easy. There is no denying that Ghalib is, on the whole, a difficult poet, and if it is true that he offers his wealth freely, it is no less true that he has laid it out behind barriers which many have not been able to pass. The most obvious and most formidable of these barriers that face the world at large is that of the two languages in which he wrote. Even in his own day much of his work was—and Ghalib knew this very well—in great measure inaccessible to his contemporaries, and for them, too, language was one of the barriers. He wrote much of his work, both prose and verse, in Persian. In the days when Persian was the language of culture of a great part of the Islamic world, this would have given him an audience over a vast area; but in his day men beyond the borders of India had ceased to be greatly interested in what Indians produced, while within India, the country of his birth, Persian had already yielded place to Urdu as the favoured medium of poetry, and many men whose fathers and grandfathers would have approved Ghalib's choice of medium no longer possessed the literary taste, or indeed even the knowledge of the language, to appreciate what he wrote. When he wrote in Persian, then, he wrote for a few, and he never ceased to lament that, even to these few, much of what he wrote went uncomprehended and unappreciated. What he wrote in Urdu, his own and his fellows' mother tongue, sometimes struck his audience as equally difficult to follow. Both his thought and the language in which he expressed it was often complex. And finally, even when his language was clear and simple, what he had to say was often beyond the imaginative reach of the men of his own day. Here, and here alone perhaps, we in the twentieth century have the advantage over his contemporaries. For much of Ghalib's thought is remarkably modern, and there are important elements in it which we can expect to understand more readily than they could. Ghalib knew this. He prophesied the fate of his poetry in much quoted Persian lines which I have translated thus:

Today none buys my verse's wine, that it may grow in age
To make the senses reel in many a drinker yet to come
My star rose highest in the firmament before my birth
My poetry will win the world's acclaim when I am gone

In short, the barriers between Ghalib's verse and our understanding of it have not all of them arisen in the time that has elapsed between his day and ours. Some of them were always there, and even the Urdu-speakers for whom he wrote have had (to change the metaphor) to travel a long road to reach their present stage of understanding.

It is worthwhile saying something about the stages of their journey. I think it is fair to say that what has always first attracted people to Ghalib from his own lifetime up to the present day has been his personality, revealed in countless anecdotes of his wit and humour which must have circulated orally long before they were written down. In the year of his death, the publication of the first collection of his informal letters to his friends enhanced his popularity still further.

For years together these letters were the foundation of the regard in which he was increasingly held. Hali, his friend and younger contemporary, says so quite unequivocally: 'Wherever one looks, Ghalib's fame throughout India owes more to the publication of his Urdu prose [i.e. his letters] than it does to his Urdu verse or to his Persian verse or prose. True, people generally already regarded him as a very great Persian poet, and thought of his Urdu verse too as poetry of a high order beyond the comprehension of the ordinary reader; but these opinions were based on hearsay and not on their own reading.'

It was Hali's own work which carried matters a stage further. His *Yadgar-i-Ghalib* (Memoir of Ghalib), itself a book justly regarded as a classic of Urdu literature, was published in 1897, nearly a generation after Ghalib's death. It falls into two parts. In the first, which occupies something less than a third of the whole, he briefly relates the story of Ghalib's life, enlivening his account with an abundance of the anecdotes which reveal Ghalib's character and personality so vividly. In the second part, which is itself subdivided into two sections, he deals at length with Ghalib's Urdu and Persian writings. The proportion of space he sees fit to allot to each is interesting. The section on the Persian is more than double the length of that devoted to the Urdu. I shall return briefly to the Persian later. For the present it is the Urdu which concerns us. Here, for the first time, the Urdu reader was presented with a sustained essay on Ghalib's Urdu poetry, illustrated by numerous quotations with detailed explanation and comment. There must have been many of Hali's readers who, attracted by Ghalib's personality, familiar to some degree with his letters, and accepting on the authority of others that he was a great poet, now ventured with Hali's help to read some of the poetry themselves and try to understand and appreciate it.

Since then many, many others have contributed to the process which Hali started, and the twentieth century has seen the growth of a voluminous and still rapidly growing literature on every aspect of Ghalib and his works. One of the earliest studies was Abdur Rahman Bijnori's vigorous essay *Mahasin-i-Kalam-i-Ghalib* (Beauties of the Verse of Ghalib) with its oft-quoted dictum that India has produced two inspired books—the Vedas and the verse of

Ghalib. Commentaries which explain every couplet in his *divan* have long been available, and are still being written. It is safe to say that almost all who read Ghalib's verse use, and need to use, these commentaries—or at any rate needed to use them when they first began to study him.

It is a striking fact that similar treatment has only recently been accorded to Ghalib's Persian. Here Hali's labours have borne only the most meagre fruit. To most of Ghalib's admirers his Persian work is still a closed book, or to be more precise, two closed books, for his Persian verse and his Persian prose each occupies a substantial volume. True, in 1957 the centenary of the great revolt of 1857 stimulated the production of two Urdu translations of *Dastambu,* Ghalib's journal of 1857–8, one of them accompanied by an edition of the original Persian text.

In more recent years editions of the Persian verse have appeared in Pakistan, and since 1969 Urdu translations of much of his Persian prose have been published. But the task of making Ghalib's Persian verse accessible to Urdu readers whose knowledge of Persian is, at the best, too rudimentary for them to be able to read it in the original was never undertaken until Sufi Tabassum wrote his commentary on the Persian ghazals. Some years before that Khurshidul Islam had taken up this task. He has now completed, but not yet published, a selection of the Persian verse (not just the ghazals) which will give the original text, a faithful Urdu prose translation, and explanatory notes; and in my view this will fill a gap which has existed for an unpardonably long time.

When it took so long to introduce Ghalib adequately to his own intended Urdu-speaking audience, it is understandable that efforts to break through the language barrier for non-Urdu speakers came later. Most of these efforts had the aim of enabling readers to approach Ghalib through the medium of English, and their intended audience was English-educated Indians and/or Pakistanis. Let me say at once first, that I do not think that these English versions are, in general, such as would fully satisfy an English-speaking public in countries where English is the mother tongue, and secondly, that this judgement by no means implies any hostility to them on my part. On the contrary, I consider that even the least adequate of these attempts deserves praise and appreciation. The best, in my view, are those of Muhammad Mujeeb, but all who have attempted this difficult task deserve praise, and all have contributed something to the task of bringing Ghalib to a wider audience. An interesting work is that of J. L. Kaul, whose *Interpretations of Ghalib* was published in Delhi in 1957 with an appreciative foreword by Abul Kalam Azad. He chose 326 couplets from Ghalib's *divan* (and it is a good selection that he made), and, using a range of verse techniques extending from rhymed couplets to free verse, presented an English interpretation of them, elaborating Ghalib's meaning where he felt this to be necessary if their point were to be understood, and adding his own reflections inspired by the verse in question. It is a method which he does not always practise successfully, but nonetheless one which has much to recommend it.

These translations and interpretations into English have in practice not reached, and perhaps cannot effectively reach, an audience outside the Indo-Pakistan subcontinent. I know of only one translation by an Urdu-speaker aimed deliberately at the English-speaking world and published outside the subcontinent—that of Sufia Sadullah (*Selected Verses of Mirza Ghalib*, Beaconsfield, England, Darwen Finlayson, 1965). But over the last twenty years or so a growing awareness of and interest in what the literatures of the subcontinent have to offer has prepared the ground for attempts by Ghalib's admirers in other lands to present his work to their fellow-countrymen, and these efforts received an impetus at the time of the centenary of his death in 1969. This brings me to speak of the work of Khurshidul Islam and myself in this field.

꙳ ꙳

I first made the acquaintance of Ghalib in the years 1946–9, when I was reading for a degree in Urdu in the University of London. Although there was much in his verse that I did not understand, I liked it from the start, and from that time onwards have hoped one day to make the attempt to introduce him to the English-speaking world. I count it my great good fortune that I met Khurshidul Islam only a year or so later, in 1949, and formed the close friendship with him that continued for the most part of forty years. Our tastes and interests and judgements, and the range of our reading in literature in general were so similar that a more ideal collaboration could hardly be imagined. In addition, in translating, where every nuance of every word and phrase, in both the language of the original and that of the translation, can be important, we could do together what neither of us could do alone, for both of us know both languages well, and each of us has one of them as his mother tongue; and we could therefore hope to understand fully what the Urdu intends and to convey that intention as fully as English allows.

It has been partly by accident and partly by design that our work proceeded along much the same path as I described earlier—that is, the English reader will travel towards an understanding of Ghalib along much the same route as his fellow-countrymen traversed, from a picture of his life and personality, through his letters, and on to his poetry. The main difference is that we have made full use of his Persian prose as well as of his Urdu letters.

The result of our labours, *Ghalib: Life and Letters*, vol. I, was published in 1969, and re-published in 1994. A second volume, in which we attempted the more difficult task of presenting his Urdu and Persian ghazals, is before you now. Khurshidul Islam made a major contribution to it, but for the final form I alone am responsible.

It is of this second task that I propose to write at some length here. Ghalib is a great writer, both of prose and verse, but it is his poetry that will always be the bedrock of his fame, and it is in relation to his poetry that the major problems of translation arise. Nevertheless, I would wish to say something first about the translation of his prose, because this is relevant to the translation of his poetry too. A translator tries to get as close as he can to an unrealizable ideal, and to produce in English what Ghalib would have written himself had English, and not Urdu, been his mother tongue. The colloquial Urdu of his letters presents its own problems, which, however, I will not discuss here. What foreshadows more closely the problems of translating his verse is the similar problem of translating his Persian prose. Hali begins his review of Ghalib's Persian prose with the remark that it differs from verse in only one respect—that it lacks regular metre, and that this enables it to be called 'prose' only in the Asian sense of the term. 'Otherwise the poetic element in it appears more prominent than it does even in his verse.' There is a measure of exaggeration in the statement, but there is substance in it all the same. Ghalib imposed upon himself the most exacting standards when he sat down to write

Persian prose, and his concern for appropriate diction, rhyme, rhythm, assonance, alliteration and all kinds of verbal conceits is as evident as it is in his verse. For me it follows that they should be of concern to his translator; but this is a matter of conscious choice. The translator can, if he thinks fit, disregard all this and translate into straightforward modern English. (Robert Graves did this—'straightening out the African curls of Apuleius', as Frank Kermode put it—in his translation of *The Golden Ass*.) I have tried to do just the opposite, reproducing in my translation all those features which Ghalib valued in the original. Two examples which come to mind, and which readers may turn to if they wish to see the results, are the letter about Agra to Ziya ud Din Ahmad Khan and the letter in which he describes his reaction to his beloved's death (on pp. 38 and 51 respectively of *Ghalib, Life and Letters*).

An age-old controversy in what may be called the theory of translation is involved here, well illustrated in the various English versions of *The Thousand and One Nights*. Here I own myself an unabashed champion of Burton, who tried to give to his English readers everything which the Arab audience found admirable in the Arabic original—and succeeded astonishingly well. The rhyming prose, the delight in the sheer exuberance of language, the repeated quotation of good, bad, and indifferent verse—all are there; and to remove them is to emasculate the work no less than the removal of the ribaldry does. Let us, however, leave aside the ribaldry, in which other issues are also involved. One can understand and respect the decision of a translator who considers that it is the essential content of his original that he wants to convey, and from a fear that if this is presented in unfamiliar trappings this may prove an insuperable obstacle to his readers' appreciation adopts instead an idiom and style with which they are familiar. What one cannot excuse is the amused contempt with which such translators have tended to speak of those who find that the styles of the original also appeal to them. In medieval societies, writers and readers tended to think that written prose of the kind that moderns write, modelled essentially on the patterns of speech, was not worthy of consideration as literature. But if the modern man rightly censures this attitude as too limited, too circumscribed by an over-zealous regard for convention, he too becomes guilty of much the same sin if he in his turn rejects all literary prose not written to his approved standards. For myself, I can enjoy both kinds of writing, and it seems to me that a cultivation of the ability to enjoy both is much to be desired and encouraged. Certainly if the best products of the literature of all nations are to be enjoyed all over the world as they deserve to be, readers in both East and West will need to develop a much more catholic taste, and break through the limitations which enable them to enjoy only what they have been taught it is permissible for them to enjoy. It is these considerations which motivate me in formulating my own principles of translation. I applied these principles to the best of my ability in translating Ghalib's Persian and Urdu prose, and now do so in translating his verse.

I shall speak here particularly of his Urdu verse. Most of it is in the form of the ghazal, and the problems of translating the ghazal are formidable. It is my view that the translator ought to take into account the fact that Ghalib's Urdu verse is in ghazal form. I know that there are admirers of Ghalib who, if I understand them aright, would not agree that this is necessary in the least. In Lahore some years ago at a party where both British and Pakistani guests were present, the conversation turned at one point on the problems of translating the ghazal. I argued for the use, where possible, of rhyme—even of the strict rhyme scheme of the ghazal where this could be done successfully—and for the use of regular metre. (I shall return to these points in more detail later.) One Englishman, and more than one Pakistani, strongly disagreed, and were particularly vehement in assailing the use of rhyme. I showed them two of my translations which I felt to be adequate—one of a ghazal of Mir (in *Three Mughal Poets*, pp. 196–7) and one of a qata, in fact of Ghalib's *qata i mazirat*, translated under the heading *An Apology* in *Ghalib, Life and Letters*, pp. 83–4. They did not feel that these were successful, though they were more lenient towards the qata on the explicit ground that here in my translation the rhyme was less obtrusive than in the translation of Mir's ghazal. 'You are translating for a contemporary audience,' they argued, 'and contemporary taste doesn't like rhyme.' My answer to that is that it depends upon what contemporary audience you are aiming at. I am not aiming at people who submit, as no self-respecting person should, to the mere tyranny of what is fashionable, but at people who have sufficient confidence in themselves to allow their taste and judgement freer range. Such people will certainly accept the proposition that poetry, if it really is poetry, does not necessarily demand rhyme and regular metre; but they will also understand just as readily that neither does it necessarily demand the abandonment of these things. The contemporaries whom I have in mind like contemporary diction, but do not feel that they are moving into an alien world when they read the language of Shakespeare's sonnets or of Donne's poetry. Let me say at once that I can conceive of a good translation of Ghalib's verse which does not employ rhyme and metre, and I shall not withhold my praise from any translator who can produce one. But I would also hold that such a translation would be less adequate than one which conveys at any rate something of the regard for regular metre, rhyme, and form in general which Ghalib himself felt. The fact that Ghalib lived in a country and an age where for him there could be no question of a conscious choice between free verse and the strict form of the ghazal does not seem to me to affect the argument in any important way. Ghalib took it for granted that to write poetry meant to work within the strict forms that tradition had prescribed, and he did just that. In my view, any translator who wants to do the fullest possible justice to him cannot ignore this. We too must write as far as possible within the limits of fairly clearly defined forms.

Having said that, let me at once add that a good deal of compromise is essential. To put the point in the most general terms, you must impose the restrictions of form, but never to the point where the restrictions choke the poetry; and when in doubt you should discard the restriction rather than injure the quality of the poetry. How does this work out in translating the ghazal?

The ghazal is made up of separate couplets, independent of each other where content is concerned, but cast in identical metre and bound together by a rhyme scheme which runs AA, BA, CA, DA and so on throughout the poem. Ideally I would like to translate it into a form which maintains this rhyme scheme. But to say that this is not always possible would be a considerable understatement: it is hardly ever possible, and there is nothing to be done about it. Any translator is faced with the stubborn and unalterable fact that Urdu has rhyming words in plenty and English has not. (For some reason which I have not analysed it seems easier to find rhymes in translating those relatively few ghazals that have a certain unity of theme or of mood.) You are forced, then, in most cases to translate a poem knit together by a unity of rhyme into one where this kind of unity cannot be maintained.

Metre too presents a difficulty. Urdu metre has a basis quite different from that of English metre. In English the essential determinant of metrical pattern is the inherent stress pattern in each English word. In Urdu, metre is essentially based upon quantity (as is Greek, Latin, and Sanskrit verse), considerably modified, however, by the incidence of a sort of stress comparable to the beat in music. (I am here expressing my own views. The traditional analysis of Urdu metre is in quite other terms, while Grahame Bailey's attempted analysis in purely quantitative terms is in my view quite inadequate.) All the same I believe that one can, and generally should, convey something of the effect of the Urdu metre in English verse translation, even allowing that the basis of the metres of the two languages is appreciably different. A few examples will perhaps illustrate my point.

In each case I write first the Urdu verse, in Roman transcription, writing the words, however, as they would be read in strict accordance with the scansion pattern. For example, *intizar* except at the end of a couplet or before a pronounced caesura scans *intizara*, and I have written it accordingly, except that I have enclosed the final 'a' in brackets, thus: *intizar(a)*. (Of course, Urdu speakers do not *recite* poetry with a mechanical adherence to scansion, any more than English speakers do with English poetry.) Then I give a statement of the metre, both in terms of longs and shorts which I hope will help English readers, and also in terms of the traditional system for those readers who are familiar with it.

> hān vuh nahīn khudā parast; jāo, vuh be-vafā sahi
> jis ko ho dīn o dil azīz, us ki galī men jāe kyon?
>
>   mufta'ilun mafā'ilun mufta'ilun mafā'ilun
>   — ᵕ ᵕ —|ᵕ — ᵕ —|— ᵕ ᵕ — |ᵕ — ᵕ —

No, she does not bow down to God; yes, she is faithless too—now go!
If I had prized my heart and faith would I have gone into her lane?
(Sixteen syllables to the lines in each case. Similar rhythms.)

> har ek(a) bāt(a) pa kahte ho tum ki 'tū kya hai?'
> tumhīn kaho ki yih andāz i guftagū kya hai?
>
>   mafā'ilun fa'ilātun mafā'ilun fa'lun
>   ᵕ — ᵕ —|ᵕ ᵕ — —|ᵕ — ᵕ —|— —

To every word that I utter you answer, 'What are you?'
You tell me: Is this the way, then, I should be spoken to?
(Fourteen syllables. Similar rhythm.)

In other verses the rhythm of the original is not, to my mind, adaptable to any natural English pattern. Here the best one can do is to produce an English line which has the same number of syllables, and moves with a discernible rhythm, but not to attempt anything approaching any more closely the rhythm of the original lines. For example:

husn(a) ghamze ki kashākash se chutā mere bād
bāre ārām(a) se hain ahl i jafā mere bād

fā'ilātun fā'ilātun fā'ilātun fa'lun
— ⏑ — —|— ⏑ — —|— ⏑ — —|— —

Beauty will rest, its war of glances cease, now I am gone
Fair cruel mistresses will live at peace now I am gone

(Same number of syllables [14], but a different rhythm.)

There are cases where translation seems to flow naturally into a pattern close to the original but in some marked respect different from it. I have found, for instance, that there are ghazals where the unit line is one of 16 syllables, with a rhythmic pattern to which English can approximate without violence to the language, but where an English pattern of a line of 16 syllables followed by one of 14 seems to serve better than the Urdu pattern of 16 and 16. This is especially so where the Urdu couplets are of a kind that deliver their main impact in the second line. For example:

sitāish-gar hai zāhid is qadar jis bāgh i Rizvān ka
vuh ik guldasta hai ham be-khudon ke tāq i nisyān ka

mafā'ilun mafā'ilun mafā'ilun mafā'ilun
⏑ — — —|⏑ — — —|⏑ — — —|⏑ — — —

The shaikh sings loud the praises of the gardens of Rizwan: to us
They lie, a bunch of faded flowers, upon oblivion's shelf

Here the shortening of the second English line increases the impact and so reproduces the force of the structure of the original couplet.

Where the translation of a line seems to go well into familiar English metres like the iambic pentameter of blank verse, there is no reason to reject it simply because the rhythm of the original is different. Thus the lines:

nahīn nigār(a) ko ulfat, na ho; nigār(a) to hai—
ravāni e ravish o masti e adā kahiye

nahīn bahār(a) ko fursat, na ho: bahār(a) to hai
tarāvat e caman o khūbi e havā kahiye

scan

    mafā'ilun fa'ilātun mafā'ilun fa'ilun
    ◡ — ◡ — | ◡ ◡ — — | ◡ — ◡ — | ◡ ◡ —

but translate naturally as

The fair are cruel? What of it? They are fair
Sing of their grace, their swaying symmetry
Spring is soon fled? What of it? It is spring
Sing of its breezes, of its greenery

Only where a possible translation with a rhythm close to the
original metre seems just as acceptable as one with a different
rhythm is there point in giving it preference. Look for example at
this couplet:

sunte hain jo bahisht(a) ki tārīf(a), sab durust—
lekin khudā kare vuh tyrī jalvagāh(a) ho

    maf'ūlu fā'ilātu mafā'īlu fā'ilun
    — — ◡ | — ◡ — ◡ | ◡ — — ◡ | — ◡ —

All that they say in praise of Paradise is true, I know
God grant, though, that it be illumined by your radiance

(Fourteen syllables. Similar rhythm.)

It could also be translated

All that they say of Paradise is true—and yet
God grant it be illumined by *your* radiance

But the first version has the advantage that it reads just as well, and
also matches the length and general rhythm of the Urdu verse.

When you have translated the verses of a particular ghazal, then
you have before you a number of couplets without rhyme, but
sharing the same rhythmic pattern. In most cases you have selected
for translation what you feel to be the best verses, and have left
the rest. Does this matter? I think not. Ghalib himself treated his
ghazals in the same way, discarding in later years verses which his
mature judgement rejected as inadequate; and the residue still
formed a ghazal. There is no good reason why we should not do
the same. Nor is the absence of rhyme, imposed though it is by

necessity and not by choice, much of a disadvantage. My practice is to try to reproduce rhyme—even, if possible, both *qafia* (rhyme) and *radif* (end rhyme) where the two lines of a single couplet rhyme together, and not elsewhere—or, sometimes, where an unrhymed Urdu couplet goes well into a rhymed English one and a rhymed Urdu one does not, to, trade the one for the other, so to speak, so that at any rate the proportion of rhymed to unrhymed couplets is about the same. Linking rhyme throughout the ghazal was, and is, important in the context of the *mushaira*, the symposium at which poets recite their ghazals. But it is much less so, even to Urdu readers, when they approach poetry outside that context, reading it at home, or quoting the occasional couplet in conversation with friends. Each couplet is separate; in everyday practice each couplet is quoted separately and appreciated separately; and only if the couplet quoted is the first one of its ghazal does rhyme feature. To an English-speaking audience which in general does not listen to its poetry recited live, but reads it, and which knows that each couplet now being presented to it in translation is to be taken separately, the absence of rhyme is of no great moment.

All the same, to return to the point I made when I began my discussion of the translation of the ghazal, I think I should try to give at least one or two translations which as nearly as possible reproduce the ghazal form, even if only by way of sample. And here, I think, I am entitled—bound, even—in at least one case to present the ghazal as it is, 'warts and all'. Very few ghazals maintain a uniform level of excellence throughout. It is not only that the mood may change drastically from one couplet to the next: some of the couplets will themselves be of very indifferent quality. Hali, the first sober critic to bring to Urdu poetry both the expertise of an accomplished poet and the courage to assess his poetic heritage in the light of freshly thought-out general values—however limited and pedestrian his attitudes may seem to us today—was quite right when he said bluntly that Urdu ghazal poets were generally satisfied if they could compose two or three good verses to a ghazal, and were content not to spend much effort upon the rest. The tradition of the *mushaira* has a good deal to do with this. These points are illustrated by one of Ghalib's best ghazals—that which begins:

kahun jo hāl(a) to kahte ho 'muddaā kahiye'
tumhīn kaho, ki jo tum yun kaho to kyā kahiye?

It has 11 couplets, and every one of them has a certain charm; but the moods vary greatly, and so does the standard of the poetry. Three couplets I have not translated—two because they are of no special merit and another because it cannot be translated to my satisfaction in a form which fits the rhyme scheme of the rest. Here are my translations of the rest of the ghazal. I have not attempted to imitate either the metre or length of the original lines. Nor have I achieved a reproduction of both rhyme and end-rhyme. (Here, and in the longer pieces that follow, I have not thought it necessary to give Roman transliteration.)

> I tell my plight: you tell me, 'Tell your plea'
> Now what am I to tell you? *You* tell *me*
>
> It pierces to my heart; so why not say
> Her glance of pride is bosom friend to me?
>
> Sing now your sickness unto death; tell now
> How ill-adapted is its remedy
>
> Sing now the burden of your heavy grief
> Now of your patience, that would ever flee
>
> The fair are cruel? What of it? They are fair
> Sing of their grace, their swaying symmetry
>
> Spring is soon fled? What of it? It is spring
> Sing of its breezes, of its greenery
>
> Your ship has reached the shore: why cry to God
> Against your captain's cruel tyranny?

As you see, it is a ghazal with warts; but then so is the original.

The first couplet is relatively light—the vehicle of humorous, slightly impudent remonstrance with an imperious beloved. Then comes a rather clever-clever conceit expressing the serious, but within the ghazal tradition unremarkable, point that the lover welcomes the wounds that his beloved inflicts on him. The next two outline some of the common themes of which a poet should sing. And finally there are three excellent, forceful verses well above the level of all that have preceded them. Together the translation of these seven verses form a ghazal, with all the unevenness of tone and quality of the original. Where the aim is to present not the whole of Ghalib but the best of him, I think one would not include all these verses.

There are cases where, I feel, a whole series of verses can be trans-
lated in a continuous piece of verse adequate to convey something
of the effect of the original and to appeal to the English reader. For
example,

> Now let me go away, and live somewhere where no man else will be
> Where there is none that knows my tongue, where there is none to
>   speak with me
> There let me build myself a house with, so to say, no doors, no
>   walls
> And live there without neighbours and with no one to keep watch
>   for me
> If I fall ill, then there should be no one to come and visit me
> And if I die let none be there to weep and wail and mourn for me

Here the translation has a long line, as in the original (15
syllables in Urdu, 16 in the English translation). The original has
rhyme and end-rhyme; the English only hints at this effect by the
recurrence of the word 'me'. Both original and translation are of
three couplets, with a continuous theme throughout.

Here is another example, a connected series of verses from one
of the most famous ghazals:

> Newcomers to the assembly of the heart's desires
> Beware, if it is wine and music that you seek
> Look well at me, if only you have eyes to see
> Listen to me, if you have ears to hear me speak
> The saqi's charm will steal away your faith, your wits
> The minstrel's song will rob you of your sense, your powers
> At night you see the carpet laden all with bloom—
> A gardener's apron, filled with fresh, sweet-scented flowers
> The saqi walks, the flute plays on enchantingly
> Heaven to the eyes, paradise to the ears of all
> Come in the morning: Look at the assembly then
> Life, joy, wine, music—all are gone beyond recall
> Bearing the scar of parting from its erstwhile friends,
> One silent candle, burnt out, shows you how it ends.

In this ghazal I have not attempted to echo the metre of the
original 14-syllable line, but have used what is essentially an iambic
pattern (commoner in classical Greek than in English) of 12–13
syllables. Nor have I reproduced the original scheme (seven
couplets rhyming AB, CB, DB, EB, FB, GB, HB), grouping the
seven couplets instead into three units of two each and a final single

couplet in which the climax of the whole piece is expressed—so that the grouping and rhyme scheme is ABCB, DEFE, GHIH, JJ.

And finally, in the following example, I have tried to give something of the flavour of a ghazal closer to the standard pattern. It translates couplets 1, 2, 3, 4, 6, 7, 8 and 9 of the famous ghazal:...*mere bad*.

> Beauty will rest, its war of glances cease, now I am gone
> Fair cruel mistresses will live at peace now I am gone
> Love's throne will seek in vain a lover worthy of my place—
> And beauty's airs, and beauty's graces, fail now I am gone
> The candle is put out; smoke from it rises in the air
> Love's flame dons black to mourn my memory now I am gone
> Laid in the dust, my heart is crushed to blood, because I know
> The fair will not find henna for their hands now I am gone
> Love's frenzy clasps its lovers in a last farewell embrace
> And lovers' garments will no more be rent now that I am gone
> Who now takes up the challenge of love's wine? Who drains the cup?
> This is a cry the saqi must repeat now I am gone
> I die of grief, for now the world will not bring forth a man
> To mourn the death of love and loyalty now I am gone
> Ghalib, I see love's helplessness, and weep to see it so
> Whose home will its destroying flood turn to now I am gone?

The original and the translation both have a unit line of 14 syllables, but no attempt has been made to reproduce the rhythm of the original. The first couplet, as in the original, employs both rhyme and end-rhyme:

> ...cease/now I am gone
> ...peace/now I am gone

but this is not maintained, the recurring 'now I am gone' alone being used to convey something of the same effect. Some of these lines will not be fully intelligible to an English audience without some added explanation. I shall return to this point later.

You will have seen from these examples how I interpret the need for compromise in presenting the ghazal. But all of them maintain what I regard as the essentials: regular metre, rhyme (or at least the hint of rhyme) and a clearly discernible regular form.

All the same I feel that in one case I only just escape the charge of being an attempt by the translator to 'improve upon' the original. It seems to me most important to resist and defeat any temptation

to do this. Such temptations do arise. For instance, I felt sorely
tempted to translate the couplet

> nākarda gunāhon ki bhi hasrat ki mile dād
> ya rab, agar in karda gunāhon ki sazā hai
>
> O Lord, if You would punish me for these committed sins
> Note too how I regret the sins that I could not commit

—that is, reversing the order of the two lines of the original.
Ghalib-worshippers will be shocked at my impertinence, but I
cannot help thinking that in the original too the couplet would
strike the reader with greater force if the punch came in the second,
and not in the first, line. (In that case, of course, the line could
not find a place in this particular ghazal, but I am speaking of it
for the moment as an isolated couplet.) However, the order that
I prefer is not the one which Ghalib preferred, and as a translator
of Ghalib I do not consider myself entitled to assert my preference
against his. I therefore keep the original order, and translate

> Note too how I regret the sins that I could not commit
> O Lord, if you would punish me for these committed sins

Nor do I think it is any part of the translator's job to explain
what Ghalib does not choose to explain. He, like all the great ghazal
poets, is often at pains to say little and suggest much, and the
translation should do the same. Any necessary explanation should
be given separately.

I made the point earlier that, for reasons which I have not
analysed, I find the typical ghazal, with its diversity of themes,
difficult to translate into comparable English form. You will have
noticed that all three of the examples I have just quoted possess
at least a unity of mood. I would like to present a ghazal with a
more typical diversity of moods, but consisting of couplets of a
more or less uniformly high standard, in an English translation
which reproduces the ghazal form, but so far I have not been able
to produce any example that satisfies me. I sometimes think that
I could produce much the same effect by putting together a sort
of composite ghazal, going through my translations, picking out
couplets which happen to have a common metre and a common
rhyme, and stringing them together in a single poem. I have not
made this experiment yet, but provided that you tell your reader
what it is you have done I see no objection to it in principle.

Up to this point I have been speaking of problems relating to the presentation of a whole poem, or to abridgements which nevertheless in effect constitute a whole poem. I should now say something of the more general principle of translation. My own is to try to reproduce in translation everything I can which I find in the original—rhythm, assonance, alliteration, and even word order where the different natural patterns of word order in the two languages do not preclude this. In short I aim to change Urdu into English, but otherwise to change nothing that does not need to be changed. It would take too long to illustrate here how I have attempted to carry over into English all the features that I have mentioned, but I will give two examples of the kind of translation which satisfies me most because they seem to me to convey all the essentials of the original Urdu with only minimal change.

> rāt(a) pī Zamzam pa mai aur subh(a) dam
> dhoye dhabbe jāma i ahrām(a) ke

> At night I drank by Zamzam, and as morning dawned
> I washed the wine-stains from the robes of Pilgrimage

> Yā rab, vuh na samjhe hain na samjhenge miri bāt—
> de aur(a) dil un ko jo na de mujh ko zabān aur

> O Lord, they do not understand, nor *will* they understand, my words
> Give them another heart, or else give me another tongue

Practically nothing is changed here except the number of syllables to the line.

It hardly needs saying that in translating, some imaginative compromise is necessary more often than not. Look, for instance, at the following couplet:

> khushī kyā? khet(a) par mere agar sau bār(a) abr āve
> samajhtā hūn ki dhūnde hai abhī se barq(a) khirman ko

> I feel no joy, though clouds should mass a hundred times above my
>   fields
> To me it means that lightning seeks already to find out my crop

Here 'come', the literal translation of *ave*, could serve as its translation but for the fact that in most of the English-speaking world there is nearly always cloud in the sky, and English needs 'though clouds should mass' to convey what is conveyed to the Indian and Pakistani reader by 'though clouds should come'. Another example is in the couplet quoted earlier (p. 526), where 'faith and heart' would reproduce the order of the Urdu, but 'heart and faith' seems to me the natural English order, though I could not say quite why. Similarly, English idiom is 'No, she does not', not 'Yes, she does not'. In the last couplet on p. 47, 'shaikh' fits the rhythm where 'ascetic' would not, and the overall sense is not affected. 'Gardens' here sounds, to me more natural in English than 'garden'.

Sometimes one has to make significant changes in the obvious wording of the translation to convey more adequately the tone and emphasis of the original. In the following example the repetition of 'waiting' is an attempt to do this:

yih na thī hamāri qismat ki visāl i yār(a) hota
agar aur(a) jīte rahte yihi intizār(a) hota

This was not to be my fate, that all should end in lovers' meeting
Even had I gone on living I should still be waiting, waiting

I could have translated the second line

If I could have gone on living, I should even now be waiting

but 'I should even now be waiting' seems to me weak and lame in comparison with *yihi intizar(a) hota*. The English word 'waiting' cannot carry the load that the long, single drawn-out *intizar(a)* can, and I think that 'I should still be waiting, waiting' is a truer equivalent.

✤ ✤

Let me in concluding this discussion of the principles of translation that guide me say that I am fully aware that there are areas in which my personal tastes—prejudices, if you like—operate. For example, I don't like 'thou's and 'thee's, though I think a hypothetical English-writing Ghalib might well have used them. I don't say that I would never use them: there are contexts which would seem to demand them, and there I would meet that demand. On the other hand (if it is the other hand) I don't much like 'I'll', 'you'll', 'he'll' and so on, preferring 'I will', etc. except where the language of the original is quite obviously, markedly, and deliberately colloquial. Most of all, perhaps, I dislike disturbing the natural order of words, especially where this is done solely for the purpose of making a rhyme. Here again Ghalib feels no particular inhibition about this.

(Nor do Urdu poets in general.) But I cannot overcome my own dislike of it in English. I may remark in passing here that I think that the cardinal linguistic sin committed by Indian and Pakistani translators of Ghalib into English is a disregard of the need for a measure of consistency of diction. By all means use 'thou' and 'thee' if your taste inclines you that way, but don't use 'thou art' and 'you are' quite indiscriminately and interchangeably, or the colloquial 'I'll go' and the archaic ' 'Twas not' in the same couplet. I know that the range of diction of the ghazal is wide. Again, if I am not mistaken, this is the impact of the *mushaira* tradition. Poets at a *mushaira* are speaking classical verse with an ancient pedigree; hence they can use archaic, gorgeous language. They are reciting, often in a gathering of people all of whom they know personally; hence they can lapse into informal colloquial. And if you translate, as you should, matching like with like, the language of your translation will show the same wide range. But this does not give you the licence to juxtapose widely differing styles in the cheek-by-jowl way that some translators do.

I have explained at length what I have tried to do. I have indicated earlier that I think I should respect what others have tried to do, even when they have chosen ways of doing it which are not my ways. But a proviso needs to be added. Respect is due only to those who have worked honestly and conscientiously at their task, with the sole desire to be true to Ghalib and enable him to speak to the new audience to whom they are presenting him.

And one hopes also that no one will condemn either these versions or others in other styles simply because they are not to his own particular taste. Ghalib has something to say to many different audiences, each of which perhaps requires its own interpreter— English-knowing Indians or Pakistanis who like rhyme, people who want interpretation rather than translation, those who will not accept verse translation by anyone who is not a poet in his/her own right, and so on. It is right too that Ghalib should reach others through the poetry he inspires in his fellow poets; the method is a good one and deserves support. In short, there is abundant room for many workers in the field, all pursuing their aims according to their own understanding. And it seems to me that Ghalib's greatness demands of us all that we feel a common bond, and, subject to the proviso of which I have spoken, honour and respect each other's efforts to present his work to ever new audiences.

Select Index to
Life and Letters

I have not indexed themes which are dealt with in relatively long continuous passages—e.g. Ghalib's relations with Bahadur Shah Zafar and the Mughal court, his attitude to the revolt of 1857 and so on. Nor are the items indexed exhaustive. For example, the references to Tufta are simply those which indicate Ghalib's exceptional closeness to him.

Explanatory Index
to the Verse

This index is intended to serve more than one purpose.

First, it is designed to obviate the need for constant repetition in the notes of explanations of words, concepts and literary allusions which occur repeatedly in the poems.

Second, it gives key words to help you find a verse which you do not remember in full.

And third, since readers will, I hope, include those who already have some acquaintance with the Urdu and Persian originals, I include, though more sparingly, key words in the original text which may serve the same purpose for them.

Quotations from the Quran are from Abdullah Yusuf Ali's translation.

In explaining literary allusions, I have not explained everything which might have needed explaining in a work of wider range, but only those relevant to the couplets in this selection.

Finding key words for important recurring concepts is not easy and if you cannot find an entry under the word you would have used, look for others of similar meaning. I have not aimed to include every possible key word or every possible reference but I hope that you will find here, if not all, at any rate most of what you are looking for.

Number refer to ghazals, not to pages.

P = Persian   U = Urdu

Mountains; but they refused to undertake it, being afraid thereof; but Man undertook it...' This is generally understood to mean that man alone of God's creation had the courage to accept the responsibility to carry out God's will, knowing that he would be punished if he failed. There is no direct reference to this in my selection but references to Adam and to humankind would carry an awareness of it.

ambition, should be limited, P. 142
anchor, P. 87 (4)
angels
    are not to be envied, P. 331 (3)
    see also Iblis, nakirain
angels, recording—two angels stationed at the left and right shoulder of everyone. The angel on the right records all the good deeds and the one on the left all the bad deeds of the person over whom they watch. These together form the record on which judgement will be passed on the Last Day.
    These angels are called kiramun katibin, U. 41 (5)
angel's song, U. 199 (13)
anger, P. 269 (2)
anqa—a mythical bird which is believed to exist, although no one has seen it, P. 233 (2)
apprehensions, U. 170
apron, U. 20 (2)
Asad—the takhallus (poetic name) which Ghalib originally used in his Urdu verse, U. 29 (8), 33 (2), 78 (7), 82 (2), 91 (2), 100 (3), 101 (2), 182 (10), 186 (2), 191 (4)
Asadullah
    'Lion of God'—(1) a title of 'Ali

(q.v.); (2) Ghalib's name, U. 69 (4) 205; P. 243 (3); Asadullah's man, P. 243 (3)
    see also Asad
ash, U. 26 (1, 2)
ashes of the lover's home, P. 184 (1)
assembly, U. 29 (2), 56, 118 (3)
atom, P. 63 (1); atom and sun, P. 69 (3)
autumn, U. 129, 181
autumn endures, spring passes, U. 14 (2)
autumn eternal, P. 82 (4)
autumn, a reflection of the beloved, P. 192 (1)
avaragi, U. 21 (3)
'Awake!', P. 49 (whole ghazal)
awareness, P. 255 (1)
    the desire for more awareness, acquired through pain, P. 200 (whole ghazal), P. 255 (1)
    awareness of the potentialities of everything, P. 82 (7), 331 (1)
awareness of self
    regret is not permanently banished, P. 245
    must be destroyed, U. 65 (3), 182 (5); P. 130 (5)
    is a source of loss, P. 214 (7)
    see also self-oblivion
Azar—a famous sculptor and idolator, the father of Ibrahim (q.v.). His son, who was prophet of Islam, tried without success to convert him to the true faith. Azar is often praised for the beauty of the idols he made, P. 112 (6), 175, 331 (1)
azizan, P. 184 (2), 219 (7), 278 (5)

Babylon, P. 103 (1)
Baghdad, P. 89 (5)
Bahadur Shah Zafar—last Mughal king, tried by the British after the

of water is the ocean and the grain
of sand the desert in microcosm.
Love gives the lover the power to
see the whole within its smallest
part and to *see* the potentiality of
the smallest part to become the
whole. Often the drop/the grain
of sand is the symbol of the lover,
whose highest aspiration is to
merge in his human or divine
beloved as the drop is lost in the
ocean or the grain of sand in the
desert, U. 21 (2), 38 (6), 48 (2, 5);
P. 21, 38 (2), 82 (5), 214 (2), 306
(2)
drop and pearl, *see* pearl
drunk (=*rind*, q.v.), P. 89 (1)
dua, *see* prayer

ecstasy, P. 214 (7)
effort, the need for, P. 205 (1)
effort, *see* constant...
egg, U. 171
eglantine, U. 180 (4)
egoism, egotism, *see* awareness of self
eight gardens of paradise, P. 333 (2)
eloquence, insincere, U. 99
embrace, P. 33, 116 (3), 239 (whole
ghazal), 287
emerald, P. 71 (2)
endless, *see* constant...
enemies, good news for, P. 250 (1)
enemies and friends, P. 332
enmity
beloved's enmity acceptable,
U. 182 (2)
the price you get for talent,
U. 227 (2)
envy, *see also* jealousy
'the penalty you pay for poetry',
U. 227 (2)
the cure for, U. 117 (1)
essence more important than form,
U. 123 (3), 149 (3), 187 (2)

everything perishes, P. 95 (2)
evil returned for good, U. 132 (2)
excellence unappreciated, U. 111 (4)
fated to penalised, U. 42 (3)
of Ghalib's verse, U. 108 (9)
execution of the lover—the readi-
ness of the lover to sacrifice even
his life for love is expressed in the
metaphor of the beloved as his
executioner, U. 20 (2) and *passim*
exile, *see* country, one's own...
experience
imaginative experience of what
has not yet happened, P. 16
(3), 163, 331 (1)
expiation, U. 20 (1)
expression, everything worthwhile
should find expression, U. 48 (2)
exuberance of the lover, U. 200 (2)
eye(s)
eye's lustre is born of watching, P.
49 (6)
eyes are for looking for ways to
serve friends, P. 49 (7)
the seeing eye, U. 48 (5); P. 63 (3),
331 (1)
see also seeing
eyebrow and eye, U. 180 (1)
eyelashes, are like sharp daggers that
pierce the lover's heart, U. 114
(5), 190 (2)

Fadak, P. 64 (6)
failure, both in love and in life,
U. 47 (6)
faith—i.e. the belief in God and his
prophet Muhammad—the first of
the 'five pillars' of Islam.
faith, in payment for wine, P. 77
(1)
faith and unbelief, U. 229 (5)
'the grime of...', P. 138 (4);
P. 256 (3), 299 (1)
fame, P. 150 (2), *see also* reputation

glass
  as a metaphor sensitivity, P. 5 (1)
  see also rock...
glass-maker, transforms rock into
    glass, P. 308 (1)
gleaning, P. 73 (1)
goal and starting point, P. 154
God, *see also* Ghalib and God
  God's grace, P. 299 (1)
  is merciful U. 20 (1)
  is merciful (He justifies wine-
    drinking), P. 129 (3)
  is inscrutable and self-sufficient,
    P. 1 (whole ghazal), 109 (2),
    182 (2, 4)
  our last refuge, U. 179 (2)
  must be loved unconditionally,
    P. 1 (6)
God criticised/complained of/re-
    buked, U. 41 (5), 47 (5), 110 (2),
    113 (1, 2), 207, 215 (4–7), 222
    (2); P. 94 (6), 158 (3), 237 (5, 6),
    306 (3, 4), 331 (4)
God and beloved, P. 158 (3)
'good', the (= *zahid*), P. 14 (2)
good fortune, U. 41 (2)
'good sir' (=*khaja*), P. 86 (1)
goodness and beauty, U. 45 (3)
gourd, P. 14 (1), 142, 198 (4)
governor, P. 64 (4), 232 (2), 265 (4)
grain of sand and the desert, *see* drop
    of water...
granaries, U. 124 (4), *see also* crop(s),
    fields, harvest
grapes and wine, P. 256 (2)
grass, U. 129, 204
grave, U. 37 (4), 45 (3)
great man of the past, P. 286 (4)
greed, U. 124 (2), 225 (3)
green waterweed, U. 60, 232 (3)
grief—commonly means the grief
    and suffering which love inevita-
    bly brings, or love itself, or sym-
    pathy with all who suffer. It is

therefore something to be sought
    and valued, U. 43 (5), 87, 139,
    149 (2, 5); P. 180, 219 (5), 233
    (4)
  'grief' in its simple sense, U. 98
    (4), 114 (9), 118 (5), 222 (2)
  grief is best not expressed, U. 133
    (1)
  grief is life-long, U. 78 (7)
  grief of living, U. 43 (5)
  should be only momentary, U. 82
    (1)
  freedom from, P. 121 (1)
grime, P. 138 (4)
guest, P. 133 (1)
  inopportune arrival, U. 47 (4);
    P. 77 (2)
guest and host in the realm of love,
    P. 214 (10), 291 (2)
gul as a musical term, P. 121 (3)
Gulistan, P. 150 (1)
  see also Sadi
gulkhan, U. 91 (1), 102 (4); P. 82 (4)
  see also bonfire, furnace

...hacked in little pieces, U. 48 (6)
haj, see Pilgrimage
halal o haram, P. 94 (3)
'Half a loaf...', U. 149 (2, 7), 228
    (3, 4); P. 45 (6), 200 (8)
Hali, U. 57 (6)
Hamza, Amir, U. 48 (4)
Hamza, the Tale of, U. 48 (4)
hand the lover's, P. 124 (2)
hands cut off, U. 191 (3)
hangama, U. 149 (5); P. 68 (2), 138
    (2), 327 (3)
hangover, U. 145
happiness, create it from your own
    resources, drawing on *all* your
    experience, P. 112 (whole ghazal)
haqiqat, P. 130 (1)
haram o halal, P. 94 (3)
harp, U. 218 (2)

God commanded him to sacrifice Ismail. Both father and son gladly prepared themselves to obey but at the last moment God substituted a ram for sacrifice, P. 127 (3, 4)

Isra'il, tribe of, P. 1 (4)

jabr, ikhtiyar, P. 316 (3)

Jacob, see Yaqub

jah, P. 64 (3)

Jam—another name for Jamshed (q.v.)

Jamal, P. 64 (6)

Jamshed—a legendary king of ancient Iran. He is said to have invented wine and the wine cup. He had (and is said by some to have invented) a wonderful wine cup in the depths of which he could see everything that went on in the world, U. 217 (1); P. 19 (3), 95 (3), 103 (2), 205 (2)

jannat, see paradise

jealousy, U. 63 (2), 118 (2), 219 (2); P. 184 (2)
  contradicted by reason, U. 21 (1)
  even of God, U. 189 (4)
  impossible, P. 272 (1)

Jesus, see Isa

jewels
  less precious than poetry, U. 126 (7)
  in the mine of the heart, P. 276 (4)

jeweller, U. 199 (4)

Jibril (Gabriel)—the angel who conveys God's messages to mankind. He conveyed the word of God, the Quran, to the Prophet. He is himself renowned for his eloquence, U. 108 (9)

journeying, see constant...

Joseph, see Yusuf

joy
  extreme joy and extreme sorrow, U. 33 (1)
  joy needs something to be contrasted with, U. 38 (1)
  'one that knows no joy', U. 115 (3)
  joy that never dies, P. 74 (1)
  see also zest for life

'Judge not...', U. 29 (4)

Judgement Day—the day when, at the sound of the trumpet, all will assemble before God on a great plain to be judged. Its turmoil and the awe which it inspires make it a metaphor for any awesome or terrible occasion, P. 204 (3)
  beloved on Judgement Day, U. 123 (2), 223 (4); P. 83 (3), 319 (4)
  a day on which one forgives, P. 329 (3)
  see also doomsday(s); day of reckoning

Junaid, P. 89 (5)

jur'at e rindana, U. 155 (2)

justice, U. 41 (5); P. 206 (5)

Kaba—the holy place in Mecca toward which Muslims turn when they pray. Muslim tradition says it was built by Ibrahim (q.v.) and his son, Ismail (q.v.). By Muhammad's time it had become a place in which idols were worshipped. When the Meccans accepted Islam, the idols were removed from the Kaba. Ghalib has numerous verses about it and while some of these (U. 214 (7), 225 (5), 229 (5); P. 87 (8), 89 (4), 162 (1), 242 (4), 323 (6)) say nothing very controversial, most of them express dissatisfaction about the Kaba and what it represents. He expects it to be open to him when he reaches it and will at once turn back if it is not (U. 48 (1)). Idols once dwelt in it and 'idolatry' still has its importance for the true worshipper (U. 124 (1), 223 (6); P. 299 (3)). The religion of love is more powerful than that centred on the Kaba (P. 320 (1)). A Hindu priest who is constant to his religion deserves burial in it (U. 126 (4)). It is too cramped a space to meet Ghalib's needs (P. 178 (1)). In any case, one needs to go beyond the Kaba, which to those who know this, simply indicates the way forward (U. 107 (4); P. 214 (11), 221 (2), 247 (4)). And anyway, says Ghalib, the Kaba is in *me* (P. 205 (3)).

kafir, kafar, see also infidel, P. 281 (3), 299 (1)

kai, U. 232 (3)

Kalim, *see* Tur, Musa

kalisa, U. 229 (5)

Karbala, *see* Husain

katan, P. 32

Kausar—the name of a stream in paradise in which 'the wine of purity' will flow, U. 110 (1); P. 83 (4), 205 (3), 213 (1), 223 (2), 242 (6), 331 (5)
    see also paradise

Kerbala (Karbala), *see* Husain

khair o shar, P. 244 (4)

khaja, P. 86 (1), 147 (1)

Khalil, *see* Ibrahim

khas o khar, P. 219 (4)

Khizr, Khizar—an ancient prophet of Islam who never dies because he found and drank the water of life (*ab e hayat*). He lives away from people and appears to travellers who have lost their way and guides them onto the right path. When he went into the pitch darkness in which the water of life was hidden, he took Sikandar (q.v.) with him. Some traditions suggest that he tricked Sikandar and so deprived him of the opportunity to drink the water of life (U. 220 (3))

Ghalib often belittles him, condemning him for avoiding the company of people (U. 211 (1)), rejecting the view that his guidance is especially valuable (U. 212 (2)), and arguing that he has not used his endless life to any good effect (U. 221 (1); P. 69 (1)), In any case, he had been deprived of the joy of dying (for love) and is therefore not to be envied (P. 6 (1)).

Other references, U. 68; P. 1 (2), 87 (1), 205 (2)

khubi e taqdir, U. 41 (2)

khuld, see paradise, P. 205 (3)

Khusrau, *see* Farhad

khvaja, see khaja

'...kill me then', P. 278 (whole ghazal)

'kindness to myself', P. 280 (1)

king, the, *see* Bahadur Shah Zafar

king(s). P. 307 (3)
    kings and justice, P. 206 (5)
    their company to be avoided, P. 87 (6)
    their gifts to be rejected, P. 265 (4)
    king's spies, P. 239 (8)
    king's beloved in Ghalib's embrace, P. 239 (6)

movement
 the mark of every living heart,
  P. 49 (6)
 see also constant...
muezzin, P. 210 (2)
muft, U. 215 (11)
'munificent' the, U. 191 (4)
Musa, *see* Tur
Musalman, is true to his word,
 U. 13
music, U. 87, 199 (6–12); P. 127 (1),
 179, 198 (6)
 music of God's secrets, U. 34 (1)
 wrongly believed to be a cure for
  sorrow, U. 107 (3)
musk, U. 219 (4); P. 277 (3, 4, 5)
muvahhid, U. 114 (8)
'My lord' (=*khaja*), U. 147 (1)
myself, P. 262 (1)
mysticism, U. 43 (6), *see also* sufism

nails, finger, U. 34 (2)
naivety, *see* simplicity
nakedness (of beloved), P. 239 (3)
nakhuda, U. 228 (5); P. 257 (4)
nakirain, U. 216
namabar, *see* letter-bearer, messenger
name, beloved's, U. 231 (1)
Namrud—a legendary king of an-
 cient Iraq who claimed that he
 was God. Ibrahim (q.v.) rejected
 his claim and Namrud had him
 thrown into a great fire, where-
 upon the fire become a bed of
 flowers, U. 47 (5); P. 127 (3, 4),
 237 (1)
narcissus, U. 232 (4); P. 121 (3)
narrowmindedness, a source of se-
 curity, U. 40 (2)
nasih, *see* counsellor, preacher,
 U. 35 (3), 59 (3); P. 57 (2)
 a true friend does not become a
  nasih, U. 43 (3)
navigate, U. 276 (3)

Naziri—a Persian poet whom Ghalib
 much admires, P. 237 (6)
necessity of opposites, U. 19 (1)
need to speak, at any cost, P. 268 (2)
net, snare, P. 183 (2)
 see also bird/snare/cage
new earth, new heavens, P. 320 (2)
nib, U. 124 (3)
nigah, U. 195 (1)
night, beauty of, U. 45 (1)
night of separation, P. 321 (2)
night of union, P. 202 (2)
nightingale—the symbol of the
 lover and of the lover-poet, whose
 verse is as beautiful as the nigh-
 tingale's song, U. 22 (1), 114 (4),
 153, 176 (1), 223 (5); P. 157 (3),
 247 (5)
 see also bird/snare/cage
Nile—in Muslim tradition, it was
 the Nile in which Pharoah's
 armies were drowned when they
 were pursuing the children of
 Israel, P. 237 (3)
'...no longer there', U. 67 (1, 2, 3)
nobles, P. 316 (5)
nonentities, P. 90 (1)
nooses, U. 224 (2)
nostalgia, U. 190 (whole ghazal)
'...now I am gone', U. 57 (whole
 ghazal)

oblivion, U. 37 (1), 114 (2)
observation unflinching, U. 36 (2),
 117 (1)
ocean, *see also* drop of water...,
 U. 14 (1), 38 (5); P. 255 (2)
'...of no account', P. 109 (1, 2, 3, 4)
ok, U. 187 (2)
old age, U. 96 (whole ghazal)
old-fashioned people, U. 107 (3)
oneness of all true lovers of God,
 U. 114 (8); P. 256 (3)
opposite, U. 200 (2)

opposites—the existence of contrast-
ing opposites essential in life,
U. 19 (1), 38 (1); P. 45 (5)
opposites are linked, U. 19 (1);
P. 75 (1)
ore, U. 126 (2)
outworn norms, P. 219 (7)
owl, P. 219 (5)

pain of love is incurable, U. 5 (1), 47
(1), 195
painting, U. 180 (2)
palaces, P. 284
paradise—in paradise (called in Per-
sian and Urdu *bahisht, firdaus,
jannat, khuld*) virtuous Muslims
will reap heavenly reward for their
good deeds on earth. Its
gatekeeper, Rizvan (q.v.), tends its
eight gardens (P. 333 (2)). There
will be milk and honey in abun-
dance (P. 95 (5)). The 'wine of
purity' will flow in the stream of
Kausar and the Tuba tree will
offer its delicious fruits. Beautiful
women (*houris*) will gratify every
desire. The orthodox present the
prospect of paradise as an incen-
tive in this life to do God's will.
True lovers of God reject this
concept with contempt; you do
His will because you love Him
and for no other reason (U. 124
(2), 225 (3)).
There are couplets in which
Ghalib speaks of paradise in a
conventional sense, without mak-
ing any comment on it (U. 45 (3);
P. 34, 147 (1), 208, 295 (2), 327
(2), 333 (2)). But there are many
more in which he is sceptical
about its supposed joys, though
the idea of it is sometimes com-
forting (U, 217 (4)). Of all its

promised joys, only the prospect
of abundant wine evokes his en-
thusiasm (U. 219 (4); P. 71 (2), 95
(6), 281 (1)). And it will be at best
inadequate to compensate for
suffering in this life (U. 145; P. 51
(3)). The pleasures that can be
experienced here and now, in this
life, are certain. They are no less
than the promised pleasures of
paradise and sometimes surpass
them (U. 27 (4), 37 (1), 104 (4),
123 (4), 212 (1); P. 68 (2), 94 (2),
205 (3)). The prospect of con-
tinuing, unalloyed pleasures is not
an attractive one (U. 214 (4); P. 68
(2)) and 'the spice of fear' will be
lacking (P. 298 (4)). The *houris*
come in for much critical com-
ment (U. 212 (1); P. 94 (2), 277
(1), 316 (1)). In any case, 'you can
yourself be paradise' (P. 116 (2)).
Or, says Ghalib, you may 'savour
[it] in me' (P. 205 (3))
parting and meeting, P. 17 (5)
Parvez—another name for Khusrau
(see Farhad), P. 71 (3)
passion in love, U. 155 (1, 2)
past, the, U. 107 (3)
time past, U. 105
days past, P. 84 (1)
past and present continuity of,
P. 103 (2)
patience, U. 78 (3); P. 74 (1)
the bonds of, P. 299 (5)
pawning, P. 89 (4)
peace, sense of, P. 37 (1)
pearl—during the Persian month of
Naisan (April–May) a raindrop
that falls into an oyster becomes
a pearl. Only a few drops attain to
this and only after passing through
many dangers, U. 78 (2); P. 255
(2), 272 (3)

pearls are often a symbol of the lover's tears, P. 199 (4)

the pearl and the lover's heart, U. 14 (1)

pearls contrasted with tears, U. 28 (1)

in royal banners, P. 122 (3)

peasant, U. 37 (3)

pen, 'the pen that wrote my fate', U. 124 (3)

perception, see experience

perceptiveness, P. 88 (2)

persecution, not testing, U. 127 (7)

Persian, Ghalib's command of, P. 122 (6)

persuasiveness of rival, U. 99

Pharoah, P. 237 (3)

philosophy, P. 103 (1)

Pilgrimage—the Pilgrimage to Mecca is one of the 'five pillars' of Islam. Every Muslim who can afford it must make the journey at least once during his life-time. The pilgrim wears special robes of pilgrimage (q.v) called *ahram* and drinks from the well of Zamzam (q.v.) before proceeding to the Kaba (q.v.), U. 223 (8)

pilot, P. 257 (4)

pious, pious friend, P. 14 (2), 208, 249 (1), 256 (2), 329 (1)

play on words, U. 191 (3), 224 (1)

poetry, poets, see Ghalib on poetry, poets…

poison, U. 109 (1)

polo, P. 299 (4)

poor, shun their company, P. 41, 90 (1)

prayer (*namaz*)—one of the 'five pillars' of Islam, 'Prayer' would be more accurately defined as 'worship', for while one may pray to God for favours, this may not be done in any of the five prayers

which together constitute a 'pillar'. Each of these is said at each of five closely defined times during the twenty-four hours in prescribed Arabic words and said with the bodily postures prescribed for each stage of the prayer.

prayer (*dua*), P. 295 (1)

is fruitless, U. 68

'do not ask', U. 79 (1)

prayer-mat, P. 87 (5)

preacher, U. 35 (3), 43 (3), 178, 223 (3); P. 83 (5), 127 (1), 206 (3) see also nasih, vaiz

preaching (*mauizat*), P. 211 (1)

predecessors, to be revered and followed, P. 286 (4)

present and past continuity of, P. 103 (2)

pretence of clemency, P. 298 (2)

pretexts for cruelty, P. 161 (2)

pride, U. 21 (2) see also sin

pride of fulfilled love, U. 114 (3)

priest (Brahman), U. 126 (4)

prison, U. 35 (4), 41 (3) see also bondage of love

prison-house, of my heart, U. 82 (2)

promises, the beloved's, U. 43 (2), 221 (3); P. 219 (2)

protest to the beloved, U. 219 (1); P. 11

pure, man of pure heart (=*rind*, q.v.), P. 137

Qais, see Majnun, U. 149 (4), 224 (1)

qalam, U. 191 (3)

Qarun—a legendary miser of enormous wealth, P. 185

Qatil—an Indian poet and scholar of Persian of whom Ghalib held a very poor opinion, P. 237 (6)

qatra, see drop

107 (1), 118 (2), 123 (1), 182 (4),
219 (2); P. 307 (2, 4)

messenger becomes rival, U. 227
(1)

confidant becomes rival, U. 42 (1)

river, P. 20, 21

its reaction to the beloved's beauty,
P. 66 (1)

riyayat e lafzi, U. 191 (3), 224 (1)

Rizvan—the gatekeeper of paradise
and keeper of its gardens, U. 27
(4), 37 (1), 40 (3); P. 95 (5),
223 (8)

robber(s), U. 62, 126 (6); P. 67 (3),
87 (5), 223 (3)

see also highwayman

robes of pilgrimage, U. 225 (5), 231
(2); P. 89 (4)

see also Pilgrimage

rock, mountain, flint, stone—rock is
hard and strong but is also a
source of beauty. Sparks leap from
it when it is struck. Beautiful
sculptures are 'locked within it'.
It is the raw material of delicate
glass, glass which will hold wine,
U. 171; P. 145 (2), 202 (3), 236
(4), 308 (1), 331 (1)

Ghalib has the qualities of both
rock and glass, U. 43 (4); P. 5
(1)

roof where the beloved stands,
U. 190 (7)

rosary, U. 37 (2), 63 (3), 224 (2);
P. 87 (5), 220 (2), 257 (1)

rose—sometimes the symbol of
beauty, sometimes of the passing
of spring (while the rosebud
marks the coming of spring). Also
very commonly the symbol of the
beautiful but indifferent beloved
of the nightingale, U. 20 (2), 22
(1), 36 (2), 93, 102 (3), 114 (1),
153, 170, 180 (4), 185 (2)

rose and poetry, U. 11

rose growing and rose plucked,
P. 240

rose's debt, P. 308 (2)

rebuked by the beloved, P. 95 (1)

roses surge within the branch,
P. 82 (7)

rosebed, P. 240

rosebud, *see also* rose, U. 152

roza, P. 305 (2)

sacking of city, U. 15 (2)

sacred thread, U. 63 (3), 224 (2)

Sadi—great thirteenth-century Per-
sian poet and prose writer, espe-
cially famous for his *Gulistan*, a
collection of short humorous and
moral anecdotes, P. 150 (1)

'saintliness', U. 43 (6)

saki—the beautiful youth who pours
the wine for you. The symbol of
your beloved (human or divine),
of love, of beauty and of any ideal
that inspires you. Ghalib some-
times criticises him for not play-
ing the role he should, U. 16 (2),
19 (2), 38 (5), 39, 57 (6), 109 (1),
133 (2), 149 (3), 187 (2), 199 (8),
225 (1); P. 28 (1), 39, 84 (1), 116
(1)

Saki of Kausar—a title of 'Ali (q.v.),
who, it is believed, will pour the
'wine of purity' for the faithful in
paradise

see also Kausar

salamander—a mythical animal that
lives in fire, P. 19 (1), 83 (2), 213
(4, 5), 247 (5)

Salsabil, a fountain in paradise,
p. 59

sand *see* drop of water...

saqi, see saki

sarsar, P. 184 (1), 329 (2)

Satan, *see* Adam

could fly through the air and who
knew the language of birds, ani-
mals and jinns and had power
over them, U. 229 (2)
sun, U. 59 (1), 78 (5), 140 (1); P. 200
(2), 250 (3)
will perish, U. 95 (2)
and the beloved, U. 102 (2)
and particle/atom, U. 98 (2), 102
(1), 135 (1)
see also dew, drop of
sun's course, U. 140 (1)
sunset, U. 59 (2)
supplication, P. 295 (3)
survivors of a former age, U. 107 (3)
suspicion
lover's suspicion of the beloved,
U. 109 (2)
sweat, P. 239 (2)
sweetness, beloved's, P. 321 (1)
symbolic love (majaz), P. 130 (1)
symbolism of the ghazal, U. 64
(6, 7)
sympathy
for all who strive, U. 113 (2)
demand for sympathy, P. 277 (4)
see also identification...

takalluf bartaraf, P. 33
talent
develop your own talent,
U. 217 (3)
is 'rewarded' by punishment,
U. 42 (3)
is 'rewarded' by enmity, U. 227
(2)
tapestry, P. 127 (5)
Tartary, P. 89 (5)
tasavvuf, see sufism, U. 43 (6)
task, 'I put my heart into my task',
P. 244 (5)
taslim ki khu, U. 182 (9)
tauhid, U. 144 (8)
taunting, U. 127 (9)

tavern
tavern and mosque, U. 123 (3),
180 (1); P. 260 (2)
love's silent tavern, U. 199 (5)
tears of blood, see blood
tears better than pearls, U. 28 (1)
temple, the home of idols (i.e. be-
loved) and of beauty, U. 124 (1),
126 (4); P. 178 (1), 221 (2), 242
(6), 247 (4)
temple doors, U. 45 (1)
'this ancient temple', P. 89 (1)
be the temple's guest, P. 299 (3)
testing and persecution, U. 127 (7)
tests, P. 259 (2)
theologians, P. 162 (2)
thief, P. 133 (2)
thirst, thirsty, P. 233 (1), 237 (2), 277
(3)
thorns, P. 65 (1), 163, 252 (3)
'Those days are gone...', P. 323
(whole ghazal)
'a thousand times, P. 17 (5)
thousand years of life, P. 28 (2)
threshold of the beloved's house,
U. 46 (5); P. 63 (5)
never leaving the beloved's thresh-
old is symbolic of constant,
unfailing love for her
throne of God, U. 42 (2)
time is out of joint, P. 88 (1)
'time past', U. 105
tolerance, U. 126 (1)
touchstone, P. 64 (3)
tradition must be revered, P. 286 (4)
transcience
of all created things, U. 95 (2)
of beauty, U. 114 (1)
of spring, U. 14 (2), 153, 176 (1),
228 (4)
of life, U. 78 (6), 118 (5)
transparency, P. 210 (10)
travellers, P. 25
travelling fast, P. 83 (4)